Symbol	Chapter where introduced	Explanation
d	18	Depreciation rate.
D	14	Replacement investment.
D	16	Total demand deposits (checking accounts).
DD	6	Aggregate demand curve.
DG	8	Demand growth line.
e	7	Superscript e means "expected."
e	5–appendix	Response of money demand to a \$1 change in income at a fixed interest rate.
e	16	Fraction of deposits that banks hold as reserves.
E	2	Real expenditures: $E = C + I + G$
E_p	3	Planned real expenditures: $E_p = C + I_p + G$
ECS	11	Extra convenience services of money.
f	5–appendix	Response of money demand to a 1 percent change in the interest rate.
f	19	Rate of change of foreign exchange rate.
F	19	Foreign exchange rate.
F	2	Real government transfer payments.
F_G	2	Real government transfer payments.
F_p	2	Real interest paid by consumers to business.
g	9	Slope of the short-run Phillips curve (SP).
G	2	Real government purchases of goods and services.
GNP	1	Gross national product, either nominal or real.
h	3–appendix	Marginal propensity to import.
H	3–appendix	Real imports.
H	16	High-powered money.
i	11	Nominal or market interest rate.
I	2	Real gross private investment.
I_n	14, 18	Net investment.
I_p	3	Planned real gross private investment.
I_U	3	Real unintended inventory investment: $I_U = E - E_p$
IS	4	Commodity market equilibrium curve.
j	7	Coefficient of adjustment of expectations.
k	3	Spending multiplier.
K	14	Capital stock of investment goods.
K^*	14	Desired capital stock.
LM	4	Money-market equilibrium curve.
LP	8	Long-run Phillips curve.
M	16	Total money supply.
M^d	4	Nominal money demand.
M^s	4	Nominal money supply.
MMC	16	Money-market certificate.
MPK	14	Expected marginal product of capital.
n	18	Growth rate of employment.

(continued inside back cover)

Macroeconomics

Macroeconomics

Second Edition

Robert J. Gordon

Professor of Economics
Northwestern University

Little, Brown and Company
Boston   Toronto

HAL

Published simultaneously in Canada
by Little, Brown & Company (Canada) Limited

Printed in the United States of America

with love,
for Julie

Summary Table of Contents

APPENDIXES

Detailed Table
of Contents

Preface:
To the Instructor

January 1980 marked the beginning of the seventh postwar recession. In some ways a mirror image of the previous 1973–75 recession, the economic slump of 1980 was largely a consequence of the oil price "shock" of 1979, just as the previous recession had been caused partly by the initial OPEC price increase of 1973–74. The events of 1979–80 once again demonstrated the obsolescence of the traditional macroeconomic textbooks, in which most of the exposition is devoted to the determination of real aggregate demand, and in which inflation is an afterthought and aggregate supply is rarely mentioned.

Students in the 1980s come to their macroeconomics class eager to understand why both inflation and unemployment have been so high and so volatile during the past decade. They will not be satisfied by the traditional "demand-only" textbooks, since these cannot explain why inflation has fluctuated so much more than nominal demand since 1971, and why inflation and growth in real output have moved in opposite directions most of the time. Supply shifts, and the reaction of demand-management policy to those shifts, must be the centerpiece of the analysis.

MACROECONOMICS IS ABOUT BOTH SUPPLY AND DEMAND

The events of the past decade have taught us that macroeconomics is about aggregate supply, not just aggregate demand. This intermediate macro text is the first to focus on inflation and unemployment as core topics rather than treating them as appendages and afterthoughts as in traditional books. The tried-and-true *IS-LM* theory of income determination is presented concisely and then linked clearly to the causes of inflation and unemployment.

Students are shown that inflation and recessions can be caused not only by shifts in aggregate demand but also by supply shifts, including changes in the relative prices of food and oil, and the introduction and termination of price controls.

UNIQUE CONTENT AND ORGANIZATION

The book is organized according to a simple principle, "Put the important things first." The first six chapters teach what every macro student must understand, the essentials of the *IS-LM* model and the effects of monetary and fiscal policy under conditions of fixed and perfectly flexible prices. But then both content and organization diverge from the traditional treatment in order to bring "up front" the essential causes and cures of inflation and unemployment. *By the end of Chapter 9 the student will fully understand the causes of the 1980 recession and what could have been done to prevent it.*

This early treatment of inflation and unemployment is achieved by devoting Chapters 7 through 11, the book's "core," to the causes, cures, and consequences of inflation and unemployment. The details of income determination—for instance, the permanent-income theory of consumption, the accelerator theory of investment, and the details of money-demand theory—are moved to later in the book, since a too-early introduction of these secondary elements diverts the student's attention from the fundamental macro relationships between aggregate demand and supply. This allows Chapters 7 through 11 to be devoted, respectively, to the static theory of aggregate supply and demand, the causes and cures of demand inflation, the causes and cures of supply inflation, the causes and cures of high unemployment, and, finally, the effects of inflation.

Then Chapters 12 through 17 turn to the controversy over demand management and policy activism. This book is neither monetarist nor non-monetarist in orientation. Instead, a new interpretation of the debate between the two camps in Chapter 12 provides a unique focus for the last part of the book. Not only the chapters on monetary and fiscal policy but also those on consumption, investment, and money demand are written with the goal of locating the major sources of instability in the economy. Can the private economy achieve stable growth in aggregate demand without government interference? Have past shifts in monetary and fiscal policy done more harm than good? A mixed picture emerges with plenty of evidence provided to support both opponents and proponents of activist stabilization policy.

CASE STUDIES AND PEDAGOGICAL TOOLS

This book is the first to introduce case studies into the intermediate macroeconomics course. Almost every chapter contains at least one case study that analyzes particular historical episodes from the point of view of the theory. Case studies treat not just recent macroeconomic events; they also illustrate interesting features of the Great Depression of the 1930s. The case studies help give the student a breather from the theory. Once per chapter, and sometimes more often, he or she is reminded that the theoretical curves do not describe an ivory-tower dream world but are actually useful in explaining major episodes of economic history and of the recent past.

Many other learning devices are included to aid student comprehension. Color is used consistently in diagrams. Each chapter ends with a summary, a list of concepts for the student to identify, and a set of discussion questions. Equations are always accompanied by numerical examples. A glossary of terms is included in the back of the book. Historical data are listed in Appendix B. A full list of these pedagogical aids is presented below.

IMPROVEMENTS IN THE SECOND EDITION

Despite the success of the first edition, extensive changes have been made in this edition to satisfy further the requirements and desires of instructors and students. Changes have been based on scores of letters received and, in addition, on more than one hundred responses to a questionnaire directed to users and non-users of the first edition.

These responses uniformly endorsed the main innovations of the first edition, including the central emphasis on inflation and unemployment, the new treatment of the monetarist-nonmonetarist debate, and the use of case studies. But there were two complaints. "Please simplify the core theory of inflation and unemployment in Chapter 8 [of the first edition]." "And please simplify the diagrams to eliminate clutter."

This second edition has been extensively changed in answer to these requests. The core theory of inflation and unemployment has been simplified, while retaining its basic content. Every diagram in the book has been redrawn to provide large, bold, uncluttered figures that aid student comprehension. And the topic coverage is even more complete than before.

THE THEORY OF INFLATION AND UNEMPLOYMENT: MUCH EASIER TO LEARN

The simplification of the inflation theory is based on three key improvements. First, the old Chapter 8 has been split in two. The new Chapter 8 is on demand inflation, both its causes and cures. The student now becomes thoroughly acquainted with accelerations and decelerations of aggregate demand growth and with adjustments of inflation expectations as causes of and cures for inflation before any mention is made of supply shifts. The innovative material from the old Chapter 8 on the economy's response to supply shocks has been moved into the new Chapter 9, which is now completely devoted to supply inflation, both its causes and cures. Material from the old Chapter 11 on stopping demand inflation has been moved to Chapter 8, and the discussion of stopping supply inflation (including the sections on price controls) has been moved to Chapter 9. The elimination of the old Chapter 11 allows the old Chapter 9 (on unemployment) to become the new Chapter 10, and the old Chapter 10 (on effects of inflation) to become the new Chapter 11.

A second key ingredient in the simplification process is the elimination of any discussion of unemployment or Okun's law from Chapters 8 and 9. The horizontal axis remains the level of real GNP (or the ratio of actual to natural real GNP), the same as in Chapters 3 through 7. An expansion in aggregate demand thus continues to move the economy to the right, in contrast to the old presentation when a student was suddenly told that an expansion meant moving to the left. The student now gains a full understanding of supply-shock inflation in Chapter 9, and why this can cause a recession, before turning to Okun's law and unemployment in Chapter 10.

Third, the dynamic aggregate demand schedule in Chapters 8 and 9, previously labeled the "BC line," has been renamed "DG," standing for demand growth. The DG line slopes downward, since real output is on the horizontal axis, thus providing a clearer link to the downward sloping static DD demand schedule of Chapters 6 and 7, and pointing out that DG is just a dynamic version of DD.

Another simplification is the elimination of the labor demand and supply curves from Chapter 7. Now the supply curve for the individual firm is derived directly from the principle of diminishing returns, just as in good principles texts. This change frees space in Chapter 7 for a more realistic treatment of aggregate supply and business fluctuations. No longer must workers be "fooled" for fluctuations to occur. New attention is also given to the advantages of long-term wage contracts for workers and firms and the consequences of these contracts for business cycles.

Finally, in response to many requests for a detailed mathematical statement of the inflation-unemployment theory of Chapters 8 and 9, a new appendix has been added at the end of Chapter 9, "The Elementary Algebra of Inflation, Real GNP, and Unemployment." Equations are presented that show students how to work through numerical exercises that trace the economy's adjustment to demand and supply shocks and to alternative policy responses.

THE NEW DIAGRAMS: LARGE, NEAT, AND UNCLUTTERED

Users of the first edition will find little resemblance between the new diagrams and the old. Compare, for instance, the new Figure 3-6 on p. 75 with the corresponding Figure 3-4 from p. 66 of the first edition. This and every other diagram is larger and bolder. The page itself is wider. The diagrams now extend to the edge of the page, using space that was wasted in the earlier design. Schedules are now drawn as wider lines, with bolder type used to identify intersection and equilibrium points. Irrelevant sections of the horizontal axis have been eliminated, thus allowing the relevant sections to be magnified. Overall, these changes have allowed the scale of Figure 3-6 to be "blown up" by a factor of 3.5 compared to the corresponding figure in the first edition.

Other changes have been made to simplify the graphs. Complex diagrams dealing with the liquidity trap and the real balance effect have been eliminated (Figures 5-3, 5-5, 6-3, and 6-4 in the first edition). Diagrams no longer introduce a curve and shift its position in the same figure; any shift in a curve is now introduced in a separate figure (notice especially the new sequences of diagrams from 3-1 to 3-6 and from 4-1 to 4-4). Now many diagrams illustrating new schedules are introduced with an accompanying table, as in some economic principles textbooks (see, for instance, Figure 3-1 and accompanying Table 3-1, or Figure 7-2 and Table 7-1).

NEW TOPIC COVERAGE OF BOTH THE DEMAND AND SUPPLY SIDE

Beyond the continuing unemployment-inflation dilemma, the most important new macroeconomic problem to emerge in the past few years has been the slowdown in productivity growth, both in the United States and worldwide. Chapter 18 is now devoted to the theory of economic growth and the productivity slowdown, and the material on fiscal policy previously in Chapter 18 has been condensed and moved to Chapter 17 and its appendix.

Much recent academic research in macroeconomics has revolved around the debate between the "new classical macroeconomics" or "rational expectations hypothesis" of Robert E. Lucas, Jr., and Thomas Sargent, and the traditional approach to macroeconomics which emphasizes a non-market-clearing analysis of labor markets. This debate is now brought into the second edition in Chapters 7 and 8. Section 7-6 on "How Long Is the Short Run?" analyzes the factors that lead firms and workers to enter into long-term price and wage contracts, thus causing price "stickiness." Section 8-10, "Stopping Inflation," examines the rational expectations and credibility hypotheses that criticize the conventional framework for underestimating the downward responsiveness of inflation to a fully anticipated change in monetary policy.

This edition contains a much more complete analysis of policy responses to supply shocks than was included in the first edition. Section 9-4 discusses a number of obstacles to the accommodation of supply shocks, including effects of reduced oil supplies on productivity, problems introduced by cost-of-living escalators, and differing policy responses in other major industrialized countries. In keeping with the theme that macroeconomics now must concern itself with supply-side problems, Section 9-8 contains a review of policy solutions to the problem of excessive U.S. oil imports.

The soaring Consumer Price Index made headlines in early 1980, and yet an increasing number of economists (both inside and outside the Bureau of Labor Statistics) have become convinced that the CPI is a misleading indicator of inflation. The reasons for this skepticism and a comparison of the CPI and personal consumption deflator are contained in section 2-10, "Measuring Prices."

NEW AND UPDATED CASE STUDIES

Any student of macroeconomics in the early 1980s will expect the course to present an application of theory to the 1980 recession. What caused the recession and how did it differ from the 1973–75 episode? Section 9-2 provides a new case study that shows a broad overview of the behavior of nominal GNP growth and inflation during the 1970–80 decade. Then detailed analysis of the late 1970s is presented in the case study of section 9-7, "Supply Shocks Strike Again." The case studies covering the early and late 1970s in sections 9-6 and 9-7 contain a detailed treatment of both the reasons for supply shocks and the response of aggregate demand policy.

Two other puzzles emerged in the late 1970s that warrant new case studies, the low 1979–80 level of the saving rate (section 13-7), and the slow growth of productivity (sections 18-4 and 18-5). Other case studies have been revised, updated, and in some cases amplified, including the new attention to the effects of inflation on corporate profits (section 11-6). All case studies involving the behavior of money now incorporate the new definitions of the money supply announced in early 1980.

PEDAGOGICAL FEATURES

As in the first edition, this book contains an unusual number of pedagogical features that have been designed to aid student comprehension.

Color. Color is used throughout to make the diagrams clear: red lines identify demand curves, and black lines identify supply curves. Shading is used liberally to mark off important features of diagrams. In theoretical diagrams involving shifts of curves, new equilibrium points are identified in red on the axes. And color is used frequently for emphasis in tables.

Summary and A Look Ahead. Each chapter ends with a summary and then a paragraph called "A Look Ahead," which explains how the next chapter is related to the present one.

Diagrams. Except for the standard Keynesian multiplier equations in Chapter 3 (and a few sections of Chapters 13–15), most of the theory is presented graphically, freeing the text from the clutter of algebra. The variables that make each curve shift are always written next to each curve, giving students a firm handle on the old bugaboo—the confusion between movement along a curve and a shift in a curve. Student review is aided by a concise caption explaining what is going on in every graph and by a headline for each graph that explains the main point in colloquial language.

Concept Boxes. There is no separate chapter on concepts; everything is explained as it is used. Background information is given in separate boxes, such as one explaining why bond prices and interest rates are inversely related and another showing how to read vertical and horizontal lines in economic diagrams.

Footnotes. Rather than a bibliography at the end of each chapter with no indication of the importance, usefulness, or relevance of each item, frequent footnote references are provided to supporting and related literature. Additional suggestions for supplemental reading are provided in the *Instructor's Manual.*

Identifications. For students' benefit the end of each chapter contains a list of important new terms introduced in the chapter, including some that are not in the Glossary.

Biographies. Short biographies of four major protagonists—Keynes, Friedman, Tobin, and Modigliani—are included in Chapters 6 and 12.

Numerical Examples. To aid the student's comprehension of the few equations included, each equation is presented twice—in its general form and with a numerical example. A single running numerical example guides the student through Chapters 3–6. All diagrams in these chapters have numbers on the axes and the slopes of all curves correspond to the numerical examples in the text.

Questions and Answers. Each chapter ends with a set of discussion questions of varying difficulty. Answers to all questions are provided in the *Instructor's Manual.*

Glossary. A glossary of terms is included in the back of the book with a cross-reference to the section where the term is first introduced. Terms with glossary definitions are identified in boldface type when first introduced.

Historical Data. Appendix B presents annual data on key variables for 1900–79 and quarterly data for 1947:Q1–1980:Q2. This is intended as a handy reference for instructors and for use in student projects or term papers.

Student Workbook. A new feature of the second edition is the availability of a workbook for student purchase. Written by John Gemello and Newby Schweitzer of San Francisco State, the *Student Workbook* contains both short objective questions and long numerical exercises. Blank grids are provided to encourage students to work out graphical solutions to numerical problems.

Instructor's Manual. The new *Instructor's Manual* includes suggestions on how to use the book and how to teach each chapter, answers to all questions in the text, and numerous objective and numerical questions for use in class exercises or tests. The introduction also suggests supplemental readings.

The "Gordon Update." A short supplemental newsletter will be issued early in the spring and fall semesters, beginning in Spring 1981, to provide a review of recent events in the context of the appropriate sections of the text. Data will be provided to update 1979–80 case studies and the figures in Appendix B.

ACKNOWLEDGMENTS

I remain grateful to all those who were thanked in the preface to the first edition. Space limitations prevent me from repeating all of those acknowledgments.

My greatest debt in preparing the second edition goes to the reviewers, who I hope will be pleasantly surprised to see how many of their suggestions have been incorporated in the published version: Burton A. Abrams (University of Delaware), Shirley Cassing (University of Pittsburgh), Glenn Hueckel (Purdue University), John S. Pettengill (University of Virginia), David Small (University of Wisconsin), and Richard E. Towey (Oregon State).

Over the past few years a number of teachers have written me with their questions and protests about the first edition. These comments were instrumental in convincing me to make many of the changes that appear here. In addition to the above-listed reviewers, some of whom had written earlier, particularly useful were the comments of H. Sonmez Atesoglu (Clarkson College), Jose Carvalho (Fundacao Getulio Vargas, Brazil), Charles Lieberman (Federal Reserve Bank of New York), Thomas S. McCaleb (Rice University), Jacob B. Michaelsen (University of California at Santa Cruz), Jeffrey B. Miller (University of Delaware), Dean Paxson (University of Manchester Business School, United Kingdom), J. Kirker Stephens (University of Oklahoma at Norman), and Donald R. Wells (Memphis State University).

Another important source of suggestions for the second edition was the set of responses to two questionnaires sent out in September 1979. Names of respondents are too numerous to be listed separately here, but I am grateful to each of them for taking the time to provide their answers.

A particularly helpful set of reactions to the first edition came directly from students. Among those who wrote to me with their suggestions were Yoo Soo Hong (a Northwestern graduate student), Eunice Lee Morris (Washington University at St. Louis), and Thomas Yee (Stony Brook).

Perhaps most useful of all was the set of student reviews of the book, assigned as a class project by Herbert D. Werner (University of Missouri at St. Louis). Among the student responses that led directly to changes in the second edition were those of Eric Archer, Peter E. Bay, John Dohr, Brian E. Harper, Kathy Higgs, Patricia A. Hogan, Richard Olszewski, Ron O'Reilly, Joan E. Schneider, Johnny Webb, and Russell L. Wertz.

This book contains a great deal of data, some of it original, both in Appendix B and in the individual case studies. The student assistants who communicated with the computer to produce the data and graphs were Jon Frye, Ross Newman, and Don Williams. George Kahn produced the index.

The new sections of the book were typed with perfect accuracy, efficiency, and a high degree of cheerfulness by my secretary Joan Robinson. I am grateful also to Elizabeth H. Johnson for her help in meeting deadline crises.

Thanks go to Al Hockwalt, the Little, Brown economics editor, for nagging me to get the second edition finished and for organizing the production of the accompanying *Student Workbook*. Garret White, Editor-in-Chief of Little, Brown's College Division, was responsible not only for coordinating production in Boston but also for many of the detailed improvements that make the second edition a more attractive book than the first. The book editor, Elizabeth Schaaf, tied together all the elements of the production process with great efficiency and considerable patience.

Finally, thanks go to my wife Julie for putting up with a book that filled our luggage on vacations, created the litter of manuscript and galley proof in the house for days on end, and caused clatter to come from the typewriter too late on too many evenings. As always, her unfailing encouragement and welcome diversions made the book possible.

Robert J. Gordon

Evanston, Illinois
September 1980

Preface:
To the Student

Macroeconomics is one of the most important topics for college students, because the health of the economy will have an influence on your whole life. The overall level of employment and unemployment will determine the ease with which you find a job after college and with which you will be able to change jobs or obtain promotions in the future. The inflation rate will influence the interest rate you receive on your savings and pay when you borrow money, and also the extent to which the purchasing power of your savings will be eroded by higher prices.

This macroeconomics text will equip you with the principles you need to make sense out of the conflicting and contradictory discussions of economic conditions and policies in newspapers and news magazines. You will be better able to appraise the performance of the president and Congress, and to predict the impact of their policy actions on your family and business.

WHO SHOULD READ THIS BOOK?

Most college students taking this course will have taken a course in economic principles. But this book has been written to be read by *all* students, even those who have not previously enrolled in an economics course. How is this possible? In Chapters 1–3 we review material which is in every principles course. By the end of Chapter 3, all students will have learned the essential concepts they need to understand the material to be developed.

This book has been carefully designed to look and read like a principles book. The entire presentation is graphic, with simple ninth-grade algebra used only in the review of elementary ideas in Chapter 3. Examples are used frequently. Most chapters have one or more case studies to give you a breather from the analysis and to show how the ideas of the chapter can be applied to real-world episodes. New words are set off in boldface type and defined in the Glossary in the back of the book, thus easing vocabulary problems. And the diagrams in the first part of the book as well as the text description itself use numerical examples instead of mathematical symbols to show movement of the economy from one situation to another.

HOW TO READ THIS BOOK

Each chapter begins with an introduction, linking it to previous chapters, and ends with a "Summary" and "A Look Ahead," which link it to subsequent chapters. When you begin a chapter, first read the introduction to make sure you understand how the chapter differs from the previous ones. Then plan to read each chapter twice, first for the main points. After the first reading, study the summary and then try to answer the questions, marking those points which you do not understand. Finally, go back for a second reading, paying special attention to the discussion of issues which you may not have grasped fully at first.

Always try to write out answers to the questions. Another aid to comprehension is to try to work through the chapter and substitute a different numerical example for the one used in the text. Those of you who have purchased the accompanying *Student Workbook* will find that the path to greater comprehension has been laid out for you in detail.

If you should get lost in the course of reading the text, remember that there are built-in study aids to help. If you don't understand a particular section, turn to the Summary at the end of the chapter. If you forget the meaning of a word, turn to the Glossary at the back of the book. (The Glossary will also help you tackle assigned outside readings.) And there is a Guide to Symbols on the endpapers of the book to help you with the alphabetical symbols that are used in equations or in diagrams as labels.

OPTIONAL MATERIAL

Footnotes and chapter appendices have been provided as a place to put more difficult or less important material. Your instructor will decide whether or not an appendix is to be assigned, but even if not assigned, feel free to tackle it on your own when you have mastered the ideas in the body of the chapter. Footnotes contain qualifications, bibliographical references (valuable if you ever need to write a term paper on these topics), and cross-references to related material and diagrams elsewhere in the book.

Finally, notice that tables in the back of the book contain historical data starting with the year 1900 and updated to mid-1980. These figures can help you determine what was going on in periods not covered by the case studies or can be used in outside assignments and term papers. Don't forget possible applications in history, political science, and sociology courses.

Macroeconomics

Part I

Introduction and Measurement

1

What Is Macroeconomics?

The cruel choice between two evils—
unemployment and inflation—has become
the major economic issue of the day.

—James Tobin and Leonard Ross[1]

1-1 THE PUZZLES TO BE EXPLAINED

HOW MACROECONOMIC CONDITIONS DETERMINE OUR WELL-BEING

Macroeconomics is about the big economic issues that determine your own economic well-being, as well as that of your family and everyone you know.[2] *Macro* comes from a Greek word meaning "large." Just as a "macrocosm" is the universe itself, macroeconomics is the study of the major economic "totals" or **aggregates.** Among these crucial economic aggregates that determine our well-being are total wealth, money, income, unemployment, inflation, and the value of the dollar when we exchange it for other currencies abroad.

Each of these aggregates shares the feature that it is an amount that is summed up or "aggregated" over all U.S. households and firms. We ask not about the income of Tom Jones or Ron Smith, but about the total national income of all U.S. citizens. We do not ask whether Tom or Ron is unemployed, nor do we inquire into their individual circumstances. Instead, we want to learn why the *total* number of unemployed individuals is so large, why that number is higher now than in earlier decades, and how some other countries manage to have a smaller number of unemployed in relation to their populations. We do not concern ourselves with the prices of *individual* products such as peanuts and lettuce but rather with the rate at which the average price level of *all* goods and services is increasing.

---

[1] "Living with Inflation," *The New York Review of Books*, vol. 16 (May 6, 1971), p. 23.
[2] Terms set in bold type are defined in the Glossary at the back of the book.

It is easy to be interested in macroeconomics. Newspapers and popular magazines, as well as radio and television programs, offer discussions of macroeconomic issues every day. Why? Because macroeconomic conditions determine how much the average family has to spend, and whether that family can make economic progress or will fall behind. When total income and production are rising, business firms can afford to pay higher wages without charging higher prices. When total employment is rising, unemployed people find it relatively easy to obtain jobs, and family members who have been at home have ample opportunities to obtain extra income by taking full-time or part-time jobs. But when inflation is high, individuals and institutions find that the value of their savings is eroding and that their income buys less and less, so it is no wonder everyone abhors inflation and hopes for stable prices.

High and rising incomes, full employment, and price stability—these objectives have been official goals of government policy since the passage of the Employment Act of 1946, a landmark piece of legislation that reflected the nation's determination never again to suffer a Great Depression. Ever since the passage of the Employment Act, the subject area of macroeconomics has included the study of government policy. How successful has the government been in its attempt to achieve the goals of high and rising incomes, full employment, and price stability? We shall see that the government has made many mistakes, and by attempting to understand *why* these mistakes occurred, we will be able to decide whether an improved performance in the future by government policymakers is possible or likely.

HOW MACROECONOMICS DIFFERS FROM MICROECONOMICS

Most topics in economics can be placed in one of two categories: macroeconomics and microeconomics. Just as *macro* comes from a Greek word meaning "large," so *micro* comes from a Greek word meaning "small." A microscope is an instrument for inspecting small things, and microeconomics is devoted to the study of relationships among individual households, firms, and products. Microeconomics is concerned with the determination of the price of one product in relation to another—for example, why does a Cadillac cost 10,000 times as much as a package of razor blades? It also attempts to explain differences in individual incomes and the sources of income inequality—for example, why is a professor's salary more than that of a secretary but less than that of a university president?

Macroeconomics is neither more nor less important than microeconomics, and it is not necessary to study one before the other. The main areas of macroeconomic concern—total income, unemployment, and inflation—are more familiar to the public because of continuing political debate, media attention, and our group experience of their influence. Macroeconomic analysis has developed as an independent subject, free of the need to base its conclusions on microeconomics. Nevertheless, a full understanding of several macroeconomic topics requires examination of their "microeconomic foundations." Among these topics are the reasons why wages and prices do not respond instantly to changes in economic conditions, why the demand for money depends on the interest rate, and why total consumption spending depends on total income.

Economic theory attempts to reach an understanding of the economy by a process of simplification. Among the millions of individuals, firms, and products in the economy, theory throws a spotlight on just a few key relations. There is no conflict between microeconomics and macroeconomics; instead, they differ by throwing their spotlight on different relationships. Microeconomics would examine the impact of a change in the personal income tax on an individual household by making the simplifying assumption that total national income and employment remain constant. Macroeconomics would examine the impact of a change in the personal income tax on these national aggregates, while ignoring differences between individual households.

It is this process of simplification that makes the study of economics so exciting. By learning a few basic relations, we can ignore hundreds of irrelevant details in the news and notice a few key items that contain hints of where the economy is going. We also begin to understand which of our national and personal economic goals can be attained, which are incompatible, and which are "pie-in-the-sky."

1-2 NOMINAL GNP, REAL GNP, AND THE GNP DEFLATOR

WHAT IS GROSS NATIONAL PRODUCT?

Probably the most frequently used abbreviation in macroeconomics is GNP, which stands for **gross national product,** the value of all currently produced goods and services sold on the market during a particular time interval. Gross national product or GNP includes consumer purchases of food, clothing, gasoline, new automobiles, and haircuts and other services; includes purchases of machinery and equipment by business firms; includes residential structures bought by households and firms as well as non-residential structures (shopping centers, factories, office buildings, warehouses); and also includes purchases of goods and services by government (federal, state, and local) as well as the excess of our exports over our imports. GNP can be most easily thought of as the *total amount of current production.*

GNP is computed by a process of adding up all the different types of current production. When we add up the actual amount of production, we call this **nominal GNP.** The word **nominal** means the actual amount purchased at current prices.

REAL AND NOMINAL MAGNITUDES

Nominal amounts are not very useful for economic analysis because they can increase either when people buy more physical goods and services

—more cars, steaks, and haircuts—or when prices rise. An increase in my nominal spending on consumption goods from $20,000 in 1981 to $25,000 in 1982 might indicate that I became able to buy more items, or it could simply reflect an increase in prices for the same type and number of items purchased in 1981.

Are we better off? Or have price increases chewed up all our higher spending, leaving us no better off than before? Changes in nominal magnitudes cannot answer these questions; they hide more than they reveal. So economists concentrate on changes in real magnitudes, which eliminate the influence of year-to-year changes in prices and reflect true changes in the number, size, and quality of items purchased.

A **real** magnitude is the value expressed in the price of an arbitrarily chosen "base year." If the base year is 1972, my real 1981 consumption "in 1972 prices" represents the amount my actual 1981 purchases would have cost if I had been able to buy each item at its 1972 price. For instance, if all prices doubled between 1972 and 1981, then my 1981 purchases of $20,000 would have cost only $10,000 in 1972 prices. Thus my real consumption in 1981 measured in 1972 prices is $10,000.

Any "real" concept measured in the prices of a single **base year** is adjusted for the effects of year-to-year changes in prices. The real gross national product (GNP) line in Figure 1-1 for each year (for instance, 1910 = $185.6 billion) is measured in 1972 prices and expresses what the production of each year would have cost at 1972 prices. **Real GNP** is sometimes called **real "output"** or "production." Because the prices of most items were higher in 1972 than in 1910, as a result of inflation, real 1910 GNP in 1972 prices is a larger number ($185.6 billion) than the number of dollars people actually spent on GNP in 1910 (nominal 1910 GNP = $35.4 billion).

Later on we will discuss other real magnitudes, such as real consumption and the real money supply. An alternate label for real magnitudes is "constant-dollar," in contrast to nominal magnitudes, which are usually called "current-dollar." In other words:

	Alternate labels for magnitudes		
Items measured in prices of a single year; for instance, 1972	Constant-dollar	or	Real
Items measured in actual prices paid in each separate year	Current-dollar	or	Nominal

The thin black line labeled nominal GNP in Figure 1-1 indicates the actual number of dollars spent on goods and services in 1910 and all other

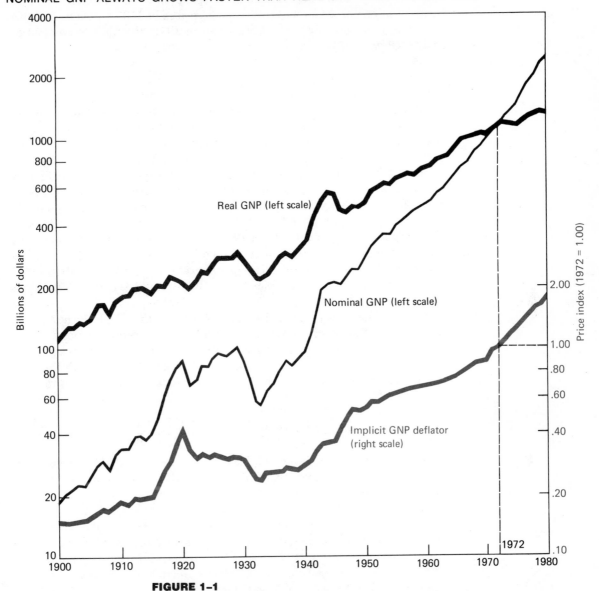

FIGURE 1–1

Nominal GNP, Real GNP, and the Implicit GNP Deflator, 1900–80

Notice how the nominal GNP line lies below the real GNP line before 1972 but lies above the real GNP line after 1972. This reflects the fact that the current prices used to measure nominal GNP were lower before 1972 than the 1972 prices used to measure real GNP. After 1972 the current prices used to measure nominal GNP were higher than the 1972 prices used to measure real GNP. For instance, the price level in 1980 was 80 percent higher than in 1972. Notice how the nominal GNP line crosses the real GNP line in 1972, the same year that the GNP deflator attains the value of 1.00. This occurs because in 1972 (and no other year) the prices used to measure nominal GNP and real GNP are the same.

Nominal GNP, Real GNP, and the GNP Deflator **7**

years of this century.[3] Actual nominal spending in 1910 was only $35.4 billion, as compared to real GNP in 1972 prices of $185.6 billion. Because prices in 1910 were so much lower than in 1972, the ratio of nominal to real GNP was only a small fraction.

THE GNP DEFLATOR

An extremely important feature of the relation between nominal and real GNP is evident in Figure 1-1. Before 1972 nominal GNP is lower than real GNP, because of the simple fact that prices have generally risen from year to year. Thus in years before 1972 prices were lower than in 1972. So nominal GNP expressed in the actual prices of years before 1972 is a smaller magnitude than real GNP expressed in the prices of 1972. As an example, consider spending on round steak, which cost $0.20 per pound in 1910 but $1.00 per pound in 1972. If every other product exhibited a similar increase in price between 1910 and 1972, we would find that 1910 real GNP measured in 1972 prices would be *five times* larger than nominal GNP for 1910. And indeed this happens to be true, with real 1910 GNP ($185.6 billion) about five times higher than nominal 1910 GNP ($35.4 billion).

A special name is given to the ratio of nominal to real GNP; it is called the **implicit GNP deflator.** The deflator tells us the ratio of prices in any single year (say, 1910) to the price level in 1972. For instance, the implicit GNP deflator in 1910 was 0.191 — the ratio of actual nominal GNP ($35.4 billion) to spending for the same year measured in 1972 prices ($185.6 billion):

$$\text{implicit GNP deflator for 1910} = 0.191 = \frac{\$35.4 \text{ billion}}{\$185.6 \text{ billion}} = \frac{\text{nominal GNP}}{\text{real GNP}}$$

Notice in Figure 1-1 that the red line displays the implicit GNP deflator for every year since 1900; you will find that the 1910 value of the GNP deflator is approximately 0.191 (read this off the right-hand red vertical scale in Figure 1-1).

There is only one year when nominal GNP and real GNP are the same. Which year? Only during 1972, when the actual prices used to measure nominal GNP equal the 1972 prices that are always used to measure real GNP. It is easy to see that the GNP deflator in 1972 must be 1.00, the ratio of nominal to real GNP, and you will find in Figure 1-1 that the GNP deflator is exactly 1.00 in 1972:

$$\text{implicit GNP deflator for 1972} = 1.00 = \frac{\$1171.1 \text{ billion}}{\$1171.1 \text{ billion}} = \frac{\text{nominal GNP}}{\text{real GNP}}$$

---

[3] The vertical scale in Figure 1-1 is called "logarithmic" and makes increases of an equal *percentage* amount appear as the same vertical distance on the graph. For more on logarithmic scales, which are used throughout this book, see the first question for discussion at the end of Chapter 1.

Prices in every year since 1972 have been higher than the prices registered in 1972—this is the phenomenon we call **inflation,** a steady rise in the GNP deflator that is shared by most products. For instance, the GNP deflator in 1980 was 1.81, indicating that on average prices were *81 percent higher* than in the 1972 base year. Since the GNP deflator in 1980 was 1.81, this means that nominal GNP in 1980 was $2561 billion, or 81 percent higher than the real 1980 GNP of $1415 billion:

$$\text{implicit GNP deflator for 1980} = 1.81 = \frac{\$2561 \text{ billion}}{\$1415 \text{ billion}} = \frac{\text{nominal GNP}}{\text{real GNP}}$$

A crucial feature of Figure 1-1 is *economic instability.* Before the 1950s both nominal GNP and real GNP went down as well as up, especially during the Great Depression of the 1930s. Even during the postwar years—the last three decades—real GNP has behaved very erratically. In some years real GNP has increased rapidly, providing higher incomes and ample job opportunities, as in 1955, 1965, and 1978. In other years real GNP has actually fallen, reducing average family income and throwing many individuals out of work, as in 1958, 1970, 1975, and 1980. A major task for anyone studying macroeconomics is to understand the causes of economic instability and to assess alternative cures.

1-3 INFLATION, "NATURAL" REAL GNP, AND THE "NATURAL" UNEMPLOYMENT RATE

THE INFLATION RATE

Recall that the implicit GNP deflator is the average price level in the economy, defined as the ratio of prices actually charged each year to those charged in 1972. Inflation is a sustained upward movement in the aggregate price level; thus when the GNP deflator in Figure 1-1 increases, we have inflation. Only rarely in the twentieth century has the GNP deflator fallen, and this is called **deflation.** To calculate the **inflation rate** we simply compute the percentage rate of change of the GNP deflator. For instance, the GNP deflator was 1.00 in 1972 and 1.058 in 1973, and its percentage change between 1972 and 1973 was:

$$\frac{1973 \text{ GNP deflator} - 1972 \text{ GNP deflator}}{1972 \text{ GNP deflator}} = \frac{1.058 - 1.00}{1.00} = .058$$

or 5.8 percent.

WHY TOO MUCH OR TOO LITTLE REAL GNP IS UNDESIRABLE

When we examine the wiggling real GNP line of Figure 1-1, we naturally search for a standard of comparison. Was real GNP too high or too low in 1980? We need to decide on a criterion for a "normal" or "desirable" level of real GNP. Later we shall study the "activist" view that the main task of government policy is to stimulate real GNP when it is below this normal level, and to try to depress real GNP when it is above this normal level. We shall also ask with critics of the activists whether it is wise for government policy to undertake this ambitious objective.

To decide what is normal, we need to ask why real GNP changes so much. As is evident in Figure 1-1, real GNP grows from year to year on average. This occurs because more people are born each year than die (and also in the United States more people immigrate than emigrate). Thus each year there is a growing number of people who can contribute to total production, or GNP. In addition, each year business firms build more structures and machinery than wear out, further adding to the capacity to produce real GNP. Finally, innovations and research yield new methods of production and new products that raise the amount the economy can produce. Thus a basic feature of "normal" production is that it grows from year to year.

Why can't the economy simply produce as much as possible each year? Unfortunately, maximum production tends to make inflation worse. When business firms are producing "flat out," they need workers desperately and are willing to pay large wage increases to entice new workers to join their firms and to keep existing workers from quitting. But these wage increases raise business costs and lead business firms to raise prices.[4] Thus too much production is inflationary and must be avoided if the overall inflation rate is to be kept from accelerating.

It is also easy to see that too little production is undesirable as well. Low levels of production mean layoffs, unemployment, low incomes for employees on commission, and a decline in the overall standard of living. Below a certain level, a low real GNP also tends to make the inflation rate slow down. A drop in real GNP and an increase in the number of unemployed may succeed in cutting the overall rate of inflation (rate of increase in prices) from, let us say, 9 percent per year to 8 percent per year.

REAL GNP: ACTUAL AND NATURAL

Between a high production level that causes the inflation rate to speed up, and a low production level that causes the inflation rate to slow down, there is some intermediate "compromise level" that keeps the inflation rate

---

[4] As we shall learn, another reason that high production causes inflation has to do with the foreign exchange rate. When production and income inside the United States are high, we purchase more goods from abroad. Foreigners find themselves with a greater supply of dollars received as payment by U.S. importers. As with any commodity in excess supply, the price of the dollar then declines. Americans find that their dollar buys less abroad, and that foreign products (French wine, Japanese automobiles) cost more. This tendency for the prices of foreign products to rise adds to domestic U.S. inflation and leads to a regular tendency for high U.S. levels of production and income to aggravate U.S. inflation.

constant. This intermediate level of real GNP has been called "natural," a situation in which there is no tendency for inflation to accelerate or decelerate. It is important to remember that the natural level of real GNP is compatible with *any* inflation rate, but an inflation inherited from the past will show no tendency to speed up or slow down as long as real GNP is maintained at its natural level.[5] For instance, if we inherit an inflation rate of 8 percent, then the inflation rate will remain at 8 percent if actual real GNP is equal to **"natural" real GNP.** If actual real GNP is higher than this, inflation will speed up, say to 9 or 10 percent. If actual real GNP is less than this, inflation will slow down, say to 7 or 6 percent.

The top frame of Figure 1-2 illustrates this basic relationship between actual and natural real GNP. The black solid line is natural real GNP and rises steadily as population growth, added factories and equipment, and innovations raise the economy's capacity to produce real GNP. The red line is actual real GNP. Starting at time period t_0, actual real GNP is equal to natural real GNP, then falls below, and finally rises above natural real GNP. During the period of low actual real GNP, designated by the gray area, the inflation rate slows down. During the period of high actual real GNP, designated by the pink area, the inflation rate accelerates. Sometimes the condition of excessive actual real GNP is called "an overheated economy," a designation you can link to the pink area on the diagram.

UNEMPLOYMENT: ACTUAL AND NATURAL

When actual production is low, people lose their jobs, and the unemployment rate is high. This is shown in the bottom frame of Figure 1-2, where the red line shows the actual **unemployment rate,** the percent of the labor force that is unemployed, and the black line shows the **natural rate of unemployment** that is compatible with steady inflation.

Notice that the period of low production, shown by the gray area in the upper frame, occurs at the same time as the period of high unemployment, shown by the gray area in the lower frame. Then the period of high real GNP when the economy is "overheated," designated by the pink area in the top frame, occurs at the same time as a period of low unemployment, shown by the pink area in the lower frame.

This diagram is an unhappy one, because it summarizes a basic dilemma faced by policymakers who are struggling to meet the goals of full employment and price stability. If the inflation rate is higher than they would like, they can slow it down only by trying to achieve a lower level of actual real GNP and higher unemployment. If they try to provide jobs for everyone, and keep the unemployment rate low, then inflation will accelerate. Much of America's inflation problem originated in the late 1960s, when policymakers allowed the actual unemployment rate to stay below the natural unemployment rate for five straight years.

---

[5] The phrase *natural rate of unemployment* was introduced in Milton Friedman, "The Role of Monetary Policy," *American Economic Review*, vol. 58 (March 1968), pp. 1–17.

TOO MUCH REAL GNP MAKES INFLATION ACCELERATE, BUT TOO LITTLE REAL GNP
CREATES HIGH UNEMPLOYMENT

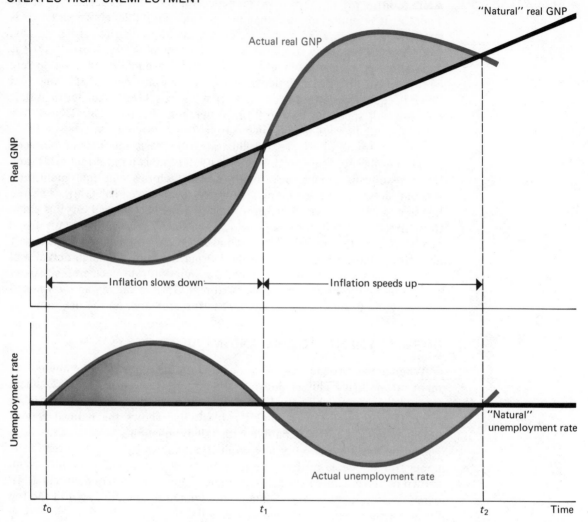

FIGURE 1–2

The Relation between "Natural" and Actual Real GNP
and Unemployment

In the upper frame the solid black line shows the steady growth of "natural" real
GNP, the amount the economy can produce without causing an acceleration of
inflation. The red line shows the path of actual real GNP, which first declines,
then rises rapidly, and finally levels off. In the region designated by the gray area,
actual real GNP is below natural real GNP, so inflation slows down. But in the
region designated by the pink area, actual real GNP is higher than natural real
GNP, so inflation speeds up. The bottom frame shows that whenever real GNP is
high, unemployment is low, and vice versa. Notice also that when actual and
natural real GNP are equal in the top frame (at time periods t_0, t_1, and t_2), the
actual and natural unemployment rates are equal in the lower frame.

1-4 THE HISTORICAL RECORD: REAL GNP, UNEMPLOYMENT, AND INFLATION

REAL GNP

Figure 1-3 is arranged just like Figure 1-2. But whereas Figure 1-2 shows hypothetical relationships, Figure 1-3 shows the actual historical record for the twentieth century. In the top frame the solid black line is natural real GNP, an estimate of the amount the economy could have produced each year without causing an acceleration of inflation.

Natural real output in the United States has grown steadily throughout this century for two basic reasons. First, attainable employment has increased as a result of immigration and a birth rate higher than the death rate. Second, each worker has become more productive, thanks to investment in machines, plants, education, and research. Chapter 18 discusses the slowdown in U.S. growth after 1973.

The red line in the top frame plots actual real GNP, the total production of goods and services each year measured in the constant prices of 1972. The red actual real GNP line in Figure 1-3 is identical to the real GNP line in Figure 1-1. See if you can pick out those years when actual and natural real GNP are roughly equal. Some of these years were 1902, 1911, 1924, 1964, 1972, and 1978.

In years marked by gray shading, actual real GNP fell below natural real GNP. A maximum deficiency occurred in 1933 when actual real GNP was only 64.2 percent of natural, and about 35.8 percent of natural was wasted. Factories were idle, many workers were unemployed, and even employed workers were less productive because they had less to do. Before 1929 and since 1950 these intervals of substantial output deficiency, shown by gray shading, have been much less serious than in the Great Depression, but nevertheless have added up to billions in lost output.

In some years actual real GNP exceeded natural real GNP, as marked off by the shaded pink areas. This occurred mainly in wartime periods, particularly during World War I (1917–18), World War II (1942–45), the Korean War (1951–53), and the first half of the U.S. involvement in the Vietnam War (1965–69).

UNEMPLOYMENT

In the bottom frame of Figure 1-3 the red line plots the actual unemployment rate. By far the most extreme episode was the Great Depression, when the actual unemployment rate remained above 10 percent for ten straight years, 1931–40. It is not surprising that the Depression left such a profound mark on economic theory, government policy, and political alignments; the masses of unemployed of the 1930s had no welfare programs or unemployment insurance to ease their misery.

The trauma of the Great Depression led Congress to pass the Employment Act of 1946, which pledged to maintain both full employment and

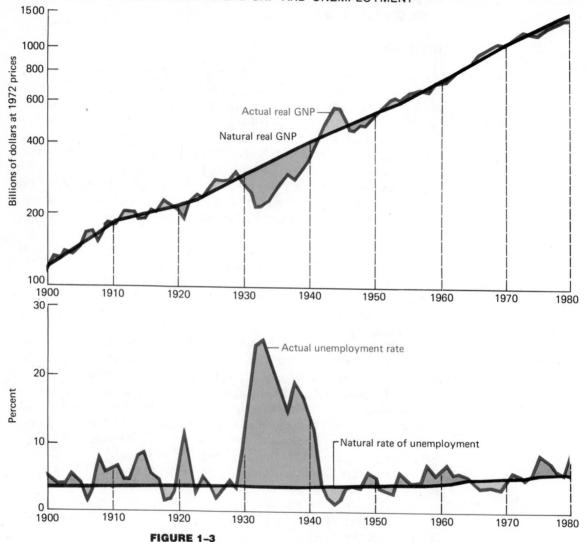

FIGURE 1–3

Real GNP and Unemployment, 1900–80

A historical report card for two important economic magnitudes during this century. In the top frame the black line indicates natural real GNP, which has grown throughout this century. The red line shows actual real GNP, which was well below natural real GNP during the Great Depression of the 1930s and well above it during World War II. In the bottom frame the black line indicates the natural rate of unemployment, and the red line indicates the actual unemployment rate. Actual unemployment was much higher during the Great Depression of the 1930s than at any other time during the century. Notice how periods of high actual unemployment like the 1930s are designated by gray areas in the bottom frame that occur simultaneously with periods of low actual real GNP in the top frame. Pink areas indicate times when the economy was "overheated," with high actual real GNP and low unemployment.

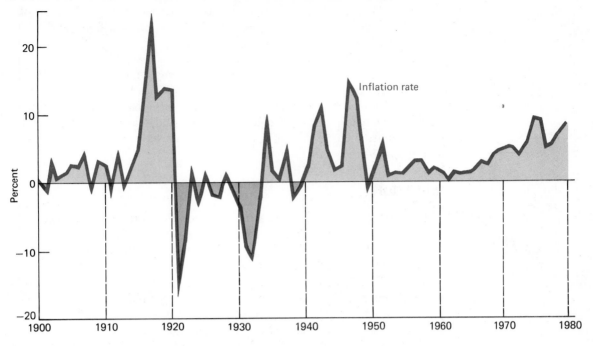

FIGURE 1–4

The Inflation Rate, 1900–80

A historical report card on the rate of change of the GNP deflator during this century. During the periods designated by the pink areas, the inflation rate was positive, and the GNP deflator rose. During the periods designated by the gray areas, the inflation rate was negative, and the GNP deflator fell. Before World War II prices both rose and fell, with no clear tendency to go in one direction or another. But since World War II the inflation rate has been positive every year but one (1949). Inflation has clearly become a much more serious problem since 1966.

stable prices. Since 1946 the unemployment rate has never been zero, but it has been lower on the average, and also considerably more stable, than during either the Great Depression or the earlier period 1900–29. Even in the 1974–75 recession, the worst period for unemployment since World War II, the peak rate for any month was 9.0 percent, lower than in recessions occurring between 1900 and 1921. But an unfortunate accompaniment to this relatively favorable level of unemployment has been steady and persistent inflation, especially since 1965.

The black line in the bottom frame of Figure 1-3 estimates the natural rate of unemployment, the minimum attainable level of unemployment that is compatible with avoiding an acceleration of inflation. The natural unemployment rate is a "danger zone" that sets a lower limit on the level of actual unemployment that can be attained without accelerating inflation. The pink shaded areas mark years when unemployment fell below the natural rate, as in 1917–19 and 1966–69. The gray shaded areas mark years when unemployment exceeded the natural rate.

Notice now the relationship between the top and bottom frames of Figure 1-3. The gray areas in both frames designate periods of low production and real GNP, and high unemployment, such as the Great Depression of the 1930s and the "Great Recession" of 1975. The pink areas in both frames designate periods of high production and real GNP, and low unemployment, such as World War II and other wartime periods (1951–53 and 1965–69).

INFLATION

Figure 1-4 illustrates the year-to-year change in the GNP deflator since 1900 — that is, the percentage inflation rate. The red inflation rate line in Figure 1-4 shows the percentage rate of change in the red implicit GNP deflator line in Figure 1-1. When the deflator rises rapidly, as in 1917–18 or 1973–74 (Figure 1-1), its rate of change is high (Figure 1-4). The inflation rate has fluctuated widely. Some periods have been marked by nearly stable prices — an inflation rate close to zero — as in 1900–14, 1923–29, and 1958–63. Other periods have exhibited short, sharp extremes of price movement, especially during and after World War I (1916–19), before and after World War II (1941–42 and 1946–48), at the outbreak of the Korean War (1951), and, more recently, in 1973–74 and 1979–80.

Let us now compare the historical record of inflation displayed in Figure 1-4 with that for unemployment and real GNP in Figure 1-3. We would expect that when real GNP was high and unemployment low — in those periods designated by pink shading in Figure 1-3 — inflation would speed up. If you look closely, you will find that the period between 1965 and 1969 (the peak years of spending on the Vietnam War) is characterized by pink shading on the real output and unemployment diagrams, and an acceleration of inflation from about 2 percent to 5 percent per year. Similarly, real output was relatively low from 1958 to 1963, as shown by the gray shading on the output diagram, and inflation slowed down from about 3 percent to 1 percent per year over the same period.

But there are other years when the relationship between inflation and real output is different. In 1973–74, for instance, inflation worsened while real output fell. The same thing happened again in 1979–80. One of the most important questions to be explained in this book is why in the 1970s both inflation and unemployment became worse at the same time. Much of the problem, we shall find, has been due to the higher oil prices charged by the Organization of Petroleum Exporting Countries (**OPEC**).

Other puzzling features of the U.S. inflation experience need to be explained. For instance, real GNP was very low and unemployment very high during the Great Depression, as shown by the large gray area in Figure 1-3 for the 1930s. Yet prices did not continually fall throughout the 1930s;

after an initial drop from 1929 to 1933, the price level rose from 1933 to 1937. Economists are still debating the reasons why prices rose after 1933 despite widespread joblessness.[6]

1-5 AGGREGATE DEMAND AND SUPPLY

In our attempt to gain an understanding of the causes of unemployment and inflation, we shall find it very helpful to distinguish between **aggregate demand** and **aggregate supply.** Aggregate demand is simply the total amount of spending on goods and services measured in current prices; thus aggregate demand is just another name for nominal GNP. A fundamental proposition of macroeconomics is that changes in aggregate demand—that is, in total nominal spending on goods and services—are the key to explaining why actual output and unemployment deviated from their natural (best attainable) levels in the periods marked by the gray and pink shaded areas in Figure 1-3. Since *unstable* aggregate demand is the basic macroeconomic problem—with undesired decreases in demand causing excessive unemployment and undesired increases in demand causing excessive inflation—the basic task of macroeconomic policy is to stabilize aggregate demand.

WHY SUPPLY-SIDE ECONOMICS HAS BECOME SO IMPORTANT

But even if aggregate demand could be made to grow at a steady rate, we still might have economic problems. An ideal world would be one with stable prices, so that every increase in nominal spending on goods and services would be automatically translated to an increase in real GNP. But the same increase in nominal spending might also be fully absorbed by price increases, leaving nothing left over to provide real GNP growth. Our study of aggregate supply asks how changes in nominal GNP are divided up between changes in prices and in real GNP. When something happens to raise the cost of production without changing aggregate demand conditions—for instance, a decision by the OPEC countries to raise the price of oil—we may find that prices rise and real GNP falls even though aggregate demand may be completely stable. This type of event, called a **supply shock,** was very infrequent before 1973. But since that date supply shocks have been important, and the need to understand these events and design policy procedures to minimize their harmful impact has caused a revolution in macroeconomic thinking.

Macroeconomics courses used to concentrate almost exclusively on aggregate demand. When total spending was too low, policymakers were

---

[6] An attempt to explain the ups and downs of the inflation rate in Figure 1-4 is contained in Robert J. Gordon, "A Consistent Characterization of a Near-Century of Price Behavior," *American Economic Review,* vol. 70 (May 1980), pp. 243–249. While this paper is short and not difficult, the student will find it easier to read after mastering Chapters 8 and 9 of this book.

called upon to raise aggregate demand. When total spending was too high, restrictive policy actions were required. It was assumed that the supply of goods and services would automatically respond to changes in aggregate demand.

But in the 1970s this convenient assumption began to lose validity. Not only did the oil price increases engineered by the OPEC cartel worsen both inflation and unemployment, but the overall increase in the U.S. standard of living was held down by sluggish productivity growth and inadequate investment in new plants and equipment. This new concern with the inadequate growth in America's capacity to produce goods and services has also encouraged U.S. economists to pay more attention to the performance of other industrialized nations abroad, especially Japan, Germany, and France. While some foreign nations share many of America's problems, in others there has been a superior record of achieving low inflation and low unemployment during the 1970s, as well as faster productivity growth than recorded in the United States.

1-6 STABILIZATION POLICY AND CONFLICTING GOALS

Macroeconomic analysis has two tasks: to analyze the causes of changes in important aggregates and to predict the consequences of alternative policy changes. In policy discussions the group of aggregates that society cares most about—inflation, unemployment, the long-term growth rate of natural output—are called "goals" or **target variables.** When the target variables deviate from desired values, alternative **policy instruments** can be used in an attempt to achieve needed changes. Instruments fall into three broad categories: **monetary policies,** which include control of the money supply and interest rates; **fiscal policies,** which include changes in government expenditures and tax rates; and a third miscellaneous group, which includes wage and price controls and manpower policy.

THE ROLE OF STABILIZATION POLICY

Macroeconomic analysis begins with a simple message: either type of **stabilization policy,** monetary or fiscal, can be used to control aggregate demand and to offset undesired changes in private spending. The effects of monetary and fiscal policy on the price level and on real aggregate output (real GNP) are the main subject of Part II. Fiscal policy can raise output and employment by increasing government spending that creates jobs through government hiring. Or fiscal policy can stimulate private spending by cutting tax rates, thus inducing a higher level of private purchases, production, and employment. A monetary policy stimulus to output and employment takes the form of an increase in the money supply, which reduces interest rates and may in turn boost stock prices and make lending institutions more willing to grant credit.

This initial message of macroeconomics, that stabilization policy can smooth undesired fluctuations in aggregate demand, is only part of the story. We can assume that policy stimulus should be applied in a recession when unemployment is high and inflation is absent and that policy restraint is required when inflation is raging and unemployment is low, but we must go further. What is to be done when *both* unemployment and inflation are excessive? The price level increased throughout the recessions of 1969–70, 1973–75, and 1980. In the midst of such stagflation, should stabilization policy adopt a stance of stimulus to fight unemployment or restraint to fight inflation? Why inflation and unemployment coexist and some possible solutions are discussed in Part III. We will learn, for instance, that the natural levels of unemployment and output in Figure 1-3 are neither optimal nor immutable, but can be improved by application of particular policy innovations *that influence aggregate supply.*

There are further problems in applying stabilization policy. It may not be possible to control aggregate demand instantly and precisely. A policy stimulus intended to fight current unemployment might boost aggregate demand only after a long and uncertain delay, by which time the stimulus might not be needed. The impact of different policy changes may also be highly uncertain. Some economists argue that the lags and uncertainties inherent in stabilization policy are such serious obstacles that policymakers should avoid "fine tuning," which shifts the setting of policy back and forth frequently between stimulus and restraint, and follow a "rule" requiring a constant growth rate of the money supply. The debate between policy "fine tuning" or "activism" on the one hand and a monetary "rule" on the other is a central theme in our consideration of monetary and fiscal policy in Parts IV and V.

RELATION BETWEEN THEORY AND POLICY

The first third of this book uses economic theory to examine the causes of changes in output, unemployment, and the price level. Instead of just describing a collection of unrelated economic facts, theory isolates the important economic variables that help explain inflation and unemployment. Theory also creates useful generalizations to describe the relationships between groups of variables, such as consumption and income or money and interest rates. We can then look at the facts to test whether the generalizations of theory have predictive power.

Economists use theory for two quite separate purposes: for **"positive"** economics — *explaining* the behavior of important variables — and for **"normative"** economics — *recommending* changes in economic policy. Economists have developed theories that explain most of the changes observed in the national unemployment rate or the rate of inflation and why interest rates are now higher than they were twenty years ago. Most disagreements among economists no longer focus on different explanations of these major phenomena; rather they center on the proper conduct of economic policy, a normative issue.

Most policy disagreements stem from the incompatibility of worthy economic goals. Most people would like the price level to be stable and the unemployment rate to be close to zero. But this state of nirvana cannot be achieved instantly, if ever. Macroeconomics, like economics in general, is the science of *choice* in the face of limitations for each of the possible alternatives. For example, economists differ on the relative importance of reducing inflation versus the alternative of reducing unemployment.

CLOSED AND OPEN ECONOMIES

Most of the macroeconomic analysis developed in this book applies to a **closed economy,** which ignores the flow of labor, goods, and money to and from other nations. Although U.S. foreign trade is immense, with exports and imports of more than $250 billion, most U.S. macroeconomic problems can be understood adequately without special consideration of international trade and payments. The domestic part of our economy is so huge that interactions with foreign nations are of secondary importance. The major exception has been the profound influence on the U.S. economy of sharp increases in the prices of imported products, such as oil in 1973–74 and 1979–80 (less important examples are price increases for sugar in 1974 and coffee in 1976–77).

Although international complications play a relatively minor role in U.S. macroeconomics, a discussion of international economic policy can be found in Chapter 19, which examines the determinants of the exchange rate for U.S. dollars, Canadian dollars, British pounds sterling, Japanese yen, and other currencies. We will learn how foreign trade weakens the effects of domestic stabilization policy in an **open economy,** and in some cases may render it completely impotent. Small nations like the Netherlands and Belgium, where more than half of the GNP consists of exports, cannot stabilize their economies as easily as the United States. But U.S. policymakers can benefit from knowledge of international economics. For instance, they can discover that changing foreign exchange rates will alter the impact of both monetary and fiscal policy on real output and on the domestic price level.

1-7 DEVELOPMENT OF MODERN MACROECONOMICS: POST-KEYNESIANS AND MONETARISTS

Most of the analysis in this book has been developed by economists writing since the 1936 publication of John Maynard Keynes' revolutionary *The General Theory of Employment, Interest and Money.* Keynes broke a new trail, discarding obsolete theories that had no explanation for unemployment (a rather glaring defect in the conditions of 1936!).[7] The de-

---

[7] When the U.S. unemployment rate was 17.0 percent; see Figure 1-3.

velopment of macroeconomic theory since the Keynesian revolution has emphasized the inherent instability of a private economy operating free of government control and the need for countercyclical government intervention to stabilize trends toward booms and recessions.[8] The Keynesian revolution was a revolt against an outmoded "classical" (pre-Keynesian) approach. "Classical" thinking led to policy actions in the Great Depression that are presently condemned by economists of all schools of thought. Under Herbert Hoover, fiscal policy aggravated the Depression by *raising* taxes 50 percent, directly opposite to the modern recommendation of fiscal stimulus in a recession.[9] Even worse, the money supply was allowed to decline by 31 percent between 1929 and 1933, and nothing was done to stop the panic and loss of confidence caused by repeated waves of bank failures.

You may well ask: "What has gone wrong? If all this post-Keynesian economic thinking is so great, why were the problems of unemployment and inflation more serious in the 1970s than in any period since World War II? Has economic theory been proved wrong?"

After the tools of post-Keynesian macroeconomic analysis have been explained, you will see that they are powerful instruments for diagnosing the underlying causes of changes in output and spotlighting the effects of changes in government monetary, expenditure, or tax policies on output. The major problems of the 1960s and 1970s were caused not by the inability to understand what determined changes in output, but by three other factors: an overly optimistic approach to inflation, the impact of supply shocks, and policy mistakes.

UNDERESTIMATING INFLATION

In the late 1960s most economists misunderstood the inflationary consequences that alternative paths of output would bring about. They thought unemployment could be pushed down to 3.5 or 4.0 percent with only minor inflationary results. A group of economists called **monetarists** protested against this sanguine assumption of post-Keynesian economists and argued that the acceleration of growth in the **money supply** needed to achieve lower unemployment would cause an acceleration of inflation. A major achievement of the monetarist counterrevolution was to show that any attempt to hold unemployment below the natural rate of unemployment would cause ever-accelerating inflation.[10] Before this contribution of the

---

[8] *Countercyclical* applies to anything that moves opposite to the business cycle in total output. A countercyclical policy can be one that stimulates the economy when output is low or one that slows down the economy when output is high.

[9] The share of tax revenues in GNP, calculated at the natural output level, increased from 3.9 percent in 1932 to 6.0 percent in 1933.

[10] The phrase *monetarist counterrevolution* originated with Harry G. Johnson in his "The Keynesian Revolution and the Monetarist Counterrevolution," *American Economic Review*, vol. 61 (May 1971), pp. 1–14. The most important manifesto of the monetarist counterrevolution was Milton Friedman's 1967 Presidential Address to the American Economic Association, "The Role of Monetary Policy," *American Economic Review*, vol. 58 (March 1968), pp. 1–17.

monetarists had been accepted by most economists, the damage had been done, and inflation was so solidly built into the expectations of firms and workers that it had become almost impossible to eliminate.

SUPPLY SHOCKS

As we have seen, supply shocks were a new phenomenon of the 1970s that added instability of aggregate supply as a new cause of economic problems. No longer was it enough to achieve the stabilization of aggregate demand. New policies were needed to stabilize supply conditions.

POLICY MISTAKES

During both the 1960s and 1970s policy mistakes occurred that many economists had foreseen and warned against. The first was the failure of the Johnson administration to raise taxes to pay for the Vietnam War in 1965–66. The resulting government deficits were the fundamental cause of the inflation that began in 1965–66 and was still going strong more than a decade later. The second mistake was the imposition of price and wage controls in 1971. This policy achieved a temporary slowdown in inflation but had no permanent effect; when controls were lifted in 1974 the price level bounced back up, aggravating the effects of the 1973–74 supply shocks. The third major mistake was the restrictive response of government monetary and fiscal policy to the events of 1973–74 and 1979–80. The policies chosen created more unemployment than was necessary and aggravated the 1974–75 and 1980 recessions. The fourth mistake was the failure in 1977–79 to adopt creative supply-side policies. Instead, the government made matters worse by instituting price-raising policies that some people have called "self-inflicted wounds"—higher payroll taxes that raised business costs and prices, as well as a higher minimum wage and higher farm price supports.

1-8 THE PARADOX OF CONVERGENCE WITHOUT AGREEMENT

Recently some broad areas of consensus have emerged. The material in Parts II and III can be learned without fear that major components will be discarded or contradicted in other courses. The leading monetarist, Milton Friedman, and several of the leading nonmonetarists, particularly Franco Modigliani, have made important recent contributions to the growth of the consensus:

1. Both monetarists and nonmonetarists are willing to discuss aggregate demand interpretation using the *IS-LM* model that we develop in Chapters 3–6. This model has long been at the center of nonmonetarist

analysis and in all but extreme situations allows both monetary and fiscal policy to influence output in the short run.

2. Nonmonetarists have accepted the major contribution of monetarist thinking. In the long run, stabilization policy cannot permanently reduce actual unemployment below the natural unemployment rate.

What then explains the paradox of convergence without agreement? Monetarists and nonmonetarists disagree sharply in their recommendations for stabilization policy. It is possible to agree on the short-run and long-run determinants of output and the price level without agreeing on the desirability of government action to interfere with the operation of the private economy. Monetarists disagree with the nonmonetarist preference for government intervention and an activist stabilization policy. Instead, they prefer a fixed-growth-rate rule for the money supply. Why? Our analysis (Chapter 12) emphasizes the monetarists' greater belief in the ability of the private economy to remain stable without government help, as well as their distrust and lack of confidence that the government is capable of doing more good than harm.

Despite my admitted nonmonetarist sympathies, I provide theories, arguments, and data (Chapters 13–17) relevant for a judgment on the dispute. A mixed picture emerges, with plenty of evidence provided to support both the opponents and proponents of an activist stabilization policy.

SUMMARY

1. We are concerned mainly with the causes, costs, and cures of inflation and unemployment. A basic problem is that an improvement in inflation may require a temporary worsening of unemployment, or the reverse may be true.

2. Nominal magnitudes, actual recorded values, combine the influence of changing physical quantities and an alteration in the price level. Real magnitudes, expressed in the constant prices of a particular base year, are corrected for the influence of price changes and reflect only changes in physical quantities.

3. In this century, U.S. inflation has fluctuated widely but has been worst during wars and after 1965. Periods of high unemployment have coincided with those of low output, with the Great Depression clearly scoring worst on both counts. There is no simple relation between unemployment and inflation.

4 Macroeconomic analysis is concerned with broad economic aggregates (inflation, unemployment) and has two tasks. It must analyze the causes of changes in the aggregates and it must predict the consequences of alternative policy changes.

5. Stabilization policy can alter the aggregate demand for goods and services. However, if both inflation and unemployment are too high, stabilization policy by itself cannot improve one without worsening the other. Stabilization policy may operate with a long delay or have effects that are highly uncertain.

6. Theory is a method of simplifying complicated problems to spotlight a few crucial relationships. A macroeconomic theory is useful only if it leads to useful generalizations that have predictive power. Policy recommendations involve not only the predictions of theory but also economic and political judgments.

7. Post-Keynesian economics supports government intervention through stabilization policy to offset the instability of the private economy. Much of the poor performance of the economy in the 1960s and 1970s reflected an overly optimistic (and now obsolete) approach to inflation, the food and oil supply shocks of 1973–74 and 1979–80, and the failure of politicians to listen to economists.

8. Much of the book (Chapters 3–11) reflects a broad consensus by monetarists and nonmonetarists on a common economic model for the determination of output, inflation, and unemployment. But an important area of disagreement remains and is the subject of Chapters 12–17. This does not involve the *effects* of monetary and fiscal policy on output or the price level but rather the *desirability* of government intervention in the economy through an activist stabilization policy.

A LOOK AHEAD

Our first task is to develop a simple theoretical model explaining real output (GNP) and the price level. Before we can turn to theory in Chapter 3, however, we must stop in Chapter 2 for a few definitions. What are GNP and the price level? How are they measured? What goods and services are included in or excluded from GNP? How are private saving, private investment, and the government deficit related to each other?

CONCEPTS

The price level versus the inflation rate

The actual unemployment rate versus the natural unemployment rate

Actual real output versus natural real output

Monetary versus fiscal policy

Stabilization policy

Closed versus open economy

Positive versus normative economics

Supply shocks

Target variables versus policy instruments

QUESTIONS FOR REVIEW

1 A notable feature of the vertical axis in Figure 1-1 is its logarithmic scale. One hundred billion dollars uses up more inches in the bottom part of the graph than in the top part. Why? The scale is chosen so that a proportional change always consumes the same number of inches. When nominal or real GNP doubles, whether from 200 to 400, from 400 to 800, or from 800 to 1600, we always move upward the same number of inches on the graph. This gives the graph a very nice property—the slope of any line drawn on the graph connecting the level of real output in two years indicates the *proportional* rate of growth between those two years.

   Now in Figure 1-1 draw a straight line with a ruler connecting the values of real GNP for 1900, 1930, 1940, 1970, and 1980. Notice that the lines you have drawn have different slopes. The interval with the steepest slope has the fastest growth rate of real GNP. Which interval has the fastest growth? The slowest?

2 If nominal GNP is 2500 and real GNP is 1250, what is the value of the implicit GNP deflator? If the implicit GNP deflator is 0.8 and the value of real GNP is 800, what is the value of nominal GNP? If the implicit GNP deflator is 1.5 and the value of nominal GNP is 3000, what is real GNP?

3 If the GNP deflator were 2.0 in 1981 and 2.2 in 1982, what would be the rate of inflation for 1982?

4 Business firms regularly reach an "all-time high" in nominal sales. Does this always mean that they have sold a larger physical quantity of goods than ever before?

5 In 1980 actual real GNP exceeded that of 1973. Why then was the actual unemployment rate higher in 1980 than in 1973?

6 Why might two economists share a common economic theory but disagree on their policy recommendations?

7 For each of the following, indicate whether the issue concerns aggregrate demand or aggregate supply:

   a. The effect of price controls in holding down the price level.

   b. The effect of the money supply on purchases of new houses.

   c. The effect of a cut in the personal income tax on purchases of consumption goods.

   d. The effect of a boost in the price of oil by the OPEC nations on the domestic price level in the United States.

   e. The effect of a drought or crop failure on the economy.

2 The Measurement of Income and Prices

True, the statistics are not as good as we
want them to be, but what would we
do without them?

—Oskar Morganstern[1]

2-1 WHY WE CARE ABOUT INCOME

A basic lesson of Figure 1-3 is that movements in the unemployment rate are closely related to the parallel movements of the gap between actual and natural real GNP. When production drops off, people are laid off and put out of work. When production is very high relative to natural output, job openings will be plentiful and unemployment will be low. So the key to understanding changes in unemployment is the total real *product*, which is equal to total real *income*.

Measures of total real income serve a second purpose. If the total amount of real income is divided by the number of people or the number of families, we obtain a measure of the relative income of one nation compared to another. For example, how well off is the average American compared to the average Norwegian or Brazilian? Further, we can chart the growth of income per person over long periods and determine whether the rate of increase of our real national product has been accelerating or decelerating and whether other nations are growing faster than the United States.

The subject of this chapter, the definition and measurement of national income—what is included and excluded and why—is an essential prelude to our study of the determinants of changes in real income and output. We will see that many of the rules governing the calculation of national income are arbitrary, that controversial choices must be made as to the proper set of ingredients in the official measure of income, and that the size of any nation's gross national product is to some degree at the dis-

---

[1] "Qui Numerare Incipit Errare Incipit," *Fortune*, vol. 68 (October 1963).

cretion of the economists and government officials who mark off the dividing lines between the included and excluded items. We will also learn how to calculate the price indexes or "deflators" that are used to convert the official current-dollar (nominal) measure of national income and product into a measure of constant-dollar (real) income and product.

2-2 THE CIRCULAR FLOW OF INCOME AND EXPENDITURE

Let us begin with a very simple economy, consisting of households and business firms. We will assume that households spend their entire income, saving nothing, and that there is no government.[2] (This is our first example of the use of theory to simplify an intricate subject by choosing a particular set of assumptions that help focus the discussion on the relevant issues.) Figure 2-1 is a picture of the operation of our simple economy, with households represented by the box on the left and business firms by the box on the right. There are two kinds of transactions between the households and the firms.

First, the firms sell goods and services (product) to the households – for instance, bread and bus rides – represented in Figure 2-1 by the lower dashed line labeled "Product." The bread and bus rides are not a gift, but are paid for by a flow of money (C), say $1,000,000 per year, represented by the solid line labeled **"Consumer expenditures."**

Second, households must work to earn the income to pay for the consumption goods. They work for the firms, selling their skills as represented by the upper dashed line labeled "Labor services." Household members are willing to work only if they receive a flow of money, usually called "wages," from the firms for each hour of work. Wages are the main component of income (Q), shown by the upper solid line.

Since households are assumed to consume all of their income, and since firms are assumed to pay out all of their sales in the form of income to households, it follows that income (Q) and consumption expenditures (C) are equal. For the same reason, the labor services provided in return for income are equal to the goods and services (product) sold by the firms to households in return for the money flow of consumer expenditures:

$$
\begin{aligned}
\text{income } (Q) &= \text{labor services} \\
&= \text{consumption expenditure } (C) \\
&= \text{product}
\end{aligned} \tag{2.1}
$$

Each of the four magnitudes in equation (2.1) is a **flow magnitude** – any money payment or physical good or service that flows from one economic unit to another. A flow of expenditure, just like a flow of water through a pipe, can be measured only if we first specify the length of time

---

[2] Because households do no saving, there is no capital or wealth, and all household income is in the form of wages for labor services.

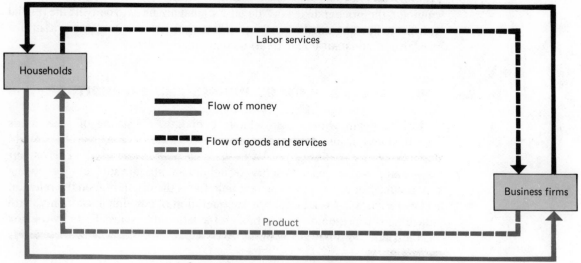

Income (Q = $1,000,000)

Labor services

Households

Flow of money

Flow of goods and services

Business firms

Product

Consumer expenditures (C = $1,000,000)

FIGURE 2–1

The Circular Flow of Income and Consumer Expenditure

Circular flow of income and expenditure in a simple imaginary economy in which households consume their entire income. There are no taxes, no government spending, no saving, and no investment.

over which the flow is measured. Thus U.S. gross national product (= income = expenditure = factor services) in 1979 was $2369 billion *per year*. Most flow magnitudes in the United States are measured at annual rates. If the flow of GNP in a quarter-year ("quarter") is $750 billion, this amounts to $3000 billion at an annual rate.

A flow is distinguished from a stock, which is an economic magnitude in the possession of a single unit at a particular moment of time. The stock of money, savings accounts, business equipment, or government debt can be measured by adding up its value at a given point in time, for instance, midnight on December 31, 1980. Measurement of a stock is like taking a flash snapshot, and it does not require specification of a unit of time.

2-3 WHAT TRANSACTIONS SHOULD BE INCLUDED IN INCOME AND EXPENDITURE?

The **National Income and Product Accounts (NIPA)** is an official U.S. government accounting of all the millions of flows of income and expenditure in the United States. The basic ideas and methods used in the NIPA were originally developed in the 1930s by economists working at the National Bureau of Economic Research, including Simon Kuznets (one of the first winners of the Nobel Prize in economics). During World War II, the U.S. Department of Commerce took over the task of computing the NIPA, and it has gradually refined and updated the procedures.[3] The latest NIPA statistics can be found in the monthly periodical, *Survey of Current Business*.

Those responsible for counting up gross national income and product do not mindlessly add up every figure on every piece of paper mailed to the government by private households and business firms. Instead, they have a set of rules to determine which items to include.

DEFINING GNP

In our free-market economy, the fact that a good or service is sold is usually a sign that it is capable of satisfying certain human wants and needs; otherwise people would not be willing to pay a price for it. So by including in the gross national product only things that are sold through the market for a price, we can be fairly sure that most of the components of GNP do contribute to human satisfaction. There are three major requirements in the rule for including items in the total final product, or GNP:

Final product consists of all currently produced goods and services that are sold through the market but not resold.

The first part of the rule—*to be included in final product a good must be currently produced*—obviously excludes sales of any used items such as houses and cars, since they are not currently produced. It also excludes any transaction in which money is transferred without any accompanying good or service in return. Among the transfer payments excluded from national income in the United States are gifts from one person to another and "gifts" from the government to persons, such as social security, unemployment, and welfare benefits. Also excluded are capital gains accruing to persons as the prices of their assets increase.

The second part of the rule—*goods included in the final product must be sold on the market and are valued at market prices*—means that we measure the value of final product by the market prices that people are willing to pay for goods and services. We assume that a Cadillac gives 10,000 times as much satisfaction as a can of shaving cream for the simple reason that it costs about 10,000 times as much. Of course, it is impossible to compare the satisfaction that an item gives to two people. Presumably a loaf of bread gives more pleasure to a poor Appalachian schoolchild than to a rich New York banker, but if the price of the bread is the same, its

---

[3] The latest methodological revisions are described in George Jaszi and Carol S. Carson, "The National Income and Product Accounts of the United States: Revised Estimates, 1929–74," *Survey of Current Business*, vol. 56 (January 1976), pp. 1–38.

contribution to the nation's GNP is considered to be the same no matter who buys it.

The criterion of market price is also a faulty measure of welfare, because it does not take account of the annoyances that are created by some market transactions. Thus the value of a factory's output of goods is included in final product, but we do not subtract from final product the dissatisfaction caused by its output of pollutants into a nearby river.[4]

The third part of the rule — *to be included in final product a good must not be resold in the current period* — further limits the acceptability of items. The many different goods and services produced in the economy are used in two different ways. Some goods, like wheat, are mainly used as ingredients in the making of other goods, in this case, bread. Any good resold by its purchaser, rather than used as is, goes by the name **intermediate good.**

The opposite of an intermediate good is a **final good**, one that is not resold. Bread located at the grocery is a final good, used by consumers, as are shoes, clothes, haircuts, and everything else the consumer buys directly.

WHY INTERMEDIATE GOODS ARE EXCLUDED FROM GNP

Why can't we just add up all transactions in the economy and call that total GNP, instead of taking the trouble to exclude intermediate goods? Look at Figure 2-2, which shows how the $.50 that a consumer spends for a loaf of bread is divided among the four firms that produce the bread. The bars on the left side of the diagram show the receipts of each of the firms involved in making and selling the bread, and the right side shows the income of the firms' workers, managers, and stockholders *after* the purchase of the intermediate goods.

For instance, the baker adds $.18 of income to the $.21 he pays to the miller for the flour, and the grocer adds $.11 to the $.39 he pays to the baker for the bread. The total paid by the consumer to the grocer, $.50, exactly equals the total income created by all four firms (.09 + .12 + .18 + .11 = .50). By excluding from final product all goods that are resold (the intermediate goods) and including only the final purchase of $.50 by the consumer who actually uses the bread, we automatically guarantee that final product ($C = \$.50$) equals total income created or **value added** ($Q = \$.50$).

The $.50 paid by the consumer for the bread is an ingredient in the lower loop of consumer expenditure (C) in Figure 2-1. The $.50 of income created is part of the upper loop of income (Q) in Figure 2-1. Now we can see why, by definition, both loops are equal in size.

---

[4] Irritants, such as water pollution and the noise of jet airplanes, for which no charge is made on the market, are called external diseconomies. An external economy is a benefit for which no charge is made, like the pollen supplied to a honeygrower's bees from a farmer's nearby orchard.

FINAL PRODUCT EQUALS TOTAL INCOME CREATED

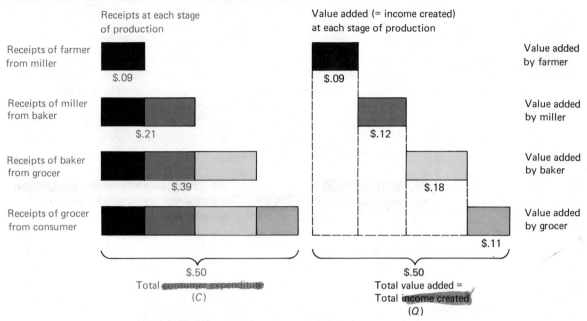

FIGURE 2–2

The Contribution of One Loaf of Bread to Consumer Expenditure and Income Created

The left side shows the amount that each firm—farmer, miller, baker, and grocer—receives in the process of producing one loaf of bread. These total receipts are used for two purposes. First, part of the receipts of each firm are used to pay for the intermediate goods purchased from the firm listed directly above (for instance, the miller pays $.09 to the farmer for the wheat). Second, what is left over—shown on the right side of the diagram—is the income created or value added (such as wages, salaries, profits; $.12 in the case of the miller).

2-4 INVESTMENT AND SAVING

The goods and services purchased by business firms that are not resold as intermediate goods to other firms or consumers during the current period qualify by our rule as final product. But the business firm does not consume them. Final goods that business firms keep for themselves are called "private **investment**" or private capital formation. They add to the nation's stock of income-yielding assets. Private investment consists of:

1. **Inventory investment.** Bread purchased by the grocer but not resold to consumers in the current period stays on the shelves, raising the inventory level. Inventories of raw materials, parts, and finished goods are

an essential form of income-yielding assets for businesses, since goods immediately available "on the shelf" help satisfy customers and make sales.

> **Example:** The grocer has ten loaves of bread at the close of business on December 31, 1980. His inventory of bread is $3.90 (ten loaves times the wholesale baker's price of $.39). At the close of business on March 31, 1981, he has 15 loaves of bread ($5.85). Inventory investment in the first quarter of 1981 is the *change* in his inventory ($5.85 − $3.90 = $1.95). If the level of inventories had fallen, then inventory investment would have been negative.

2. **Fixed investment.** This includes all final goods purchased by business other than additions to inventory intended for eventual resale. The main types of fixed investment are structures (factories, office buildings, shopping centers, apartments, houses) and equipment (cash registers, computers, trucks). Newly produced houses and condominiums sold to individuals are also counted as fixed investment—homeowners are treated in the national accounts as business firms that own their house as an asset and rent the house to themselves.[5]

Figure 2-1 described a simple imaginary economy in which households consumed their total income. Figure 2-3 introduces investment into that economy. Total expenditures on final product are once again $1,000,000, but this time they are divided into $750,000 for household purchases of consumption goods (C) and $250,000 for business purchases of investment goods (I). The $1,000,000 of total expenditures flowing to the business firms from the lower loops generates $1,000,000 in income for households shown in the top loop, just as before. Households take their $1,000,000 in income and spend $750,000 on purchases of consumption goods. Where does the remaining $250,000 go?

The portion of household income that is not consumed is called **personal saving.** What happens to income that is saved? The funds are channeled to business firms in two basic ways:

1. Households buy bonds and stocks issued by the firms, and the firms then use the money to buy investment goods.
2. Households leave the unused income (saving) in banks. The banks then lend the money to the firms, which use it to buy investment goods.

---

[5] An individual who owns a house is treated as a schizophrenic in the national accounts: as a business firm *and* as a consuming household. My left side is a businessman who owns my house and receives imaginary rent payments from my right side, the consumer who lives in my house. The NIPA identifies these imaginary rent payments as "imputed rent on owner-occupied dwellings," and they are the most important exception to the rule that a good must be sold on the market to be counted in GNP.

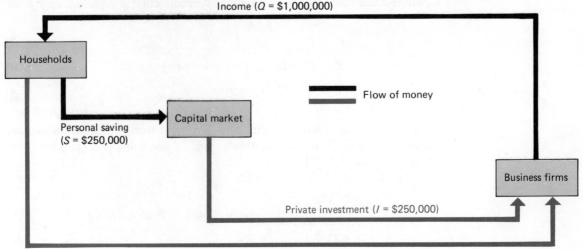

SAVING LEAKS OUT OF THE SPENDING STREAM BUT REAPPEARS AS INVESTMENT

Income (Q = $1,000,000)

Households

Flow of money

Personal saving
(S = $250,000)

Capital market

Business firms

Private investment (I = $250,000)

Consumption expenditure (C = $750,000)

FIGURE 2–3

Introduction of Saving and Investment to the Circular Flow Diagram

Our simple imaginary economy (Figure 2–1) when households save 25 percent of their income. Business firms' investment accounts for 25 percent of total expenditure. Again, we are assuming that there are no taxes and no government spending.

Whether households channel their saving to firms directly (through purchases of bonds and stock) or indirectly (through banks), the effect is the same: business firms obtain funds to purchase investment goods. The box labeled "capital market" in Figure 2-3 symbolizes the transfer of personal saving to business firms for the purpose of investment. Just as total expenditure on final product is equal by definition to income created, investment purchases must be equal to saving. Why? This conclusion follows from the definitions of three concepts just introduced:[6]

$$\text{income } (Q) \equiv \text{expenditure } (E) \qquad (2.2)$$

$$\text{expenditure } (E) \equiv \text{consumption } (C) + \text{investment } (I) \qquad (2.3)$$

$$\text{saving } (S) \equiv \text{income } (Q) - \text{consumption } (C) \qquad (2.4)$$

---

[6] A three-bar equality sign is an identity and means that the relationship is true by definition.

It is customary in economics to eliminate unnecessary words by writing equations like these using alphabetical symbols only:

$$Q \equiv E \qquad (2.2)$$

$$E \equiv C + I \qquad (2.3)$$

$$S \equiv Q - C \quad \text{or rearranging,} \quad Q \equiv C + S \qquad (2.4)$$

Now we can see why saving and investment must be equal. Substitute equation (2.3) for E on the right side of (2.2) and substitute (2.4) for Q on the left side of (2.2). The result:

$$
\begin{array}{rl}
C + S \equiv & C + I \\
\underline{-C \qquad} & \underline{-C} \qquad \text{(subtracting C from both sides)} \qquad (2.5) \\
S \equiv & I
\end{array}
$$

Since income is equal to expenditure, the portion of income not consumed (saving) must be equal to the nonconsumption portion of expenditure (investment).

In other words, saving is a "leakage" from the income spent on consumption goods. This leakage from the spending stream must be balanced by an "injection" of nonconsumption spending in the form of private investment.

Why do we bother to distinguish between consumption and investment? One reason is that expenditure plans for the two are made by different economic units. Households decide how much of their incomes they want to consume and save; business firms decide how much they want to invest. The mismatch between household saving plans and business investment plans has been a major source of instability in U.S. output and income.

A second reason for distinguishing between consumption and investment is the different implications of the two types of spending for the economy's potential to produce output in the future. An economy that consumes a small portion of its income has a large portion left over for saving and investment—that is, for the formation of capital assets. It can build a relatively large number of factories, office buildings, computers, or other business equipment, and those capital assets add to the nation's "natural" real GNP for next year and the years to follow. As Table 2-1 shows, Japan devotes a very high proportion of its income to investment, and its output growth rate has been correspondingly high throughout the postwar period. The United Kingdom and the United States have consumed a greater share of income at the sacrifice of a smaller increase in the stock of capital assets. Therefore, they have a smaller increase in output each year.

TABLE 2-1

1970 Investment Shares and Postwar Growth Rates for Major
Developed Countries, 1959–78

	Ratio of investment to GNP, 1970	*Growth rate of real GNP, 1959–78*
High-investment countries		
Japan	39	8.8
West Germany	35	4.0
France	32	5.1
Low-investment countries		
United Kingdom	22	2.6
United States	19	3.5

Source: See Appendix C for ratio of investment to GNP. Real GNP growth from the Federal Reserve Bank of St. Louis.

2-5 NET EXPORTS AND FOREIGN INVESTMENT

Exports are expenditures for goods and services produced in the United States and sent to other countries. Such expenditures create income in the United States but are not part of the consumption or investment spending of U.S. residents. **Imports** are expenditures by U.S. residents for goods and services produced elsewhere, which thus do *not* create domestic income. For instance, an American-made Chevrolet exported to Canada is part of U.S. production and income but is Canadian consumption. A German-made Mercedes imported to the United States is part of German production and income but is U.S. consumption. If income created from exports is greater than income spent on imported goods, the net effect is an increase in domestic production and income. Thus the difference between exports and imports, **net exports,** is a component of final product and GNP.[7]

Net exports can also be **net foreign investment** and given the same economic interpretation as domestic investment. Why? Both domestic and foreign investment raise domestic production and income created. Domestic investment creates domestic capital assets; foreign investment creates U.S. claims on foreigners that likewise yield us future flows of income. An American export to Japan is paid for by Japanese yen, which

---

[7] Thus equation (2.3) above can be rewritten

$$E = C + I + X - H$$

where X equals exports and H equals imports.

can be used to buy a Japanese asset (a Japanese bank account or part of a Japanese factory).[8]

2-6

THE GOVERNMENT SECTOR

Up to this point we have described an economy consisting only of private households and business firms. Now we introduce the government, which collects taxes from the private sector and makes two kinds of expenditures. Government purchases of goods and services (tanks, fighter planes, schoolbooks) generate production and create income. The government can also make payments directly to households without any production of goods and services in return. Social security, unemployment compensation, and welfare benefits are examples of these transfer payments.

Figure 2-4 adds the government (federal, state, and local) to our imaginary economy of Figures 2-1 and 2-3. A flow of tax revenue ($R = \$100,000$) flows from the households to the government.[9] The government buys $100,000 of goods and services (G), raising total expenditures on GNP and income created from the $1,000,000 of Figure 2-3 to $1,100,000. So far the government's budget is balanced. But in addition the government sends $50,000 back to the households in the form of transfer payments (F), such as welfare payments, leaving a deficit of $50,000 that must be financed. The government sells $50,000 of bonds to private households through the capital market, just as business firms sell bonds and stock to households to finance their investment projects.

As before, total income created (Q) is equal to total expenditure on final product (E):

$$Q \equiv E$$

Now there are three types of expenditure on final product: consumption (C); private investment, both domestic and foreign (I); and government purchases of goods and services (G):[10]

$$E \equiv C + I + G \qquad (2.6)$$

---

[8] There is an additional alternative. An American exporter may not want a Japanese asset but may want his payment in U.S. dollars. He can obtain U.S. dollars from the U.S. government in trade for his yen. The increased U.S. government holdings of yen and other currencies can be kept, thus counting as a foreign capital asset, or can be used to pay off U.S. debts, reducing U.S. liabilities to foreigners.

[9] In the "real world" that will be described in Figure 2-6, both households and business firms pay taxes. Here we keep things simple by limiting tax payments to personal income taxes.

[10] In an open economy with exports (X) and imports (H), equation (2.6) can be replaced with:

$$E = C + I + G + X - H$$

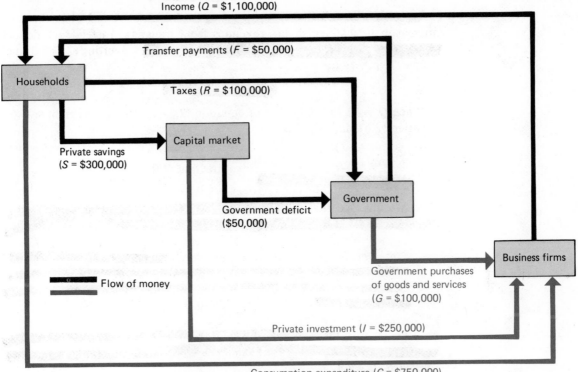

FIGURE 2–4

Introduction of Taxation and Government Spending to the Circular Flow Diagram

Our simple imaginary economy with the addition of a government collecting $100,000 in tax revenue, paying households $50,000 in transfer payments, and purchasing $100,000 of goods and services. Its total expenditures ($150,000) exceed its tax revenues ($100,000), leaving a $50,000 deficit that is financed by selling government bonds to the households.

The total personal income that households receive consists of the income created from production (Q) and transfer payments from the government (F). This total ($Q + F$) is available for the purchase of consumption goods (C), saving (S), and the payment of taxes:

$$Q + F \equiv C + S + R$$

An equivalent expression is obtained if we subtract F from both sides:

$$Q \equiv C + S + R - F \qquad (2.7)$$

Transfer payments (F) can be treated as negative taxes. Thus there is no reason to distinguish tax revenues from transfers. Instead, we define **net tax revenue** (T) as taxes (R) minus transfers (F), converting (2.7) into the simpler expression:

$$Q \equiv C + S + T \qquad (2.8)$$

Since $Q \equiv E$, the right side of equation (2.8) is equal to the right side of equation (2.6), and we obtain:

$$
\begin{aligned}
C + S + T &\equiv C + I + G \\
-C &\qquad -C \\
\hline
S + T &\equiv I + G
\end{aligned}
\qquad \text{(subtracting } C \text{ from both sides)}
$$

$$(2.9)$$

Now we can see that saving and investment do not always have to be equal, as they were in equation (2.5). Instead, we have a more general rule:

> *Since income is equal to expenditure, the portion of income not consumed (saving plus net taxes) must be equal to the nonconsumption portion of expenditure on final product (investment plus government spending).*

In other words, **leakages** out of the income available for consumption goods ($S + T$) must be exactly balanced by **injections** of nonconsumption spending ($I + G$).

This rule helps explain how the economy finances the **government deficit.** Subtracting S and G from both sides of equation (2.9), we have:

$$T - G \equiv I - S \qquad (2.10)$$

The left side of the equation is the government surplus — net tax revenues (T) minus expenditures (G). Whenever the government runs a surplus, the private economy must adjust to make private investment exceed private saving. When the left side of (2.10) is negative, the government is running a deficit and the private economy must adjust to make private saving exceed private investment.

2-7 CASE STUDY: SAVING, INVESTMENT, AND GOVERNMENT DEFICITS

Figure 2-5 illustrates the workings of equation (2.10) for the postwar period 1946–79. The top section of the illustration shows the annual values of real private investment (I) and saving (S). The bottom section shows the government surplus ($T - G$). As required by equation (2.10), years in which investment fell short of saving were also years in which the government ran a deficit.

PRIVATE INVESTMENT MINUS PRIVATE SAVING EQUALS THE GOVERNMENT SURPLUS

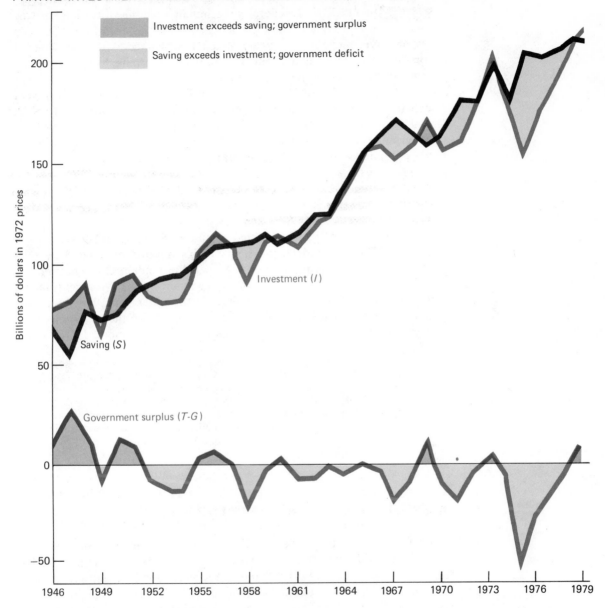

FIGURE 2–5

Private Saving and Investment and the Government Surplus, 1946–79

In the top part of the diagram, the pink shaded area indicates that S exceeds I. In the bottom part, the pink area shows that G exceeds T and that the government is running a deficit. By definition—equation (2.10)—the top and bottom pink areas are equal. The same goes for the gray areas: in the top part I exceeds S, in the bottom part T exceeds G, and the government is running a surplus.

Source: Economic Report of the President, January 1980, p. 230.

Case Study: Saving, Investment, and Government Deficits **39**

Deficits imply an excess of saving over investment as well as the reverse. In 1967, U.S. federal government spending for Vietnam was high. As a consequence the private economy had to adjust to reduce private investment below private saving, as indicated by the pink shading for 1967. In this instance, the behavior of government caused private investment to fall below private saving.

But exactly the same situation (low investment with a government deficit) can occur for a different reason. In 1949, 1954, 1958, 1961, 1970, and again in 1975–76, a marked drop in private investment caused the government to run a deficit, by weakening the economy and causing net tax revenue (T) to fall below government expenditure (G).

There is no way to tell from Figure 2-5 whether a government deficit is caused by high government spending, as in the Vietnam War, or by a weak economy, as in years 1975–76. The economy influences the government budget, and vice versa.

Figure 2-5 can also be viewed as summarizing the relation between household saving and business spending. In years designated by pink shading, business firms did not invest all the funds that the households saved, leaving a remainder available to finance the government deficit. In years designated by gray shading, on the other hand, business firms invested more than households saved, requiring that the government run a surplus to provide the extra funds needed by business. James Tobin sums up the relation this way:

> The moral is inescapable, if startling. If you would like the federal deficit to be smaller, the deficits of business must be bigger. Would you like the federal government to run a surplus and reduce its debt? Then business deficits must be big enough to absorb that surplus as well as the funds available from households and financial institutions.[11]

2-8 A SUMMARY OF TYPES OF SPENDING

The NIPA treatment of the different types of expenditures is summarized in Table 2-2. The top part of the table splits total expenditures on final goods and services (GNP) into three basic components: private consumption, private investment (both domestic and foreign), and government spending. Private consumption and investment exclude purchases of intermediate goods, which are listed separately at the bottom of the table on line C.

---

[11] James Tobin, "Deficit, Deficit, Who's Got the Deficit," *National Economic Policy* (New Haven: Yale University Press, 1966), p. 52.

TABLE 2-2

Items Included in and Excluded from GNP

Type of expenditure	Included in GNP?	1979 spending, $ billions	Examples
A. Final goods and services (GNP)	Yes	2368.5	
1. Consumer expenditures (C)	Yes	1509.8	
a. Durable goods	Yes	212.8	Autos, TV sets
b. Nondurable goods	Yes	597.0	Food, clothes, shoes
c. Services	Yes	700.0	Haircuts, airline trips
2. Private investment (I)	Yes	382.7	
a. Change in business inventories	Yes	18.4	
b. Producers' durable equipment	Yes	163.6	Computers, tractors
c. Structures	Yes	204.2	
i. Nonresidential	Yes	92.3	Factories, office buildings, shopping centers
ii. Residential	Yes	111.9	Houses, condominiums
d. Foreign (exports minus imports)	Yes	−3.5	*Exports:* tractors, computers *Imports:* coffee, bananas, wine
3. Government purchases of goods and services (G)	Yes	476.1	
a. Intermediate	Yes	–	Fire fighters, police officers
b. Consumption	Yes	–	City parks, street cleaners
c. Investment	Yes	–	Airports, university dormitories, hospitals
B. Government interest and transfer payments	No	293.6	Social security, welfare, unemployment benefits
C. Private intermediate goods	No	–	Wheat, iron ore
D. Private purchases of used assets	No	–	Purchases of used houses, used cars
E. Nonmarket activities[a]			
1. Value of leisure time	No	–	Watching television, playing tennis
2. Services from existing consumer durables	No	–	Value of use of auto, dishwasher
3. Costs of pollution	No	–	Costs of smog, water pollution
4. Illegal activities	No	–	Earnings from theft, rackets

[a] See the discussion of these categories in Appendix A.
Source: Economic Report of the President (January 1980).

A Summary of Types of Spending **41**

The treatment of government spending is different. All government purchases of goods and services, whether intermediate or final, are included in the GNP and on line A.3. Many government purchases, such as wages paid to police officers, do not create assets and are not investment. They are not consumption either, because they are not desired for their own sake. Police protection is an intermediate good, a necessary ingredient in maintaining an orderly society and protecting the value of private property, just as coal and iron ore are necessary ingredients in making steel.

There is an interesting inconsistency in the accounting system. When the crime rate goes up, private businesses hire more security guards, who are counted as an intermediate good, because they are a business expense. The GNP remains the same, because there has been no increase in expenditures on final product. When the crime rate goes up and the government hires more police, however, GNP goes up by the increase in wages paid to the new government policemen.

Why are government expenditures on fire fighting, police protection, the court system, and other intermediate goods counted as part of GNP? The problem is the difficulty in finding an easy-to-use criterion for the government intermediate goods to be excluded. Private intermediate goods are excluded whenever they are business expenses incurred in making a product that is sold in the current period. But government goods such as police and fire protection are not sold; it would be difficult to prevent individuals who do not agree to buy a given government service from receiving the same fire and police protection as everyone else. This is why basic government services are financed by taxes everyone is required to pay.

Although all government spending on goods and services is included in GNP, government expenditures in the form of transfer payments are not included. Government transfer payments (Table 2-2, line B), private intermediate purchases (line C), and private purchases of used assets (line D) are three of the most important exclusions of expenditures from the final product as defined in the NIPA accounts.

2-9 THE CIRCULAR FLOW IN 1979: LEAKAGES FROM THE SPENDING STREAM

Figure 2-6 is a more realistic version of Figure 2-4, showing the relation of the spending streams between households, business firms, the capital market, and the government, using actual data on spending and income from 1979. The width of the "pipes" flowing among the sectors is scaled to be proportional to the actual 1979 flows of spending, income, taxes, and so on.

Start in the lower right corner, where business firms produce three basic types of final product: consumption goods, investment goods, and government purchases. Expenditures (E) on these three categories are shown as wide red pipes flowing to the right from households, the capital market, and the government to the business firms box.

Let us look at how the income created from the sale of final output is distributed. The first deduction is for **depreciation (capital consumption allowances)** charged by business firms (saving for *de*preciation, thus S_D). This S_D is shown flowing through a gray pipe from the business firms to the capital market box at the left.

When new output is produced, a part of the nation's capital equipment is worn out, and business firms deduct a capital consumption allowance from their income to provide funds to replace worn-out equipment. To this extent a part of total output and spending does not represent net income paid to factors of production but is used to *replace* capital goods used up in the process of production. This portion of output, capital consumption allowances, must be included in GNP if we are to show the expenditures of final users on the national output. But, at the same time, capital consumption allowances must be excluded from **net national product (NNP)** if we are to show the incomes actually earned by the factors of production.

The terms **gross** *and* **net** *in economics usually refer to the inclusion or exclusion of capital consumption allowances. Thus the difference between "gross investment" and "net investment," or between "gross saving" and "net saving," is exactly the same as that between GNP and NNP.*

The next leakage is the collection by the government (federal, state, and local) of **indirect business taxes** (taxes on business, hence R_B). These taxes — for instance, state or city excise and sales taxes — are included in the prices paid by the consumer but are not available for payment as income to workers or firms. Indirect business taxes are shown flowing from the NNP box to the government sector. With the deduction of R_B we move up above NNP to **national income** (Q_N), the sum of all net incomes earned by the factors of production (labor and capital) in producing current output.

But not all of the national income is paid out to individuals. Corporations withhold part of their income as **undistributed corporate profits**, shown in Figure 2-6 as a leakage flowing from the national income box to the capital market. This is saving by incorporated business (S_B). In addition, a substantial amount "leaks out" to the government as corporate income taxes (R_C) and social security taxes (R_S) — both employer and employee contributions. Finally, what remains of national income after deducting undistributed corporate profits, corporation income taxes, and social security taxes paid by business is paid out to persons in the form of wages, salaries, rent, interest dividends, and the profits of unincorporated enterprises (for example, the income of small shopkeepers and farmers).

Some individuals receive incomes that are not a payment for any productive service and therefore are not included in GNP, NNP, or the national income. Part of these payments are government transfers and interest payments on the government debt (F_G), shown flowing from the government sector in the middle of Figure 2-6 to the personal income box at the upper left, bypassing GNP, NNP, and national income on the way.

Additional "nonproductive" transfer payments of installment and mortgage interest payments by consumers (F_p) are shown flowing away from the household sector and then back again.

The total we now arrive at is **personal income** (Q_P), the sum of all income payments to individuals. This represents the current flow of purchasing power to individuals through the workings of the productive system plus the transfers from the government and personal sectors. If we now deduct personal tax payments (R_p), we obtain one of the most important totals in national income accounting. This remainder is **personal disposable income** (Q_p), which is the amount of income that individuals as consumers have available to spend or save.

We see three different flows emerging below the personal sector box: personal consumption expenditure (C), which flows around to the right to be spent on GNP; interest paid by consumers (F_p), which is a transfer payment and flows back to households; and the final leakage from the spending stream, personal savings (S_p).[12] The flow of consumption expenditure to the business firms brings us full circle.

Taking an overall view of Figure 2-6, we can see that there is a series of leakages flowing through gray pipes (taxes and saving of various types minus transfer payments) that reduces the amount spent on GNP ($2368.5 billion) to the total disposable income of persons, $1623.2 billion. A further diversion, in the form of personal saving and interest payments, results in consumer expenditures of $1509.8 billion. The total of the leakages, after the necessary adjustments, is exactly equal to the sum of investment (including net exports) and government spending. We can now rewrite equation

---

[12] The Department of Commerce has labeled consumer expenditures plus interest payments ($C + F_p$) as "personal outlays." In practice, disposable income and personal outlays are directly estimated, and personal saving is obtained as a residual.

FIGURE 2–6 (facing page)

Income, Product, and Transfer Flows in the 1979 U.S. Economy

An elaboration of Figure 2–4 showing that much of the income created in producing GNP (lower right corner) "leaks out" of the white income flow through the gray pipes into saving ($S_D + S_B + S_P$) and into taxes ($R_B + R_C + R_S + R_P$). Government transfer payments (F_G) are a negative leakage adding to personal income. Only the remaining portion of GNP net of all the leakages is available for the red consumption pipe. In addition, total expenditures on GNP include the red expenditure pipes representing private investment and government spending, which are financed by the gray tax and saving leakages.

Source: Economic Report of the President, January 1980. Some minor flows, including the statistical discrepancy, are included as part of R_B, S_B, and F_G to improve legibility.

A "PLUMBING" DIAGRAM FOR THE U.S. ECONOMY IN 1979

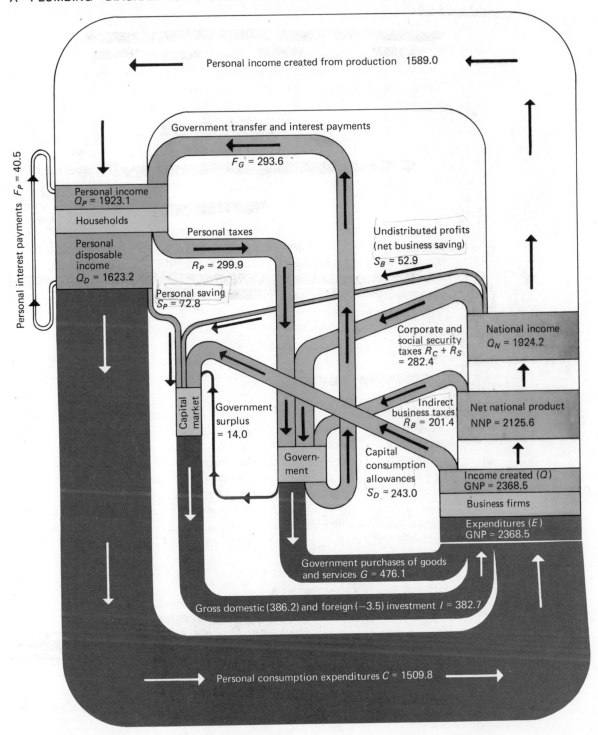

(2.9) using the specific symbols of the actual U.S. economy as described in Figure 2-6:

$$(S_D + S_B + S_P) + (R_B + R_C + R_S + R_P) - F_G \equiv I + G \qquad (2.11)$$

Saving   Taxes   Transfers   Injections

or, once again, the more general form (2.9) that combines all the saving terms into one symbol (S) and lets T stand for all tax receipts minus transfers:

$$S + T \equiv I + G \qquad (2.9)$$

Equations (2.11) and (2.9) both summarize the main lesson of Figure 2-6: *leakages must be equal to injections, by definition.* Transposing (2.9), we have once again:

$$T - G \equiv I - S \qquad (2.10)$$

The government surplus is written on the left-hand side of (2.10) and is shown as the black line flowing from the government sector leftward up to the capital market. Equation (2.10) illustrates the second lesson of Figure 2-6: *the government surplus must be equal to the difference between total investment (including net exports) and total private saving.*

2-10 MEASURING PRICES

For most problems in economic analysis, we are interested in comparing measurements of income and expenditures at different times. Hence we must measure these magnitudes in "real terms"—that is, terms adjusted for the effects of price changes. The illustration of actual and natural GNP in Figure 1-3, and of saving, investment, and the government surplus in Figure 2-5, shows these magnitudes in real terms. How do the national income accountants take the recorded nominal income and expenditure (Y) of two years in which prices were very different—say 1972 and 1980—and compute real GNP (Q) adjusted for all effects of price changes?

IMPLICIT GNP DEFLATOR

Real GNP (Q) is the value of expenditures for *each year* (say, 1980) when each separate good or service is measured in the prices of a *single year,* say 1972. The implicit GNP deflator, in turn, is the ratio of nominal to real GNP:

$$P \equiv \frac{Y}{Q}$$

TABLE 2-3

Calculation of Nominal GNP, Real GNP, and the Implicit GNP
Deflator in an Imaginary Economy Producing Only Round Steak
and Eggs

	1972	1980
1. Prices		
a. Round steak, pound	$ 1.00	$ 2.00
b. Eggs, dozen	.50	.75
2. Production in physical units		
a. Round steak, pounds	10	8
b. Eggs, dozens	10	12
3. Production in current prices of each year		
a. Round steak (1a times 2a)	$10.00	$16.00
b. Eggs (1b times 2b)	5.00	9.00
c. Nominal GNP (3a plus 3b)	15.00	25.00
4. Real production in constant 1972 prices		
a. Round steak (1a for 1972 times 2a for each year)	$10.00	$ 8.00
b. Eggs (1b for 1972 times 2b for each year)	5.00	6.00
c. Real GNP (4a plus 4b)	15.00	14.00
5. GNP deflator, 1972 base (3c/4c)	1.000	1.786

The **implicit GNP deflator** *(P) is the ratio of nominal GNP (Y) to real GNP measured in constant dollars (Q).*

Table 2-3 works through an example of the calculation of nominal GNP, real GNP, and the GNP deflator for a hypothetical economy in 1972 and 1980 producing only round steak and eggs. Nominal GNP (line 3c) is the sum of expenditures on the two products in the two years at the actual prices paid. Real GNP (line 4c) is the sum of expenditures on the two products in the two years in both cases measured at 1972 prices. The GNP deflator (line 5) is the ratio of nominal to real GNP (1.786), which indicates that the average price level in 1980 was 78.6 percent higher than the level in 1972.

The calculation of the GNP deflator in the imaginary world of Table 2-3 is mere child's play compared to the real world with its thousands of individual products. This complex job requires not only the use of a large computer for all the arithmetic but also diligent legwork and many difficult choices. The GNP deflator is just one **price index** among the several published by the U.S. government. Of the others, the most important is the Consumer Price Index.

THE CONSUMER PRICE INDEX (CPI)

The Department of Commerce, which compiles and publishes the quarterly figures on nominal GNP, real GNP, and the implicit GNP deflator, does not actually collect the individual prices of round steak, eggs, and other products. This job of collection is performed by the U.S. Bureau of Labor Statistics (BLS), which also publishes two price indexes of its own, the Consumer Price Index (CPI) and the Producer Price Index (PPI).

The CPI, which is published monthly, is based on the prices of several thousand products. Prices paid by consumers are recorded by 250 price collectors who call or visit about 18,000 stores monthly in 56 cities, obtaining about 125,000 prices each month. Then the average prices for individual products, say round steak and eggs, are combined by the BLS into group indexes — for instance, "food and beverages." Then the group indexes are combined into the "all-items CPI." The weights used to combine the different product prices into group indexes and to arrive at the all-items index are based on the proportions of these items in consumer expenditures as recorded in a survey taken in 1972–73.

The Department of Commerce takes the group indexes of the CPI and puts them together according to a different set of rules when it computes the consumption component of the implicit GNP deflator. The importance of the differing rules used by Commerce and BLS became evident in 1979, when the two different price indexes for consumption goods differed by a major amount:

Quarterly percentage changes at annual rates

Year and quarter	Implicit GNP deflator for consumption	CPI
1978:Q1	8.07	7.09
1978:Q2	8.49	10.58
1978:Q3	6.89	9.64
1978:Q4	6.78	8.34
1979:Q1	10.82	10.71
1979:Q2	9.17	14.44
1979:Q3	9.76	13.73
1979:Q4	9.79	12.29
1980:Q1	12.37	17.07
1980:Q2	10.00	15.37

One important reason for the greater inflation recorded in 1978 and 1979 by the CPI was the use of obsolete 1972–73 expenditure weights. Since that date, for instance, energy prices have increased much faster than other prices, and so consumers have cut their consumption of energy. The current expenditure weights used by the Department of Commerce thus attach a lesser importance to the rising price of energy and yield an overall index that records a slower rate of inflation.

Another important difference between the Department of Commerce and BLS rules concerns the treatment of housing. The BLS procedures used in the CPI attach an excessive weight to current changes in mortgage rates, based on an unrealistic estimate of the proportion of households actually taking out new "mortgages" each month. The Department of Commerce, in contrast, uses the CPI group index for rent to give a rough indication of increases in the cost of home ownership. Although the Commerce method also has flaws, many observers think that the implicit GNP deflator for consumption is a more reliable indicator of inflation than the CPI for years such as 1979, when mortgage rates were rising rapidly. The only real advantage of the CPI has been its publication monthly (unlike the implicit GNP deflator, which was published quarterly). But in late 1979 the Department of Commerce began to publish a monthly consumption deflator, thus eliminating the last advantage of the CPI.[13]

Unfortunately, the CPI is used widely as a cost-of-living escalator in wage contracts as well as for many government transfer programs, including food stamps and social security. If the CPI erroneously measures too much inflation, then this tends to push up wages and to add to the government deficit, making inflation worse.

THE PRODUCER PRICE INDEX (PPI)

Another BLS price index, the Producer Price Index (PPI), collects prices on a large number of commodities that are not purchased directly by consumers. These include raw materials such as coal and crude oil, intermediate products such as flour and steel, and many types of machinery purchased by businesses (cash registers, tractors). The actual price data are recorded on mail questionnaires submitted monthly by thousands of firms that sell these goods. Just as the group indexes of the CPI are used for the consumption part of the implicit price deflator by the Department of Commerce, so product and group indexes of the PPI are used to create other components of the implicit GNP deflator, including producers' durable equipment and inventory investment.

Even after using the available information in the individual and group indexes in the CPI and PPI, the Department of Commerce still must make many difficult choices to obtain estimates of price change for goods that are not included in the BLS price-collection program, including electronic computers, jet aircraft, ships, and buildings.[14]

---

[13] The monthly implicit GNP deflator for personal consumption expenditures was introduced in James C. Byrnes et. al., "Monthly Estimates of Personal Income, Taxes, and Outlays," *Survey of Current Business* (November 1979), pp. 18–38. Differences between the CPI and personal consumption deflator are discussed in "Reconciliation of Quarterly Changes in Measures of Prices Paid by Consumers," *Survey of Current Business,* vol. 58, no. 3 (March 1978).

[14] Appendix A in the back of the book explores a few of the main flaws in the present techniques used to estimate the CPI, PPI, and implicit GNP deflator.

SUMMARY

1. This chapter is concerned with the definition and measurement of national income – what is included and excluded and why. Since many of the rules governing the calculation of national income are arbitrary, the size of any nation's GNP is at the discretion of its economists and government officials who mark off the dividing lines between the included and excluded items.

2. A flow magnitude is any money payment, physical good, or service that flows from one economic unit to another per unit of time. Examples are income, consumption, saving, and investment. A flow must be distinguished from a stock, which is an economic magnitude in the possession of an individual or firm at a moment of time. Examples are the stock of money, savings accounts, and capital equipment.

3. Final product (GNP) consists of all currently produced goods and services sold through the market but not resold. By counting intermediate goods only once, and by including only final purchases, we avoid double counting and ensure that the value of final product and total income created (value added) are equal.

4. Leakages out of income available for consumption goods are by definition exactly balanced by injections of nonconsumption spending. This equality of leakages and injections is guaranteed by the accounting methods used.

5. In the same way, by definition total income (consumption plus leakages) equals total expenditure (consumption plus injections). Injections of nonconsumption spending fall into three categories – private domestic investment (on business equipment and structures, residential housing, and inventory accumulation); foreign investment or net exports; and government spending on goods and services. The definitions require private investment (including domestic and foreign) to exceed private saving by the amount of the government surplus.

6. Net national product (NNP) is obtained by deducting depreciation from GNP. Deduction of indirect business taxes from NNP yields national income, the sum of all net incomes earned by factors of production in producing current output. If we deduct corporate undistributed profits, corporate income taxes and social security taxes, and add in transfer payments, we arrive at personal income, the sum of all income payments to individuals. Personal disposable income is simply personal income after the deduction of personal income taxes.

7. The implicit GNP deflator, the economy's aggregate price index (P), is defined as nominal GNP in actual current prices (Y) divided by real GNP measured in prices of a base year (Q). Other price indexes are the CPI and PPI.

A LOOK AHEAD

This completes our explanation of the government's measure of total income and product and its measure of the price deflator. The BLS has another branch that computes the monthly figures on employment and unemployment. We examine *its* methods in Section 10-2. In the next chapter we will turn to the elements of the theory of how real GNP (Q) is determined. The causes of changes in the GNP deflator (the price index P) are explored in Chapters 7 and 8. Combining the two theories, we will be able to explain nominal income (Y) through the definition $Y \equiv PQ$.

CONCEPTS

GNP, NNP, national income, personal income, personal disposable income

Implicit GNP deflator

Circular flow of income and expenditure

Value added

Final and intermediate goods

Transfer payments

Consumption expenditures

Inventory investment and fixed investment

Net foreign investment

Leakages and injections

Capital consumption allowances

Gross and net magnitudes

Undistributed corporate profits

CPI and PPI

QUESTIONS FOR REVIEW

1   Why is double counting a problem? How is the problem avoided in the U.S. national accounts (NIPA)?

2   How could a major disaster appear to make the economy seem better off under our current national accounts system?

3   How are government purchases treated differently from purchases by firms?

4   What is the difference between GNP and NNP? Between gross investment and net investment? Why are we interested in net magnitudes?

5   For a hypothetical country, the implicit GNP deflator for 1980 on a 1970 base is 1.50, and GNP in current dollars for 1980 is $750 million. What is real GNP for 1980 in constant 1970 dollars?

6   Indicate whether or not each of the following items is included in GNP, national income, and personal income:
a. Social security contributions.
b. Capital consumption allowances.

c. The increase in value of a house brought about by general inflation.

d. Salary of a city police officer protecting against vandalism.

e. Payment by a consumer for guards to protect against vandalism.

f. Five percent Illinois state sales tax.

7 Which flow pipe in Figure 2-6 contains dividends paid by corporations to households?

8 Three loaves of bread are produced by a bakery on December 31, 1980, and sold to a grocery store for 39 cents each. They are not sold until January 1, 1981, when consumers purchase them for 50 cents each. How much do the three loaves contribute to 1980 GNP? 1981 GNP?

9 Calculate nominal GNP, real GNP, and the implicit GNP deflator on a 1958 base in 1967, using the following information. The only products sold in the economy are electronic computers and haircuts.

		1958	1967
Computers:	Quantity	1	8
	Price	$500,000	$250,000
Haircuts:	Quantity	500,000	500,000
	Price	$1.00	$2.00

Part II

Determination of Real Output and the Price Level

3 Commodity-Market Equilibrium and the Multiplier

In those days, Roosevelt had to save his country from a tremendous economic crisis, perhaps the worst crisis that any modern country has ever faced.
—A. J. P. Taylor[1]

3-1 INCOME DETERMINATION AS AN EXPLANATION OF UNEMPLOYMENT

Figure 1-3 provides a convincing demonstration that unemployment is closely related to the gap between actual real GNP and natural real GNP. Understanding the causes of movements in actual real GNP is the key to understanding movements in the unemployment rate. This chapter sets out the elementary theory of how actual real GNP is determined and helps us explain modern recessions, the Great Depression of the 1930s, and the operation of fiscal policy. In subsequent chapters the elementary theory will be supplemented by elements that add to its realism without destroying its basic validity.

In this chapter we will make two important simplifying assumptions. First, the interest rate (and thus monetary policy) is not allowed to influence desired spending. We will focus on "equilibrium" in the commodity market, the market for goods and services. In the next chapter we will introduce an additional market for money. Changes in private spending will then be linked to the interest rate, allowing us to establish a connection between monetary policy and output.

The second assumption is that the price level is constant. Thus all changes in real income are also changes in nominal income of the same amount. For Chapters 3–5 we will maintain the assumption of "rigid" prices. Not until Chapter 6 will we begin our examination of the effects of private spending decisions and government policy on the price level.

---

[1] A. J. P. Taylor, *The War Lords* (New York: Penguin, 1978), p. 128.

3-2 THE DIVISION OF DISPOSABLE INCOME BETWEEN CONSUMPTION AND SAVING

To determine real income (which is the same as real GNP) we naturally start with the most important component of aggregate demand—personal consumption expenditures. By definition household disposable income (Q_D) is divided between consumption expenditures (C) and saving (S).[2] If additional dollars of income are mainly spent on consumption goods, then any initial boost in income (caused, let us say, by a sudden jump in investment) will cause a further increase in spending, production, and income. Since the initial jump in income causes further increases in income in this case, it thus destabilizes the economy. If, on the other hand, extra income is mainly saved rather than spent, the economy will tend to be more stable.

How do households divide their disposable income between consumption and saving? One possibility is that all disposable income is spent on consumption purchases. If this were the case, the relation between consumption and disposable income would be depicted by the thick black upward-sloping line in Figure 3-1 labeled $C = Q_D$. Because this line rises in a vertical direction by one dollar of consumption for each dollar of disposable income measured in the horizontal direction, it is sometimes called the "45-degree line." *Along this line, every dollar of disposable income is consumed.* Saving, the amount left over out of disposable income after consumption purchases are made, must therefore be zero. For instance, in Figure 3-1 find point F—here consumption and disposable income are both 400, so saving is zero.

THE CONSUMPTION FUNCTION AND THE MARGINAL PROPENSITY TO CONSUME

There are other possible relationships to consider. Let us imagine that households always spend $100 billion on consumption spending at every level of income, an amount we shall call **autonomous** consumption. The word *autonomous* means "completely independent of income." If autonomous consumption were the only form of consumption, then consumption expenditures (C) would simply be:

$$C = 100 \tag{3.1}$$

But we know that people tend to consume more as their disposable income increases. The amount by which consumption expenditures increase for each extra dollar of disposable income is a fraction called the **marginal propensity to consume.** For instance, we shall assume as an example that households consume 75 cents more for each extra dollar of disposable income they receive. This component of consumption is called **induced**

---

[2] For the rest of the chapter we consider only personal saving and ignore business saving. Thus personal saving is labeled S in this chapter instead of S_P as in Figure 2-6.

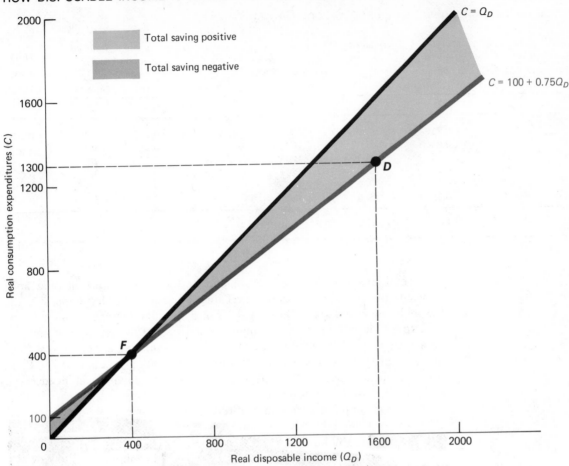

FIGURE 3–1

A Simple Hypothesis Regarding Consumption Behavior

Along the black upward-sloping line consumption equals disposable income.
The red line passing through F and D illustrates a more realistic possibility, that
consumption is 75 percent of disposable income plus an "autonomous" component of $100 billion that is spent regardless of the level of disposable income.
The pink area shows the amount of positive saving that occurs when income exceeds consumption; the gray area shows the amount of negative saving ("dissaving") that occurs when consumption exceeds income.

consumption. If induced consumption were the only form of consumption,
then consumption expenditures (C) would simply be the marginal propensity
to consume (0.75) times disposable income (Q_D):

$$C = 0.75Q_D \qquad (3.2)$$

TABLE 3-1

A Hypothetical Schedule of Consumption and Saving Behavior

Point in Figure 3-1	Disposable income ($ billions) (Q_D)	Marginal propensity to consume (c)	Induced consumption (cQ_D) (2) × (1)	Autonomous consumption (a)	Total consumption $a + cQ_D$ (4) + (3)	Marginal propensity to save (s)	Induced saving (sQ_D) (6) × (1)	Total saving $-a + sQ_D$ $-(4) + (7)$
	(1)	(2)	(3)	(4)	(5)	(6)	(7)	(8)
	0	0.75	0	100	100	0.25	0	−100
F	400	0.75	300	100	400	0.25	100	0
	800	0.75	600	100	700	0.25	200	100
	1200	0.75	900	100	1000	0.25	300	200
D	1600	0.75	1200	100	1300	0.25	400	300
	2000	0.75	1500	100	1600	0.25	500	400

Several examples of the relationship between disposable income and induced consumption are shown in Table 3-1. Along the left-hand side of the table are listed six different values of disposable income, ranging from zero to $2000 billion. Next, column (2) shows that the fraction of any increase in disposable income devoted to consumption expenditures (the marginal propensity to consume) is always an identical fraction, 0.75. This fraction times each level of disposable income is equal to induced consumption, as shown in column (3).

Total consumption is neither entirely induced nor entirely autonomous. Column (4) of the table shows that autonomous consumption is always the same amount ($100 billion) at every level of income. Total consumption in column (5) is the sum of autonomous consumption in column (4) and induced consumption in column (3).

The relationship between disposable income and the alternative levels of total consumption listed in column (5) is plotted as the thick red line in Figure 3-1. Look first to the left vertical axis of the diagram, where disposable income is zero. Total consumption here consists entirely of autonomous consumption ($100 billion). In addition, for every dollar of extra disposable income as we move to the right in the diagram, induced consumption rises by 75 percent of that amount. For instance, at point D disposable income is $1600 billion, induced consumption is three-quarters of that amount ($1200 billion), and autonomous consumption is $100 billion as always, leading to a total consumption level of $1300 billion.

The red line is called a **consumption function.** It shows the amount of total consumption spending for each level of disposable income. The consumption function can also be written as an equation. One way to write this equation is to use the specific numerical examples written in equations (3.1) and (3.2). Another way would be more general, using the alphabetical symbols a for autonomous consumption, c for the marginal propensity to consume, and cQ_D for induced consumption:

GENERAL FORM   NUMERICAL EXAMPLE

$$C = a + cQ_D \qquad\qquad C = 100 + 0.75Q_D \qquad (3.3)$$

Either way of writing the consumption function states that total consumption is the sum of autonomous consumption and induced consumption. The only difference is that the general form is always true, whereas the specific numerical example is only true in the particular case considered here. For instance, if autonomous consumption were to be 50 and the marginal propensity to consume were to be 0.5, the numerical example would change to $C = 50 + 0.5Q_D$.

THE SAVING FUNCTION AND INDUCED SAVING

The simplest way to show the amount of saving is to use a graph like Figure 3-1. The thick black line shows the amount of disposable income in both a horizontal and a vertical direction. Since the thick red line shows the consumption function, the distance between the two lines indicates the total amount of saving. To the right of point F total saving is positive because disposable income exceeds consumption; this is indicated by the pink shading. To the left of point F total saving is negative because consumption exceeds disposable income; this is indicated by the gray shading. How can saving be negative? Individuals can consume more than they earn, at least for a while, by withdrawing funds from a savings account, by selling stocks and bonds, or by borrowing. Negative saving is quite typical for many students who borrow to finance their education.

Table 3-1 also illustrates the determination of saving. The fraction of an extra dollar of disposable income that is not consumed is the **marginal propensity to save**, for which we use the abbreviation s. By definition each extra dollar of income must be consumed or saved, so the marginal propensities to consume and to save must add up to unity:

GENERAL FORM   NUMERICAL EXAMPLE

$$c + s = 1.0 \qquad\qquad 0.75 + 0.25 = 1.0 \qquad (3.4)$$

In column (6) of Table 3-1 we find that the marginal propensity to save is always the fraction 0.25 at every level of disposable income. **Induced saving** is the marginal propensity to save times disposable income, as shown in column (7). Total saving in column (8) is induced saving *minus* the amount of autonomous consumption, $100 billion at every level of disposable income. For instance, when disposable income is zero, induced saving must also be zero, and total saving is equal to minus $100 billion, the amount of autonomous consumption.

This relationship between induced saving, autonomous consumption, and total saving is illustrated in Figure 3-2. The top frame duplicates Figure

3-1 but emphasizes the division of disposable income between induced consumption ($0.75Q_D$) and induced saving ($0.25Q_D$). The red line indicates the consumption function, induced consumption plus $100 billion of autonomous consumption. The bottom frame subtracts induced consumption from the top frame and isolates the relationship between autonomous consumption and induced saving. As in Figure 3-1, the pink and gray shaded areas show the amount of total saving.

The *saving function* is just disposable income minus the consumption function. It is also equal to the amount of induced saving minus autonomous consumption:

GENERAL FORM	NUMERICAL EXAMPLE
$S = -a + sQ_D$	$S = -100 + 0.25Q_D$

It is easy to see that the saving function plus the consumption function must add up to disposable income:

$$S + C = -a + sQ_D + a + cQ_D$$
$$= (s + c)Q_D$$
$$= Q_D$$

THE AVERAGE PROPENSITIES TO CONSUME AND TO SAVE

The ratio of total consumption to disposable income (C/Q_D) is also called the **average propensity to consume**, and it is always equal to the consumption function divided by disposable income:

GENERAL FORM	NUMERICAL EXAMPLE
$\dfrac{C}{Q_D} = \dfrac{a}{Q_D} + c$	$\dfrac{C}{Q_D} = \dfrac{100}{Q_D} + 0.75$

FIGURE 3-2 (facing page)

The Relation between Induced Consumption, Induced Saving, and the Consumption Function

The upper frame duplicates Figure 3-1. The upward-sloping red line is exactly the same consumption function that was depicted in Figure 3-1, $C = 100 + 0.75Q_D$. Along the thick black line the vertical and horizontal dimensions are identical (this is a "45-degree line"), so we can read off disposable income in a vertical direction. The thin black line shows the dividing line between induced saving and induced consumption. Starting at zero disposable income, each extra dollar of disposable income is divided between 75 cents of induced consumption and 25 cents of induced saving. The consumption function is simply induced consumption plus the $100 billion of autonomous consumption. The lower frame subtracts induced consumption from the upper frame. It shows the relation between induced saving and autonomous consumption. Total saving in both parts of the diagram is shown by the pink and gray shading and equals induced saving minus autonomous consumption.

ANY CHANGE IN DISPOSABLE INCOME IS DIVIDED BETWEEN INDUCED CONSUMPTION AND INDUCED SAVING

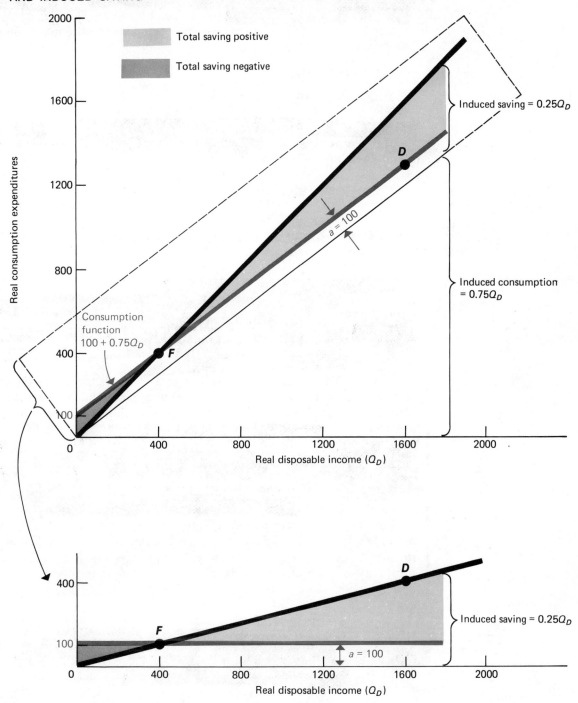

It is easy to see from the numerical example that the average propensity to consume is always larger than the marginal propensity, as long as autonomous consumption is positive. For instance, at point D in Figure 3-2 disposable income is $1600 billion, and the average propensity to consume is $1300/1600 = 0.8125$, or

$$\frac{C}{Q_D} = \frac{100}{1600} + 0.75 = 0.0625 + 0.75 = 0.8125$$

The average propensity to save is the ratio of total saving to disposable income. It is always equal to 1.0 minus the average propensity to consume. At point D in Figure 3-2 the average propensity to save is $300/1600$, or 0.1875.

3-3 CASE STUDY: ACTUAL U.S. CONSUMPTION AND SAVING BEHAVIOR

When disposable income falls very low, as it did during the Great Depression, households take money out of their savings accounts or borrow in order to buy the basic necessities of life.[3] Saving is negative (dissaving), because consumers must draw on their savings accounts and other assets in order to purchase the consumption goods that their disposable income alone can no longer purchase.

Figure 3-3, arranged exactly like Figure 3-1, shows the actual values of disposable income, consumption, and saving in the United States during the years 1929–79. Three major conclusions can be drawn from the evidence. First, both consumption and saving have increased as disposable income has grown during the years since World War II. Second, in the worst year of the Great Depression, households consumed more than their incomes, so that saving was slightly negative in 1933. Third, these usual peacetime relationships were interrupted during World War II (1942–45), when consumer goods were unavailable or rationed. In that period households were forced to consume much less and save much more than is normal in peacetime. After the war, consumers rushed out to spend their accumulated savings accounts, helping to maintain prosperity in spite of the drastic drop in government spending that occurred in 1945–46.

---

[3] Be careful to distinguish between "savings" (with a terminal "s"), which is the stock of assets that households have in savings accounts or under the mattress, from "saving" (without a terminal "s"), which is the *flow* per unit of time that leaks out of disposable income (see Figure 2-6) and is unavailable for purchases of consumption goods. It is the flow of *saving* that is designated by the symbol S.

HOW ACTUAL U.S. DISPOSABLE INCOME HAS BEEN SPLIT BETWEEN CONSUMPTION
AND SAVING

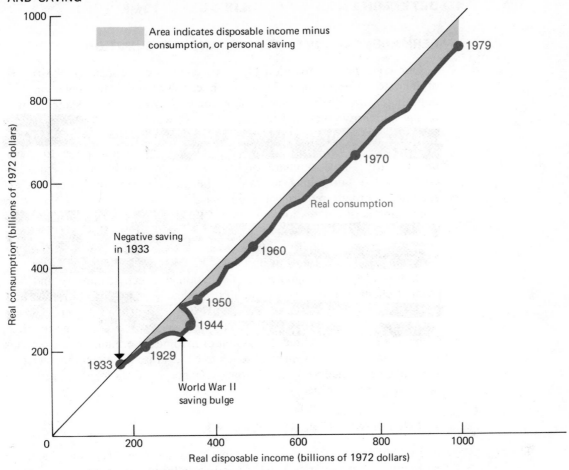

FIGURE 3-3

Consumption, Saving, and Disposable Income, 1929–79

Notice that in 1933 U.S. saving was negative. In 1979 saving was positive and
amounted to 4.5 percent of disposable income, leaving the remaining 95.5 percent
for consumption (93.0 percent) and interest payments (2.5 percent). Saving was
unusually high during World War II because consumer goods were rationed.

Source: Economic Report of the President (January 1980), and Supplements to the *Survey
of Current Business.*

3-4 DETERMINATION OF EQUILIBRIUM INCOME

PERMANENT INCOME, WEALTH, AND CONSUMPTION

Our consumption function (3.3) is a central component of the theory of income determination. How much can we trust its implication that households alter their consumption purchases by exactly the same fraction of any increase in income? In Chapter 13 we will find that households base their consumption purchases not on their current income, but on their perception of "permanent" or "lifetime" income. They prefer to maintain a fairly stable standard of living consistent with their average income over a fairly long interval, rather than raising or lowering their spending (perhaps requiring the purchase or sale of a house or car) with every short-term fluctuation in income. For this reason, a temporary change in income (caused, for instance, by an income tax rebate or a short-term layoff) may cause only a minor change in consumption compared to a change in income perceived to be permanent (for instance, a job promotion).

In this chapter we ignore the distinction between temporary and permanent changes in income to simplify the theory. The marginal propensity to consume (c) is assumed to be the same for all changes of disposable income, regardless of their source or expected duration.[4] This assumption helps to simplify our initial discussion of income determination but implies that our analysis in this chapter tends to exaggerate the effect on consumption and total income of temporary changes in investment, government spending, and tax rates.

PLANNED INVESTMENT SPENDING

In addition to our neglect of interest rates and monetary policy, and our assumption that the price level is fixed, initially in this chapter we examine the determination of real GNP in a simple economy in which both government expenditures and tax revenues are equal to zero. Thus total expenditures on GNP include only consumption and investment.

Total domestic investment includes business purchases of new structures and equipment, expenditures on residential apartments and houses by individuals and firms, and changes in business inventories. We saw in Figure 2-5 that investment expenditures have been extremely variable over most of the postwar period. For instance, between 1974 and 1975 real investment dropped from $183.6 to $142.6 billion, for a decline of 22 percent. In the Great Depression of the 1930s, between 1929 and 1933 investment declined by over 80 percent.

---

[4] All of any dollar of disposable income must be either consumed or saved. Thus the marginal propensity to save (s) is equal to the fraction of a dollar not consumed ($s = 1 - c$).

Our task in this chapter is not to explain the causes of fluctuations in private investment (we turn to this question in Chapter 4). Instead, we attempt to answer a more limited question. *Given* the level of investment, what determines the total level of real GNP and real income? Throughout the chapter, the level of planned investment will be an assumed **parameter**, taken as given or known within a given analysis. For instance, initially we shall assume that planned autonomous investment (I_p) is $200 billion:

$$I_p = 200 \qquad (3.5)$$

So far we have encountered two other parameters in our analysis, the level of autonomous consumption (a = $100 billion) and the marginal propensity to consume ($c = 0.75$). As in the case of planned investment, these values are assumed to be given within a particular analysis and not to respond to changes in income. Instead, our task is to determine the level of real GNP for given values of these parameters. Then, once we know real GNP, we can ask how much real GNP would change if we were to allow *one* of the parameters to change; for instance, to allow planned autonomous investment to rise from $200 to $300 billion.

TOTAL PLANNED EXPENDITURES

The total of household and business purchases, or planned expenditures (E_p), is the amount of household consumption (C) plus business planned investment (I_p):

$$E_p = C + I_p \qquad (3.6)$$

Substituting the consumption function (3.3) for C, (3.6) becomes:[5]

GENERAL FORM   NUMERICAL EXAMPLE

$$E_p = a + cQ + I_p \qquad E_p = 100 + 0.75Q + 200 \qquad (3.7)$$

In Figure 3-4 the red planned expenditure (E_p) line plots the numerical example in equation (3.7). The E_p line lies above the red consumption function line by exactly $200 billion, the amount of planned investment.

The lower frame of Figure 3-4 starts with the horizontal red autonomous consumption line that was drawn in Figure 3-2. Then, when $200 billion of planned autonomous investment is added, we obtain the total $300 billion level of "planned autonomous spending" (A_p). The upper red horizontal line in the lower frame shows that the level of A_p is independent of the level of income. If *either* planned autonomous investment (I_p) or autonomous consumption (a) were to increase, this red line would shift upward, as would the total planned expenditures (E_p) line in the top frame of the diagram.

---

[5] The consumption function depends on disposable income (Q_D) in Figure 3-1 and equation (3.3). But in Figure 3-4 and equation (3.7) the consumption function depends on total real income (Q). This makes no difference because $Q = Q_D$ under our current assumption in this chapter that there is no business saving and no tax collections by the government.

WHEN IS THE ECONOMY IN EQUILIBRIUM?

A basic lesson of Chapter 2 was that *actual* expenditures (E) and total income (Q) are always equal by definition. But there is no reason for income (Q) always to equal *planned* expenditures (E_p). The main principle of this chapter is that the economy is in **equilibrium** when income is equal to planned expenditures. Only then do households and business firms want to spend exactly the amount of income that is being generated by the current level of production, all of which can be sold to households and firms.

Equilibrium is *a situation in which there is no pressure for change*. When the economy is out of equilibrium, production and income are out of line with expenditures, and business firms will be forced to raise or lower production.

This central idea is illustrated in Figure 3-5. The thick black line in the top frame has a slope of 45 degrees; everywhere along it the level of income plotted on the horizontal axis is equal to the level of expenditures plotted on the vertical axis. Hence the black line is labeled $E = Q$. The red line is the total level of planned expenditures (E_p) and is copied directly from Figure 3-4. Only where the black and red lines cross at point B is income equal to planned expenditure. Only point B represents a situation of equilibrium in which there is no pressure for change. Households and business firms want to spend $1200 billion when income is $1200 billion, which is created by the $1200 billion of production to produce the goods and services that households and business firms want to buy.

WHAT HAPPENS OUT OF EQUILIBRIUM?

The economy is out of equilibrium at all other points along the 45-degree income line. For instance, at point J, income (which always equals production) is $1600 billion. How much do households and business firms want to spend? The three components of planned expenditures are:

FIGURE 3-4 (facing page)

Planned Autonomous Investment and the Level of Total Planned Expenditures

In the upper frame the lower red line repeats the red consumption function from Figure 3-1. When we add $200 billion of planned autonomous investment, we obtain total planned expenditures as illustrated by the upper red line. The lower frame repeats the red autonomous consumption line from Figure 3-2 and adds to the $100 billion of autonomous consumption the $200 billion of planned autonomous investment. The total of these two, $300 billion, is shown by the upper horizontal red line and is called "planned autonomous spending" (A_p).

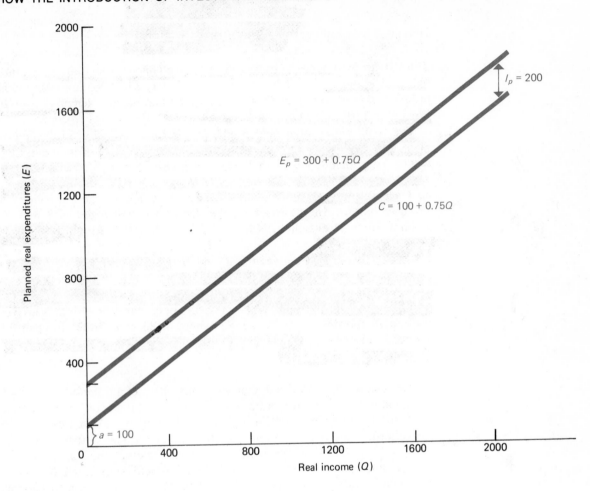

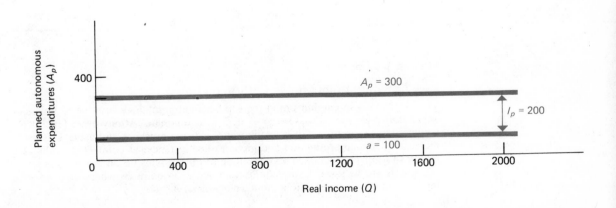

$$\begin{array}{rl}
\text{Planned autonomous investment } (I_p) = & 200 \\
\text{Induced consumption } (0.75Q) = & 1200 \\
\text{Autonomous consumption } (a) = & 100 \\
\hline
\text{Planned expenditures } (E_p) = & 1500
\end{array}$$

Thus at an income level of $1600 billion, planned expenditures (E_p) are only $1500 billion (point H on the E_p line). Only $1500 billion of the total production (= income) level of $1600 billion can be sold, leaving business firms with $100 billion of unsold merchandise.

The $100 billion of unsold production is counted as inventory investment, but businesses do not desire this inventory buildup (if they did, they would have included it in their planned investment, I_p). To bring inventories back to the original desired level, businesses react to the situation at J by cutting production and income, which moves the economy left toward point B. In the diagram, the distance between points J and H, amounting to $100 billion, is labeled I_u, which stands for **unintended inventory investment.**

The triangular area between B, J, and H measures the excess of income over planned expenditures—that is, the positive value of I_u. Production and income will be cut until this area disappears and the unwanted inventory buildup ceases ($I_u = 0$). This occurs only when the economy arrives back at B, the only level of income where no force operates to push the economy elsewhere. Only at B are businesses producing exactly the amount that can be sold.

Example: In early 1980, consumer purchases of automobiles declined, and industry found itself producing more cars than consumers wanted to buy. The Chrysler Corporation had so many unsold cars in stock that it ran out of room to store them. Since this inventory accumulation by Chrysler was unplanned and undesired, the company's reaction was a drastic cut in production and substantial layoffs of employees, which meant a cut in Chrysler's contribution to national income and national product. The whole auto industry's contribution

---

FIGURE 3–5 (facing page)

How Equilibrium Income Is Determined

The economy is in equilibrium in the top frame at point B, where the red planned expenditures (E_p) line crosses the 45-degree income line. At any other level of income, the economy is out of equilibrium, causing pressure on business firms to increase or reduce production and income. For instance, at point H, E_p falls $100 billion short of production, so $100 billion of output piles up on the shelves unsold ($I_u = 100$). In the lower frame equilibrium occurs at point B, where induced saving (sQ) equals planned autonomous spending (A_p).

THE ECONOMY IS IN EQUILIBRIUM ONLY WHERE THE RED AND BLACK LINES CROSS

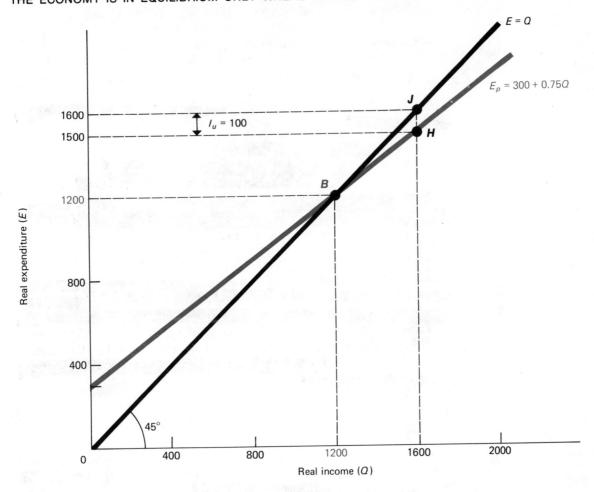

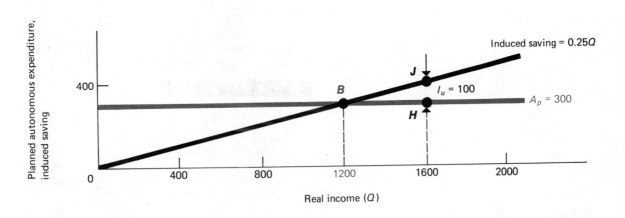

Determination of Equilibrium Income **69**

to GNP fell from $58.1 billion in the first quarter of 1979 to 36.9 billion in the second quarter of 1980, a decline of 37 percent.[6]

Exercise: What happens in the top frame of Figure 3-5 when income is only $800 billion? Describe the forces that move the economy back to equilibrium at B.

At point J, as in every situation, income and actual expenditures are equal by definition:

$$\text{income } (Q) \equiv \text{expenditures } (E)$$
$$\equiv \text{desired spending } (E_p = C + I_p) +$$
$$\text{unintended inventory accumulation } (I_u) \qquad (3.8)$$

By contrast, the economy is in equilibrium only when unintended inventory accumulation or decumulation is equal to zero $(I_u = 0)$. Equation (3.8) can be rewritten to describe the economy's equilibrium situation:[7]

$$Q = E_p \qquad (3.9)$$

Economists sometimes use the Latin phrase **ex post** to describe the total expenditure that is actually made "after the fact" $(E_p + I_u)$. **Ex ante** describes the expenditure that is desired or planned "before the fact" (E_p). In Table 3-2 the definitional requirement of equation (3.8) — that income is always equal to *ex post* spending — is compared with the statement of equation (3.9) — that the economy is in equilibrium only when income is equal to *ex ante* spending.

AUTONOMOUS PLANNED SPENDING EQUALS INDUCED SAVING

The lower frame of Figure 3-5 illustrates the determination of equilibrium income in a slightly different way. It subtracts induced consumption from both income and planned expenditure. The red horizontal line is total planned autonomous spending (A_p), which includes the $100 billion of autonomous consumption (a), plus the $200 billion in planned autonomous investment (I_p).

Take the definition of equilibrium in equation (3.9) and subtract induced consumption (cQ) from both sides of that equation:

$$Q - cQ = E_p - cQ$$

---

[6] Seasonally adjusted totals at annual rates in constant 1972 prices.

[7] Another requirement for equilibrium, assumed throughout this chapter, is that there is no unintended consumption or saving. In other words, households are always "on" their consumption function, consuming exactly the fraction of saving that they desire.

TABLE 3-2

Comparison of the Economy's "Always True"
and Equilibrium Situations

	Always true by definition	True only in equilibrium
1. What concept of expenditures is equal to income?	Actual (*ex post*) expenditures including unintended inventory accumulation	Planned (*ex ante*) expenditures
2. Amount of unintended inventory accumulation (I_u)?	Can be any amount, positive or negative	Must be zero
3. Which equation is valid, (3.8) or (3.9)?	(3.8) $Q = E = E_p + I_u$	(3.9) $Q = E_p$
4. Described by which point in top frame of Figure 3-5?	Any point on 45-degree income line (example: point J)	Only at point where E_p line crosses 45-degree income line
5. Numerical example in Figure 3-5?	At point J, $Q(1600) = E(1600)$ $= E_p(1500) + I_u(100)$	At point B, $Q(1200) = E_p(1200)$

We can replace $E_p - cQ$ on the right-hand side by its equivalent, A_p:[8]

$$(1 - c)Q = A_p \tag{3.10}$$

Because the marginal propensity to save equals 1.0 minus the marginal propensity to consume ($s = 1 - c$), we can rewrite (3.10) as:

GENERAL FORM	NUMERICAL EXAMPLE	
$sQ = A_p$	$0.25Q = 300$	(3.11)

Thus the definition of equilibrium requires induced saving (sQ) to equal planned autonomous spending (A_p). The black sloped induced saving line in the lower frame of Figure 3-5 rises by $0.25 per $1.00 of income and crosses the red A_p line at point B, which is at an income level of $1200 billion and lies directly beneath the top frame's point B. The economy is in equilibrium at B in the top frame because production (Q) equals planned

---

[8] Because $E_p = a + cQ + I_p$ in equation (3.7), it follows that $E_p - cQ = a + I_p$. When we define total planned autonomous spending (A_p) as equal to $a + I_p$, we obtain the right-hand side of (3.10).

spending (E_p). When this occurs, point B in the lower frame shows that the induced leakage out of the spending stream into saving (sQ) just balances the planned autonomous spending (A_p) injected back into the spending stream by autonomous consumption (a) and planned investment (I_p).

The equilibrium level of income is always equal to planned autonomous spending (A_p) divided by the marginal propensity to save (s), as we can see when both sides of (3.11) are divided by s:

GENERAL FORM   NUMERICAL EXAMPLE

$$Q = \frac{A_p}{s} \qquad\qquad Q = \frac{300}{0.25} = 1200 \qquad\qquad (3.12)$$

Equilibrium income must be high enough to generate enough induced saving to balance planned autonomous spending. In our numerical example, \$1.00 of income generates \$0.25 of induced saving. This means \$1200 billion of income is required to generate the \$300 billion of induced saving needed to balance \$300 billion of planned autonomous spending.

GENERAL METHOD FOR DETERMINING EQUILIBRIUM INCOME

The lower frame of Figure 3-5 and equation (3.12) both illustrate the two-step method used throughout the chapter for determining income. To represent this in a graph, first draw a horizontal line at a height equal to planned autonomous spending (A_p). Then plot a line with a slope equal to the marginal propensity to save (s). The point where the horizontal A_p line crosses the sloped sQ line indicates the equilibrium level of income. At any other point, for instance, J, sQ does not balance A_p, indicating an unplanned increase or decrease in inventories.

Income equilibrium can be determined using the same technique with the symbols in equation (3.12). The numerator is A_p and corresponds to the horizontal A_p line in the figure. The denominator is the fraction of income that leaks out of the spending stream into saving, corresponding to the slope of the induced saving line in the figure.

3-5 THE MULTIPLIER EFFECT

The conclusion of section 3-4, that equilibrium income equals \$1200 billion, is absolutely dependent on the assumption that planned autonomous spending (A_p) equals \$300 billion. It is clear that any change in autonomous spending will cause a change in equilibrium income. To illustrate the consequences of a change in A_p, assume that business people become more optimistic, raising their guess as to the likely profitability of new investment projects. They increase their investment spending by \$100 billion, boosting A_p from \$300 billion to \$400 billion.[9] In each situation where a change is described, a numbered subscript is used to distinguish the original from the new situation. Thus A_{p0} denotes the original level of A_p (\$300 billion), and A_{p1} denotes the new level (\$400 billion).

Economic theorists typically examine the effects of a change in one parameter on the assumption that all other things are equal. This technique of analysis is sometimes described by the Latin phrase, *ceteris paribus*, abbreviated *cet. par.*, which means "other things being equal." Therefore, in equation (3.12) where the only "other thing" besides A_p determining income is s (the marginal propensity to save), we assume in this section that s is constant. The equilibrium level of income in the new and old situations can be immediately calculated from equation (3.12):

	GENERAL FORM	NUMERICAL EXAMPLE	
Take new situation	$Q_1 = \dfrac{A_{p1}}{s}$	$Q_1 = \dfrac{400}{0.25} = 1600$	
Subtract old situation	$Q_0 = \dfrac{A_{p0}}{s}$	$Q_1 = \dfrac{300}{0.25} = 1200$	
Equals change in income	$\Delta Q = \dfrac{\Delta A_p}{s}$	$\Delta Q = \dfrac{100}{0.25} = 400$	(3.13)

The top line of the table calculates the new level of income when $A_{p1} = 400$. The second line calculates the original level of income when $A_{p0} = 300$. The change in income, abbreviated ΔQ, is simply the first line minus the second. The autonomous spending multiplier (k) is defined as the ratio of the change in income (ΔQ) to the change in planned autonomous spending (ΔA_p) that causes it:

$$\text{Multiplier } (k) = \frac{\Delta Q}{\Delta A_p} = \frac{1}{s} \qquad \frac{\Delta Q}{\Delta A_p} = \frac{1}{0.25} = 4.0$$

In Figure 3-6 we can see why the multiplier (k) is $1/s$, or 4.0. Each frame of 3-6 reproduces from Figure 3-5 the "original situation," with A_p at its original value of \$300 billion. In the top frame the original equilibrium occurs at point B, where the dashed red original planned expenditure (E_p) line crosses the black 45-degree income line. Now a new red E_p line is drawn exactly \$100 billion above the original E_p line. Point B clearly no longer represents equilibrium, since planned expenditures have risen to \$1300, exceeding income at B by \$100 billion. The \$100 billion excess of desired spending, distance RB, causes an undesired \$100 billion drop in inventories ($I_u = -100$). In order to restock their shelves businesses raise production

---

[9] Increased business investment raises I_p from \$200 billion to \$300 billion. Since autonomous consumption (a) is unchanged at \$100 billion, A_p, the sum of the two, increases by \$100 billion from \$300 billion to \$400 billion.

and income until they equal spending. The economy moves right from *B* to *J*, which ends unintended inventory decumulation.

The lower frame of Figure 3-6 shows the same $400 billion increase in income caused by the $100 billion increase in A_p. The A_p line shifts upward by $100 billion and intersects the fixed induced saving line at point *J*. Since in equilibrium—see equation (3.11)—induced saving (sQ) equals A_p, induced saving must increase by $100 billion. Because only 25 percent of extra income is saved, income must rise by $400 billion to generate the required $100 billion increase in induced saving. In terms of the line segments in the lower frame:

$$\text{Multiplier } (k) = \frac{\Delta Q}{\Delta A_p} = \frac{RJ}{RB} = \frac{1}{s}, \quad \text{since } s = \frac{RB}{RJ}$$

What actually happens in the real world when the multiplier effect is in operation? Figure 3-7 magnifies the triangle *RBJ* in the top frame of Figure 3-6 in order to show what happens during the transition between the original equilibrium at *B* and the new equilibrium at *J*. The vertical line segment extending from *B* to *R* shows the initial $100 billion increase in A_p. Because production and income have not yet been increased to satisfy the higher sales, all added autonomous spending must be supplied by drawing down inventories. Thus the segment *BR* also represents inventory decumulation of $100 billion ($I_u = -100$).

To adjust, business firms must increase production and income (ΔQ) by just enough to restock their inventories. Along the line segment from *R* to *d* the horizontal movement (ΔQ) is exactly the same distance as the previous inventory decumulation. The consumption function states that 0.75 of the extra income, or $75 billion, will be spent on consumption purchases, which is indicated by the vertical expenditure increase along line segment *de*. But production has gone up only by enough to supply the initial extra demand for A_p. The $75 billion of extra consumption spending can only be supplied by drawing inventories again by $75 billion.

FIGURE 3–6 (facing page)

The Change in Equilibrium Income Caused by a $100 Billion Increase in Autonomous Planned Spending

Increasing planned autonomous spending (A_p) by $100 billion raises the planned expenditures (E_p) line in the top frame up vertically by $100 billion. The economy's equilibrium position where the red E_p line crosses the black 45-degree income line shifts from point *B* to point *J*. Thus the change in A_p has a multiplier effect, raising income by $400 billion. In the lower frame the horizontal red A_p line shifts up by $100 billion, also moving the equilibrium position from *B* to *J*, and also showing the operation of the multiplier effect.

HOW HIGHER AUTONOMOUS PLANNED SPENDING RAISES INCOME

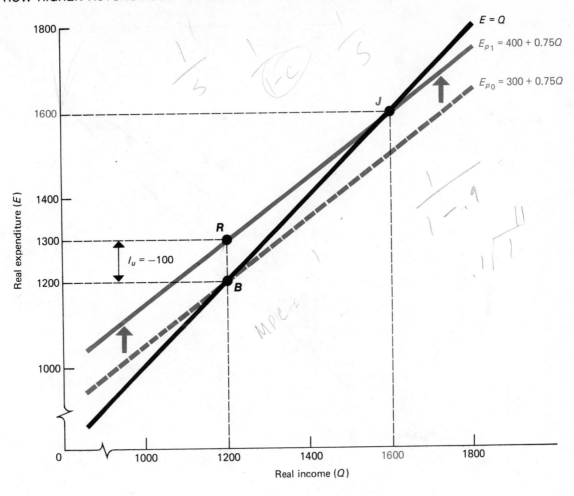

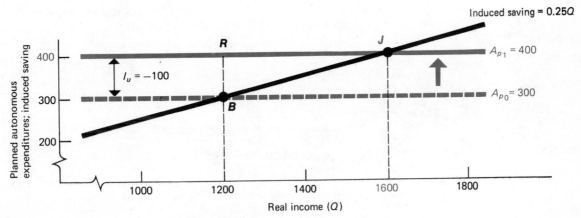

HOW HIGHER A_p SPURS CONSUMPTION SPENDING

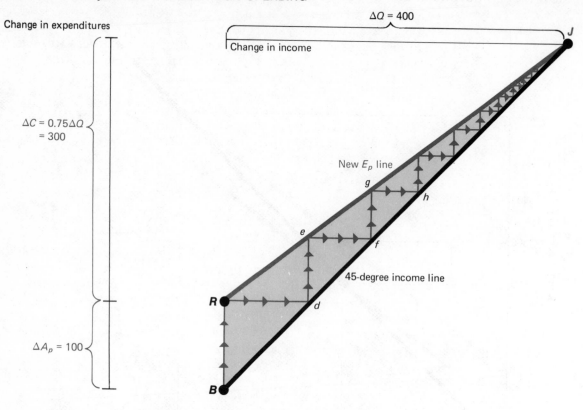

Change in expenditures

$\Delta Q = 400$

Change in income

$\Delta C = 0.75 \Delta Q$
$= 300$

New E_p line

g

h

e

f

45-degree income line

R

d

$\Delta A_p = 100$

B

J

FIGURE 3–7

The Effect of a $100 Billion Increase in A_p on Consumption and Income

The table below provides a detailed explanation of each line segment, starting with the inventory decumulation of $100 billion (the segment RB) caused by the initial $100 billion boost in planned autonomous spending.

(1) Line segment	(2) ΔA_p	(3) $\Delta E_p = \Delta A_p + c \Delta Q$	(4) $I_u = -\Delta E_p$	(5) $\Delta Q = -I_u$
B to R	100	$100 = 100$	-100	—
R to d	—	—	—	100
d to e	0	$75 = 0 + 0.75\,(100)$	-75	—
e to f	—	—	—	75
f to g	0	$56.25 = 0 + 0.75\,(75)$	-56.25	—
g to h	—	—	—	56.25
Cumulative from B to J	100	$400 = 100 + 0.75\,(300)$	—	400

At the next stage the adjustment continues. Once again business firms increase production (the segment *ef*) to restock their inventories, once again consumption spending is induced (*f* to *g*), and once again inventories are decumulated. Notice that the amount of inventory decumulation becomes less and less at each stage, until finally at *J* it stops, and the economy returns to equilibrium. The total horizontal movement is the change in production and income, and the vertical movement is the sum of ΔA_p plus the induced consumption at each stage.[10] Higher investment starts off the multiplier expansion, and the induced consumption expenditures of income recipients keep the expansion going until total income and production once again equal planned expenditures.

3-6 RECESSIONS AND FISCAL POLICY

Is a multiplier expansion or contraction of output following a change in planned autonomous spending desirable or not? The answer depends on the desired level of total real income. In section 1-3 we defined natural real GNP as the highest level of real GNP attainable without causing an accelerating inflation. A multiplier expansion or contraction of output is favorable if it moves the economy closer to its natural real GNP and is unfavorable if it pushes the economy away from natural real GNP.

Assume that the level of natural real GNP is $1600 billion. In the bottom frame of Figure 3-6 a level of planned autonomous spending (A_p) of $400 billion would be perfect, for it would bring about an equilibrium level of actual real GNP of $1600 billion at point *J*, the desired level. On the other

---

[10] It is possible to use an algebraic trick to prove that the sum of ΔA_p plus the induced consumption at each stage is exactly equal to the multiplier $(1/s)$ times ΔA_p. The first round of consumption is $c\Delta A_p$. The second is c times the first, $c(C\Delta A_p)$, or $c^2 A_p$. Thus the total ΔQ is the series:

$$\Delta Q = \Delta A_p \quad + c\Delta A_p + c^2\Delta A_p + \cdots + c^n\Delta A_p \tag{a}$$

"Factor out" the common element ΔA_p on the right-hand side of equation (a):

$$\Delta Q = \Delta A_p(1.0 + c \quad + c^2 \quad + \cdots + c^n \quad) \tag{b}$$

Subtract c times both sides of equation (b):

$$-c\Delta Q = \Delta A_p(\quad - c \quad - c^2 \quad - \cdots - c^n - c^{n+1}) \tag{c}$$

The difference between line (b) and (c) is:

$$(1 - c)\Delta Q = \Delta A_p(1.0 \qquad\qquad - c^{n+1}) \tag{d}$$

Since c^{n+1} is almost zero (because c is a fraction and $n + 1$ is large), we can neglect it. Dividing both sides of equation (d) by $(1 - c)$, we obtain the familiar:

$$\Delta Q = \frac{\Delta A_p}{1 - c} = \frac{\Delta A_p}{s}$$

hand, a decline in A_p by \$100 billion would cut equilibrium income to \$1200 billion at B and would open up a gap of \$400 billion between actual and natural GNP.

What might cause actual real GNP to decline below natural real GNP? A drop in planned investment (I_p), a major component of A_p, can be and has been a major cause of recessions and depressions. In the Great Depression, for instance, fixed investment dropped by 74 percent, and this contributed to the 29 percent decline in actual real GNP between those years.[11] But the changing plans of business firms are not the only possible cause of a change in planned autonomous spending. Changes in household autonomous consumption (a) can cause exactly the same kinds of effects on income as changes in the level of planned investment.

GOVERNMENT SPENDING AND TAXATION

The government can adjust its expenditures on goods and services as well as its tax revenues in an attempt to offset fluctuations in autonomous investment and consumption. Thus far our simple economic model in this chapter has excluded any consideration of the government sector. Now it is time to introduce government spending and taxation, which alter the economy in two ways. We will see that an increase in government spending can raise total income through the multiplier effect, and how an increase in tax revenue has the opposite impact.

First, government spending on goods and services (G) is part of planned expenditures. Thus equation (3.6) is modified:

$$E_p = C + I_p + G \qquad (3.14)$$

Second, a positive level of tax revenues (T) reduces disposable income (Q_D) below total actual income (Q):

$$Q_D = Q - T \qquad (3.15)$$

Inserting (3.15) into the consumption function makes the level of consumption spending depend on tax revenues:

$$C = a + cQ_D = a + c(Q - T) \qquad (3.16)$$

We have previously developed a simple theory stating that equilibrium income equals planned autonomous spending (A_p) divided by the marginal propensity to save (s). What is A_p in an economy influenced by the government? Substituting the definition of consumption in (3.16) into the definition of planned spending in (3.14), we have:

$$E_p = a + cQ - cT + I_p + G \qquad (3.17)$$

---

[11] These figures are discussed further and their sources are identified in Figure 3-8.

Planned autonomous spending (A_p) is simply E_p minus induced consumption (cQ), if total tax revenues (T) can be treated as autonomous:

$$A_p = a - c\bar{T} + I_p + G \qquad (3.18)$$

We have converted (3.17) into (3.18) by subtracting cQ and by writing a "bar" on top of $\bar{T}$. The bar reminds us that tax revenues are assumed to be *autonomous*—that is, they do not change automatically with income. Examples of autonomous taxes are local dog licenses and property taxes.[12]

Now we are equipped with a complete theory of income determination that takes into account government spending (G) and autonomous tax revenue ($\bar{T}$). Equation (3.18) implies that the change in planned autonomous spending equals the change in four components. If we insert the symbol "Δ," which means "change in," in front of each element in equation (3.18), we have an exact statement of the four different events that can cause a change in planned autonomous spending. The only element that does not have the "change in" symbol written in front is the marginal propensity to consume (c), which we are assuming to be fixed throughout this discussion:

$$\Delta A_p = \Delta a - c\Delta\bar{T} + \Delta I_p + \Delta G \qquad (3.19)$$

In other words, the four causes of changes in A_p are:

1. A $1 change in autonomous consumption (a) changes A_p by $1 in the same direction.
2. A $1 change in autonomous tax revenue ($\bar{T}$) changes A_p by c (the marginal propensity to consume) times $1 in the opposite direction. For example, a $100 billion increase in $\bar{T}$ would reduce A_p by $75 billion if c were 0.75. How do households pay for the other $25 billion in higher tax revenue? They obtain the $25 billion by reducing their saving.
3. A $1 change in planned investment (I_p) changes A_p by $1 in the same direction.
4. A $1 change in government spending (G) changes A_p by $1 in the same direction.

Summary: Real income can be raised or lowered by a change in autonomous consumption (a), tax revenues ($\bar{T}$), planned investment (I_p), or government spending (G). The job of government fiscal policy is to control tax revenues and government spending to offset undesired changes in private autonomous spending (a and I_p).

Once the change in A_p has been calculated from this list, our basic multi-

---

[12] The value of property subject to taxation does not increase immediately as income goes up because most local governments perform the laborious task of property assessment only at infrequent intervals.

plier expression from (3.13) determines the resulting change in equilibrium income:

$$\Delta Q = \frac{\Delta A_p}{s} \tag{3.13}$$

FISCAL EXPANSION AND THE GOVERNMENT DEFICIT

To provide an example of a situation in which higher government spending can expand real income, let us assume that initially the level of private autonomous planned spending (A_p) is 300. This means that the level of real income will be 1200, as shown at point B in the top frame of Figure 3-8. If natural real GNP were 1200, then point B would be satisfactory, but we are assuming that natural real GNP is at the level of $1600 billion. Thus point B represents a situation in which actual real GNP and real income are $400 billion too low, and in which many members of the labor force are jobless. How can government fiscal policy correct this situation through its control over the level of government expenditures?

It is clear from our basic income-determination formula (3.13) that the required $400 billion increase in real income and real GNP can be achieved by any action that can raise autonomous spending (A_p) by $100 billion. Two possibilities are (1) a $100 billion increase in G (government spending on goods and services) and (2) a $133 billion reduction in autonomous tax revenue.[13]

The $100 billion change in government spending ($\Delta G = 100$) in Figure 3-8 has exactly the same effect on income as any other $100 billion increase in A_p. The economy reaches a new equilibrium at point J, just as it did in Figure 3-6. The multiplier (k) for ΔG is also the same. As before, we calculate the multiplier by taking the change in income (ΔQ) and dividing it by the thing that is changing (ΔG in this case):

GENERAL FORM   NUMERICAL EXAMPLE

$$k = \frac{\Delta Q}{\Delta G} = \frac{\Delta Q}{\Delta A_p} = \frac{1}{s} \qquad k = \frac{\Delta Q}{\Delta G} = \frac{1}{0.25} = 4.0 \tag{3.20}$$

In the top frame of Figure 3-8 the government manages to push total income up from $1200 billion at point B to $1600 billion at point J by making $100 billion of purchases. Since its tax revenues remain at zero, the government's purchases cause a government deficit of $100 billion:

$$\text{government deficit} = G - T = \$100 \text{ billion}$$

---

[13] Why $133 billion? Because according to equation (3.19), a reduction in taxes raises A_p by c times the reduction, where c is the marginal propensity to consume. If $c = 0.75$, as in our numerical example, then

$$\Delta A_p = c\Delta T = -0.75(-133) = 100$$

Recall that transfer payments are equivalent to negative taxes, so that a $133 billion reduction in taxes has the same impact on A_p as a $133 billion increase in transfer payments (welfare, social security, or such).

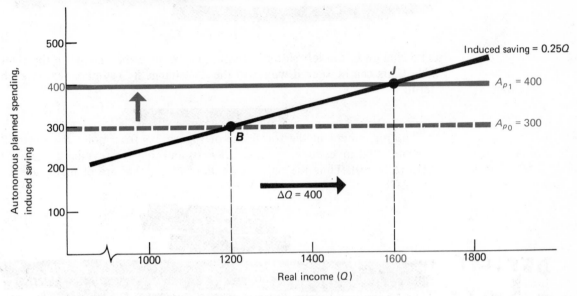

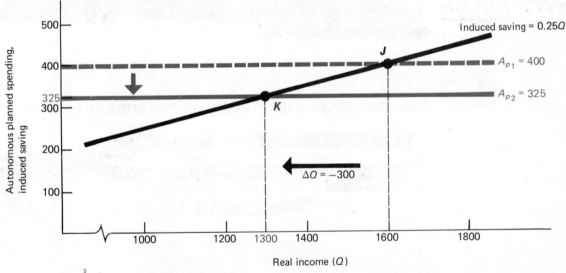

FIGURE 3-8

Effect on Income of a $100 Billion Increase in Government Spending
Followed by a $100 Billion Increase in Autonomous Tax Revenue

The top frame is identical to the lower frame of Figure 3–6. It shows that a $100
billion increase in government spending moves the economy from B to J, having
the same multiplier impact on equilibrium income as a $100 billion increase in A_p
caused by alterations in private spending decisions. In the lower frame the $100
billion tax increase only reduces A_p by $75 billion, since the remaining $25 billion
of tax revenue is paid for by higher saving. The economy moves from point J
down to point K.

How is this deficit financed? A relationship in Chapter 2 (which was illustrated in Figure 2-5) sets the difference between private saving and investment $(S - I)$ equal to the government deficit.

$$S - I \equiv G - T \tag{2.12}$$

The change in the left side of (2.12) must balance the change in the right side. This can be seen if we insert the Δ ("change in") symbol next to each term:

$$\Delta S - \Delta I \equiv \Delta G - \Delta T \tag{3.21}$$

The movement in the top frame of Figure 3-8 from point B to point J assumes that investment is fixed $(\Delta I = 0)$ and that tax revenue remains at zero $(\Delta T = 0)$. Thus the only elements of (3.21) that are changing are ΔS and ΔG:

$$\Delta S - \Delta I \equiv \Delta G - \Delta T$$
$$s\Delta Q - 0 \equiv 100 - 0$$
$$0.25(400) \equiv 100$$

DEFICIT

GOVT. SELLS

The $400 billion increase in output induces $100 billion of extra saving, but there is no extra private investment for the extra saving to finance $(\Delta I = 0)$. Thus each extra dollar of saving is available for households to purchase the $100 billion of government bonds that the government must sell when it runs its $100 billion deficit.

3-7 TAX INCREASES AND THE BALANCED-BUDGET MULTIPLIER

The government may prefer not to run a deficit. If equilibrium was at point J, with $G = \$100$ billion, what happens if autonomous tax revenues (T) are raised from zero to $100 billion $(\Delta \bar{T} = 100)$ and everything else remains the same (ceteris paribus)? Once again we use our basic two-step method to calculate the change in income. First, the change in A_p in equation (3.19) is:

$$\begin{aligned}
\Delta A_p &= \Delta a - c\Delta T + \Delta I_p + \Delta G \\
&= 0 - c\Delta T + 0 + 0 \\
&= -0.75(100) \\
&= -75
\end{aligned} \tag{3.19}$$

A $100 billion increase in autonomous tax revenues $(\Delta \bar{T} = 100)$ reduces autonomous planned spending by only $75 billion because households "pay" the remaining $25 billion of higher taxation by saving less than they otherwise would.

The effect of the tax increase on income is illustrated in the lower frame of Figure 3-8. Autonomous spending drops by $75 billion from $400 billion to $325 billion, and equilibrium income drops from $1600 billion to $1300 billion (point K).

What is the corresponding multiplier expression for a change in autonomous tax revenues? In this case the only component of autonomous spending that is changing is tax revenues. Thus we can take our general expression used to calculate income change (3.13) and substitute for ΔA_p the expression $-c\Delta \bar{T}$ that indicates the response of A_p to the tax change:

GENERAL FORM   NUMERICAL EXAMPLE

$$\Delta Q = \frac{\Delta A_p}{s} = \frac{-c\Delta \bar{T}}{s} \qquad \Delta Q = \frac{-(0.75)100}{0.25} = -300 \qquad (3.22)$$

The multiplier for an increase in taxes is the income change in equation (3.22) divided by $\Delta \bar{T}$. We always calculate the multiplier by taking income change and dividing by the parameter that is changing:

GENERAL FORM   NUMERICAL EXAMPLE

$$\frac{\Delta Q}{\Delta \bar{T}} = \frac{\Delta A_p}{s\Delta \bar{T}} = \frac{-c\Delta \bar{T}}{s\Delta \bar{T}} = \frac{-c}{s} \qquad \frac{\Delta Q}{\Delta \bar{T}} = \frac{-0.75}{0.25} = -3.0 \qquad (3.23)$$

The top and lower frames of Figure 3-8 show that the government can influence total income even if it maintains a balanced budget. In the top frame the $100 billion increase in G moves the economy from B to J; in the lower frame the $100 billion increase in $\bar{T}$ that balances the budget moves the economy from J to K (but *not* all the way to B). Why? The **balanced-budget multiplier** is the government spending multiplier ($1/s$) in (3.20) plus the autonomous tax multiplier ($-c/s$) in (3.23):

$$\text{balanced-budget multiplier} = \frac{\Delta Q}{\Delta G} + \frac{\Delta Q}{\Delta \bar{T}} = \frac{1}{s} - \frac{c}{s} = \frac{1-c}{s} = 1 \qquad (3.24)$$

Caution: The balanced-budget multiplier is $(1-c)/s$. If all taxes are autonomous, the balanced-budget multiplier is 1.0. Thus in Figure 3-8 a $100 billion increase in G balanced by a $100 billion increase in tax revenues leads to a $100 billion increase in income as the economy moves from B to K. But, as demonstrated in the appendix to this chapter, when the government collects part of its revenue in the form of an *income tax,* the denominator of all multipliers is higher than it is in this section, reducing all the multipliers. Thus in general the balanced budget multiplier is less than 1.0.

Exercise: Notice that, starting from point B in Figure 3-8, a balanced-budget expansion of $100 billion in both G and $\bar{T}$ is too small to cure the recession. The economy moves only to K, and it fails to reach the desired level of natural real GNP at $1600 billion (point J). What is the size of the balanced budget expansion in both G and $\bar{T}$ that would be necessary to raise income from $1200 to $1600 billion without causing a government deficit?

Our analysis of fiscal policy has been conducted by holding other things constant, including the marginal propensity to save (s). But changes in s can cause major changes in equilibrium income. If $A_p = 400$ and $s = 0.25$, equilibrium income is at the desired level of $1600 billion. If all households were to save more, raising their marginal propensity to save from 0.25 to 0.40, equilibrium income would drop from $1600 to $1000 billion:

$$Q = \frac{A_p}{s} = \frac{400}{0.4} = 1000$$

With $s = 0.4$, the multiplier for any change in A_p is $1/s$ or 2.5. The larger is s, the smaller is the spending multiplier.

Thus households through their spending and saving decisions can alter equilibrium income in two ways, by changing autonomous consumption (a) or the marginal propensity to save (s). Consumer attitudes, then, are a major source of economic instability, and a sufficient degree of consumer pessimism can bring about a recession.

The appendix to this chapter contains a more complete model, which shows that the denominator of the multiplier is the fraction of income that leaks out of the spending stream (the **marginal leakage rate**), whether into saving, income tax revenue, or imports. The higher the leakage rate grows, the lower the multiplier for changes in A_p and the lower the equilibrium income for any given A_p. Thus the government can influence spending by raising or lowering the income tax rate, which is part of the leakage rate and hence influences equilibrium income.

3-8 CASE STUDY: SPENDING, LEAKAGES, AND THE MULTIPLIER IN THE GREAT DEPRESSION

The most traumatic economic event in U.S. history was the Great Depression. Actual real GNP, roughly equal to natural real GNP in 1929, fell precipitously to a level almost 40 percent below natural output in 1933. The unemployment rate rose from a modest 3.2 percent in 1929 to an unprecedented 25.2 percent in 1933.[14] When Franklin D. Roosevelt was inaugurated as president on March 4, 1933, the U.S. economy was almost at a standstill. One of every three workers was unemployed. Almost every bank in the country was closed. And, to make matters worse, no unemployment compensation, national welfare, or social security was available to cushion the blow of lost jobs and income.[15]

---

[14] See Figure 1-3.

[15] A vivid, detailed, and exciting narrative of daily life in the 1930s, and of the first attempts of the New Deal to cope with the Great Depression, is contained in William Manchester,

Figure 3-9 summarizes the main features of the first phase of the Great Depression (1929–33) in terms of the analytical framework of this chapter. The main components of planned autonomous spending are listed under Figure 3-9. Clearly the cause of the problem was investment, which declined by 85 percent, or $49.5 billion in 1972 prices. Investment was 18.7 percent of natural GNP in 1929, but only 2.5 percent of natural output in 1933. We do not yet have a clue as to the possible causes of the decline in investment, because we have been assuming that planned investment is autonomous. But we can analyze the effects of the investment collapse on GNP.

First we must calculate the change in planned autonomous spending.[16] Although autonomous consumption did not change, government spending increased between 1929 and 1933 and offset part of the decline in investment.[17] But this was offset by an increase in taxation; as a result planned autonomous spending declined by $49.6 billion, about the same as the decline in investment. The decline in A_p amounted to 29.4 percent of the level of A_p in 1929. Assuming that total income was in equilibrium in both 1929 and 1933, induced saving must have equaled A_p in both 1929 and 1933, and thus it must have fallen by the same amount in the interim.[18]

The net result of the $49.6 billion collapse in planned autonomous spending was a $92.6 billion decline in real GNP. The multiplier in this case was 1.9 (92.6/49.6). The government may be able to prevent recessions and depressions by regulating G and T to offset reductions in private planned autonomous spending. Figure 3-9 plainly shows that the government deserves a grade of "D−" for its performance in the first four years of the Great Depression. First, although government spending increased by $1.9 billion between 1929 and 1933, this amount was only 4 percent of the increase that would have been necessary to offset the effect of the

---

The Glory and the Dream: A Narrative History of America, 1932–1972 (Boston: Little, Brown, 1974), pp. 3–171. A thorough immersion in these pages is almost guaranteed to "turn the student on" to macroeconomics as an important and relevant subject. It will also explain why the Keynesian solution to mass unemployment, first published in J. M. Keynes, *The General Theory of Employment, Interest, and Money* (London: Macmillan, 1936), was so revolutionary in comparison to the doctrines then in vogue.

[16] This discussion simplifies the true situation in 1933 by ignoring the substantial amount of unintended inventory change in that year and thus treats all investment in 1933 as planned.

[17] Actually, the decline in consumption during the Great Depression, although mainly induced, appears partly to have been autonomous, particularly in 1930. See Peter Temin, *Did Monetary Forces Cause the Great Depression?* (New York: Norton, 1976), especially pp. 68–75.

[18] Another simplification in Figure 3-9 is that all tax revenues during this period were autonomous. The bulk of tax revenues during this period was collected from state and local property taxes, which actually increased in real terms between 1929 and 1933.

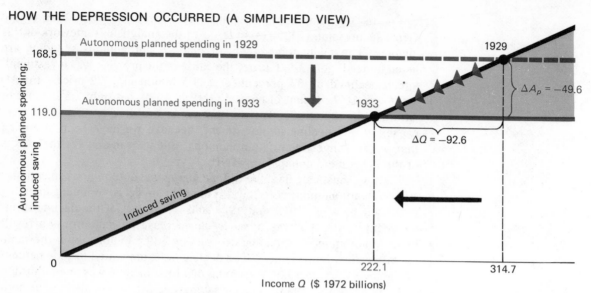

FIGURE 3-9

An Interpretation of Induced Leakages and Autonomous Planned
Spending in the Great Depression

INGREDIENTS IN FIGURE 3-9

	Q	A_p =	I_p +	a +	G	$-c\bar{T}$	Deficit $G - T = S - I$
1929	314.7	168.6	58.1	103.0	40.9	−33.4	−4.6
1933	222.1	119.0	8.6	103.0	42.8	−35.4	7.3
Δ = 1933−29	−92.6	−49.6	−49.5	0.0	+ 1.9	− 2.0	11.9

Source: Economic Report of the President, January 1977. I_p includes foreign investment.
$-c\bar{T}$ is 95 percent of real state and local government receipts.

$49.5 billion collapse in private investment. Second, the total amount of
tax revenue collected actually increased, adding to the depressing effect
of the investment collapse.

Why did the government make matters worse in this way? The accepted doctrine of the day, later made obsolete by the Keynesian revolution, claimed that a balanced government budget was necessary to "restore investor confidence." Thus tax rates were raised, although not
enough to prevent the government deficit from increasing by $11.9 billion

(see the far-right column of the table with Figure 3-9). Furthermore, the government allowed the money supply to decline substantially between 1929 and 1933, which compounded and aggravated the collapse in investment. In Chapter 4 we will examine how planned spending is influenced by monetary policy.

SUMMARY

1. This chapter presents a simple theory for determining real income. Important simplifying assumptions include the independence of planned spending from the interest rate and the rigidity of the price level.

2. By definition we divide disposable income between consumption and saving. Throughout the chapter consumption is assumed to be a fixed autonomous amount, $100 billion in the numerical example, plus 0.75 of disposable income. Saving is the remaining 0.25 of disposable income minus the $100 billion of autonomous consumption.

3. During the 1929–79 period, U.S. consumption was a roughly constant fraction of disposable income. Exceptions were during the worst year of the Great Depression, when consumption exceeded income, and during World War II, when rationing prevented households from obtaining the goods they desired and forced them to save an abnormal fraction of their income.

4. Output and income (Q) are equal by definition to total expenditures (E), which in turn can be divided up between planned expenditures (E_p) and unintended inventory accumulation (I_u). We convert this definition into a theory by assuming that business firms adjust production whenever I_u is not zero. The economy is in equilibrium, with no pressure for production to change, only when there is no unintended inventory accumulation or decumulation ($I_u = 0$).

5. Planned autonomous spending (A_p) equals total planned expenditures minus induced consumption. The four components of planned autonomous expenditures are autonomous consumption (a), planned investment (I_p), government spending (G), and the effect on consumption of autonomous tax revenue ($-c\bar{T}$). Any change in planned autonomous spending (ΔA_p) has a multiplier effect; an increase raises income and induces consumption over and above the initial boost in A_p. Income must increase until enough extra saving has been induced ($s\Delta Q$) to balance the injection of extra planned autonomous spending (ΔA_p). For this reason the multiplier, the ratio of the change in income to the change in planned autonomous spending ($\Delta Q/\Delta A_p$), is the inverse of the marginal propensity to save ($1/s$).

6. The same multiplier is valid for a change in any component in A_p. Thus if private spending components of A_p are weak, the government can raise its spending (G) or cut taxes ($\bar{T}$) to maintain stability in A_p and thus in real output.

7. The multiplier for a balanced-budget government operation that raises spending and tax revenues by the same amount is positive, because the impact of government spending on A_p outweighs the effect of higher tax revenue, since only a fraction (c) of the change in tax revenue influences expenditures.

A LOOK AHEAD

Throughout this chapter we have assumed that planned autonomous spending is not influenced by changes in the interest rate and that the price level is fixed. The first section of the next chapter allows private planned spending to be influenced by the interest rate (a high interest rate causes a reduction in spending). In order to determine simultaneously both equilibrium income and the interest rate, we must introduce an additional "market," that for money. Through its control over the money supply, the government gains an additional method of simultaneously influencing equilibrium real income and the interest rate.

CONCEPTS

Consumption function
Saving function
Average propensity to consume and to save
Planned expenditures
Unintended inventory accumulation
Marginal leakage rate
Equilibrium
Ex ante and *ex post*

Marginal propensity to consume and to save
Autonomous planned spending
Induced saving
The multiplier
Ceteris paribus
Autonomous tax revenue
Government deficit
Balanced-budget multiplier

QUESTIONS FOR REVIEW

1   Under what condition are the average and marginal propensities to consume equal to each other?

2   An increase in government spending causes a government deficit when tax revenues are fixed. How is the deficit financed in the new equilibrium (that is, who buys government bonds issued as a consequence of the deficit)? How is the deficit financed after the increase in spending but before income has had time to adjust?

Assume the following model of the economy:

$$C = 60 + 0.8Q_D \qquad I_p = 100$$
$$Q_D = Q - \bar{T} \qquad\qquad G = 200$$
$$\bar{T} = 200$$

3   What is the saving function implied by this model?

4   When $Q_D = 300$, what are the marginal and average propensities to save and consume?

5   With no government sector ($G = \bar{T} = 0$), what is the equilibrium level of income? If I_p increases to 200, what is the new equilibrium level of income? What is the value of the multiplier for a change in I_p? Do the same for an increase of 100 in the autonomous component of consumption. Compare.

6   Now, with the government sector included ($G = \bar{T} = 200$) and $I_p = 100$, what is the equilibrium level of income? What is the value of the multiplier for the introduction of the government sector?

7   How do you account for the difference between the multipliers in question 5 and question 6?

8   Suppose that the government wants to stabilize income at the equilibrium level you calculated in question 6. If I_p were to increase by 40 (to 140), the government must then offset this increase. It may change G or $\bar{T}$ or both to do this. If the government wants to change one policy instrument to offset the increase of 40 in I_p, what will be the required change in G? in $\bar{T}$? Describe how the economy will move back to equilibrium in each case.

APPENDIX TO CHAPTER 3
Income Taxes, Foreign Trade, and the Multiplier

EFFECT OF INCOME TAXES

When the government raises some of its tax revenue (T) from an income tax, in addition to the autonomous tax ($\bar{T}$), its total tax revenue is:

$$T = \bar{T} + \bar{i}Q \tag{1}$$

The first component, as before, is the autonomous tax (revenue from the property tax, dog licenses, and other revenue sources that do not vary automatically with income). The second component is income tax revenue, the tax rate ($\bar{i}$) times income (Q). Disposable income (Q_D) is total income minus tax revenue:

$$Q_D = Q - T = Q - \bar{T} - \bar{i}Q = (1 - \bar{i})Q - \bar{T} \tag{2}$$

Following any change in total income (Q), disposable income changes by only a fraction $(1 - \bar{t})$ as much. For instance, if the tax rate ($\bar{t}$) is 0.2, then disposable income changes by 80 percent of the change in total income. Any change in total income (ΔQ) is now divided into induced consumption, induced saving, and induced income tax revenue. The fraction of ΔQ going into consumption is the marginal propensity to consume disposable income (c) times the fraction of income going into disposable income $(1 - \bar{t})$. Thus the change in total income is divided up as follows:

Fraction going to:	GENERAL FORM	NUMERICAL EXAMPLE
1. Induced consumption	$c(1 - \bar{t})$	$0.75(1 - 0.2) = 0.6$
2. Induced saving	$s(1 - \bar{t})$	$0.25(1 - 0.2) = 0.2$
3. Income tax revenue	$\bar{t}$	0.2
Total	$(c + s)(1 - \bar{t}) + \bar{t}$ $= 1 - \bar{t} + \bar{t} = 1.0$	1.0

As before, the economy is in equilibrium when income equals planned expenditures:

$$Q = E_p \tag{3}$$

We found it useful in Chapter 3 to subtract induced consumption from both sides of the equilibrium condition. According to the table above, income (Q) minus induced consumption is the total of induced saving plus induced tax revenue. Planned expenditures (E_p) minus induced consumption is planned autonomous spending (A_p). Thus the equilibrium condition is:

$$Q - \text{induced consumption} = E_p - \text{induced consumption}$$

and is equivalent to:

Induced saving + induced tax revenue =
$$\text{planned autonomous spending } (A_p) \tag{4}$$

From the above table, (4) can be written in symbols as:

$$[s(1 - \bar{t}) + \bar{t}]Q = A_p \tag{5}$$

The term in brackets on the left-hand side is the fraction of a change in income that does not go into induced consumption — that is, the sum of the fraction going to induced saving $s(1 - \bar{t})$ and the fraction going to the government as income tax revenue ($\bar{t}$). The sum of these two fractions within the brackets is called the **marginal leakage rate.** Equilibrium income is determined when we divide both sides of (5) by the term in brackets:

GENERAL FORM   NUMERICAL EXAMPLE

$$Q = \frac{A_p}{s(1 - \bar{t}) + \bar{t}} \qquad Q = \frac{400}{0.25(0.8) + 0.2} = \frac{400}{0.4} = 1000 \tag{6}$$

The numerical example shows that if planned autonomous spending (A_p) is $400 billion, income will be only $1000 billion, rather than $1600 billion.

Why? A greater fraction of each dollar of income now leaks out of the spending stream – 0.4 in this numerical example – than occurred due to the saving rate alone, 0.25 in the example used in Chapter 3. This allows the injection of planned autonomous spending ($A_p = 400$) to be balanced by leakages out of the spending stream at a lower level of income.

How can the government raise equilibrium income from $1000 billion in equation (6) to the desired level of $1600 billion? One alternative would be to cut the income tax rate from 0.2 to zero. Then income would be simply A_p/s, or 400/0.25 = 1600. Another alternative would be to maintain the income tax rate at 0.2, but to raise A_p by higher spending (G) or reduced autonomous tax revenue ($\bar{T}$). How much must A_p be raised to achieve the desired $600 billion increase in income, from $1000 to $1600 billion? The multiplier is no longer $1/s$ (4.0), but rather:

$$\text{multiplier} = \frac{\Delta Q}{\Delta A_p} = \frac{1}{s(1 - \bar{t}) + \bar{t}} = \frac{1}{0.4} = 2.5 \tag{7}$$

Thus A_p must be increased by $240 billion to achieve the desired income increase of $600 billion, since 600/240 = 2.5, the new multiplier. When A_p is increased to $640 billion, equilibrium income is determined by equation (6).

$$Q = \frac{A_p}{s(1 - \bar{t}) + \bar{t}} = \frac{640}{0.25(0.8) + 0.2} = \frac{640}{0.4} = 1600$$

Summary: Introducing the income tax has two implications for the theory in Chapter 3:

1. Introducing the income tax increases leakages out of the spending stream and reduces the multiplier (from 4.0 to 2.5 in our example). With an income tax, changes in A_p have a weaker effect on income than without it. This feature of the income tax is sometimes called **automatic stabilization,** because the lower multiplier insulates the economy from the adverse effects of fluctuations in A_p.
2. The government gains a new tool for stabilizing income. Changes in the income tax rate can alter equilibrium – in equation (6) an increase in $\bar{t}$ raises the denominator and reduces income. Thus the government can cut the tax rate when it wants to stimulate the economy (as occurred in 1975), and it can raise the tax rate when it wants to restrain the economy (as occurred in 1968).

Exercise: If $s = 0.2$, $\bar{t} = 0.2$, and $A_p = 400$, all of which is government spending, is the government's budget balanced?[1] If not, how is the surplus or deficit financed?

---

[1] $A_p = G = 400$, and $a = I_p = \bar{T} = 0$.

EFFECT OF FOREIGN TRADE

Our more general theory of income determination in equation (6) states that equilibrium income equals planned autonomous spending (A_p) divided by the marginal leakage rate. When we trade with nations abroad, U.S. producers sell part of domestic output as exports. Households and business firms purchase imports from abroad, so part of U.S. expenditures does not generate U.S. production.

How do exports and imports affect the determination of income? Since the demand for exports depends on the income level of foreign nations, not the income level of the United States, we can treat exports as a part of planned autonomous spending (recall that *autonomous* means "independent of U.S. income").[2] Thus in place of equation (3.18) we can define A_p as:

$$A_p = a - c\bar{T} + I_p + G + X \qquad (8)$$

where X is the abbreviation for the real value of exports.

The level of imports does depend on total U.S. income. When U.S. income is high, households and firms purchase more imported goods than when it is low. Assume that the total level of imports (H) is a fixed fraction (h) of total U.S. income (Q):

$$H = hQ \qquad (9)$$

Imports have exactly the same effect on equilibrium income and the multiplier as does the income tax. Imports represent a leakage from the spending stream, a portion of a change in income that is not part of the disposable income of U.S. citizens and thus not available for consumption. The fraction of a change in income that is spent on imports (h) is part of the economy's marginal leakage rate.

Types of leakages	Marginal leakage rate
Saving only	s
Saving and income tax	$s(1 - \bar{t}) + \bar{t}$
Saving, income tax, and imports	$s(1 - \bar{t}) + \bar{t} + h$

When we combine (6), (8), and the table, equilibrium income becomes:

$$Q = \frac{A_p}{\text{marginal leakage rate}} = \frac{a - c\bar{T} + I_p + G + X}{s(1 - \bar{t}) + \bar{t} + h} \qquad (10)$$

Exercise: In Belgium both exports and imports are a much higher fraction of income than in the United States. Which country has the higher multiplier for changes in government spending, Belgium or the United States? Do you think that the city of Chicago has a high or low multiplier for changes in Chicago income induced by changes in Chicago city government spending?

---

[2] Since the United States has such a large economy and buys from other countries, the level of income in the rest of the world is partly dependent on the level of U.S. income.

4 Spending, the Interest Rate, and Money

I still feel that the (*IS–LM*) diagram gives the most convenient summary of the Keynesian theory of Interest and Money which has yet been produced.

— J. R. Hicks[1]

4-1 INTRODUCTION

The basic theme of the last chapter was that income and real GNP change by a *multiple* of any change in planned autonomous spending. But changes in planned autonomous spending (ΔA_p) were assumed to be already known and were not explained. In this chapter we accept everything in Chapter 3 as valid. But we go further by relating the level of private planned autonomous investment and autonomous consumption ($I_p + a$) to the level of the interest rate. Business firms pay interest when they finance investment projects by borrowing from banks and by selling bonds to households and other business firms. Banks pay interest to households to induce them to hold deposits. We will simplify the discussion by assuming that there is only one interest rate paid on loans and bonds, though in the real world interest rates differ.

If private planned spending depends partly on the interest rate, what determines the interest rate? First we will explore the connection between the interest rate and the supply of money the government provides in the form of currency and checking accounts. Then we will see how the government uses its control over the money supply to influence the interest rate, and thus the equilibrium level of income.

This chapter adds to our understanding of the process of income determination, and begins our investigation of the key questions at the heart of recent economic debates:

1. What factors make the interest rate for borrowing higher in some periods

---

[1] *A Contribution to the Theory of the Trade Cycle* (Oxford, Eng.: Oxford University Press, Clarendon Press, 1950), chap. 11.

than in others? Why, for instance, did the interest rate on short-term loans reach 17.2 percent in March 1980? Why was the same rate as low as 0.5 percent in early 1958?[2]

2. Is it correct to consider planned investment (I_p) and government purchases (G) as being determined independently of each other, as in Chapter 3? Or does an increase in government spending partially or totally "crowd out" planned investment, leaving no net effect on the total of planned autonomous spending (A_p)? What determines the size of this crowding-out effect?

3. Which is more advantageous: a stimulus to the economy provided by fiscal policy—that is, an increase in government spending (G) or a reduction in tax revenues (T); or a stimulus provided by monetary policy—that is, an increase in the supply of money?

In this chapter, as in Chapter 3, we will assume that the price level is fixed. All changes in real income and GNP are accompanied by the same change in nominal income and GNP. All effects of spending on inflation, and of inflation on the interest rate, are postponed for treatment later.

4-2 THE RELATION OF PRIVATE AUTONOMOUS PLANNED SPENDING TO THE INTEREST RATE

Why should private planned investment and autonomous consumption ($I_p + a$) depend on the interest rate? Business firms attempt to profit by borrowing funds to buy investment goods—office buildings, shopping centers, factories, machine tools, computers, airplanes. Obviously, firms can stay in business only if the earnings of investment goods are at least enough to pay the interest on the borrowed funds.

Example: United Airlines calculates that it can earn $8 million per year from one additional DC-10 jet airliner after paying all expenses for employee salaries, fuel, food, and airplane maintenance—that is, all expenses besides interest payments on borrowed funds. If the DC-10 costs $40 million, that level of earnings represents a 20 percent **rate of return** ($8,000,000/40,000,000 = 0.20$), defined as annual dollar earnings divided by the dollar cost of the airplane. If United must pay 10 percent interest to obtain the funds for the airplane, the rate of return of 20 percent is more than sufficient to pay the interest expense.

In the top frame of Figure 4-1, point A shows that the 20 percent rate of return on the first DC-10 exceeds the 10 percent interest rate

---

[2] Figures refer to the federal funds rate, the rate on overnight loans of bank reserves between one bank and another.

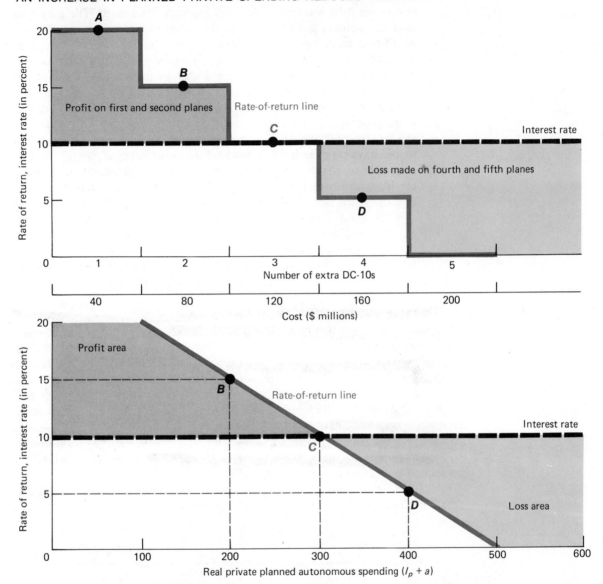

AN INCREASE IN PLANNED PRIVATE SPENDING REDUCES THE RATE OF RETURN

FIGURE 4–1

The Payoff to Investment for an Airline and the Economy

The red steplike line in the top frame shows the rate of return to United Airlines for purchases of additional DC-10s. If the interest rate is 10 percent, a profit is made by purchasing the first two planes, and the company breaks even by buying the third plane. Purchase of a fourth or fifth plane would be a mistake, because the planes would not generate enough profit to pay for the cost of borrowing the money to buy them. The bottom frame shows the same phenomenon for the economy as a whole.

on borrowed funds. The steplike red line in the top frame of Figure 4-1 shows the rate of return on the first through fifth planes. The gray area between point A and the 10 percent interest rate represents the annual profit rate made on the first plane. Point B for the second plane also indicates a profit. Point C shows that purchase of a third extra DC-10 earns only a 10 percent rate of return or $4 million in extra earnings after payment of all noninterest expenses. Why do the second and third planes earn less than the first? The first plane is operated on the most profitable routes; the second and third must fly on routes that are less likely to yield full passenger loads. A fourth plane (at point D) would have an even lower rate of return, insufficient to pay the interest cost of borrowed funds. A fifth plane earns nothing because its passenger loads are even lighter. The pink area between the interest rate and rate-of-return line shows the loss made on the fourth and fifth plane.

How many planes will be purchased? The third can pay its interest expense and will be purchased, but the fourth will not. If the interest cost of borrowed funds were to rise above 10 percent, purchases would be cut from three planes to two, but if the interest rate were to fall to or below 5 percent, then four planes would be purchased.

The interest rate not only influences the level of business investment, but also affects the level of household consumption. For instance, households deciding whether to purchase a dishwasher or a second automobile are influenced by the size of the monthly payment, which depends on the interest rate.[3] In the bottom frame of Figure 4-1 the rate-of-return line shows that the return on planned investment and autonomous consumption spending $(I_p + a)$ decline as the level of spending increases. As for United Airlines, each successive investment good purchased by business firms is less profitable than the last. Similarly, each successive consumption good purchased by households provides fewer services than the last (for instance, a family's second car is less essential and useful than its first car).

The rates of return for three alternative quantities of $I_p + a$ are plotted along the rate-of-return line in the bottom frame of Figure 4-1. The three are:

Point	$I_p + a$	Rate of return	Interest rate	Profit
B	200	15	10	5
C	300	10	10	0
D	400	5	10	−5

The gray area shows that if the interest rate is 10 percent, a profit will be made on the first $300 billion of $I_p + a$. However, the rate of return of

---

[3] The interest rate also influences households who pay "cash" for the automobile or dishwasher, since they lose the interest that they would have earned if they had refrained from buying and had instead kept the funds in a savings account.

further spending is below the interest rate and creates the losses indicated by the pink area.

The rate-of-return line shows how profitable firms expect additional investment to be, and how useful households expect additional consumption goods to be. How much will actually be spent? The answer depends on the interest rate, since firms will not be willing to incur losses by entering the pink-shaded region where the rate of return is below the interest rate.

Thus, determination of the level of $I_p + a$ is a two-step process. First we plot the rate-of-return line representing firms' and consumers' expectations of the benefit of additional purchases. Second, we find the level of $I_p + a$ at the point where the rate-of-return line crosses the interest rate level.

When the interest rate is 10 percent as in Figure 4-1, $I_p + a$ spending will be $300 billion at point C, as long as the level of business and consumer optimism remains constant (*ceteris paribus*). A decrease in the interest rate will increase purchases ($I_p + a$); for instance, a decrease from 10 percent to 5 percent moves purchases from $300 billion at C to $400 billion at D.

Can purchases ever change when the interest rate is held constant at 10 percent? Certainly—an increase in business and consumer optimism about the expected payoff of additional purchases can shift the entire rate-of-return line to the right, as indicated by the red "New rate-of-return line" in Figure 4-2. This shifts to the right (to point F) the intersection of the rate-of-return line with the fixed horizontal interest-rate line.

Summarizing, we can show the amount of $I_p + a$ spending that would occur at different interest rates and different levels of confidence.

	Demand for $I_p + a$	
Interest rate	Original rate-of-return line (expectations pessimistic)	New higher rate-of-return line (expectations optimistic)
15	200 (at B)	300
10	300 (at C)	400 (at F)
5	400 (at D)	500

This table shows the demand for private planned autonomous spending ($I_p + a$) for different levels of confidence and different interest rates. The left-hand column (expectations pessimistic) is plotted as the "Original rate-of-return line" (red dashes) in Figure 4-2. The right-hand column (expectations optimistic) is plotted as the solid red "New rate-of-return line."

Although $I_p + a$ spending is negatively related to the interest rate, it is still completely autonomous—that is, independent of income. Why? This is a restriction we have imposed to simplify the analysis, but it is not completely realistic. The rate-of-return line in Figure 4-2 shifts right or left as expectations of profitability are altered, and those expectations are surely influenced by actual production and income.

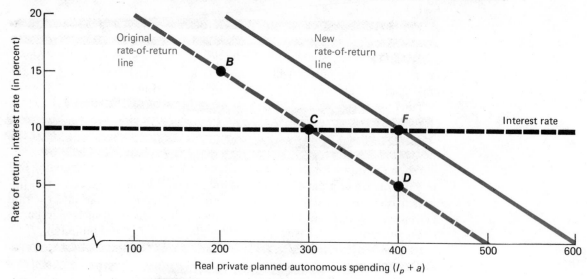

FIGURE 4–2

Effect on Planned Autonomous Spending of an Increase in Business and Consumer Confidence

The dashed red "Original rate-of-return line" is an exact copy of the solid red "Rate-of-return line" in Figure 4–1. If the level of business and consumer confidence were to increase, perhaps because of higher expected profits and income, the spending schedule would shift rightward to the solid red "New rate-of-return line." If the interest rate were to stay constant at 10 percent, as indicated by the dashed black "Interest-rate" line, then planned autonomous spending (A_p) would increase from $300 billion at point C to $400 billion at point F.

Recall from Chapter 3 that there are four different components of planned autonomous spending (A_p) — autonomous consumption (a), planned investment (I_p), government spending (G), and the effect on consumption of autonomous tax revenues ($-c\bar{T}$). So far in this chapter we have seen that the two private components, $I_p + a$, are sensitive to the interest rate. When the interest rate is high, $I_p + a$ spending is relatively low, and vice versa. Even though government spending and autonomous tax revenues may not depend at all on the interest rate, the sensitivity of private planned autonomous spending to the interest rate means that the *total* of all planned autonomous spending (A_p) — including both private spending ($I_p + a$) and government spending and taxes ($G - c\bar{T}$) — must depend on the interest rate.

4-3 THE *IS* CURVE

We have now learned that total planned autonomous spending (A_p) depends on the interest rate. And in Chapter 3 we learned that the total level of real GNP and real income depend on the total level of planned autonomous spending. Now, if we put two and two together, we conclude that total real GNP and real income must depend on the interest rate. In this section we derive a graphical schedule called the *IS curve* that shows the different combinations of the interest rate and real income that are compatible with a given state of business and consumer confidence and a given marginal propensity to save.

The first ingredient in the derivation of the *IS* curve is shown in the lower left-hand corner of Figure 4-3. This "A_p line" shows the demand for planned autonomous spending at different levels of the interest rate and is copied from the "Original rate-of-return line" in Figure 4-2. Notice that at a 10 percent interest rate (point C), A_p will be $300 billion, just the same as in Figure 4-2 at point C. Initially we assume that there is no government spending or tax revenue, so total autonomous spending consists simply of its two private components ($I_p + a$).

What will be the equilibrium level of real income if A_p equals $300 billion? We answer this question just as in Chapter 3 by plotting the level of A_p in the upper right-hand corner of Figure 4-3 as the horizontal red line (with a height of $300 billion). Where the $A_p = 300$ line crosses the upward-sloping "Induced-saving" line at point C, equilibrium real income is $1200 billion. Once again, we arrive at this conclusion because we continue to assume that the marginal propensity to save is 0.25, so that a real income level of $1200 billion generates $300 billion of induced saving—exactly the amount needed to balance the $300 billion of autonomous planned spending.

In the lower right-hand side of Figure 4-3 we plot the equilibrium level of real income of $1200 billion against the assumed 10 percent level of the interest rate. We also show two other possibilities. At point B the interest rate is 15 percent. Along the A_p line in the lower left-hand frame, only $200 billion of A_p will be demanded. In the upper right-hand frame A_p must equal an induced saving level of $200 billion, which occurs only when real income is $800 billion. Thus at point B in the lower right-hand frame the assumed 15 percent interest rate is plotted against the $800 billion level of real income that is compatible with it.

> **Exercise:** Be sure you can explain why a 5 percent interest rate at point D is compatible with a $1600 billion level of equilibrium real income.

Because A_p depends on the interest rate, equilibrium income does also. The "*IS* curve" in Figure 4-3 plots the values of equilibrium real income when the marginal propensity to save is 0.25 and the multiplier is 4.0, as in

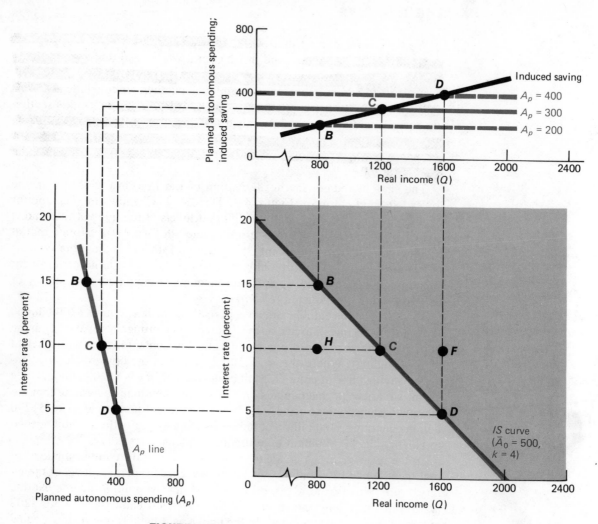

FIGURE 4–3

Relation of the *IS* Curve to the Demand for Autonomous Spending and the Amount of Induced Saving

In the lower left frame the "A_p line" is copied from Figure 4–2. It shows that the demand for autonomous planned spending depends on the interest rate. For instance, at a 10 percent interest rate the level of A_p is $300 billion at point C. Following the thin dashed black line up above point C and over to the upper right frame, we see that the economy is in equilibrium at point C, where both A_p and induced saving are equal. This equilibrium level of income is $1200 billion and is plotted directly below in the lower right-hand frame, opposite the 10 percent interest rate that we assumed at the beginning. Make sure you understand why equilibrium income is lower at point B and higher at point D.

the last chapter. Notice that points B, C, and D along the IS curve are all plotted at a horizontal distance exactly 4.0 times the value of the A_p line in the lower left-hand frame.

The IS curve shows all the different combinations of the interest rate (r) and income (Q) at which the economy's market for commodities (goods and services) is in equilibrium, which occurs only when income equals planned expenditures with no unintended inventory accumulation or decumulation. At any point off the IS curve the economy is out of equilibrium. The pink region to the left of the IS curve, for instance, at point H, shows unintended inventory decumulation, resulting from real GNP too low for the spending induced by a 10 percent interest rate. The gray region to the right of the IS curve, for instance, at point F, shows unintended inventory accumulation, resulting from real GNP too high for the spending induced by a 10 percent interest rate.

We have already seen that a shift toward greater consumer and business optimism will shift the rate-of-return line in Figure 4-2 and thus the A_p line in the lower left of Figure 4-3. It will be convenient to have a label for the horizontal position of the A_p line, since this will in turn affect the horizontal position of the IS curve.[4] *Let us define $\bar{A}$ as the value of planned autonomous spending that would take place at an interest rate of zero*. In Figure 4-3 the A_p line intersects the horizontal axis at \$500 billion, so our label for this A_p line will be $\bar{A}_0 = 500$. The IS curve always lies at a horizontal distance 4.0 times the A_p line, because the multiplier (k) is 4.0, the inverse of the marginal propensity to save of 0.25. Notice in Figure 4-3 that the IS curve intersects the horizontal axis at \$2000 billion, exactly 4.0 times the level of $\bar{A}_0 = 500$.

4-4 LEARNING TO SHIFT AND TILT THE *IS* CURVE

Since the IS curve is so important and useful, we need to pause here and study it more closely.[5]

---

[4] We call the IS schedule a "curve," even though we have drawn it as a straight line, because in the real world the relationship might be a curve. Also, "IS curve" has been familiar terminology to generations of economists since its invention by Sir John Hicks in a classic article, "Mr. Keynes and the 'Classics': A Suggested Interpretation," *Econometrica*, vol. 5 (April 1937) pp. 147–159. Its name comes from the fact that when there is no government, the economy is in equilibrium when planned investment equals planned saving—or, in our language, when planned private autonomous spending ($I_p + a$) equals induced saving (sQ).

[5] Despite its name, the IS curve has no unique connection with investment (I) or saving (S). It shifts whenever $\bar{A}$ changes, which can be caused by a change in government spending or in tax rates as well as by changes in business and consumer confidence.

1. WHY DOES THE *IS* CURVE SLANT DOWN TO THE RIGHT?

A lower interest rate raises A_p, and a higher level of A_p raises equilibrium Q by k times as much. This is the multiplier process discussed in Chapter 3.

2. WHAT SHIFTS THE *IS* CURVE?

Figure 4-3 demonstrates that the horizontal intercept of the *IS* curve is always equal to the multiplier (k) times $\bar{A}$, the amount of planned autonomous spending that would occur at a zero interest rate. For instance, the IS_0 curve has a horizontal intercept at $2000 billion, equal to 4.0 (k) times $500 billion ($\bar{A}_0$). Anything that changes the multiplier (k) or $\bar{A}$ will shift the *IS* curve.

The Multiplier. The position of the *IS* curve will rotate relative to that of the A_p line in Figure 4-3 if the marginal propensity to save changes, since this will rotate the black "Induced-saving" line in the upper right-hand frame. An increase in the marginal propensity to save will rotate the Induced-saving line up, thus shifting leftward the level of equilibrium income compatible with any given amount of A_p. Stated another way, an increase in the marginal propensity to save will reduce the multiplier (its inverse, $k = 1/s$), thus shifting the *IS* curve leftward for any given A_p line and any given level of $\bar{A}$. A decrease in the marginal propensity to save will have the opposite effect, raising the multiplier and shifting the *IS* curve to the right.

Business and Consumer Confidence. Both the A_p line and the *IS* curve will shift if businesses and consumers become more optimistic and raise the amount they desire to spend for any given interest rate. For instance, bank failures in the Great Depression may have shifted the *IS* curve to the left, and the inauguration of President Roosevelt in March 1933 may have helped to restore confidence and shift the *IS* curve to the right.

In Figure 4-4 the left-hand frame shows two A_p lines. Along the left-hand "Old A_p line" confidence is relatively low, but the "New A_p line" reflects a higher level of confidence and lies everywhere exactly $100 billion further to the right. For instance, when the interest rate is 10 percent, planned autonomous spending is $300 billion at point C along the old line and $400 billion at point F along the new line. Since the multiplier is 4.0, every point on the "Old *IS* curve" is four times as great as along the "Old A_p line," and with an interest rate of 10 percent, equilibrium real income is $1200 billion at point C. The "New *IS* curve" lies $400 billion to the right, so that with an interest rate of 10 percent, equilibrium real income is $1600 billion at point F.

Once again, it is convenient to label each *IS* curve by the amount of autonomous planned spending that would occur at an interest rate of zero — that is, $\bar{A}_0 = 500$ along the "Old A_p line" and $\bar{A}_1 = 600$ along the "New A_p line."

Government Actions. So far we have assumed that there is no government spending or tax revenue. But a $100 billion increase in government

HOW INCREASED CONFIDENCE SHIFTS THE *IS* CURVE

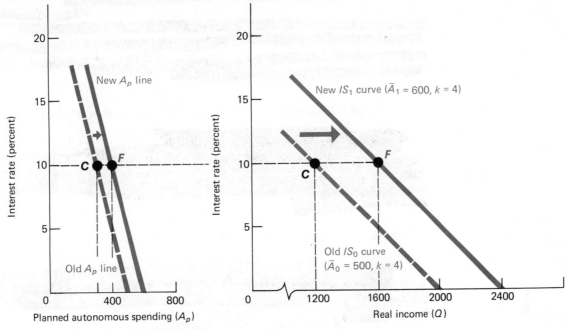

FIGURE 4–4

Effect on the *IS* Curve of a Rightward Shift in the Demand for Planned Autonomous Spending

The "old" A_p line and *IS* curve are copied from Figure 4–3. Now we assume that an increase in the level of business and consumer confidence shifts the A_p line $100 billion to the right, just as occurred in Figure 4–2. The *IS* curve shifts to the right by four times as much. Notice that the horizontal intercept of the new *IS* curve is four times the horizontal intercept of the A_p line—that is, $\bar{A}_1 = 600$.

spending would raise planned autonomous spending by $100 billion. Starting from the "Old A_p line," the addition of $100 billion of government spending would move us to the "New A_p line" and would cause the *IS* curve to shift in just the way depicted in Figure 4-4.

Thus the rightward shift in Figure 4-4 of $100 billion in the A_p line and of $400 billion in the *IS* curve can be caused by any event that raises by $100 billion the amount of autonomous spending desired at a zero interest rate, $\bar{A}$. These events include an increase in business or consumer confidence, an increase in government spending, or a reduction in autonomous tax revenue.[6]

---

[6] The appendix to Chapter 3 showed that the multiplier itself depends on income tax rates, giving the government a third way to shift the *IS* curve.

Learning to Shift and Tilt the *IS* Curve **103**

Because the position of the IS line depends on both k and $\bar{A}$, the value of both is always given next to each IS line, as in Figure 4-4. Does a change in the interest rate (r) cause IS to shift? No. When there is a change in a variable already plotted on the axes, Q and r in this case, we move along the line. If a change occurs in an element relevant to the graph but *not* on the axes, the line shifts. This is true of any graphic line or curve.[7]

3. WHAT IS TRUE OF POINTS THAT ARE OFF THE *IS* CURVE?

The entire area to the left of each IS curve, for example, point H in Figure 4-3, is characterized by an *excess demand for commodities*. All points in the region to the right of an IS curve are characterized by purchases below production, which means undesired inventory accumulation and an *excess supply of commodities*.

4. WHAT CHANGES THE SLOPE OF THE *IS* CURVE?

How is the responsiveness of spending related to changes in the interest rate? **Spending responsiveness** or "A_p responsiveness" refers to the change in autonomous spending (ΔA_p) divided by the change in the interest rate (Δr) that causes it. Along the original A_p line in the left frame of Figure 4-4, for instance, a $100 billion increase in planned autonomous spending (ΔA_p) is caused by a 5 percent drop in the interest rate (Δr). Thus A_p responsiveness is 100/5, a $20 billion increase in A_p per 1 percentage point drop in r.

The change in output (ΔQ) per dollar of change in A_p is the multiplier (k), 4.0 in our numerical example.[8] Thus the responsiveness of the IS curve to a change in the interest rate is the multiplier (k) times the induced change in A_p. In the numerical example, a 5 percent drop in r increases equilibrium Q by $400 billion. In the right frame of Figure 4-4, the responsiveness of the IS curve is 400/5 = 80.

The IS curve becomes flatter either when the multiplier (k) becomes larger (as, for instance, when the marginal propensity to save declines) or when A_p responsiveness increases. If the rate of return of additional investment projects declines only slightly as extra projects are built, any decline in the interest rate will generate a large increase in A_p, so that the slope of IS will be flatter. The IS curve becomes steep if either the multiplier or A_p responsiveness is small. When businesses and households fail to raise spending in response to a lower interest rate, then the IS curve is vertical.

---

[7] The line shifts only if the change is in a variable not on the axes that matters for the relationship being plotted. Here, for instance, a change in $\bar{A}$ or k will shift IS, but a change in the money supply will not.

[8] In the text of Chapter 3 the multiplier of 4.0 was the inverse of the propensity to save (4.0 = 1/0.25). In the appendix to Chapter 3 a 20 percent income tax rate reduced the multiplier from $k = 4.0$ to $k = 2.5$.

Value of A_p responsiveness for a given multiplier	Slope of IS curve
0	Vertical
Small	Steep
Large	Flat
Infinity	Horizontal

In the next chapter we shall see that a steep *IS* curve (small A_p responsiveness) makes fiscal policy more potent and monetary policy less potent.

THE SCOPE FOR GOVERNMENT ACTION

Our study of the *IS* curve leaves two major questions unanswered. First, will $\bar{A}$ be at the right level to achieve target income and, if not, can $\bar{A}$ be controlled by the government? Second, will the interest rate (r) be at the right level to achieve target income and, if not, can r be controlled by the government? The answer to the first question follows from the definition that the change in $\bar{A}$ is the sum of the changes of its three elements: (1) the change in private planned investment and autonomous consumption that would occur at a constant interest rate, (2) the change in government purchases, and (3) the change in consumption induced by a change in autonomous tax revenue.

A basic rationale for fiscal policy is that the government can increase purchases or decrease tax revenues in periods of business and consumer pessimism in order to keep $\bar{A}$ constant and thus insulate income and the *IS* curve from any effects of the change in business and consumer attitudes. Most economists agree that prompt and vigorous government action would have greatly reduced the extent of the drastic fall in income that occurred during the Great Depression.

4-5 THE MONEY MARKET AND THE *LM* CURVE

An alternative strategy would be for the government to allow business and consumer pessimism to reduce $\bar{A}$ (shifting the *IS* curve to the left) and then offset the decline in income by reducing the interest rate. How could such a change in the interest rate be engineered? The government can control the interest rate indirectly by its control over the supply of money.

The **money supply** (M^s) consists of two parts, currency and demand deposits (checking accounts at banks). In the United States both are controlled by the Federal Reserve Board, or "Fed" for short. Currency is directly controlled by the Fed, which prints most of it; demand deposits are indirectly controlled by the Fed, which makes regulations for the reserves that banks must keep to back up demand deposits. At this stage the money supply may be considered as a policy instrument that the government can set exactly at any desired value, just as we have been assuming that the government can precisely set the level of its fiscal policy instruments—that is, purchases of goods and services and tax rates.

INCOME AND THE DEMAND FOR MONEY

The hypothesis that links the money supply, income, and the interest rate states that *the amount of money that people demand in real terms depends not only on income but also on the interest rate*. To appreciate the importance of this hypothesis, imagine individuals always holding a fixed fraction of income in the form of money. Households do not desire money for itself, but for the goods and services it can buy (you can't stay healthy eating dollar bills). Holding large balances of currency and demand deposits is not without cost, since that money could be used to buy desirable consumption goods instead of remaining idle. Why do households give up consumption goods to hold money balances that pay no interest? The main reason is that at least *some* holding of money is necessary to facilitate transactions.

Funds held in the form of stocks, bonds, or saving accounts pay interest but cannot be used for transactions. Before the invention of the credit card, people had to carry currency in their pockets or have money in their bank accounts to back up a check before they could buy anything. Because rich people make more purchases, they generally need a larger amount of currency and larger bank deposits. Thus the demand for real money balances increases when everyone becomes richer—that is, when the total of real income increases.

It is customary to discuss the demand for money in real terms—that is, adjusted for changes in the price level. Let us assume that the demand for real money balances (M/P) equals half of real income (Q):

$$\left(\frac{M}{P}\right)^d = 0.5Q$$

The superscript d means "the demand for."

If real income (Q) is at \$1600 billion, the demand for real money balances $(M/P)^d$ will be \$800 billion, as shown in Figure 4-5 by the vertical line (L') drawn at \$800 billion. The line is vertical because we are assuming initially that the demand for real balances $(M/P)^d$ does not depend on the interest rate (r).

THE INTEREST RATE AND THE DEMAND FOR MONEY

The L' line is unrealistic, however, because individuals will not hold as much money at a 10 percent interest rate as at a zero interest rate. Why? Because the interest rate plotted on the vertical axis is paid on assets other than money, such as bonds and savings accounts. The higher the reward (r) for holding bonds and savings accounts, which are not money, the less money will be held, because money does not pay interest.

HOW INCOME AND THE INTEREST RATE SHIFT THE DEMAND FOR REAL BALANCES

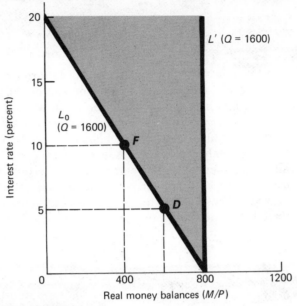

FIGURE 4–5

The Demand for Money, the Interest Rate, and Real Income

The vertical line L' is drawn on the unrealistic assumption that the demand for real balances is equal to half of real income ($1600 billion in this case), but does not depend on the interest rate. The L_0 curve maintains income at $1600, but it allows the demand for real balances to decrease by $200 billion for each 5 percent increase in the interest rate. What happens to the $200 billion that is released by each 5 percent increase in the interest rate? It is used to purchase assets that (unlike money) can earn this higher interest rate, including savings accounts, money-market mutual funds, bonds, and stocks. The gray area shows the amount shifted into these other assets, an amount that grows as the interest rate rises, leaving a smaller and smaller amount to be held as money (checking accounts and currency).

If the interest rate (r) paid by these nonmoney assets (bonds, savings accounts) were zero, there would be no point in holding them. Individuals would hold all of their financial assets in the form of money to take advantage of its convenience. But if the interest rate on them were 10 percent, individuals would be willing to inconvenience themselves by cutting down on their average money holding in order to earn the higher interest available on alternative assets. Sufficient money would be available for transactions, even if smaller average balances of currency and demand deposits were held, only if individuals were willing to suffer the inconvenience of more frequent trips to the broker or the bank to obtain money from sales of stocks and bonds and from transfers out of savings accounts. This inconvenience would be judged worthwhile if the interest earnings on the alternative assets were high enough to compensate individuals for the nuisance of periodically converting these assets into money.

In Figure 4-5 the downward slope of L_0 through points F and D indicates that when real income is $1600 billion and the interest rate is zero, the demand for real balances is $800 billion. But when the interest rate rises from zero to 5 percent, people suffer inconvenience to cut down their money holdings from $800 billion to $600 billion (point D). When the interest rate is 10 percent, only $400 billion is demanded (point F) because individuals are willing to suffer the inconvenience of converting their money into savings accounts, stocks, and bonds even more often. The new L_0 line can be summarized as showing that the real demand for money $(M/P)^d$ is half of income minus $40 billion times the interest rate:

$$\left(\frac{M}{P}\right)^d = 0.5Q - 40r$$

A change in the interest rate moves the economy up and down its real money demand schedule. But if real output (Q) falls, for instance, from $1600 billion to $1200 billion, then the curve shifts left from L_0 to L_1 as shown in Figure 4-6. People with a lower level of real income hold less money at any given level of the interest rate. The distance of the leftward horizontal shift between L_0 and L_1 is $200 billion, exactly half the assumed decline in real income of $400 billion in Figure 4-6.

THE *LM* SCHEDULE

To have equilibrium in the money market the real supply of money (M^s/P) must equal the demand for real balances $(M/P)^d$:

$$\left(\frac{M^s}{P}\right) = \left(\frac{M}{P}\right)^d = 0.5Q - 40r \tag{4.1}$$

If the amount of money supplied by the government is $400 billion, and the price index (P) is set at a constant value of 1.0, then (M^s/P) equals $400 billion. Since we assume for now that the supply of money does not depend on the interest rate, (M^s/P) is drawn in the left frame of Figure 4-7 as a vertical line at a level of $400 billion for every interest rate. The two demand schedules, L_0 and L_1, are copied from Figure 4-6.

The sloped demand line L_0, drawn for an income of $1600 billion, crosses the M^s/P line at point F, where the interest rate is 10 percent. The demand for money at F is $400 billion, and the supply of money is also $400 billion. Because the two are equal, the money market is in equilibrium when $Q =$

A DROP IN THE LEVEL OF INCOME SHIFTS THE MONEY DEMAND
SCHEDULE TO THE LEFT

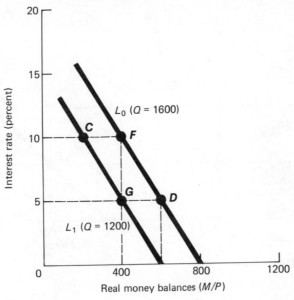

FIGURE 4–6

Effect on the Money Demand Schedule of a Decline in Real Income
from $1600 to $1200 Billion

The L_0 line is copied from Figure 4–5 and shows the demand for real balances at
different interest rates on the assumption that real income is $1600 billion. A $400
billion drop in the level of income to $1200 billion causes the demand for real
balances to drop by half as much, or $200 billion, at each interest rate. For in-
stance, at a 10 percent interest rate the demand for real balances falls from $400
billion at point F to $200 billion at point C.

1600 (assumed in drawing the L_0 line) and $r = 10$ percent. This equilibrium
combination of values is plotted at point F in the right frame of Figure 4-7.[9]

  If income is $1200 billion instead of $1600 billion, the demand for money
is smaller at every interest rate, as indicated by the parallel schedule L_1
passing through points C and G. When the income level is only $1200
billion, the demand for real money balances can be equal to the fixed $400

---

[9] Thus in equation (4.1)

$$400 = 0.5(1600) - 40(10)$$
$$= 800 - 400$$
$$= 400$$

A FIXED MONEY SUPPLY IS CONSISTENT WITH MANY DIFFERENT LEVELS OF INCOME

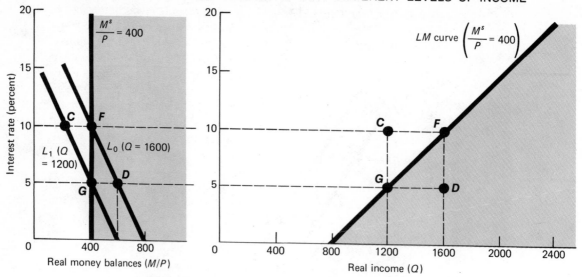

FIGURE 4–7

Derivation of the *LM* Curve

In the left frame the L_0 schedule is copied from the previous figure and assumes that $Q = 1600$. The L_1 schedule shows the demand for money when income is at the lower level of $1200 billion. The vertical M^s/P line shows the available supply of money provided by the government. The money market is in equilibrium where the supply line (M^s/P) crosses the demand line (L_0 or L_1). When income is $1600 billion, equilibrium occurs at point F, plotted again in the right frame. When income is $1200 billion, equilibrium occurs where L_1 crosses M^s/P at point G, also plotted in the right frame. The *LM* curve or schedule shows all combinations of Q and r consistent with equilibrium in the money market.

---

billion real supply of money only at point G, where the interest rate is 5 percent. Thus $Q = 1200$ and $r = 5$ is another combination consistent with equilibrium in the money market, and it is plotted at point G in the right frame of Figure 4-7. Although the lower income level of $1200 billion cuts the money needed for the transaction purposes, the lower interest rate at G counteracts this by raising the portion of financial assets that people choose to hold in the form of money.[10]

---

[10] Thus in equation (4.1)

$$400 = 0.5(1200) - 40(5)$$
$$= 600 - 200$$
$$= 400$$

The line connecting points G and F in the right-hand frame of Figure 4-7 is called the *LM* **curve**. The *LM* curve represents all combinations of income (Q) and interest rate (r) where the money market is in equilibrium—that is, where the real supply of money equals the real demand for money.

Points on the lower left portion of the *LM* curve have a low level of income and a correspondingly low demand for money for transaction purposes. The only way the total demand for money can be kept equal to the fixed supply is for a low interest rate to induce individuals to hold most of their assets in the form of money. The upper right portion of the *LM* curve shows a high transaction demand for money caused by high income, requiring a high interest rate to induce individuals to keep only a small share of their assets in the form of money.

At any point off the *LM* curve, say point D, the money market is not in equilibrium. The problem at D and all other points in the pink area is that the demand for real money exceeds the available supply. Point D is located at an income level of $1600 billion and an interest rate of 5 percent, which creates a money demand of $600 billion (see D in the frame on the left). This exceeds the available $400 billion supply by $200 billion. Similarly, point C, at an income level of $1200 billion and an interest rate of 10, generates too small a demand for money, only $200 billion instead of the required $400 billion. At point C and all other points in the white area there is an excess supply of money that exceeds the demand.

How does the economy adjust to guarantee that the given supply of money created by the government is exactly equal to the demand when the money market is out of equilibrium, as at point D? One possible adjustment, a reduction in the price level, will be considered later. In this chapter we assume the price index (P) to be equal to 1.0. Without changing prices, the economy might achieve money market equilibrium from point D by increasing the interest rate from 5 to 10 percent. This would move it to point F, cutting the demand for money from $600 to $400 billion. Or, instead, income might fall from $1600 billion to $1200 billion while the interest rate remains fixed. This would cause a movement to point G and would cut the demand for money from $600 billion to $400 billion. Or some other combination might occur, with a partial drop in income and partial increase in the interest rate.

4-6 LEARNING TO SHIFT AND TILT THE *LM* CURVE

1. WHY DOES THE *LM* CURVE SLOPE UP?

When the real money supply (M^s/P) is fixed, an increase in the interest rate leads people to put up with the inconvenience of carrying less money per dollar of income. The higher interest rate has the effect of "stretching" the available real money supply to support a higher level of real income.

For instance, along the LM line in Figure 4-7 the real money supply is assumed to be $400 billion. If the interest rate is zero, real income is only $800 billion. But each percentage point increase in the interest rate stretches the available money and makes possible an extra $80 billion of income. Thus an increase in the interest rate from zero to 5 percent at point A makes possible an increase in real income by $400 billion, from $800 to $1200 billion.

Along any given LM curve the level of real money balances (M^s/P) is fixed, but real income (Q) varies. The ratio of real income to real balances is called the **velocity** of money (V):

$$\text{velocity } (V) = \frac{Q}{M^s/P} = \frac{PQ}{M^s}$$

The right-hand expression states that velocity is also equal to nominal income (PQ) divided by the nominal supply M^s. The higher the interest rate, the higher is velocity, as the available money is "stretched" to support a higher level of income and transactions. Anything that can cause the economy to move back and forth along a fixed LM curve achieves a change of velocity by altering Q while M^s/P is fixed.

2. WHAT MAKES THE LM CURVE SHIFT?

The Fed can make a monetary policy decision to alter M^s, the nominal money supply. If the price level P is fixed, this will alter the real money supply (M^s/P). In Figure 4-8, for instance, a $200 billion increase in the money supply from $400 to $600 billion shifts the LM curve from the left-hand dashed line LM_0 to the right-hand solid line LM_1. Since each dollar of extra available money makes possible 2.0 extra dollars of income, the LM curve shifts horizontally by $400 billion.

3. WHAT ALTERS THE SLOPE OF LM?

The slope of LM measures the extra dollars of income made possible by a higher interest rate, $80 billion per each 1 percent increase in the interest rate in our example. This is the product of two components, the money-demand responsiveness to a higher interest rate ($40 billion per percentage point) along either the L_0 or L_1 line in Figure 4-7, and the number of dollars of extra income made possible by each dollar of money released by the higher interest rate (2.0). Thus a change in either factor will rotate the LM curve.

Particularly interesting is the extreme case when the demand for money does not depend on the interest rate at all, which would cause the LM curve

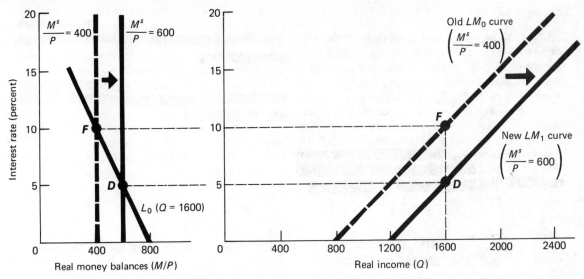

FIGURE 4-8

The Effect on the *LM* Curve of an Increase in the Real Money Supply from $400 Billion to $600 Billion

The dashed LM_0 line in the figure is identical to LM in the previous figure. When the money supply is increased, the money available to support output increases, and the LM curve shifts rightward by 2.0 dollars per dollar of extra money to the new line LM_1.

to be vertical.[11] We will see in the next chapter that fiscal policy loses its potency when the *LM* curve is vertical. The slope of *LM* depends on the responsiveness of money demand to a higher interest rate in the following way:

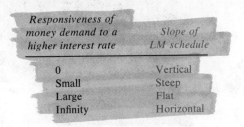

Responsiveness of money demand to a higher interest rate	Slope of LM schedule
0	Vertical
Small	Steep
Large	Flat
Infinity	Horizontal

[11] In the numerical example the *LM* curve would be a vertical line at a horizontal position exactly two times the current real money supply (M^s/P).

Finding a Solution in Economics

The LM curve by itself cannot tell us the level of both income and the interest rate. Why? You cannot find a city like Des Moines on a map if you are given only the number of a road passing through it, say Interstate 80. The city could be anywhere between New York and San Francisco! Instead, one needs to know two roads that intersect at Des Moines, say Interstate 80 and Interstate 35. In exactly the same way, the LM curve is a single line, like a highway, and is not enough by itself to determine the two unknown magnitudes (Q and r).

The other line relating the interest rate and income is the IS curve of section 4-3. Together, the IS and LM curves can determine both income and the interest rate, just as two crossing highways can determine a location on a two-dimensional map. In more formal language, it takes two schedules—the IS curve and the LM curve—to determine two unknowns (Q and r). If there were three unknowns, three schedules on a three-dimensional graph would be necessary, just as it is necessary to know latitude, longitude, and altitude to find an airplane in a three-dimensional sky.

4-7 SIMULTANEOUS EQUILIBRIUM IN THE COMMODITY AND MONEY MARKETS

Equilibrium in the commodity market for any given value of $\bar{A}$ occurs only at points on the IS curve. Figure 4-9 copies the IS_0 schedule from Figure 4-4, drawn for a value of $\bar{A} = 500$. At any point off the IS_0 curve, for instance, G and F, the economy is out of equilibrium. At F production is too high, and unintended inventory accumulation occurs. At G production is too low, and unintended inventory decumulation occurs.

Equilibrium in the commodity market occurs along the IS_0 curve at points C, D, and E_0. These three points represent different combinations of income and the interest rate, all of which are compatible with commodity-market equilibrium. At which equilibrium point will the economy come to rest? The single IS_0 schedule does not provide enough information to determine *both* income and the interest rate. An additional schedule is needed, since *two* schedules are needed to pin down the equilibrium values of *two* unknown variables.

The necessary additional information is provided by the LM curve, showing all combinations of income and the interest rate at which the money market is in equilibrium for a given real money supply—in this case, $400 billion. Figure 4-9 copies the LM_0 schedule from Figure 4-8 drawn for a value of $M_0^s/P = 400$. At any point off the LM_0 curve—for instance, points C and D—the money market is out of equilibrium. At D income is too high and the real demand for money exceeds the real supply. At C income is too low and the real demand for money is below the real supply. Equilibrium in the money market occurs only at points G, F, and E_0, each representing combinations of income and the interest rate at which the real demand for money is equal to a real money supply of $400 billion.

At what point is the entire economy, consisting of the commodity and money markets together, in equilibrium? Equilibrium occurs only at the

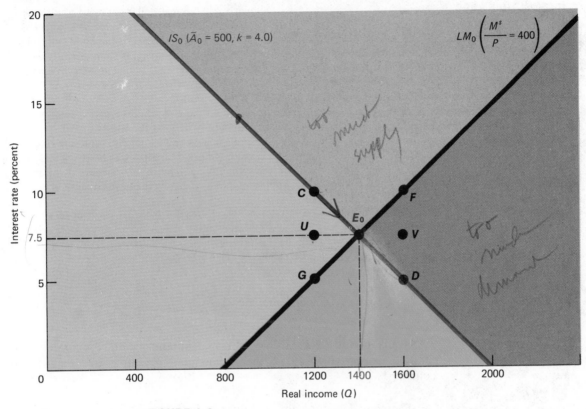

FIGURE 4-9

The *IS* and *LM* Schedules Cross at Last

The IS_0 schedule is copied from Figure 4–4; the LM_0 schedule from Figure 4–8. Only at the red point E_0 is the economy in a "general" equilibrium, with the conditions for equilibrium attained in both the commodity market (along *IS*) and the money market (along *LM*). At points *U*, *V*, *G*, and *F* the commodity market is out of equilibrium. Can you describe which way—excess demand or supply? At points *U*, *V*, *C*, and *D* the money market is out of equilibrium. Is the problem too much supply of money or too much demand for money?

point where the *IS* and *LM* curves cross, point E_0 in Figure 4-9. Why is the economy out of equilibrium at every other point? Consider these examples:

At *C* the commodity market is in equilibrium, but the demand for real money balances is below the real supply of money.

At *D* the commodity market is in equilibrium, but the demand for real money balances exceeds the real supply of money.

At *G* the money market is in equilibrium, but the demand for commodities exceeds production, so that unintended inventory decumulation is occurring.

Interest Rates and Bond and Stock Prices

Whenever individuals have more money than they desire to hold at the present income and interest-rate level, they are likely to use the extra unwanted money to buy stocks and bonds and other assets. Any increase in the demand for stocks and bonds drives up their prices. This simultaneously reduces the interest rate. Why? The interest rate on a stock is its dividend yield, the dollar dividend divided by the stock's price. Let us assume that initially the price of a stock paying a $5 dividend is $50, so that the dividend yield is 0.10, or 10 percent (= 5/50). If, however, an increase in the demand for stocks drives the stock price up to $100, the dividend yield drops from 0.10 (= 5/50) to 0.05 (= 5/100), because the $5 dividend payment in this example is unaffected by movements in stock prices.

Similarly, the annual dollar payment of interest on a long-term bond, say $5 per year, is unaffected by movements in bond prices. If the bond's price is initially $50, the bond pays a 0.10 interest "yield" or interest "rate." When the bond price is driven up to $100, the interest yield or rate drops from 0.10 (5/50) to 0.05 (5/100).

In short, if there is an excess real supply of money—a supply beyond the needs of individuals at the present level of income and interest rate—stock and bond prices are likely to be rising and interest rates falling. The reverse occurs if the real supply of money is below the needs of individuals.[a]

_____

[a] Later we will see that an excess supply of money reduces the interest rate only in the short run. Once prices are allowed to change, an excess supply of money can create inflation and raise the nominal interest rate.

At F the money market is in equilibrium, but the demand for commodities falls short of production, so that unintended inventory accumulation is occurring.

Exercise: Describe the situation in both the commodity and money market at U and V in Figure 4-9.

How does the economy arrive at its **general equilibrium** at point E_0 if it starts out at the wrong place, as at points U or V? If the commodity market is out of equilibrium and involuntary inventory decumulation or accumulation occurs, firms will step up or cut production, pushing the economy in the direction needed to reach E_0. If the money market is out of equilibrium, there will be pressure on interest rates to adjust. For instance, at point D the real demand for money is higher than the real supply. Individuals cannot obtain enough money to satisfy their demand at an interest rate of 5 percent and an income level of $1600 billion, so that they sell stocks and bonds to obtain the needed money. This drives down stock and bond prices, increasing the interest rate. Similarly, if there is too little demand for money, as at C, people will use the extra unwanted portion of the real supply of money to buy bonds and stocks, thus driving up bond and stock prices and driving down the interest rate. Either way, the economy arrives at E_0—from above if it starts at point C and from below if it starts at point D.

The IS and LM curves are the basic tools that allow us to study the effects of fiscal and monetary policy when both the commodity market and money market are in equilibrium. Can the Fed by its monetary policy decisions off-set or cancel the stimulative impact of higher government spending or lower tax rates? What difference does it make if the government decides to stimulate the economy by means of fiscal or monetary policy? As we will see, both fiscal and monetary policy can affect income, but the level of the interest rate will depend on which policy instrument is used.

SUMMARY

1. Private planned autonomous spending (A_p) depends partly on the interest rate. We cannot know the total level of A_p, hence the level of income (A_p times the multiplier k), until we know the level of the interest rate. The higher the interest rate, the lower is A_p.

2. Private planned autonomous spending (A_p) depends also on the profitability firms expect from additional investment and the utility households expect from additional consumption goods. When firms and consumers become more optimistic about the payoff of additional purchases, A_p tends to increase for any given level of the interest rate.

3. The *IS* curve indicates all the combinations of the interest rate and income at which the economy's market for commodities is in equilibrium. At any point off the *IS* curve the economy is out of equilibrium: to the right of the *IS* curve, purchases lag behind production, and unintended inventory accumulation is occurring; to the left, purchases exceed production, and inventory decumulation is occurring.

4. The real quantity of money that people demand depends both on total real income and on the interest rate. Equilibrium in the money market requires that the real supply of money equal the demand for real money balances. The *LM* curve represents all the combinations of real income and of the interest rate where the money market is in equilibrium. To the right of the *LM* curve money demand exceeds the money supply; to the left, the money supply exceeds money demand.

5. Neither the *IS* nor the *LM* schedule alone provides enough information to determine the equilibrium values for both income and the interest rate. Since there are two unknown variables, the situation of "general equilibrium" must be determined using both schedules simultaneously. This simultaneous equilibrium occurs only at the point where the *IS* and *LM* curves intersect. At any other point, one or both markets are out of equilibrium.

A LOOK AHEAD

Now we have determined simultaneously the levels of equilibrium income and the interest rate. Both depend on the variables that establish the positions of the *IS* and the *LM* curves: the multiplier, business and consumer confidence, fiscal policy, and monetary policy. But can monetary and fiscal policy maintain control over the economy under all conditions? In Chapter 5 we examine the effects of changes in policy and establish several extreme situations in which either fiscal or monetary policy is impotent.

CONCEPTS

Rate of return
Interest rate
Business and consumer confidence
IS curve
LM curve
Federal Reserve control over the
    money supply

Demand for real money balances
Equilibrium in the commodity
    market
Equilibrium in the money market
Simultaneous general equilibrium
    for the entire economy

QUESTIONS FOR REVIEW

1   Why do private planned investment and autonomous consumer spending depend on the interest rate? What types of purchases would be most sensitive to interest rate changes? Why?

2   What are the costs of holding money? Given these costs, why do people hold money?

3   Which factors shift the position of the *IS* curve and which change the slope?

4   Which factors shift the position of the *LM* curve and which change the slope?

5   To achieve maximum responsiveness of income to changes in the money supply, what should the *LM* curve look like? What does this imply about the underlying money demand curve?

6   Would the response of income to a change in the money supply be greater if the *IS* curve were completely vertical or completely horizontal?

7   How can the Federal Reserve Board use monetary policy to offset the impact on income of higher government spending? Of higher tax rates?

8   To raise output toward the full employment level, either a monetary or a fiscal policy stimulus may be used. While both can raise total output to the same level, other variables may not be the same. Which variables would you expect to be different? The interest rate? The share of private sector spending in total GNP?

5 Strong and Weak Effects of Monetary and Fiscal Policy

First, let me explain what *I* thought the main issue was. In terms of the Hicksian language of Friedman's article, I thought (and I still think) it was the shape of the *LM* locus.

—James Tobin[1]

5-1 INTRODUCTION

The last chapter introduced the *IS* and *LM* curves, the tools necessary to determine the economy's level of equilibrium real income and its interest rate, as well as the effect of monetary and fiscal policy on both real income and the interest rate. We will now use these tools to find the strength or weakness of monetary and fiscal policy, still assuming that the price level is fixed. Under some circumstances monetary policy may be powerful, creating large changes in real income with relatively small shifts in the real money supply. But under other circumstances, real income may get "stuck" at an unsatisfactory level, and even massive increases in the real money supply may not be able to raise real income. Similarly, fiscal policy (changes in government purchases or tax rates) may or may not be a potent instrument for controlling real income.

As we have learned, the *IS* curve shows all the combinations of real income and the interest rate that keep the commodity market in equilibrium, with production equal to planned expenditures. The *IS* curve slopes downward because a lower interest rate raises planned investment and consumption spending, requiring higher production to avoid involuntary inventory decumulation. The position of the *IS* curve shifts whenever there is a change in the autonomous spending planned at a zero interest rate ($\Delta \bar{A}$); this could occur because of a change in consumer or business optimism *or* because of a change in government purchases or autonomous tax revenue. In addition,

---

[1] "Friedman's Theoretical Framework," in Robert J. Gordon (ed.), *Milton Friedman's Monetary Framework: A Debate with His Critics* (Chicago: University of Chicago Press, 1974), p. 77.

the *IS* curve is rotated around its vertical intercept whenever the multiplier (k) is changed by an alteration in the household saving rate or in the income tax rate.

The *LM* curve shows all the combinations of real income and the interest rate that keep the money market in equilibrium, with the demand for real money balances equal to a given real money supply (M^s/P). The *LM* curve slopes upward because an increase in the interest rate reduces the demand for money by inducing people to shift more of their funds into savings accounts. This shift requires an offsetting increase in real income to generate a higher demand for money for transactions, thus keeping the total demand for money equal to a fixed supply. The *LM* curve shifts its position whenever there is a change in the real money supply, requiring a corresponding change in real money demand to maintain equilibrium in the money market. Each *LM* curve is labeled with the value of the real money supply that fixes its position.

5-2 STRONG EFFECTS OF AN INCREASE IN THE REAL MONEY SUPPLY

In Figure 4-8 we saw that an increase in the real money supply reduces the interest rate. Our more general analysis, which combines the money market and the commodity market, shows that most increases in the real money supply not only reduce the interest rate but also cause an increase in real income. The top frame of Figure 5-1 repeats the LM_0 curve of Figures 4-8 and 4-9, drawn on the assumption that the real money supply is $400 billion. Also repeated is the IS_0 curve of Figures 4-4 and 4-9, which assumes that $\bar{A} = 500$ and $k = 4.0$. The economy's general equilibrium, the

WHY A VERTICAL *LM* CURVE MAKES MONETARY POLICY MORE POTENT

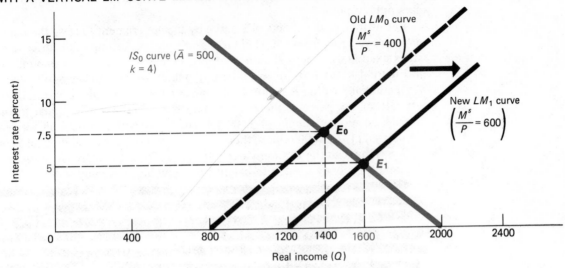

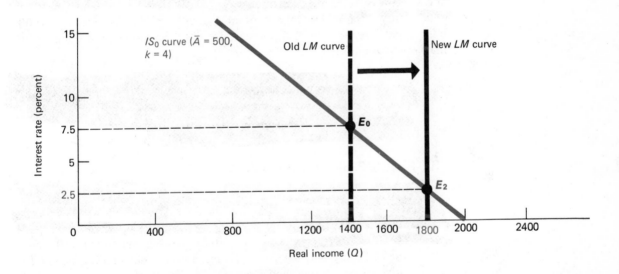

FIGURE 5–1

The Effect of a $200 Billion Increase in the Money Supply with a Normal *LM* Curve and a Vertical *LM* Curve

The top frame repeats the $200 billion increase in the money supply that was shown in Figure 4–8. In order to maintain equilibrium in both the commodity and money markets here, two effects occur; equilibrium income rises and the interest rate declines, as indicated by the movement from E_0 to E_1. In the bottom frame, the *LM* curve is vertical and the same $200 billion increase in the money supply shifts the *LM* curve to the right by $400 billion, leading to a greater drop in the interest rate and a greater increase in equilibrium income.

Strong Effects of an Increase in the Real Money Supply **121**

point where both the money and commodity markets are in equilibrium, occurs only at point E_0.

Let us look at the effects of a move by the government to raise the nominal money supply from $400 billion to $600 billion. As long as the price level stays fixed at 1.0, the real money supply increases by the same amount. As in Figure 4-8, the LM curve shifts horizontally to the right by $400 billion. At the initial position E_0, with an income level of $1400 billion, and an interest rate of 7.5 percent, the real demand for money remains equal to the initial real money supply of $400 billion. Now, with the new higher real money supply of $600 billion, there is an "excess supply of money" of $200 billion. How can the economy generate the $200 billion increase in the real demand for money needed to balance the new higher supply?

Finding themselves with more money than they desire, individuals do not merely let it rest idle in their pockets or in checking accounts that pay no interest. Instead, they transfer some into savings accounts and use some to buy stocks, bonds, and commodities. This new higher demand raises the prices of bonds and stocks and reduces the interest rate, and this is sometimes called the "liquidity effect" of a monetary expansion. The lower interest rate raises the desired level of autonomous consumption and investment spending, requiring an increase in production. This is the "income effect" of a monetary expansion. Only at point E_1, with an income level of $1600 billion and interest rate of 5 percent, are both the money and commodity markets in equilibrium.

> **Summary:** Compared to the starting point E_0, the increase in the real money supply has caused both an increase in real income and a reduction in the interest rate to the new equilibrium point E_1, due to the combined impact of the liquidity and income effects.

THE PULL OF HIGHER INCOME ON THE INTEREST RATE

The size of the drop in the interest rate depends on the interest responsiveness of the demand for money. For instance, if this is very small, then it takes a very large drop in the interest rate to induce individuals to hold the higher money supply voluntarily. An extreme case is illustrated in the bottom frame of Figure 5-1, where we assume that the demand for money depends only on real income and does not depend on the interest rate at all (as signified by the vertical LM curve). Here no interest rate will raise the demand for money even one cent above its initial level at E_0 in response to a $200 billion increase in the real money supply. Because the demand for money depends only on income, then the only way for the demand for money to rise by the necessary $200 billion is for real income to rise by $400 billion (recall that the demand for money increases by half of the increase in real income). If involuntary accumulation of inventories is to be avoided, the interest rate must decline enough to induce $1800 billion of desired expenditures, which requires that we move down the IS curve to a new equilibrium at point E_2.

Now compare the top and bottom frames of Figure 5-1. In both, the real money supply increases by $200 billion. Yet in the top frame income increases by only $200 billion, whereas in the bottom frame income increases by $400 billion, or twice as much. Why? The supply of money has increased by the same amount, $200 billion, in both cases, and the demand for money must increase the same $200 billion in both diagrams. In the top diagram the responsibility for increasing the demand for money by $200 billion between equilibrium points E_0 and E_1 is shared — half is accomplished by the drop in the interest rate from 7.5 to 5 percent, and the remaining half is accomplished by the $200 billion increase in income. But in the bottom diagram the interest rate cannot contribute to raising money demand because the demand for money is completely independent of the interest rate, requiring that the entire responsibility for raising money demand be shouldered by an increase in income.

> **Summary:** If the demand for money is independent of the interest rate, the *LM* curve is vertical and an increase in the money supply has a potent effect on real income. When the demand for money is responsive to the interest rate, the *LM* curve is flatter, and the impact of the money supply on real income is less potent.

5-3 WEAK EFFECTS OF MONETARY POLICY: UNRESPONSIVE EXPENDITURES AND THE LIQUIDITY TRAP

If, as we assumed in Chapter 3, natural real GNP (Q^N) equals $1600 billion, then the initial position at E_0 in Figure 5-1, with an income level of only $1400 billion, would be considered unsatisfactory by government policy-makers.[2] The **GNP "gap"** would be $200 billion ($1600 - 1400$), and the unemployment rate would be high. The previous section demonstrated that the Federal Reserve will be able to raise real income by raising the real money supply if:

1. The price level is fixed,
2. The *IS* curve is negatively sloped, and
3. The *LM* curve is positively sloped or vertical.

Now we examine two situations in which the Federal Reserve *cannot raise the level of actual real income*. The first, illustrated in Figure 5-2, occurs if planned expenditures do not respond to the interest rate. In this case the *IS* curve is vertical (parallel to the vertical interest-rate axis). The position of the *IS* curve and the level of income in this case depend *only* on the level of $\bar{A}$ (autonomous expenditures planned at a zero interest rate), and of k (the multiplier). Since income is *independent* of the interest rate, changes in the real money supply have no effect on real income.

---

[2] **Review:** Real GNP, real output, and real income are the same thing, as we learned in Chapter 2.

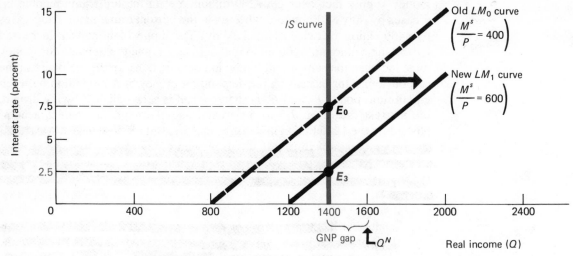

FIGURE 5–2

Effect of a $200 Billion Increase in the Real Money Supply When the Interest Responsiveness of A_p Is Zero

The higher money supply forces a reduction in the interest rate to maintain equilibrium in the money market. But the lower interest rate does nothing to stimulate expenditures, because autonomous planned spending (A_p) is now assumed to be independent of the interest rate, as indicated by the vertical *IS* curve. Notice that the interest rate must fall more here than in the top frame of Figure 5–1. Why?

Now an increase in the money supply from $400 to $600 billion has absolutely no effect on real income, which remains "stuck" at $1400 billion. The equilibrium position does shift down vertically from E_0 to E_3, because at E_0 the higher money supply throws the money market out of equilibrium. A $200 billion increase in money demand is required, and the interest rate must drop from 7.5 percent at E_0 to 2.5 percent at E_3 to induce households to shift funds out of stocks, bonds, and savings accounts into money (cash and checking accounts). The vertical *IS* curve means that planned expenditures are not stimulated by the lower interest rate at E_3, there is no change in planned expenditures, and no change in production or income.

Thus, even if the Federal Reserve wants to raise the level of income above $1400 billion to Q^N, $1600 billion, it is powerless to do so in a situation with a zero interest response of planned expenditures. This does *not* mean that the fiscal branch of government is powerless to raise output, however. It can increase Q by raising $\bar{A}$ with higher government purchases or lower autonomous tax revenues, or it can lower income tax rates, increasing the multiplier. Only monetary expansion is rendered impotent, not fiscal policy.

THE LIQUIDITY TRAP

Even with the normal, negatively sloped *IS* curve, the Federal Reserve may be unable to push real income as high as natural real GNP. This case of monetary impotence may occur if there is a lower limit to the interest rate. The Fed does not control the interest rate directly; it influences only the supply of money. An increase in the money supply usually reduces the interest rate, because individuals try to get rid of their excess holdings of money by buying stocks and bonds, which drives up stock and bond prices and drives down the interest rate.[3] But if this effect is to work, some individuals must be willing to buy stocks and bonds. If, on the other hand, *every* individual were convinced that stock and bond prices were so far above "normal" that they could not rise further, and could only fall, no individuals would hold or be willing to buy stocks or bonds. The Federal Reserve would be unable to push up stock and bond prices (or reduce the interest rate), no matter how much money it was willing to create.[4] People who believe stock and bond prices will go down are often called **bears**. As Keynes remarked, the minimum interest rate is reached when all investors have joined the "bear brigade."

The theory of the minimum interest rate requires for its validity both a constant "normal" interest rate and agreement among all individuals that the current interest rate is so far below normal that the holding of stocks and bonds can lead only to capital losses. Some writers have held that the **liquidity trap**, a phrase sometimes used to describe the minimum-interest-rate situation, is an essential part of Keynes' case for downgrading monetary policy and emphasizing fiscal policy. But, as we will see, the liquidity trap did not occur in the 1930s, Keynes never claimed that it did occur, and there is no reason why individuals would ever maintain a constant immutable view of the normal interest rate in the face of the massive economic changes that occur in a depression.

Figure 5-3 depicts an economy in a liquidity trap. The *LM* curve is shown as a horizontal line, indicating that changes in the money supply no longer cause changes in the interest rate. The minimum interest rate attainable is 2.5 percent, and we call this interest rate along the flat *LM* curve "r_{min}."

---

[3] Throughout we adopt the simplification of referring to the interest yield on bonds and the dividend yield on stocks as "the interest rate." To review the reasons for the inverse relationship between stock and bond prices and the interest rate, turn back to the boxed explanation in section 4-7 on p. 116.

[4] The theory of the speculative motive for money demand was developed by Keynes in the *General Theory* and is compared with postwar developments in the theory of money demand in Axel Leijonhufvud, *On Keynesian Economics and the Economics of Keynes* (New York: Oxford University Press, 1968), pp. 354–386.

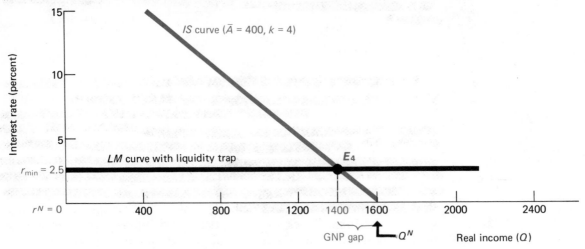

FIGURE 5–3

Illustration of an Economy in a "Liquidity Trap"

Two elements are necessary. First, businessmen and consumers must be pessimistic so that the IS curve is relatively far to the left. Notice that the $\bar{A}$ used to draw this IS curve is only \$400 billion, less than assumed previously. The interest rate (r^N) where the IS curve crosses natural real GNP of \$1600 billion (Q^N) is zero. The second element is that this value of r^N is below the minimum interest rate attainable along the horizontal LM curve, owing to the effect of the "liquidity trap." The economy is stuck at point E_4, with a GNP gap of \$200 billion.

Whether or not the economy has trouble achieving its natural level of real GNP at $Q^N = \$1600$ billion depends on the position of the IS curve. If the IS curve were to cross the flat LM curve at an income level of \$1600 billion, there would be no problem. But we have assumed that $\bar{A}$ is only \$400 billion, and so the IS curve in Figure 5-3 touches the horizontal axis at an income level of \$1600 billion (the multiplier of 4 times $\bar{A}$). Since the minimum interest rate attainable along the LM curve is 2.5 percent, the maximum income level along the IS curve is \$1400 billion. This represents a "GNP gap" of \$200 billion, in comparison to the desired goal of \$1600 billion.

We use the symbol r^N to designate the **"natural rate of interest"** at which the IS curve crosses the natural real GNP level of \$1600 billion. In Figure 5-3 r^N is zero. If the IS curve were drawn further to the right, r^N would be higher. For instance, in Figure 5-1 the IS curve crosses the \$1600 billion income level at an interest rate of 5 percent, so in that diagram $r^N = 5$.

GENERAL RULE FOR MONETARY IMPOTENCE

The general rule that applies is:

When r^N is greater than or equal to r_{min}, the monetary authority (the Fed) is capable of stimulating the economy by enough to return actual real income to the level of natural real GNP if IS is not vertical. But when r^N is less than r_{min} (as is true in Figure 5-3), the monetary authority is incapable of stimulating the economy by enough unless it can find some way to raise r^N directly.

Notice that the general rule applies even if there is no liquidity trap. It is impossible for the interest rate to be negative. (Why? Banks would pay you interest to borrow money, so that you would instantly borrow infinity dollars.) Thus the lowest possible value of r_{min} is zero. In this case, the general rule says that monetary policy cannot achieve natural output (Q^N) if r^N is negative. Monetary policy can succeed only if it can operate directly on r^N and raise it above r_{min}.

Belief in the weakness of monetary policy reached its peak of popularity among economists in the 1940s and 1950s, summarized in the saying "You can take a horse to water but you can't make it drink." The Fed can create all the money it wants, but it can't force the economy to use it for consumption and investment purchases.

5-4 CASE STUDY: WAS THERE A LIQUIDITY TRAP DURING THE GREAT DEPRESSION?

In Figure 5-4 the interest rate is once again drawn on the vertical axis. Instead of plotting the real money supply by itself on the horizontal axis, we have plotted data for the real money supply divided by real income (M^s/PQ).[5] This technique makes a rough correction for the effect on money demand of changing real income, and it allows us to concentrate on the relationship between money demand (holding income constant) and the interest rate.

The annual data for (M^s/PQ) and for the interest rate on long-term government bonds have been plotted for each year between 1929 and 1940. A line connecting the 1929 and 1940 points has been added. The points for most of the years lie fairly close to the line, although between 1931 and 1934 they are too high, suggesting that in the darkest days of the Great Depression individuals were so pessimistic that they held more money, particularly in the form of cash, than would normally have been warranted at the prevailing interest rate.

---

[5] The data refer to $M1$, which includes currency and checking accounts at commercial banks.

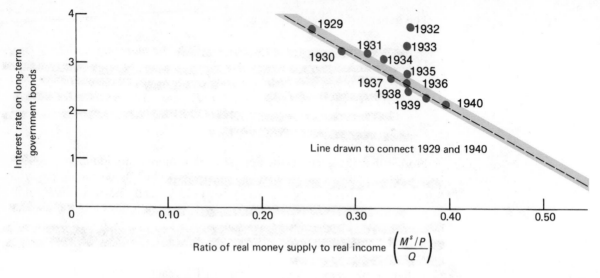

FIGURE 5-4

The Effect of a Higher Money Supply Relative to Income on the Long-Term Interest Rate, 1929–40

For a liquidity trap to have occurred during the Great Depression, we should find evidence that the Fed was unable to push down the interest rate by raising the money supply. Although the relationship between money and the interest rate does not fall along the pink line in every year, most of the years do fall quite close to the line except for 1932 and 1933, the worst years of economic collapse. This suggests that the liquidity trap did not occur during the Great Depression, so that monetary policy was not rendered impotent.

Source: M^s/PQ from Appendix B. Interest rate is Series B–73 in *Long Term Economic Growth 1860–1970* (U.S. Department of Commerce, 1973).

But certainly the observations between 1935 and 1940 are consistent with the hypothesis that the demand for money depends inversely on the interest rate. There is no sign at all that the interest rate hit a minimum level at any time during the latter half of the Great Depression. If the Fed had created more money, it is likely that the long-term interest rate would have fallen further and provided at least some additional stimulus to planned expenditures.

The verdict taken from these data did not surprise Keynes, who was not an apostle of the liquidity trap. As of the publication of his book in 1936, Keynes knew "no example of it hitherto," although he was willing to concede that the trap "might become important in the future."[6] He

---

[6] J. M. Keynes, *The General Theory of Employment, Interest and Money* (London: Macmillan, 1936), p. 207.

TABLE 5-1

Money, Output, and Unemployment in the Great Depression, 1929–40

Year	Real money supply	Real GNP	GNP gap (percent)	Unemployment rate (percent)
	($ billions, 1972 prices)			
1929	81.1	314.7	−1.4	3.2
1930	81.0	285.2	10.5	8.9
1931	83.5	263.3	19.6	16.3
1932	82.1	226.8	32.6	24.1
1933	79.2	222.1	35.8	25.2
1934	80.1	239.4	32.6	22.0
1935	93.1	260.8	28.5	20.3
1936	105.8	296.1	21.0	17.0
1937	105.6	309.8	19.6	14.3
1938	106.7	297.1	24.9	19.1
1939	120.2	319.7	21.5	17.2
1940	136.2	343.6	17.8	14.6
1941	147.7	396.6	7.7	9.9

Sources: See Appendix B.

recognized that the logical assumptions necessary for the liquidity trap were unlikely to occur, primarily because the "normal" expected interest rate was likely to drift downward in a continuing state of depression.[7] In fact, the long-term government bond rate drifted even lower in 1941, despite the increase in output connected with the beginning of World War II, suggesting that investors had substantially revised downward the interest rate they considered normal.

Although there does not appear to have been a liquidity trap during the 1930s, the beneficial effects of a higher real money supply were quite weak. As illustrated in Table 5-1, the real money supply was increased between 1929 and 1939 by 48 percent, and yet real GNP in the latter year was only 1.6 percent higher than in the former.[8] Because natural real GNP had grown in the meantime, the GNP gap between actual and natural output grew from −1.4 to 21.5 percent and the unemployment rate from 3.2 to 17.2 percent.

In recent years there has been a lively debate regarding the relative role of monetary and nonmonetary factors in causing the Great Depres-

[7] Leijonhufvud, *op. cit.*, pp. 202–203.

[8] The sources of the 1929–39 increase in the money supply are identified in the case study in section 16–5. For a recent statistical study that finds no evidence of a liquidity trap, see John L. Scadding, "An Annual Money Demand and Supply Model for the U.S.: 1924–1940/1949–1966," *Journal of Monetary Economics*, vol. 3 (January 1977), pp. 41–58. See also Karl Brunner and Alan Meltzer, "Liquidity Traps for Money, Bank Credit, and Interest Rates," *Journal of Political Economy*, vol. 76 (January/February 1968), pp. 1–35.

sion, particularly the collapse of nominal and real GNP between 1929 and 1933. In an extensive statistical study of the data with James A. Wilcox, I recently concluded that both monetary and nonmonetary factors were important, but at different times.[9] For instance, in the first two years of the contraction (1929–31) the decline in the money supply was much too small to account for the drop in spending, which must be attributed mainly to nonmonetary factors (including overbuilding in the 1920s and the impact of the 1929 stock market crash on consumption). But after September 1931 the contraction was caused mainly by monetary factors, including the enormous loss of lifetime savings in bank failures.

The 1933–37 recovery and 1937–38 recession also seem compatible with a prominent role for money. It is mainly for the 1938–41 period that a case for monetary impotence can be made. The money supply grew very rapidly between early 1938 and 1941, but the economy was very sluggish until mid-1940. At that time expansive fiscal policy, in the form of expanded production of military equipment for the United States and United Kingdom, caused the growth of real GNP to "take off." This conclusion is more obvious in quarterly data than in the annual data of Table 5-1.

5-5 WEAK MONETARY EFFECTS: QUALIFICATIONS TO THE GENERAL RULE

The general rule in section 5-3 states that monetary policy cannot by itself push the economy out of a recession or depression when r^N, the natural rate of interest, is below r_{min}. Even when there is no liquidity trap, and hence the minimum interest rate (r_{min}) is zero rather than a positive number, the Fed may be incapable of achieving higher output if r^N is negative, as when businesses and consumers are pessimistic. When this kind of pessimism is pervasive, it may well take a negative interest rate to induce more spending by businesses and consumers.

The negative value of r^N does not mean that the entire government is incapable of ending the depression or recession; it is just that the Fed by shifting the LM curve has no power. The fiscal policymakers (Congress and the president) are still able to raise $\bar{A}$ and hence shift the IS curve to the right as far as necessary to bring the economy back to its natural level of output (Q^N) and full employment. Another technique for shifting the IS curve to the right would be a cut in the income tax rate.

Another possibility is that the Fed can directly influence r^N without help from the fiscal branch of government. It can do so if planned autonomous expenditure depends not just on the interest rate but also on the current value of real balances (the real money supply — M^s/P). In this case the IS curve shifts not only when $\bar{A}$ changes but also whenever the Fed changes

[9] Robert J. Gordon and James A. Wilcox, "Monetarist Interpretations of the Great Depression: An Evaluation and Critique," in Karl Brunner (ed.), *Contemporary Views of the Great Depression* (Hingham, Mass.: Martinus Nijhoff, 1980).

M^s/P. Why? Because an increase in the real money supply increases household wealth, which in turn induces households to purchase more consumption goods. Imagine two households, A and B, with exactly the same real income but with household A owning ten times as much money (cash and checking accounts) as household B. It is likely that household A would consume more than household B because its "cushion of cash" would free it from the need to save as much as household B.

The addition of the real money supply to the list of determinants of the IS schedule (along with $\bar{A}$ and k) is usually called the **real balance effect** or the **Pigou effect,** after the British economist who first recognized its implications.[10] The real balance effect rescues monetary policy in situations when r^N is less than r_{min} by giving the monetary authority a direct lever to control r^N.

5-6 PURE FISCAL EXPANSION AND THE CROWDING OUT EFFECT

We have so far examined **pure monetary policy shifts,** those which hold fiscal variables constant. Now we turn from pure monetary to pure fiscal policy. Because our purpose is to study the effects of monetary and fiscal policy separately, our subject here is **pure fiscal policy shifts** – that is, changes in government spending or taxes while the money supply is held constant. Once we understand pure monetary and fiscal operations separately, we can easily carry out combined monetary-fiscal changes.

Under what circumstances are the effects of a pure fiscal stimulus strong or weak? The normal situation is depicted in Figure 5-5, where we begin at the original equilibrium point E_0, the crossing point of the LM_0 and IS_0 curves. A \$100 billion increase in government purchases (ΔG) raises $\bar{A}$ by the same amount and shifts the IS curve to the right by \$400 billion, from the old IS_0 schedule drawn for $\bar{A} = \$500$ billion to the new IS_1 schedule drawn for $\bar{A} = \$600$ billion.

In Figure 5-5 we see that the fiscal policy multiplier is reduced when the money market is taken into consideration. The full fiscal multiplier of $k = 4.0$ would move the economy horizontally from the initial equilibrium position at E_0 to point E_6, where income is \$400 billion higher. But at E_6 the money market is not in equilibrium. Income is higher than at E_0, raising the transaction demand for money, but the money supply remains unchanged, so that there is an excess demand for money. To cut the demand for money back to the level of the fixed supply, the interest rate must rise. But an increase in the interest rate makes point E_6 untenable by reducing planned consumption and investment expenditures. Only at point E_5 are both the commodity and money markets in equilibrium. Real income does not increase by the fully multiplied \$400 billion, but only by half as much, \$200 billion.

---

[10] A. C. Pigou, "The Classical Stationary State," *Economic Journal,* vol. 53 (1943), pp. 343–351.

THE CROWDING OUT EFFECT CUTS THE FISCAL MULTIPLIER

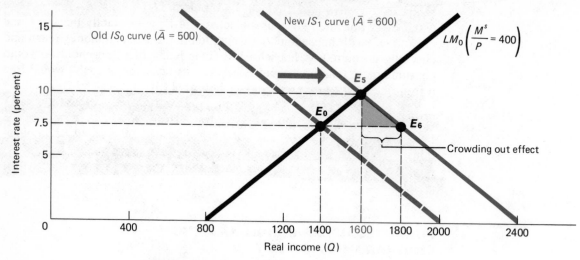

FIGURE 5–5

The Effect on the Interest Rate and Real Income of a $100 Billion Increase in Government Spending

Along the original IS_0 curve autonomous spending desired at a zero interest rate ($\bar{A}$) is 500, and the economy's equilibrium occurs at point E_0. A $100 billion increase in government spending boosts $\bar{A}$ from 500 to 600, and shifts the IS curve rightward to IS_1. The economy's equilibrium slides up the LM curve from point E_0 to point E_5. In contrast to Chapter 3's multiplier of 4.0, now the government spending multiplier is only 2.0 (the $200 billion increase in real income between E_0 and E_5 divided by the $100 billion boost in government spending that causes it).

The higher interest rate accounts for the reduction in the fiscal policy multiplier from 4.0 to 2.0. The increase in the interest rate from 7.5 to 10 percent cuts private autonomous planned consumption and investment spending by $50 billion, fully half of the $100 billion increase in government spending. Thus fully half of the original multiplier of 4.0 is "crowded out."

COMPARISON OF EQUILIBRIUM POSITIONS E_0 AND E_5

	Initial E_0	New E_5
Interest rate (r)	7.5	10.0
Private autonomous spending	350	300
($I_p + a = 500 - 20r$)		
Government spending (G)	0	100
Total autonomous spending	350	400
($A_p = I_p + a + G$)		
Income ($Q = 4.0A_p$)	1400	1600

132 Strong and Weak Effects of Monetary and Fiscal Policy

Some economists and journalists use the phrase **crowding out effect** to compare points such as E_0 and E_5 in Figure 5-5. If the interest rate were to remain constant, the higher government spending would shift real income from $1400 billion at point E_0 to $1800 billion at point E_6. But the interest rate cannot stay fixed so long as the unchanged $400 billion real money supply pins the economy to the LM_0 curve and leads to an equilibrium position with a $1600 billion level of real income at point E_5. The difference, the $200 billion difference in real income between points E_6 and E_5, represents the investment and consumption spending "crowded out" by the higher interest rate.

Point E_6, used in calculating the size of the crowding out effect, is a purely hypothetical position that the economy cannot and does not reach. Actually, far from being crowded out, total private spending is higher in the new equilibrium situation at E_5 than at the original situation at E_0 — real income has increased by $200 billion, of which only $100 billion represents higher government purchases, leaving the remaining $100 billion for extra private expenditures. The composition of private spending changes, however, as a result of the higher interest rate. Induced consumption spending increases, but autonomous spending decreases. Expenditures are divided up as follows in the two situations:

	At E_0	At E_5
Government purchases	0	100
Autonomous private spending ($I_p + a$)	350	300
Induced consumption	1050	1200
Total real expenditures	1400	1600

Summary: Higher government spending raises real output, but not by as much as implied by the simple multiplier of Chapter 3. The steeper the LM curve, the more powerful the crowding out effect, and the smaller the fiscal policy multiplier.

5-7 CASE STUDY: INTEREST RATES AND THE EXPANSION OF VIETNAM SPENDING

The 1965–67 period, during which U.S. government spending was expanding rapidly as our involvement in the Vietnam War deepened, provides an unusual case study of the consequences of fiscal expansion while the real money supply remains fixed. In the fourth quarter of 1966 (October through December), which we write as 1966:Q4, the real money supply was almost exactly the same as five quarters earlier, in 1965:Q3. An LM curve corresponding to this fixed level of M^s/P is drawn in Figure 5-6. During this five-quarter interval the level of real government purchases grew by 12.9 percent, represented in Figure 5-6 by the rightward shift in the IS curve from IS_0 to IS_1.

How did real income and the interest rate behave over the five-quarter interval? Real income increased by $60.4 billion, more than the $27.3 billion increase in government spending, because of the multiplier effect.[11] And the higher transaction demand for money forced an increase in the interest rate from 4.5 to 5.4 percent to keep the total demand for money equal to the fixed real money supply.

The immediate victim of the higher interest rates was investment in residential housing. By 1966:Q4 this component of investment had declined 23 percent from its level reached in 1965:Q3. We shall learn later (in Chapter 16) that high interest rates discourage residential investment, not only because individuals try to avoid committing themselves to expensive mortgages when interest rates are high, but also because savings institutions tend to lose funds to other assets that can boost their interest payments more promptly. Thus the savings institutions tend to have few funds available to lend for residential mortgages during a period of high interest rates such as late 1966. In fact, between December 1965 and December 1966 the monthly growth in mortgage debt dropped by 65 percent (see Table 16-2).

As shown in the table under Figure 5-6, nonresidential investment — including inventory change and expenditures on plant and equipment — continued to grow despite the increase in interest rates through 1966:Q4. The reason for this growth, rather than the "crowding out" that our theory predicts, stems from a factor our *IS–LM* model does not take into account. That factor is the *delay* between the increase in the interest rate and the subsequent decline in nonresidential investment. The table shows that in the subsequent two quarters, between 1966:Q4 and 1967:Q2, nonresidential investment dropped back almost to its original level of 1965:Q3, despite the fact that the real money supply began to grow again and the interest rate declined a bit from its peak level.

There is an old saying that a wartime economy cannot boost military spending and still keep civilian expenditures at their previous high level; that is, the economy "cannot have both guns and butter." Through the end of 1966 this age-old rule was enforced by the tightness of monetary policy through high interest rates and the stable level of the real money supply. Another way this discipline could have been enforced would have been for the higher wartime expenditures to be "paid for" by an increase in government tax rates, particularly those on personal and corporate income. Although the Council of Economic Advisers — then chaired by Professor Gardner Ackley of the University of Michigan — strongly recommended a tax increase in early 1966, President Lyndon Johnson refused to accept their recommendation. Why? Johnson may have been afraid to raise taxes, fearing defeat for Democratic members of Congress in the upcoming congressional elections of November 1966.

As a result of Johnson's delay in approving a tax increase, which was not finally approved by Congress until July 1968, the economy went

---

[11] The real-world multiplier is slightly larger than the 2.0 multiplier assumed in the hypothetical example of Figure 5-5.

THE CROWDING OUT EFFECT IN ACTION

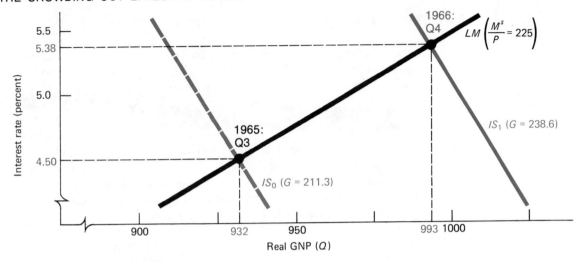

FIGURE 5–6

Real Income and the Interest Rate During a Period of Expanding
Government Expenditures, 1965:Q3 to 1966:Q4

In both 1965:Q3 and 1966:Q4 the economy was on the same *LM* curve because
the real money supply was identical in both periods. But government spending
was much higher in the second period, so that the *IS* curve was much farther to
the right. One consequence of the rightward shift of the *IS* curve was to raise the
interest rate in order to release extra money to support the higher level of transactions in 1966:Q4.

	Real income	Real government expenditures	Real residential investment	Real nonresidential investment	Real money supply	Interest rate, Moody's Aaa (percent)
1965:Q3	932.3	211.3	43.0	108.5	224.9	4.50
1966:Q4	992.8	238.6	33.3	126.9	225.4	5.38
1967:Q2	1001.3	247.3	36.3	110.8	228.7	5.26

Note: All real magnitudes in 1972 prices.
Source: Supplement to the *Survey of Current Business: Business Statistics: 1975 Biennial
Edition.*

through a period in 1967 and early 1968 when it tried to have *both* "guns
and butter." The money supply began to grow rapidly, and this allowed
private spending to grow in addition to the ongoing rapid increases in defense expenditures. The excessive spending growth of 1967–68 in an
economy that was straining at the limit of its productive capacity unleashed a serious inflation. Many analysts think that an underlying cause
of the chronic inflation suffered by the United States in the 1970s dates
back to Johnson's refusal to "pay for" the Vietnam War in 1966.

5-8 STRONG AND WEAK EFFECTS OF FISCAL POLICY

The effect of a fiscal policy stimulus on real income may be either greater or less than in our numerical example of Figure 5-5, depending on the assumed values of the multiplier and the interest responsiveness of money demand and of autonomous private spending. Fiscal policy is strong when the demand for money is highly interest responsive, as illustrated in the top frame of Figure 5-7, where we choose the largest possible responsiveness, infinity. This makes the *LM* curve horizontal, so that the multiplier becomes just the simple multiplier (4.0) of Chapter 3. Just as in Chapter 3 we ignored the effect of a changing interest rate, we can ignore the interest-rate effect in exactly the same way here so long as the interest responsiveness of money demand is infinity, because this means that the interest rate is fixed.

The opposite situation occurs when the interest responsiveness of money demand is zero, which makes the *LM* curve vertical. An increase in government spending by $100 billion shifts the *IS* curve to the right in the bottom frame of Figure 5-7 exactly as in the top frame, but real income cannot increase without throwing the money market out of equilibrium. Even $1 of extra income above $1400 billion raises money demand, but because of the zero interest responsiveness of money demand, there is no increase in the interest rate that can bring money demand back into balance with the fixed money supply. In this case, the only effect of a fiscal stimulus is to raise the interest rate. The crowding out effect is complete, with the higher interest rate cutting autonomous private spending by exactly the amount by which government spending increases.

In recent years, the possibility of a vertical *LM* curve has received considerable attention as a result of the claim by some monetarists that the stimulative effect of fiscal policy on real output is negligible or even zero.[12] All recent statistical studies are unanimous in concluding that the interest responsiveness is not even close to zero.[13] As will be seen in the next chapter, fiscal effects can be weak despite a positively sloped *LM* curve if the fiscal stimulus raises the price level and causes the real money supply to

---

[12] One source of this assertion is the empirical result obtained in L. C. Andersen and J. L. Jordan, "Monetary and Fiscal Actions: A Test of Their Relative Importance in Economic Stabilization," *Review — Federal Reserve Bank of St. Louis* (November 1968), pp. 11–23, that the fiscal effect vanishes after four quarters. For a summary of the debate on this issue, and some different results, see Robert J. Gordon, "Perspectives on Monetarism," in Jerome L. Stein (ed.), *Monetarism: Studies in Monetary Economics* (Amsterdam: North-Holland, 1976), and other papers in the same volume. The best analysis of the methodological defects of the Andersen-Jordan approach is Stephen M. Goldfeld and Alan S. Blinder, "Some Implications of Endogenous Stabilization Policy," *Brookings Papers on Economic Activity*, vol. 3, no. 3 (1972), pp. 585–640.

[13] See, for instance, Stephen Goldfeld, "The Demand for Money Revisited," *Brookings Papers on Economic Activity*, vol. 4, no. 3 (1973), pp. 577–646.

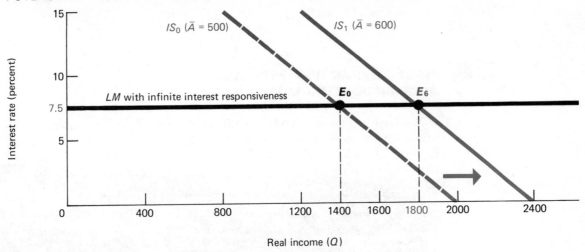

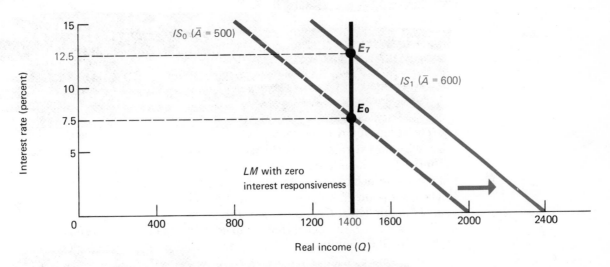

FIGURE 5–7

Effect of a $100 Billion Fiscal Stimulus When Money Demand Has an Infinite and a Zero Interest Responsiveness

In the top frame an increase in government spending has exactly the same effect as in Figure 3–8, with the full multiplier effect of 4.0. An infinite interest responsiveness means only that the interest rate is fixed, and no crowding out can occur. In contrast, the same fiscal stimulus has no effect on income when the interest responsiveness is zero (bottom frame), because then a higher interest rate releases no extra money to support higher income, and the income level is completely determined by the size of the real money supply.

shrink, shifting the *LM* curve to the left. Thus the demonstration that the *LM* curve is positively sloped is not by itself a logical proof that fiscal policy can raise real income.[14]

5-9 FISCAL EXPANSION WITH AN ACCOMMODATING MONEY SUPPLY

We have been considering the effects of a pure fiscal expansion that involves no change in the money supply. Because both the money supply and the price level have been held fixed, the *LM* curve in Figures 5-5 and 5-7 has remained stationary as the *IS* curve has shifted rightward. But there may be a possibility of interaction between fiscal and monetary expansion. If the sole policy goal of the monetary authority is to hold the interest rate constant, then the fiscal branch of government automatically gains indirect control of the money supply. Any type of fiscal expansion, whether an increase in government expenditures or a cut in tax rates, will lead to monetary accommodation—the monetary authority increases the money supply to prevent an increase in the interest rate.

Figure 5-8 illustrates again the same rightward shift in the *IS* curve caused by a $100 billion increase in real government purchases. Previously, however, the real money supply was kept constant, and as a result the interest rate was forced to rise to keep the demand for money equal to the fixed supply. If the goal of the monetary authority is not to keep the money supply fixed but to keep the interest rate fixed, the money supply must be allowed to change automatically whenever there is a shift in the *IS* curve.

The result of any fiscal change when the monetary authority acts to stabilize the interest rate is exactly the same as the result of the same fiscal change when the interest responsiveness equals infinity. No increase in the interest rate occurs, and the economy's equilibrium moves directly to the right from point E_0 to point E_6. The multiplier for the fiscal change is the simple multiplier of Chapter 3, $k = 4.0$.

It was not clearly recognized by all economists in the mid-1960s that the full fiscal policy multipliers of Chapter 3 required the tacit cooperation or accommodation of the monetary authority. If the Fed refuses to allow the money supply to be influenced by the position of the *IS* curve, and instead holds the money supply constant, the fiscal policy multipliers (as in Figure 5-5) are smaller than if the monetary authority accommodates the fiscal change by holding the interest rate constant (as in Figure 5-8). Policymakers

---

[14] On this issue, see the exchange between James Tobin and Milton Friedman in Robert J. Gordon (ed.), *Milton Friedman's Monetary Framework: A Debate with His Critics* (Chicago: University of Chicago Press, 1974). Because of the possibility of changing prices the Tobin quote that begins this chapter is not strictly valid.

FISCAL POLICY GAINS CONTROL OF THE MONEY SUPPLY IF THE MONETARY AUTHORITIES
ATTEMPT TO STABILIZE INTEREST RATES

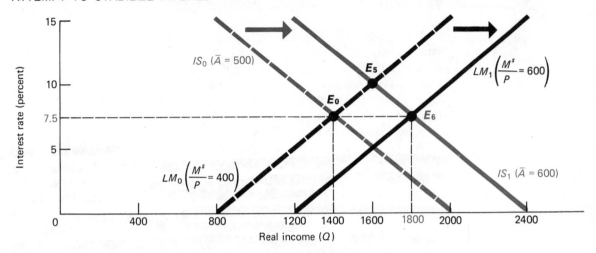

FIGURE 5–8

Effect on Real Income of a $100 Billion Fiscal Stimulus When the Fed
Acts to Keep the Interest Rate Constant

If the money supply were to remain constant in the face of the $100 billion fiscal
stimulus, the economy would move from E_0 to E_5, just as in Figure 5–5. Now,
however, the monetary authority (the Fed) attempts to keep the interest rate constant. The money supply must be increased by exactly enough to support the
higher level of income. Because $1 of extra money is needed for each $2 of extra
income, the money supply must be raised $200 billion to allow income to grow
$400 billion in response to the fiscal stimulus.

were surprised by the relatively small effect on spending of the temporary
income tax increase of 1968 because they had judged the effect of the 1964
tax cut to be quite substantial. But the tax cut in 1964 was accompanied by
an accommodating monetary policy that held the interest rate constant between late 1963 and mid-1965, whereas in the 1968 tax surcharge case the
Fed counteracted the fiscal change, moving the *LM* curve opposite to the *IS*
curve instead of in the same direction.[15]

Summary: An accommodating monetary policy eliminates the crowding out effect and leads once again to the simple fiscal policy multiplier
of Chapter 3.

---

[15] These two episodes are considered in more detail in the case studies of sections 13-6 and
16-6.

5-10 THE MONETARY-FISCAL POLICY MIX

Throughout this chapter, we have taken the starting point to be an unsatisfactorily low level of real output, $1400 billion, instead of the desired natural output (Q^N) level of $1600 billion. Two methods of reaching $1600 billion have been examined, a pure expansion of the money supply to point E_1 in the top frame of Figure 5-1 and a pure fiscal expansion of point E_5 in Figure 5-5. Does the choice between these two alternatives for the monetary-fiscal mix make any difference?

Figure 5-9 compares points E_1 and E_5. In both cases the total level of real income is identical and equal to Q^N, $1600 billion. We can assume that the total level of employment and unemployment would also be identical. What are the differences? Point E_5 has a lower money supply and, in order to keep money demand equal to money supply, also has a higher interest rate. This can be described as the "tight money, easy fiscal" position. Point E_1, on the other hand, is the "easy money, tight fiscal" position, with a higher money supply and a lower interest rate to stimulate a demand for money equal to the supply.[16] The higher interest rate at point E_5 cuts planned private autonomous spending, both investment and consumption, below that at point E_1, to make room for the government spending. Induced consumption is the same at both E_1 and E_5.

Which position, E_1 or E_5, should society prefer? At point E_1 investment is higher, and thus the economy's rate of natural real GNP growth is likely to be higher. This growth does not benefit us today but will help us in future years and future generations as well. At point E_5, government spending is higher than at point E_1. The government purchases may be currently consumed government services (national defense, police and fire protection, education, or health) or government investment (school buildings, hospitals). Should society prefer the faster output growth of point E_1 to the higher level of public services of point E_5? This is a difficult problem to which we will return. Its solution depends partly on society's preference for public versus private goods and partly on its taste for present goods and services versus those obtained in the future.

The fiscal stimulus that takes the economy to the tight money, easy fiscal point E_5 is assumed in line 2 of the table accompanying Figure 5-9 to take the form of $100 billion of government purchases. But we learned in section 3-7 that a $133 billion cut in autonomous tax revenue, or a $133 billion increase in autonomous government transfer payments, has exactly the same effect on autonomous planned spending (A) as a $100 billion increase in government purchases. Line 3 of the table gives the consequences of achieving point E_5 by means of a $133 billion transfer payment, such as

---

[16] On May 11, 1978, the Chairman of the Federal Reserve Board, G. William Miller, decried the size of the Federal budget deficit and urged a "shift to a tighter fiscal and a relaxed monetary policy." *Wall Street Journal*, May 12, 1978, p. 2.

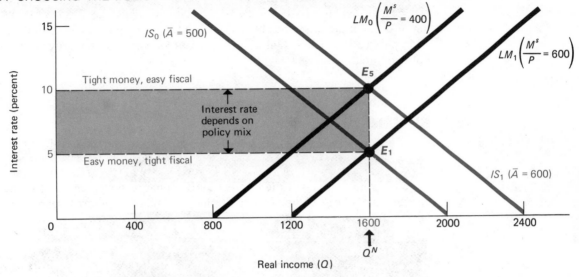

POLICYMAKERS CAN ALTER THE INTEREST RATE WITHOUT CHANGING INCOME
BY CHOOSING THE POLICY MIX

FIGURE 5-9

Two Alternative Methods of Achieving the Natural Level of Output
(Q^N = $1600 Billion)

The IS_0, IS_1, LM_0, and LM_1 curves are the same as we have encountered earlier
in this chapter. The combination at E_1 achieves target income with a low interest
rate by avoiding a government deficit. At E_5 the same income level implies
a higher interest rate because the government deficit requires sales of bonds
to households and a higher interest rate to "bribe" them to buy the bonds. The
table shows that E_5 can be achieved either by raising government spending (line 2)
or by raising consumption expenditures through higher government transfer payments (a reduction in net autonomous taxation).

Line	Position	Real money supply	Real money demand	Real income	Real government spending	Real investment	Real autonomous consumption	Real induced consumption
1.	E_1	600	600	1600	0	300	100	1200
2.	} E_5 {	400	400	1600	100	225	75	1200
3.		400	400	1600	0	225	175	1200

Social Security payments, instead of by $100 billion in government pur-
chases.[17] The interest rate and money demand are identical at point E_5
whether achieved by higher government purchases or by transfer payments.

---

[17] Why does the lump-sum transfer payment have to increase by $133 billion to raise $\bar{A}$ by
$100 billion? The $133 billion transfer raises autonomous consumption spending by $100
billion [$c\Delta T = 0.75(133) = 100$]. **Review:** section 3-7.

The difference is that under the transfer payment scheme, $100 billion is spent on private consumption purchases rather than on government purchases. The debate between fiscal stimulus in the form of government spending or transfer increases has been going on for a long time, at least since the 1958 publication of J. K. Galbraith's *Affluent Society,* and is mainly political, not economic.[18]

SUMMARY

1. In most cases, an increase in the real money supply not only reduces the interest rate but also causes an increase in real income. That increase is large for *small* values of the interest and income responsiveness of money demand and a *large* value of the multiplier (k), and of the interest responsiveness of planned private spending.

2. The monetary authority (Federal Reserve or Fed) can increase real income by raising the money supply if the price level is fixed, the *IS* curve is negatively sloped, and the *LM* curve is positively sloped or vertical. Two situations in which the Fed cannot raise the level of actual real income are (1) if planned expenditures do not respond to the interest rate (a vertical *IS* curve) and (2) if the economy is operating in a liquidity trap.

3. When r^N (the interest rate where the *IS* curve intersects natural output) is greater than or equal to r_{min} (the lower limit to the interest rate), the Fed is capable of stimulating the economy by enough to return actual real income to the level of natural real income. But when r^N is less than r_{min}, the Fed is incapable of stimulating the economy by enough unless it can find some way to directly raise r^N.

4. In the latter case, monetary stimulation succeeds only if planned autonomous expenditure depends not just on the interest rate but also on the current value of real money balances. This real balance effect rescues monetary policy in situations where r_{min} exceeds r^N, because the monetary authority can now shift the *IS* curve by altering the real money supply.

5. Large fiscal policy multipliers are associated with small values of the interest responsiveness of spending, and the income responsiveness of money demand and with large values of the multiplier and of the interest responsiveness of money demand. At one extreme, when the *LM* curve is horizontal, the fiscal multiplier becomes the simple multiplier of Chapter 3. At the other extreme, when the *LM* curve is vertical, the fiscal multiplier is zero and the crowding out effect is complete; the higher interest rate cuts private planned spending by exactly the same amount as the increase in government spending.

---

[18] Galbraith argued that a basic weakness of the United States was "private affluence and public squalor," too much spending on personal automobiles and dishwashers with too little spending on public parks, schools, and other government programs.

6. The size of the fiscal policy multipliers depends on whether the monetary authority holds the money supply constant or accommodates the fiscal changes by holding the interest rate constant. In the first instance, the crowding out effect can occur, but in the latter instance, output is raised by the full multiplier effect.

7. The composition of total expenditures depends on the mix of monetary and fiscal policy. The tight money, easy fiscal policy combination has a low money supply and a high government deficit, and the easy money, tight fiscal combination has the reverse. The interest rate is lower in the second combination, and investment is stimulated by the lower interest rate, raising the economy's rate of natural real GNP growth. In the first combination, government spending or private consumption purchases crowd out investment, cutting the growth of natural real GNP. The choice between the two policy combinations depends on the relative attractiveness of investment, consumption, and government spending.

A LOOK AHEAD

In the last three chapters the price level has been assumed to be fixed. Several determinants of the level of real output, and hence employment and unemployment, have been identified—business and consumer confidence, government spending and taxation, and the money supply. But as yet we have not begun to deal with inflation. Nor can we answer a critic who claims "government policy is not necessary, because the economy can get itself out of a recession without help through the stimulating effects on aggregate demand of a declining price level."

Now we switch hats and examine the consequences for the price level of changes in the demand for commodities, assuming that the price level adjusts to keep real GNP constant. We will find that under some conditions, but not others, the private economy can maintain its natural level of real GNP through price flexibility without help from the government. Only in Chapter 7 will we be ready to wear both hats at once and to allow the price level and real GNP to change simultaneously.

CONCEPTS

Interest responsiveness of the demand for money
Interest responsiveness of planned expenditures
Liquidity trap
r^N and r_{min}

The "normal" interest rate
Real balance effect
Pigou effect
Crowding out effect
Monetary accommodation
Monetary-fiscal policy mix

QUESTIONS FOR REVIEW

Are the following statements true, false, or uncertain? Be sure you can give a clear explanation of your answer.

1   The size of the increase in real income resulting from a given increase in the real money supply depends only on the slope of the *LM* curve.

2   An increase in government expenditures results in an increase in the equilibrium level of real income and of the interest rate.

3   A fiscal multiplier of the simple form of Chapter 3 requires that the economy must be operating in a liquidity trap.

4   *Crowding out* refers to the decline in total private spending that occurs when government expenditure is increased.

5   Monetary policy is impotent when the *LM* schedule is a horizontal line.

6   If r^N is below r_{min}, the monetary authority is incapable of stimulating the economy back to the level of real potential output.

7   An increase in the real money supply results in a lower equilibrium level of real income and a lower rate of interest.

APPENDIX TO CHAPTER 5
The Elementary Algebra of Equilibrium Income

When you see an *IS* curve crossing an *LM* curve, as in Figure 4-9 and in all of Chapter 5, you know that the equilibrium level of income (Q) and the interest rate (r) occurs at the point of crossing, as at point E_0 in Figure 4-9 or 5-1. But how can the equilibrium level of income and the interest rate be calculated without going to the trouble of making careful drawings of the *IS* and *LM* curves? Wherever you see two lines crossing to determine the values of two variables, such as Q and r, exactly the same solution can be obtained by solving together the two equations describing the two lines.

In Chapter 3 we found that equilibrium income was equal to autonomous planned spending (A_p) divided by the saving rate (s), so that the multiplier (k) was $1/s$. Then in the appendix to Chapter 3 we found that more generally the multiplier (k) is equal to 1.0 divided by whatever fraction of income leaks out of the spending stream into saving, the government's income tax revenue, and imports. Once we have determined Chapter 3's multiplier (k), income can be written simply as:

GENERAL FORM   NUMERICAL EXAMPLE

$$Q = kA_p \qquad\qquad Q = 4.0A_p \qquad\qquad (1)$$

At the beginning of Chapter 4 (Figures 4-1 and 4-2), we introduced the assumption that autonomous planned spending (A_p) declines when there is an increase in the interest rate (r). If the amount of A_p at a zero interest rate is written as $\bar{A}$, then the value of A_p can be written:

GENERAL FORM   NUMERICAL EXAMPLE

$$A_p = \bar{A} - br \qquad A_p = \bar{A} - 20r \qquad (2)$$

where b is the interest responsiveness of A_p, in our example \$20 billion of decline in A_p per one percentage point increase in the interest rate. Substituting (2) into (1), we obtain the equation for the *IS* schedule:

GENERAL FORM   NUMERICAL EXAMPLE

$$Q = k(\bar{A} - br) \qquad Q = 4.0\bar{A} - 80r \qquad (3)$$

Thus if $\bar{A}$ is 500 and $r = 0$, the IS_0 curve intersects the horizontal axis at 2000, as in Chapters 4 and 5.

The *LM* curve shows all combinations of income (Q) and the interest rate (r) where the real money supply (M^s/P) equals the real demand for money $(M/P)^d$, which in turn depends on Q and r. This situation of equilibrium in the money market was previously written as equation 4.1 in the text:

GENERAL FORM   NUMERICAL EXAMPLE

$$\left(\frac{M^s}{P}\right) = \left(\frac{M}{P}\right)^d = eQ - fr \qquad \left(\frac{M^s}{P}\right) = 0.5Q - 40r \qquad (4)$$

where e is the responsiveness of real money demand to higher real income, 0.5 in our example, and f is the interest responsiveness of real money demand, in the example a \$40 billion decline in real money demand per one percentage point increase in the interest rate. Adding fr (or $40r$) to both sides of (4), and then dividing by e (or 0.5), we obtain the equation for the *LM* schedule:

GENERAL FORM   NUMERICAL EXAMPLE

$$Q = \frac{\dfrac{M^s}{P} + fr}{e} \qquad Q = \frac{400 + 40r}{0.5} \qquad (5)$$

We are assured that the commodity market is in equilibrium whenever Q is related to r by equation (3) and that the money market is in equilibrium whenever Q is related to r by equation (5). To make sure that both markets are in equilibrium, both equations must be satisfied at once.

Equations (3) and (5) together constitute an **economic model.** Finding the value of two unknown variables in economics is very much like baking a cake. One starts with a list of ingredients, the **parameters,** or knowns, of the model: $\bar{A}$, M^s/P, b, e, f, and k. Then one stirs the ingredients together using the "instructions of the recipe," in this case equations (3) and (5). The outcome is the value of the unknown variables, Q and r. The main rule in economic cake-baking is that the number of equations, the instructions of the recipe, must be equal to the number of unknowns to be determined. In this example there are two equations and two unknowns (Q and r). There is no limit on the number of ingredients known in advance, the parameters. Here we have six parameters, but we could have seven, ten, or any number.

To convert the two equations of the model into one equation specifying the value of unknown Q in terms of the six known parameters, we simply substitute (5) into (3). To do this, we rearrange (5) to place the interest rate on the left side of the equation, and then we substitute the resulting expression for r in (3). First, rearrange (5) to move r to the left side:[1]

$$r = \frac{eQ - \dfrac{M^s}{P}}{f} \tag{5a}$$

Second, substitute the right side of (5a) for r in (3):

$$Q = k(\bar{A} - br) = k\left[\bar{A} - \frac{beQ}{f} + \frac{b}{f}\left(\frac{M^s}{P}\right)\right] \tag{6}$$

Now (6) can be solved for Q by adding $kbeQ/f$ to both sides and dividing both sides by k:

$$Q\left(\frac{1}{k} + \frac{be}{f}\right) = \bar{A} + \frac{b}{f}\left(\frac{M^s}{P}\right)$$

Finally, both sides are divided by the left term in parentheses:

$$Q = \frac{\bar{A} + \dfrac{b}{f}\left(\dfrac{M^s}{P}\right)}{\dfrac{1}{k} + \dfrac{be}{f}} \tag{7}$$

Equation (7) is our master general equilibrium income equation and combines all the information in the *IS* and *LM* curves together; when (7) is satisfied, both the commodity market and money markets are in equilibrium. It can be used in any situation to calculate the level of real income by simply substituting into (7) the particular values of the six known right-hand

---

[1] First multiply both sides of (5) by e:

$$eQ = \frac{M^s}{P} + fr$$

Then subtract M^s/P from both sides:

$$eQ - \frac{M^s}{P} = fr$$

Now divide both sides by f:

$$\frac{eQ - \dfrac{M^s}{P}}{f} = r$$

Equation (5a) is then obtained by reversing the two sides of this equation.

parameters in order to calculate unknown income.[2] Because we are interested primarily in the effect on income of a change in $\bar{A}$ or M^s/P, we can simplify (7):

$$Q = k_1 \bar{A} + k_2 \left(\frac{M^s}{P}\right) \tag{8}$$

All we have done in converting (7) into (8) is to give new names, k_1 and k_2, to the multiplier effects of $\bar{A}$ and M^s/P on income. The definitions and numerical values of k_1 and k_2 are:

GENERAL FORM   NUMERICAL EXAMPLE

$$k_1 = \frac{1}{\dfrac{1}{k} + \dfrac{be}{f}} \qquad\qquad \frac{1}{\dfrac{1}{4.0} + \dfrac{20(0.5)}{40}} = 2.0 \tag{9}$$

$$k_2 = \frac{b/f}{\dfrac{1}{k} + \dfrac{be}{f}} = \left(\frac{b}{f}\right)k_1 \qquad\qquad \frac{20(2.0)}{40} = 1.0 \tag{10}$$

Using the numerical values in (9) and (10), the simplified equation (8) can be used to calculate the value of real income illustrated by E_0 in Figure 4-9 and in several figures of Chapter 5.

$$Q = k_1 \bar{A} + k_2 \left(\frac{M^s}{P}\right) = 2.0(500) + 1.0(400) = 1400 \tag{11}$$

With this equation it is extremely easy to calculate the new value of Q whenever there is a change in $\bar{A}$ caused by government fiscal policy, or by a change in business and consumer confidence, and whenever there is a change in M^s/P caused by a change in the nominal money supply.[3] Remember, however, that the definitions of k_1 and k_2 in (9) and (10) do depend on particular assumptions about the value of parameters $b, e, f,$ and k.

The main point of Chapter 5 is that changes in fiscal and monetary policy may have either strong or weak effects on income, depending on the answers to these questions.

1. How does the effect of a change in $\bar{A}$ on income, the multiplier k_1, depend on the values of b and f (the interest responsiveness of the demand for commodities and money)?

---

[2] A parameter is taken as given or known within a given exercise. Parameters include not just the small letters denoting the multiplier (k), and the interest and income responsiveness of planned autonomous expenditures and money demand ($b, e,$ and f), but also planned autonomous expenditures at a zero interest rate ($\bar{A}$) and the real money supply (M^s/P). Most exercises involve examining the effects of a change in a single parameter, as in $\bar{A}$ or in M^s/P.

[3] The equilibrium interest rate illustrated in Figure 4-9 can be calculated in the same way by substituting the numerical values into equation (5a):

$$r = \frac{0.5(1400) - 400}{40} = \frac{300}{40} = 7.5 \text{ percent}$$

2. How does the effect of a change in M^s/P on income, the multiplier k_2, depend on the values of b and f?

You should work through Chapter 5 to see if you can derive each of the diagrammatic results by substituting the appropriate definition of k_1 and k_2 into the simplified general equilibrium equation (8).

Example: If we work through Figure 5-1, the value of k_1 is, using (9):

$$k_1 = \frac{1}{\frac{1}{k} + \frac{be}{f}} = \frac{1}{\left(\frac{1}{4}\right) + \left(\frac{20}{40}\right)(0.5)} = 2.0$$

The value of k_2 is, using (10):

$$k_2 = \frac{b}{f} k_1 = \left(\frac{20}{40}\right)(2.0) = 1.0$$

Thus income in the new situation at point E_1 in the top frame of Figure 5-1, using equation (8), is:

$$Q = k_1\bar{A} + k_2\left(\frac{M^s}{P}\right) = 2.0(500) + 1.0(600) = 1600$$

In the bottom frame, $f = 0$, and so:

$$k_1 = \frac{1}{\frac{1}{k} + \frac{be}{f}} = \frac{1}{\frac{1}{4} + \frac{20(0.5)}{0}} = 0$$

$$k_2 = \frac{b}{\frac{f}{k} + be} = \frac{20}{0(0.25) + 20(0.5)} = 2.0$$

Thus in the bottom frame of Figure 5-1, the new equilibrium situation at point E_2 is as follows when the real money supply rises from 700 along the left-hand LM line to 900 along the right-hand LM line.[4]

$$Q = k_1\bar{A} + k_2\left(\frac{M^s}{P}\right) = 0(500) + 2.0(900) = 1800$$

Exercise: Assume the following simple model with the price level fixed at 1.00:

$$IS \text{ curve:} \quad Q = k(\bar{A} - br)$$

$$LM \text{ curve:} \quad Q = \frac{\frac{M^s}{P} + fr}{e}$$

---

[4] These assumed numerical values for the real money supply were not used as labels for the bottom frame of Figure 5-1 to avoid complicating the exposition in the text.

With the following parameter values:

$$\bar{A} = 600 \qquad \frac{M^s}{P} = 600$$

$$b = 20 \qquad f = 20$$

$$k = 5.0 \qquad e = 0.40$$

1. Plot the *IS* and the *LM* curves. What are the equilibrium values for *Q* and *r*? Why do these values of *Q* and *r* differ from those in Figure 4-9?

2. Now suppose $\bar{A}$ declines from 600 to 450. What are the new equilibrium values for *Q* and *r*? What kind of event might cause $\bar{A}$ to decline in this way?

3. Suppose that the Federal Reserve wanted to offset this decline in $\bar{A}$ by using monetary policy. To regain the initial income level, what is the required real money supply? What will be the new equilibrium interest rate?

4. Assuming the initial set of parameters, describe the situation at a point such as $Q = 1500$, $r = 8$. Which market or markets are out of equilibrium? Describe the adjustment to the equilibrium point.

5. Describe what happens when the Federal Reserve uses monetary policy to raise the equilibrium real income level back to its original value.

6 Flexible Prices and the Self-Correcting Economy

It is, therefore, on the effect of a falling wage- and price-level on the demand for money that those who believe in the self-adjusting quality of the economic system must rest the weight of the argument.

—John Maynard Keynes[1]

6-1 INTRODUCTION

Today's aggregate price index or **deflator** is simply an economywide weighted average of the prices of goods today compared to the prices of the same goods in a base year, say 1967 or 1972. When the prices of most goods are rising, the aggregate deflator (P) increases and we have inflation, whereas **deflation** describes a situation in which the prices of most goods and hence the aggregate deflator are falling. During a period of aggregate price stability, the prices of some goods increase, some decrease, but the average of all prices (P) stays approximately steady.

Throughout Chapters 3, 4, and 5 all our analysis has held the price level fixed for simplicity. Now that we are ready to allow the price level to vary, we find that the basic tools developed so far retain their usefulness. When we allow the price level to be perfectly (instantly) flexible in this chapter, we find that shifts in monetary and fiscal policy that previously caused real income to vary now cause the price level to change in the same direction.

During the first part of this chapter, we assume that P is perfectly flexible and examine the conditions under which that flexibility automatically maintains a stable level of real output, making monetary and fiscal policy unnecessary. When can the governors of the Federal Reserve "go fishing," confident that any change in business and consumer confidence will be automatically counteracted by the economy's **self-correcting forces?** Can a shift in the price level maintain the stability of real output and employment? We will see now that a decline in the price level plays the same role as an increase in the money supply in Chapter 5.

---

[1] Keynes, *The General Theory of Employment, Interest and Money* (New York: Harcourt, Brace and Company, 1936).

In the previous chapters we artificially held P constant to examine the forces that can vary real income (Q). Through much of this chapter we do just the opposite, holding Q constant and examining the same forces that can vary P. Only in the next chapter will we be ready to enter fully into the real world in which Q and P can and do change together.

6-2 FLEXIBLE PRICES, THE REAL MONEY SUPPLY, AND THE *DD* CURVE

In this section we develop a new tool, the aggregate demand (*DD*) curve, which summarizes the stimulating effect of lower prices on the level of real output. It can be used to illustrate the operation of the economy's self-correcting forces, which stabilize the level of real output when prices are flexible.

We already know that the *LM* curve shifts its position whenever there is a change in the real money supply. Until now every *LM* shift has resulted from a change in the nominal money supply, while the price level has been held fixed at a constant level. The price level has been treated as a parameter, or a known variable, allowing us to concentrate on the determination of the two unknowns, real income (Q) and the interest rate (r).

There is no reason, however, why the *LM* curve could not shift in exactly the same way when a change in the real money supply M^s/P is caused by a change in the price level P, while the nominal money supply M^s remains fixed at a single value, say \$400 billion. The top frame of Figure 6-1 illustrates three *LM* curves drawn for three values of P and M^s/P, each assuming that $M^s = 400$. For instance, the middle curve LM_0 is identical to LM_0 in the previous chapter. The price index is 1.0, and because $M^s = 400$, M^s/P also equals 400. A doubling of the price level to $P = 2.0$ would cut the real money supply in half to $M^s/P = 400/2.0 = 200$. For the real demand for money to be equal to the smaller real supply of money, some combination of lower real income and a higher interest rate is needed, as along the left-hand curve LM_1. Similarly, if the price level is very low, only 0.5, the real money supply is a large $M^s/P = 400/0.5 = 800$, and equilibrium in the money market occurs along the right-hand curve LM_2.

What is the level of real income if the nominal money supply remains fixed at \$400 billion? The answer depends not only on which price level and *LM* curve is valid but also on the position of the *IS* curve. When $\bar{A} = 600$, the commodity market is in equilibrium anywhere along the IS_1 curve copied from Chapters 4 and 5. When $P = 1.0$ and the LM_0 curve describes money-market equilibrium, the economy's general equilibrium occurs at point E_0, where LM_0 crosses IS_1 and equilibrium real output (Q) is \$1600 billion.[2]

To show the relationship between equilibrium Q and the assumed price

---

[2] E_0 is the same as E_5 in the last chapter. We now take the opportunity to renumber the equilibrium points.

THE AGGREGATE DEMAND CURVE SHOWS THAT A DECLINE IN THE PRICE LEVEL STIMULATES REAL OUTPUT, AND VICE VERSA

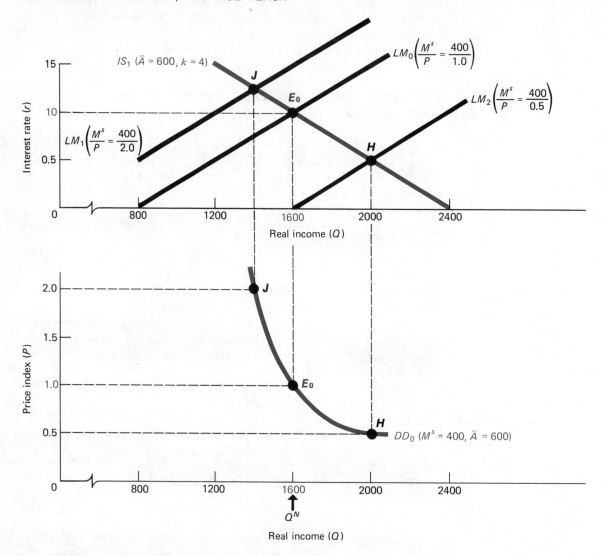

FIGURE 6–1

Effect on Real Income of Different Values of the Price Index

In the top frame three different *LM* curves are drawn for three different hypothetical values of the price index. Corresponding to the three levels of the price index are three positions of equilibrium, *J*, E_0, and *H*. These three points are drawn again in the lower frame with the same horizontal axis (real output), but the price index for the vertical axis. A drop in the price index from point *J* to E_0 and then to *H* raises the *real* money supply and stimulates real output along the aggregate demand curve DD_0.

index P, a new diagram is drawn in the bottom frame of Figure 6-1. The horizontal dimension once again is real output, and so point E_0 in the bottom frame lies just below E_0 in the upper frame. The vertical dimension in the bottom frame measures the price index P, and so E_0 is plotted at the assumed value $P = 1.0$.

Other values of real income occur if the assumed price level is higher or lower than 1.0. A price level of 2.0 cuts the real money supply in half, as shown along LM_1 in the top frame, and it reduces real output to \$1400 billion at point J. Point J is plotted in the lower frame again at a vertical height $P = 2.0$. Similarly, a lower price index of $P = 0.5$ boosts the real money supply, shifts the LM curve to LM_2, and raises output to \$2000 billion, as plotted at point H.

The curved line in the bottom frame connecting points J, E_0, and H shows all the possible combinations of P and Q consistent with a nominal money supply of \$400 billion and a value of $\bar{A}$ of \$600 billion.[3] If the assumed value of P is high, then Q is low, and vice versa. The curved line is called the **aggregate demand curve** and is abbreviated DD. The main characteristics of DD are:

1. The DD curve shows all the possible crossing points of a single IS commodity market equilibrium curve with the various LM money-market equilibrium curves drawn for each possible price level. Everywhere along the DD curve both the commodity and money markets are in equilibrium.
2. The DD curve slopes downward because a lower price index (P) raises the real money supply and stimulates planned expenditures, requiring an increase in actual real GNP (Q) to keep the commodity market in equilibrium. The steeper the IS curve, the steeper the DD curve.

   Exercise: Try to determine, without peeking at footnote 4, whether a steeper LM curve would make the DD curve steeper or flatter.[4]

3. Because it describes the economy's general equilibrium, the position of the DD curve depends on all the factors that can shift the IS and LM curves except the price level.[5] Since a shift in either M^s or $\bar{A}$ will shift DD, the assumed values of both M^s and $\bar{A}$ are always written next to each DD curve.

---

[3] Recall that the definition of $\bar{A}$ is the level of autonomous planned real spending that would occur if the interest rate were zero.

[4] **Answer:** Compare the top and bottom frames of Figure 5-1. Notice that a steep LM curve amplifies the effect on output of a higher real money supply. Thus a reduction in the price level that raises M^s/P and shifts the LM curve will raise output more and make the DD curve flatter when the LM curve is steep (the interest responsiveness of the demand for money is small).

[5] The equation of the DD curve is the master income equation (7) in the Appendix to Chapter 5. The simplified equation of the DD curve is (8), in which a change in either $\bar{A}$ or M^s clearly alters the relationship between Q and P:

$$Q = k_1 \bar{A} + k_2 \frac{M^s}{P}$$

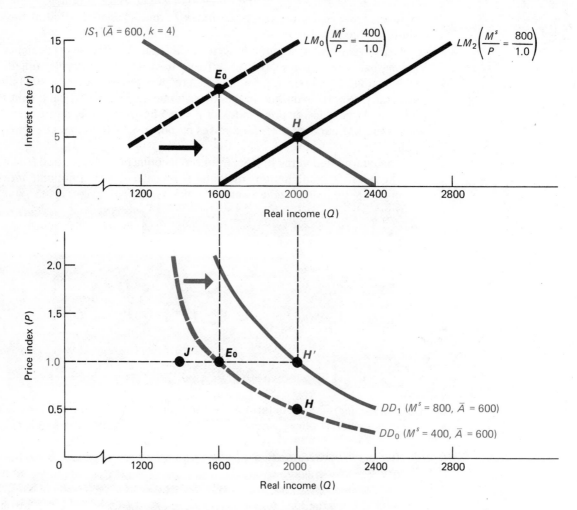

FIGURE 6–2

The Effect on the *DD* Curve of an Increase in the Nominal Money Supply from $400 to $800 Billion

In the top frame a doubling of the nominal money supply from $400 to $800 billion moves the *LM* curve rightward from LM_0 to LM_1 and the economy's general equilibrium (where *IS* crosses *LM*) from point E_0 to point *H*. In the lower frame we remain at a vertical distance of $P = 1.0$, since nothing has happened to change the price level. The higher money supply raises real output and causes the economy's equilibrium position to be at point H' rather than at point E_0. Notice that the new DD_1 curve running through point H' lies everywhere twice as high as the old DD_0 curve drawn for a nominal money supply of half the size.

4. An increase in either M^s or $\bar{A}$ will shift the DD curve to the right, and a decrease in either will shift the curve to the left.

Example: Begin at point E_0 in the upper frame of Figure 6-2 and assume that the price level equals 1.0. If the nominal money supply were raised from \$400 to \$800 billion, then M^s/P would rise to 800 and the money market would be in equilibrium along LM_2, not LM_1. General equilibrium would occur at point H in the top frame, where LM_2 crosses the fixed IS curve, at $Q = \$2000$ billion.

Looking directly below, point H' is plotted for $Q = \$2000$ billion and $P = 1.0$, the assumed value. Thus H' lies on a higher aggregate demand curve DD_1, which shows the various possible combinations of real output with various assumed price levels when $M^s = \$800$ billion. Curve DD_1 lies above the original DD_0 curve drawn for $M^s = \$400$ billion. By the same reasoning, a low assumed nominal money supply value of \$200 billion would shift the DD curve downward to a new curve (not drawn) running through point J'.

Notice that the aggregate demand schedule DD shifts up vertically in Figure 6-2 by exactly the same proportion as the nominal money supply. Along DD_1 the nominal money supply (\$800 billion) is exactly double its value along DD_0 (\$400 billion), and at H' the DD_1 curve is exactly twice as high (where $P = 1.0$) as the DD_0 curve at H (where $P = 0.5$). This occurs because a doubling of money and a doubling of prices from point H to H' leads to the same real money supply, hence the same LM curve, the same interest rate, and hence the same real GNP.

Exercise: Experiment to see how the IS and DD curves would be shifted by an increase in $\bar{A}$ from \$600 to \$800 billion.

6-3 THE SELF-CORRECTING ECONOMY: DEFLATION AS A CURE FOR RECESSION

The study of countercyclical monetary and fiscal policy began in the dark days of the Great Depression and was initiated by the publication of Keynes' *The General Theory of Employment, Interest and Money.* Why did pre-Keynesian economists minimize the need for policy? It was generally believed that the economy had sufficiently powerful self-correcting forces to guarantee full employment and to prevent actual real GNP (Q) from falling below natural real GNP (Q^N) for more than a short time.[6]

The flexibility of the price level was the automatic mechanism that was believed capable of regulating real output without help from government

---

[6] See the quotation that begins this chapter.

policymakers. In Figure 6-3 the vertical line marked QQ is plotted at an income level of \$1600 billion and shows the level of natural real GNP (Q^N) that the economy is capable of producing with its present population and stock of structures, equipment, education, and research knowledge. Any vertical line is independent of the variable plotted on the vertical axis, so that in this case the vertical QQ schedule represents the assumption that the economy's natural real GNP ($Q^N = 1600$) does not depend on the price index (P).

When actual real GNP (Q) is to the left of the QQ line, firms are producing less than the capacity for which their factories and equipment are designed, and prices will tend to be reduced in order to stimulate fuller use of plant capacity. In Figure 6-3, the price level (P) is assumed to decline continuously whenever low demand pushes the economy to the left of the QQ natural output line.

When high demand raises actual real GNP to the right of the QQ line, on the other hand, firms are working overtime to produce more than their optimal capacity. Overtime wage rates and shift differentials must be paid to obtain the necessary hours of work from employees; employees are less efficient because old, obsolete machinery must be pressed into service; and firms must pay more to suppliers to obtain extra raw materials. Firms have extra costs in periods of high production that induce them to raise prices. Thus in Figure 6-3 the price level (P) is assumed to increase whenever real output is to the right of the QQ line.

The DD_0 curve is copied from the bottom frame of Figure 6-2 and as before assumes $M^s = 400$ and $\bar{A} = 600$. Now a decline in business and consumer confidence occurs, and planned autonomous investment and consumption spending fall by \$100 billion. The position of the DD curve depends on $\bar{A}$ and the \$100 billion decline in $\bar{A}$ shifts the aggregate demand curve left from DD_0 to DD_1. The economy's equilibrium shifts from E_0 to F as long as the price index remains at 1.0.

But in this chapter we no longer assume that the price level is fixed, and so the economy will not move to point F. Instead, we assume that real GNP is fixed, and that any leftward shift in the aggregate demand curve will put downward pressure on the price level. The price level falls until the economy arrives at point E_1, where the price index has reached 0.67. How can the economy maintain its original level of real GNP, \$1600 billion, when $\bar{A}$ has fallen? The answer is that the lower price level (P) boosts the level of real balances (M^s/P) and moves Chapter 5's LM curve to the right by exactly the amount by which the drop in $\bar{A}$ shifts the IS curve to the left.

Summary: Whenever the initial price level crosses the DD curve to the left of the vertical QQ line, the price level declines to the crossing point of DD and QQ, as at point E_1. The reverse is also true: when the initial price level crosses the DD curve to the right of the vertical QQ line, the price level rises. Thus when we allow for price flexibility we see that the economy can be in equilibrium, with no tendency for the price level to either rise or fall, only at the single point where DD and

HOW FLEXIBLE PRICES INSULATE REAL OUTPUT FROM THE IMPACT OF A DECLINE
IN AUTONOMOUS SPENDING

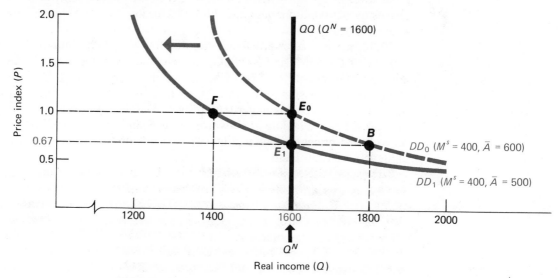

FIGURE 6–3

Effect of a $100 Billion Decline in Planned Autonomous Spending
When the Price Level Is Perfectly Flexible

Starting from point E_0, the equilibrium position when $\bar{A} = \$600$ billion, a drop in
$\bar{A}$ to $500 billion would move the economy to point F if the price index were to
remain constant, as in earlier chapters. But now at any point to the left of QQ the
price index declines. A drop in the price index from 1.0 to 0.67 raises the real
money supply from the initial $400 billion to $600 billion, enough to push the
economy's real output equilibrium to point E_1.

QQ cross. Anything that cuts aggregate demand, whether a drop in
business and consumer confidence, a cut in government expenditures
or the nominal money supply, or an increase in taxes, will shift the DD
curve left and reduce the price level.

*There is no need for stimulative monetary or fiscal policy, because the
economy has managed to correct the drop in real GNP without government interference.*

6-4 FLEXIBLE PRICES AND FISCAL POLICY: REAL VERSUS NOMINAL CROWDING OUT

The positively sloped LM curve that we assumed in deriving the DD
curve does not guarantee that a fiscal policy stimulus can raise real output.
An illustration is provided by Figure 6-3. Imagine that $\bar{A} = \$500$ billion and

that the economy starts at point E_1, with a real income level of \$1600 and a price level of 0.67. Now let us assume that the government raises its purchases by \$100 billion, boosting $\bar{A}$ to \$600 billion. The DD curve shifts from DD_1 to DD_0.

If the price level were fixed, the economy's equilibrium would move from point E_1 to B. The \$100 billion increase in government spending would increase real income by \$200 billion, exactly as in Figure 5-5. But in this chapter we are assuming that the price level does not stay fixed. Instead, the price level rises whenever the DD schedule moves rightward relative to the vertical QQ schedule. P rises from B to E_0 in Figure 6-3 and stops rising only when real equilibrium income arrives back on the QQ curve at its starting level of \$1600 billion.

Now allowing for price flexibility, the \$100 billion expansion of government spending has a zero multiplier. Crowding out has become complete. With total real GNP unchanged, and government purchases increased by \$100 billion, fully \$100 billion of autonomous investment and consumption spending $(I_p + a)$ must have been crowded out by the fiscal expansion. Complete crowding out, therefore, is not ruled out as a logical possibility by the demonstration that the LM curve is positively sloped, as we assumed in deriving the DD curve.[7]

> **Summary:** When prices are completely flexible, shifts in the IS curve — whether caused by fiscal policy or by changes in business or consumer confidence — have no effect on real output. Rightward shifts in the IS curve move DD rightward and raise the price level, whereas leftward shifts in IS have the opposite effect.

6-5 THE FAILURE OF DEFLATION IN EXTREME CASES: THE GENERAL RULE REVISITED

Price deflation can automatically equate equilibrium real GNP (Q) to its natural level (Q^N) in all situations in which a change in the real money supply is capable of raising equilibrium real GNP. In Chapter 5 we learned a general rule that this capability of the real money supply requires r^N, the "natural rate of interest" at which the IS curve crosses Q^N, to be equal to or

---

[7] In 1966, Milton Friedman understood this point completely when he wrote that "no fundamental issues in either monetary theory or monetary policy hinge on whether" the interest responsiveness of the demand for real money balances is zero or a positive number, so long as it is "seldom capable of being approximated by infinity." But as late as 1972 James Tobin wrote, "First, let me explain what *I* thought the main issue was. . . . I thought (and I still think) it was the shape of the LM locus." Quotations and context may be found in Robert J. Gordon (ed.), *Milton Friedman's Monetary Framework: A Debate with His Critics* (Chicago: University of Chicago Press, 1974), pp. 138 and 77, respectively. The second quote began Chapter 5.

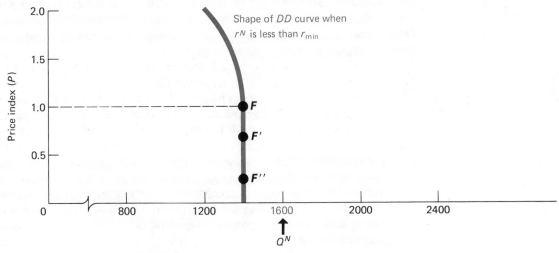

FIGURE 6–4

The Lack of Effect of a Drop in the Price Index When r^N Is Less Than r_{min}

Turn back to Figure 5–3 and notice that r^N below r_{min} means that real GNP cannot rise above $1400 billion. This diagram shows the same thing, but in this case it is a fall in the price level that is being used to achieve higher real money balances (M/P). Because of the inability of the higher real money supply to reduce the actual interest rate to the level r^N, the *DD* curve cannot extend to the right of the maximum attainable output level, $1400 billion in the case of Figure 5–3 and this figure.

greater than r_{min}, the minimum interest rate along the *LM* curve. Figure 5-3 examined a case when monetary expansion failed, when r^N was well below r_{min}.

In this case the reason for the failure of monetary expansion was simple. To achieve Q^N a particular level of A_p was required, and this could occur only if the interest rate were as low as r^N. Instead, the interest rate was prevented from falling below r_{min}, either because of a liquidity trap or because r^N was a negative value. Thus an interest rate low enough to stimulate the spending sufficient to reach the natural output level (Q^N) could not be achieved, and the economy was forced to suffer a GNP gap, with real GNP below natural real GNP.

Exactly the same problem might arise with a constant money supply when the downward movement of the price index is the mechanism for maintaining Q^N. When r^N is below r_{min}, this means that *no* increase in the real money supply, even if achieved by a drop in prices, can push the economy to its natural level of real GNP. In Figure 6-4 the vertical portion of the *DD* curve shows that a drop in prices from 1.0 to 0.67 to 0.25 and below will not boost real GNP above $1400 billion, well below the Q^N level of $1600 billion. This occurs because the resulting increase in M/P cannot push the interest rate below r_{min}, and this is not low enough to achieve output Q^N, which requires an interest rate of r^N.

As in Figure 6-3, the price level declines continuously whenever we are to the left of the vertical QQ natural real GNP schedule. But now the DD curve does not intersect QQ. The price level never stops falling and real output cannot equal Q^N. No equilibrium is possible because there is continuous and unending pressure on P to fall. Our general rule is amended:

> *Whenever the natural rate of interest (r^N) is less than r_{min}, and the position of the IS curve does not depend on the price level, then the DD curve becomes a vertical line to the left of QQ. There is no point of intersection between DD and QQ and thus no possibility of a stable-price, full-employment equilibrium where actual and natural real GNP are equal.*

6-6 TWO SOLUTIONS TO CONTROL r^N: FISCAL POLICY AND THE REAL BALANCE EFFECT

In Chapter 12 we will study more closely the differences between the modern economic Keynesians, or nonmonetarists, who support active government use of policy tools, particularly fiscal policy, to stabilize the economy, and the monetarists, who support fixed settings for the policy tools and trust the economy's self-correcting forces to keep private output on target. The present-day Keynesian position originates in the dilemma of Figure 6-4, where the private economy cannot cure a depression by itself through price deflation because r^N falls short of r_{min}. It was Keynes who first pointed out the possibility that r^N might be negative and that r_{min} might (but was not likely to) be some positive number.[8] And it was Keynes who pointed to fiscal policy as a way out of the dilemma.

The crucial problem in Figure 6-4 is not the liquidity trap, the positive value of r_{min}. The dilemma would persist even if there were no liquidity trap and r_{min} were at zero, its normal level, if r^N were negative, owing to a low level of $\bar{A}$ caused by a collapse in business and consumer confidence.

How can estimates of the future rate of return be raised to revive the economy? All problems disappear if $\bar{A}$ can be raised back by enough to make r^N equal or exceed r_{min}. For this reason fiscal policy, which can shift $\bar{A}$ through increases in government expenditure and transfer payments and reductions in tax rates, is the obvious antidepression tool to use. In fact, fiscal policy might avert the depression entirely if government policymakers could

---

[8] Neither the *IS-LM* nor the *DD-QQ* diagrams appeared in Keynes' book. The *IS* and *LM* curves were invented soon afterward by John Hicks and published as part of his article "Mr. Keynes and the Classics," *Econometrica* (April 1937).

accurately forecast the drop in business and consumer confidence and could instantly raise $\bar{A}$ by \$1 for each dollar decline in $\bar{A}$ caused by reduced confidence.

In fact, however, government action may not be necessary. A. C. Pigou originally pointed out (as we learned in section 5-5) that the Keynesian dilemma illustrated in Figure 6-4 is not a dilemma at all if the demand for commodities depends directly on the level of real money balances. The IS curve would then shift not only when $\bar{A}$ changes, as in Figure 6-4, but also whenever the price level changes. Thus a sufficient drop in the price level could raise real balances as high as necessary to move the IS curve rightward and raise r^N up to r_{min}.

> **Summary:** The real balance effect completely changes the slope of the DD curve: in Figure 6-4 the DD curve is vertical below point F because price deflation has no stimulative effect on real output, but with the real balance effect the DD curve is always negatively sloped, and a price deflation can achieve any desired real GNP level if prices fall far enough.

Why is the real balance effect so powerful when the price level is flexible? Imagine yourself owning only a \$5 bill. You would not be able to consider purchasing a \$12,000 Cadillac. But there is some price level at which your money would have more impressive buying power. If the price index were to decline from 1.0 to 0.0001, the price of the Cadillac would fall from \$12,000 to \$1.20, and your \$5 would be more than ample to buy the Cadillac, leaving \$3.80 in change! Although the numbers in this illustration are extreme, they forcefully illustrate the logic of the real balance effect. A fixed nominal amount of money buys more when the price level falls, so that individuals are bound to find some portion of their previous money balances excessive and to spend more on real commodities.

When the price level is perfectly flexible and the real balance effect is in operation, no monetary or fiscal policy is necessary. The Federal Reserve Governors and the President's Council of Economic Advisers can "go fishing," confident that the DD curve crosses the QQ curve.

We have now identified two stimulative effects of price deflation:

1. The **Keynes effect** is the stimulus to aggregate demand (both consumption and investment) due to a decline in the rate of interest, which in turn is brought about by an increase in the real money supply (M^s/P) caused either by an increase in the nominal money supply or by price deflation. The Keynes effect brings the economy from point F to E_1 in Figure 6-3. It is the Keynes effect that is cut off and rendered ineffective when r^N falls below r_{min}.
2. The **Pigou effect (real balance effect)** is the direct stimulus to consumption spending that occurs when a price deflation causes an increase in the real money supply; this stimulus does not require a reduction in the interest rate.

John Maynard Keynes
(1883–1946)

John Maynard Keynes' *The General Theory of Employment, Interest and Money* (1936) is one of the two or three most influential economics books of the twentieth century. It sets out explicitly the story that has been called the Keynesian Revolution.

The book ended the reign of the prevailing classical orthodoxy, which viewed the economy as having an automatic self-correcting mechanism that maintained prosperity and full employment. Instead, Keynes argued, the propensity of firms to invest may be too low compared to that of households to save, leading to endemic depression. Lacking forces sufficiently powerful to restore full employment, the private sector may need help from government fiscal policy in the form of lower taxes and higher government spending.

Keynes was a distinguished economist, intellectual leader, and member of the upper crust of England's literary and artistic establishment long before 1936. He was born into economics, the son of Neville Keynes, a Cambridge don who specialized in economics and logic. By the time World War I broke out, young Keynes had written most

The Bettmann Archive, Inc.

of two books, *Indian Currency and Finance* (1913) and *A Treatise on Probability* (1921). During the war, he rose rapidly as an official in the British Treasury handling external finance, and eventually resigned from the British negotiating team at the 1919 Paris Peace Conference in protest against the stiff reparation payments the victors were demand-

Unfortunately, the stimulative effects of price deflation are not always favorable, even when the Pigou effect is in operation. The two major unfavorable effects of deflation are:

1. The **expectations effect.** When people expect prices to continue to fall, they realize that goods will cost less to buy next week and next year, and they will tend to postpone purchases as much as possible to take advantage of lower prices in the future. This decline in the demand for commodities may be strong enough to offset the stimulus of the Pigou effect. Later (in Figure 11-1) we shall see how the expectations effect can be incorporated into the *IS-LM* diagram.

2. The **redistribution effect** may be more important. Deflation causes a redistribution of income from debtors to creditors. Why? Debt repayments are usually fixed in dollar value, so that a uniform deflation in all prices causes an increase in the real value of mortgage and installment repayments from debtors to creditors (banks, and ultimately, savers).

ing from the Germans. He put his objections into writing in *The Economic Consequences of the Peace,* one of the finest pieces of polemic writing of his generation.

The first postwar decade was Keynes' heyday as a multifaceted financier, journalist, academic, editor, socialite, and farmer. He spent half an hour in bed each morning making investment decisions and was able to convert a small loan from members of his family into a fortune of half a million pounds, largely by speculating in foreign exchange. He was Bursar of King's College, Cambridge, increasing its endowment by a factor of ten. He wrote frequent essays for newspapers and magazines, and published collections in *Essays in Biography* and *Essays in Persuasion.* Married to a famous Russian ballerina, he was a member of the "Bloomsbury Circle," a group of England's best-known and most colorful artists and authors, including E. M. Forster, Virginia Woolf, and Lytton Strachey. He spent much of his time on a small country farm that he worked to improve, and—as if all this were not enough—found time to be the editor of the prestigious *Economic Journal* (England's equivalent of the *American Economic Review*) from 1911 to 1945.

In addition to the *General Theory,* Keynes wrote two earlier and more orthodox books on monetary economics, *A Tract on Monetary Reform* (1923), and *A Treatise on Money* (1930). Since 1936, however, the word "Keynesian" has been synonymous with support of an activist government policy that intervenes to offset the economy's tendency to slip into episodes of depression and inflation. Until the mid-1960s, the Keynesians ruled macroeconomics, but more recently the Monetarist Counterrevolution has gained many adherents to the view that partly returns to the pre-Keynesian orthodoxy—that the private economy's self-correcting forces have been underestimated, and that government intervention may do more harm than good.[a]

---

[a] Monetarism is the subject of Chapter 12. For more reading on Keynes, see R. F. Harrod's *The Life of John Maynard Keynes* (New York: St. Martins, 1951). A short but brilliant comparison of the two revolutions is Harry G. Johnson, "The Keynesian Revolution and the Monetarist Counter-Revolution," *American Economic Review,* vol. 61 (May 1971), pp. 1–14. For the recent state of the debate among prominent economists on what Keynes really meant, see Robert J. Gordon (ed.), *Milton Friedman's Monetary Framework* (Chicago: University of Chicago Press, 1974).

Example: Imagine an individual who originally earns $100 per week and pays $25 per week in debt repayment (not an unusual situation). A drop in the price level from 1.00 to 0.25 will cut his earnings from $100 to $25 per week (assuming the deflation reduces all prices and wages uniformly). All his $25 earnings will be required for the fixed $25 debt repayment, reducing to zero the income available for current consumption. The debtor's consumption may be cut by far more than the increase in the consumption of the creditor who receives the debt repayment, because rich creditors may consume less of their incomes than do poor debtors. The net effect on total economywide spending may be negative, further depressing r^N.[9]

---

[9] A relatively advanced discussion of the consequences of these effects on the economy's self-correcting mechanism is contained in James Tobin, "Keynesian Models of Recession and Depression," *American Economic Review,* vol. 65 (May 1975), pp. 195–202. See also Axel Leijonhufvud, *On Keynesian Economics and the Economics of Keynes* (New York: Oxford University Press, 1968), pp. 315–331.

During the Great Depression deflation of 1929–33, for instance, the GNP price deflator fell from an initial 0.329 to 0.251 in 1933 (1972 = 1.0), a decline of 23.7 percent. Yet the interest income of creditors hardly fell at all, from \$4.7 to \$4.6 billion (current dollars). Farmers were hit worst by falling prices — their current-dollar income fell by two-thirds, from \$6.2 to \$2.1 billion — and many lost their farms through foreclosures as a result of this heavy debt burden. Although many factors were at work in the collapse of real autonomous spending during the Great Depression, it appears that the negative expectations and redistribution effects of the 1929–33 deflation may have dominated the stimulative Keynes effect and Pigou effect.

6-7 SUMMARY AND EVALUATION OF DEPRESSION ECONOMICS

The main thrust of the mid-1930s Keynesian revolution in economics was a denial that the economy's self-correcting forces unleashed by a price deflation are always strong enough in every situation to maintain full employment ($Q = Q^N$). Beyond that, at least two interpretations of Keynes' position are possible:

1. *Hard-line fiscalists.* Not only is a price deflation incapable in every situation of raising Q to Q^N, but monetary policy is ineffective as well. This position is summarized by the saying that "You can take a horse to water but you can't make it drink," meaning that the Fed can make money available but can't force businesses to spend it on new investment projects. The only salvation is fiscal policy, which can add \$1 to $\bar{A}$ for every dollar subtracted during a decline in business and consumer confidence.
2. *Soft-line Keynesians.* A price deflation might raise output enough if prices were sufficiently flexible to fall instantly and steeply, but in fact prices decline relatively slowly, if at all. Government action is necessary to counteract the inflexibility of prices, but either monetary or fiscal policy is capable of achieving the natural level of employment ($Q = Q^N$).

Table 6-1 helps to sort out the assumptions necessary for either the hard-line or soft-line view to be valid. The hard-liners must believe in the assumptions listed under item 3, that there is no real balance effect and that it is possible for r^N to fall below r_{min}. Those who take this position find fiscal policy necessary whether or not the price level is flexible.

Soft-liners do not find the universal denial of the real balance effect, as in line 3, to be an appealing assumption, and they regard lines 1 and 2 to be more accurate. But they reject perfect price flexibility as unrealistic, and, though not willing to claim that the price level is completely fixed, they find the assumption of price fixity closer to reality than that of perfect price flexibility, at least for discussions of policy in the short run. The implications of their view are listed in the two identical items in column (b), lines 1 and 2.

A large number of U.S. economists today, probably a majority, hold

TABLE 6-1

Summary of Depression Economics: Starting from a Large GNP Gap, Can Actual Real GNP (Q) Be Raised Back to Equal Natural Real GNP (Q^N)?

Case	(a) Price level perfectly flexible	(b) Price level fixed
1. Normal case: r^N equal to or greater than r_{min}	Yes: government policy-makers can go fishing[a] (Example: Figure 6-3)	No: without government action Yes: with enough monetary or fiscal stimulus (Examples: Monetary: Figure 5-1 Fiscal: Figure 5-5)
2. r^N less than r_{min}; real balance effect exists	Yes: government policy-makers can go fishing[a]	No: without government action Yes: with enough monetary or fiscal stimulus
3. r^N less than r_{min}; but no real balance effect	No: without government fiscal action; monetary policy ineffectual (Example: Figure 6-4)	No: without government fiscal action; monetary policy ineffectual (Example: Figure 5-3)

[a] Ignores expectation and redistribution effects of a price deflation.

views that can be described as "soft-line Keynesian." Both monetary and fiscal policy are considered important, and the private economy cannot keep itself on course without help from the government. Most of the remaining U.S. economists are monetarists, who generally attribute more flexibility to the price level and who tend to oppose countercyclical policy activism as undesirable and unnecessary. We will return to the Keynesian-monetarist debate and identify some issues where the two schools of thought have converged, and others where disagreement continues today (Chapter 12).

6-8 CASE STUDY: PRICES AND OUTPUT DURING THE GREAT DEPRESSION

It is an outstanding characteristic of the economic system in which we live that . . . it seems capable of remaining in a chronic condition of sub-normal activity for a considerable period without any marked tendency either towards recovery or towards complete collapse.

Keynes, *General Theory*, p. 249

Does the behavior of output and the price level in the Great Depression tend to support the hard-line fiscalists, the soft-line Keynesians, or neither? For neither to be correct we should be able to find evidence of the economy's self-correcting forces at work through price deflation. Turning back to Figure 6-3, we notice that when price deflation works in a stabilizing direction, the economy slides down a DD curve to the southeast toward the QQ curve, as from point F to point E_1.

Now compare these theoretical diagrams to a graph of the actual data plotted in the top frame of Figure 6-5. To eliminate the effect of growth in natural real GNP (Q^N), the horizontal axis is measured as the ratio of actual to natural real GNP (Q/Q^N). Starting on the vertical QQ schedule at natural real GNP in 1929, with a price index of 1.0 (on a 1929 base), the economy moved rapidly to the southwest until 1933. Then a recovery to the northeast began, interrupted briefly in 1938. We can view the decline of output up to 1933 as caused by several factors that shifted DD to the left: a collapse in confidence, a major decline in the money supply, and an ineptly timed move to fiscal restraint in 1932.[10]

In 1933 a recovery began, under the combined influence of an increase in the real money supply, a fiscal stimulus, and a revival of confidence. The recovery got stuck around 1936, with no progress between 1936 and 1939, and the massive monetary and fiscal expansion induced by the outbreak of World War II was required before the economy was able to regain its starting position in early 1942.

The story of the Great Depression appears to lie in shifts in the DD curve to the left and then back to the right. There is no evidence at all of a movement southeast along a given DD curve, as would have occurred had price deflation played a major role in stimulating the recovery. The economy moved southeast only between 1938 and 1939, and then only slightly. Particularly important is the fact that there was no deflation at all between 1936 and 1940, even though Q/Q^N remained at or below 82 percent throughout that five-year interval. Thus the evidence appears quite conclusive that the government cannot rely on rapid and massive price deflation to revive the economy, at least if the price level today is as sluggish as it was in the late 1930s.

Despite the absence of perfect price flexibility, however, it is also clear from the top frame of Figure 6-5 that the price level was not rigid at all during the Great Depression and did drop 24 percent between 1929 and 1933. The path from northeast to southwest to northeast reflects a regularity, as if the DD curve were following a well-marked highway. The bottom frame of Figure 6-5 represents a hypothetical interpretation of

---

[10] We have not yet attempted to explain why confidence fell so low. Monetary policy and the collapse of the banking system played a role after autumn 1931, but it is difficult to explain the initial 1929–31 period as a monetary phenomenon. See Peter Temin, *Did Monetary Forces Cause the Great Depression?* (New York: Norton, 1975), and Robert J. Gordon and James A. Wilcox, "Monetarist Interpretations of the Great Depression," *op. cit.*

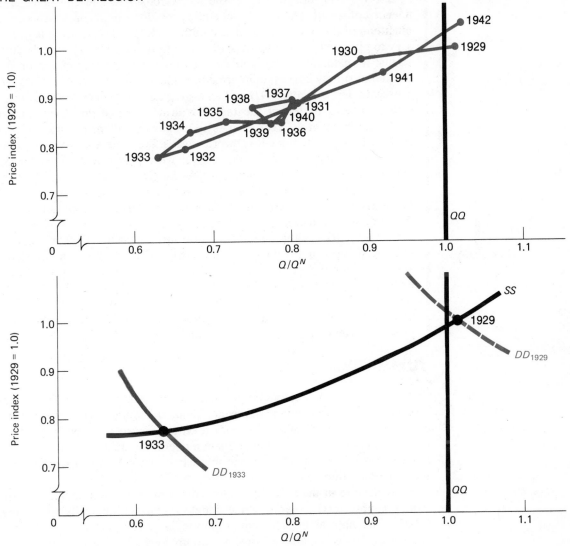

FIGURE 6–5

The Price Level (P) and the Ratio of Actual to Natural Output (Q/Q^N)
during the Great Depression, 1929–42

The upper frame illustrates the actual values of the implicit GNP deflator (P) and
an estimate of the ratio of actual to natural output during the Great Depression
era, 1929–42. The remarkable fact in the top frame is that the economy returned
to natural output in 1942 with a price level that was actually higher than in 1929,
despite the intervening decade that should have pushed the price level down. The
bottom frame illustrates a hypothetical interpretation of what happened. A drop in
the economy's aggregate demand curve (DD) moved the economy along its aggregate supply curve (SS), a concept to be discussed fully in the next chapter.

Case Study: Prices and Output during the Great Depression **167**

what happened. The DD curve in 1929 was close to the QQ schedule, but by 1933 it had moved well to the left as business and consumer confidence collapsed. The DD_{1933} schedule provides a menu of possible combinations of the price level and real output. An additional curve is necessary to pin down the economy's 1933 location along the DD_{1933} schedule.

Just as elementary economic principles place great emphasis on demand and supply curves, in intermediate macroeconomics we employ the aggregate demand curve DD and an **aggregate supply curve** SS. Curve SS slopes upward to reflect the fact that firms can and do charge higher prices in a prosperous year such as 1929 than they do in a depressed year such as 1933. If the price level were always fixed, the SS curve would be a horizontal line, and if the price level were perfectly flexible, the SS curve would be a vertical line, just like the QQ schedule. The SS curve drawn in the bottom frame of Figure 6-5 is intermediate between these two extremes: when demand declines and the DD curve shifts leftward, the price level falls, but not continuously and without limit.

The SS curve is the major new tool introduced in Chapter 7. As we will see, SS is a supply curve for the short run and assumes that business and consumer expectations of the normal price level are fixed. Whenever expectations change, the SS curve shifts its position. A chief puzzle of the Great Depression is why the SS curve remained so stable, and why expectations of the normal level of prices did not decline in light of the prolonged reduction in prices that actually occurred.[11]

SUMMARY

1. In the previous chapters we assumed that the price level (P) is constant and that any change in aggregate demand is completely reflected in a change in real GNP. When the price level is allowed to be perfectly flexible in this chapter, we find that shifts in monetary and fiscal policy that previously caused real GNP to vary now cause the price level to change in the same direction.

2. A decline in the price level plays the same role as an increase in the money supply in Chapter 5. Price deflation can automatically return real GNP to its natural level in any situation in which a change in the real money supply is capable of raising output. Perfect price flexibility automatically maintains a stable level of real GNP, making changes in monetary and fiscal policy unnecessary.

3. The aggregate demand curve (DD) shows all the possible combinations of the price deflator (P) and of real output (Q) consistent with a fixed nominal money supply and a fixed autonomous spending schedule ($\bar{A}$). Everywhere along the DD curve both the commodity and money markets are in equilibrium.

---

[11] An attempt to explain changes in the price index during the period before World War II is Robert J. Gordon, "A Consistent Explanation of a Near-Century of Price Behavior," *American Economic Review*, vol. 70 (May 1980), pp. 243–249.

4. The *DD* curve is steep when the *IS* curve is steep and the *LM* curve is flat. An increase either in the nominal money supply or in the autonomous spending schedule shifts the *DD* curve to the right.

5. The price level declines whenever real GNP is less than natural real GNP (Q^N) and rises when real GNP exceeds natural real GNP. With flexible prices the economy can be in equilibrium with no tendency for price-level movements only at the point where *DD* intersects the vertical natural real GNP line (*QQ*); that is, when actual real GNP (*Q*) equals natural real GNP (Q^N).

6. Whenever r^N is less than r_{min} and the position of the *IS* curve does not depend on the price level, the *DD* curve becomes a vertical line, allowing no possibility of a stable-price, full-employment equilibrium when the *IS* curve is depressed. But with a real balance effect a sufficient drop in *P* can move the *IS* curve to the right and raise r^N to r_{min}. Thus when the price level is perfectly flexible and the real balance effect is in operation, no monetary or fiscal policy is necessary.

7. The Keynes effect is the stimulus to aggregate demand that occurs when price deflation raises the real money supply and reduces the rate of interest. It is this effect that is rendered ineffective when r^N falls below r_{min}.

8. The Pigou effect or real balance effect is the direct stimulus to autonomous consumption spending of an increase in the real money supply. The stimulative effects of price deflation may not always be favorable, even when the Pigou effect is in operation, if the expectations effect and the redistribution effect are sufficiently strong.

9. Hard-line fiscalists find fiscal policy necessary whether or not the price level is flexible. Soft-line Keynesians reject perfect price flexibility as unrealistic, and, although not willing to claim that the price level is completely fixed, they find the assumption of short-run price fixity closer to reality. In this case the economy can get stuck with a low level of real and substantial unemployment unless a monetary or fiscal stimulus is applied.

A LOOK AHEAD

The case study of the Great Depression in section 6-8 suggests that in reality the price level is neither perfectly fixed nor perfectly flexible. Thus the real world cannot be adequately described by our theory in Chapters 3–5, which assumes that the price level is completely fixed, nor by that in Chapter 6, which assumes that the price level is perfectly and instantly flexible.

Our next task is to maintain intact our theory of the determinants of the aggregate demand curve (*DD*) and add a theory of the supply curve that explains how a shift in aggregate demand is divided between output and price changes in the short run. We will find that under most conditions an increase in aggregate demand is accompanied by both higher prices and higher output. Eventually, as expectations adjust to the initial price increase, most or all of the effect takes the form of higher prices; changes in aggregate demand then have little if any effect on real output.

CONCEPTS

Implicit price deflator

Aggregate demand curve

Self-correcting forces

Perfect flexibility

Keynes effect

Pigou effect

Expectations effect

Redistribution effect

r^N and r_{min}

QUESTIONS FOR REVIEW

Are the following statements true, false, or uncertain? Be sure you can give a clear explanation of your answer.

1   A liquidity trap always prevents $Q = Q^N$ from being attained even if prices are perfectly flexible.

2   The Keynes effect is operative except when the economy is in a liquidity trap.

3   A fall in the rate of interest is necessary for the operation of the Pigou effect.

4   A change in prices shifts the *IS* curve, but not the *LM* curve, when the real balance effect is in operation.

5   A change in prices shifts the *LM* curve, but not the *IS* curve, when the real balance effect is not in operation.

6   A fiscal stimulus always raises real output as long as the *LM* curve is positively sloped.

7   The price level fell continuously during the Great Depression in response to a large GNP gap and high unemployment.

8   Evidence from the Great Depression supports the proposition that any unexpected demand shock—that is, drop in demand growth relative to expected demand growth—has its main short-run impact on output behavior rather than on price behavior.

Part III

Inflation and Unemployment

7 Allowing Both Prices and Output to Change Together

Inflation is always and everywhere a
monetary phenomenon.
—Milton Friedman[1]

7-1 THE CENTRAL IMPORTANCE OF AGGREGATE SUPPLY

In the last two chapters we have explored the determinants of the economy's general equilibrium in which both the commodity market and money market are simultaneously in equilibrium. We have been particularly interested in the effect on aggregate demand of changes in business and consumer confidence, in government fiscal variables, and in the money supply. We were able to link changes in aggregate demand to changes in real output only by assuming that the price level was fixed (Chapter 5). Exactly the opposite assumption, that changes in aggregate demand influence the price level while maintaining real output fixed, was made in Chapter 6. Now it is time to allow the price level and real output to change simultaneously.

Neither the fixed-price approach of Chapter 5 nor the fixed-output approach of Chapter 6 is adequate. Why? Neither extreme assumption is derived from any basic theoretical analysis, and neither is valid in reality. In Figure 7-1 the rightward shift from DD_0 to DD_1 occurs as the result of a higher level of aggregate demand, resulting from a higher nominal money supply, a higher level of government spending, a reduction in tax rates, or an increase in business and consumer confidence. In Chapters 3–5 we assumed that any such increase in aggregate demand would *not* be accompanied by an increase in the price level; thus we were assuming that the economy moved from its initial position E_0 directly rightward to point E_1 along the "horizontal aggregate supply curve" in Figure 7-1. In Chapter 6 we switched assumptions and fixed real GNP at its "natural" level Q^N, so that the same increase in aggregate demand now had no effect at all on real

---

[1] "Inflation: Causes and Consequences" (New York: Asia Publishing House, 1963), reprinted in *Dollars and Deficits* (Englewood Cliffs, N.J.: Prentice-Hall, 1968), p. 39.

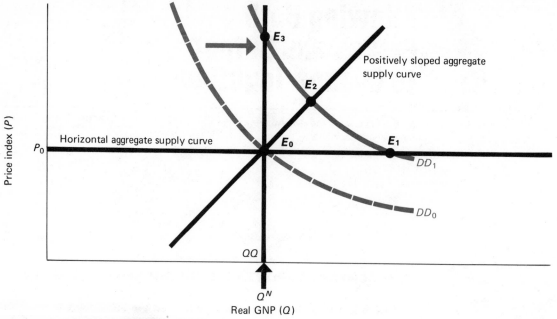

FIGURE 7-1

Effect of a Rightward Shift in the *DD* Curve with Three Alternative
Aggregate Supply Curves

The horizontal supply curve at the price level P_0 reflects the "fixed price" assumption of Chapters 3–5. An increase in aggregate demand that shifts the DD_0 curve to DD_1 will move the economy from its initial position E_0 to new position E_1. In contrast, the "fixed output with flexible prices" assumption of Chapter 6 makes the supply curve vertical and causes higher aggregate demand to push the economy from point E_0 to E_3. In Chapter 7 we will study an intermediate possibility—that both output and prices rise in the short run to a point such as E_2, and that in the long run the boost in real GNP gradually disappears until we arrive at E_3.

GNP and simply raised the price level from P_0 to a higher price level at point E_3 along the vertical QQ supply curve in Figure 7-1.

Now in this chapter we are prepared to be more realistic and allow the higher level of aggregate demand to boost both real GNP and the price level in the short run to a point such as E_2. We shall see that the increase in real output that occurs is only temporary, however, and that eventually in the long run the impact of higher aggregate demand is to raise prices to point E_3. Our new analysis is more realistic than before because it is consistent with the fact that *both* real GNP and the price level vary in real-world business cycles.

This analysis shares with previous chapters the approach of **comparative statics.** Our basic diagram measures the level, not the rate of change, of real output and the price level. Our analysis is just like a show of photographic slides—we show one slide in the form of a single static equilibrium position, we turn out the lights, and, when the lights come back on, the economy has moved to a new static equilibrium position such as point E_2 in Figure 7-1. Our comparative static slide-show method of analysis cannot tell us anything about economic dynamics—how long does it take output and the price level to change? What is the rate of price change (the inflation rate) per year or per month? Only in Chapter 8 will we be able to examine the dynamic relationship between the rate of inflation and real GNP.

7-2 THE AGGREGATE SUPPLY CURVE WHEN THE WAGE RATE IS CONSTANT

SUPPLY CURVE FOR THE INDIVIDUAL FIRM

A basic tool of macroeconomics, introduced in every elementary economics course, is the supply curve for the individual business firm. We shall briefly examine the factors that account for the positive slope of the firm's supply curve, and then assume that the economy's aggregate supply curve has the same positive slope.

The firm makes production decisions by comparing the price of a good with its marginal cost—that is, the extra cost the firm incurs by producing an extra unit of output. Because firms are in business to make a profit, they will not produce extra output unless the extra revenue they receive from selling an extra unit is *at least as high* as the extra cost they incur in producing that unit.

We analyze the firm's production decision over a short period (the "short run") during which its stock of machines, its factory, and its land are assumed to be fixed. Starting on the first line of Table 7-1, the firm hires one worker, who is paid a fixed wage of $80 per day and who is able to produce ten units of output. The "marginal cost" of these ten units is $8, the $80 wage divided by the ten units produced.

When a second worker is hired, only eight extra units are produced, and since the wage paid to the second worker is the same $80, the marginal cost of the extra output is $10, or the $80 wage divided by the eight units produced. Why is the second worker less productive then the first? The available machinery and land now have to be "stretched" over two workers, rather than just one, and each worker has less machinery to work with. The same principle of a diminishing **marginal product of labor** is evident when the third and fourth workers are hired. Again the stock of equipment, buildings, and land is fixed, and each existing worker has to share the fixed stock of capital when a new worker is hired. Thus the third worker only adds six units of output, costing $13.33 extra per unit (the $80 wage divided by the

TABLE 7-1

Derivation of the Aggregate Supply Curve
for an Individual Firm

Point in Figure 7-2	Workers hired	Marginal labor cost per extra worker	Extra units of output produced	Marginal labor cost per extra unit of output	Total output	Selling price required to produce this amount
(1)	(2)	(3)	(4)	(5)	(6)	(7)
A	1	$80	10	$ 8.00	10	$ 8.00
B	2	80	8	10.00	18	10.00
C	3	80	6	13.33	24	13.33
D	4	80	4	20.00	28	20.00

six extra units). The fourth worker adds only four units of output, costing $20 extra per unit.

Now that we know the firm's marginal cost schedule as written in column (5) of Table 7-1, we know its supply schedule, because the firm will be willing to produce only up to the point where the price of the product equals its marginal cost. To produce more than this would mean expanding into the region where marginal cost exceeds price and a loss is made on extra output. To produce less would mean giving up the chance to add extra units on which a profit is earned because the marginal cost is less than the price. In the classic agricultural example often used to illustrate this idea, the farmer decides how much wheat to plant on the basis of the market price he expects to receive for his wheat. The firm's aggregate supply curve can be drawn as in Figure 7-2, which simply plots the total level of output in column (6) against the price the firm must receive to be willing to produce this amount from column (7).

THE AGGREGATE SUPPLY CURVE WITH A FIXED NOMINAL WAGE

The firm in Figure 7-2 has a positively sloped supply curve even though it pays a fixed wage rate of $80 per day. In the same way, the economy as a whole would have a positively sloped aggregate supply curve as drawn in Figure 7-3 even if the economywide wage rate were fixed. The aggregate supply curve is just the horizontal sum of the supply curves for the individual firms, although we have simplified a bit by drawing the supply curve in Figure 7-3 as a straight line rather than the curve shown for the individual firm in Figure 7-2.

Notice that in Figures 7-1 and 7-3, for the first time, we have discontinued writing specific numerical values on the horizontal axis. We do not indicate

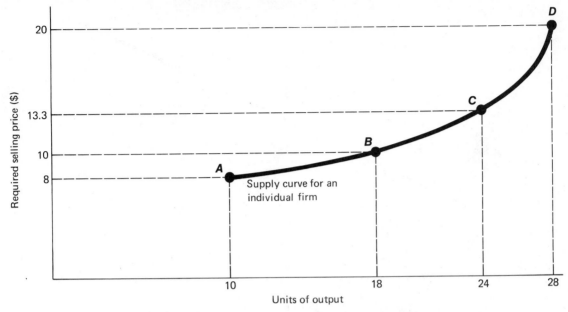

FIGURE 7–2

The Relation between Total Output and the Price the Firm
Must Charge

This figure illustrates the relationship between total output and the required selling
price derived in Table 7–1. Because each additional worker is paid the same daily
wage but produces less and less output, the marginal cost of each additional unit
of output rises.

the exact index or level of real GNP but label points only by general desig-
nations; for instance, P_0 in Figure 7-1. Why? From here on, with only a few
exceptions, specific numbers on the axes would add unnecessary arithmetic
without contributing anything essential to understanding. The main thing to
notice about a diagram such as Figure 7-3 is the direction of the relation
being discussed. The supply of output depends positively on the price index.
Exactly how much is not important; it is only necessary to note that the relationship is positive.

7-3 DETERMINANTS OF THE NOMINAL WAGE RATE

So far we have learned that the aggregate supply curve slopes upward
even if the wage rate is fixed. But surely the wage rate will not stay at the
same level forever. The factors that determine the nominal wage rate (the

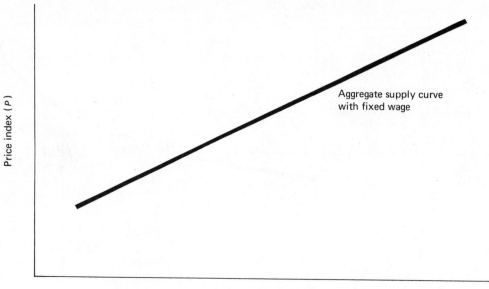

FIGURE 7–3

The Aggregate Supply Curve with a Fixed Nominal Wage

The aggregate supply curve is derived by horizontally summing up all the individual firm supply curves, such as that drawn in Figure 7–2. We draw the aggregate supply curve as a straight line to simplify the discussion.

actual wage rate paid) have a crucial effect on the nature of the economy's response to a change in aggregate demand. Will an increase in aggregate demand mainly boost real GNP or prices? How rapidly will the price level respond? The answers to these questions depend on how wages are set.

THE EQUILIBRIUM EXPECTED REAL WAGE

Just as the price of most products depends on the interaction of supply and demand, so the wage rate depends on the determinants of both the demand for and supply of labor. An important determinant of the wage rate is the price level that is expected by workers to occur over the period of work, usually called the "expected price level" (P^e). The higher the expected price level, the higher will be the wage rate that workers will require to be willing to work. The upper left-hand frame in Figure 7-4 illustrates the dependence of the wage rate on the expected price level. At point E_0 the expected price level on the horizontal axis is P_0^e, and the nominal wage rate on the vertical axis is W_0. If the expected price level were higher than P_0^e, say P_1^e, the nominal wage rate would be higher also at W_1, as shown by the point E_0'.

The line connecting points E_0 and E_0' is called the "equilibrium expected real wage line" and shows how high will be the nominal wage rate (W) for any given expected price level (P^e). The equilibrium expected real wage is simply the slope of the line — that is, the nominal wage rate divided by the expected price level (W/P^e). What determines the slope of the equilibrium expected real wage?

1. The demand for labor. Just as the demand for a consumer good depends on how useful it is to a consumer, so the demand for labor depends on how useful labor is to the business firm — that is, on how much labor can produce. The productivity of a worker, in turn, depends on education and acquired skills, as well as on the amount of capital equipment, research and development, and managerial and organizational ability that the firm combines with the worker in the production process. The real wage of workers in the United States is much higher than in less developed countries in Asia and Africa because of the much higher quantity of all these factors (education, skills, capital, research, and managerial ability) per worker in the United States. Over time the real wage tends to grow as the quantity of these factors increases, and in Chapter 18 we will try to determine why the growth in worker productivity and the real wage has been considerably slower since 1973 than before.

2. The supply of labor. Several factors influence the number of workers willing to work at any given real wage. Most obvious is the size of the population and the proportion of the total population of working age. An increase in the birth rate, like that in the United States in the late 1940s and 1950s, raised the number of young workers in the 1970s and held down their real wage. The birth rate slump of the 1970s will hold down the number of young workers in the 1990s and help boost their real wage. The influx of females into the labor force has also raised the number of people seeking work and has tended to hold down the real wage. There are several other important determinants of the equilibrium expected real wage. Unemployment benefits enable individuals to survive (at least temporarily) without jobs and thus to be less desperate to accept the first available low-paying job; thus the existence of unemployment benefits tends to boost the real wage. An increase in the minimum wage, as occurred in 1978–80, also tends to boost the real wage. Finally, taxation may influence the real wage by making individuals less willing to work or to hold second jobs.

It is possible to illustrate the determination of the equilibrium real wage on a supply-demand diagram, but this is a needless distraction for our purposes. Instead, we shall concentrate on the determination of real GNP (Q) and the price level (P) in a short period, usually called the "short run," during which we assume to be fixed all the determinants of the equilibrium expected real wage line in the upper left-hand frame of Figure 7-4.

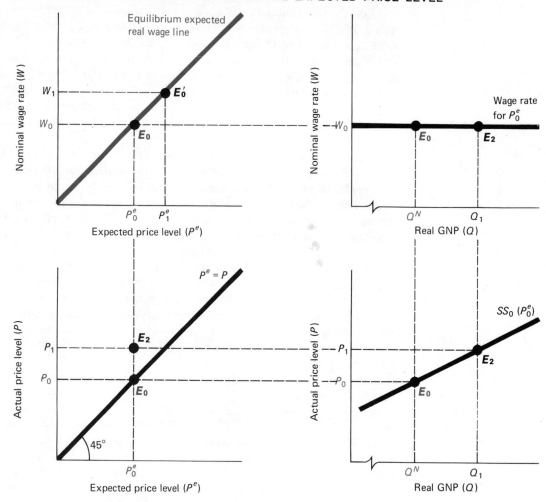

FIGURE 7–4

The Relation of the Nominal Wage Rate, the Actual and Expected Price Level, and the Aggregate Supply Curve

The slope of the red upward sloping line in the upper left-hand frame shows the equilibrium expected real wage. If the expected price level is P_0^e, point E_0 indicates that the nominal wage rate will be W_0. With a fixed W_0, however, the aggregate supply curve is the same as that drawn in Figure 7–3 and is labeled as SS_0 in the lower right-hand frame. The 45-degree line in the lower left-hand frame shows all the possible combinations of P and P^e where expectations are accurate. One such combination, $P_0^e = P_0$, is shown at point E_0, and at E_0 in the lower right-hand frame the aggregate supply curve shows that the economy's level of real GNP is Q^N. If the price level rises to P_1 while expectations remain at P_0^e, the economy moves to point E_2, and the nominal wage rate remains fixed.

THE EXPECTED PRICE LEVEL, THE WAGE RATE, AND THE SHORT-RUN AGGREGATE SUPPLY CURVE

First we examine the determination of real GNP (Q) and the actual price level (P) on the assumption that the expected price level (P^e) is fixed at an initial level, say P_0^e. Because the equilibrium expected real wage line is also assumed to be fixed in the upper left-hand frame of Figure 7-4, the actual wage rate is fixed at W_0, and *does not depend on the level of real GNP*. This fixity of W_0 at every level of Q is shown by the horizontal line in the upper right-hand frame of Figure 7-4.

Because the wage rate is fixed at W_0, we can copy in the lower right-hand frame of Figure 7-4 our aggregate supply curve from Figure 7-3, which also assumed a fixed wage rate. Now we label the aggregate supply curve SS, which stands for Short-run Supply, and write in parentheses the value of the expected price level (P_0^e), which determines the level of the fixed nominal wage rate (W_0). This helps to remind us that any change in P^e would change W and hence shift the position of the SS line.

Where will the economy produce along its short-run supply curve SS? This depends on the relation between the actual and expected price level, as depicted in the lower left-hand frame of Figure 7-4. Here a 45-degree line shows all the different possible situations in which the actual price level is equal to the expected price level. For instance, point E_0 shows where our assumed value of the expected price level, P_0^e, is equal to the actual price level P_0. Point E_0 in the lower right-hand quadrant lies on the short-run supply line SS_0 and shows how much real GNP will be produced at an actual price level P_0 and an expected price level P_0^e.

The horizontal intercept below point E_0 in the lower right-hand frame is labeled Q^N, standing for the "natural" level of real GNP. Why? Q^N is defined as that level of real GNP which will be produced when expectations are accurate; that is, when the expected price level (P^e) equals the actual price level (P).

> *Only when the economy is operating at its natural level of real GNP is the actual price level equal to the expected price level ($P = P^e$). At a higher level of real GNP the actual price level is above what people expect, while at a lower level of GNP the actual price level turns out to be less than what people expect. Thus fluctuations in real GNP are accompanied by fluctuations in the price level about the level that people expect.*

Point E_2 in Figure 7-4 illustrates a situation in which the price level is P_1, rather than P_0. If the expected price level remains fixed at its initial value (P_0^e), then the SS line also remains fixed. Point E_2 in the lower right-hand frame shows that the higher price level P_1 will induce firms to hire more workers and produce the higher level of real GNP Q_1. Why? Because firms produce up to the point where price equals marginal cost, as in Table 7-1, and the higher price level P_1 allows firms to pay the higher marginal cost of hiring additional workers. At point E_2, since the price level is higher than at E_0 but the wage rate is fixed at W_0, the actual real wage (W_0/P_1) has fallen, compensating for the lower productivity of the additional workers who are hired. **Review:** Each additional worker hired produces less than the last one hired, as shown in column (4) of Table 7-1.

In the lower left-hand frame, point E_2 shows that the higher price level P_1 has moved the economy off its 45-degree "$P^e = P$" line as long as the expected price level remains at P_0^e. Why should expectations of the price level (P^e) ever differ from the actual price level (P), and how will expectations adjust if they turn out to be incorrect?

7-4   EXPECTATIONS, WAGE CONTRACTS, AND SHIFTS IN THE AGGREGATE SUPPLY CURVE

So far we have learned that real GNP can rise above its natural level (Q^N) only when the price level rises above the expected price level at a point like E_2 in Figure 7-4. But one ingredient is missing. We do not know the position of the SS line until we know what price level is expected by the workers. How are their expectations formed? And why would their expectation (P^e) diverge from the actual price level for any significant period of time?

ADAPTIVE EXPECTATIONS AND WAGE CONTRACTS

One particularly simple hypothesis, described in Figure 7-5, plots the path of the expected price level along the black line on the assumption that workers always set P^e at last period's actual value of the price level (P_{-1}):

$$P^e = P_{-1}$$

Thus when the price level follows the hypothetical path plotted by the red line starting from the initial position E_0, the expected price level "tags along" one period later.

The hypothesis that the expected price level is based on past values of the actual price level is called **adaptive expectations.** In general, expectations do not necessarily adjust fully to an increase in the price level because workers may believe that some part of a price increase is temporary. For instance, they might adjust their expectations by only a fraction (j) of any change in the price level from what they previously expected:

$$P^e - P^e_{-1} = j(P_{-1} - P^e_{-1})$$

Example: Assume that $j = 0.5$. What will be the expected price level in period 2 in Figure 7-5? In the previous period the actual price level (P_{-1}) exceeded the expected price level (P^e_{-1}) by the vertical distance indicated by the first pink box. If the current expected price level were

THE EXPECTED PRICE LEVEL LAGS BEHIND THE ACTUAL PRICE LEVEL

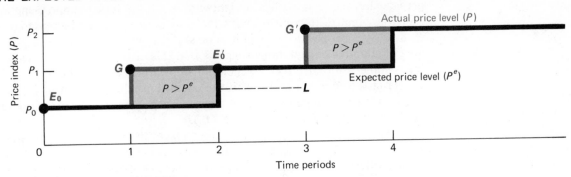

FIGURE 7–5

The Path of the Expected Price Level When Expectations Lag
One Period behind Actual Events

The behavior of the actual price level (P) is assumed to follow the red line. The
black line shows the behavior of the expected price level (P^e), if the latter is
always set equal to last period's actual price level. If errors in forecasting the
price level are not completely made up in each period, then expected prices do
not rise by the full amount of the previous error, as indicated by the dashed line
at point L.

to adjust upward by half of the pink expectational error, then the new
level of the expected price in period 2 would be indicated by the
dashed line at point L. When $j = 1.0$, as assumed in Figure 7-5, the expected price in period 2 rises by the full amount of the pink error to
point E_0', correcting the full amount of the previous error.

In general, the higher the value of j, the coefficient of adjustment of expectations, the shorter is any temporary boom in output before workers
catch on and shift the economy back to natural real GNP.

EFFECT OF AN ADJUSTMENT IN THE EXPECTED PRICE LEVEL
ON THE AGGREGATE SUPPLY CURVE

Until now our aggregate supply curve, which shows the amount of real
GNP firms will be willing to produce at different levels of the aggregate price
index, has been fixed in position by the underlying assumption that firms
and workers expect the future price level to be a constant value, P_0^e. Thus if
the actual price level is P_0, then it is exactly at the value that people expect,
P_0^e. When the actual price level rises above the level people expect, their expectations are in error, and they must decide how much to revise their expectations.

Now imagine in Figure 7-6 that the economy experiences a boom in aggregate demand that pushes it rightward along the initial supply schedule SS_0 from point E_0 to point E_2. Now the actual price level has increased from P_0 to P_1, yet people still expect it to be at its initial expected level (P_0^e). The idea of adaptive expectations suggests that this error will not last long, and that people will revise their expectations upward to take account of the increase in the actual price level. If the coefficient of adjustment of expectations (j) is 1.0, then people will set their *new* expected price level at P_1^e, equal to the new higher actual price level (P_1).

Once this shift in expectations takes place, the aggregate supply curve shifts up from SS_0 to SS_1. Why? The answer is based on the upper left-hand frame, where we see that the wage rate increases from W_0 to W_1 in exact proportion to the increase in the expected price level from P_0^e to P_1^e. We know that point E_0', just like point E_0, is a point of equilibrium, because it lies on the "equilibrium expected real wage" line.

The increase in the wage rate from W_0 to W_1 means that the horizontal wage line in the upper right-hand frame shifts upward. Point E_0' in the lower left-hand frame shows that now that expectations are accurate, the new higher expected price level P_1^e is equal to the actual price level P_1. And directly to the right the price level P_1 intersects the new aggregate supply schedule SS_1 at the natural level of real GNP (Q^N), since the economy always produces at the real GNP level Q^N when expectations are correct.

CHARACTERISTICS OF THE SS CURVE

Now we can summarize the characteristics of the economy's short-run aggregate supply curve SS:

1. The SS curve slopes up, because when the expected price level is constant at P_0^e, a higher actual price level will induce firms to hire more workers and produce more output.
2. Everywhere along any SS curve, the expected price level is fixed. For SS_0 in Figure 7-6, the expected price level is P_0^e.
3. At the initial real GNP level Q^N, expectations of the price level are correct. The expected price level (P_0^e) is exactly the same as the actual price level (P_0). Thus the price level that workers are anticipating along an SS curve is always measured by the vertical height of the intersection of that SS curve with the vertical QQ line.
4. When workers catch on that the price level has in fact risen, they will adjust their expectations (P^e) upward. The SS curve will shift upward whenever P^e rises.

THE LONG-RUN SUPPLY SCHEDULE QQ

The new SS_1 line drawn through point E_0' lies above the original SS_0 curve by exactly the amount by which the expected price level has risen. As al-

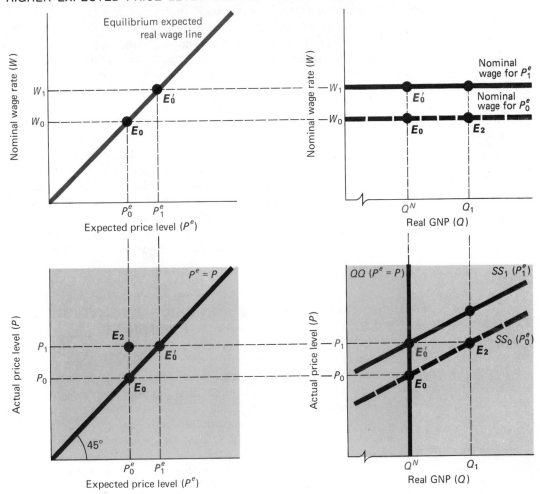

FIGURE 7–6

The Short-run Aggregate Supply Curve with Two Different Expected Price Levels

In the top right-hand frame the lower wage curve is copied from Figure 7–4, as is the aggregate supply curve SS_0. Both are drawn on the assumption that the price level is expected to be P_0^e. But a higher expected price level (P_1^e) will shift up both the wage curve and the aggregate supply curve in the same proportion. The two left-hand frames show the relation of the higher expected price level (P_1^e) to the nominal wage rate and the actual price level.

ways, the expected price level is measured by the vertical distance of the SS curve above the point marked Q^N on the horizontal axis. This vertical distance is equal to the new price level P_1. The black vertical QQ line running up above Q^N through E_0 and E_0' shows the different points where expectations of the price level are correct ($P^e = P$). Only if the price level once again increases above P_1, while expectations remain at P_1^e, can real GNP increase along the SS_1 curve to the right of the vertical QQ line.

Summary: When worker expectations of the future price level are correct ($P^e = P$), there is only one possible natural level of real GNP (Q^N). Only when the actual price level exceeds the expected price level, everywhere in the pink area to the right of Q^N, can actual real GNP exceed natural real GNP. Only when the actual price level is below expectations in the gray area can actual real GNP fall below natural real GNP. A real GNP level differing from Q^N is not a long-run equilibrium situation, since there is upward or downward pressure on the price level caused by the inevitable adjustment of expectations toward reality.

7-5 SHORT-RUN OUTPUT AND PRICE EFFECTS OF FISCAL AND MONETARY EXPANSION

We have examined the effect of fiscal stimulus, such as a $100 billion increase in planned autonomous spending caused by higher government purchases. In Chapter 5 we assumed that the price level was fixed, and that the fiscal stimulus raised real output; in Chapter 6 we assumed that real output was fixed, and that the fiscal stimulus simply raised the price level. Now we find that both output and the price level are increased simultaneously in the short run.

In Figure 7-7, we begin in equilibrium at point E_0 with an actual price level equal to P_0.

INITIAL SHORT-RUN EFFECT OF A FISCAL EXPANSION

Now a fiscal stimulus is introduced, in the form of an increase in government purchases that raises autonomous planned spending from $\bar{A}_0$ to $\bar{A}_1$. Where do we find the new equilibrium levels of output and the price index? If the price level were to remain constant, we would move straight to the right in Figure 7-7 from point E_0 to point E_1. But the price level cannot remain fixed because firms will insist on an increase in the price level to cover the higher costs of the increased production. In short, point E_1 is off the short-run supply curve SS_0 and is not a point at which firms will be willing to produce.

Point E_2 is the crossing point of the SS_0 schedule with the new DD_1 schedule, where businesses are willing to produce. The increase in government

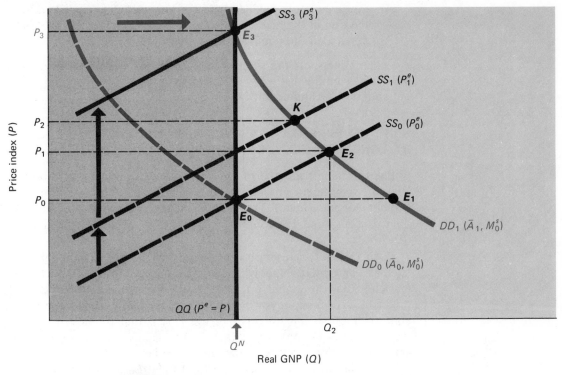

FIGURE 7–7

Effects on the Price Index and Real Income of an Increase in Planned Autonomous Spending from $\bar{A}_0$ to $\bar{A}_1$

Higher planned autonomous spending shifts the economy's equilibrium position from the initial point E_0 to E_2, where both the price level and real output have increased. Point E_2 is not a sustainable position, however, because the actual price level P_1 exceeds the expected price level P_0^e. Only at point E_3 does the expected price level finally catch up to the actual price level.

purchases has raised the price level and increased output at the same time. But output has not increased by the full Chapter 5 multiplier based on a fixed price level, the horizontal distance between E_0 and E_1. Instead, point E_2 lies northwest of the constant price point E_1, because the higher price level at E_2 reduces the real money supply and hence the demand for commodities.

The situation illustrated in Figure 7-7 at point E_2 would result from any stimulative factor that raises aggregate demand — not only an increase in government purchases, but also:

1. An increase in autonomous transfer payments or a reduction in autonomous taxes that raises $\bar{A}$.
2. An improvement in business and consumer confidence that raises $\bar{A}$.
3. A reduction in the income tax rate that raises the multiplier.
4. An increase in the nominal money supply.

As long as the short-run supply curve SS slopes upward to the right, any of the changes on this list will shift the DD curve rightward and raise both output and prices simultaneously to point E_2.

SHIFTING EXPECTATIONS AND THE ARRIVAL AT LONG-RUN EQUILIBRIUM

Point E_2 is not the end of the adjustment of the economy to the higher level of government purchases, however, because business firms are satisfied but workers are not. The price level has risen from P_0 at point E_0 to P_1 at point E_2, but point E_2 assumes that the expected price level is unchanged (P_0^e).

Each SS (short-run supply) curve assumes that the expected price level is fixed at a particular value, which is P_0^e for the supply curve SS_0. Once workers learn that the actual price index has risen higher than the level they originally expected, they will revise their expectations upward. One reasonable assumption, illustrated in Figure 7-7, is that the new expected price level in the current pay period (P_1^e) is estimated by workers to be equal to the actual price level reached at the end of the last pay period (P_1).

When the price level rises from P_0 at point E_0 to P_1 at point E_2, workers revise the price level expected for the next period upward to P_1^e. Since the position of the SS curve depends on the expected price level, the SS curve shifts up from the initial position SS_0, drawn for P_0^e, to the new position SS_1, drawn for P_1^e. As before, the equilibrium price level occurs at the point of intersection between the DD_1 curve and the SS curve, now at point K.

Workers expected the price level to be P_1, and it turns out to be P_2 at point K. What is the problem? The actual price level along any SS curve equals the expected price level (P^e) on which that SS curve is based only when actual output equals natural output $(Q = Q^N)$—that is, only at points on the vertical QQ curve. Since the SS curve slopes up to the right of the QQ curve, the actual price level is higher than expected whenever the economy is to the right of the QQ schedule in the pink area on the diagram.

The only place where the economy can be on its DD curve and simultaneously where price expectations are accurate is at the point of crossing of DD and QQ. For instance, initially in Figure 7-7 the economy was in equilibrium at point E_0. Now, however, with the rightward shift in the DD_1 curve, the full "no fooling" equilibrium can occur only at point E_3, where DD_1 intersects the vertical QQ schedule. Only at point E_3 does the price level turn out to be just what workers expect, so that they no longer are forced to revise their expectations, and the economy can stay put.

SHORT-RUN AND LONG-RUN EQUILIBRIUM

The economy is in **short-run equilibrium** when two conditions are satisfied. First, the level of output produced must be enough to balance the demand for commodities without any involuntary accumulation or decumulation of inventory—this first condition is satisfied at any point along the appropriate DD curve. Second, the price level P must be sufficient to make firms both able and willing to produce the level of output specified along the DD curve; this can happen only along a short-run supply curve (SS) specified for a particular set of expectations about the price level (P^e). The equilibrium at the crossing point of the DD and SS curves, however, is not permanent if the actual price level differs from that which had been expected, since expectations will be revised.

The economy is in **long-run equilibrium** only when all the conditions for a short-run equilibrium are satisfied, and, in addition, the actual price level turns out to be exactly equal to what individuals expect for the current period. In Figure 7-7, long-run equilibrium occurs only where all three schedules (DD, SS, and QQ) intersect.

> **Summary:** In the long run, any change in aggregate demand (shift in the DD curve), whether caused by monetary, fiscal, or confidence factors, changes the price level without causing any change in real GNP. Real GNP can change in short-run equilibrium but not in long-run equilibrium.

The effect of a shift in aggregate demand in long-run equilibrium in this chapter is thus exactly the same as the perfectly flexible price case of Chapter 6. The difference now is that we have carefully specified an intermediate step, short-run equilibrium, and we have introduced the state of expectations of the future price level as a central element in the process of price adjustment that takes the economy from point E_0 to point E_3.

7-6 HOW LONG IS THE SHORT RUN?

The preceding theory of price and output adjustment contains a troubling element that many students have rightly questioned. An increase in aggregate demand can raise real GNP to the right of the vertical QQ line in Figure 7-7 only if the actual price level exceeds the price level that workers expect. Thus, in a sense, workers must be "fooled" for an increase in real GNP to occur. Does it make sense to have a theory of output fluctuations based on the "fooling" of workers?

SOURCES OF PRICE INFORMATION FOR WORKERS

The deviation between the actual price level (P) and the expected price level (P^e) requires that firms have more accurate information than that available to workers, since in Figure 7-7 at point E_2 firms are willing to produce Q_1 only if the price is P_1, while the workers still expect the price to be P_0^e. Such an information advantage for firms is the basis of the best-known model of output fluctuations based on the "fooling of workers," that contained in Milton Friedman's Presidential Address to the American Economic Association.[2] Friedman's idea is that firms have a concentrated interest in a small number of prices of their products and monitor them continuously. Workers, on the other hand, are interested in a wide variety of prices of the things they buy and have insufficient time to keep careful track. Thus workers do not notice immediately when the price level rises.

But three important questions can be raised about Friedman's model. First, workers and their families buy many goods, particularly gasoline, food, and drug items, on a weekly basis and would discover almost immediately if the prices of these items had risen. Second, workers could easily discover within a month or two that the aggregate price level had risen, since reports on the monthly change in the Consumer Price Index are featured prominently in newspapers and television news shows. Third, if periods of high real GNP had always been accompanied by an increase in the aggregate price level, then workers would become suspicious that a new interval of high production and easily available job opportunities would also be accompanied by an increase in the price level.

Thus some economists believe that Friedman's model is incapable of explaining the way the economy behaves. Increases in the level of actual real GNP above natural real GNP could not last more than a month or two, the time needed for information on higher prices to be included in the monthly Consumer Price Index and publicized. How can the long-time duration of actual high-output periods be explained?

LONG-TERM WAGE AND PRICE AGREEMENTS

An alternative approach is to take note of the advantages to firms and workers of long-term agreements involving wages and prices that are set over substantial intervals and do not change on a daily or weekly basis. Advocates of this view do not claim that long-term agreements are universal, nor do they deny that prices of raw commodities such as wheat and gold traded in "auction markets" are extremely volatile from day to day. Rather, they analyze factors that cause price adjustment in some product and labor markets to be slower than in others.

---

[2] Milton Friedman, "The Role of Monetary Policy," *American Economic Review,* vol. 58 (March 1968), pp. 1–17.

In labor markets differences among workers and firms create an incentive for firms to keep existing employees content and for workers to avoid unnecessary job changes. Because job holders have received training and acquired skills that are not possessed by unemployed individuals, firms are willing to pay job holders more than they would pay a new hire "off the street." In turn, existing employees return the favor by refusing to quit their existing jobs in response to fluctuations in aggregate demand that may increase the wage rate of jobs available elsewhere.[3] By quitting to take another job, workers would lose the wage premium that they are paid as a reward for their special skills, and they also would be taking a risk that working conditions at the new job might not match their present situation.

CHARACTERISTICS OF LABOR CONTRACTS

Long-term attachments between firms and workers would tend to introduce time lags in the adjustment of wage rates to changes in aggregate demand, even in the absence of labor unions. But about one-quarter of all workers in private industry belong to labor unions and have their wage rates determined by a formal "collective bargaining" contract between their union and employer. A number of important characteristics of labor union contracts contribute to the "stickiness" of wage rates.

First, the majority of labor union contracts last for three years, so that the agreed-upon wage rate remains in effect even if there is a substantial rise or fall in aggregate demand. Both firms and workers desire long contracts in order to avoid strikes. Second, labor contracts in the United States do not all expire simultaneously but rather on a staggered schedule. Thus an auto firm facing a 10 percent drop in the demand for its product cannot reduce the price of autos proportionately even if it could talk the auto union into a 10 percent wage cut, because the preexisting wage contract for steel workers would hold up the price of steel.

Third, although many labor contracts allow for **cost-of-living agreements** (often called "COLA" clauses) that escalate wages automatically in response to monthly increases in the Consumer Price Index, the responsiveness of wages to prices is rarely allowed to be complete. Firms resist contracts with full price escalation in order to avoid a situation in which higher consumer prices caused by external forces (e.g., higher oil prices charged by foreign nations) would boost their wage costs without any commensurate increase in the nominal demand for their product.

---

[3] Arthur Okun's analysis of career labor markets is contained in his "Inflation: Its Mechanics and Welfare Costs," *Brookings Papers on Economic Activity,* vol. 6, no. 2 (1975), pp. 351–390. An accessible discussion of career labor markets in a world of differences ("idiosyncrasies") among workers is Oliver E. Williamson, Michael L. Wachter, and Jeffrey E. Harris, "Understanding the Employment Relation: The Analysis of Idiosyncratic Exchange," *Bell Journal of Economics,* vol. 6 (Spring 1975), pp. 250–278.

Fourth, and perhaps most important, contracts are never written to make wage rates dependent on the state of aggregate demand. An auto firm would resist a contract calling for an increase of 10 percent in wages in response to a 10 percent increase in aggregate demand, because the demand for autos might increase by a lesser amount or might even fall. A union would resist a wage contract calling for a boost in wages in proportion to auto sales, since they would fear that auto sales might fall relative to aggregate demand as a whole, and they might also fear that auto companies would understate their sales figures in order to cut their wage payments. What we observe almost universally is that the amount people are paid per hour is negotiated for the life of the contract, subject only to partial cost-of-living escalation.[4]

In short, the temporary fixity of the nominal wage and the SS curve in Figure 7-6 does not require that workers be fooled. All that is necessary is that firms and workers find it mutually advantageous to enter into long-term labor contracts.

CONSEQUENCES OF A DECLINE IN AGGREGATE DEMAND WITH SLOW ADJUSTMENT OF WAGES AND PRICES

Let us now examine the consequences of a drop in aggregate demand from curve DD_2 to curve DD_0 in Figure 7-8, caused by a decline in the money supply from M_1^S to M_0^S. If all prices and wages were completely flexible, and if all firms and workers were aware of the decline in demand, the economy would move from the initial point E_3 to a new equilibrium at point E_0. Real GNP would remain at the natural level (Q^N) while the price level would decline in proportion to the money supply.

But if wages and prices adjust sluggishly, the economy moves initially to a point such as E_4 in Figure 7-8. Because the price level does not drop in proportion to the decline in the money supply, the level of real money (M_0^s/P_4) has fallen, and real GNP drops.

Firms cannot afford to drop prices to E_0 because their wage costs are held up by existing wage contracts. Even nonunion workers do not renegotiate their wages daily but rather have wage rates set by their employers for six months or a year at a time.

Further, unions whose contracts are expiring refuse to agree to a drop in the wage rate by the full percentage of the drop in the money supply, since they know that their cost of living will be held up by the large number of products being produced by workers whose wage contracts are still in force.

Thus we conclude that, while the price level does not remain fixed at P_3 in response to the drop in the money supply, it does not fall instantly to P_0. It first reaches an intermediate position at P_4. Workers and firms can be completely aware of the exact extent of the fall in the money supply, and yet they

---

[4] A relatively advanced theoretical explanation of important features of labor contracts is contained in Robert E. Hall and David M. Lilien, "Efficient Wage Bargains under Uncertain Supply and Demand," *American Economic Review*, vol. 69 (December 1979), pp. 868–879.

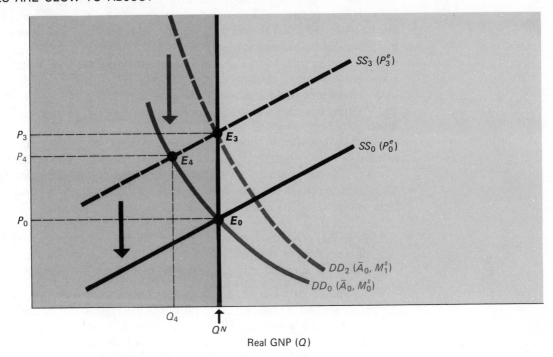

FIGURE 7–8

Effect of a Decline in the Money Supply from M_1^S to M_0^S on the Price Level and Real GNP

If the price level were perfectly flexible, the economy would move from its initial equilibrium position at point E_3 to a new equilibrium position at E_0. But the sluggish downward adjustment of wages and prices, which is due to long-term relationships between firms and both their customers and their workers as well as to the influence of labor contracts, causes the economy to move to point E_4 in the short run. Real GNP falls from Q^N to Q_4, and the price level falls from P_3 to P_4.

do not reduce their price expectations immediately to P_0, because *they are well aware of all of the features of the economy that inhibit rapid price adjustment.* Thus the aggregate supply curve does not drop immediately from SS_3 to SS_0, but rather falls only slowly as the expected price level drifts lower.[5]

_____

[5] Much has been made in the recent macroeconomics literature of the implications for economic policy of the idea that expectations are "rational." Yet the radical policy analysis of this framework hinges not on the assumption of rational expectations but on the unrealistic assumption that prices and wages are perfectly flexible. See section 8-10.

During the protracted period when the price level is adjusting downward to a drop in aggregate demand, real GNP is below the natural real GNP level (Q^N). This happens, not because there is any "fooling" of workers or firms, but because they find the advantages of long-term wage and price arrangements and of labor contracts sufficiently advantageous to outweigh the loss in sales and employment that such arrangements entail. The state of the economy at point E_4 is better described not as a "short-run equilibrium" but as a situation of **disequilibrium**.[6] The economy cannot be said to be in an equilibrium, because there is downward pressure for change on the price level.

It is only a matter of time, albeit perhaps a long time, before the economy eventually arrives at its long-run equilibrium at point E_0. The problem is that much real GNP and employment is lost to society in the transition from E_4 to E_0 as a result of the private advantages of long-term firm-customer and firm-worker relations and of long-term labor contracts.

Summary: Our discussion of long-term wage and price agreements and of labor contracts introduces a new, more realistic interpretation of the short-run aggregate supply curve SS in Figures 7-7 and 7-8.

1. The SS curve slopes up, as we concluded previously, because higher real GNP reduces worker productivity, raising the marginal cost of production and thus the price that business firms must charge.

2. Along any SS curve, the expected price level is fixed, and the actual price level is equal to the expected price level only at the natural level of real GNP (Q^N).

3. The expected price level upon which the SS curve is based (for instance, P_3^e for curve SS_3 in Figure 7-8) reflects what firms and workers expected *when their long-term agreements and contracts were first entered into.* At a higher or lower level of real GNP, workers can be quite aware that the price level has changed but be unable to reachieve the previous equilibrium real wage immediately; rather they must wait until their agreement or contract expires.

4. Whenever real GNP exceeds Q^N, the price level has increased above that upon which wage contracts were initially based, and wages will increase when contracts expire. New contracts and agreements cause the SS curve to shift up. This upward pressure on wages and prices continues until real GNP returns to the Q^N level. When real GNP is below Q^N, there is downward pressure in the same way. *Only along the vertical long-run supply line QQ is there no pressure for change in the price level.*

---

[6] The pioneering analysis of the workings of an economy in disequilibrium is Robert J. Barro and Herschel Grossman, "A General Disequilibrium Model of Income and Employment," *American Economic Review,* vol. 61 (March 1971), pp. 82–93.

7-7 CONDITIONS REQUIRED FOR A CONTINUING DEMAND-PULL INFLATION

Inflation is an upward movement in prices that (1) is shared by all components of the price deflator and (2) is sustained. Thus an increase in the price of haircuts and other services during the early years of the 1960s was not considered as an episode of inflation, because at the same time other prices (particularly television sets and other durable goods) were falling. The average price index, the GNP deflator, hardly increased at all. Part (1) of our definition of inflation was violated; the relative price of haircuts increased, but the upward movement in this price was not shared by all components of the price deflator. Since 1965, however, almost all prices have increased in the United States, and we have had what almost everyone describes as an inflation.

Part (2) of the definition requires that a general upward movement of prices be sustained to be called an inflation. An upward movement in prices is not generally classified as inflation if it lasts for only six months or a year and then stops or is followed by a general decline in prices. If the price index were to increase in some years and decrease in others, ending the decade roughly where it began, there would be no serious consequences and no one would describe the situation as an era of inflation.

Just as a fiscal stimulus can shift the DD curve and raise the price level, so too can a monetary stimulus. Figure 7-9 depicts an initial long-run equilibrium situation at point E_0, just as in Figure 7-7, with an initial level of $\bar{A}_0$ and M_0^s. The DD curve is now shifted up by an increase in the money supply from M_0^s to M_1^s. The results are just the same as when a fiscal stimulus is applied in Figure 7-7: first both output and the price level increase as the economy moves northeast of point E_0 to point E_2. But then, as the price level gradually adjusts upward and price expectations respond to this upward movement, the economy eventually attains a new long-run equilibrium at point E_3, where there is no further upward pressure on the price level.

EVERY INFLATION HAS A MONETARY CONNECTION

So far our conclusion is exactly the same as in Figure 7-7. A demand-pull increase in the price level can be initiated by any event that raises aggregate demand, thus pulling upward on the price level. A one-shot monetary stimulus, an increase in real government spending, a cut in taxes, or an increase in business and consumer confidence are all capable of shifting DD and so initiating a demand-pull increase in the price level. But for a **demand-pull inflation** to occur—that is, a sustained continuous increase in the price level—something more is necessary. A continuous upward shift in DD must occur. Since there is a natural limit on the size of a fiscal stimulus, only a continuous increase in the nominal money supply can fuel a sustained inflation.

This is illustrated in Figure 7-9, where the money supply grows first from

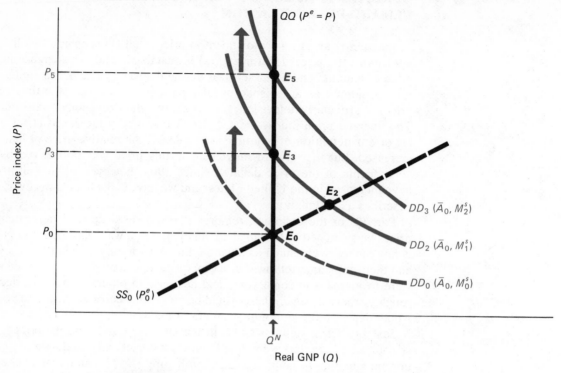

FIGURE 7–9

Effects in the Short Run and the Long Run of an Increase in the
Money Supply

At first output rises above Q^N from point E_0 to E_2, owing to the gradual adjustment of prices and wages. But as price expectations adjust, the economy moves
toward point E_3, with a higher price level and a return of real GNP to its natural
level (Q^N). A steady inflation of prices from E_0 to E_3 to E_5 requires a steady
increase in the money supply from M_0^s to M_1^s to M_2^s.

M_0^s to M_1^s. If the nominal money supply were to grow further to M_2^s and even
higher amounts, it would shift the DD curve continuously upward and carry
the price level with it from P_0 at point E_0 to P_3 at point E_3 to P_5 at point E_5
and so on to points further north of E_5. A sustained, continuous inflation requires the continuous expansion of the nominal money supply. This is what
Milton Friedman meant when he issued his famous dictum that "inflation is
always and everywhere a monetary phenomenon."[7] This does not mean that
an increase in M^s is the cause of every one-shot increase in the price level,

---

[7] See the quote that began this chapter.

because a fiscal stimulus or a change in business and consumer confidence can shift the DD curve as well. But these stimuli have natural limits that prevent them from shifting the DD curve to the right continuously, whereas there is no natural limit to an increase in the money supply.

The word *inflation* carries with it the idea of a "blowing up" of prices, as when one blows up a balloon. And, just as air is required to blow up a balloon, so an inflation requires that prices be "blown up" by a continuous increase in the nominal money supply.

Every sustained inflation has a monetary connection. But this does not mean that the branch of government responsible for the creation of money, the Federal Reserve Board, always initiates every episode of inflation. Instead, the Fed may be induced to raise the money supply if it attempts to keep the interest rate constant when the administration and Congress provide a fiscal stimulus, a situation illustrated in Figure 5-8. The Fed may also be induced to raise the money supply by other events that cause an autonomous shift in the short-run supply curve SS.

SUPPLY-SHOCK INFLATION

So far all upward shifts in the short-run supply curve SS have resulted from upward adjustments in the expected price level, stemming from the response of expectations to the increase in the actual price level caused by higher aggregate demand. But an increase in the price level can also be caused by a spontaneous upward shift in SS that is not initiated by the response of expectations to an aggregate demand boost. This spontaneous upward shift in SS, not initiated directly or indirectly by higher aggregate demand, is often called a **supply shock.** The most common and important type of supply shock in the 1970s was the spontaneous boost in oil prices by the Organization of Petroleum Exporting Countries, better known as **OPEC,** first in 1973–74 and then again in 1979-80. But a supply shock can also be caused by a crop failure that reduces the supply of food and boosts its price, or by a spontaneous decision by workers to demand a higher real wage—as occurred in some European countries in the 1968–70 period.

In Figure 7-10, starting from an initial equilibrium at E_0, let us imagine that the price of oil increases enough to boost the aggregate short-run supply curve from SS_0 to SS'. This happens despite the fact that the expected price level remains at P_0^e along SS', because higher oil prices have raised the marginal costs of production for many business firms (especially airlines, trucking firms, gas and electric utilities, and the neighborhood service station). If aggregate demand remains unchanged along the initial curve DD_0, the economy will move initially to point H.

Because the Fed has held the nominal money supply constant at M_0^s along the initial DD_0 curve, the higher price level at H has caused a decline in the real money supply, a drop in real GNP, and the laying off of some workers. The price level has increased, but not to the full extent of the upward shift in the supply curve. Notice that point H exhibits an imbalance between the

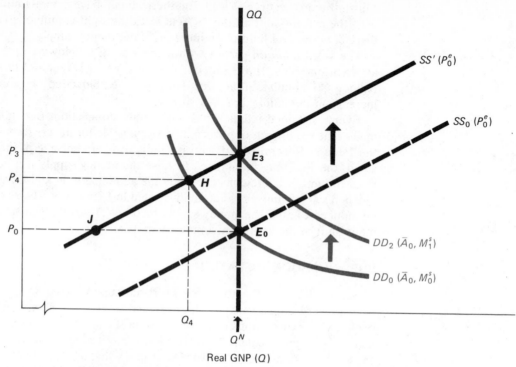

FIGURE 7–10

Effect on Real GNP and the Price Level of a Higher Oil Price That Shifts the Short-run Supply Curve from SS_0 to SS'

Initially the higher oil prices will shift the economy from point E_0 to point H if the nominal money supply is left unchanged at M_0^s. A monetary policy that cuts the money supply will push the economy to point J, whereas an accommodating monetary policy will push the economy to point E_3.

actual price level P_4 and the original expected price level (along curve SS') of P_0^e. To bring the actual price level and expected price level back into balance, the Federal Reserve would have to reduce the nominal money supply enough to bring the economy to point J.[8]

But the Federal Reserve may not depress aggregate demand and cause the economy to move to point J. Instead, the Fed may choose to maintain the previous level of real GNP by allowing the money supply to increase,

---

[8] How much does the supply shock reduce Q^N? This depends on the flexibility of wages and prices. If wages and prices are perfectly flexible, the reduction in Q^N depends on the elasticity of output to the factor input that has been affected by the shock (e.g., oil), on the responsiveness of labor supply to the lower equilibrium real wage that will occur, and on the responsiveness of the capital stock to the new situation.

shifting the aggregate demand curve up from DD_0 to DD_2. At point E_3 the price level and the money supply have doubled, leaving the real money supply unchanged and avoiding the need for any decline in real GNP. The Fed, by preventing the supply shock from reducing real GNP, is said to have "accommodated" the supply shock.

Point E_3, however, is not likely to be the end of the story. The contradiction between the price level at P_3 and the expected price level at P_0^e (the assumption upon which the supply curves SS_0 and SS' are based) makes an upward adjustment of the expected price level a certainty unless the supply shock is expected to be reversed. While a reversal might be plausible in the case of a temporary agricultural crop failure, it has not proved to be realistic for the OPEC manipulation of oil prices. Thus the SS curve will shift up in response to a higher expected price level, again forcing the Fed to push up the money supply if it wants to avoid a drop in real GNP.

PASSIVE MONETARY ACCOMMODATION

In moving from point E_0 to point E_3, both the price level and the money supply have doubled. But does this mean that the Fed has caused the inflation? The ultimate cause of the higher price level is the initiator of the supply shock—for instance, the OPEC oil sheikhs. The Fed plays the role of passive "ratifier" of the higher prices by allowing the money supply to increase. In the same way, an inflation may be initiated by a fiscal policy action that shifts the DD curve when government purchases increase; if the Fed wants to keep the interest rate from rising, it allows the money supply to increase and thus accommodates or ratifies the fiscal stimulus. An increase in government purchases, creating a continuous deficit financed by printing money, can cause a continuing inflation unless the Fed refuses to print the money. Similarly, a supply shock can cause a continuing inflation if ratified by the Fed.

A shift in either SS or DD moves the equilibrium position of the economy from point E_0 to E_3 and further points north. The only difference is that initially a demand-pull inflation raises output along path $E_0 E_2 E_3$ in Figure 7-9 if expectations are slow to adjust, and a supply-shock inflation reduces output along path $E_0 H E_3$ in Figure 7-10 if the Fed is slow to raise the level of the nominal money supply. But to be sustained and continuous, the increase in prices must be accompanied by an increase in the money supply, once again confirming that "inflation is always and everywhere a monetary phenomenon."

A Keynesian demand inflation generated by shifts in fiscal policy or in business or consumer optimism, or a supply-shock inflation, has to be validated by the monetary authority. Can one argue, therefore, that a distinction should be made not between demand and supply inflation but rather between inflations in which the role of money is active versus passive? Even this potential basis for classification becomes blurred when one recognizes that, even in most classic wartime or postwar money-fueled inflations, the role of the monetary authority has been passively to finance deficits arising from the unwillingness or inability of politicians to finance expenditures through increases in conventional taxes. Keynesian fiscal-induced, money-accommodated inflation and "pure" money-initiated inflation have in almost all historical cases amounted to one and the same thing.

> *Thus, a more general view is that inflation results from the passivity of the monetary authority in the face of pressures emanating from all groups in society — workers, firms, setters of oil and food prices, and government.*[9]

7-8 CASE STUDY: INFLATION IN HISTORY — DEMAND OR SUPPLY INDUCED?

Comparing the northward movement of the economy from point E_0 to E_3 in Figures 7-9 and 7-10, we see that prices, wages, and the money supply all increase together, preventing any easy statement that inflation is caused by a supply shock or by overly stimulative Federal Reserve policy. But there is a difference between the two figures. If expectations are slow to adjust, then a demand-pull inflation initiated by a rightward shift in DD is accompanied by an increase in output from point E_0 to point E_1, followed by a decrease in output from E_1 to E_3 when expectations begin to adjust. The line connecting E_0, E_1, and E_3 in Figure 7-9 can be thought of as a counterclockwise loop:

An inflation initiated by a supply shock differs. If the monetary authority either does not accommodate the shock or delays its accommodation, then the increase in prices initiated by a leftward shift in SS is initially accompanied by a decrease in output from point E_0 to point H, followed by an increase in output from point H to E_3 if the Fed raises the money supply. The line connecting E_0, H, and E_3 can be thought of as a clockwise loop:

---

[9] The notion that the Federal Reserve (or any central bank) is operating under a tripartite set of pressures from labor, management, and the fiscal side of government was originated in a classic article by Melvin W. Reder, "The Theoretical Problems of a National Wage-Price Policy," *Canadian Journal of Economics and Political Science* (February 1948), pp. 46–61.

Figures 7-11 and 7-12 plot data for P and Q/Q^N for the major U.S. episodes of inflation in the twentieth century. We can examine the economy's path in each case to see whether a counterclockwise (demand-pull) or clockwise (cost-push) route is followed. Figure 7-11 shows the inflations connected with World Wars I and II. In both the increase in prices was initially accompanied by an increase in output, as one would expect in the classic wartime inflation in which the government runs a large deficit and finances the deficit by printing money.[10] In both, the initial increase in Q/Q^N was followed by the inevitable decline as wartime expenditures wound down after the war, and in both cases the price level continued to rise after the termination of hostilities in 1918 and in 1945.

The main differences between the two wartime episodes are, first, that the price level fell substantially between 1920 and 1922 but did not fall at all after World War II. One obvious explanation is that prices were set freely by business firms during World War I, but during World War II prices were tightly controlled by the government. After the termination of controls in mid-1946, prices jumped rapidly and wound up about 70 percent higher than at the beginning of the war, very similar to the 60 percent net increase between 1915 and 1923. This similarity between the two episodes is somewhat surprising, given the much more nearly total production effort in the second war and much higher share of total production purchased by the government.[11]

Figure 7-12 plots data for indexes of P and Q/Q^N in the five major episodes of postwar inflation. The first two episodes (1950–54 and 1954–58) resulted in an increase in the price level of about 10 percent. Both loops are counterclockwise, with the main differences limited to the timing of price and output increases. In the first episode Q/Q^N remained high for three straight years, 1951–53, whereas in the second episode Q/Q^N increased for only one year, 1955, and then fell for three years. In the first episode, almost all the price increase occurred immediately, whereas in the second episode most of the price increase occurred relatively late, possibly because of a delayed upward shift in the expected price level (P^e).

The third episode, 1964–70, also follows a counterclockwise course, consistent with the hypothesis that the major cause of higher prices was the rightward DD shift caused by the combined monetary–fiscal expansion that began in 1965 when the United States entered active Vietnam combat. The 1964–70 counterclockwise path is very smooth and regular in appearance: the economy in 1970 arrived back at exactly the same

---

[10] Thus the wartime economic stimulus is neither pure monetary nor pure fiscal policy. but mixed monetary and fiscal expansion.

[11] Equations that explain the timing of price change in both wars are contained in Robert J. Gordon, "A Consistent Characterization of a Near-Century of Aggregate Price Behavior," *American Economic Review,* vol. 70 (May 1980), pp. 243–249.

INFLATION IN WORLD WARS I AND II FOLLOWED THE CLASSIC DEMAND-PULL PATTERN

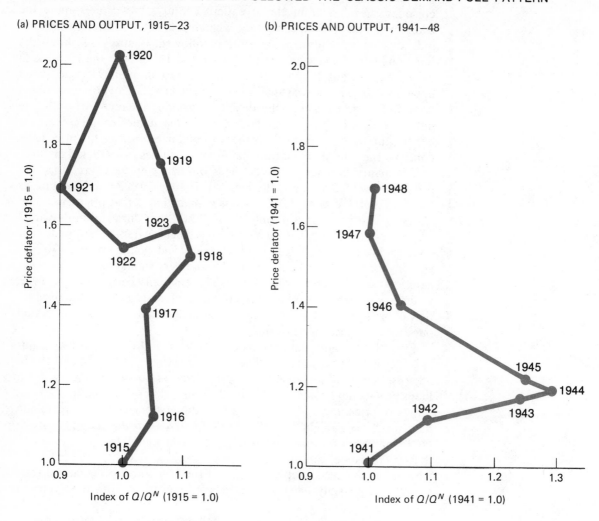

(a) PRICES AND OUTPUT, 1915–23

(b) PRICES AND OUTPUT, 1941–48

FIGURE 7–11

The Behavior of the Price Deflator and the Ratio of Actual to Natural Real Output (Q/Q^N) in Two Wartime and Postwar Episodes, 1915–23 and 1941–48

In both episodes both the price level and the output ratio increased together, but the timing was different. The increase in the price level during World War II in 1942–45 was moderated by controls on prices and wages, whereas in World War I (1916–18) there were no controls. The postwar experience also differed. There was an overshooting of the price level in 1919–20, followed by a drastic deflation in 1921 and 1922, which returned prices to the 1918 level. In contrast, prices shot up at the end of World War II (1946–48) when price controls were terminated.

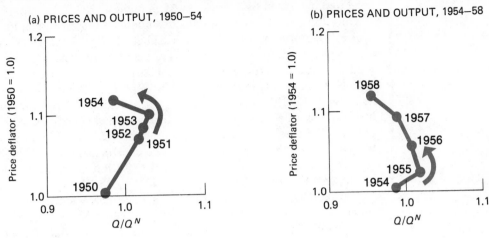

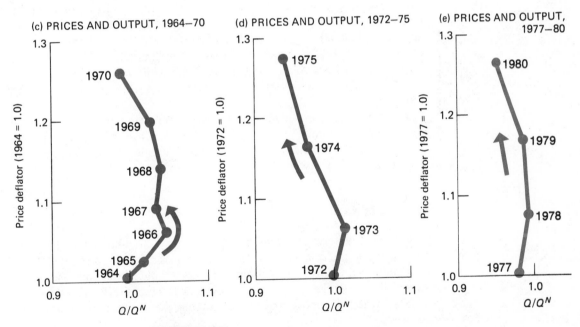

FIGURE 7–12

The Behavior of the Price Deflator and the Ratio of Actual to Natural Real GNP (Q/Q^N) in Five Postwar Episodes, 1950–54, 1954–58, 1964–70, 1972–75, and 1977–80

In the first three episodes the price deflator and the output ratio increased together, a sign of demand-pull inflation. But between 1973 and 1975 and again in 1977–80 a dramatic increase in the price level was accompanied by a decline in the output ratio, the result of cost-push in the form of higher oil and food prices.

Q/Q^N value achieved in 1964, but over the intervening six years the price level had increased by more than 25 percent.

Only the two most recent episodes qualify for a cost-push interpretation. After a brief movement northeast between 1972 and 1973, the economy moved rapidly northwest in 1974 and 1975. The higher prices of food, oil, and imports in general pushed the SS curve leftward, while a tight Federal Reserve monetary policy kept the DD curve approximately constant. The 1973–75 inflation was aggravated by the termination in mid-1974 of the wage and price controls that had been in effect under the different "phases" of the control program between 1971 and 1974. It has been estimated that the removal of price controls subtracted about 2 percent from the price level in 1971 and 1972 but added about the same amount back to the price level in 1974.[12]

During 1978–80 the economy was once again subjected to supply shocks. In 1978 the relative price of food began to rise again, and then in 1979–80 the price of oil jumped, raising gasoline prices from 60 cents to well over \$1.25 per gallon. At first the higher oil and food prices did not cause as prompt or sharp a reduction in real GNP as in 1974–75, because through most of 1978 and 1979 the Federal Reserve allowed aggregate demand to grow rapidly. The ratio Q/Q^N slipped only a moderate amount in 1979 but then much more substantially in 1980, as monetary tightness held down the growth of M^s while the continuing effects of rapid inflation raised the price level and further reduced the real money supply, M^s/P.

Our conclusion is that five of the seven major inflationary episodes in the twentieth century were demand-pull in origin rather than cost-push. We will next look further into the causes of inflation and begin to explore the policy options available to fight inflation.

SUMMARY

1. In this chapter real GNP and the price level are allowed to change together in the short run. We take into account the effect on real GNP and prices of the anticipations workers and firms hold about the price level. Along a single aggregate supply curve (SS), actual real GNP exceeds natural real GNP when the actual price level exceeds the expected price level, and vice versa.

2. For real GNP to rise above natural real GNP, the price level tends to rise. Just as the price level is likely to rise above initial expectations when actual real output increases, the price level will fall relative to the expected price level when aggregate demand declines.

3. A fiscal or monetary stimulus shifts the aggregate demand (DD) curve

---

[12] Robert J. Gordon, "Can the Inflation of the 1970s Be Explained?" *Brookings Papers on Economic Activity*, vol. 8, no. 1 (1977), pp. 253–278.

to the right and raises both real GNP and prices simultaneously in the short run as long as price expectations are fixed. Equilibrium at the intersection of the DD and SS curves is necessarily temporary and unstable if actual real output is either above or below natural output (Q^N). The actual price level then differs from that which has been expected, leading to a revision of price expectations and a shift of the SS curve.

4. An increase in real GNP can occur even without "fooling" of workers. Higher aggregate demand does not tend to boost the price level instantly, because of long-term wage and price agreements and the influence of labor contracts. But a situation with real GNP differing from natural real GNP sets up a series of adjustments to prices and wages as existing price agreements and labor contracts expire.

5. The economy is in long-run equilibrium only at a single level of natural real GNP where there is no upward or downward pressure on the price level, and when price expectations turn out to be accurate. In the long run, any change in aggregate demand changes the price level without causing a change in real GNP, the same result as in Chapter 6.

6. Inflation is a sustained upward movement in prices that is shared by all components of the price deflator. A demand-pull increase in the price level results from a rightward shift of the DD curve. An autonomous supply shock, resulting from higher oil or food prices, or from a demand by workers for a higher real wage unjustified by higher productivity, shifts the SS curve upward.

7. An upward shift in either the SS or the DD curve raises prices. The distinguishing difference is that initially a demand-pull inflation raises real GNP if expectations are slow to adjust, whereas a supply-shock inflation initially reduces real GNP if the Fed is slow to raise the level of the nominal money supply. But to be sustained and continuous, any increase in prices must be accompanied by a continuous increase in the money supply.

8. Until 1973, each major episode of accelerating inflation in the United States had been initiated by an increase in aggregate demand. But in 1973–75, higher oil and food prices, together with the end of price controls, boosted the price level and depressed real GNP simultaneously. In 1978–80, higher food and oil prices caused another acceleration of inflation, and another recession occurred in 1980 that repeated the basic pattern of 1974–75.

A LOOK AHEAD

We have now been introduced to the basic factors that cause prices to rise. But our attention has been limited to a series of static equilibrium situations, and we do not yet have much understanding of the dynamics of inflation. We also need to study alternative cures for inflation. The next chapter presents a thorough study of demand-pull inflation—its causes and cures—whereas a treatment of supply-shock inflation is reserved for Chapter 9.

CONCEPTS

Comparative statics
Short-run aggregate supply curve
Expected price level
Equilibrium expected real wage
Short-run equilibrium
Cost-of-living adjustment

Long-run equilibrium
Inflation
Demand-pull inflation
Supply-shock inflation
Monetary accommodation
Supply shock

QUESTIONS FOR REVIEW

1   Assume that the daily wage rate is $50. The addition of one worker adds 20 units of output, of a second worker adds 10 units, and of a third worker adds 5 units. Plot the individual firm's supply curve, using Table 7-1 and Figure 7-2 as a model.

2   Do the following events increase or decrease the equilibrium expected real wage (W/P^e)?
    a. An increase in worker productivity due to the introduction of new computerized machinery.
    b. A decrease in worker productivity due to lowered winter thermostats, as firms attempt to save energy in response to higher oil prices.
    c. Higher unemployment benefits available to individuals who do not work.
    d. Increased immigration of refugees from Cuba, who are willing to work for less than present American residents.

3   When real GNP increases above natural real GNP (Q^N) in Figure 7-4 from point E_0 to E_2, describe whether the following variables increase or decrease:
    a. The price level (P).
    b. The wage rate (W).
    c. The actual real wage rate (W/P).
    d. The expected price level (P^e).
    e. The equilibrium real wage rate (W/P^e).

4   Is a sustainable long-run equilibrium always reached when the DD and SS curves intersect? If not, why not?

5   In the spring of 1980 Chrysler Corporation offered rebates of up to $1000 to induce customers to purchase some of its automobile models that had been manufactured in excess quantities and remained unsold. What factors prevented Chrysler from offering rebates of $4000? $2000?

6   Imagine that Chicago bus drivers are paid $10 per hour. A cost-of-living-adjustment ("COLA") clause in their contract states that an in-

crease of 1 percent in the Consumer Price Index (CPI) raises their wage rate by 10 cents per hour. What happens to the nominal wage rate and real wage rate of Chicago bus drivers when the CPI increases by 1 percent?

7   Is the initial effect of the following events to increase or decrease real GNP? To increase or decrease the aggregate price level?
a. An increase in the nominal money supply.
b. A decrease in government spending.
c. A decrease in government autonomous tax revenue.
d. Bumper crops that reduce the relative price of food.
e. Another OPEC increase in the relative price of oil.

8   A supply shock may reduce real GNP without raising the price level, raise the price level without reducing real GNP, or produce some combination of lower real GNP and a higher price level. Explain the main factor upon which the outcome depends.

8
Demand Inflation:
Its Causes and Cures

Why is our money ever less valuable?
Perhaps it is simply that we have inflation
because we expect inflation, and we
expect inflation because we've had it.
—Robert M. Solow[1]

8-1 INTRODUCTION

We are now ready to study the fundamental causes of inflation, and the determinants of the responsiveness of inflation to shifts in aggregate demand and supply. Does faster growth in the money supply cause faster inflation instantly, or only after some time has passed? Does the government, through its monetary and fiscal policy, bear the blame for the faster inflation experienced in the United States since 1965 than previously? Is there any way that government management of aggregate demand can end inflation and return the nation to price stability?

Inflation describes a sustained continuous upward movement in prices shared by all components of the aggregate price index (or GNP deflator). In Chapter 7 we studied the determinants of the level of the price index. We learned that any event that can cause a single rightward shift in the economy's aggregate demand schedule (*DD* curve) can cause at the same time a single upward jump in the price index.

But inflation is a continuous increase in the price index, not a single jump. Thus a sustained inflation requires a continuous increase in aggregate demand. To focus on the determinants of inflation, we now shift from the diagrams of Chapter 7, which measure the level of the price index on the vertical axis, to related diagrams that measure vertically the percentage rate of change of the price index — that is, the inflation rate itself. In Chapter 7, a continuous inflation results in a steady upward movement of the economy's equilibrium position so that the economy eventually moves off the upper

---

[1] *Technology Review,* December/January 1979, p. 31.

edge of the page. Now, as we shift to the rate of inflation, the equilibrium position of an economy experiencing a steady inflation of, say, 6 percent remains fixed on the page.

In this chapter we study the relationship between inflation and the level of real GNP. In the absence of supply shocks, shifts in aggregate demand are the main cause of swings in real GNP and the rate of inflation. We shall see that a level of real GNP above the natural level of real GNP cannot be sustained permanently without a continuous acceleration of inflation. We shall also examine the unfortunate corollary to this fact, that a reduction of inflation cannot be achieved by aggregate demand policy without also involving a transition period of recession, with real GNP below natural real GNP.

Because inflation caused by supply shocks, such as an increase in the price of oil by the OPEC nations, raises somewhat different issues and requires different policy responses, we postpone until Chapter 9 a full treatment of supply-shock inflation. We also simplify our discussion by postponing until Chapter 10 an analysis of the relationship between inflation and unemployment.

8-2 THE SHORT-RUN PHILLIPS CURVE

Just as we found in Chapter 7 that a *single* upward shift in the economy's aggregate demand schedule can cause a *one-time* increase in the price level, now we will see that a *continuous* increase in demand pulls the price level up *continuously*. This kind of inflationary process is sometimes called demand-pull inflation, describing the role of rising aggregate demand as the factor "pulling up" on the price level.

This type of inflation is depicted in Figure 8-1. Here the top frame repeats the last chapter's aggregate supply and demand schedules, with the minor changes that (for expositional simplicity) we have drawn the aggregate demand curves as straight lines, and we have introduced specific numbers on the vertical and horizontal axes. For instance, the natural level of real GNP is assumed to be 100 on the horizontal axis, and the economy is assumed to be at that level of output initially at point E_0, where the SS_0 and DD_0 curves cross. The initial values of the price index (P) and expected price index (P^e) are both 1.0.

EFFECTS OF AN INCREASE IN AGGREGATE DEMAND

If there should be a rightward shift in the aggregate demand curve from DD_0 to DD_1, because of an increase in the money supply or in government spending, the economy would move initially to point E_1, where the price level is $P_1 = 1.03$. Everywhere to the right of the vertical QQ line the price level exceeds what people expected when they entered into their current set

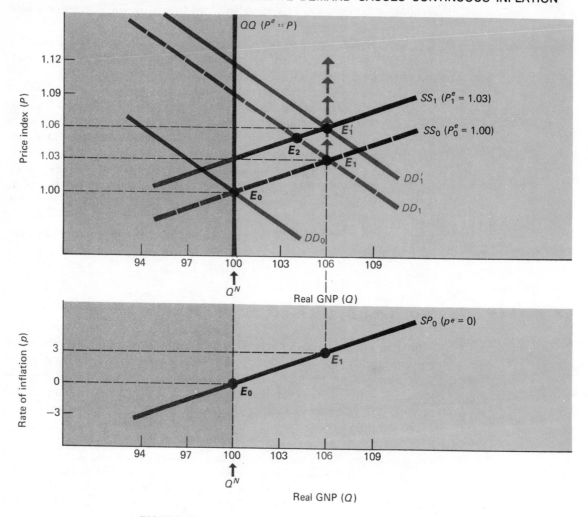

FIGURE 8–1

Relationship of the Short-run Aggregate Supply Curve (*SS*) to the Short-run Phillips Curve (*SP*)

In the top frame the economy is in long-run equilibrium at point E_0. When aggregate demand shifts up from the DD_0 curve to the DD_1 curve, the price level moves to point E_1 and exceeds the expected price level. The economy can stay to the right of the QQ line in the pink area only if aggregate demand shifts up continuously from DD_1 to DD_1' to even higher levels of aggregate demand. Because expectations of the price level adjust upward whenever P exceeds P^e, aggregate demand must keep ahead of the upward adjustment of expectations, shown by the vertical path marked by red arrows. This continuous inflation of 3 percent per period is represented directly below in the lower frame at point E_1.

of long-term wage agreements and contracts. As these contracts expire, naturally expectations for the future will adjust in response to the actual price level at 1.03, and thus point E_1 and all other points to the right of the QQ line are not positions of long-run equilibrium.

What happens when people have the opportunity to renegotiate contracts? If their new contracts are based on expectations that the new price level of 1.03 will continue ($P_1^e = 1.03$), the aggregate supply curve will shift upward by the amount by which the expected price level has increased. Thus the SS_1 curve drawn for the new expected price level lies everywhere exactly 3 percent higher than the old SS_0 curve.

WHY HIGHER REAL GNP MUST BE SUSTAINED BY A CONTINUOUS UPWARD SHIFT IN *DD*.

What happens to real GNP and the price level as the result of the upward adjustment of expectations from $P_0^e = 1.00$ to $P_1^e = 1.03$? There are two possibilities, both illustrated in the top frame of Figure 8-1.

The first possibility is that aggregate demand stays at the level indicated by the DD_1 schedule. Then the upward shift of the supply curve to SS_1 would shift the economy from E_1 northwest to point E_2. What must happen if the level of output is to be prevented from declining? The aggregate demand schedule DD must shift upward by exactly the same amount as the supply schedule SS. Thus if the expected price level increases from 1.00 to 1.03, shifting supply up from SS_0 to SS_1, output can remain fixed only if the demand curve shifts up again, this time from DD_1 to DD_1'. Once again people are fooled, because again the price level at E_1' ($P_1' = 1.06$) turns out to be higher than they expected ($P_1^e = 1.03$).

To keep output from declining, aggregate demand must continuously increase; the economy will move straight upward along the path depicted by the red arrows in the top frame. The bottom frame shows the same process in a much simpler way. In the bottom frame the horizontal axis is the same as in the top frame, but now the vertical axis measures not the price level but its rate of change. Thus in the top frame when the price level is fixed in long-run equilibrium, as at point E_0, the percentage rate of change of prices (or the rate of inflation) in the bottom frame is zero, as at point E_0. Throughout the book we will write percentage rates of change as lowercase letters, p in the case of inflation, and so the vertical axis measures off the zero rate of inflation occurring at point E_0 as $p = 0$.

The maintenance of a higher level of output requires a continuous increase in aggregate demand and in the price level, as depicted by the vertical path followed by the red arrows in the top frame. This same process of continuous inflation in the bottom frame occurs at the single point E_1, where each period the rate of change of the price level is 3 percent (just as in the top frame the price level rises by 3 percent between points E_1 and E_1').

The upward-sloping schedule connecting points E_0 and E_1 in the bottom frame of Figure 8-1 is called the **short-run Phillips curve,** abbreviated SP. The curve is named after A. W. H. Phillips, who first discovered the statistical relationship between real GNP and the inflation rate (p).[2] Just as each short-run supply curve assumes that the price level people expect is the same everywhere along that curve (for instance, $P_0^e = 1.00$ is expected everywhere along the SS_0 curve in the top frame of Figure 8-1), so the short-run Phillips curve assumes a single anticipated rate of inflation (p^e). For instance, people do not anticipate inflation at all along the SP_0 curve drawn in the bottom frame of Figure 8-1, and so the assumption of a zero anticipated inflation rate $(p^e = 0)$ is written next to that curve.

8-3 THE EXPECTED PRICE LEVEL AND THE ANTICIPATED RATE OF INFLATION

The remarkable thing about the inflation process illustrated in Figure 8-1 is that people never learn to anticipate the inflation *in advance* when they negotiate their long-term wage and price agreements and labor contracts. Each period the price level races ahead of the expected price level along the path shown by the red arrows, but people fail to build this inflation into their price and wage agreements ahead of time.

The left frame of Figure 8-2 depicts exactly the same relationship between the actual and expected price levels as plotted in the top frame of Figure 8-1. Notice how the price level (P) follows the red line and each period stays ahead of the black line representing the expected price level (P^e). For instance, at point E_1 (which corresponds to E_1 in Figure 8-1) the excess of the price level over the expected price level is indicated by the first pink rectangle.[3]

FORMING ANTICIPATIONS OF INFLATION

People are not likely to remain unaware of inflation for very long. If a 3 percent inflation has been going on for a while, they will begin to anticipate

---

[2] Phillips showed that over 100 years of British history the rate of change of wage rates was related to the level of unemployment. Because the change in wage rates in turn is related to inflation, and unemployment is related to real GNP, the research of Phillips popularized the idea depicted by the SP curve in Figure 8-1, that a high level of output is associated with a high inflation rate. See A. W. H. Phillips, "The Relation Between Unemployment and the Rate of Change of Money Wage Rates in the United Kingdom, 1861–1967," *Economica* (November 1958), pp. 283–299. The curve should actually be called the "Fisher curve," since the relationship between the unemployment and inflation rates had been pointed out much earlier in Irving Fisher, "A Statistical Relation between Unemployment and Price Changes," *International Labour Review* (June 1926), pp. 785–792, reprinted in *Journal of Political Economy* (March/April 1973), pp. 596–602.

[3] The labels on the vertical axis of Figure 8-2 ignore the effect of compound interest. A steady 3 percent inflation would raise the price level to 1.030, 1.062, 1.094, 1.127, and so on.

ADJUSTING THE EXPECTED PRICE LEVEL IS NOT THE SAME AS ANTICIPATING A CONTINUOUS INFLATION

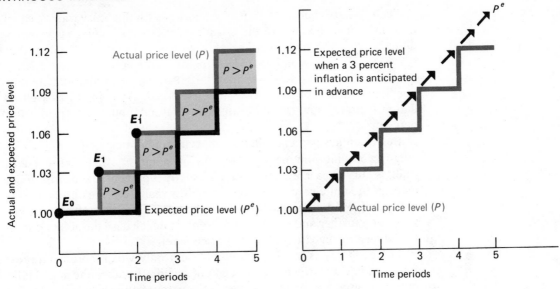

FIGURE 8–2

The Adjustment of the Expected Price Level (P^e) Contrasted to Accurate Anticipation of Inflation (p^e)

The left frame shows the relationship assumed in Figure 8–1 between the actual price level (P), depicted by the red line, and the expected price level (P^e), depicted by the black line. Because P^e always is assumed to adjust upward one period later than P, the pink shaded rectangles indicate the disequilibrium excess of P over P^e at points E_1 and E_1' in the top frame of Figure 8–1. The problem is that a continuing inflation is not anticipated. A contrasting adjustment is illustrated in the right frame. Line P^e always keeps up with P, because P^e is always set at last period's value of P plus an extra 3 percent upward adjustment to reflect the anticipated inflation rate of 3 percent.

that it will occur again next period. Their expected price level (P^e) will be adjusted upward from last period's actual price level (P) by the percentage inflation rate they anticipate (p^e). If initially the price level is $P_0 = 1.00$ and people anticipate an inflation of 3 percent, then the price level expected for the subsequent period is not 1.00, but 1.03. The more reasonable upward adjustment of the expected price level, when the anticipated inflation rate is 3, is illustrated by the black arrows in the right frame of Figure 8-2. There the price level (P) follows the same red path as in the left frame, but the expected price level never falls behind. Instead, each period people raise their expected price level in advance, and the actual price level always turns out to be exactly what they expect.

CHANGING INFLATION ANTICIPATIONS SHIFT THE *SP* CURVE

Such "smart" behavior shifts the short-run Phillips curve, as we can illustrate in Figure 8-3, where the lower SP_0 short-run Phillips curve is copied directly from the bottom frame of Figure 8-1. Everywhere along the SP_0 curve no inflation is anticipated. At point E_0 the actual inflation rate is just what is anticipated—zero—and so the economy is in a long-run equilibrium position with the price level completely fixed. At point E_1 as well no inflation is anticipated ($p^e = 0$), but the actual inflation rate turns out to be 3 percent.

But when a 3 percent inflation is accurately anticipated ($p = p^e = 3$), the long-run equilibrium position occurs at point E_3. The entire short-run Phillips curve has shifted upward by exactly 3 percent, the degree of adjustment of the anticipated inflation rate. Now real GNP greater than 100 cannot be achieved along the new SP_1 schedule unless the actual inflation rate speeds up further and exceeds 3 percent, in which case the actual price level would again exceed the expected price level.

The economy is in long-run equilibrium only when there is no pressure for change. Point E_1 certainly does not qualify, because the actual inflation rate of 3 percent at point E_1 exceeds the zero inflation rate anticipated along the SP_0 curve, and there is pressure for people to adjust their erroneous expectation ($p^e = 0$) to take account of the continuing inflation. At point E_3 the pressure for change ceases because anticipated inflation has been boosted enough ($p^e = 3$). Thus point E_3 qualifies as a point of long-run equilibrium because anticipations turn out to be correct, just as does E_0. The only difference between points E_0 and E_3 is the inflation rate that is correctly anticipated, zero at E_0 versus 3 percent at E_3; otherwise the two points share the correctness of anticipations and the same real GNP level of 100, equal to natural real GNP (Q^N).

THE *LP* "CORRECT ANTICIPATIONS" LINE

The vertical *LP* line connects E_0 and E_3 and shows all possible points where the anticipated inflation rate turns out to be correct. The *LP* stands for Long-run Phillips curve and can be thought of as the "correct anticipations" line. Everywhere to the right of the *LP* line (indicated by the pink shading) inflation turns out to be faster than anticipated, and the anticipated inflation rate will be raised. Everywhere to the left (indicated by gray shading) inflation turns out to be slower than anticipated and the anticipated inflation rate will be reduced. The vertical *LP* line showing all possible positions of long-run equilibrium is completely analogous to the vertical *QQ* long-run supply schedule of Chapters 6 and 7. Its message is the same: real GNP (Q) cannot be pushed permanently above its long-run natural level (Q^N).

The message of Figure 8-3 as a whole is simply that the combination of real GNP and inflation that the economy can achieve depends on the antici-

THE RELATION BETWEEN OUTPUT AND INFLATION DEPENDS ON THE RATE OF ANTICIPATED INFLATION (p^e)

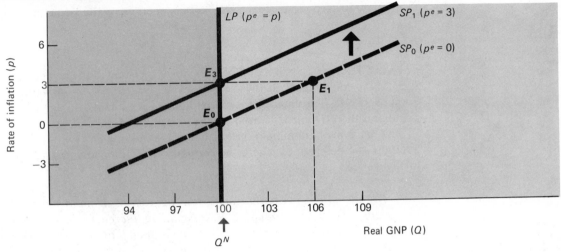

FIGURE 8–3

Effect on the Short-run Phillips Curve of an Increase in the Anticipated Inflation Rate (p^e) from Zero to 3 Percent

The lower SP_0 curve is copied directly from the bottom frame of Figure 8–1 and shows the relation between output and inflation when no inflation is anticipated ($p^e = 0$). Real GNP equals Q^N at 100 when the inflation rate is zero at point E_0, and it is raised higher when inflation is 3 percent at point E_1. But when people begin to anticipate fully the 3 percent inflation, now the 3 percent actual inflation yields only the level of real GNP at E_3. The short-run Phillips curve has shifted upward by exactly 3 percent, the amount by which people have raised their anticipated inflation rate. The vertical LP line running through points E_0 and E_3 shows all the possible positions of long-run equilibrium where the actual and anticipated inflation rates are equal ($p = p^e$).

pated rate of inflation (p^e). For any level of real GNP, the actual rate of inflation will be higher, the higher is the inflation rate that is anticipated. In this sense inflation is self-propelling—if people expect it, it will occur, even if output is at its long-run natural level. A cure for inflation cannot be successful without cutting the inflation rate that people anticipate.

8-4 NOMINAL GNP GROWTH AND INFLATION

Throughout our discussion of the last few chapters, nominal GNP has remained on the sidelines. In Chapters 3 through 5, where we held the price level fixed, every movement in real GNP was duplicated by exactly the same movement of nominal GNP. This occurred because by definition nominal GNP (Y), sometimes called current-dollar GNP, is equal to the GNP deflator (P) times real GNP (Q), sometimes called constant-dollar GNP:

$$Y \equiv PQ \tag{8.1}$$

Then in Chapter 6, when real GNP remained constant at the level of natural real GNP, movements in the price level were mirrored by movements in nominal GNP. Throughout these chapters every change in aggregate demand and the DD curve caused a shift in nominal GNP.

The behavior of nominal GNP provides the missing link for our theory of inflation and determines where the economy will be on any given SP curve in Figure 8-3.

> *Any economic event that shifts the aggregate demand curve to the right will raise nominal GNP, including increases in the nominal money supply, higher real government spending, lower autonomous tax revenues, and increases in business and consumer confidence. As we shall see in this section, any sustained increase in the growth rate of nominal GNP will raise the inflation rate.*

The relationship between nominal GNP growth and inflation is based on an extremely simple piece of arithmetic: the growth rate of any product of two numbers, such as P times Q in equation (8.1), is equal to the sum of the separate growth rates of the two numbers. Writing the growth rates of nominal GNP, the price deflator, and real GNP, respectively, as y, p, and q, (8.1) implies:

$$y = p + q \tag{8.2}$$

In words, this equation says that the growth rate of nominal GNP (y) equals the inflation rate (p) plus the growth rate of real GNP (q). If the level of nominal GNP starts out at 100, as in period 0 in Table 8-1, then a growth rate of 6 percent will bring the level to 106 in period 1. As shown in the table, several different combinations of inflation and real GNP growth are compatible with a 6 percent growth rate for nominal GNP ($y = 6$).

THE ECONOMY'S DEMAND GROWTH LINE

The three alternative ways in Table 8-1 of dividing nominal GNP growth of 6 percent are illustrated in Figure 8-4. Notice that the axes in this diagram are identical to Figure 8-3. On the vertical axis we plot the rate of inflation. On the horizontal axis we plot the level of real GNP in period 1. Thus if the level of real GNP in period 0 is 100, and its growth rate in alternative C in Table 8-1 is 3 percent, the level of real GNP in period 1 is plotted as 103 at point C.

TABLE 8-1

Alternative Divisions of 6 Percent Nominal GNP Growth
between Inflation and Real GNP Growth

	Period	Level of variable			Growth rate of variable between periods 0 and 1		
		Nominal GNP (Y)	Real GNP (Q)	GNP deflator (P)	Nominal GNP (y)	Real GNP (q)	GNP deflator (p)
Alternative A: Inflation at 9 percent							
	0	100	100	1.00	6	−3	9
	1	106	97	1.09			
Alternative B: Inflation at 6 percent							
	0	100	100	1.00	6	0	6
	1	106	100	1.06			
Alternative C: Inflation at 3 percent							
	0	100	100	1.00	6	3	3
	1	106	103	1.03			

The importance of the downward-sloping red line in Figure 8-4 is that it shows the conditions under which real GNP will grow or shrink from the starting value of 100 in period 0, depending on the assumed inflation rate. The assumed 6 percent rate of nominal GNP growth ($y = 6$) is the economy's "demand growth" — the growth rate of aggregate demand — that sets a limit on the sum of inflation (p) plus real GNP growth (q). Thus "demand growth" accounts for the name of the red line, the "*DG* line." It slopes downward, exactly like the *DD* line of Chapters 6 and 7.

If inflation is greater than 6 percent, as at point *A*, the assumed demand growth ($y = 6$) does not provide enough aggregate demand to "pay for" both high inflation and constant real GNP. Instead, the extra inflation, over and above the 6 percent demand growth, must be "paid for" by a negative value of q, meaning that real GNP must fall from its initial value, $Q_0 = 100$, to its next-period value at point *A* of 97. If, on the other hand, inflation is 6 percent, exactly equal to demand growth ($y = 6$), then exactly nothing remains for real GNP growth. *Thus the DG line always intersects the same inflation*

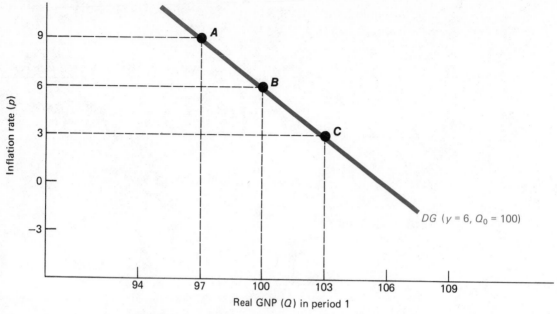

FIGURE 8–4

Alternative Combinations of Inflation and Real GNP Compatible
with a 6 Percent Growth Rate of Nominal GNP

This figure plots all the alternative ways in which a 6 percent growth rate of
nominal GNP ($y = 6$) can be divided between inflation and the level of real GNP
in period 1 *when real GNP starts at 100 in period 0* ($Q_0 = 100$). Points A, B, and
C plot the assumed inflation rates of Table 8–1 against the value of real GNP in
period 1.

rate on the vertical axis as the assumed growth rate of nominal GNP, directly above the initial period's level of real GNP. Point B in Figure 8-4 lies
at the point where $p = y = 6$, and real GNP remains at its initial period value
of 100. Finally, a low rate of inflation means that less nominal GNP growth
is needed to "pay for" inflation and more is available to support higher
real GNP.

Summary: Figure 8-4 conveys the message that for any given growth
rate of nominal GNP, an increase in inflation above that rate causes
real GNP to drop, whereas an inflation rate lower than y allows real
GNP to increase above its starting level in the previous period.

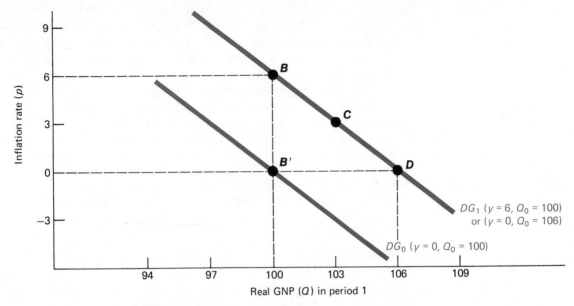

FIGURE 8-5

Two Alternative *DG* Lines Drawn for Assumed Nominal GNP Growth
Rates of Zero and 6 Percent

The DG_1 line is drawn for an assumed $y = 6$ and is copied directly from Figure
8–4. The DG_0 line is drawn for an assumed $y = 0$ and lies everywhere exactly 6
percentage points below DG_1. Both lines are drawn on the assumption that the
initial value of real GNP is 100.

SHIFTS IN THE *DG* LINE

The red *DG* line in Figure 8-4 was drawn on the basis of two assumptions.
First, demand (nominal GNP) growth was assumed to be 6 percent ($y = 6$).
Second, in the first period real GNP was assumed to start out at 100 ($Q_0 =$
100). A change in either assumption will cause the *DG* line to shift its
position:

1. A smaller value of demand growth, say $y = 0$, caused by slower growth in
   the money supply, by tighter fiscal policy, or by consumer and business
   pessimism, would cause the *DG* line to shift downward. This is shown in
   Figure 8-5, where the DG_0 line, drawn for $y = 0$, lies exactly 6 percentage
   points lower than the DG_1 line, drawn for $y = 6$ and copied from Figure
   8-4.

2. A different starting value of real GNP would shift the DG line. Up to this point we have always started with real GNP at 100 ($Q_0 = 100$). But if real GNP should start at a different value, the DG line would shift. The rule for plotting the DG line is simple: *the vertical position of the DG line directly above the starting value of real GNP is always equal to the assumed rate of demand growth.* For example:

Point B in Figure 8-5 lies directly above the starting value of $Q_0 = 100$, so its vertical position on the inflation rate axis, $p = 6$, equals the value of demand growth assumed along DG_1, $y = 6$.

Point B' lies directly above the starting value of $Q_0 = 100$, so its vertical intercept of $p = 0$ equals the value of nominal GNP growth assumed along DG_0, $y = 0$.

What does point D represent if the starting value of Q_0 is 106 instead of 100? The vertical intercept at point D, $p = 0$, must lie on a DG line drawn for $y = 0$ and a starting value of Q of 106, and this is an alternative interpretation of the DG_1 line.

Another important fact about the DG line stands out as well in Figure 8-5. When the inflation rate is equal to the rate of demand growth, the DG line intersects the initial value of real GNP; for example, at point B on the DG_1 line. Thus there is no change in real GNP between its initial value of $Q_0 = 100$ and its new value of $Q_1 = 100$. But at any other point on the DG line, when inflation is either greater or less than nominal GNP growth, the new value of Q_1 will differ from the initial value, and this means that the analysis of the next period must be based on a new starting value of real GNP. For instance, if inflation should turn out to be 3 percent and nominal GNP growth is 6 percent, we would be at point C on the DG_1 line. Real GNP would grow from $Q_0 = 100$ to $Q_1 = 103$. The DG line for the subsequent period would have to be redrawn, so that the vertical intercept of $p = y = 6$ lies above $Q_1 = 103$. This new DG line, not drawn in Figure 8-5, would lie exactly three units to the right of DG_1.

> *In short, when inflation turns out to be less than nominal GNP growth, real GNP grows, and next period's DG line shifts to the right. When inflation turns out to be more than nominal GNP growth, real GNP must shrink, and the next period's DG line shifts to the left.*

8-5 EFFECTS OF AN ACCELERATION IN NOMINAL GNP GROWTH

The DG line shows all the combinations of inflation and real GNP that are compatible with given demand growth and an initial starting point for real GNP. But which of these various combinations describes where the economy actually comes to rest?

THE IMPACT ON INFLATION AND REAL GNP OF FASTER NOMINAL GNP GROWTH WHEN THE
ANTICIPATED RATE OF INFLATION FAILS TO ADJUST

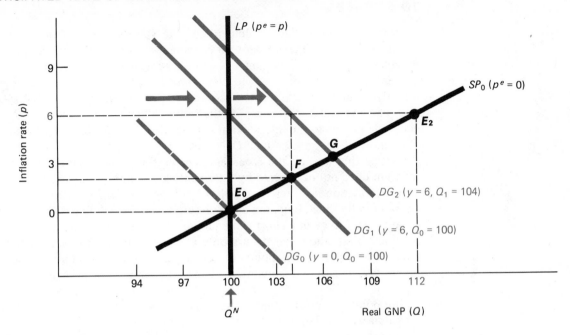

FIGURE 8-6

The Adjustment Path of Inflation and Real GNP to an Acceleration
of Demand Growth from Zero to 6 Percent

The economy initially is at point E_0, the crossing point of the SP_0 curve copied
from Figure 8–3 and the DG_0 line copied from Figure 8–5. A 6 percent acceleration in nominal GNP growth first shifts the DG line directly up by 6 percentage
points to DG_1, and the economy moves to point F. Then, since the economy's
starting point in period 1 is a real GNP level of 104, the DG line shifts rightward
by four units to DG_2. The rightward shift in DG continues until the economy
arrives at point E_2.

The SP curve from Figure 8-3 is needed to pin down the economy's position along the DG line. In the same way, the DG line is needed to determine
where the economy rests on its SP short-run Phillips curve. The two lines,
DG and SP, are needed to determine the two variables, inflation and current
real GNP.

Figure 8-6 shows at point E_0 an initial long-run equilibrium consistent
with demand growth of zero. If policymakers initially set $y = 0$, then the
initial inflation rate of zero allows the economy to remain forever at its initial real GNP level of 100, the assumed natural level of real GNP (Q^N).

EFFECTS IN PERIOD 2 OF A BOOST IN DEMAND GROWTH TO 6 PERCENT

What happens initially if demand growth speeds up, say from $y = 0$ to $y = 6$, as a result either of buoyant consumer and business confidence or of monetary or fiscal policy stimulus? The DG line instantly shifts upward by 6 percentage points from DG_0 to DG_1. The DG_1 line, which is also copied directly from Figure 8-5, intersects the starting value of real GNP ($Q_0 = 100$) at a vertical intercept $p = 6$, the same as the assumed value of y. The economy moves to the intersection at point F of the SP_0 line, which remains fixed in position, and the new DG_1 line.

Notice that despite the 6 percent acceleration of nominal GNP growth, inflation does not accelerate by 6 percentage points right away. Instead, at point F inflation has increased only from 0 percent to 2 percent. Why? Because initially the anticipated inflation rate along the SP_0 line is $p^e = 0$, so for the economy to be in a short-run equilibrium, it must be on both its DG and SP lines, a situation that occurs only at point F. What happens to the remaining four percentage points of demand growth, over and above the two points devoted to faster inflation? These remaining four percentage points boost real GNP from $Q_0 = 100$ to $Q_1 = 104$.

But point F is not the end of the story. Even if everyone continues to anticipate a zero inflation so that the SP_0 line remains valid, the DG line will shift to the right because of the new higher value of real GNP. Because DG always intersects the inflation rate equal to the assumed value of demand growth directly above the starting value of real GNP, a new DG_2 line must now be drawn that intersects $p = y = 6$ directly above the new real GNP value of $Q_1 = 104$. Notice that the DG_2 line is labeled with the two assumptions on which it is based, $y = 6$ and $Q_1 = 104$.

THE CONTINUING ADJUSTMENT

What happens next? Again the economy shifts northeastward to the intersection at point G of the fixed SP_0 line and new DG_2 line. Again the starting value of real GNP has shifted, and again the DG line will shift to the right (not shown separately on the graph). The DG line will stop shifting only when *inflation totally exhausts demand growth,* which occurs only when inflation reaches 6 percent at point E_2.

But point E_2 is not satisfactory either. Granted that it lies on both the DG and SP lines, satisfying the requirements for a short-run equilibrium. But, alas, the economy cannot stay at point E_2. Why? Because at E_2 inflation is racing along at 6 percent, yet anticipations of inflation remain at zero along SP_0. It is inevitable that people will adjust their anticipations of inflation to take account of the unfortunate reality of 6 percent inflation, causing the SP curve to shift upward. And once this occurs, the economy cannot sustain the high values of real GNP reached in Figure 8-6. A long-run equilibrium can be attained only where actual and anticipated inflation are equal—that is, along the vertical LP line. This happens only when real GNP returns to its natural level, Q^N.

How high can real GNP be pushed, and for how long? Everything depends on the speed at which expectations are adjusted. This depends in turn on how aware people are of what is going on, and also what fraction of wage and price agreements are set every day as opposed to being tied down by long-term contracts. The slower anticipations adjust, the longer a high level of real GNP can persist.

8-6 ADAPTIVE EXPECTATIONS AND THE INFLATION CYCLE

A hypothesis of how expectations are formed, which has been widely studied and verified, is called **adaptive expectations**.[4] The idea is simply that when people find that actual events do not turn out as they expected, they adjust their expectations to bring them closer to reality. A simple way of writing the adaptive expectations hypothesis for inflation is that the expected (or anticipated) rate of inflation (p^e) is set as an average of last period's actual inflation (p_{-1}) and last period's expected inflation rate (p^e_{-1}):

$$p^e = jp_{-1} + (1-j)p^e_{-1} \tag{8.4}$$

Here j represents the weight put on last period's actual inflation; j could be any fraction between zero and 1.0.

Here are examples showing how the expected inflation rate is formed when j takes on different hypothetical values:

Value of j	Calculation of p^e	Example when $p_{-1} = 2$ and $p^e_{1} = 0$
0	$p^e = (0)p_{-1} + (1)p^e_{-1} = p^e_{-1}$	$p^e = 0$
0.25	$p^e = 0.25p_{-1} + 0.75p^e_{-1}$	$p^e = 0.5$
1	$p^e = (1)p_{-1} + (0)p^e_{-1} = p_{-1}$	$p^e = 2$

In the first line of the table, j is zero. People do not adjust their expectations at all to the actual behavior of inflation, but instead they maintain their expectation (p^e) at its value in the previous period (p^e_{-1}). This behavior, which is not very realistic, is the same as in Figure 8-6, where the SP_0 curve remains in effect as a result of the failure by people to raise their anticipation of inflation above $p^e = 0$.

---

[4] The idea of adaptive expectations was first used in macroeconomics in a paper that has become a classic, Phillip Cagan, "The Monetary Dynamics of Hyperinflation," in Milton Friedman (ed.), *Studies in the Quantity Theory of Money* (Chicago: University of Chicago Press, 1956), pp. 25–117.

In the second line of the table, j is at the intermediate value of 0.25. People compromise, basing part of their estimate of expected inflation on what actually happened last period (p_{-1}) and the remainder (0.75) on what they previously expected. Why is this compromise approach plausible? Last period's actual inflation may not be a very good guide to what will happen this period. If inflation has been running at a zero rate, and people have been expecting a zero rate ($p^e_{-1} = 0$), then a sudden acceleration to 2 percent ($p_{-1} = 2$) might not necessarily continue into the future. A value of j equal to 0.25 indicates that people believe that there is a one-quarter chance that the new rate of inflation will continue and a greater three-quarter chance that inflation will return to what they previously expected.

The third line of the table shows the extreme case of $j = 1.0$, which means that the expected inflation rate is always set equal to what actually happened last period. In Figure 8-6, the acceleration of nominal GNP growth, which raises actual inflation from zero to 2 percent as the economy moves from point E_0 to point F, would cause next period's expected inflation rate to rise by the same amount, to 2 percent.

The economy's response to higher demand growth is quite different, depending on j, the coefficient of adjustment of expectations. In Figure 8-7 three responses are plotted, corresponding to each of the three values of j assumed in the table: zero, 0.25, and 1.0. The black line moving straight northeast from point E_0 through points F and G to E_2 duplicates Figure 8-6. Since j is zero, expectations do not adjust at all and the economy remains on its original SP_0 curve.

The other black line shows the opposite extreme of rapid adjustment of expectations when $j = 1.0$. In each period the SP curve shifts upward by exactly the previous period's increase in actual inflation. Because actual inflation increases by 2 percentage points in going from E_0 to point G, in the next period the SP curve shifts upward by 2 percentage points and takes the economy northward from F to H. At point H the economy is on its DG_2 line (see Figure 8-6), but then expectations adjust upward again. Eventually, after looping around the long-run equilibrium point E_3, the economy arrives there.

When the expected inflation rate adjusts by only part of the difference between last period's actual and expected inflation, in the example of $j = 0.25$, the economy follows the red path in Figure 8-7. This lies between the two black paths and illustrates a slower adjustment.

Both the red path for $j = 0.25$ and the black path for $j = 1.0$ share several basic characteristics of the inflation process:

1. An acceleration of demand growth as in Figures 8-6 and 8-7 raises the inflation rate and real GNP in the short run.
2. In the long run, if expectations adjust even partially to the actual behavior of inflation, the inflation rate rises by exactly the same amount as y, and the increase in Q is only temporary. The economy eventually arrives at point E_3.

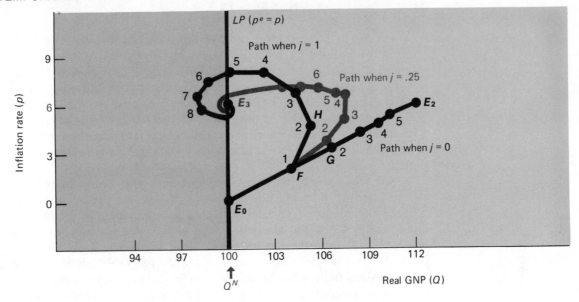

FIGURE 8–7

Effect on Inflation and Real GNP of an Acceleration of Demand
Growth from Zero to 6 Percent, Under Alternative Assumptions
of Expectation Adjustment

When expectations do not adjust at all, the economy follows the black path northeast from E_0 to E_2, exactly as in Figure 8–6. An adjustment coefficient of 0.25
causes expectations to shift upward slowly, pushing the economy onto the higher
adjustment path indicated in red. When expectations adjust fully to last period's
actual inflation ($j = 1.0$), the economy moves upward even faster, as shown by
the black path going northwest from point H.

3. Inflation always "overshoots" its final equilibrium value of 6 percent,
   rising temporarily above 6 percent and then returning to 6 percent. Along
   the upper black path inflation reaches 8 percent in periods 4 and 5. Along
   the red path inflation reaches a peak of 7.15 percent in period 7. The
   reason for the overshooting is that the economy initially arrives at its
   long-run 6 percent inflation rate before expected inflation has caught up
   with actual inflation. The subsequent points that lie above 6 percent reflect the combined influence on inflation of (1) the upward adjustment of
   expectations and (2) the continued upward demand pressure that raises
   actual inflation above expected inflation whenever the economy is to the
   right of its long-run LP line.

8-7 CASE STUDY: THE U.S. INFLATION CYCLE AND STAGFLATION, 1964–71

For too long in the 1960s, economists preached that there was a trade-off between inflation and unemployment. Along any SP curve, the enjoyment of higher real GNP requires tolerating more inflation. But no SP curve is likely to stay fixed for long if the inflation rate differs substantially from the expected rate of inflation. There is no positive relation between inflation and real GNP in the long run when expectations have adjusted to the actual inflation experience. The natural rate hypothesis states that in the long run real GNP is at a natural value (Q^N) independent of the inflation rate.

Some journalists and critics have claimed that "economics is bankrupt" because it could not explain stagflation, the simultaneous occurrence of inflation, recession, and high unemployment in the late 1960s and early 1970s. But stagflation is precisely what we have generated in Figure 8-7! Both the red and upper black adjustment paths display segments in which the inflation rate is rising and real GNP falling at the same time. Along both paths the economy suffers through several periods when inflation is higher than its long-run 6 percent value, while simultaneously real GNP is lower than its natural level, Q^N.

The real world never precisely duplicates any simple textbook model, but the U.S. rate of inflation and level of real output during the period 1964–71 provide a classic example of the effects of an acceleration in nominal GNP growth. If we compare the annual growth rate of nominal GNP (y) during the four-year interval 1960–63 in the first line of Table 8-2 with its growth rate during the three-year interval 1964–66, we observe an acceleration of 3.1 percentage points from 5.1 percent to 8.2 percent. And in the third line of Table 8-2, we see that the inflation rate accelerated steadily, from an average rate of 1.5 percent during 1960–63, to 2.4 percent during 1964–66, to 4.5 percent during 1967–70.

The table shows that the response of inflation to faster nominal GNP growth was not immediate, just as we learned in Figure 8-7 that it takes time for inflation to respond to an acceleration of nominal GNP growth. During the intermediate interval 1964–66, nominal GNP growth accelerated from 5.1 percent to 8.2 percent, but inflation only speeded up from 1.5 to 2.4 percent. This "left room" during 1964–66 for the growth of real GNP ($q = y - p$) to speed up from 3.6 to 5.7 percent, as shown on line 2.

ADJUSTING NOMINAL AND REAL GNP FOR GROWTH IN NATURAL REAL GNP

So far there is one major difference between the U.S. inflation experience summarized in Table 8-2 and our theoretical diagram of inflation

TABLE 8-2

Annual Growth Rates of Important Variables During
Selected Intervals, 1960–70

	1960–63	1964–66 (in percent)	1967–70
Growth rate of:			
1. Nominal GNP (y)	5.1	8.2	6.9
2. Real GNP (q)	3.6	5.7	2.3
3. GNP deflator ($p = y - q$)	1.5	2.4[a]	4.5[a]
4. Natural real GNP (q^N)	3.6	3.8	3.5
5. "Adjusted" nominal GNP ($\hat{y} = y - q^N$)	1.5	4.4	3.4
6. "Adjusted" real GNP ($\hat{q} = q - q^N$)	0.0	1.9	−1.2
7. Ratio of actual real GNP to natural real GNP in last year of interval (Q/Q^N)	.987	1.041	.993

[a] Lines 2 and 3 do not add precisely to line 1, because the exact formula is $y = q + p + pq$; for instance, (using decimals) in the third column, we have $.069 = .023 + .045 + .001$. The same factor also explains why lines 3 and 6 do not add up exactly to line 5.
Source: Appendix B.

adjustment in Figure 8-7. In that diagram inflation started out at zero, the same as nominal GNP growth. Yet in Table 8-2 in the initial period (1960–63) inflation (1.5 percent) does not proceed at the same rate as nominal GNP growth (5.1 percent). Why? In our theoretical model we assumed that the economy's growth in natural real GNP (q^N) was zero. But in the real world of Table 8-2, we must recognize that, in fact, natural real GNP grows each year.[5]

Because natural real GNP growth occurs each year in the economy, we must modify our theoretical model slightly. In our theoretical diagrams such as Figure 8-7, real GNP remained constant when inflation (p) equaled nominal GNP growth (y). Now, taking account of growth in natural real GNP, the modified rule is:

The ratio of real GNP to natural real GNP (Q/Q^N) remains constant when inflation (p) is equal to the excess of demand growth over natural real GNP growth ($y - q^N$).

In line 5 we calculate the difference between demand growth and natural real GNP growth and label this difference **adjusted demand**

---

[5] The determinants of q^N are considered in more detail in Chapter 18 and include the growth in the population of working age, trends in hours per person, and changes in education, the stock of capital equipment and structures, and the level of technology.

Case Study: The U.S. Inflation Cycle and Stagflation, 1964–71 **227** growth or, as another name for the same concept, **adjusted nominal GNP growth** ($\hat{y} = y - q^N$). This equals $5.1 - 3.6$, or 1.5 percent, during 1960–63. On line 3 we can see that inflation (p) is exactly the same figure, 1.5 percent. Thus the 1960–63 period was characterized by constancy in the ratio of real GNP to natural real GNP (Q/Q^N). Since natural real GNP growth was proceeding at 3.6 percent per year, clearly the growth of actual real GNP must have been the same 3.6 percent per year for the ratio of the two real GNP concepts (Q/Q^N) to have remained constant. The last line in Table 8-2 confirms that the difference in the growth rates of Q and Q^N, which we label **adjusted real GNP growth** ($\hat{q} = q - q^N$), was zero.

We can summarize the effect of allowing for growth in natural real GNP in the following way:

	True in Figure 8-7 at point E_0 with natural real GNP growth (q^N) assumed to be zero	*True in Table 8-2 with natural real GNP growth (q^N) positive*	*Numerical example for 1960–63*
1. Relation of inflation (p) to demand growth (y) and natural real GNP growth (q^N)	$p = y$	$p = \hat{y} = y - q^N$	$1.5 = 5.1 - 3.6$
2. Real GNP concept assumed to be constant	Q	Q/Q^N	.987
3. Implication of line 2 for the growth of actual real GNP (q)	$q = 0$	$\hat{q} = q - q^N = 0$	$3.6 - 3.6 = 0$

What happens in a period when there is an acceleration in demand growth minus natural real GNP growth, or "adjusted demand growth" ($\hat{y} = y - q^N$)? Such an acceleration occurred in the 1964–66 period. As shown on line 1 of Table 8-2, actual demand growth (y) accelerated from 5.1 to 8.2 percent. Adjusted demand growth ($\hat{y}$) as shown in line 5 accelerated by almost as much, from 1.5 to 4.4 percent. However, inflation did not immediately adjust to the faster growth in $\hat{y}$. Instead during the 1964–66 interval the inflation rate averaged 2.4 percent. This "left room" for the remaining growth in $\hat{y}$ to take the form of rapid real GNP growth. The growth of actual real GNP during this period ($q = 5.7$ percent) raced ahead of the growth in natural real GNP ($q^N = 3.8$ percent), so that adjusted real GNP growth was 1.9 percent per year ($\hat{q} = q - q^N = 1.9$).

In previous sections, when we neglected growth in natural real GNP, we learned that growth in nominal GNP must be divided between inflation and actual real GNP growth ($y = p + q$). Now, taking account of growth in natural real GNP, we have a modified rule:

Adjusted demand growth must be divided between inflation and adjusted growth in real GNP ($\hat{y} = p + \hat{q}$).[6] This means that when inflation (p) is less than adjusted demand growth ($\hat{y}$), adjusted real GNP growth is positive. Real GNP grows faster than natural real GNP, and the ratio Q/Q^N rises. If inflation exceeds adjusted demand growth, on the other hand, then adjusted real GNP growth is negative, and the ratio Q/Q^N must decline.

What is the importance of adjusted real GNP growth ($\hat{q}$)? In long-run equilibrium, along the vertical *LP* line of Figure 8-7, actual and natural real GNP must be equal ($Q = Q^N$). This means that the ratio of the two must be equal to unity ($Q/Q^N = 1.0$). Adjusted real GNP growth ($\hat{q}$) simply tells us whether the ratio Q/Q^N is growing, shrinking, or staying the same:

$\hat{q}$ greater than zero means q greater than q^N, so Q/Q^N rises
$\hat{q}$ less than zero means q less than q^N, so Q/Q^N falls
$\hat{q}$ equal to zero means q equals q^N, and Q/Q^N stays constant

Thus, for the economy to be in long-run equilibrium with Q/Q^N continuously equal to 1.0, the Q/Q^N ratio must stay constant, and so $\hat{q}$ must be equal to zero. Any other situation — for instance, the situation of $\hat{q} = 1.9$ during 1964–66 — can only be temporary.

In the theoretical diagram, Figure 8-7, an acceleration in demand growth initially is accompanied by only a partial adjustment of inflation, so that real GNP rises temporarily above natural real GNP. But then inflation begins to accelerate and eventually "overshoots" its long-run equilibrium value.

Exactly the same events occurred in the United States during the late

---

[6] Because $y = p + q$ by definition, as we originally learned in equation (8.2), it must be true that adjusted demand growth equals inflation plus adjusted real GNP growth ($\hat{y} \equiv p + \hat{q}$). Why? We start with equation (8.2):

$$y \equiv p + q \qquad \text{(a)}$$

Then we subtract q^N from each side of equation (a):

$$y - q^N \equiv p + q - q^N \qquad \text{(b)}$$

But since $\hat{y}$ is defined as $y - q^N$, and $\hat{q}$ is defined as $q - q^N$, the substitution of these definitions into (b) gives us:

$$\hat{y} \equiv p + \hat{q} \qquad \text{(c)}$$

In the example for 1960–63 in Table 8-2, the actual figures are:

$$1.5 = 1.5 + 0.0$$

In the example for 1964–66, the actual figures are:

$$4.4 = 2.4 + 1.9$$

In this case p and $\hat{q}$ do not add up exactly to $\hat{y}$, for the reason explained in note *a* of Table 8-2.

1960s. As shown in the final column of Table 8-2, during 1967–70 inflation accelerated to an average 4.5 percent rate, faster than adjusted nominal GNP growth ($\hat{y} = 3.4$) during the same interval. As a result, adjusted real GNP growth was negative ($\hat{q} = -1.2$), and the ratio Q/Q^N fell from its high 1966 level back below unity. By 1970 the United States was experiencing **"stagflation,"** the combination of a declining real GNP ratio (Q/Q^N) and accelerating inflation.[7]

THE ACCELERATION OF INFLATION, 1964–71

The quarter-by-quarter evolution of the inflation rate (p) and the ratio Q/Q^N during the period 1964–71 is traced in Figure 8-8. Here we see that the actual U.S. behavior of inflation and real GNP almost precisely mirrors the theoretical diagram, Figure 8-7. At first, in 1965 and 1966, the acceleration of nominal GNP growth caused the DG line to move rightward along a relatively fixed SP schedule, and a substantial increase in the Q/Q^N ratio was achieved at the cost of only a moderate acceleration in the inflation rate. After 1966, however, expectations of inflation appear to have begun a rapid adjustment upward, shifting up the SP schedule. As a result inflation accelerated to about 5 percent without any further increase in the Q/Q^N ratio after early 1966.[8]

But 1969 was not the end of the story. Expected inflation had not yet caught up with actual inflation, and the continuing adjustment of expectations shifted up the SP schedule even further. Inflation "overshot" its long-run equilibrium value and "used up" so much of nominal GNP growth that the output ratio Q/Q^N began to fall. The government added to the downward pressure on Q/Q^N by reducing nominal GNP growth substantially in 1970–71. By early 1971 the economy's real GNP level had fallen to only .983 of natural real GNP, lower than in early 1964, but now with an inflation rate of 5 percent instead of the initial 1.5 percent.

---

[7] *Stagflation* is a combination of the two words *stagnation* and *inflation*. A stagnation, or halting, of real GNP growth will cause the Q/Q^N ratio to fall if growth in natural real GNP proceeds uninterrupted.

[8] All inflation figures in Figure 8-8 refer to the rate of change of the GNP deflator over the previous four quarters. This four-quarter rate of change of the GNP deflator is equivalent to a four-quarter average of the one-quarter annual rate of change of the GNP deflator. The following shows the one-quarter rate of change of the GNP deflator during each quarter of 1969, and the rate of change in the four quarters ending in the last quarter of the year (1969:Q4):

	One-quarter rate of change at annual rate	Four-quarter rate of change
1969:Q1	4.28	
1969:Q2	5.18	
1969:Q3	6.51	
1969:Q4	5.03	5.25

INFLATION ACCELERATED IN THE 1960s AS THE THEORETICAL MODEL
WOULD HAVE PREDICTED

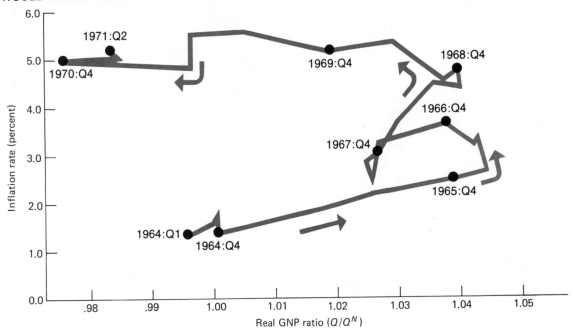

FIGURE 8–8

Inflation and the Output Ratio in the United States, 1964–71

Notice how faster demand growth initially raised the real GNP ratio, Q/Q^N. But
then in 1967 and 1968 expectations adjusted upward and the economy moved almost straight up until a reduction of demand growth brought about the recession
of 1970–71.

Source: Appendix B.

8-8 RECESSION AS A CURE FOR INFLATION

In our theoretical model as summarized in Figure 8-7, an increase in demand (nominal GNP) growth causes an acceleration of inflation. Eventually,
the inflation rate speeds up by as much as demand growth. In the same way
in the United States between 1964 and 1971 an acceleration in nominal
GNP growth caused inflation gradually to accelerate from 1.5 percent per
year in the early 1960s to about 5 percent per year in 1970–71.

It seems obvious that the most straightforward way of eliminating inflation would be to set the same process into reverse. By causing demand
growth (y) to slow down, the government could cause inflation to decelerate.

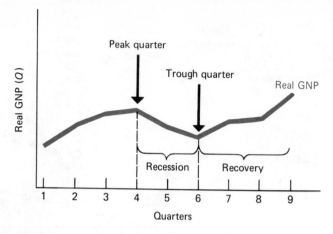

FIGURE 8–9

The Behavior of Real GNP During a Recession and Recovery

In every postwar recession real GNP has declined for at least two quarters, shown to occur in the diagram between quarters 4 and 6. Quarter 4 is called the "peak quarter" and quarter 6 is called the "trough quarter." The phase of the business cycle that begins after the trough quarter is called the "recovery," occurring here in quarters 7 through 9. Notice that in quarters 7 and 8 of the recovery the level of real GNP remains below the previous peak.

Inflation would not respond immediately by the full amount of the slowdown in y, just as inflation did not instantly respond to faster demand growth in 1964–66. But eventually a policy of "slow y" would lead to low inflation.

WHAT IS A RECESSION?

Yet such a policy was not put into effect in 1971, or indeed at any point during the 1970s. Why not? Because the slowness of the downward responsiveness of inflation to a deceleration in demand growth means that *during the transition period real GNP growth must be low*. It is quite possible that real GNP could actually decline, in which case the economy would be said to experience a **recession**.

The last quarter before the recession begins is called the cyclical "peak." The recession is said to begin in the first quarter in which real GNP declines (providing the decline lasts at least two quarters). The recession is said to end in the quarter when real GNP hits bottom, called the cyclical "trough." Once the economy has passed the "trough quarter," it is said to experience a "recovery." The relationships of these concepts can be depicted diagrammatically as in Figure 8-9.

THE "COLD TURKEY" REMEDY FOR INFLATION

The essential problem in stopping inflation is the slowness of adjustment of inflation to a deceleration in demand growth. If inflation responded instantly to a slowdown in nominal GNP growth, the elimination of inflation would be a painless process. The fact that policymakers have not carried out a sustained policy of substantially cutting demand growth in the 1970s suggests that the costs of stopping inflation are perceived to be substantial.

The response of inflation to a slowdown in nominal GNP growth can be explored in Figure 8-10. This figure is a "twin" of Figure 8-6 and shares its simplifying assumption that growth in natural real GNP is zero ($q^N = 0$). Thus actual demand growth (y) and "adjusted" demand growth ($\hat{y} = y - q^N$) are assumed to be the same. On the horizontal axis we plot actual real GNP (Q) and assume that natural real GNP (Q^N) remains fixed at a value of 100. In the case of this diagram, along the SP_2 line expected inflation is assumed to be 6 percent, the same as the actual inflation rate at point E_3.

The downward sloping red DG lines are drawn for an assumed fixed demand growth rate (y) and for an initial starting value of real GNP, $Q_0 = 100$. When demand growth is 6 percent, the upper red DG_1 line intersects the SP_2 and LP lines at point E_3, and the economy is in long-run equilibrium.

In Figure 8-10 we assume that the government introduces a policy sometimes called "cold turkey," suddenly reducing demand growth (y) from 6 percent to zero. The DG line, whose position depends on the value of y, instantly shifts downward by 6 percentage points from DG_1 to DG_0. If the position of the SP_2 line remains fixed, with people expecting inflation of 6 percent because inflation last period was 6 percent, then the economy will move to point K, the crossing point of the fixed SP_2 line with the new DG_0 line. The government's policy cuts inflation from 6 percent at point E_3 to 4 percent at K, but at the cost of a recession as real GNP falls from 100 to 96.

Notice that the move from E_3 to point K in Figure 8-10 represents an exact reversal of the adjustment from E_0 to point F in Figure 8-6. In both cases, the initial reaction of the economy is for the 6 percent change in nominal GNP (up in Figure 8-6, down here in Figure 8-10) to be divided into 2 percentage points of adjustment of inflation and 4 percentage points of adjustment in real GNP.

THE PERIOD OF ADJUSTMENT TO THE NEW LONG-RUN EQUILIBRIUM

When does the process of adjustment end? The vertical LP line shows all the different combinations of inflation and real GNP where expectations are correct. One such point on LP is at point E_0, where inflation is zero and thus is compatible in the long run with nominal GNP growth of zero. But to reach E_0, the SP line must go through that point, which requires that expected inflation fall to zero, and this is unlikely to occur until people see an inflation rate of zero actually occur.

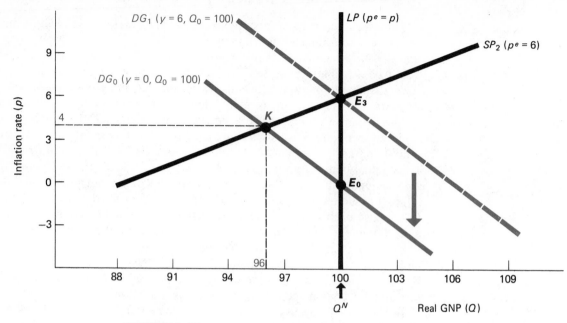

FIGURE 8-10

Effect on Inflation and Real GNP of a Slowdown in Demand Growth
from 6 Percent to Zero

Initially the economy is in a long-run equilibrium at point E_3, with expected inflation (p^e) equal to the actual inflation rate (p) of 6 percent. Demand growth is also
at 6 percent, and the relevant DG line is DG_1. A slowdown in demand growth to
zero shifts the DG line down by exactly 6 percentage points to DG_0. The various
possible combinations of inflation and next period's real GNP are shown along
DG_0. If the SP line stays fixed, with expected inflation remaining at 6 percent,
then the economy goes to point K, with a 2 percent drop in the inflation rate and
a 4 percent drop in real GNP from 100 to 96. Only if expected inflation dropped
instantly would the economy go immediately to a new long-run equilibrium position at point E_0.

Because individual households and firms are likely to take a "show me"
attitude, refusing to believe that inflation will slow down until they see such
a slowdown actually occur, the "cold turkey" cure for inflation is likely to
be a long and drawn-out process. Even if we make the optimistic assumption
that the weight (j) put on last period's inflation in forming expectations is 1.0
on an annual basis (that is, treating each "period" as lasting one year), the
economy's arrival at point E_0 would take more than a decade, as illustrated
in Figure 8-11.

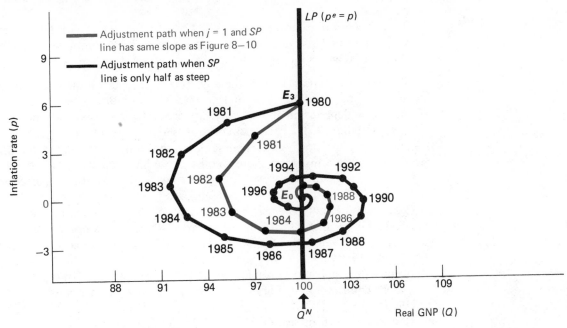

FIGURE 8–11

Alternative Adjustment Paths of Inflation and Real GNP to a Policy
That Cuts Demand Growth from 6 Percent in 1980 to Zero in
1981 and Thereafter

The red line between 1980 and 1981 traces exactly the same path as between E_3
and K in Figure 8–10. The black line shares the assumption of an expectation
adjustment coefficient (j) of unity, but as an alternative assumes that the SP line
is only half as steep as in previous diagrams in this chapter. The flatter the SP
line, the longer it takes for the economy to approach long-run equilibrium.

Why does the economy's period of adjustment last so long? Running our
eye along the red path in Figure 8-11, we note several phases of the adjustment process.

1. Between 1980 and 1982, both real GNP and the inflation rate decline.
   Because demand growth of zero is divided up between inflation and the
   change in real GNP ($y = p + q$), real GNP growth must be negative (real
   GNP must drop) as long as inflation is positive.
2. Starting in 1983, inflation along the red line becomes negative. Prices
   begin to fall. Thus real GNP can rise and still leave nominal GNP (aggregate demand) unchanged. This occurs between 1983 and 1987, as the

negative inflation rate allows real GNP to rise from about 95 to 101.5. Then in 1988 inflation becomes positive again, and real GNP again declines.

3. This process of alternating phases of positive inflation with falling real GNP, and negative inflation with rising real GNP, continues until the economy reaches its long-run equilibrium at point E_0.

The length of time taken for the adjustment depends on the speed of adjustment of expectations toward the long-run equilibrium value, $p^e = 0$. This, in turn, depends on how quickly expected inflation responds to changes in actual inflation. If the coefficient of adjustment of expectations (j) is unity, so that last period's change in the inflation rate is fully incorporated into this period's expectations, then the economy can adjust rapidly. But if the adjustment coefficient is only $j = 0.25$, for example, the adjustment period involves a slower response of inflation and a larger recession in real GNP.

The second factor determining the length of the adjustment period is the slope of the *SP* line itself. Since expected inflation does not respond (regardless of the value of j) until *actual* inflation responds to slower nominal GNP growth, everything depends on how the drop in y is initially divided between a drop in p and a drop in the real GNP growth rate q. In Figure 8-10 and along the red line in Figure 8-11, the initial drop from $y = 6$ to $y = 0$ is accompanied by a 2-percentage-point drop in inflation (p) and a 4-percentage-point drop in real GNP from 100 to 96. But what if the *SP* line is only half as steep, so that the same nominal GNP deceleration is divided with only a 1.2-percentage-point drop of inflation and 4.8 in real GNP? Along this hypothetical flatter *SP* line (which rises 1 unit for each rightward movement of 4 units in contrast to the 1-for-2 slope of the SP_2 line in Figure 8-10) the economy will suffer through a more prolonged adjustment path, as illustrated by the black line in Figure 8-11. Two decades will be required for the full adjustment to occur, instead of "only" one decade along the red path.

To summarize, the major obstacles to stopping inflation by a policy of dropping nominal GNP growth to zero are the following:

1. Inflation can't be ended without a recession unless expected inflation can be caused to drop suddenly. This is unlikely to occur, because people will wait for evidence that inflation is actually slowing down. The reduction of actual inflation below what people expect, in turn, requires a recession during which real GNP drops below natural real GNP. Only then will expectations of inflation begin to be adjusted downward.

2. In Figure 8-11 the recession phase of declining real GNP lasts two years along the red path and three years along the black path. But real GNP remains below natural real GNP for four years along the red path and six years along the black path. As we will learn in Chapter 10, the unemployment rate will remain high throughout this period when Q is below Q^N. Many people will lose their jobs as a cost of the government's anti-inflation policy, a reason that helps to explain why governments rarely have the courage to sustain such a policy for long.

8-9 CASE STUDY: THE BEHAVIOR OF WAGES IN POSTWAR RECESSIONS

A major point of the previous section was that the downward response of inflation to slower demand growth takes time, both because expectations are unlikely to adjust until people see actual inflation slow down, and because the slowing down of actual inflation initially is only a small fraction of the drop in demand growth. Why doesn't actual inflation respond fully to a change in demand growth? This question asks why Chapter 7's *SS* short-run supply schedule, and the *SP* short-run Phillips curve of Chapter 8, are positively sloped rather than vertical. One of the major reasons cited in Chapter 7 to explain why prices react slowly to shifts in demand growth was the existence of long-term wage agreements between firms and workers.

How are wages and prices related? On average over the years a firm can afford to boost wages faster than the increase in prices only if labor **productivity** is increasing. Over the period 1973–79, labor productivity in the United States increased at the annual rate of only about 1 percent. Thus the following would be possible combinations of inflation and wage growth:

	At point E_0 in Figure 8-11 (percent per annum)	At point E_3 in Figure 8-11 (percent per annum)
Inflation rate	0	6
Growth of labor productivity	1	1
Total, equals possible growth in wage rate	1	7

Notice that the growth of labor productivity is independent of the inflation rate. In short, firms could not afford an inflation rate of zero at point E_0 if the growth of wage rates were to remain at 7 percent while labor productivity grew only at 1 percent. Firms would gradually be bankrupted by the fast growth in wages unaccompanied by an offsetting growth in prices.

Inflation does not follow in the footsteps of wage rates every quarter. But over several years inflation does not deviate very far from wage growth minus productivity growth. Thus,

A good test of the ability of a recession to cause a lasting drop in inflation is to examine whether actual postwar recessions succeeded in cutting wage growth.

Figure 8-12 consists of five separate diagrams showing the adjustment of wage growth in each of the five postwar recessions (the 1980 recession had not proceeded far enough at press time to be included). Before examining each episode closely, let us stop and ask ourselves how we would expect wages to behave, on the basis of the previous sections.

1. In a short, sharp recession we would expect lower real GNP to cut wage growth as the economy moves southwest along its initial SP curve. But if policymakers end the recession before expectations have begun to adjust downward, the economy will move back up to the northeast along its original SP curve and wind up with as much wage growth as before the recession. The first two episodes in Figure 8-12, the 1948–50 and 1953–55 recessions, appear to have been too short to result in a substantial permanent downward movement of wage growth. Instead, wage growth dropped temporarily and then jumped back up as the economy neared a real GNP ratio (Q/Q^N) of unity.

2. In a long recession, we should expect to see a steady reduction in wage growth as expectations of inflation gradually decline. During the long period between 1957 and 1964 the economy remained below $Q/Q^N = 1.0$; a recovery during 1958–60 aborted and a second recession occurred in 1960–61. There appears to have been some decline in expectations of inflation. For instance, wage growth in the 1960–61 recession in Figure 8-12 appears to have been about 0.7 percentage point lower than in the same stage of the 1957–58 recession. By early 1964 wage growth was only about 2.5 percent, compared to 5.2 percent in 1957. The most notable aspect of the 1957–65 episode is the amazing slowness of the downward adjustment, less than 3 percentage points in seven years. This pace was even slower than the black path in Figure 8-11.

3. The fourth episode in 1970–72 was different. Inflation expectations continuously increased during the 1965–71 period. Thus in the 1970–71 recession wage growth actually increased, apparently indicating that the SP curve was still shifting up in response to higher inflation expectations, as people attempted to adjust to the acceleration of inflation that had surprised them in the previous five years. Unfor-

---

FIGURE 8–12 (facing page)

The Relationship between Wage Growth and the Real GNP Ratio (Q/Q^N) in Five Postwar Recessions

Each of the five frames of the diagram plots the rate of change of wages (over the preceding four quarters) against the real GNP ratio (Q/Q^N). The five frames correspond to the five postwar recessions. The main conclusion is that wage change responds in a highly variable manner to recessions. In 1949 and 1954 there was a sharp and prompt downward adjustment of wage rates. During the long period of low Q/Q^N between 1957 and 1964, there was a prompt downward response in 1958 but then little further downward adjustment between 1960 and 1964. In 1970–71 wage growth actually accelerated during the recession. In the final episode wage growth slowed down markedly, but much of this seems to have been due to the end of temporary supply shocks rather than to the impact of the recession itself.

RECESSIONS HAVE HELD DOWN WAGE GROWTH, BUT BY A HIGHLY VARIABLE AMOUNT

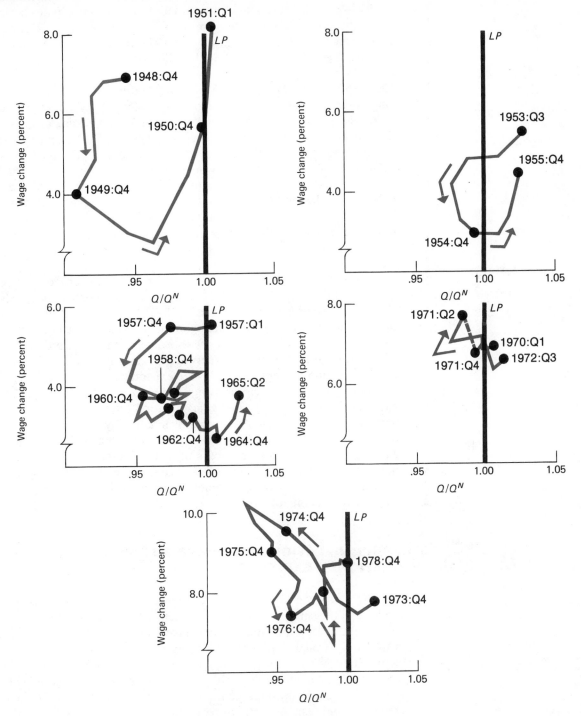

tunately, we do not know what would have happened to wage growth in 1971–72 if the economy had been left alone to adjust by itself, because the Nixon administration introduced wage and price controls on August 15, 1971. The data for late 1971 and 1972 show a sudden drop in wage growth, suggesting that the primary cause was the control program.

4. 1974–76 was another period of low Q/Q^N. But wage growth slowed much more rapidly than in the earlier recessions. Why? Inflation and wage change were both abnormally high in 1974 because of the coincidence of two unprecedented events: the oil and food supply shocks and the termination of the Nixon wage-price control program in May 1974. In short, the 1974–76 slowdown in inflation expectations, which allowed the SP curve and wage growth both to drop substantially, can be partly explained by the realization of ordinary people that the supply shocks were over, abnormal times had ended, and more normal times were ahead. We discuss this period more fully in the next chapter.

Summary: Wage growth has behaved differently in each postwar recession, mainly because inflation expectations responded to the special circumstances of each episode. In 1948–50 and 1953–55, the recessions were too short to allow enough time for a substantial downward adjustment in expectations. In 1970–71, expectations were still adjusting upward to the previous years of accelerating inflation caused by too-low unemployment. In 1974–76 expectations dropped rapidly, mainly because of the abnormal wage and price behavior in 1974. Thus we are left with the long, slow adjustment of 1957–65 as perhaps the best evidence of the potential for curing inflation by deliberate creation of high unemployment. That episode suggests that inflation can be cured only by causing many years of lost real GNP. And the task is now even more difficult than in 1957 because the rate of wage growth in early 1980 was 9 percent, much faster than the 1 percent rate of wage growth compatible with zero inflation.

8-10 STOPPING INFLATION, THE "CREDIBILITY EFFECT," AND RATIONAL EXPECTATIONS

For many years the argument of the preceding two sections has been effectively used to scare off policymakers intent on stopping inflation. "Any serious attempt to stop inflation," policymakers are warned, "will force the nation to suffer through a protracted period of low output and high unemployment. Hundreds of billions of dollars of real GNP will be lost during the period of adjustment, as along the red and black paths in Figure 8-11." The key ingredients in this argument are the assumption that the SP line is relatively flat, and that expectations of future inflation adjust only after actual inflation has begun to slow down.

THE "CREDIBILITY EFFECT"

But in recent years another group of economists has balked at accepting the conclusion of sections 8-8 and 8-9 that stopping inflation must involve a protracted loss of real GNP. William Fellner, a former Yale professor now at the American Enterprise Institute, argues that prices respond slowly to slow demand growth because the *public has come to expect policymakers to reverse themselves quickly*.[9] Firms cut prices in recessions less than they used to before the past decade because they expect policymakers to over-react to declining real GNP, and thus to boost nominal GNP growth after only a short recession. If the government were only to adopt a "credible" policy of consistent aggregate demand restraint and hold down the growth of nominal GNP for five years or more, Fellner argues, firms and workers would adapt. Seeing that government nominal GNP creation would not bail them out, firms and workers would be more willing to accept price and wage cuts in a recession.

The most important and valid ingredient in the credibility hypothesis is the idea that the slopes of schedules such as *SP* are not fixed and immutable. Rather, the behavior of workers and firms that generates these slopes will be sensitive to perceptions about future government policy. If we take a long historical view and look back to the period before World War I, it is clear that prices responded much more promptly to swings in nominal GNP growth than they have in the postwar period. Thus in principle the credibility hypothesis makes sense, for if people believed that policymakers now would keep nominal GNP growth (adjusted for natural real GNP growth) rigidly at zero, and would not allow nominal GNP growth to accelerate again (as during 1967–68, 1972–73, and 1977–79), they would change their wage- and price-setting behavior.

THE RATIONAL EXPECTATIONS HYPOTHESIS

The hypothesis that expectations are formed "rationally" simply means that people form their expectations on the basis of all information, including any available information on the probable future actions of policymakers.[10]

---

[9] A short and readable statement is William Fellner, "The Credibility Effect and Rational Expectations: Implications of the Gramlich Study," *Brookings Papers on Economic Activity*, vol. 10, no. 1 (1979), pp. 167–178. The argument is developed more fully in William Fellner, *Towards a Reconstruction of Macroeconomics: Problems of Theory and Policy* (Washington: American Enterprise Institute, 1976).

[10] A readable introduction to the rational expectations approach is contained in Bennett T. McCallum, "The Significance of Rational Expectations Theory," *Challenge* (January/February 1980), pp. 37–43. Most of the original articles on the rational expectations hypothesis are quite technical. See, for instance, Thomas J. Sargent and Neil Wallace, "Rational Expectations and the Theory of Economic Policy," *Journal of Monetary Economics*, vol. 2 (April 1976), pp. 169–183. A number of recent papers, and a discussion of important issues, are contained in Stanley Fischer, *Rational Expectations and Economic Policy* (Chicago: University of Chicago Press for the National Bureau of Economic Research, 1980).

Thus, when people see policymakers slow down nominal GNP growth, they form inflation expectations on the basis of (a) their knowledge of how inflation reacted to swings in nominal GNP growth in previous historical episodes, and (b) their knowledge of whether policymakers allowed a temporary slowdown in nominal GNP growth to be reversed in order to end a recession *or* whether policymakers maintained their policy for a long time.

For instance, if people knew that a slowdown in adjusted nominal GNP growth from 6 to zero percent caused inflation to slow down to zero, and if they expected policymakers to maintain zero adjusted demand growth forever, they would instantly drop their expected rate of inflation from 6 to zero. Instead of suffering through a protracted recession, with slumping real GNP, the economy would instantly adjust downward vertically from E_3 to E_0 in Figure 8-11. This would be made possible by an instant 6-percentage-point downward movement in the SP line immediately following the 6-percentage-point downward movement in the DG line.

CRITICISMS OF THE CREDIBILITY HYPOTHESIS

The skeptics divide their criticism of Fellner's credibility hypothesis into two parts. First, they argue, the government has no way to convince the public that its determination to stop inflation is now more serious than in the past, and only the passage of time can allow the public to judge the government's claims of credibility. Second, the historical evidence suggests that the behavior of wages and prices was not very different under the restrictive monetary policy pursued by policymakers in the late 1950s than under the overly expansive policy pursued since 1967.

The first argument of the skeptics deals with the fundamental nature of the government policymaking process. The monetary and fiscal policies that help to determine whether demand growth is 6 or zero percent per annum are not set by a permanent dictator. Instead, they result from the decisions of numerous individuals in Washington, D.C., many of whom will hold their jobs for only a year or two, and whose current attempts to appear "credible" do not bind the decisions of their successors.

The second argument is that even a wide belief that the government will maintain a tight aggregate demand policy does not guarantee instant responsiveness of prices and wages. The best evidence of this comes from the 1957–64 period. In rapid succession the 1957–58 recession was followed by another recession in 1960. Slow monetary growth in 1959–60 and a tight lid on government spending were the direct causes of the 1960 recession. Particularly after creating the second recession in three years, policymakers had proved the credibility of their determination to maintain slow nominal GNP growth. And yet we have seen in Figure 8-12 that four years were necessary between 1957 and 1961 to reduce wage growth by just 2 percentage points, from 5.0 to 3.0 percent per year. This historical episode is the basis for the claim by the skeptics that even a credible government cannot convince individuals to cut the rate of wage and price growth rapidly. And in fact the problem of introducing a credible anti-inflation policy in the 1980s is a much more difficult one than in 1957, both because inflation is so much higher now and because in the 1960s and 1970s people have seen many episodes of the government's reversing itself within a short period.

CRITICISMS OF THE RATIONAL EXPECTATIONS HYPOTHESIS

The assumption that people use all available information when forming expectations is very convincing, but its implications depend entirely on the kind of market being discussed. "Auction" prices—for instance, those on the New York Stock Exchange or Chicago Board of Trade—are free to move from day to day and hour to hour. All available information is already incorporated into these prices, including the best guess of purchasers regarding the likely next step of government policy. If someone knew for certain that the government was going to slow monetary growth, and that this would boost stock market prices, he would be needlessly wasting the chance to make a profit if he did not take advantage of his knowledge.

But stopping inflation is different. As we have seen, inflation cannot be halted unless wage growth slows down to the modest rate of 1 percent per year compatible with zero inflation. Yet wages are not like stock prices. They do not rise and fall from day to day and hour to hour. Instead, many unionized workers enter into contracts that last for three years, each contract having a different expiration date. Imagine a situation in which the government has slowed adjusted demand growth to zero, but inflation is proceeding at 6 percent and wage growth at 7 percent. Will a union such as the Teamsters at the expiration of its contract be willing to settle for an annual wage increase of only 1 percent, when other recently negotiated contracts have called for a 7 percent wage increase? The Teamsters will be unwilling to make this sacrifice by themselves, because they know that the 7 percent wage increases built into contracts with one or two more years left to run will make it impossible for inflation to reach zero over that time period. No single union or group of workers will be willing to make this sacrifice when other unions are enjoying rapid wage increases under previously negotiated contracts.

> *Thus it is the U.S. system of three-year decentralized wage bargaining with staggered contract expiration dates that makes stopping inflation such a prolonged process. And although unionized workers are only a minority, the wage patterns set in their negotiations have an important effect on nonunionized workers as well.*

In short, the rational expectations approach, while perfectly valid for auction markets such as the New York Stock Exchange, cannot be applied to the problem of macroeconomic adjustment of inflation and real GNP. For its validity depends on the perfect flexibility of wages and prices, since it is based on the assumption that individuals will instantly adjust wages and prices in response to policy actions they expect the government to take. The institutions of long-term labor contracts and of price agreements between firms that last for several weeks or months undermine the attempt to apply rational expectations to macroeconomic policy.[11]

SUMMARY

1. The fundamental cause of inflation is excessive growth in aggregate demand, or nominal GNP. In long-run equilibrium, when actual inflation turns out to be exactly what people anticipate, the pace of that inflation depends only on the growth rate of aggregate demand adjusted for the growth of natural real GNP. Zero adjusted demand growth ($\hat{y}$) is necessary for the economy to be in long-run equilibrium with zero inflation.

2. Because a high rate of demand growth is sustainable only if it is fueled by a continuous increase in the nominal money supply, in the long run inflation is a monetary phenomenon. The Federal Reserve, by choosing growth rates for the money supply over a decade, determines roughly what the inflation rate will be over that decade.

3. In the short run actual inflation may be higher or lower than expected, and real GNP can differ from long-run equilibrium natural real GNP. An acceleration of demand growth in the short run goes partially into an acceleration of inflation, but also partly into an acceleration of growth in real GNP. But when expectations of inflation catch up to actual inflation, the economy will return to natural real GNP.

4. The response of inflation to an acceleration in demand growth depends on the slope of the short-run Phillips curve (SP) and the speed with which expectations of inflation respond to changes in the actual inflation rate. The flatter is SP, and the slower is the adjustment of expectations, the longer it takes for inflation to respond to faster nominal GNP growth, and the longer is the temporary expansion of real GNP.

5. The 1964–70 period in the United States provides the classic example of the gradual response of inflation to a permanent acceleration in demand growth. Inflation in 1960–63 averaged 1.5 percent per annum but by 1970

---

[11] For a short discussion of these issues, see Robert J. Gordon, "The Theory of Domestic Inflation," *American Economic Review,* vol. 67 (February 1977), pp. 128–134. Also see Robert J. Gordon, "Recent Developments in the Theory of Inflation and Unemployment," *Journal of Monetary Economics,* vol. 2 (April 1976), pp. 185–220. Another critique is Franco Modigliani, "The Monetarist Controversy or, Should We Forsake Stabilization Policies?" *American Economic Review,* vol. 67 (March 1977), pp. 1–19. McCallum's article in footnote 10 questions whether it is efficient for workers to agree to long-term labor contracts but does not contradict our conclusion that slow wage adjustment undermines the rational expectations argument.

had accelerated to about 5 percent. And, after a temporary boom, real GNP by 1970 had fallen below natural real GNP.

6. A permanent end to inflation requires that adjusted demand growth return to zero. But this will cause a temporary recession in real GNP, the length and intensity of which will depend on the slope of the SP curve and the speed of adjustment of expectations.

7. The slow downward adjustment of wage growth during 1957–61 is important evidence that a substantial time period is required for inflation to adjust downward.

8. Some economists argue that past historical evidence is no guide to the consequences of a "credible" government policy to stop inflation, but people will take some time before they will believe that the new government policy is here to stay. And the slow response of wages during 1957–61 did occur when the government was pursuing a widely perceived anti-inflationary policy.

9. Some economists have argued that expectations are formed rationally, and that prices respond promptly to government policy changes that people anticipate in advance. But this hypothesis neglects the role of long-term wage contracts, which prevent quick price adjustment even if everyone knows exactly what the government is doing.

A LOOK AHEAD

An acceleration in demand growth is not the only cause of inflation. In the 1970s nominal GNP growth was quite stable, yet inflation exhibited volatile accelerations and decelerations. In Chapter 9 we learn how to use the SP and DG lines to analyze "supply-shock" inflation caused by a jump in oil prices and by other causes. Whereas in Chapter 8 an acceleration in demand growth causes the inflation rate and real GNP to rise initially, in Chapter 9 we find that supply inflation is accompanied by a fall in real GNP. Chapter 9 will also examine price controls and other policies for stopping inflation that do not rely on manipulating demand growth.

CONCEPTS

Inflation rate
Short-run Phillips curve (SP)
Long-run Phillips curve (LP)
Expected rate of inflation
Demand growth schedule (DG)
Adaptive expectations
Adjusted demand growth ($\hat{y}$)
Adjusted real GNP growth ($\hat{q}$)

Stagflation
Recession
Recovery
Productivity
Cyclical peak and trough
Credibility hypothesis
Rational expectations hypothesis

QUESTIONS FOR REVIEW

1 Explain why the *SP* curve slopes upward to the right.

2 What is the main factor discussed in this chapter that shifts the *SP* curve?

3 What is the difference between the *SS* curve of Chapter 7 and the *SP* curve of Chapter 8? Between the factors that shift the two curves?

4 What is true at every point along the *LP* line?

5 How does the *LP* line relate to the *QQ* line of Chapter 7?

6 Why must the rate of adjusted demand growth ($\hat{y}$) be equal to the rate of inflation (p) in the long run?

7 If real GNP in the initial period is $Q_0 = 97$, what will be the level of real GNP in the next period (Q_1) for the following combinations of demand growth and inflation rates?

$\hat{y}$	p	Q_1 (fill in)
0	0	_____
6	6	_____
0	3	_____
3	0	_____

Indicate how your answers would change if Q_0 were initially 100 instead of 97.

8 In which direction will the following events shift the *DG* schedule? Will the shift be temporary or permanent?

a. A permanent one-step increase in the level of the nominal money supply.
b. A permanent increase in the rate of growth of the nominal money supply.
c. A one-step increase in the level of real government spending.
d. An increase in the personal income tax from one rate to another higher rate.

9 When there is an increase in adjusted demand growth from zero to three percent, and there is no adjustment of the expected rate of inflation ($g = 0$), what is the inflation rate after one period? What is the increase in the inflation rate and the level of real GNP in the long run after the process of adjustment has been completed? (**Hint:** Assume that the *SP* schedule has the same slope as in the diagrams of Chapter 8).

10 When there is an increase in adjusted demand growth from zero to 3 percent, and the coefficient of adjustment of expectations is unity ($g = 1$), what is the inflation rate after one period? During the process of adjustment, does the inflation rate ever rise above 3 percent? Why?

What is the level of real GNP in the long run after the process of adjustment has been completed? Compare your answers with those to question 9.

11 In deciding whether or not to attempt to reduce the inflation rate by restricting the rate of demand growth, the president of the United States must weigh the short-run loss of output and employment against the long-run gain to society of having lower inflation. Explain why his choice is likely to be influenced by (a) the slope of the SP line and (b) the coefficient of adjustment of expectations (j).

9 Supply Inflation: Its Causes and Cures

Since 1970 the Phillips curve has
become an unidentified flying object.

—Arthur M Okun[1]

9-1 THE NEW IMPORTANCE OF SUPPLY-SIDE ECONOMICS

In the previous chapter our explanation of inflation focused on the behavior of nominal GNP growth, which can be controlled (within limits) by monetary and fiscal policy. Let nominal GNP growth accelerate permanently, from one rate to a new higher rate, and inflation will exhibit a gradual but permanent acceleration. If inflation is to be slowed down permanently, nominal GNP growth must lead the way by experiencing a permanent deceleration.

Yet this approach, while yielding a remarkably accurate explanation of the acceleration of inflation in the United States during the years 1964–70, cannot by itself explain the highly variable inflation experience of the United States since 1970. In the decade of the 1970s adjusted nominal GNP growth ($\hat{y}$) has averaged 7.0 percent, providing a good guide to the average rate of inflation (p) over the same 1970–79 period, 6.8 percent.[2] But the *timing* of fluctuations in $\hat{y}$ was a poor guide to fluctuations in p. In fact, the lowest $\hat{y}$ of the decade was experienced in early 1975, when p was fastest.

In this chapter we introduce new factors that can explain why the inflation rate was so unstable in the 1970s. In Chapter 8 the only cause of shifts in the SP schedule was changing expectations of inflation. But now we will see that there is an additional source of SP shifts, which we call "supply shocks." These can take the form of a boost in oil prices engineered by the

---

[1] "Postwar Macroeconomic Performance," in M. S. Feldstein (ed.), *The American Economy in Transition* (Chicago: University of Chicago Press, 1980).

[2] The average figures for 1970–79 were $y = 10.27$ percent, $p = 6.82$ percent, $q = 3.22$ percent, and $q^N = 3.32$ percent. The sum of $p + q$ is slightly less than y, for reasons explained in note a to Table 8-2.

OPEC nations, or a jump in farm prices caused by a poor harvest—both events that shift the *SP* line upward even if inflation expectations remain the same. Tax increases and other cost-increasing government policies can also shift *SP* upward. Other events can shift the *SP* line downward, including price controls, tax reductions, and decreases in the relative price of oil or farm products.

The initial impact of a shift in *SP* is generally to raise inflation and reduce real GNP, assuming that the growth of nominal GNP remains the same. After that, the response of the economy depends on how nominal GNP responds, and how expectations adjust to the supply shock. In this chapter we will examine alternative responses that policymakers may adopt and examine the effect of supply shocks on the economy in the 1970s. We will also discuss several suggested cures for inflation that do not rely on control of nominal GNP growth.

9-2 CASE STUDY: INFLATION AND ADJUSTED NOMINAL GNP GROWTH IN THE 1970s

In this section we look in more detail at the basic behavior of nominal GNP (demand) growth and inflation in the 1970s. By definition demand growth adjusted for growth in natural real GNP ($\hat{y} = y - q^N$) must be divided between inflation (p) and growth in real GNP relative to natural real GNP ($\hat{q} = q - q^N$).[3] When $\hat{y}$ exceeds p, $\hat{q}$ is positive, and the rapid growth of real GNP relative to natural real GNP allows the ratio Q/Q^N to increase. The reverse occurs when p exceeds $\hat{y}$. In Figure 9-1 we see that $\hat{y}$ and p were roughly similar on average during the 1970–80 period, but this similarity disguises the ups and downs of $\hat{y}$ and p in particular episodes.

As the decade of the 1970s began, $\hat{y}$ was low, reflecting the restrictive monetary policy introduced in 1969 to fight inflation. But inflation did not respond immediately. In frustration, the Nixon administration introduced wage and price controls in August 1971, and we can see the modest downward response of inflation between late 1971 and early 1973. Perhaps because they thought that inflation was now freed from dependence on nominal GNP growth, policymakers allowed $\hat{y}$ to rise to the highest rate experienced in the previous twenty years. The pink-shaded gap between $\hat{y}$ and p during 1972 allowed for a large positive value of $\hat{q}$, real GNP (Q) rose relative to natural real GNP (Q^N), and the ratio Q/Q^N rose well above unity. Because a presidential election was held in November 1972, many critics have accused the Nixon administration of "engineering a reelection economic boom."

Starting in early 1973, the inflation rate (p) and adjusted nominal GNP growth ($\hat{y}$) began moving in opposite directions. Inflation was stimulated

---

[3] **Review:** See section 8-7, especially pp. 227–229.

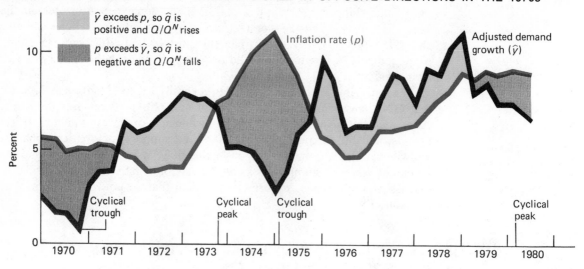

FIGURE 9–1

Four-Quarter Growth Rates of the GNP Deflator and Nominal GNP
Adjusted for Natural Real GNP, 1970–80

This figure compares the inflation rate (p) with adjusted demand growth ($\hat{y}$) over
the interval between 1970:Q1 and 1980:Q2. At the beginning of the decade $\hat{y}$ was
low, reflecting the desire of policymakers to restrain inflation. But inflation did
not decline until 1971:Q3, when wage and price controls were introduced. Rapid $\hat{y}$
and slow inflation in 1972 created a real GNP boom. But $\hat{y}$ decelerated during
1973–75 while inflation climbed to unprecedented heights as a result of higher oil
and food prices and the end of price controls. These temporary factors ended in
1976–77, allowing inflation to abate while nominal GNP growth accelerated. Further supply shocks in 1978–79 boosted inflation, but continued high $\hat{y}$ delayed the
subsequent recession until 1980.

by the loosening of price controls in early 1973 and their complete removal in May 1974; by a doubling of farm prices between mid-1972 and
early 1974; and by a quadrupling of the price of oil by the OPEC oil
cartel in late 1973 and early 1974. The combined effect of these supply
shocks, together with the high level of the real GNP ratio Q/Q^N experienced in early 1973, caused inflation to accelerate from less than 4 percent in late 1972 to almost 12 percent in early 1975.

Each of the supply-shock factors, however, was temporary. This, together with the direct effect of the recession on inflation (moving the
economy leftward along the SP schedule), caused inflation to decline to
about 6 percent in 1977.

Beginning in 1978:Q1 inflation began to accelerate, and this acceleration continued through early 1980. Faster inflation surprised many ob-

servers, who expected that inflation would continue to slow down as long as the Q/Q^N ratio remained below unity. Both demand and supply factors can help to explain faster inflation in 1978–80, as we shall see later in this chapter.

9-3 THE ADJUSTMENT OF INFLATION AND REAL GNP TO A SUPPLY SHOCK

This brief review of economic events in the 1970s suggests that a supply shock, as occurred in 1973–75 and again in 1978–80, will make inflation accelerate. But what happens to real GNP? This depends on whether adjusted nominal GNP growth ($\hat{y}$) stays the same, falls as in 1974 and 1979–80, or rises as in 1978. The relationship between supply shocks, inflation, and real GNP can be illustrated on the same theoretical diagram that we developed in Chapter 8.

INITIAL EFFECTS OF AN UPWARD SHIFT IN *SP*

Point E_3 in Figure 9-2 depicts a situation of long-run equilibrium. Expected inflation and actual inflation are both equal to nominal GNP growth. Once again, to keep the diagram simple, we assume that natural real GNP growth is zero, so that actual and adjusted nominal GNP growth (y and $\hat{y}$) are the same. The upward-sloping SP_2 schedule assumes that expected inflation is 6 percent. The downward-sloping DG_1 line reflects both the assumed 6 percent growth rate of demand (nominal GNP), and the economy's initial position at $Q_0 = 100$. Starting from that level of real GNP at point E_3, higher inflation will "use up" more of demand growth and force real GNP to fall along the DG_1 line; lower inflation will leave more of demand growth "left over" and allow real GNP to increase.

Now let us assume that the OPEC oil cartel suddenly doubles the price of oil over the course of a year, as occurred in 1979, and let us assume that its action is sufficient *to add 3 extra percentage points to the inflation rate at any given level of real GNP*. The 3 extra points of inflation are reflected in the upward shift of *SP* from SP_2 to SP_3. This increase occurs because more expensive oil not only raises the price of gasoline and heating oil to consumers, but also raises the price of competing sources of energy (electricity, coal, natural gas).

Any supply shock—for instance, the increasing relative price of oil in this case—shifts the *SP* curve.[4] The upward shift in *SP* in Figure 9-2 reflects our

---

[4] The phrase *relative price* means the price of a particular product *relative* to the GNP deflator. If we designate the price of oil as P^O, then the relative price of oil is P^O/P. Starting from an initial situation with both the price of oil and GNP deflator equal to 1.0, a doubling of the price of oil to 2.0, together with an increase in the GNP deflator to 1.08 (as at point L in Figure 9-2) would raise the relative price P^O/P to $2.0/1.08 = 1.85$.

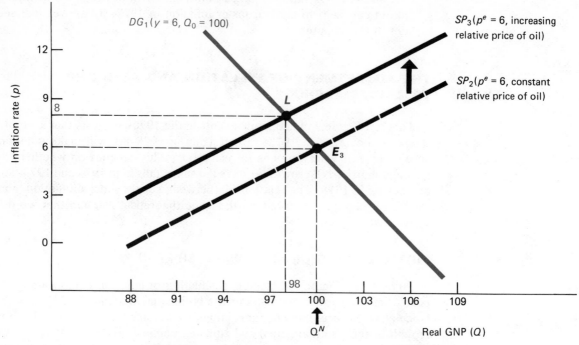

FIGURE 9–2

Effect on Inflation and Real GNP of a Supply Shock
That Shifts up the *SP* Line by 3 Percentage Points

The economy is assumed to start at point E_3, with an initial real GNP of
$Q_0 = 100$, an expected inflation equal to nominal GNP growth, and an initial
inflation rate of 6 percent. Assuming that nominal GNP growth remains at 6 percent, the red DG_1 line is a menu of possible ways that nominal GNP growth can
be divided. If the *SP* line is shifted up 3 percentage points by an increase in the
relative price of oil, the economy goes in the next period to point *L*, where inflation has risen by 2 percent to 8 percent, and real GNP has experienced an exactly
offsetting drop of 2 percent.

assumption that the oil price increases sufficiently to boost inflation by 3 percentage points *at any given level of real GNP.* But real GNP does not stay
unchanged. The economy moves to a new short-run equilibrium at point *L*,
with 6 percent nominal GNP growth divided between an 8 percent inflation
rate and a −2 percent growth in real GNP. That is, real GNP *falls* by 2 percent from 100 to 98.

POLICY RESPONSES TO SUPPLY SHOCKS

Does the government have any way to escape the simultaneous worsening of inflation and decline in real GNP? It can keep real GNP fixed if it is willing to accept more inflation. It can keep inflation from accelerating if it is willing to accept a greater decline in real GNP. Or, as at point L, it can reach a "compromise solution," accepting somewhat more inflation and less real GNP. Each of the three options has a name, as illustrated in Figure 9-3.

A *neutral policy* is one that maintains fixed demand growth (y). Because the supply shock boosts inflation, and inflation takes up a larger amount of demand growth, real GNP must fall, as at point L in Figures 9-2 and 9-3. If we allow for growth in natural real GNP, the ratio Q/Q^N must fall.

An *extinguishing policy* is one that attempts to eliminate entirely the extra inflation caused by the supply shock.[5] This requires cutting demand growth and thus causing the DG line to shift down vertically until it intersects the SP line at point M, where the inflation rate is 6 percent, the same as at point E_3. But notice that real GNP must now decline from 100 to 94 at point M, in contrast to the neutral policy that causes real GNP to decline only to 98 at point L. Why is the extra 4 percent decline in Q necessary? To "extinguish" the extra 2 percentage points of inflation that occur at L compared to M, real GNP must be cut by 4 percentage points, because the slope of the SP line is assumed to be 4 units in the horizontal direction for every 2 units in the vertical direction.

An *accommodating policy* is one that attempts to maintain real GNP intact at point N. To do this, inflation must be allowed to rise by the full extent of the vertical shift in SP, so that inflation jumps from 6 to 9 percent per year.

Summary: A supply shock causes the SP curve to shift up vertically — in the example of Figures 9-2 and 9-3, by 3 percentage points. If the economy remains in the same horizontal position with real GNP unchanged, as at point N, demand growth must increase, and inflation will accelerate by the full 3 percentage points. For policymakers to achieve a lesser acceleration of inflation at point L, demand growth must remain constant. To achieve no acceleration of inflation at point M, real GNP must be allowed to fall, and demand growth must slow to zero.

THE RESPONSE OF EXPECTED INFLATION

We are not yet in a position to decide whether an extinguishing, neutral, or accommodative policy is "best," because we have not yet examined the

---

[5] The phrase *extinguishing policy* was introduced in Edward M. Gramlich, "Macro Policy Responses to Price Shocks," *Brookings Papers on Economic Activity,* vol. 10, no. 1 (1979), pp. 125–178.

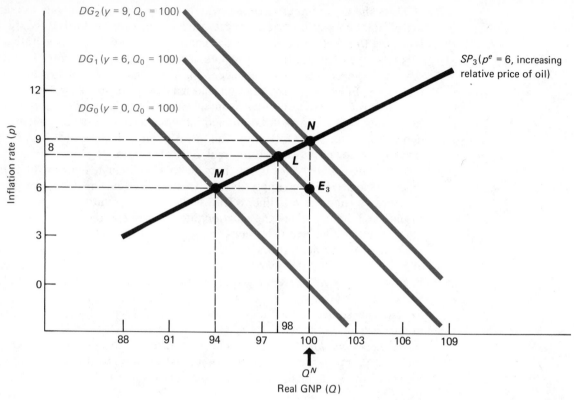

FIGURE 9–3

Alternative Effects of a Supply Shock with Alternative Nominal GNP Growth Rates of 9, 6, and Zero Percent

The SP_3 line is identical to that in Figure 9–2 and represents the same assumption that an increasing relative price of oil has pushed up the inflation rate by 3 percent at each level of real GNP. The three red DG lines show alternative responses of policymakers. DG_1 assumes a 6 percent value of y and is copied from Figure 9–2. This represents a "neutral policy," and the economy goes to point L. DG_0 assumes a zero percent value of y and represents an "extinguishing policy," causing the economy to go to point M. DG_2 assumes a 9 percent value of y and represents an "accommodative policy," causing the economy to go to point N.

adjustment of the economy in subsequent periods after the supply shock has occurred. Along the SP_3 line inflation is 3 percentage points higher than along the SP_2 line in Figure 9-2, because of the inflationary effect of the higher relative price of oil, but *expected inflation has not changed and still remains at 6 percent.* This causes no problems under the extinguishing policy option, because the actual inflation rate at point *M* in Figure 9-3 is equal to the 6 percent inflation that people expect. But at points *L* and *N*, the neutral and accommodating policy options, inflation turns out to be faster than people expect. Will expected inflation adjust upward, further shifting the *SP* upward in a vertical direction?

Temporary Supply Shock. One type of supply shock is a crop failure, caused by an untimely freeze or drought. The result is likely to be a temporary increase in the level of prices, followed by a return in the price index to its previous level. This occurred in the winter of 1977, when an unusually severe freeze ruined fruit and vegetable crops in Florida at the end of January, causing an increase in prices in February and March. But then normal weather returned and the price index for these products dropped to its initial level. The following diagram assumes that initially the inflation rate is zero:

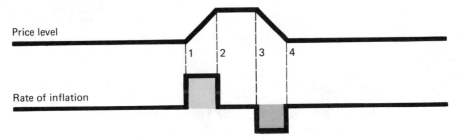

In the diagram, at time 1 the price level begins to rise, increasing the rate of inflation (which is, after all, just the rate of change of the price level). At time 2 the price index levels off, so that the rate of inflation returns to zero. At time 3 the price level begins to fall, so that the rate of inflation becomes negative, and finally both the price level and rate of inflation return at time 4 to their initial values. This type of supply shock is unlikely to cause any adjustment of the expected inflation rate, because most people will correctly view the initial inflation (indicated by the pink-shaded area) as a temporary phenomenon.

Permanent Supply Shock. The OPEC oil price increases of 1974 and 1979 permanently raised the level of oil prices. Increasing energy prices pushed up the rate of inflation as firms adjusted to the higher price of oil, but then no further direct impact was felt on the price level. This type of "permanent" supply shock can be depicted as follows:

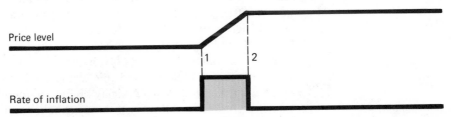

This diagram duplicates the previous one for the first two time periods during which the price index rises to a new higher level. The difference is that no subsequent drop in the price level occurs; the OPEC oil cartel did not allow the price of oil to return to its pre-1973 level, unlike the co-operative Florida fruits and vegetables that were willing to renew themselves after the freeze of 1977.

Even the permanent supply shock, such as the steplike increase in the price of oil by the OPEC oil cartel, may not cause the expected rate of inflation (p^e) to shift upward if people think that the shock is a one-time-only event. If there is no shift in p^e, then after the shock has occurred the short-run Phillips curve shifts back down from SP_3 to SP_2 in Figure 9-2, and real GNP shifts back up to its initial value at $Q = 100$. In this fortunate situation, policymakers are free to eliminate the temporary drop in real GNP from point E_3 to point L or point M by temporarily raising demand growth. In this case of full accommodation the economy would move from the initial point E_3 up to point N in Figure 9-3, and then back to point E_3 after the end of the effect of the rising relative oil price. Demand growth would temporarily rise while the SP curve is at SP_3, and then go back to the initial rate when the SP curve returns to SP_2.

9-4 OBSTACLES TO ACCOMMODATION OF SUPPLY SHOCKS

The conclusion that demand growth should be temporarily raised in response to a supply shock, in order to minimize the temporary decline in real GNP that would otherwise occur, is subject to a number of important qualifications. These refer to reduced productivity, the cost-of-living escalation of wages, and international repercussions.

REDUCED PRODUCTIVITY

Energy is an input into the production process, along with capital and labor. When the price of energy increases as the result of an OPEC oil shock, business firms will naturally try to economize on the use of energy. Temperatures in buildings may be lowered, perhaps reducing the efficiency of employees; bakers may lower the temperatures in their ovens; some equipment that uses a relatively large amount of fuel may be discarded, thus reducing the total amount that a factory can produce. All these factors may tend to reduce the economy's level of natural real GNP (Q^N), in contrast to Figures 9-2 and 9-3, which assume an unchanged level of Q^N. Any attempt by policymakers to maintain the original level of real GNP (Q), when Q^N had fallen, would imply a higher level of the real GNP ratio Q/Q^N than in the initial situation, and this would tend to put upward pressure on the inflation rate. Policymakers may be forced, therefore, to allow real GNP to decline somewhat following a supply shock, but there is no simple way for them to determine how much Q^N has fallen.

COST-OF-LIVING ESCALATORS

Many labor contracts in the United States and other countries include "cost-of-living escalators," sometimes called "COLA" clauses (for cost-of-living adjustment). Another name for COLA is "wage indexation." These COLA clauses call for wage rates to go up automatically in response to an increase in the Consumer Price Index (CPI).[6] Usually the extent of the COLA escalation is partial—that is, a 1-percentage-point increase in the CPI causes an automatic increase in wage rates of somewhat less than 1 percentage point in wages, perhaps as little as half a percentage point.

COLA clauses complicate the task of policymakers. In Figure 9-3 an attempt to minimize the real GNP loss by accommodating the supply shock, moving the economy to point N during the period of rising relative oil prices, will cause an acceleration of inflation as measured by the CPI. COLA clauses then will call for an acceleration in wage increases. As a result, after the end of the increase of the relative price of oil, when the SP curve would ordinarily return to its initial position, the growth of wage costs has permanently accelerated. Table 9-1 shows how a policy of accommodation of supply shocks endows the economy with a permanent acceleration of inflation when wages are subject to COLA escalation.

The top section of the table, case 1, traces the movement of the economy in Figure 9-3 from point E_3 to M back to E_3 in the case of an "extinguishing policy" that drops real GNP by enough to keep inflation from rising at all in response to the supply shock. Line (a) under case 1 shows the assumed growth of wages, which drops from 7 to 4 percent in response to the drastic drop of real GNP during the period of the supply shock. Line (b) assumes that productivity growth is constant each period at 1 percent. Line (c) subtracts productivity growth in line (b) from wage growth on line (a), yielding the growth of "labor cost." Inflation on line (e) is assumed to be the sum of the growth of labor cost and the effect of the supply shock itself, listed on line (d). Recall that it is the entry on line (d) that accounts for the upward shift of the SP line from SP_2 to SP_3 in Figure 9-2 and Figure 9-3. The extinguishing policy at the top of the table drops real GNP sufficiently to cause wage growth to slow down by 3 percent, exactly offsetting the 3 percent impact of the supply shock. When the supply shock ends, real GNP and wage growth can be allowed to return to the original level.

In case 2, in the middle of Table 9-1, we see exactly the same transition as from point E_3 to point N in Figure 9-3, followed by a movement back to point E_3. Inflation speeds up by exactly the amount of the supply shock, and then returns to its original level. Because wage growth is assumed to be totally unaffected by the supply shock, wage growth is listed on line (a) under case 2 as 7 percent in each period.

Contrast this with case 3, where the supply shock has a delayed effect that raises wage growth from 7 to 8 percent in the third column. Thus in-

---

[6] **Review:** COLA clauses are also discussed in section 7-6.

TABLE 9-1

Alternative Policy Responses to Supply Shocks

	Situation before supply shock	Situation during supply shock	Situation after supply shock
	(All numbers are percentage changes at annual rate)		
Case 1. Extinguishing policy			
a. Growth of wage rates	7	4	7
b. Less: productivity growth	−1	−1	−1
c. Equals: growth of labor cost	6	3	6
d. Effect of supply shock	0	3	0
e. Inflation [total of (c) and (d)]	6	6	6
Case 2. Accommodative policy with no response of wage growth to supply shock			
a. Growth of wage rates	7	7	7
b. Less: productivity growth	−1	−1	−1
c. Equals: growth of labor cost	6	6	6
d. Effect of supply shock	0	3	0
e. Inflation [total of (c) and (d)]	6	9	6
Case 3. Accommodative policy with COLA clauses causing partial response of wage growth to supply shock in subsequent period			
a. Growth of wage rates	7	7	8
b. Less: productivity growth	−1	−1	−1
c. Equals: growth of labor cost	6	6	7
d. Effect of supply shock	0	3	0
e. Inflation [total of (c) and (d)]	6	9	7

flation does not return to the original 6 percent rate after the supply shock ends. Instead, inflation is 7 percent in the third column, and policymakers will have to decide whether to accept this 7 percent inflation permanently by maintaining adjusted nominal GNP growth at 7 percent.

Now we can see that in case 3 the policy of accommodating the supply shock leaves the economy with a permanent acceleration of inflation. Notice that COLA clauses will cause wages to speed up if supply shocks are allowed to have *any* effect on inflation. Even the neutral policy, which causes the economy to go to point *L* in Figure 9-3 during the supply shock, will cause a permanent acceleration of inflation. The more real GNP is caused to decline during the period of the supply shock, the less of a permanent acceleration in inflation will occur.

THE NEED FOR REAL-WAGE FLEXIBILITY

The lesson of this section can be restated in another way.

Workers must be willing to accept the drop in real wages caused by the supply shock. If they try to maintain the previous rate of real wage growth, either by full COLA protection or by demanding faster wage growth directly, policymakers will be forced to choose between a permanent acceleration of inflation and a permanent drop in real GNP.

The growth in real wages is simply the growth in nominal wages [line (a) for each case in Table 9-1] minus inflation [line (e)]. In each case real wage growth is +1 percent initially, −2 percent in the middle column when the supply shock occurs, and +1 percent thereafter. The effect of the COLA clause is to partially compensate workers for the loss of real wages caused by the supply shock, but since inflation responds completely to any acceleration in wage growth, the workers do not actually gain anything. All that COLA adjustment accomplishes is to create a permanently faster inflation.

In Table 9-1 it is assumed that a 3 percent temporary loss in real wages causes wage growth to accelerate by only 1 percent in case 3; that is, the COLA clause calls for only a partial response of wages to the supply shock. If the COLA clause called for fixed 1 percent growth in real wages, plus a *full* 3 percent adjustment of wage growth to the 3 percent acceleration of inflation, then the situation would be even worse. The 3 percent loss of real wage growth caused by the supply shock would lead to a 3 percent acceleration of wage growth in the final period, and inflation would be permanently raised to 9 percent.

REAL-WAGE RIGIDITY AND THE EXAMPLE OF ISRAEL

In 1978 and 1979 inflation in Israel accelerated and reached a rate of more than 100 percent per year. Part of the reason for rapid inflation originated in rapid demand growth, caused by large government budget deficits and rapid monetary growth. But in part supply shocks played a role in explaining why inflation was so much more rapid in 1979 than earlier in the 1970s, when inflation had been "only" 10 or 15 percent per year. As a reaction to earlier inflation, Israeli workers and savers had demanded and received virtually complete protection from inflation. As of late 1979, wage rates were adjusted for 70 percent of the rise in consumer prices, and the government was expected to increase the extent of the adjustment even further. Savers could buy indexed bonds, which offered a return that was geared to the inflation rate and left savers' assets intact in real terms. Thus when the OPEC nations almost doubled oil prices in 1979, the economy of Israel was vulnerable to an acceleration of inflation. Since wage indexation caused higher oil prices to flow through promptly to wages, the government had to choose between creating a recession to push down wage rates and adopting an accommodative policy that would cause an acceleration of inflation. The latter course was chosen, and the growth in both wages and prices speeded up to more than 100 percent per year: "triple-digit inflation."

INTERNATIONAL REPERCUSSIONS

The United States policymakers' choice of the degree of accommodation of supply shocks is made more difficult by the possibility that other nations may make different choices. Imagine that the United States decided to accommodate supply shocks, while West Germany and Japan decided to adopt an extinguishing policy. United States demand growth would accelerate, while demand growth in Germany and Japan would slow down. Americans would want to buy more imported goods with their higher incomes, while German and Japanese consumers would want to buy fewer American goods. The demand for dollars by foreigners would decline, while the demand for German marks and Japanese yen would increase. As a result, the dollar would *depreciate*. Initially, for instance, the dollar might be worth 2.0 German marks. But after the relative demand for dollars had declined, the dollar might slip in value to 1.8 German marks.

Why would a **depreciation** of the dollar matter to policymakers? Because a declining dollar makes imported goods more expensive and boosts the U.S. rate of inflation as measured by the prices of goods (both domestic and imported) that U.S. consumers purchase.[7] The CPI would increase faster, and this (through COLA clauses) would raise the growth of U.S. wages and prices. Thus an accommodative policy by the United States might create a permanent acceleration of inflation in the United States that would be even more pronounced than in case 3 in Table 9-1.

The issue of real wage flexibility, discussed in the last two sections, is related to international repercussions. Imagine that in Germany, after a supply shock, workers make higher wage demands in an attempt to restore their previous real wage. To avoid the resulting permanent acceleration of inflation, German policymakers may choose to reduce real GNP, say from 100 to 94. Then let us assume that as a result of three-year wage contracts and incomplete COLA protection against inflation, American workers accept most of the reduction in the real wage caused by the supply shock. This allows U.S. policymakers to choose a higher real GNP target, say 98 or 100. But the increase in American real GNP relative to German real GNP will raise U.S. imports of German products, cut German imports of U.S. prod-

---

[7] Thus the CPI and the deflator for personal consumption expenditures would both increase. The GNP deflator would be unaffected, since imports are subtracted from GNP (see section 2-5), unless the higher prices of imported goods caused price increases by domestic firms whose goods competed with imports.

ucts, and cause the dollar to depreciate. As a result, inflation is aggravated in the United States.[8]

9-5 EFFECTS OF PRICE CONTROLS AND FAVORABLE SUPPLY SHOCKS

We have seen how the responses of inflation and real GNP to adverse supply shocks depend on the actions of policymakers. Is the growth of nominal GNP left unaffected, increased, or decreased in response to an event that shifts the SP curve upward? Exactly the same analysis can be used to predict the effects of a favorable supply shock, one that causes the SP curve to shift downward. Just as a crop failure or freeze in Florida can shift SP up, so bumper crops that lower relative farm prices could shift SP down.

PRICE CONTROLS SHIFT *SP* DOWNWARD

Another factor that could cause SP to shift downward is a program of price controls like that instituted by the Nixon administration on August 15, 1971. While the controls were not successful on a permanent basis, they did have the effect of temporarily holding down prices. The effect of price controls can be interpreted with the help of Figure 9-4. The decline from SP_2 to SP_4 reflects the assumption that the favorable supply shock, the effect either of lower relative farm prices or of price controls, *reduces inflation by 3 percent at each level of real GNP.*[9]

Our entire analysis of adverse supply shocks remains valid for this case of a "favorable supply shock," except that *everything happens in reverse.* If demand growth is held at the original 6 percent rate, along the DG_1 line in Figure 9-4, then the economy will move from E_3 to L'. Inflation will slow by 2 percent, and there will be an exactly offsetting increase in real GNP from 100 to 102. If policymakers want to avoid this increase in real GNP, demand growth can be reduced by 3 percentage points. This would shift the DG line down (not shown) by enough to intersect the new SP_4 line at point N'.

Developments in subsequent periods depend on the adjustment of expectations. Along SP_4 it is assumed that the expected inflation rate remains

---

[8] The interrelations between real wage flexibility and macroeconomic adjustment in the 1970s are explored in Jeffrey Sachs, "Wages, Profits, and Macroeconomic Adjustment: A Comparative Study," *Brookings Papers on Economic Activity,* vol. 10, no. 2 (1979), pp. 269–319.

[9] An alternative assumption, not shown in Figure 9-4, would be that the price controls hold down inflation to a certain amount and make inflation independent of real GNP, thus converting SP into a horizontal line.

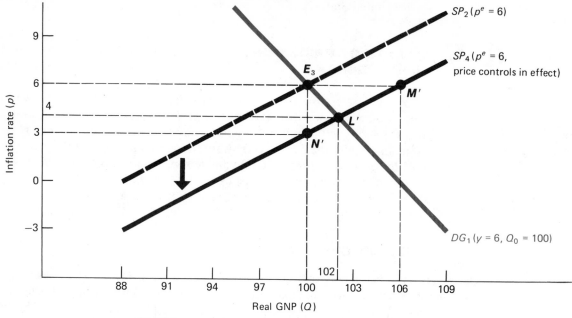

FIGURE 9–4

Effect on Inflation and Real GNP of a Price Control Program
That Shifts the *SP* Line Down by 3 Percentage Points

The economy is assumed to start at point E_3, with an initial real GNP of $Q_0 = 100$, expected inflation equal to demand growth, and an initial inflation rate of 6 percent. If the *SP* line is shifted down by 3 percentage points by a price control program (or by a decline in the relative price of food or oil), the economy goes in the next period to point L' on the assumption that demand growth remains at 6 percent. Inflation falls by 2 percent to 4 percent, and real GNP experiences an exactly offsetting rise from 100 to 102. If an accommodating demand growth reduction is chosen by policymakers, the economy goes to N', whereas an "extinguishing" policy that boosts demand growth enough to move the economy to M' can eliminate all of the price-reducing effects of price controls.

at 6 percent. If people begin to adjust their expectations of inflation downward in response to the reduction in actual inflation, then the *SP* line will shift down further. On the other hand, if people think that the effect of the price controls is strictly temporary, they may refuse to adjust their expectations. If so, and if the price controls are soon discontinued, the economy will eventually return to point E_3. But the period when price controls are discontinued may cause a jump in the price level as firms try to reestablish former pricing patterns. This postcontrols "rebound" jump in the price level is exactly like an adverse supply shock and can be analyzed as in Figures 9-2 and 9-3. We shall see in the case study in the next section that the behavior of inflation and real GNP in the first half of the 1970s can be understood in terms of our simple model of supply shocks.[10]

THE CASE AGAINST PRICE CONTROLS AS A CURE FOR INFLATION

We learned in the last chapter that one cure for inflation is a recession that may last from several years to a decade. Because a recession is painful, it is not surprising to find that some economists and politicians periodically turn to price controls as a "way out." In August 1971 the Nixon administration turned to controls in frustration at the failure of the 1970 recession to achieve any significant slowing of inflation. More recently, on January 28, 1980, presidential candidate Edward Kennedy called for a six-month price freeze to be followed by mandatory wage and price controls.

Controls are not a new idea. The Roman Emperor Diocletian imposed a comprehensive control program in 301 A.D. Offenders who violated the edict by charging prices or paying wages differing from those decreed by the emperor were sentenced to death! The program was abandoned as a failure after thirteen years.[11] The United States had a comprehensive and compulsory system of wage and price controls during World War II, a more limited system during the Korean War, a period of voluntary wage-price guidelines in the Kennedy-Johnson administrations during 1962–66, and, finally, a full-fledged control program in the Nixon administration between August 1971 and April 1974.

In the example of Figure 9-4, price controls shift down the *SP* schedule. But if expectations do not adjust downward, then the termination of price controls will cause a rebound in the price level. Thus the long-run success of controls depends on the adjustment of expectations, and yet this adjustment may not occur. Because there is a long historical record that price controls are abandoned sooner or later, expectations may fail to adjust because people *expect the controls to fail*. Why not just announce that controls will be imposed permanently? Few would believe such a promise, because controls are always abandoned eventually as a result of the harm they do *by interfering with the efficiency of the private economy, which depends on the flexibility of relative prices to allocate resources.*

---

[10] The analysis of supply shocks in this chapter was introduced in two papers. See Robert J. Gordon, "Alternative Responses of Policy to External Supply Shocks," *Brookings Papers on Economic Activity,* vol. 6, no. 1 (1975), pp. 183–206, and Edmund S. Phelps, "Commodity Supply Shocks and Full-Employment Monetary Policy," *Journal of Money, Credit, and Banking,* vol. 10 (May 1978), pp. 206–221.

[11] This and other examples are reviewed in C. Jackson Grayson, "Controls Are Not the Answer," *Challenge* (November/December 1974), pp. 9–12, which contains a good introduction to the major arguments against controls. See also the debate between David Lewis and Myron E. Sharpe, "The Great Debate on Wage-Price Controls," *Challenge* (January/February 1975), pp. 26–32.

If controls could reduce the growth rate of all wages and prices by the same percentage, without having any effect on the flexibility of relative prices or relative real wages, they would not be so harmful. Unfortunately, the relative prices of different products and the real wages of different groups of workers are continually changing as the private marketplace uses the price system to allocate resources. Because government officials running the control program cannot possibly know how relative prices and real wages would be moving each day in the absence of controls, they have no way to *decree* exactly the same changes in relative prices and real wages by the use of controls. Instead, all actual control programs tend to impose simple rules, particularly on the growth of wage rates.

For instance, the attempt to impose the same wage rule on all employees may create shortages of some employees in growing occupations. Firms may be unable to attract computer programmers without an above-average wage offer, but that is prohibited by the controls. As a result firms selling computer programming services will be unable to supply the demand for their product, causing a shortage, and they will be unable to increase the price to eliminate the shortage. The danger of shortages of products or labor skills is the chief argument against controls.

Some economists agree that controls would be harmful in a competitive economy. But they claim that prices and wages are jacked up by powerful large corporations and large unions.[12] In this view the enforced control of union wages would be beneficial even if real wage rates were reduced, because the supply of workers would still exceed the demand and firms could hire more unemployed workers. Enforced control over the prices of large corporations would be beneficial, even if corporate profits were reduced, by reducing misallocation of resources caused by corporate monopoly profits.

A control program limited to large unions and corporations would be easier to administer than a universal program. But large corporations produce thousands of products. Some relative prices would surely be pushed out of line. Controls may cause quality to be reduced, warranties to be shortened, or financing terms to be stiffened. A more efficient method of reducing monopoly profits would be for the government to encourage competition by better enforcement of the antitrust laws.

Concentrating controls on large corporations also leaves the large service sector uncontrolled. A price lid on General Motors' automobiles will not automatically prevent the television repairer from raising his charge. This leaves us with wage controls on large unions as the least harmful system, but labor unions are unlikely to welcome being selected as the sole victim of the control program. "Where are the controls," they will ask, "on the rent, interest, and dividend checks that rich people receive and on executive stock options and bonuses?"

---

[12] See especially John Kenneth Galbraith, *The New Industrial State* (Boston: Houghton Mifflin, 1967).

EFFECTS OF THE 1971–74 PRICE CONTROL PROGRAM

We shall see in the case study in the next section that the controls program failed to reduce inflation permanently and destabilized the economy, aggravating the real GNP boom of 1972 and deepening the recession of 1974–75. But the harm done by the controls program goes further than this. By preventing relative price adjustments during the 1971–72 period, the controls program caused shortages of several products to develop.

Controls on the price of lumber in 1972 began to curtail the supply of lumber and caused sawmills to shut down operations. Shortages of molasses, fertilizer, and logs appeared because higher world prices pulled domestic supplies abroad while domestic producers were forbidden from raising prices within the United States. Reinforcing steel bars fell under the controls, but the steel scrap used in making the bars was excluded from the controls and shot up in price, squeezing the profits of the makers of steel bars, causing their production to shrink, and interfering with construction projects. Baling wire used by farmers to bundle crops also was in short supply because steel companies found that they were losing $100 on every ton of baling wire at the low controlled price.[13]

The control officials can attempt to deal with some of these problem areas by devising exceptions and special rules, but soon producers of similar products protest that they have been treated unfairly. The Nixon controls exempted raw farm products, which normally exhibit volatile ups and downs in prices and would have been almost impossible to control without creating havoc in the nation's wholesale and retail food markets. But then problems of definition arose. What is a raw farm product?

> Was honey a "raw" food — or processed by the busy bees? What if the honey were strained or drained? What about fish and other seafood when "shelled, shucked, skinned, or scaled"? Cucumbers went up but pickles were controlled; popped corn was controlled, raw corn was not. Since chicken broilers were cut up and packaged before being sold, they were considered a processed food, and their price was frozen. When the price of feed went up, the farmer simply discontinued production; the nation was shocked at pictures of thousands of chicks being drowned.[14]

INNOVATIVE PROPOSALS TO CONTROL WAGES

Considerable attention was centered in the late 1970s on proposals for innovative methods to slow the inflation rate. These involved using the tax system to induce workers to accept lower wage increases, which (assuming

---

[13] These examples are from C. Jackson Grayson, "Controls Are Not the Answer," *Challenge* (November/December 1974), pp. 9–12; and Walter Guzzardi, Jr., "What We Should Have Learned about Controls," *Fortune* (March 1975), p. 105.

[14] Guzzardi, *op. cit.*

prices respond in a regular way to wages) would allow the inflation rate to slow down. One version, independently invented about a decade ago by Pennsylvania's Sydney Weintraub and Governor Henry Wallich of the Federal Reserve System, is called "tax-based incomes policy" (TIP for short). TIP plans operate by a system of penalties (the "stick") or of rewards (the "carrot"). Under a penalty version a firm pays a corporate income tax that depends on the wage increase it grants. For instance, it might pay 48 percent of its profits in tax if it granted a 6 percent wage increase, 52 percent if it granted 7 percent, and so on. Because the firm would find its after-tax profit eroded when it granted high wage increases, its resistance to union demands would be stiffer than otherwise.

Proponents of TIP do not deny that excessive aggregate demand growth is a fundamental cause of inflation. Rather, they point to the reasoning (like that contained in section 8-8) that a slowdown in aggregate demand growth will slow inflation only at the cost of a prolonged recession. They see TIP as a means of shifting the *SP* curve down in response to a demand deceleration more rapidly than would occur otherwise.

Unions and firms were both opposed to TIP, and as a result the idea never made any headway among politicians in Washington. Unions viewed TIP as equivalent to wage controls, an anathema that implies that only workers are to blame for inflation and fails to provide any restraint on profits, dividends, or rents. Firms dislike TIP because it attempts to impose a uniform rate of wage increase on every firm, neglecting the need for relative wages to rise in some occupations where workers are scarce and to fall in others where jobs are scarce. Firms also feared that the penalty form of TIP, which counts on increased firm resistance to hold down wage increases, would simply lead to longer and more bitter strikes. Any form of wage control, including TIP, also must face the problem of three-year contracts that were negotiated before the program began; would firms be penalized for wage increases negotiated before the inception of the program? Further limitations of TIP, pointed out by experts on the administration of the federal tax system, derive from administrative difficulties in measuring wages, taxable income, and profits.[15]

In early 1979 the Carter administration proposed another version of TIP, which was called "real wage insurance." Workers and unions that agreed to hold down wages to a given rate of increase would be "insured" against a loss of real income if firms failed to reduce prices in response to wage moderation, or if external supply shocks caused prices to increase relative to wages. The "insurance" would be a government payment to offset part of the real wage loss. The Carter administration proposal was not enacted by Congress, which feared that government payments would be much larger than the administration predicted, thus causing larger deficits. The unexpected doubling of the price of oil in 1979 would have made real wage insurance extremely expensive, and in fact the moderate behavior of wages

---

[15] A full discussion of these issues is contained in *Brookings Papers on Economic Activity*, vol. 9, no. 2 (1978).

in response to rapid 1979 inflation demonstrated that gradual wage adjustment in the United States (owing to three-year wage contracts) helps to minimize the long-run inflationary consequences of supply shocks.

9-6 CASE STUDY: INFLATION TRIGGERS RECESSION, 1971–76

In mid-1976 the *New York Times* announced "A New Theory: Inflation Triggers Recession."[16] But this idea is nothing new to readers of the previous sections. Any upward shift in SP, whether caused by an upward revision in the expected rate of inflation, by the termination of price controls, or by a supply shock can both raise the actual inflation rate and trigger a recession as long as adjusted demand growth ($\hat{y}$) is held constant by monetary and fiscal policymakers.

PROSPERITY 1971–73

The story of inflation and recession in the United States in the early 1970s is a dramatic one. In the four quarters of 1974 the deflator for personal consumption expenditures increased at an annual rate of 11.4 percent, faster than in any year since 1948. And in the first quarter of 1975 the real GNP ratio (Q/Q^N) was only 0.928, the lowest rate of any quarter since 1949.

The behavior of inflation and Q/Q^N can be explained in terms of shifts in the SP line along a relatively fixed DG schedule. Movements in the DG line, upward in 1972–73 and downward in 1974–75, served mainly to amplify the instability of real GNP that was caused primarily by supply shocks.

In Figure 9-5 the vertical axis is the inflation rate, as in Figures 9-2, 9-3 and 9-4. Now, to take account of growth in natural real GNP (Q^N), we plot on the horizontal axis the real GNP ratio, Q/Q^N. When the inflation rate (p) falls short of adjusted demand growth ($\hat{y}$), we know that the growth of real GNP adjusted for growth in natural GNP ($\hat{q}$) is positive, and the Q/Q^N ratio rises.[17] Just this event occurred, starting after 1971:Q2, as a result of the program of wage and price controls introduced by the Nixon administration on August 15, 1971.

We can interpret the effect of the controls with the help of Figure 9-4, which shows a downward movement of the SP curve in response to the controls that moves the economy southeast from point E_3 to point L'. The real-world economy behaved similarly, as shown in Figure 9-5, moving southeast from the point marked 1971:Q2 (the second quarter of 1971), when the four-quarter inflation rate was 5.1 percent, to that marked 1973:Q1, with a four-quarter inflation rate of only 2.7 percent.

---

[16] *New York Times*, July 18, 1976, Section F 13.

[17] **Review:** Section 8-7 and Figure 8-8, where the axes correspond exactly to Figure 9-5.

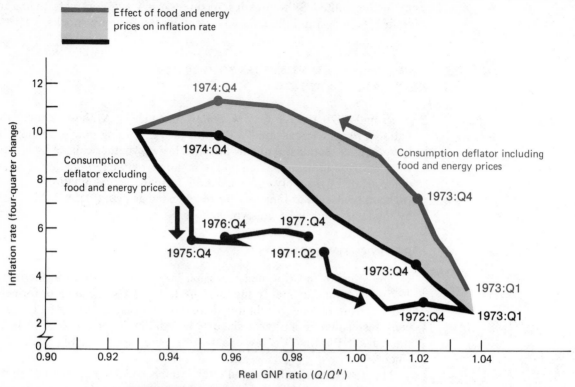

FIGURE 9–5

The Real GNP Ratio Q/Q^N and the Inflation Rate, Both Including and Excluding Food and Energy Prices, 1971–77

The black line traces the relation between the real GNP ratio (Q/Q^N) and inflation, excluding food and energy prices. Notice the southeast movement in 1971–72, when prices were controlled, and the northwest movement in 1974, when controls were terminated. The upper red line shows total inflation, including food and energy prices, and the pink area measures the impact on inflation of food and energy prices between early 1973 and early 1975.

Source: Same as Table 9–2. The inflation rate refers to personal consumption expenditures, not total GNP. The inflation rate is measured as a four-quarter change ending in the designated quarter.

The main difference between the theoretical diagram in Figure 9-4 and the real-world diagram in Figure 9-5 occurs because adjusted demand growth ($\hat{y}$) did not remain constant. Instead, there was an acceleration in $\hat{y}$ from a four-quarter rate of 3.9 percent in 1971:Q2 to 7.9 percent in 1973:Q1. This accounts for the fact that the economy moved so far to the right, with an increase in Q/Q^N over this period much greater than the decline in the inflation rate. Put another way, the DG line shifted up and the SP line shifted down at the same time.

Notice how in 1973:Q4 the black inflation line still remains below its 1971:Q2 starting value. But then the black inflation line shows how inflation surged between 1973:Q1 and 1974:Q4. Everything in Figure 9-5 seems compatible with the interpretation that controls held down the inflation rate in 1971–73, but then contributed to high inflation in 1974–75 as firms tried to reestablish the no-controls level of prices.[18]

THE INCREASE IN THE RELATIVE PRICES OF FOOD AND ENERGY

Figure 9-5 separates the effect of price controls and their removal from the separate supply shock caused by the increase in the relative prices of food and energy. This is done by plotting two lines between early 1973 and early 1975. The continuous black loop shows the relation between the Q/Q^N ratio on the horizontal axis and the rate of inflation of consumer prices *excluding consumer expenditures on food and energy*, sometimes called the "stripped" inflation rate. If the relative prices of food and energy had remained constant, then the black line would show total inflation as well.

But 1973 and 1974 were years of dramatic jumps in the relative prices of food and energy. As a result the total inflation rate, shown by the red line in Figure 9-5, considerably exceeded the "stripped" inflation rate excluding food and energy products. The pink area shows the contribution of food and energy prices to overall inflation. We conclude that there would have been an acceleration of inflation in 1974 anyway as a result of the termination of controls, but that this acceleration was aggravated considerably by the food and oil supply shocks.

In terms of our theoretical diagrams in Figures 9-3 and 9-4, the SP line shifted down from SP_2 to SP_4 in 1972 as a result of controls. Then in 1973–74 the SP line shifted up from SP_4 to SP_2 and further up to SP_3 as a result of the combined influence of the termination of controls and the food and oil supply shocks. At the same time in 1974 the DG line, instead of remaining fixed as on our theoretical diagrams, shifted down. Adjusted demand growth ($\hat{y}$) slowed from a peak of 7.9 percent in the four quarters ending in 1973:Q1 to a low of 2.8 percent in the four quarters ending in 1975:Q1. Because inflation (p) exceeded $\hat{y}$ throughout 1973 and 1974, $\hat{q}$ ($= \hat{y} - p$) was negative, and the real GNP ratio Q/Q^N fell precipitously from a peak of 1.035 to a trough of 0.928.

---

[18] I first reached this finding in 1972 and confirmed it in 1977. See Robert J. Gordon, "Wage-Price Controls and the Shifting Phillips Curve," *Brookings Papers on Economic Activity,* vol. 3, no. 2 (1972), pp. 385–421, and "Can the Inflation of the 1970s Be Explained?" *Brookings Papers on Economic Activity,* vol. 8, no. 1 (1977), pp. 253–277. For a similar interpretation with considerably more background detail, see Alan S. Blinder, *Economic Policy and the Great Stagflation* (New York: Academic Press, 1979).

Table 9-2 illustrates the effect of the supply shocks in more detail. The top part of the table shows the *level* of several price deflators, those for all consumption goods (line A1), food (line A2), and energy (line A3). The relative price of food is the price deflator for food divided by the total deflator, as shown on line A4. The relative price of energy is shown on line A5.

Four-quarter growth rates are shown in the bottom part of the table, for food prices (line B1), energy prices (line B2), the total consumption deflator (line B3, same as the red line in Figure 9-5), and the consumption deflator net of food and energy (line B4, same as the black line in Figure 9-5).

THE 1972–73 FOOD PRICE SHOCK

We note that the big jump in the relative price of food (line A4) came in 1973. Why? A coincidence of unfortunate events, beginning in the last half of 1972, caused farm prices almost to double over a short two-year period. The adverse events include:

1. Peruvian anchovies disappeared from their normal feeding grounds, causing a drop in the anchovy catch to only one-tenth of normal. Because anchovies are normally made into fish meal that is fed to livestock, their disappearance caused a jump in the prices of other types of livestock feed, particularly corn and soybeans.
2. The U.S. crop in 1972–73 was below normal because of poor growing weather.
3. Crop failures and droughts occurred elsewhere, particularly in the USSR. To feed its population, the Russian government was forced to buy from the United States over 20 million tons of wheat and feed grains.
4. The dollar depreciated in value in early 1973, making U.S. farm exports less expensive in terms of foreign currencies. This tended to raise foreign demand and boost farm prices in terms of dollars.
5. A worldwide economic boom occurred simultaneously in most industrialized countries. This also boosted the demand for farm products.

THE 1973–74 OIL PRICE SHOCK

Notice on line A5 that the relative price of energy increased by about 25 percent between 1972 and 1975 and then leveled off before jumping even more in 1979 and 1980. The initial surge of energy prices was caused in 1973–74 by the new assertiveness of the OPEC oil cartel. Oil supplies from Arab countries were embargoed during the Arab-Israeli War that began in October 1973, and then oil prices were quadrupled from about $3 per barrel in early 1973 to about $12 per barrel in March 1974. The price of energy paid by U.S. consumers did not increase by

TABLE 9-2

Inflation and the Relative Price of Food and Energy, 1971–80

	1971: Q2	1972: Q4	1973: Q4	1974: Q4	1975: Q4	1976: Q4	1977: Q4	1978: Q4	1979: Q4	1980: Q2
	(1)	(2)	(3)	(4)	(5)	(6)	(7)	(8)	(9)	(10)
A. Price deflators, 1972 = 1.00										
1. Personal consumption expenditures	0.96	1.01	1.09	1.22	1.29	1.35	1.43	1.54	1.69	1.78
2. Consumer expenditures on food	0.95	1.02	1.19	1.33	1.42	1.43	1.51	1.68	1.83	1.89
3. Consumer expenditures on energy	0.96	1.02	1.16	1.46	1.62	1.71	1.82	1.95	2.67	3.10
4. Relative price of food (A2 ÷ A1)	0.99	1.01	1.09	1.10	1.10	1.06	1.06	1.09	1.08	1.06
5. Relative price of energy (A3 ÷ A1)	1.00	1.01	1.07	1.20	1.26	1.26	1.28	1.27	1.58	1.74
B. Four-quarter percentage rate of change[a]										
1. Food price deflator (line A2)	3.0	4.8	16.3	12.5	6.2	0.7	5.7	11.7	8.8	6.4
2. Energy price deflator (line A3)	2.6	3.9	14.2	25.3	11.3	5.3	6.7	6.9	37.1	35.1
3. Consumption deflator (line A1)	4.5	3.5	7.3	11.4	6.0	4.7	5.6	7.4	9.9	11.2
4. Consumption deflator excluding food and energy	5.1	3.1	4.5	9.8	5.7	5.6	5.7	6.5	7.7	9.8
5. Effect of food and energy (B3 minus B4)	−0.6	0.4	2.8	1.6	0.3	−0.9	−0.1	0.9	2.2	1.4

[a] Four-quarter percentage rate of change in designated quarter, except for column (2), which is a six-quarter rate of change at an annual rate, and column (10), which is a two-quarter rate of change at an annual rate.

Source: National Income and Product Accounts. Tables 2.3 and 2.4.

nearly this percentage, as a result of price controls on oil and natural gas, as well as the requirement that electric utilities had to win approval of local regulatory commissions before being allowed to raise electricity prices.

As shown on lines A4 and A5 of Table 9-2, the year 1976 brought relief from supply shocks. There was no further increase in the relative price of energy during 1976, while the relative price of food actually dropped. And the temporary price-boosting effect of the termination of controls had ended. Thus the SP line dropped from SP_3 back to SP_2, in terms of the diagram in Figure 9-2. By late 1977 the economy had returned almost exactly to where it was in 1971:Q2, with about the same real GNP ratio Q/Q^N, and only about half a percentage point additional inflation. Since inflation was roughly constant during 1976 and 1977 at about 5.5 percent per year, we may assume that expectations of inflation had settled down to about the same rate.

As 1977 ended, many economists had concluded that inflation had "settled down" to a "basic rate" of about 6 percent. Since estimates of the natural level of real GNP were considerably more optimistic at that time than now, it was thought that the Q/Q^N ratio was still around 0.95 and that there was still considerable room for expansive policy.[19] Few economists would have predicted that by the end of 1979 inflation would once again have reached 10 percent with little change in the Q/Q^N ratio between late 1977 and late 1979.

AGGREGATE DEMAND GROWTH DURING 1971–76

Most of the story of the early 1970s can be understood in terms of a downward and then an upward movement of the SP schedule along a fixed DG schedule. But it is also true that swings in the rate of demand growth aggravated the instability of real GNP. An acceleration in y between early 1971 and early 1973 amplified the increase in real GNP stimulated by the effect of the price controls, whereas a deceleration in y between early 1973 and early 1975 aggravated the recession of 1974–75.

We learned in Chapters 3–5 that swings in aggregate demand can be caused by monetary policy, fiscal policy, and shifts in business and consumer confidence. All these elements contributed to the behavior of demand growth in the early 1970s, but certainly the most important element was the acceleration of the growth of the money supply during 1971–73 and deceleration during 1973–75. Notice how closely the behavior of y

---

[19] In 1976 the Council of Economic Advisers (CEA) estimate of Q^N, which they called "potential real GNP," was about $1425 billion, with the implication that the 1976 Q/Q^N ratio was only 0.895. In 1977 and again in 1979 the CEA estimate of Q^N was revised down and thus the Q/Q^N ratio was revised up. For instance, Q^N for 1976 is listed in the 1979 *Economic Report of the President* (p. 75) as $1341 billion, almost the same as in the first edition of this textbook. Our current estimate for 1976 is even lower, $1324 billion (see Appendix B).

parallels that of monetary growth over these two successive two-year intervals:

	Percentage rate of change at annual rate over period indicated	
	Nominal GNP	*Money supply (new M_2)*
1969:Q1–1971:Q1	6.4	5.9
1971:Q1–1973:Q1	10.6	12.7
1973:Q1–1975:Q1	7.8	6.3

Other factors added to the impact of the acceleration and deceleration in monetary growth. The federal government budget measured for a given level of Q/Q^N became more stimulative in 1971–72 and less stimulative in 1973–74. Inflation in 1974, by moving people into higher tax brackets, caused federal personal income tax receipts to increase at almost double the rate of nominal GNP growth. In addition, the price controls bolstered consumer confidence in 1971–72 and led to a buying spree of consumer durable goods that peaked in 1973:Q1, whereas the 1974 increase in oil prices dampened business and consumer confidence and led to a slump in consumer spending and business investment. We will examine the behavior of aggregate demand in the 1970s more closely in Chapters 13, 16, and 17.

9-7 CASE STUDY: SUPPLY SHOCKS STRIKE AGAIN, 1977–80

The behavior of the U.S. economy in the late 1970s mirrored some of the main elements of the early 1970s. Once again supply shocks in 1978–80 caused inflation to accelerate and the real GNP ratio Q/Q^N to fall, as had occurred in 1973–74.

A crucial difference between the early and late 1970s was the absence of price controls in the more recent period. Thus a major element that contributed to the instability of inflation and real GNP during 1971–75 was not repeated during 1977–80. As a result, the acceleration of inflation that occurred in 1978–80 was more moderate than in 1973–75.

Figure 9-6 plots data for the inflation rate and the real GNP ratio (Q/Q^N) for the period between the end of 1976 and early 1980. The size and scale of the diagram are identical to Figure 9-5, and so a comparison of the two figures helps to identify the unique features of the more recent episode:

1. Unlike the 1971–73 period, when the economy moved southeast owing to price controls, the expansion of real GNP in 1977–78 was accompanied by a northeast movement along the solid black line in

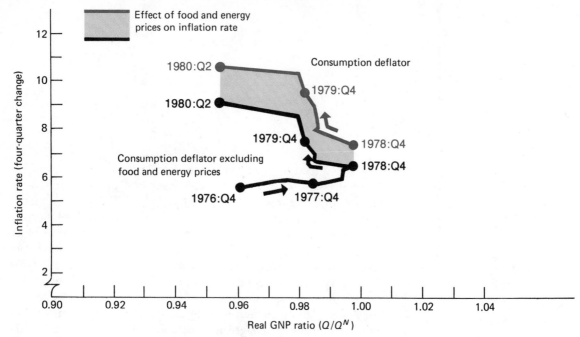

FIGURE 9–6

The Real GNP Ratio Q/Q^N and the Inflation Rate, Both Including and Excluding Food and Energy Prices, 1976–80

The black line traces the relation between the real GNP ratio (Q/Q^N) and inflation excluding food and energy prices. The black line suggests that one reason for faster inflation in 1978–79 was an acceleration in demand growth, since the black line describes a loop that looks much like that in Figure 8–7. The upper red line shows total inflation, including food and energy prices, and the pink area measures the impact on inflation of food and energy prices between late 1978 and early 1980.

Source: Same as Figure 9–5.

Figure 9-6. In this period the economy can be viewed as moving up a relatively fixed *SP* schedule, just as in the 1965–66 period graphed in Figure 8-8.

2. Starting in early 1978, an increase in the relative price of food (see Table 9-2, line A4) began to cause a divergence between total inflation and the "stripped" inflation rate net of food and energy prices. By 1978:Q4 this divergence had reached almost a percentage point, as shown by the distance between the black and red lines for 1978:Q4. During 1979 the divergence widened to about 2.5 percentage points as

the increasing relative price of food was joined by a dramatic jump in the relative price of oil.

3. The 1979 supply shock pushed the economy to the northwest, just as in 1973–74. But the speed of the leftward movement in 1979 was not as swift or pronounced as in 1973–74, both because there was not any post-termination effect of price controls and because the slowdown in demand growth in 1979 was much milder than that of 1973–74. The really rapid leftward movement of the economy beginning in 1980:Q2 was due more to perversely restrictive demand policy than to the intensity of the supply shock.

THE 1978–79 FOOD PRICE SHOCK

The primary source of the 1972–74 jump in the relative price of food had originated in the market for grains, with both lower supply and higher demand contributing to a higher relative price. In that episode beef prices rose substantially, since the cost of producing beef depends partly on the prices of feed grains. But in 1977–79 it was the price of beef that led the way for inflation in food prices.

Why was livestock such a problem? During 1971–74 the price of grain increased much more than the price of livestock, putting a squeeze on the profits of cattle raisers. Cattlemen became pessimistic about future profit opportunities and in 1974 began to liquidate their herds. The number of cattle and calves on U.S. farms declined from 132 million head in January 1975 to about 111 million at the end of 1978. This 16 percent drop was the sharpest ever recorded. Since there was no offsetting increase in the production of pork, rising consumer demand combined with shrinking supply caused a dramatic jump in meat prices.

THE 1979–80 OIL PRICE SHOCK

In 1973 the leap in oil prices was initiated by a political event, the Yom Kippur War. Saudi Arabia, which had helped to moderate oil price increases until that time, objected to American aid to Israel during the October 1973 war with Egypt and Syria and led other Arab members of OPEC in an oil embargo. The embargo, in turn, led to a series of OPEC decisions that boosted the price of a barrel of oil from $3 in mid-1973 to $11.65 in January 1974. Then for five years the price of oil remained roughly constant, increasing only to $13.30 in January 1979.

But then another political event intervened: the revolution in Iran that overthrew the Shah in January 1979. Oil production in Iran dropped, causing a significant cut in the overall world supply of oil. This would have driven up the price in any case, but the upward pressure on prices was aggravated by panic stockpiling of crude oil. Over the subsequent year the price of Saudi Arabian crude oil more than doubled, from $13.30 to $28, and most other members of OPEC were charging between $30 and $34 per barrel.

Together, increases in the relative prices of food and energy contributed about 2.2 percent to inflation in the four quarters ending in 1979:Q4. It was expected that the United States would gain some relief from this source of inflation in late 1980 and 1981, but the continued impact of the decontrol of domestic oil prices would guarantee a further increase in the relative price of energy.

"SELF-INFLICTED WOUNDS"

So far we have treated supply-shock inflation as if it were a curse inflicted on the United States in the 1970s without any recourse for policymakers except to choose whether to accommodate or extinguish the impact of the supply shock. Yet in the late 1970s there was a growing awareness that government policies were available to reduce the instability in the *SP* curve stemming from supply shocks, and that some supply shocks had actually been initiated by the government.

The Minimum Wage. Although the Carter administration knew about the inflationary consequences of a higher minimum wage, nevertheless it bowed to political pressures from labor unions and put into effect an increase from $2.30 an hour in 1977 to $2.65 in 1978, $2.90 in 1979, $3.10 in 1980, and $3.35 in 1981. This increase of 46 percent in the minimum wage rate over four years put considerable upward pressure on other wages and prices. For instance, it has been estimated that the 1978 increase alone caused a speed-up in the rate of increase of the average hourly wage rate by between 0.2 and 0.4 percentage points, and this increase in the growth of labor costs put pressure on firms to raise prices faster.[20] A number of economists have concluded also that an increase in the minimum wage (relative to other wages) aggravates the teenage unemployment problem.[21]

The Social Security Payroll Tax. In the United States social security benefits are financed out of a payroll tax on labor earnings, half of which is paid by the employee and half by the employer.[22] Even if the employee bears the burden of the tax without demanding offsetting wage increases, it is very likely that employers will pass on some or all of their tax bill to consumers by raising prices. Significant increases in social security tax rates were put into effect in early 1978 and 1979 that raised the ratio of social security tax collections to total wage and salary income from 14.2 percent in 1977:Q4 to 15.5 percent in 1979:Q1. This may have added 0.5 to 0.7 percentage points of extra inflation over the same interval.

Direct Government Price-raising Policies. Some government programs contribute directly to higher prices. For instance, import fees on foreign sugar boost the price consumers pay for sugar in U.S. super-

---

[20] *Economic Report of the President,* January 1979, p. 66.
[21] Edward M. Gramlich, "Impact of Minimum Wages on Other Wages, Employment, and Family Incomes," *Brookings Papers on Economic Activity,* vol. 7, no. 2 (1976), pp. 409–451.
[22] This is the paycheck deduction you see in the box labeled "F.I.C.A."

markets, and grain reserve programs lead to higher wheat and flour prices while reserves are being built up. Protection of domestic industries against foreign competition also tends to increase prices to American consumers. For instance, in 1978 the U.S. government instituted a "trigger price" program that established minimum prices for the sales of foreign steel in the United States as a way of protecting the U.S. steel industry against foreign competition that it claimed was "unfair."

Government Cost-raising Regulations. Throughout this century, the U.S. government has engaged in economic regulation, particularly of the transportation industry. In the late 1970s there was a growing consensus that this form of regulation should end. Airlines were deregulated in late 1978, and there were signs at the end of the decade that the regulation of trucking and railroads would be loosened or eliminated.

While economic regulation has a long history, social regulation was a new phenomenon of the 1970s. Health, safety, and environmental regulations contributed significantly to the costs of numerous industries. This tends to be inflationary, both because Congress has introduced regulations that may have costs significantly higher than their benefits, and also because the benefits (safer jobs, cleaner water and air) are not included in GNP. The estimation of the effects on inflation of these regulations, and the potential for reducing inflation by eliminating or weakening some regulations, is a complex task. But there is widespread agreement that there is substantial scope for anti-inflationary policy in this area.[23]

AGGREGATE DEMAND GROWTH IN THE LATE 1970s

We have now established that there were supply shocks during the 1978–80 period that pushed up the rate of inflation at any given level of real GNP—that is, that pushed up the *SP* schedule. But we learned in Figure 9-3 that the effect of supply shocks on inflation and real GNP depends on the response of aggregate demand growth, which could speed up to "accommodate" the supply shocks or slow down to "extinguish" the shocks. Thus a full understanding of the 1978–80 period must include a discussion of the behavior of demand growth.

Figure 9-7 contrasts the behavior of adjusted demand growth ($\hat{y}$), inflation (p), and adjusted real GNP growth ($\hat{q} = \hat{y} - p$) during the 1971–75 and 1977–80 periods. The diagram is arranged so that the peak quarter of Q/Q^N in each period occurs at the same horizontal position on each frame of the figure, as indicated by the vertical black line marked "peak quarter in Q/Q^N."

The middle frame repeats information we have already studied in Figures 9-5 and 9-6. The red line shows total inflation of the deflator for consumption expenditures for 1971–75 (dashed red line) and 1977–80

---

[23] A comprehensive and readable introduction to this area is Robert W. Crandall, "Federal Government Initiatives to Reduce the Price Level," *Brookings Papers on Economic Activity*, vol. 9, no. 2 (1978), pp. 401–440.

(solid red line). The black lines in the same frame show inflation "stripped" of food and energy prices. We see that in each period, at about the same stage in the business cycle, there was a growing divergence between the black and red lines, owing to food and energy supply shocks. But we also see that there was a much greater acceleration in the black "stripped" inflation rate line in the 1971–75 interval than in 1977–80, owing to the influence of the price controls in holding down prices in 1971–73 and boosting prices in 1974.

The top frame compares adjusted demand growth ($\hat{y}$) in the two periods. In each interval there was an acceleration of demand growth followed by a deceleration. On average $\hat{y}$ was higher in 1977–80 than in 1971–75, and the 10 percent rate for $\hat{y}$ achieved in the four quarters ending in 1979:Q1 set a postwar record.

In 1971–75 the slowdown in $\hat{y}$, combined with the dramatic 1973–74 acceleration of inflation, meant negative values for $\hat{q}$ that had no precedent in the postwar era, and a decline in Q/Q^N from 1.035 in 1973:Q1 to 0.928 in 1975:Q1. In 1977–80 $\hat{q}$ also experienced a slowdown, but this deceleration initially was milder than in 1973–75, primarily because the acceleration of inflation was less pronounced. Nevertheless, as of mid-1980, the slowdown in $\hat{y}$ was proceeding at about the same pace as in 1973–74, and it seemed possible that the recession in 1980–81 would push Q/Q^N as low as in 1975:Q1.

In retrospect economic policy can be criticized. Nominal GNP growth was too rapid in 1978, just as in 1972. A substantial part of the 1977–79 acceleration in the "stripped" inflation rate (net of food and energy prices) must be blamed on excessive aggregate demand growth, although another portion must be attributed to the "self-inflicted wounds" of 1978–79, particularly the influence of the higher minimum wage and payroll tax. The net result of misguided demand and supply policies was to endow the economy in 1980 with an underlying inflation rate of about 8 percent net of any influence of rising food or energy prices. Thus the task of policy at the beginning of the decade of the 1980s was tougher than at the beginning of the 1970s, since the "basic" inflation rate had increased in the interim from 5 to 8 percent.

FIGURE 9-7 (facing page)

Comparison of Inflation Rate and Adjusted Growth Rates of Nominal GNP and Real GNP, 1971–75 Versus 1977–80

In each frame of the diagram the horizontal axis is aligned so that the peak quarter of Q/Q^N in the early 1970s (1973:Q1) occurs at the same horizontal position as the peak quarter of Q/Q^N in the late 1970s. We can see that a major difference between the early 1970s (dashed lines) and late 1970s (solid lines) was the effect of price controls in holding down inflation during 1971–73 and allowing for a very rapid $\hat{q}$ (bottom frame). Then, when price controls were terminated, inflation accelerated much more than in the late 1970s and pushed $\hat{q}$ to record negative rates.

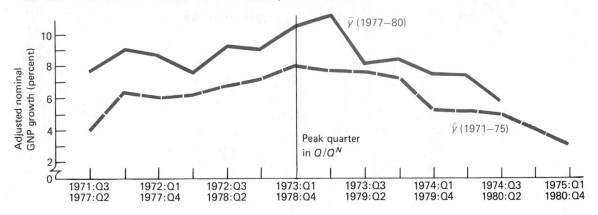

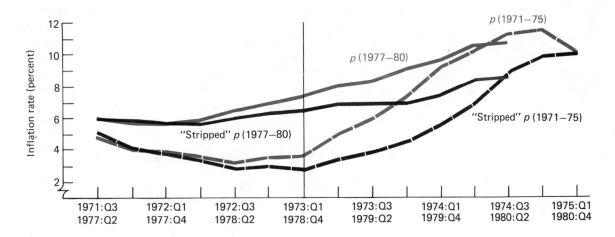

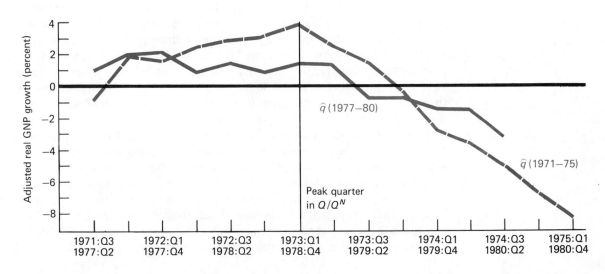

9-8

POLICY SOLUTIONS TO THE OIL PRICE PROBLEM

Because changes in the relative price of energy have had a major impact on macroeconomic policy in the 1970s, "energy policy" has now become a part of the subject of macroeconomics. Until now we have assumed that the price set by the OPEC oil nations is beyond the control of U.S. policy-makers, and that their only reaction is to choose the degree of "accommodative" or "extinguishing" aggregate demand response. But there is more that the United States can do. By devising means of holding down imports of oil, the United States can improve its inflation rate in two ways:

1. There is a direct dampening of U.S. inflation when imports are reduced, since there tends to be an appreciation of the dollar. As the dollar becomes more valuable, U.S. imports of all products from abroad become cheaper, and this puts downward pressure on U.S. domestic prices.
2. By cutting oil imports, the United States may be able to directly influence the price set by the OPEC nations. If they have agreed among themselves on a total annual volume of oil production, then the price at which they can sell that oil depends on the total demand from oil-consuming nations. Anything that the oil-consuming nations can do to reduce their oil imports will tend to limit the price increases that can be enforced by the OPEC cartel.

EFFECT OF PRICE CONTROLS ON DOMESTIC OIL

Thus the U.S. debate on energy policy has centered on means of reducing oil imports. Various policy options can be illustrated with the simple supply-and-demand diagram provided in Figure 9-8. The upward-sloping black line is the "Domestic supply curve," showing the different quantities of oil on the horizontal axis that would be produced at different price levels on the vertical axis. A higher price encourages domestic producers to search harder for oil and to produce types of energy that are uneconomic at lower prices. The red downward-sloping "Total demand curve" shows the different quantities of oil that the United States will want to buy at different prices. A higher price cuts consumption, as people drive less, shift to smaller cars, turn down their thermostats, and find they cannot afford to take airline vacations because of high fares caused by expensive fuel.

If there were no price controls on domestic oil, and if OPEC charged a price of $30 per barrel, total demand would be at point B and the domestic supply would be at point A, so oil imports would be the difference indicated by the distance AB. But in the United States price controls have been imposed on domestic oil, and this has had the effect of raising oil imports. Imagine that all domestic oil is sold at the controlled price of $10, so that the domestic supply is shown at point C. If we assume (for simplicity) that in the initial situation half of total demand is produced domestically and half

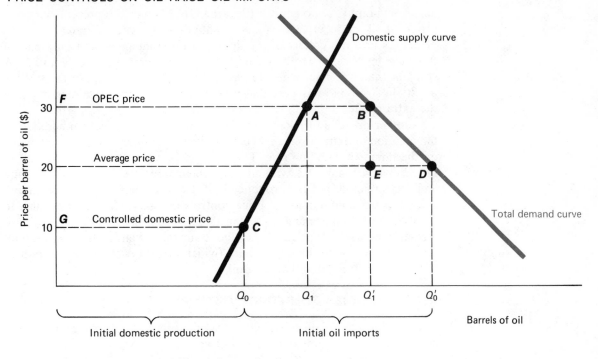

FIGURE 9–8

Effect on Oil Prices and Imports of Alternative Energy Policies

The upward-sloping black line shows the domestic supply of oil, and the down-ward-sloping red line shows the total demand. If the price is free to equal the OPEC price of $30 per barrel, oil imports will be AB. But if the domestic price is controlled at $10, and roughly half the oil is imported at a price of $30, the average price paid by consumers will be $20, and consumer demand is at point D. Then total imports will be the difference between demand and domestic supply, indicated on the horizontal axis by the distance $Q_0 Q_0'$.

is imported, then the average price paid by consumers will be $20 (the average of $10 and $30), and this is indicated at point D along the total demand curve. Oil imports will be the horizontal distance between C and D, shown by the quantity $Q_0 Q_0'$ along the horizontal axis, labeled "Initial oil imports."

Thus we see that the decontrol of domestic oil could cut oil imports from $Q_0 Q_0'$ to the distance AB, also indicated on the horizontal axis by $Q_1 Q_1'$. Why, then, was the debate on the decontrol of oil prices during 1977–79 so acrimonious? The major problem was that the decontrol of domestic oil would shift domestic oil producers from point C up to point A along their supply curve. The entire area between the supply curve and the vertical axis from point C up to point A (the area $GCAF$) would represent increased profits of oil producers. Consumers would thus be forced to transfer billions of dollars into the coffers of the domestic oil companies, and only part of this huge increase in profits would be spent on increased oil exploration. A solution that was finally enacted in early 1980 was to impose an "excess profits tax" on oil producers that would keep them from retaining much of the extra profit.

Another obvious problem with the decontrol of oil prices, in addition to the creation of extra profits, is the direct impact of higher domestic oil prices on the domestic inflation rate. There would be yet another upward shift in the SP line in Figure 9-2, with all the problems this creates for the economy and for economic policy. Proponents of decontrol have pointed out, however, that the continuation of price controls on oil would lead inevitably to increasing oil imports and a greater ability of the OPEC cartel to impose further increases in prices. Also, government revenues from a windfall profits tax do create the opportunity (which in 1980 was missed) to reduce the prices of products other than oil.

OTHER POLICIES TO REDUCE OIL IMPORTS

In addition to decontrol of oil prices, numerous other policies have been proposed. Each has advantages and disadvantages.

Import Quotas and Rationing. If price controls were retained, it would still be possible to reduce oil imports, say by the distance ED in Figure 9-8, by the direct imposition of quotas on oil imports. It would also be necessary to supplement these quotas with domestic rationing of oil products, since otherwise the demand at D would exceed the total supply at point E. Rationing, however, creates innumerable administrative problems and potential problems of unfairness. How would ration coupons be distributed?

Conservation. In the early days of his administration in 1977 President Carter urged Americans to "conserve energy"—that is, cut their demand. Minor demand reductions were achieved by various federal rules, particularly those limiting temperatures in public buildings. Yet the most effective spur to fuel conservation is a price increase, as was demonstrated in 1979–80 when a doubling in the retail price of gasoline substantially curtailed fuel consumption and led to a dramatic shift in demand toward smaller automobiles.

Synthetic Fuels. The July 1979 energy policy of the Carter administration put major emphasis on an expensive crash program to develop alternatives to oil. Skeptics pointed out, however, that the technology for these alternative forms of energy was new and might involve huge cost overruns, and that the potential savings in oil imports were minor—particularly when weighed against the enormous multibillion-dollar costs of these programs—in comparison with the savings in oil imports that would come from decontrol.

Taxes on Oil. Some proponents of raising oil prices would go beyond decontrol. They point approvingly to Europe and Japan, where heavy taxes are imposed on gasoline and other forms of energy as a means of reducing energy demand. Excise taxes on gasoline—which have raised the price per gallon to $3 in many European countries—are not necessarily inflationary because the government revenue from the tax can be used to reduce taxes on products other than energy. This is easier to accomplish in practice in Europe, where the rate on the nationwide "value-added tax" (equivalent to a national retail sales tax) can be manipulated, than in the United States. Finding an equivalent method to rebate gasoline tax revenues to the consumer has met political resistance in the United States, although no fundamental economic problems are involved. As an example of the dramatic potential for reducing energy consumption without creating extra inflation, a 50-cent federal excise tax on gasoline would raise $55 billion, enough if rebated to the states *to eliminate all state sales taxes*.[24]

9-9 RECAPITULATION OF CURES FOR INFLATION

In Chapters 8 and 9 we have learned that an acceleration of inflation can be caused both by excessive aggregate demand growth and by supply shocks that cause a jump in the price that business firms charge for a given amount of real GNP. Supply inflation and demand inflation are interrelated, because the extent and duration of extra inflation following a supply shock depends on the response of demand growth. An accommodative policy response will minimize the loss of real GNP but cause more inflation that may persist, particularly if wage rates respond to supply inflation through the effects of COLA clauses. An extinguishing policy response may be unable to eliminate all the inflationary impact of a supply shock immediately and is sure to cause a substantial loss of real GNP.

Just as excessive demand growth and adverse supply shocks are the fundamental causes of inflation, the basic cure for inflation is to turn these causes on their head. The reverse of fast demand growth is obviously slow demand growth. The reverse of adverse supply shocks is obviously favorable supply shocks. Government policy can achieve slower aggregate demand growth by slowing the growth rate of the money supply and by moving the federal budget from deficit to surplus. And government policy, while it cannot eliminate the consequences of OPEC oil price hikes, can create favorable supply shocks by eliminating or weakening price-raising and cost-raising legislation, and by creative tax and subsidy policy. The demand and

---

[24] The idea of higher oil taxes, offset by lower taxes (or subsidies) on other products, is nothing new. It was recommended after the first round of oil price increases in Robert J. Gordon, "Alternative Responses of Policy to External Supply Shocks," *Brookings Papers on Economic Activity*, vol. 6, no. 1 (1975), pp. 194–196.

supply cures for inflation are interrelated, since *any success by government policy in creating favorable price-reducing supply shocks must be backed up by accommodative policies that slow the growth of aggregate demand—* otherwise favorable supply shocks will boost real GNP and undo their own benefits by aggravating inflationary pressures.

The third traditional "cure" for inflation is to control prices or wages, either through compulsory controls or voluntary "guidelines." The abortive Nixon program of 1971–74 only served to destabilize real GNP with no permanent anti-inflationary benefit, and in fact the main benefit of the price control program was political—the reelection of the president in 1972. Price controls on domestic U.S. oil production have also been harmful by increasing U.S. dependence on oil imports and increasing the power of the OPEC cartel. Wage guidelines serve no purpose in the United States, where there is no evidence that the behavior of wages has been an independent source of inflation.

DEMAND INFLATION, MONETARY POLICY, AND THE 1980 BUDGET PANIC

Journalists frequently blame inflation on excessive government deficits. Overly influenced by journalists and political hysteria in reaction to temporarily high inflation rates in early 1980, the Carter administration scrapped its January 1980 budget after only two months and proposed a new, more restrictive budget in March 1980. How much truth is there in the accusation that budget deficits cause inflation and in the implication that the elimination of government deficits would reduce inflation? The simple answer is that government deficits are *one* source of inflation but are not unique, and that ending deficits would not necessarily end inflation.

Carter's second budget represents a classic mistake in postwar macroeconomic policy, as were the misguided credit controls introduced at the same time by the Federal Reserve with Carter's encouragement. In many previous periods, especially 1957, 1960, and late 1974, a tight fiscal or monetary policy was pursued long after it had ceased to be appropriate and in fact served mainly to worsen the subsequent recession. Carter's timing was precisely wrong—the new tight budget was introduced almost at the exact moment that the economy slipped into a precipitous decline in real GNP that marked the start of the 1980 recession. Since the reductions in expenditures and increases in tax rates on energy did not have their main effect until the last half of 1980, Carter's policy contributed directly to the extent of the increase of unemployment that occurred in 1980.

How did this mistimed policy action affect the inflation rate? A reduction in the government deficit is likely to cause a reduction in the inflation rate by shifting the DG line down temporarily along an initial SP schedule. But government deficits are not unique in this regard. Anything that shifts Chapter 4's IS curve leftward will cut aggregate demand and shift the DG line down temporarily. For instance, if a firm postpones an investment project and the issue of bonds intended to finance it, it simultaneously has a smaller deficit for itself and tends to reduce the national rate of inflation.

Government deficits may appear different from private deficits, because deficits in the government sector can be financed directly when the Federal Reserve decides to print money to cover the deficits. But this action by the Fed occurs only because government deficits push up interest rates, an event the Fed often tries to resist by allowing faster monetary expansion. There is, however, nothing special about federal government deficits. If AT&T or some other company issues more bonds to finance investment spending, interest rates will be pushed up, and the Fed may try to resist this in exactly the same way by allowing faster monetary expansion.

Thus government deficits are no more inflationary than an equal number of dollars spent on a private investment project financed by borrowing.[25] The popular myth that government deficits always are inflationary stems from the frequent episodes of huge deficits and rampant monetary expansion in wartime. But in principle, if an equally large private investment boom were to develop, private spending financed by borrowing could be equally inflationary.

It is important to recognize that inflation can be caused by supply shocks, but it is equally important to recognize that the inflationary impact of a supply shock depends on the response of aggregate demand growth, which in turn depends partly on monetary policy. As we learned in Figure 9-3, a given supply shock can cause very different responses of inflation, depending on whether the policy reaction is accommodative or extinguishing.

USING SUPPLY AND DEMAND POLICY TOGETHER TO SLOW INFLATION

In early 1980 it was easy for the president and his advisers to grow pessimistic about finding a cure for inflation. The old and traditional cures were beset by obvious problems. Price and wage controls had failed, and the innovative TIP plans seemed riddled with flaws. Restrictive aggregate demand policy depended for its success on the speed of response of inflation expectations to any achievement in reducing actual inflation, a response that might be slow to develop in light of the steady revision of inflation expectations *upward* in 1978–80. Without immediate success in reducing inflation expectations, a restrictive aggregate demand policy would have its main effect in reducing real GNP rather than inflation.

But pessimism had clearly been carried too far, because there was much

---

[25] The statement in the text refers to the short run. Later, after the private investment project has been completed and is in operation, it will raise the economy's aggregate supply of output, partially offsetting the initial inflationary effect. The major reason to oppose government deficits is that they tend to "crowd out" private investment and reduce the economy's capacity to produce in the long run, thus slowing the growth of natural real GNP (Q^N). See Chapter 18.

that government policy could achieve that would tend to shift the *SP* schedule downward. A policy stance that attempted to create favorable supply shocks would reinforce the effect of slower demand growth and reduce its impact on real GNP. Ideally a simultaneous downward shifting of the *SP* and *DG* schedules would allow a slowing of inflation without a drastic drop in the real GNP ratio Q/Q^N.

What policies were available that could create favorable supply shocks? A long list of possibilities had been proposed, and even if each item on the list might have only a minor impact, the cumulative effect of all items would be substantial:

1. Introduce a "split" minimum wage for teenagers that would allow firms to pay teenagers less than adults and that would hold down labor costs and prices in fast-food and other service industries.
2. Introduce a substantial excise tax on gasoline, which would reduce oil imports, help to hold down the OPEC price, and strengthen the dollar.
3. Use the revenue from the gasoline tax to reduce state sales taxes or to reduce the social security payroll tax.
4. Eliminate farm price support programs and deal with problems of farm poverty by supporting farm incomes, not prices.
5. Eliminate the protection from foreign competition of "lame-duck" U.S. industries (such as steel, TV, and the Chrysler Corporation). Spend government money encouraging high-technology industries rather than bailing out low-technology industries.
6. Eliminate aspects of the U.S. tax system that encourage consumption and borrowing and that depress productive investment and reduce productivity.
7. Rescind environmental, safety, and health regulation that does not pass a test comparing costs and benefits. For instance, it may be desirable to eliminate the first 90 percent of air and water pollution caused by automobiles and industrial waste but much too expensive to eliminate the last 10 percent.
8. Eliminate regulation of trucking and other forms of transportation, as was done for air transportation in 1978.
9. Eliminate the errors in the compilation of the Consumer Price Index that cause it to exaggerate inflation and then, through the feed-through of these errors via COLA clauses, to cause faster growth of wages and prices.
10. Cut the costs of the social security program to eliminate the need for increases in the payroll tax. This could be done by gradually raising the eligibility age for benefit recipients along with the increase in life expectancy made possible by improvements in medical care. Another major improvement would be to index social security benefits to average earnings instead of the erroneous Consumer Price Index (see section 2-10).

Economists had learned in the 1970s that excessive demand growth was not the only cause of inflation. And so there was no longer any reason to rely on restrictive demand growth as the only cure for inflation. Policies to reduce aggregate demand growth, *used in combination with imaginative supply-side, price-reducing, and cost-reducing policies*, would be more effective than either approach used alone.

SUMMARY

1. The highly variable inflation experience of the United States in the 1970s cannot be explained simply as the consequence of previous fluctuations in the growth of aggregate demand. Instead, "supply shocks" caused inflation to accelerate and decelerate independently of the influence of aggregate demand growth.

2. An adverse supply shock temporarily shifts upward the economy's short-run Phillips curve (*SP*). If nominal GNP growth is left unchanged, the result will be an acceleration of inflation and a reduction in the ratio Q/Q^N.

3. The response of policymakers who control nominal GNP growth determines how much inflation will result from an adverse supply shock. An "accommodative policy" keeps real GNP at its previous level but causes inflation to accelerate by the full impact of the supply shock; an "extinguishing policy" attempts to cancel out the acceleration of inflation but at the cost of a reduction in real GNP.

4. Accommodation would be an attractive policy if the upward shift in *SP* were expected to be temporary, and if expectations of inflation did not respond to the temporary jump in the inflation rate. But accommodation may cause more than a temporary increase of inflation if wage contracts have cost-of-living adjustment clauses that incorporate the supply shock into wage growth, if the supply shock causes productivity growth to decline permanently, and if a greater degree of accommodation in the United States than in other nations causes the dollar to decline in value.

5. Price controls can be treated as a favorable supply shock that shifts down the *SP* schedule, usually only temporarily. The response of inflation and real GNP depends on whether government policy accommodates the controls by slowing down aggregate demand growth. In the early 1970s controls served only to destabilize the behavior of prices and real GNP with no long-run benefit, and in addition they interfered with the efficient operation of the economy.

6. The depth of the recession of 1973–75 can be explained by three supply shocks (the termination of price controls and increases in the relative prices of food and of energy), together with an extinguishing policy that slowed aggregate demand growth in response to the supply shocks.

7. In 1978–80 the economy was again beset by adverse supply shocks, again involving an increase in the relative price of food and of energy. The response of real GNP growth was almost as severe as in 1974–75 and was aggravated by misguided government policies that restricted demand growth just as the recession began.

Policies to fight supply-shock inflation involve creating favorable supply shocks. These include policies to reduce oil imports, cut the types of taxes that tend to be passed forward to consumers, and reduce the impact on the economy of government economic and social regulations that boost prices and costs.

A LOOK AHEAD

Until now we have examined the behavior of only one measure of real activity in the economy: the ratio of actual to natural real GNP (Q/Q^N). But we are interested also in understanding the reason for fluctuations in unemployment. In the next chapter we learn that the difference between the actual unemployment rate (U) and natural unemployment rate (U^N) is very closely related to the real GNP ratio Q/Q^N. We shall also learn why the natural unemployment rate U^N is so high in the United States, and what can be done to reduce it.

CONCEPTS

Supply shock	Depreciation of the dollar
Relative price	Price controls
Neutral policy	"Stripped" inflation rate
Accommodative policy	Self-inflicted wounds
Extinguishing policy	Supply-side anti-inflation policy
Labor productivity	TIP
COLA clause	

QUESTIONS FOR REVIEW

1   Explain whether each of the following events will shift the SP curve and, if so, in what direction:
    a. An increase in the price of oil from $12 to $30 per barrel
    b. A temporary freeze in all prices
    c. The termination of a temporary freeze in all prices
    d. A slowdown in the growth rate of the money supply
    e. A freeze that kills all the oranges in Florida

2   Following an adverse supply shock, what happens to the rate of inflation and the real GNP ratio (Q/Q^N) in each of these three cases:
    a. Accommodative policy
    b. Neutral policy
    c. Extinguishing policy

3   What does it mean to "accommodate a price control program"? What

happens to the economy if a price control program is not accommodated?

4 Explain the relevance of question 3 to the presidential election of 1972.

5 Which of the following pairs represents a situation more conducive to accommodation of supply shocks?
   a. An open economy versus a closed economy
   b. Fully indexed wage contracts versus no cost-of-living escalators
   c. Fixed nominal wages versus fixed real wages

6 What happens to the real GNP ratio (Q/Q^N) in each of the following situations?
   a. Inflation exceeds adjusted demand growth.
   b. Inflation equals adjusted demand growth.
   c. Inflation is less than adjusted demand growth.

7 Use your answer in the previous question to explain the phrase, *Inflation breeds recession.*

8 If the termination of price controls on domestic oil and the introduction of an excise tax on imported oil both raise the relative price of oil, and thus create an adverse supply shock, then why do some economists recommend that these measures be taken?

9 Which of the following cures for inflation do you favor, and why?
   a. Slower demand growth
   b. Wage and price controls
   c. Policies to create cost-reducing supply shocks
   d. a and b
   e. a and c

APPENDIX TO CHAPTERS 8 AND 9
The Elementary Algebra of Inflation, Real GNP, and Unemployment

Throughout Chapters 8 and 9 we have located the short-run equilibrium rate of inflation and level of real GNP at the crossing point of a *DG* line and an *SP* line, as at point E_3 of Figures 9-2 or 9-5. Now we learn how to calculate the inflation rate and level of real GNP without going to the trouble of making drawings of the *DG* and *SP* lines. We do this by solving together the equations that describe the *DG* and *SP* lines, just as we did in the Appendix to Chapter 5, where we learned the equivalent in algebra to the *IS* and *LM* curves.

EQUATION FOR THE *SP* LINE

The *SP* line of Chapters 8 and 9 can be written as a relationship between the actual inflation rate (p), the expected inflation rate (p^e), and the real GNP ratio—that is, the ratio of actual real GNP to natural real GNP (Q/Q^N):

| GENERAL FORM | NUMERICAL EXAMPLE |

$$p = p^e + g(Q/Q^N - 1) + x \qquad p = p^e + 0.5(Q/Q^N - 1) \qquad (1)$$

Here the x designates the contribution of supply shocks to inflation, and initially in the numerical example we assume that the element of supply shocks is absent ($x = 0$), so that we can concentrate initially on demand inflation. The numerical example also assumes that the slope of the SP line, designated g in the general form, is 0.5 in the numerical example as was assumed in all the figures of Chapters 8 and 9. Thus $g = 0.5$ indicates that the SP line slopes up by 1 percentage point in extra inflation for each 2 percentage points of extra real GNP relative to natural real GNP (Q/Q^N). We also note that the term in parentheses in the equation equals zero only when $Q/Q^N = 1$, in which case the economy is on its vertical LP line where actual and expected inflation are equal ($p = p^e$).

In order to understand what makes the SP line shift, we must copy here equation (8.3). This indicates that expectations of inflation (p^e) are formed adaptively as a weighted average of last period's actual inflation rate (p_{-1}) and last period's expected inflation rate (p^e_{-1}):

| GENERAL FORM | NUMERICAL EXAMPLE |

$$p^e = jp_{-1} + (1 - j)p^e_{-1} \qquad\qquad p^e = p_{-1} \qquad (2)$$

The numerical example assumes that $j = 1$; that is, that expected inflation depends simply on what the inflation rate actually turned out to be last period, with the subscript "−1" indicating "last period."

When we substitute (2) into (1), we obtain a new expression for the SP line that depends on two current-period variables (Q/Q^N and x) and two variables from last period (p_{-1} and p^e_{-1}):

GENERAL FORM

$$p = jp_{-1} + (1 - j)p^e_{-1} + g(Q/Q^N - 1) + x \qquad (3)$$

NUMERICAL EXAMPLE

$$p = p_{-1} + 0.5(Q/Q^N - 1)$$

EQUATION FOR THE *DG* LINE

But we need more information than that contained in (3) to determine both current inflation (p) and the current real GNP ratio (Q/Q^N). In other words, we have two unknown variables and just one equation to determine their equilibrium values. What is the missing equation? This is the DG line that contains the definition that adjusted real GNP growth ($\hat{q}$) is equal to adjusted nominal GNP growth ($\hat{y}$) minus the inflation rate (p):

$$\hat{q} = \hat{y} - p \qquad (4)$$

The next step is to relate $\hat{q}$ in (4) to the current real GNP ratio (Q/Q^N)

that appears in (3). This can be done by noting that $\hat{q}$ is approximately equal to the change in the real GNP ratio from last period to this period:[1]

$$\hat{q} = Q/Q^N - (Q/Q^N)_{-1} \qquad (5)$$

COMBINING THE *SP* AND *DG* EQUATIONS

Now we are ready to combine our equations for the *SP* line (3) and *DG* line (4). When (5) is substituted into the *DG* equation (4), we obtain the following:

$$Q/Q^N = (Q/Q^N)_{-1} + \hat{y} - p \qquad (6)$$

Now (6) can be substituted into the *SP* equation (3) to obtain:

$$p = jp_{-1} + (1-j)p^e_{-1} + g[(Q/Q^N)_{-1} - 1 + \hat{y} - p] + x \qquad (7)$$

This can be further simplified if we factor out p from the right-hand side of (7):[2]

GENERAL FORM

$$p = \frac{1}{1+g} \{jp_{-1} + (1-j)p^e_{-1} + g[(Q/Q^N)_{-1} - 1 + \hat{y}] + x\} \qquad (8)$$

NUMERICAL EXAMPLE

$$p = \frac{2}{3} \{p_{-1} + 0.5[(Q/Q^N)_{-1} - 1 + \hat{y}]\}$$

Now we are ready to use equation (8) to examine the consequences of any event that can alter the inflation rate and real GNP ratio in the short run and long run. The main subject of Chapter 8 was the consequences of accelerations and decelerations in adjusted demand growth ($\hat{y}$), so let us use

---

[1] **Review:** $\hat{y}$ and $\hat{q}$ are defined in section 8-7. Equation (5) is only approximately true and can be derived if we note that $\hat{q}$ is the time derivative of the log of the ratio Q/Q^N:

$$\frac{d}{dt}[\log (Q/Q^N)] = \frac{d \log (Q)}{dt} - \frac{d \log (Q^N)}{dt} = q - q^N = \hat{q} \qquad (a)$$

Here the variables written in lower-case letters, for instance q, are percentage rates of change of variables written in capital letters (Q), and can also be written as the time derivative of the log of the variable written in capital letters, $d \log (Q)/dt$.

The first term on the left of equation (a) can also be written as the percentage change in Q/Q^N between last period and this period:

$$\frac{d}{dt}[\log (Q/Q^N)] = \frac{Q/Q^N - (Q/Q^N)_{-1}}{(Q/Q^N)_{-1}} \qquad (b)$$

Thus equation (5) in the text is obtained by setting the right-hand term in (a) — that is, adjusted real GNP growth ($\hat{q}$) — equal to the right-hand side of (b). The denominator of (b) is omitted in equation (5), a valid procedure only if the ratio Q/Q^N is reasonably close to 1.0. Obviously (5) will be a rougher approximation if Q/Q^N is far from 1.0, but within the 1950–80 period Q/Q^N has ranged only from 0.93 to 1.04.

[2] To obtain (8) from (7), add gp to both sides of equation (7). Then divide both sides of the resulting equation by $1 + g$.

equation (8) to reproduce the path of adjustment plotted in Figure 8-7 on p. 225 following an acceleration in $\hat{y}$ from zero to 6 percent per annum.

EXAMPLE WHEN $\hat{y}$ RISES FROM 0 TO 6 PERCENT

We start out initially with zero inflation and with a real GNP ratio of 1.0, as at point E_0 in Figure 8-7. We also assume that there are no supply shocks ($x = 0$). Thus our initial situation begins with:

$$p_{-1} = p^e_{-1} = \hat{y} = 0 \quad \text{and} \quad Q/Q^N = 1.0$$

Substituting into the numerical example version of (8) we can confirm that these values are consistent with an initial value of zero inflation:

$$p = \frac{2}{3} [0 + 0.5(1 - 1 + 0)] = 0$$

Now there is an assumed sudden jump in $\hat{y}$ to 6 percent per year, which we will write as $\hat{y} = 0.06$. What happens to inflation in the first period? Substituting $\hat{y} = 0.06$ into the numerical example, we have:

$$p = \frac{2}{3} [0 + 0.5(1 - 1 + 0.06)] = \frac{2}{3} (0.03) = 0.02$$

The new real GNP ratio can be found by using equation (6):

$$Q/Q^N = (Q/Q^N)_{-1} + \hat{y} - p = 1.0 + 0.06 - 0.02 = 1.04$$

Thus we have derived the combination of p and Q/Q^N plotted at point F in Figure 8-7—that is, inflation of 2 percent and a real GNP ratio of 1.04.[3]
   The adjustment continues in future periods, of course. We can compute the values of p and Q/Q^N in the next few periods by substituting the correct numbers into the numerical example version of (8), using a pocket calculator. These values correspond exactly to the path labeled "$j = 1$" in Figure 8-7:

Period	p_{-1}	$(Q/Q^N)_{-1}$	$\hat{y}$	p	Q/Q^N
0	0.00	1.00	0.00	0.00	1.00
1	0.00	1.00	0.06	0.02	1.04
2	0.02	1.04	0.06	0.0467	1.0533
3	0.0467	1.0533	0.06	0.0689	1.0444
4	0.0689	1.0444	0.06	0.0807	1.0237

Exercise 1: Using the same numerical example, calculate what happens for the first four periods when the economy is in an initial long-run equilibrium at point E_3 in Figure 8-11 with $\hat{y} = p = p^e = 0.06$, and $Q/Q^N = 1.0$, and suddenly the adjusted growth rate of nominal GNP

---

[3] In Figure 8-7 we assumed for simplicity that natural real GNP was not growing. Thus any change in Q/Q^N became simply a shift in Q itself, in this case a 4 percent increase from 100 to 104 in Figure 8-7.

($\hat{y}$) falls to a new permanent value of zero. How is your answer changed if the coefficient of adjustment of expectations is assumed to be $j = 0.25$ instead of $j = 1.0$? (**Hint:** This requires that you substitute $j = 0.25$ and $g = 0.5$ into the "General Form" version of equation (8) above.)

THE CONSEQUENCES OF A SUPPLY SHOCK

We have examined the effect on inflation of an acceleration of growth in aggregate demand. But another source of inflation may be a supply shock, such as an increase in the relative price of food or energy. Let us assume that we start in long-run equilibrium at point E_3 in Figure 9-2, with $\hat{y} = p = p^e = 0.06$, and $Q/Q^N = 1.0$. Initially the supply-shock variable x is equal to zero. But now let us assume there is a jump in the relative price of oil that boosts x to a value of 0.03 for two periods, followed by a return after that to $x = 0.00$.

Our discussion of supply shocks emphasized that two crucial factors determine how the economy reacts to a supply shock. First, is $\hat{y}$ increased, decreased, or left the same by policymakers following the shock? Second, do expectations adjust to the temporary shock? Cost-of-living-adjustment clauses in wage contracts are equivalent to an adjustment of expected inflation for the influence of the supply shock.

The simplest case to analyze is one in which there is no response of either demand growth ($\hat{y}$) or expected inflation (p^e). To trace the path of inflation and the real GNP ratio, we simply use our general formula (8) with $\hat{y}$ assumed to be permanently fixed at 0.06, and $j = 0$ (representing the failure of expectations to respond at all to actual inflation). The general form for this case becomes:

$$p = \frac{1}{1+g}\{p^e_{-1} + g[(Q/Q^N)_{-1} - 1 + \hat{y}] + x\} \qquad (9)$$

$$= \frac{2}{3}\{p^e_{-1} + 0.5[Q/Q^N)_{-1} - 1 + \hat{y}] + x\}$$

Now, starting in the initial situation, we substitute the required elements into this formula for each period in succession.

Period	p^e_{-1}	$(Q/Q^N)_{-1}$	$\hat{y}$	x	p	Q/Q^N
0	0.06	1.00	0.06	0.00	0.06	1.00
1	0.06	1.00	0.06	0.03	0.08	0.98
2	0.06	0.98	0.06	0.03	0.0733	0.9667
3	0.06	0.9667	0.06	0.00	0.0489	0.9778
4	0.06	0.9778	0.06	0.00	0.0526	0.9852
5	0.06	0.9852	0.06	0.00	0.0551	0.9901

This adjustment path shows what would happen to the economy with a two-period supply shock of $x = 0.03$, with a "neutral" aggregate demand policy that maintains steady nominal GNP growth, and with no response of expectations to the effects of the supply shock. In period 1 the inflation rate jumps from 0.06 to 0.08, exactly duplicating the movement from point E_3 to point L in Figure 9-2. In the next period inflation diminishes somewhat; since the position of the DG line depends on the current period's starting value of Q/Q^N, which has fallen from 1.00 to 0.98. Thus the intersection of DG and SP slides southwest down the stationary SP_3 line to $p = 0.0733$ and $Q/Q^N = 0.9667$. Then the supply shock ends, x returns to its original zero value, and the economy gradually climbs back up the SP_2 line to its long-run equilibrium position, $p = 0.06$ and $Q/Q^N = 1.00$.

> **Exercise 2:** What rate of adjusted demand growth should policymakers choose if they want to pursue an accommodating policy? An extinguishing policy? (**Hint:** An accommodating policy means that Q/Q^N remains fixed at 1.0, which can only occur if $\hat{q} = 0$, requiring that $\hat{y} = p$. Substitute p for $\hat{y}$ in equation (9) and, in addition, note that $(Q/Q^N)_{-1} = 1$, thus obtaining $p = p^e_{-1} + x$. For an extinguishing policy take (9) and set the left-hand side (p) equal to 0.06; then solve for the required $\hat{y}$.)

> **Exercise 3:** For a neutral policy response, calculate the adjustment path of inflation and Q/Q^N in the first four periods when expectations respond fully to the extra inflation caused by the supply shock. That is, assume now that $j = 1$ instead of $j = 0$ as in the previous exercise. Next, maintaining the assumption that $j = 1$, calculate the same adjustment path when the policy response is accommodative. (See the hint for Exercise 2.) How would you describe the disadvantages of an accommodative policy when $j = 1$?

THE BEHAVIOR OF THE UNEMPLOYMENT RATE

At the beginning of Chapter 10 we shall learn that the unemployment rate (U) is very closely related to the ratio Q/Q^N. Corresponding to the natural level of real GNP (Q^N), defined as the level of real GNP at which expectations of inflation turn out to be accurate, there is a natural rate of unemployment (U^N). When real GNP is above Q^N, and inflation is accelerating, we also find that the actual unemployment rate (U) is below the natural rate of unemployment (U^N). This relationship can be written:[4]

GENERAL FORM	NUMERICAL EXAMPLE	
$U = U^N - h(Q/Q^N - 1)$	$U = U^N - 0.5(Q/Q^N - 1)$	(10)

How is this relationship to be used? First, we must determine the value of the natural rate of unemployment. In the United States in the early 1980s this appears to be approximately $U^N = 0.055$ (or 5.5 percent). Then we take

---

[4] **Caution:** In the appendix to Chapter 3 we used h to designate the response of real imports to a change in real GNP. This is the first case in the book where we have been forced by the limitations of the alphabet to repeat a letter for a second purpose.

values for Q/Q^N determined in the above examples and exercises and substitute these values into equation (10). Here are two examples:

Example 1: $Q/Q^N = 0.95$
Since $U^N = 0.055$, we use (10) to determine:

$$U = 0.055 - 0.5(0.95 - 1) = 0.055 - 0.5(-0.05) = 0.080$$

or an unemployment rate of 8 percent.

Example 2: $Q/Q^N = 1.05$

$$U = 0.055 - 0.5(1.05 - 1) = 0.055 - 0.5(0.05) = 0.030$$

or an unemployment rate of 3.0 percent. Thus we see that for every 5 percentage points by which Q/Q^N exceeds 1.0, the unemployment rate lies 2.5 percentage points below U^N, the natural unemployment rate of 5.5 percent. And for every 5 percentage points by which Q/Q^N falls short of 1.0, the unemployment rate lies 2.5 percentage points above the natural unemployment rate of 5.5 percent.

There is also a simple short-cut way of calculating the *change* in the unemployment rate from last period (U_{-1}) to this period (U):[5]

GENERAL FORM   NUMERICAL EXAMPLE

$$U = U_{-1} - h\hat{q} \qquad U = U_{-1} - 0.5\hat{q} \qquad (11)$$

Thus, starting with $U_{-1} = 0.06$, a value of $\hat{q}$ of 0.01 (one percentage point) will cause the unemployment rate to fall to $U = 0.055$.

Exercise 4: Go back through the previous exercises and calculate the unemployment rate for each period corresponding to Q/Q^N.

---

[5] How can (11) be derived from (10)? Let us write down (10) and then subtract from it the value of (10) for last period:

$$U = U^N - h(Q/Q^N - 1)$$
$$- U_{-1} = U_{-1}^N - h[(Q/Q^N)_{-1} - 1]$$

If there is no change in U^N from one period to the next, then this difference is:

$$U - U_{-1} = -h[Q/Q^N - (Q/Q_{-1}^N)]$$

But now we can substitute $\hat{q}$ into this expression, using equation (5):

$$U - U_{-1} = -h\hat{q}$$

10 Unemployment: Causes, Costs, and Policy Options

The matter of unemployment—the awful human situation that is entailed, the distressing business of a man or a woman wanting work but not finding any—is indeed a dreadful business. It would be heartless to contend that human misery is not involved.[1]

10-1 THE DILEMMA OF HIGH UNEMPLOYMENT

The average U.S. unemployment rate in the decade of the 1970s was 6.2 percent. In 1975 and 1976 the jobless rate soared to 8.5 and 7.7 percent, respectively, both figures higher than in any year since the Great Depression. In 1980 an unemployment rate of 8 percent was reached and exceeded. Why should society tolerate such high levels of unemployment, together with the waste that occurs when machines, factories, stores, and office buildings are underutilized? Should we conclude that there is some simple solution that economists understand but politicians refuse to accept? Or is the problem of high unemployment basically insoluble?

We were first introduced to the close relationship between real GNP and the unemployment rate in Figure 1-3. There we noticed that years when real GNP fell below natural real GNP were also years of high unemployment, when the actual unemployment rate exceeded the natural rate of unemployment. Our first task in this chapter is to quantify the relationship between real GNP and unemployment.

Because of the regular relation between real GNP and the unemployment rate, we have already completed the job of understanding the main causes of *fluctuations* in unemployment. In Chapter 8 we concluded that the government has the power to raise real GNP (and thus reduce unemployment) by stimulating aggregate demand growth, but only for a temporary period. In Chapter 9 we learned that supply shocks can cause inflation to worsen and real GNP to decline at the same time, thus also causing higher unemployment.

---

[1] Alfred L. Malabre, Jr., *America's Dilemma: Jobs vs. Prices* (New York: Dodd, Mead, 1978), pp. 31–32.

But what we have learned so far only helps us understand the causes of *changes* of actual unemployment above and below the natural rate of unemployment. So far we have said nothing that would explain why the natural rate of unemployment (U^N) is itself so high.

> *The first and most basic cause of high unemployment in the United States is that the natural rate of unemployment is not zero, but a much higher number, in the vicinity of 5.5 or 6.0 percent.*

We learn in the first part of this chapter why the natural rate of unemployment is not zero. We discover that at least some unemployment is not a complete waste but actually serves a social purpose. Nevertheless, the high level of the natural rate of unemployment in the United States includes a wasteful portion: the natural rate is higher than necessary as a result of discrimination against blacks and women, barriers to mobility and the acquisition of job skills, and even to some extent because of government regulations.

Thus the terminology *natural rate of unemployment* is misleading. The natural rate is not carved in stone, immutable, or desirable. It can be changed either by the actions of private firms and households (for instance, better matching of job requirements and worker skills) or by changes in government policy (for instance, changes in minimum wage rates or unemployment benefits). The rate is natural only in the sense of equilibrium—at the natural unemployment rate, whatever its value in a particular year, there is no pressure on the inflation rate to change. Any attempt to push the unemployment rate lower than this year's natural rate of unemployment causes inflation to speed up, whereas a higher unemployment rate slows inflation.

After we examine in the main portion of this chapter why the natural unemployment rate is so high, and what can be done to reduce it, in the last sections we will look closer at the costs to society of policies that allow actual unemployment to exceed the natural rate. We will measure these costs of recessions and then, in Chapter 11, for comparison examine the costs of inflation.

10-2 CASE STUDY: UNEMPLOYMENT AND THE REAL GNP RATIO

Most of our task of understanding fluctuations in unemployment has already been completed. When the real GNP ratio (Q/Q^N) rises, the unemployment rate declines, and vice versa. Although one cannot predict the unemployment rate perfectly by knowing the Q/Q^N ratio, nevertheless the unemployment rate is very closely related to Q/Q^N.

In Figure 10-1 notice the cluster of prosperous years, 1965–69, in the lower right corner, with values of Q/Q^N well above 1.0 and unusually low unemployment rates. The contrasting situation in the upper left

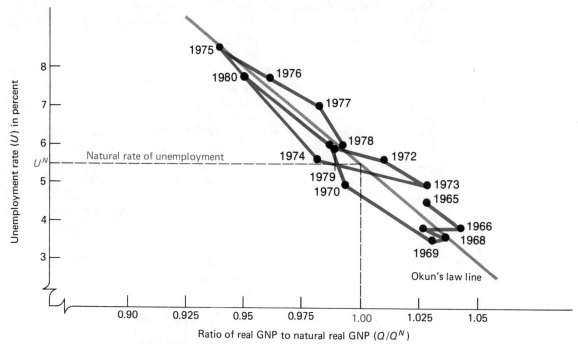

FIGURE 10–1

The U.S. Ratio of Actual to Natural Real GNP (Q/Q^N)
and the Unemployment Rate, 1965–80

This diagram illustrates that unemployment (U) moves inversely with the real
GNP ratio (Q/Q^N). In prosperous years, such as 1966–69, the observations are in
the lower right corner, with a high real GNP ratio and low unemployment. The
opposite extreme occurred in 1975 and 1980, the observations plotted at the upper
left corner. A recession occurred, the output ratio fell, and workers were laid off.
The gray line expresses the relation between U and Q/Q^N, sometimes called
Okun's law.

corner occurred in the recession year 1975, when massive layoffs caused
record unemployment, and the Q/Q^N ratio fell to only 0.939. The negative
slope of the points connected by the red line in Figure 10-1 just reflects
common sense. When sales slump, workers are laid off and the jobless
rate rises. But when sales boom and Q/Q^N is high, some of the jobless
are hired, and the unemployment rate goes down.

The close negative connection between the unemployment rate (U)
and Q/Q^N was first pointed out in the early 1960s by the late Arthur M.
Okun, formerly Chairman of the Council of Economic Advisers in the

Johnson administration.[2] Because it has held up so well, the relationship has been widely dubbed **Okun's law.** Not only does U tend to follow the major movements in Q/Q^N, but in addition the percentage-point change in the unemployment rate tends to be about one-half the percentage change in the Q/Q^N ratio, in the opposite direction. For instance, the gray line is drawn so that a real GNP ratio (Q/Q^N) of 1.0 corresponds to a natural unemployment rate of 5.5 percent, a situation in which the actual and expected rates of inflation are equal. A drop in the Q/Q^N ratio by 5 percentage points, from 1.0 to 0.95, would correspond to an increase in the unemployment rate of half as much, or 2.5 percentage points, as indicated by the gray line going through 8.0 percent unemployment on the vertical axis and 0.95 on the horizontal axis.[3]

Consider, for instance, the following examples in which a change in the real GNP ratio was accompanied by a change in the unemployment rate of about half as much in the opposite direction:

Years	Percentage change in Q/Q^N	Percentage change in U	Ratio of (2) to (1) (percent)
1969–71	−4.4	2.4	−54.5
1975–78	5.3	−2.5	−47.2

Another feature that stands out in Figure 10-1 is that the red line connecting the various annual observations tends to "loop around" the gray Okun's law line in a clockwise direction. This reflects the lag in the adjustment of unemployment to changes in Q/Q^N. In a year such as 1973 Q/Q^N expanded rapidly, but firms were slow to hire workers, delaying the decline in unemployment. In years such as 1970 and 1974, when Q/Q^N dropped sharply, firms were slow to fire workers, and so there was a delay in the increase in the unemployment rate.[4]

---

[2] Arthur M. Okun, "Potential GNP: Its Measurement and Significance," reprinted in Okun's *The Political Economy of Prosperity* (Washington, D.C.: Brookings Institution, 1970), pp. 132–145. The most recent studies of the relationship are contained in George Perry, "Potential Output and Productivity," *Brookings Papers on Economic Activity,* vol. 8, no. 1 (1977), pp. 11–47; and John A. Tatom, "Economic Growth and Unemployment: A Reappraisal of the Conventional View," *Federal Reserve Bank of St. Louis Review* (October 1978), pp. 16–22.

[3] The response of unemployment to a change in Q/Q^N is estimated to be 0.45 by Tatom, *op. cit.* This figure is rounded off to 0.50 here. The original Okun article and much of the literature on Okun's law sets the responsiveness of unemployment to Q/Q^N at 0.33, but this estimate seems to have been obsolete for many years, because the original articles on Okun's law ignored the substantial lag in the response of unemployment to Q/Q^N.

[4] The delayed response of unemployment to changes in Q/Q^N is the counterpart of the over-staffing of employees that has occurred late in each business-cycle expansion in years such as 1956–57, 1959–60, 1969–70, 1974, and 1979. See Robert J. Gordon, "The End-of-Expansion Phenomenon in Short-run Productivity Behavior," *Brookings Papers on Economic Activity,* vol. 10, no. 2 (1979), pp. 447–461.

10-3

HOW THE GOVERNMENT MEASURES UNEMPLOYMENT

Many people wonder how the government determines facts such as that "the teenage unemployment rate in May 1980 was 17.8 percent," because they themselves have never spoken to a government agent about their own experiences of employment, unemployment, and time in school. It would be too costly for everyone in the country to be contacted every month; the government attempts to reach each household to collect information only once each decade when it takes the Decennial Census of Population. On the other hand it would not be enough to collect information just once every ten years, because policymakers would have no guidance for conducting current policy.

As a compromise, the Census Bureau interviews each month about 55,000 households, or about 1 in every 1500 households in the country. Each month one-fourth of the households in the sample are replaced, so that no family is interviewed more than four months in a row. The laws of statistics imply that an average from a survey of a sample of households of this size comes very close to the true figure that would be revealed by a costly complete census.[5]

The interviewer first asks, for each separate household member, "What was he (or she) doing most of last week—working, keeping house, going to school, or something else?" The person is counted as employed if he did any work at all for pay during the past week, whether part-time, full-time, or temporary work.

For those who say they did no work, the next question is "Did he have a job from which he was temporarily absent or on layoff last week?" If the reason for job absence is that the person is awaiting recall from a layoff or has obtained a new job but is waiting for it to begin, he is counted as unemployed. If the person neither works nor is absent from a job, the next question is "Has he been looking for work in the last four weeks?" If so, "What has he been doing in the last four weeks to find work?" If the person has not been ill and has searched for a job by applying to an employer, registering with an employment agency, checking with friends, or other specified job-search activities, he is counted as unemployed. The remaining people who are neither employed nor unemployed, mainly homemakers who do not seek paid work, students at school, disabled people, and retired people, are counted as not in the labor force.

Despite the intricacy of questions asked by the interviewer, the concept is simple: "People with jobs are employed; people who do not have jobs and are looking for jobs are unemployed; people who meet neither labor market test are not in the labor force."[6] The **total labor force** is the total of the em-

---

[5] The facts in this section are taken from *How the Government Measures Unemployment*, BLS Report no. 505 (Washington, D.C.: U.S. Bureau of Labor Statistics, 1977).

[6] *How the Government Measures Unemployment*, p. 6.

ployed and the unemployed. Thus the entire population aged 16 and over falls into one of three categories:

1. Total labor force
   a. Employed (civilian employed plus members of the armed forces)
   b. Unemployed
2. Not in the labor force

The actual unemployment rate is defined as the ratio:

$$U = \frac{\text{number of unemployed}}{\text{civilian employed} + \text{unemployed}}$$

Example: In May 1980 the BLS reported an unemployment rate of 7.8 percent. This was calculated as the ratio:

$$U = \frac{\text{number of unemployed}}{\text{civilian employed} + \text{unemployed}} = \frac{8,154,000}{96,988,000 + 8,154,000}$$
$$\text{or } U = 7.8 \text{ percent}$$

The government's unemployment measure sounds relatively straightforward, but unfortunately it disguises almost as much as it reveals:

1. *The unemployment rate by itself is not a measure of the social distress caused by the loss of a job.* Each person who lacks a job and is looking for one is counted as "1.0 unemployed people," whether he is the head of a household responsible for feeding three, four, or even ten dependents or whether he is a 16-year-old looking only for a ten-hour-per-week part-time job to provide pocket money for milk shakes and rock records. Only a minority of the unemployed can be described as workers who have lost one job and are looking for another. Other important categories are those who have obtained jobs but are not at work (either because the jobs have not yet started or because of temporary layoffs); workers who are between temporary jobs; and people who are looking into the possibility of work as an alternative to household duties, school, or retirement. Only a minority of those counted as unemployed are engaged in job-seeking activities as their major use of time during the week of the household survey; the majority are keeping house, going to school, or retired.[7] Almost half the teenage unemployed, for instance, are looking for part-time jobs after school rather than full-time work.[8]
2. *The government's unemployment concept misses some of the people hurt by a recession.* Some suffer a cut in hours, being forced by their employer to shift from full-time to part-time work. Still counted as employed, they never enter the unemployment statistics.

---

[7] Robert E. Hall, "The Nature and Measurement of Unemployment," National Bureau of Economic Research working paper no. 252, July 1978.

[8] Martin S. Feldstein and David Ellwood, "Teenage Unemployment: What Is the Problem?" National Bureau of Economic Research working paper no. 393, September 1979, Table 1, p. 6.

3. *A person lacking a job must have performed particular specified actions to look for a job during the past four weeks.* What if he has looked and looked and has given up, convinced that no job is available? He is not counted as unemployed at all. He simply "disappears" from the labor force, entering the category of not in labor force. Those out of the labor force who would like to work but have given up on the job search are sometimes called discouraged workers or the disguised unemployed. They have numbered as many as 1 million in some postwar recessions.[9]

Despite the inadequacies of the government unemployment concept, our graphs and tables emphasize the total official unemployment rate because it is most widely publicized and discussed by the public.[10] To reach a better understanding of the meaning of unemployment, however, we have to probe deeper and look at some of the subtotals and supplementary figures published in government reports.

10-4 CASE STUDY: ACTUAL AND NATURAL RATES OF UNEMPLOYMENT IN THE UNITED STATES

The top frame of Figure 10-2 (p. 305) for the years since 1954 shows the Q/Q^N ratio; the middle frame compares the actual unemployment rate with an estimate of the natural rate of unemployment. The period can be divided into several major episodes, a recession in 1954, a boom in 1955–57, a long period of high unemployment and sluggish output growth between 1958 and 1964, a prolonged boom (partly caused by the Vietnam War) between 1965 and 1969, followed in the 1970s by two recessions (1970–71 and 1973–75), two periods of recovery (1972–73 and 1977–79), and then another recession in 1980. Episodes with actual unemployment above the natural rate are distinguished from episodes with actual unemployment below the natural rate by the shading on the diagram.

The natural-rate hypothesis, examined in Chapter 8, tells us that inflation increases faster than people expect when actual unemployment falls below the natural rate. Figure 10-2 illustrates the workings of the natural-rate hypothesis. The middle frame, as we have seen, plots the actual rate and estimated natural rate of unemployment. During the in-

---

[9] Two techniques have been used to estimate disguised unemployment. One is to measure how far the labor force in a recession falls below its normal growth. The second, which yields much smaller estimates of disguised unemployment, is to count those who tell the Census interviewer that their reason for being not in labor force is that they "think they cannot get a job." Why the discrepancy between the two methods? Some discouraged workers may drop out of the labor force and enter school or take up housework, and then they may tell the Census interviewer that those activities are the reason they are not in the labor force.

[10] A recent attempt to correct some of these inadequacies is Sar A. Levitan and Robert Taggart III, *Employment and Earnings Inadequacy: A New Social Indicator* (Baltimore: Johns Hopkins Press, 1974).

terval between 1954 and 1971, periods of low actual unemployment (pink shading) were also periods, denoted by pink shading in the bottom frame, when the rate of inflation exceeded the estimated expected rate.[11] In contrast to the pink-shaded periods of price acceleration, the gray shading shows periods when price change slowed. During the gray periods the actual unemployment rate was above the natural rate in the top frame of Figure 10-2.

Notice that the relation breaks down after 1971. Why? As we learned in Chapter 9, inflation and unemployment can change in the same direction if something shifts the SP or short-run Phillips curve. Two major factors interfered: (1) the food and oil supply shocks resulting from bad harvests and from the formation of the OPEC oil cartel, and (2) the imposition and termination of price controls.

Supply shocks can cause the relation between U and U^N and the inflation rate to break down in several ways. First, as we learned in Chapter 9, even if expected inflation is completely unaffected by supply shocks, supply inflation causes inflation to accelerate, and the Q/Q^N ratio to fall (so that the actual unemployment rate rises). Thus in a period such as 1974–75 inflation can speed up, as indicated by the pink shading in the bottom frame, but unemployment can also increase, as indicated by the gray shading in the middle frame.

The inflation-rate series illustrated in the bottom frame is the change in the deflator for personal consumption expenditures "stripped" of food and energy prices (the same index we examined in Figures 9-5 and 9-6). Thus we have eliminated the direct influence of food and energy supply shocks on inflation. Nevertheless, we notice that both actual and expected "stripped" inflation speeded up in the late 1970s, despite the relatively high values of the actual unemployment rate in the middle frame. Why? The primary reason is that food and energy inflation has an indirect effect on inflation in "stripped" nonfood non-energy prices, through cost-of-living escalators (COLA clauses) that make wages responsive to total inflation.

Figure 10-2 shows a gradual increase in the natural employment rate (U^N) from 4.2 percent in 1954 to 5.6 percent in 1979. This gradual upward creep in U^N has resulted from a shift in the composition of U.S. unemployment. Compared to 1955, the 1974 unemployment of adult males was about the same, but the overall unemployment rate increased from 4.2 percent in 1955 to 5.6 percent in 1974. How could it do that? The two reasons are obvious from Table 10-1 (p. 306).

1. Although the unemployment rate of adult men and women did not change between 1955 and 1974, the other two groups, male young people and female young people, suffered from much higher unemployment rates in 1974.

---

[11] The methodology of estimating the expected rate of inflation is described in Appendix C.

2. The labor force was dominated in 1955 by adult men, but by 1974 less than half the labor force consisted of adult men. Because the composition of the labor force shifted over to other groups, each having higher unemployment rates, the average unemployment rate would have increased even if the separate unemployment rates of each of the subgroups had remained absolutely unchanged. (This is true of any average: if a baseball player begins to suffer a higher fraction of bad hitless days than good two-hit days, his batting average will go down.)

Why should a shift in the composition of unemployment toward adult women and teenagers change the natural rate of unemployment? An unemployment rate of 5.0 percent in the mid-1950s included a substantial fraction of skilled and experienced adult males who were available to fill job vacancies. But in the mid-1970s the same unemployment rate included mainly adult women and teenagers, *many of whom lacked the job skills required by employers.* Although some teenagers and adult women are hired and trained to fill job vacancies, other firms find it cheaper to bribe an experienced male away from another firm by offering him a higher wage rate. This upward wage bidding plays a part in the acceleration of inflation that occurs in tight labor markets when actual unemployment (U) is below the natural rate (U^N).[12]

---

[12] A comprehensive survey of the reasons why U^N has risen since the mid-1950s, and a comparison of alternative estimates of this increase in U^N, is contained in Joseph Antos, Wesley Mellow, and Jack E. Triplett, "What Is a Current Equivalent to Unemployment Rates of the Past?" *Monthly Labor Review*, vol. 102 (March 1979), pp. 36–46.

FIGURE 10-2 (facing page)

The Real GNP Ratio, the Actual and Natural Unemployment Rates, and the Actual and Expected Inflation Rates in the United States, 1954–80

In the top and middle frames the pink and gray shading shows the close relation between the Q/Q^N ratio and the relation of the actual and natural unemployment rates. Thus Okun's law has continued to remain valid throughout this period. Comparing the middle and bottom frames, notice that before 1971 during the two main intervals of low unemployment (1955–57 and 1965–69) the inflation rate accelerated ahead of what people expected. During the long period of high unemployment between 1958 and 1964, the inflation rate decelerated (although not by much). Supply shocks and the effects of price controls caused the relation to break down after 1971.

Source: The inflation rate is the change in the personal consumption deflator "stripped" of food and energy prices, the same index used in Figures 9–5 and 9–6. Details on the estimation of U^N and p^e are contained in Appendix C. Official unemployment-rate figures before 1967 are adjusted for changes in the method of measurement that occurred in 1967.

BEFORE 1971 INFLATION ACCELERATED WHEN UNEMPLOYMENT DIPPED BELOW THE NATURAL RATE

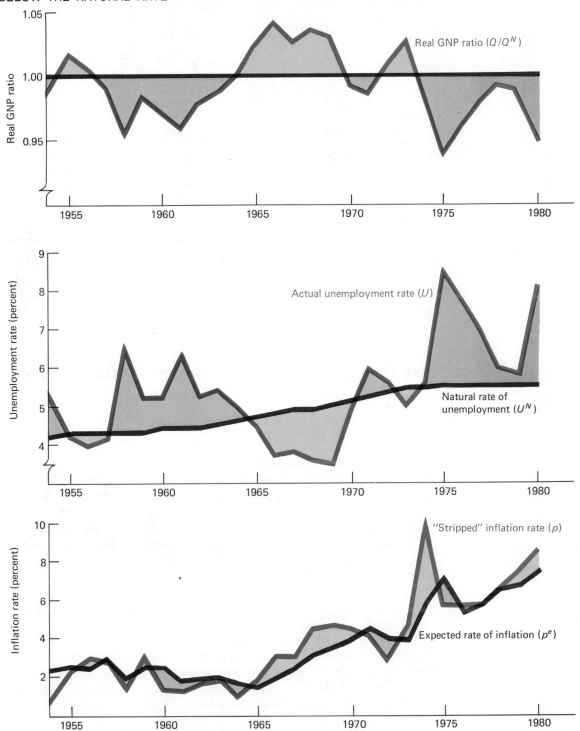

TABLE 10-1

The Structural Shift in the Composition of Unemployment,
1955 and 1974

	Unemployment rates			Shares in the labor force		
	1955[a]	1974	1955–74 change	1955	1974	1955–74 change
1. Males aged 25 and over	3.0	3.0	0.0	59.8	47.4	−12.4
2. Females aged 25 and over	4.6	4.6	0.0	25.2	28.6	+ 3.4
3. Males aged 16–24	8.7	11.4	+2.7	8.6	13.2	+ 4.6
4. Females aged 16–24	7.4	12.4	+5.0	6.4	10.8	+ 4.4
5. Total, all groups	4.2	5.6	+1.4	100.0	100.0	0.0

[a] The 1955 figures have been adjusted to reflect changes in the methods of measuring unemployment introduced in 1967. See Robert L. Stein, "New Definitions for Employment and Unemployment," *Employment and Earnings* (Washington, D.C.: U.S. Bureau of Labor Statistics, February 1967), pp. 3–27. *Source: Handbook of Labor Statistics 1975 — Reference Edition* (Washington, D.C.: Bureau of Labor Statistics, 1974), BLS Bulletin 1865.

10-5 WHY IS THE NATURAL UNEMPLOYMENT RATE SO HIGH?

VACANCIES AND UNEMPLOYMENT IN AN IMAGINARY ECONOMY

We gain a better understanding of the natural unemployment rate (U^N) if we think of an imaginary society in which U^N is zero. All jobs are completely identical in their skill requirements, and all are located at exactly the same place. All workers are completely identical, with skill requirements perfectly suited for the identical jobs, and all workers live in the same location as the jobs. We can imagine a 10-mile-high combined factory-office-apartment skyscraper with very fast elevators at the corner of State and Madison Streets in Chicago.

In this imaginary economy it is impossible for vacancies and unemployment to exist simultaneously. Why? Imagine that initially some workers are unemployed, and that the government pursues expansive monetary and fiscal policies that stimulate aggregate demand. Additional jobs open up, but the unemployed workers are in exactly the right place and possess the right skills, so that they instantly zoom up or down the speedy elevators in the 10-mile-high skyscraper to the job's location. Each job vacancy disappears immediately, and unemployment declines.

Eventually all the unemployed will have found jobs. Any further job vacancies caused by an additional aggregate demand stimulus will not disappear because there are no available jobless people to fill them. Further aggregate demand stimulus will just expand the number of job vacancies.

To be slightly more realistic, let us now assume that there are two types of jobs and workers in the 10-mile-high skyscraper, typists and computer programmers. As the economy expands, it gradually uses up its supply of trained computer programmers. Once all the computer programmers have jobs, all of the unemployment consists of jobless typists. If the government further stimulates aggregate demand, we assume that an equal number of job vacancies is created for programmers and typists. The typist vacancies disappear immediately as available typists are carried by elevator to fill the job openings. But there are no computer programmers left, and so the programmer job openings remain. *Vacancies and unemployment exist simultaneously because firms refuse to hire typists to fill programmer vacancies.* The costs of training are just too high. If training were costless, typists could fill the programmer vacancies, and there would be no remaining vacancies or unemployment.

In reality the actual economy is divided into numerous separate labor markets differing in location, working conditions, and skill requirements. If aggregate spending increases when the overall unemployment rate is 20 or 30 percent, then unemployed workers are available in almost every skill category and location, and firms do not have to raise wage rates to attract applicants. But in our economy at a 5 or 6 percent unemployment rate, any increase in aggregate spending generates job openings in some labor markets while many people remain unemployed in other markets. Some unemployed are able to fill developing job vacancies. But others are prevented from qualifying by the cost of moving to the locations of the job openings, by the cost of acquiring the required skills, and even by the "cost of information" involved in finding out what jobs are available. More machine-tool operators and computer programmers may be needed, but only unskilled bootblacks or retail salesclerks may be available among the unemployed. Or the new jobs may be created in Houston or Chicago, while the unemployed may be in Boston, New York, or Detroit.

VACANCIES AND UPWARD PRESSURE ON WAGE RATES

In our imaginary economy with all jobs and workers alike and located at the same place, policymakers could use aggregate demand stimulus to push the unemployment rate to zero. There would be no job vacancies and no tendency for firms to boost wage rates to fill empty job slots. Thus it would be possible to experience zero unemployment without upward pressure on wages.

But in the real-world economy, with numerous separate labor markets, vacancies and unemployed workers can coexist. Any attempt to use aggregate demand policy to push the total unemployment rate to zero will create numerous job vacancies for the types of skills that are in short supply and in the locations where labor is scarce. Firms will be desperate to fill the job vacancies and will boost wage rates, hoping to steal workers away from other firms. Higher wages will raise business costs and cause price increases. *Thus a situation with a low unemployment rate and lots of job vacancies maintained by rapid demand growth is one in which the inflation rate will continuously accelerate.*

How low can policymakers push the unemployment rate without causing inflation to accelerate? This depends on how much upward pressure on wages is created by each job vacancy, compared to the downward pressure on wages created by each unemployed worker. If the upward pressure of one vacant job slot exactly balanced the downward pressure of one jobless worker, then the natural rate of unemployment with no upward or downward pressure on inflation would occur when the number of job vacancies exactly equaled the number of unemployed. Clearly, the greater the mismatch in skills and location of the vacancies and jobless workers, in contrast to our imaginary economy, the higher would be the natural rate of unemployment.[13]

10-6 THE MISMATCH OF JOBS AND WORKERS

The natural rate of unemployment does not automatically occur when unemployment and vacancies are equal because the upward pressure put on wages by job vacancies may be different from the downward pressure put on wages by the existence of unemployed workers. We cannot perform careful tests of the relation between job vacancies and wage pressure because we lack comprehensive vacancy statistics suitable for comparison with our comprehensive unemployment data. Nevertheless, the previous section does summarize our basic problem, that a demand stimulus creates job openings that are not necessarily suitable for the skill endowments or locations of the unemployed, and these job slots remain unfilled and create inflationary pressure.

In early 1975, despite an unemployment rate that exceeded 8 percent, numerous jobs were vacant in the U.S. economy. *Business Week* reported:

> Help Wanted: machinists, welders, nurses, traveling salesmen, computer repairers, and many, many others. Help Wanted? With unemployment at 8.2 percent . . . jobs going begging? In brief, yes. They always do, in every recession. The unemployed do not have the right skills for the unfilled jobs. A jobless auto worker cannot step into a nurse's white shoes.[14]

---

[13] In the discussion we neglect productivity growth that allows wage rates to grow at the rate of productivity growth without causing inflation.

[14] "A Million Jobs Go Begging," *Business Week* (March 17, 1975), p. 44.

Among the occupations with unfilled jobs at the depth of the 1975 recession were some that always have had job openings in recent years—secretaries, draftsmen, X-ray technicians, machinists, television and hi-fi repairers, and electronics engineers. The 1973–74 increase in the price of oil had created a boom in oil exploration and drilling, opening up unfilled vacancies in a wide range of occupations related to energy: rig builders, dehydration plant operators, oil well drillers, piping designers, and welders. Environmental legislation had also created openings for industrial hygienists and lab technicians.

Not only do most of the teenage and adult female unemployed fail to qualify for these jobs, but in a recession many adult males have the wrong skills or are in the wrong location. Why does the job-worker mismatch occur? The explanations fall into at least seven categories:

1. INFLEXIBILITY OF RELATIVE WAGES

A basic principle of elementary economics is that a shortage of a commodity develops when its price is held too low and is prevented from rising. A surplus develops when its price is held too high. Similarly in labor markets, high unemployment for a group such as teenagers is a sign that its wage rate is too high relative to the wage rates of skilled adult men. A reduction in the teenage wage rate would induce firms to create more job openings teenagers could fill. *Government minimum wage legislation is one factor that keeps the relative wage of high-unemployment groups from declining.*

Inflexible relative wages mean that some members of disadvantaged groups are unemployed while others are employed at higher wage rates than would occur with flexible wage rates. But this factor provides no explanation at all why teenagers, women, blacks, and other groups are disadvantaged in the first place. The remaining factors help to explain the disadvantaged status that leads to high unemployment.

2. LACK OF INCENTIVES FOR FIRMS TO TRAIN WORKERS

Many skills are not taught in school. Firms must train workers on the job. When workers are new and inexperienced, their productivity often falls short of their wage, so that the firm loses money on them. After they become experienced, the firm would like to recoup its losses by making a profit on the workers. It can do so when their skills are "firm-specific"—that is, when the skills are useful only to that firm. The worker cannot quit in protest when the firm pays him a wage below his productivity because he cannot carry his job skills with him to a rival firm.

In contrast, when the worker's skills are general and can be used at several companies, the training firm loses all its investment in his training if he should quit. Many jobs that were vacant in the 1975 recession, such as electronics engineers and welders, require general skills. Firms are under-

standably unwilling to hire and train inexperienced workers who might reward the firm by a slap in the face—quitting to join a rival firm.[15]

3. "RATIONAL" EMPLOYER DISCRIMINATION

Many managerial and white-collar occupations do provide workers with
specific training that makes them more valuable to their firm than to rivals.
Because a firm takes losses on new employees, and begins to make profits
only as they become experienced, it is understandable that firms try to hire
only those job applicants who can be predicted to stay with the firm a long
time.

Employers have no way of predicting which young female employees will
continue working after a brief pregnancy leave to have children, which ones
will quit work for a substantial number of years to take care of their children
at home, and which will not have children at all. Thus, in the absence of any
information on future job tenure, employers may discriminate against *all*
young women when hiring.[16] This is unfair to young women who plan to
continue working while their children are young, and to those who plan to
remain childless. Although some discrimination against women for this
reason is inevitable, there is less of a problem in some European countries
where women are entitled to paid maternity leaves financed by the government.

Teenagers face even greater problems. They take jobs for short periods
either to make money for further schooling or to experiment with several
possible occupations. Because it is impossible for job interviewers to guess
which teenagers will be stable workers and which will quit early, they take
the easy way out and brand all applicants with the undesirable characteristics of the group to which they belong. The real losers are the young applicants who are serious in wanting to stick with a job and learn a skill.

4. "PURE" DISCRIMINATION

Some employers will not hire women, blacks, or young workers, even if
some members of these disadvantaged groups are actually more capable
than some of the adult white males who are favored. Much "pure" discrimination stems from long-standing customs and from social pressure.

---

[15] The distinction between general and specific training, or human capital, was introduced
by Gary Becker, *Human Capital* (New York: Columbia University Press, 1964, 2d ed. 1975).
Other important contributions include Jacob Mincer, "On-the-Job Training: Costs, Returns,
and Some Implications," *Journal of Political Economy,* vol. 70 (October 1962 supplement),
pp. 40–79; and Sherwin Rosen, "Learning and Experience in the Labor Market," *Journal of
Human Resources,* vol. 7 (Summer 1972), pp. 326–342. A recent survey of the state of this
litarature is Mark Blaug, "The Empirical Status of Human Capital Theory: A Slightly Jaun-
diced Survey," *Journal of Economic Literature,* vol. 14 (September 1976), pp. 827–855.

[16] Women aged 20 and over have higher rates of unemployment because of their quitting
jobs and also their "reentry" into the labor force after periods as homemakers. See Table 10-2.

Because by custom some occupations are considered better suited for women or blacks, we observe that almost all secretaries, telephone operators, elementary school teachers, nurses, and typists are women, and black workers are pushed into relatively unpleasant occupations. Although women and blacks made significant progress in the decade after 1964, many of the gains were limited to those who completed college. Less educated blacks and women are still prevented in many cases from entering unions in blue-collar trades.[17] As for teenagers, government regulations may do more harm than good, particularly the high minimum wage that makes many teenagers too expensive to hire and regulations that set age minimums for particular occupations or require bureaucratic red tape for teenage hires but not for adults.[18]

5. HIT-AND-MISS AVAILABILITY OF TRAINING IN SCHOOL

If firms are unwilling or unable to provide training, why can't the schools and community colleges equip their students with the skills needed in today's job markets? Often the curriculum lags years behind changes in skill requirements. Sometimes school systems are unwilling to spend the money for expensive equipment. High school counselors still advise teenagers to go into specialties that became obsolete long ago. Sometimes the students themselves are the problem, hoping to go to college in order to enter a "prestigious" professional field and refusing to take courses to become the technicians and skilled tradespeople that society needs.

6. DIFFICULTY OF BORROWING

Many young people would be willing to learn useful skills in community colleges or private trade schools but they cannot afford to go, either because their families are poor or because they have married early and need an immediate job to support their family. Because schooling is an investment that yields a return in the form of higher future earnings, young people should be able to borrow for their schooling and pay back the loans out of future income. State university systems are a form of borrowing, allowing a student to pay a low tuition subsidized by tax collections from state residents. The student "repays" part of the subsidy in the future as the state collects sales

---

[17] The progress of blacks is documented in Richard B. Freeman, "Changes in the Labor Market for Black Americans, 1948–72," *Brookings Papers on Economic Activity,* vol. 4, no. 1 (1973), pp. 67–120. The earnings of women have fallen relative to those of men, as shown in Robert J. Gordon, "Structural Unemployment and the Productivity of Women," *Journal of Monetary Economics* (January 1977 supplement), pp. 181–229.

[18] A high estimate of the job losses from the minimum wage is presented by Jacob Mincer, "Unemployment Effects of Minimum Wages," *Journal of Political Economy,* vol. 84, part 2 (August 1976), pp. S87–S104. A more modest effect is measured by Edward Gramlich, "The Impact of Minimum Wages on Other Wages, Employment and Family Incomes," *Brookings Papers on Economic Activity,* vol. 7, no. 2 (1976), pp. 409–451.

and income taxes from him. But state university systems are unfair, because the whole population is taxed but only the most able students with high school grade records that qualify them for entry are subsidized.

7. LONG ADJUSTMENT LAGS IN EDUCATION

In 1966, when the demand for engineers was buoyant, many students entered college and decided to major in engineering. But they found upon graduation that the demand for engineers had been dried up by the recession and the decline in government spending for the Vietnam War and for space exploration. Because college takes four years to complete, information that may have been perfectly valid when students entered as freshmen became obsolete by the time they were seniors. The long educational lag may create cycles of feast and famine. The depressed market for engineers cut the number of engineering majors in the early 1970s and created some of the shortages of engineers that surfaced in the 1974–75 recession.[19] By 1980 the problem appeared to be more general—the number of people graduating from college substantially exceeded the creation of new jobs of the type that had traditionally required a college degree.[20]

10-7   TURNOVER UNEMPLOYMENT AND JOB SEARCH

The preceding section argued that the natural rate of unemployment is high because the requirements of job openings and the qualifications of the unemployed do not mesh. Another view—partly a competing explanation and partly complementary—is that the major force maintaining a relatively high natural rate of unemployment is turnover in the labor force. In this view there is no long-run imbalance between job requirements and worker qualifications, but instead jobs and workers are highly differentiated so that unemployed workers require time to find the job that is best for them.

An individual is counted as unemployed when he lacks a job and, if not on temporary layoff, has made specific efforts to find one within the last month. Anyone who quits his old job before finding a new one, as well as any teenager entering the labor market for the first time, or any older woman reentering after her children have left home, will quite sensibly spend some time trying to find the best possible job and will be counted as unemployed while doing so.

If, for instance, every teenager left school on June 1, searched for a job for two weeks, and worked at a summer job for 12 weeks thereafter, the

[19] Richard B. Freeman, *The Market for College-trained Manpower* (Cambridge, Mass.: Harvard University Press, 1971).

[20] Richard B. Freeman, *The Over-educated American* (Washington, D.C.: Academic Press, 1976).

TABLE 10-2

Unemployment Rates by Reason, Sex, and Age in 1978

| | *1978 unemployment rate* | | | | *Percentage of 1978 group unemployment* | | | |
	Males, 20 and over	*Females, 20 and over*	*Teenagers, 16–19 years*	*All groups*	*Males, 20 and over*	*Females, 20 and over*	*Teenagers, 16–19 years*	*All groups*
1. Lost job	2.6	2.2	3.1	2.5	61.6	37.2	19.0	41.6
2. Left job	0.6	1.0	1.7	0.8	14.5	16.2	10.5	14.1
3. Reentrant	0.9	2.4	4.7	1.8	20.2	40.7	28.8	30.0
4. New entrant	0.2	0.4	6.8	0.9	3.6	6.0	41.8	14.3
5. Total for group	4.2	6.0	16.3	6.0	100.0	100.0	100.0	100.0

Source: Employment and Training Report of the President (Washington, D.C., 1979), Table A-27, p. 275.

average annual teenage unemployment rate would be 14 percent (0.14 = 2/14, the number of weeks unemployed divided by the number of weeks in the labor force).

Table 10-2 divides up the unemployed by the major reason for their unemployment: (1) people who have lost their job, mainly because of layoffs, (2) people who have left their job by quitting it, (3) people who have re-entered the labor force after a period out of the labor force at school or at home, and (4) new workers, mainly teenagers, who have never held a job before. The year illustrated in Table 10-2 is 1978, when the economy was quite close to the natural rate of unemployment. A glance at the table reveals several important differences that help to explain the higher unemployment of adult women and teenagers. The three groups are very close together on the percentage of the labor force out of work through job loss (line 1). Adult women and teenagers suffer by their higher "left job" (quit) rates and by their more frequent unemployment due to reentry. On line 4, almost 7 percentage points of the total 16 percent teenage unemployment rate appear to be due to the extra unemployment experienced by teenagers when they search for their first job ("new entrant"). Overall, perhaps the most striking contrast is between the large percentage of adult male unemployment caused by "lost job" (61.6 percent on line 1) as opposed to the small share of teenage unemployment caused by job loss (19.0 percent).

The most important novelty in the theory of "search" unemployment is the idea that an unemployed person may sometimes do better to refuse a job offer than accept it! Why? Imagine a teenager who quits school and begins to look for his first job. He walks down the street and soon encounters a restaurant displaying a sign "Dishwasher Wanted." An inquiry provides the information that the dishwasher opening is available immediately and pays $3 per hour. Will the teenager accept the job without further search? Refusal may benefit the teenager if he is able to locate a job with higher pay or better working conditions. On the other hand, refusal imposes two immediate costs: (1) the loss of the dishwasher wage during the extra days spent searching, and (2) the costs of telephone calls, bus fares, and other extra search expenses. At first the benefit of refusing a job offer may outweigh the costs, but as time goes on the advantages of job refusal decline. Either a better job does turn up that is too good to be refused or the failure to find a better offer causes the searcher to "lower the odds" on eventual success.[21]

The turnover view treats unemployment as a socially valuable, productive activity. Unemployed individuals "invest" in job search. The cost of their investment is the cost of search itself plus the loss of wages that could be earned by accepting a job immediately. The payoff to their investment is the prospect of earning a higher wage for many months or years into the future. Because people do not always want the first available job and prefer to search, the only way for the government to bring down the natural rate of unemployment is either (1) to lessen entry into job search by reducing the reasons behind quitting, reentry, and initial entry, or else (2) to change the economic incentives that unnecessarily prolong the search, particularly unemployment benefits and high taxes on the income of the employed, both of which cut the net earnings of taking a job immediately.

THE MISMATCH AND TURNOVER DEBATE

There are striking similarities between the mismatch and turnover explanations of the high U.S. natural unemployment rate. Both explain why adult women and teenagers have higher unemployment rates than do adult men. The assumption shared by both explanations is that job openings and workers are diverse. The main difference between the two views lies in the height and size of the barriers separating jobs and workers. The barrier in the turnover theory—the absence of perfect information, which makes search necessary—is eroded automatically by the passage of time. The barriers between jobs and workers in the mismatch theory—the absence of required skills and the locational concentration of the unemployed in the wrong places—are much more serious and do not necessarily fade away as time passes.

---

[21] Many of the original papers on the theory of job search are collected in Edmund S. Phelps et al., *Microeconomic Foundations of Employment and Inflation Theory* (New York: Norton, 1970). Another important early reference is Dale T. Mortensen, "Job Search, the Duration of Unemployment, and the Phillips Curve," *American Economic Review,* vol. 60 (December 1970), pp. 847–862. Unfortunately for undergraduate students, much of the early work in this field, including these two references, is quite mathematical. More comprehensible introductions to the subject are Martin S. Feldstein, "The Economics of the New Unemployment," *The Public Interest,* no. 33 (Fall 1973), pp. 3–42; and Robert E. Hall, "Why Is the Unemployment Rate So High at Full Employment?" *Brookings Papers on Economic Activity,* vol. 1, no. 3 (1970), pp. 369–402.

In an economy with no government regulations and no unions or other institutional barriers to flexible wages, there should be no unemployment caused by mismatch. Unskilled workers would simply earn low wages and skilled workers would earn high wages. Indeed, the U.S. economy succeeded in creating jobs for millions of unskilled immigrants before 1929, although the wages for those jobs were usually very low compared to the wages received by skilled workers (in 1907 the average wage rate for "helpers and laborers" in the building trades was only half the skilled wage; by 1967 the unskilled wage had climbed to three-quarters of the skilled wage, and it has retained that relative position since).

Part of the problem of unemployment among unskilled workers in the modern economy is due to government regulations, including the minimum wage laws that hold up the wage rates of unskilled workers and thereby cut the number of unskilled job openings, creating unemployment among unskilled workers who cannot improve their skills. Other barriers include legislation that limits employment in many industries and regions to union workers, whose high wage rates cut job availabilities. Without these barriers to the flexibility of relative wage rates, the mismatch problem would gradually cure itself through a reduction in the relative wages of unskilled workers. But flexibility in relative wages is a superficial solution, in the sense that it converts an unemployment problem of unskilled workers into a poverty problem. Any true solution requires an upgrading of skills.

EFFECTS OF UNEMPLOYMENT COMPENSATION

The turnover view also blames the government for making unemployment higher than necessary and advocates measures to reduce the duration in weeks of an average episode ("spell") of unemployment, as well as reducing the number of episodes per worker. In a series of articles, Martin S. Feldstein of Harvard University has focused on how the unemployment compensation system extends the duration of unemployment. A job with a before-tax wage of $200 per week may yield a worker only $146 in take-home pay. With no unemployment compensation or welfare benefits to sustain him, the worker would have an incentive to search many hours per day and take a new job quickly. But the opportunity to receive an unemployment benefit of $120 per week, as in our economy today, cuts drastically the worker's incentive to search for a new job. The combination of taxes on income from work together with unemployment compensation imposes a tax rate of 87 percent — that is, the drop in take-home pay during unemployment ($146 − $120 = $26) is only 13 percent of the before-tax original wage. Many workers on layoff do not search at all but simply wait to be recalled to their old job.[22]

---

[22] Martin S. Feldstein, "The Importance of Temporary Layoffs: An Empirical Analysis," *Brookings Papers on Economic Activity,* vol. 6, no. 3 (1975), pp. 725–744.

The incentive for temporary layoffs given by the unemployment compensation system occurs not only in recessions but also when the economy is operating at its natural rate of unemployment. The economy may be in equilibrium, with no tendency for inflation to accelerate or decelerate, and yet a firm may find that its sales have dropped temporarily. The unemployment compensation system provides an incentive for the firm to adjust by laying off workers rather than by cutting hours per employee or simply by allowing inventories to grow. Even in a relatively prosperous economy such as that of 1979, each month roughly 1 percent of manufacturing workers were laid off. This is a third factor contributing to the high natural unemployment rate (U^N) in the United States.

REFORM OF UNEMPLOYMENT COMPENSATION

Feldstein's remedy for the artificial incentive given to turnover and temporary layoff unemployment is not to eliminate the unemployment compensation system but to reform it by making the unemployment benefit check taxable, just as income from work is taxable. In the above numerical example this would cut take-home unemployment benefits from $120 per week to $100 or less and would increase the incentive for workers to search. Perhaps more important, Feldstein would penalize the worker for long periods of unemployment. When he finally returned to the job, the worker would find his take-home pay reduced by an extra "unemployment tax" proportional to the length of time spent unemployed. A worker who spent four weeks on layoff might face a 1 percent unemployment tax, whereas one out of work for twenty-six weeks might face a 10 percent unemployment tax. This would motivate many workers to seriously consider accepting a new job rather than waiting for recall to their old job.

Some economists criticize Feldstein's ideas as failing to remedy the underlying causes of unemployment. First, the entry and reentry portions of turnover unemployment are not stimulated by unemployment compensation, for which only former employees are eligible. Second, curing the unemployment problem by imposing an unemployment tax on the long-term unemployed, they reply, is like trying to cure a disease by imposing an illness tax on those who report symptoms to their doctor. The clash brings us back to the contrast between the turnover and mismatch views of unemployment.

As in many areas of economics, the truth is not as simple as either extreme view, but in fact both diagnoses are correct. Some job vacancies have high skill requirements, as emphasized by the mismatch view, but some do not, as pointed out by the turnover view. A 1975 *Wall Street Journal* story began with four sample job vacancies, the first three of which were skilled openings and the fourth a relatively "crummy" job:

> A construction outfit putting up a soda-ash plant in Wyoming is having trouble finding enough experienced pipe fitters. NCR Corporation in Dayton, Ohio, is looking for experts in developing the software for computer systems. General Dynamics Corporation's shipbuilding division, in Quincy, Mass., needs at least 200 more

welders of heavy steel plates to help build eight big liquefied-natural-gas tankers. And Mike's Cafe in Strongsville, Ohio, near Cleveland, wants a short-order cook to work from 6 A.M. to 2 P.M. But none of this helps Ernest Gardner one bit. The young Cleveland native was laid off two months ago and hasn't been able to find a job since.[23]

Feldstein may be right: Ernest Gardner might be forced to take the job at Mike's Cafe if unemployment benefits were taxed and if he eventually faced an extra unemployment tax by refusing to accept the cook's job. But the mismatch view is also right: changes in the unemployment compensation system would contribute nothing to filling the three remaining skilled job openings in the *Wall Street Journal* story and would leave plenty of unemployed workers in a worse plight after the "crummy" jobs had been filled.

10-8 POLICY SOLUTIONS: BETTER MATCHING BETWEEN JOBS AND JOBLESS

The mismatch view emphasizes two factors that prevent the unemployed from filling job openings: (1) lack of skills and (2) being in the wrong location.

LACK OF SKILLS

First Solution: Training Subsidies. At present firms lack profit incentives to train unskilled workers. Because much training is best acquired on the job, many schemes have been proposed to subsidize firms to train new workers. One idea, also proposed by Feldstein, would be to give teenagers a training voucher redeemable by employers who hire them and provide them with job skills. The main weakness of the proposal is the difficulty of monitoring the firms to make sure that they actually use the voucher money for training and to make sure that they do not fire the teenagers after the voucher money is received.[24] Also, firms would tend to hire the most able individuals possible within the rules of the program, leaving the least capable individuals without help.

Second Solution: The Teenage Minimum Wage. Some European countries have a lower minimum wage for teenagers than for adults, and, at least partly as a result, have a lower excess of the teenage unemployment rate over the adult unemployment rate. To some extent a lower teenage minimum wage simply increases the number of available "crummy" jobs and cuts the time necessary for a teenager to find such a job. But in addition a lower

---

[23] Ralph E. Winter, "Over 400,000 Jobs Go Begging in an Era of 8.5 Million Jobless," *Wall Street Journal* (June 10, 1975), p. 1.

[24] An excellent recent discussion of several of Feldstein's ideas is contained in Walter Guzzardi, Jr., "How to Deal with the 'New Unemployment,'" *Fortune* (October 1976), pp. 132ff. See also "Carter's Job Policy: A Key Role for Business," *Business Week* (December 13, 1976), pp. 63–66.

minimum wage encourages firms to train teenagers and to develop apprenticeship systems.

Third Solution: Better Schooling. Much vocational training is obsolete, partly because individual school systems do not have the funds or talent to keep up with changing training needs. It seems unlikely, however, that schools are better suited than private firms to train welders and pipefitters. Extra dollars might be more efficiently spent on subsidies to unskilled individuals than to school systems.

Fourth Solution: Training Loans. Some occupations with job openings, such as television repairers, can be entered by graduates of private training schools. Some of these schools, unfortunately, are disreputable. But a more important problem is that many students from lower-income homes cannot afford to attend them. Nor can they borrow the tuition money, because banks do not trust them. The government could bridge this shortage of loan money by lending to students who would then be billed for the repayment on their federal income tax forms (eliminating any problem of enforcing repayment). At present our society discriminates against vocational training and encourages too many young people to attend college because government loans are limited to college students and because state governments subsidize state colleges but not private vocational training institutions.[25]

Fifth Solution: Reduce Discrimination. Teenagers, blacks, and women suffer from low wages and high unemployment rates, often through no fault of their own. The basic difficulty is the economic and social barriers that keep them from entering career jobs with opportunities for promotion. Several Western European nations have helped reduce discrimination against women by subsidizing maternity leaves and providing subsidized child care, allowing women with children to maintain more stable job records. A case could be made for similar subsidies in the United States to members of minority groups who have been cheated in the past by segregated school systems, low expenditures on inner-city schools, and outright job discrimination. Some barriers, particularly the limitation of many blue-collar craft unions to white males, may require legal rather than economic remedies.

WRONG LOCATION

First Solution: A Better Employment Service. Some economists criticize the Feldstein turnover emphasis on the unemployment compensation system by pointing to West Germany and other countries that enjoy a much lower natural unemployment rate despite generous unemployment benefits. Part of the German success is due to the migrant workers from Italy, Greece, Turkey, and other countries, who fill the "crummy" jobs and are

---

[25] The bias in our system against vocational training is the theme of Edward F. Denison, "Some Reflections," *Journal of Political Economy*, vol. 80, part 2 (May/June 1972), pp. 290–292.

quietly shipped back home without entering the unemployment statistics whenever a recession strikes. But another favorable factor in Germany and other European countries is a very efficient government employment service, which has much more complete records of job openings (because employers are forced to list openings) and is able to direct workers quickly to those firms most likely to hire them. The employment service also minimizes job refusals, not by any Feldstein type of unemployment tax, but by the simple threat that unemployment benefits will be stopped should the worker refuse to accept a job.

Second Solution: Moving Subsidies or Loans. If the unemployed workers are concentrated in one part of the country and the unfilled job openings in another part, the government could cut the natural rate of unemployment by giving or lending money to jobless individuals to enable them to move. The same problem occurs within many metropolitan areas, with excess unemployment of central-city residents who lack adequate transportation to allow them to fill job openings in the suburbs. Although moving subsidies would cost money, the government would save on unemployment benefits and would collect taxes from the newly employed workers. This idea has actually been introduced in West Germany in the form of a plan to pay moving costs and a direct subsidy to encourage unemployed workers to accept job offers in distant locations.

10-9 ARE GOVERNMENT JOB PROGRAMS A SOLUTION?

If people are unemployed, why can't the government simply create jobs for them? During the Great Depression, the Roosevelt administration created millions of jobs in the Civilian Conservation Corps, the Works Progress Administration, and other agencies that put unemployed individuals to work building post offices, roads, public housing projects, improving national parks, and many other activities. The modern counterpart is Public Service Employment (PSE), a program under which the federal government pays the salaries of a specified number of workers added to state and local government payrolls. These workers include teachers' aides, clerks, janitors, security guards, bus drivers, and recreation instructors. To the outside observer they appear identical to other state and local government employees doing the same tasks; the only difference is that their paychecks are covered by federal funds rather than local funds.

Advocates have endorsed PSE as (1) a method to cure cyclical unemployment, when the actual unemployment rate exceeds the natural rate (U^N), and as (2) a method that can reduce U^N itself:

1. As a cyclical remedy PSE does not accomplish anything to raise aggregate demand that cannot be achieved by the normal monetary and fiscal policy tools of Chapters 3–5. Any type of policy stimulus in a large enough dose can raise aggregate demand and lower the actual unemploy-

ment rate to the natural rate of unemployment. The main difference between the alternative methods of stimulating the economy lies in the composition of the extra output they create. Tax reductions stimulate personal consumption; increases in the money supply mainly stimulate business investment, residential construction, and consumer purchases of durable goods, whereas increases in government expenditures expand the share of government spending in GNP. Public Service Employment simply concentrates the extra government expenditures on activities that hire employees in the state and local government sector. The main argument in favor of PSE is that it creates more jobs per dollar of spending and it creates jobs faster than do alternative methods of fiscal stimulus.

2. PSE can lower the natural rate of unemployment only if it succeeds in hiring unemployed individuals who presently cannot qualify for available job openings or who refuse offers of "crummy" jobs. Clearly, a massive PSE program limited to blacks, teenagers, and adult women would reduce the natural rate of unemployment. But such "reverse discrimination" might not be politically acceptable, and a general PSE program might well hire some skilled adults who would then be unavailable for an unfilled job in the private sector. Further, many of the PSE jobs would be "crummy" dead-end jobs without training programs or possibilities for promotion or career.

If PSE simply pays a high wage for unskilled work in local government, only a portion of the PSE expenditures will go to those presently employed. Some dollars will be paid by local governments to new employees who replace local government workers and shift the burden of unemployment to someone presently employed. Recent studies have concluded that up to half the federal funds used for PSE so far have been used to pay for local government employees who would have been hired anyway. Other dollars will be paid to new employees who are not presently employed but who are in school or doing housework. Still others will be paid to those working in low-paid private jobs, forcing an increase in wages and prices in restaurants and laundries.

In sum, PSE funds may involve substantial waste. The natural rate of unemployment might be lowered more if government funds were spent directly on programs that directly raise the skills or change the locations of unemployed workers and enable them to qualify for job openings. The actual effect of a permanent PSE program would be to raise the proportion of the labor force working in the government sector, as opposed to private firms, at any actual unemployment rate. Discussion of PSE must therefore concentrate on the familiar debate between the Galbraithites, who want cleaner parks, more paramedical personnel, more police, and more of other public services, and the Friedmanites, who want to reduce the share of the government sector. Ultimately, this choice must be made on political rather than purely economic grounds.

10-10

CASE STUDY: THE COSTS OF RECESSIONS

So far we have examined the factors that make the natural rate of unemployment so high in the United States. Some unemployment performs a valuable function by allowing individuals to explore without being forced to accept the first available job, which may pay little or have unattractive working conditions. Nevertheless, much of the unemployment that occurs at the natural rate reflects social waste. Far from refusing a wide variety of job offers, many unemployed people never have a job offer to consider.

LOSS OF REAL GNP

During a substantial part of the postwar era, actual unemployment has exceeded the natural rate. But the costs of a recession far exceed the value of the wages lost by the individuals who become unemployed. Recall that the empirical relationship called Okun's law, plotted in Figure 10-1, states that real GNP changes relative to natural real GNP by roughly two times the change in the unemployment rate.

Thus a recession that raises the unemployment rate by 1 percentage point above the natural unemployment rate cuts actual real GNP 2 percent below natural output, for an output loss of $51 billion at 1980 prices.

Why does output decline by so much?

1. The unemployed lose their wages. Although they receive unemployment benefits, taxes must still be paid to finance these benefits, and so society as a whole suffers the loss of all the earnings of the unemployed.[26]
2. Some of the unemployed become discouraged and drop out of the labor force, so that society loses the value of their wage even though they are not counted as among the unemployed.
3. Overtime hours are cut substantially, reducing the take-home pay of many of those still employed.
4. Many employees are needed to keep a business firm functioning even when its sales decline, and they must be paid (janitors, executives, maintenance workers, people with valuable skills whom the firm is

---

[26] If the unemployed person previously earned a wage W, and if his unemployment benefit is B, then society loses the taxes levied to pay for the benefit B plus the taxes levied on the previous wage (tW) plus the loss in take-home pay of the unemployed individual himself $[(1-t)W - B]$:

$$\text{total loss} = B + tW + [(1-t)W - B] = W$$

afraid to lose). Because the recession cuts a firm's sales without reducing its wage bill proportionately, its profits (part of GNP) drop precipitously.

5. All branches of government lose a substantial amount of tax revenue — sales, excise, income, payroll, and corporation taxes.

Figure 10-3 presents a magnified view of the GNP gap during the 1970s. During a recession, almost all the GNP gap is pure waste. When the actual unemployment rate is 1 percentage point above the natural rate, it is almost as if a $51 billion tax had been imposed on everyone (about $680 per household) without providing a single service in return.

Why is "almost all" the GNP gap pure waste, rather than "all"? Unemployed individuals, as well as the discouraged workers who drop out of the labor force, as well as those who work less overtime, have the partial compensation of more hours to enjoy at home. Hours of home time are valuable, but not nearly as valuable as the GNP that an hour of time produces at work. Why not?

Imagine that GNP per worker is $12 per hour on average. Before the workers are paid, some money must be left aside for sales, excise, and property taxes, for replacing worn-out capital equipment, for corporate profits, for corporate profits taxes, and for employer contributions to social security and unemployment payroll taxes. Only about $6 may be left over for payment as gross before-tax wages to workers. But then workers do not get $6 per hour, but only around $4.50, after deductions for social security and federal and state income taxes. Most workers must pay something for the expenses of working and getting to work (uniforms, bus fares, child care, lunches that cost more than eating at home), leaving perhaps $3 per hour "net spendable pay" when they finally arrive home at night.

The extra hours of time at home that people give up when they go to work cannot be worth more than net spendable pay, or about $3 per hour. Yet society gains $12 per hour when an individual goes to work. Thus the extra time at home "enjoyed" by the unemployed and by discouraged workers has only a small value and offsets only part of the GNP gap lost during a recession.[27] The dollar value of the GNP gap needs only a slight adjustment, say a downward revision of 25 percent, to be a reasonably accurate measure of the social waste society suffers during a recession.[28]

---

[27] On average, the home time regained during a recession is worth less than $3 per hour. Why? Because an individual going to work compares the value of the net spendable pay from work with the value to him of the last most valuable hour given up to go to work, say the 40th hour when the job involves 40 hours per week. The first hour given up to go to work is the least valuable and is probably worth much less than $3 per hour.

[28] The analysis of this section follows Robert J. Gordon, "The Welfare Cost of Higher Unemployment," *Brookings Papers on Economic Activity*, vol. 4, no. 1 (1973), pp. 133–195.

WHEN ACTUAL REAL GNP FALLS BELOW NATURAL REAL GNP IN A RECESSION, MOST OF THE LOSS IS PURE WASTE

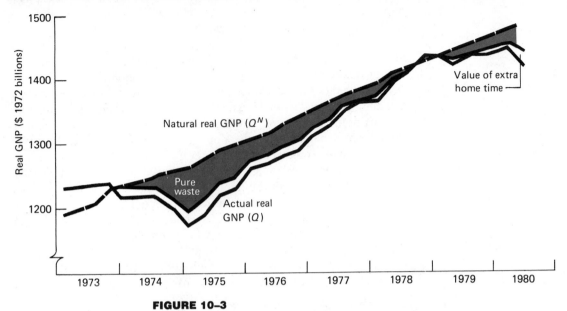

FIGURE 10–3

Natural Real GNP (Q^N), Actual Real GNP (Q), and an Estimate of the Value of Extra Home Time during 1973–80 in the U.S. Economy

The steadily growing line represents natural real GNP (Q^N), the amount the economy can produce when unemployment is equal to the natural rate of unemployment. The solid line represents actual real GNP (Q). The maximum loss of real GNP, the difference between Q^N and Q, occurred in the first quarter of 1975. The red area labeled "Pure waste" reflects the estimate, explained in the text, that about 75 percent of the loss of output in a recession is not balanced by a compensating gain of leisure or home time.

PSYCHIC COSTS OF RECESSION UNEMPLOYMENT

Numerical calculations of the cost of job loss may seem mechanical, and they are. The GNP gap underestimates the trauma of a recession, because it does not include:

1. The time wasted waiting in line at the unemployment office, when an individual neither works nor enjoys home activity.[29]
2. The insecurity caused by the loss of medical insurance by laid-off em-

---

[29] Charlayne Hunter, "Tension, Disappointment Strain West Side Unemployment Office," *The New York Times* (July 27, 1976), p. 35.

ployees whose premiums were covered by their companies.[30] The dollars of lost premiums are included in the GNP gap, but not the nervousness and insecurity of families who suddenly face the danger of health expenses without coverage.

3. The strain and tension faced by children who find their parents suddenly preoccupied by worries about money, debts, and job seeking.[31]

4. The psychological anguish faced by adults: embarrassment passing local merchants who cannot be paid, "disintegration of your confidence as a man," adding "a crushing dimension to the natural self-doubts that are part of the process of growing older."[32] "After a while, it becomes a question of personal worth. You ask yourself, 'What am I worth?' and the answer comes back, 'Apparently nothing.'"[33]

5. A deterioration in both physical and mental health. Heart disease, deaths from cirrhosis of the liver, suicide, and homicide have all been found to rise in a regular way between one and three years after the onset of a national recession. One recent study claims that a 1-percentage-point permanent increase in the unemployment rate ultimately causes 30,000 extra deaths each year.[34]

6. The increase in crime as unemployed workers turn to illegal activity, imposing on society higher expenses for police, courts, and prisons.

All these factors together have a substantial consequence. The total welfare cost of cyclical unemployment may not be an amount 25 percent less than the GNP gap, as concluded in the last section, but an amount equal to or larger than the GNP gap.

SUMMARY

1. A primary concept in this chapter is the natural rate of unemployment, abbreviated U^N. The term does not imply immutability or desirability but, rather, naturalness in the sense of equilibrium: the unemployment rate at which there is no pressure for the inflation rate to change.

2. The most important reason for high unemployment in the United

---

[30] William K. Stevens, "For the 'Hidden' Jobless, a Drastic Impact," *The New York Times* (February 8, 1975), p. 1.

[31] "Down and Out in America," *The New York Times Magazine* (February 9, 1975), p. 9.

[32] Edward B. Furey, "The Fear, the Numbing Fear," *The New York Times* (April 1, 1975), p. 35.

[33] *Newsweek* (January 20, 1975), p. 56.

[34] See M. Harvey Brenner, "Estimating the Social Costs of National Economic Policy: Implications for Mental and Physical Health, and Criminal Aggression," prepared for the use of the Joint Economic Committee, U.S. Congress (Washington, D.C.: Government Printing Office, October, 1976). See also M. Harvey Brenner, *Mental Illness and the Economy* (Cambridge, Mass.: Harvard University Press, 1973).

States is that the natural rate of unemployment is not zero but in the vicinity of 5.5 percent.

3. The actual unemployment rate falls below the natural rate of unemployment when the real GNP ratio (Q/Q^N) rises above unity, and vice versa. Thus all the factors in Chapters 8 and 9 that cause the Q/Q^N ratio to fluctuate also cause the actual unemployment rate to change in the opposite direction.

4. A gradual increase in the natural rate of unemployment over the 20 years between the mid-1950s and mid-1970s was caused by a shift in the composition of U.S. unemployment. The unemployment rate of young people has increased relative to that of adults. At the same time the composition of the labor force has shifted away from adult males toward groups that suffer higher unemployment rates, especially teenagers and adult women.

5. One explanation of a high natural rate of unemployment is called the mismatch view. It emphasizes the mismatch between the high skill requirements of available jobs and the low skills possessed by many of the unemployed. In an economy with flexible relative wages, the unskilled would be able to find jobs more easily but would receive lower wage rates. Any real cure for the problems of the unskilled—whether high unemployment, or low wages, or both—requires an increase in their skills and better matching of their locations with the locations of available job openings.

6. Among the policy proposals that have been recommended to cure mismatch unemployment are training subsidies and loans, better schooling, a lower minimum wage for teenagers, a reduction in discrimination, a better employment service, and moving subsidies or loans.

7. Another explanation of the high natural rate of unemployment emphasizes job turnover. The barrier that maintains a high natural rate is the absence of perfect information, making necessary an investment in job search to locate job openings that offer higher wage rates or better working conditions.

8. Policy solutions to reduce turnover unemployment include an improved employment service to provide better information as well as changes in the present system of unemployment compensation, which provides a subsidy to workers who turn down job offers and continue to search or to remain at home awaiting recall to their old job.

9. The increase in the official unemployment rate during a recession understates the cost to society of the recession. Typically the gap between natural output (Q^N) and actual output (Q) grows by 2 percentage points for every 1 percentage point by which the actual unemployment rate rises above the natural unemployment rate. Only a small fraction of this gap is offset by the enjoyment of time at home by the unemployed; the rest is pure waste.

10. The output gap itself may understate the true costs of a recession, because mental and physical health are not included in official measures of gross national product.

A LOOK AHEAD

We have seen that unemployment imposes major costs on society. Yet to reduce inflation, the government must slow down the growth of aggregate demand and must raise the unemployment rate temporarily. Is the benefit of lower inflation worth the cost of higher unemployment? The next chapter examines the nature of the harm done by inflation, which groups in society are losers from inflation, and how government regulation of interest rates can alter the impact of inflation on savers.

CONCEPTS

Actual rate of unemployment
Natural rate of unemployment
Okun's law
Disguised unemployment
Unemployment benefits
Firm-specific skills versus general skills

Public service employment
"Pure" versus "rational" discrimination
Mismatch versus turnover views of unemployment
Compositional (structural) shift in unemployment

QUESTIONS FOR REVIEW

1   Are government policymakers able to lower the actual unemployment rate below the natural unemployment rate? Explain.

2   Discuss what you feel are the major defects in our current measures of unemployment. Which defects do you feel are worth improving upon? Why?

3   Let us assume that the Q/Q^N ratio follows this path over six successive quarters: 0.984, 0.950, 0.900, 0.960, 1.00, 1.026, 1.040. Using Okun's law and assuming that $U^N = 5.5$ percent, calculate the corresponding path of the actual unemployment rate.

4   Why is the natural rate of unemployment higher than zero? Suggest at least two explanations.

5   Compare the mismatch and turnover views of unemployment. Which do you feel more accurately describes current unemployment in the United States?

6   Explain the connection between the amount of turnover unemployment and the following:
    a. The income tax rate levied on unemployment benefits.
    b. The income tax rate levied on income from work.
    c. Fees charged by employment agencies.
    d. Cost of a pay telephone call.

7   What is the welfare cost of a recession? Is the welfare cost greater or less than the average wage rate multiplied by the lost hours of work that would otherwise have been performed by an unemployed individual?

8   If an economy had unemployment exceeding its natural rate by 100,000 unemployed, would a policy to create 100,000 new jobs by stimulating aggregate demand solve the problem? Explain.

9   Can you suggest any reasons why Japan and the United Kingdom have on average experienced lower teenage unemployment rates than the United States?

10   Comment on these statements:
     a. "Policymakers may reduce temporarily the *natural* rate of unemployment by pursuing an expansionary monetary policy."
     b. "A reduced minimum wage rate for teenagers would be a policy measure that would simultaneously reduce inflation and the unemployment rate."

11

The Consequences
of Inflation

Inflation is the time when
those who have saved for a rainy day
get soaked.

11-1 INTRODUCTION

The U.S. economy in the early 1980s has a "built-in" inflation because individuals and firms alike expect inflation to continue. As we learned in Chapter 8, one basic method of cutting the inflation rate is deliberately to create a *recession*. How hard should the government try to eliminate the inflation? Is the benefit of lower inflation worth the cost of layoffs, unemployment, and lower incomes during the transition period? This and the previous chapter provide the raw material for our evaluation of this great policy problem. How much difference does inflation make?

At first glance, worry about inflation may appear misplaced. When inflation is zero, wages may increase at 1 percent a year. When inflation proceeds at 6 percent annually, wages may grow at 7 percent annually. Workers have little reason to be bothered about the inflation rate (p) if the growth in their wages (w) always stays the same distance ahead, as in this example:

	No inflation	*6 percent annual inflation*
Growth rate of nominal wages (w)	1	7
Growth rate of price deflator (p)	0	6
Growth rate of real wages ($w - p$)	1	1

The main point in this chapter is that inflation is felt primarily by owners of financial assets, not by workers whose only income is earned in the form of wages and who spend their entire wage income on consumption goods.[1] An unexpected "surprise" inflation hurts "ordinary people" by cutting the real value of individual saving accounts and hits particularly hard at the savings and to some extent at the pension funds of those who are retired or are about to retire. Even when inflation is fully anticipated and is no surprise, everyone notices the shrinkage in the value of the cash in their pockets and the dollars in their checking accounts, and people invest extra effort in managing their cash that would not be necessary in the absence of inflation. Furthermore, inflation creates real costs for society because of the failure of the tax system to state its rules in inflation-adjusted "real" dollars, and more generally because the capricious redistribution of income caused by inflation creates uncertainty for everyone.

11-2 NOMINAL AND REAL INTEREST RATES

As Americans have become accustomed to inflation, they have learned that the interest rates charged by banks and finance companies are not as onerous as they seem. Without any help from economics textbooks, many people understand the difference between nominal and real interest rates, even if they have not been taught the economist's jargon.

> *The* **nominal interest rate** *(i) is the rate actually quoted by banks and negotiated in financial markets. The* **expected real interest rate** *(r^e) is what people expect to pay on their borrowings or earn on their savings after deducting expected inflation ($r^e = i - p^e$). The expected real interest rate is what matters for investment and saving decisions.*

The nominal interest rate can be very different in two countries with different inflation rates, or in one country at different moments in history. But investment and saving decisions will be the same in the two situations as long as the expected real interest rate is the same. Let us consider the example of Pete Puritan and Sam Spendthrift—two boys, both broke, who both want a new ten-speed bicycle. Both plan to earn $100 at part-time jobs over the next year, exactly the price of a new bicycle, but Sam impatiently buys his bike immediately with borrowed money, whereas Pete patiently waits until the end of the year. When there is no inflation, the price of the bicycle remains constant at $100:

---

[1] The statement that workers do not lose refers to a normal inflation fueled by increasing aggregate demand. When the economy experiences a supply shock, as did the United States in 1974 and 1979 at the time of the oil price hikes, inflation experiences a temporary acceleration while real wages simultaneously decline.

	Pete Puritan	Sam Spendthrift
1. Sam purchases bicycle on January 1 with borrowed money	–	100
2. Earnings during year, put into savings account	100	100
3. Savings account on December 31, including 3 percent interest	103	103
4. Sam repays loan, including 3 percent interest	–	103
5. Pete buys bicycle	100	–
6. Balance at end of year (line 3 minus 4 and 5)	3	0

At the end of the year, each boy has his bicycle, but Pete has $3 left and Sam has nothing. Why? Pete has received a reward for his patience, the interest on his savings account. Sam has spent his interest earnings to pay the interest cost of his loan; he was not patient, and so he receives no reward for patience as does Pete.[2]

Now we consider the example again in a second situation in which inflation proceeds at a 6 percent annual rate instead of zero. If the expected real interest rate is to remain at 3 percent as in the first situation, the nominal interest rate on both savings accounts and bicycle loans must rise from 3 to 9 percent:

GENERAL FORM

$$r^e = i - p^e$$

NUMERICAL EXAMPLE

$$r^e = 9 - 6 = 3$$

With a 6 percent rate of inflation, the price of the bicycle rises from $100 to $106 by the end of the year, but the higher interest rate exactly compensates, and both boys wind up in exactly the same situation as before:

	Pete Puritan	Sam Spendthrift
1. Sam purchases bicycle on January 1 with borrowed money	–	100
2. Earnings during year, put into savings account	100	100
3. Savings account on December 31, including 9 percent interest	109	109
4. Sam repays loan, including 9 percent interest	–	109
5. Pete buys bicycle on December 31, which now costs $106	106	–
6. Balance at end of year (line 3 minus 4 and 5)	3	0

[2] Notice the simplifying assumptions introduced to keep this example manageable. First, neither boy pays taxes on his wages. Second, we pretend that interest is earned on the $100 of

As before, Pete receives a $3 reward for his patience, while Sam is compensated not by money but by the nonmonetary benefit of an extra year's enjoyment of his bicycle. The extra $6 that Sam earns on his savings account is exactly eaten up by the extra interest on his loan, whereas the extra $6 that Pete earns on his savings account is exactly eaten up by the $6 increase in the price of the bicycle.

Summary: This example was designed to illustrate an artificial situation in which inflation has no effect on economic well-being. Our current inflation would have no adverse consequences, and there would be no need for policymakers to try to reduce or stop inflation if these basic characteristics of the example were universally true in the United States.

1. Inflation is universally and accurately anticipated.
2. Inflation raises the prices of all goods by the same percentage rate (that is, any changes in the relative prices of goods are just the same as would have occurred in the absence of inflation).
3. An inflation of p_0 percent raises the market nominal interest rate (i) for both saving and borrowing by exactly p_0 percent above the no-inflation interest rate.
4. Only real (not nominal) interest income is taxable, and only the real cost of borrowing is tax deductible.
5. All savings are held in bonds, stocks, or savings accounts earning the nominal interest rate (i); no one holds money in accounts with an interest rate held below the market nominal interest rate. We will see that this condition is violated in the United States, where the interest rate on cash and checking accounts is maintained at zero and the interest rate on some types of savings accounts is held down by Regulation Q ceilings.

11-3 REDISTRIBUTIVE EFFECTS OF AN INFLATIONARY SURPRISE

Now let us violate condition 1, that inflation is accurately anticipated. In several postwar episodes, such as 1966–69, 1973–74, and 1978–80, the actual inflation rate accelerated well above the rate expected by most people. We now assume that in the bicycle example both the savings and borrowing rate stay at 3 percent, because banks expect a zero rate of inflation. Then, as a total surprise to everyone, the price of all goods jumps 6 percent on December 30, forcing Pete to pay $106 for his bicycle:

---

wage earnings throughout the year, whereas, in fact, if work is distributed evenly in each month the average balance in the savings account is only $50. Third, the borrowing interest rate and savings account interest rate are both 3 percent, whereas in the real world borrowing rates are higher to compensate banks and other lenders for risk and for administrative costs. Fourth, we disregard the depreciation on Sam's bicycle, which is one year older than Pete's.

	Pete Puritan	Sam Spendthrift
1. Sam purchases bicycle on January 1 with borrowed money	—	100
2. Earnings during year, put into savings account	100	100
3. Savings account on December 31, including 3 percent interest	103	103
4. Sam repays loan, including 3 percent interest	—	103
5. Pete buys bicycle on December 31, which now costs $106	106	—
6. Balance at end of year (line 3 minus 4 and 5)	−3	0

Poor Pete's hopes have been dashed. He would never have bothered to save if he had known that his money would lose value during the year. Pete is the classic loser from inflation, the individual who has his savings eroded by an **unanticipated inflation,** but who does not (like Sam) have debts to match. Because most people start out in life with relatively few assets, and then gradually build up savings in preparation for retirement, those hurt most by an unanticipated inflation are those who have retired or who are about to retire.

When actual inflation ($p = 6$ percent in the example) turns out to be different than expected ($p^e = 0$ in the example), the actual **real interest rate** differs from that which was expected. In the example a 3 percent real interest rate was expected ($r^e = 3$), but after the fact (*ex post*) the actual real interest (r) turned out to be much less:

GENERAL FORM   NUMERICAL EXAMPLE

$$r = i - p \qquad\qquad r = 3 - 6 = -3$$

GAINERS FROM UNANTICIPATED INFLATION

Who gains from inflation? Sam does not gain, because he has a debt and an asset to match when the price increase occurs. His bicycle has gained in value. But because all prices have increased together, his capital gain on the bicycle does him no good. If he wanted to sell his bike and buy schoolbooks, the higher price of schoolbooks would prevent him from buying any more schoolbooks than would have been possible in the absence of inflation. The real gainers from unanticipated inflation are those who are heavily in debt, but who have no financial assets, only physical assets whose prices rise with inflation. Private individuals who have just purchased houses with small down payments are among the classic gainers from an unanticipated inflation. Here is an example of Harold Homeowner, who purchases his

$100,000 house on January 1 with a 10 percent down payment.[3] His financial statement appears as follows on January 1 and December 31, when an inflationary surprise increases the price of his house by 6 percent on December 30. His increase in net worth of $6000 is a "nominal **capital gain**," and the $5094 increase in his real net worth is called his "real capital gain."

Harold Homeowner's Financial Statement, January 1 and December 31, when an inflationary surprise increases the price of his house by 6 percent on December 30

	January 1	December 31
Assets		
House	$100,000	$106,000
Liabilities		
Mortgage debt	90,000	90,000
Net worth		
= assets −		
liabilities	10,000	16,000
Real net worth		
$= \dfrac{\text{net worth}}{\text{price index}}$	$\dfrac{10,000}{1.00} = \$10,000$	$\dfrac{16,000}{1.06} = \$15,094$

Other classic gainers are corporations, whose outstanding stocks and bonds are the counterpart of household assets. The government also gains from inflation, because its outstanding liabilities are money (currency and bank reserves) and government bonds. A steady inflation can continue only if the nominal money supply grows steadily, and these extra dollars of money that the government "prints" can be used to pay for government purchases without the legislative strife required to raise tax rates. The extra revenue the government gains by increasing its liabilities (money) in response to higher prices is often called the **inflation tax.**

REDISTRIBUTIONAL CONSEQUENCES

The best known extreme of the redistributional consequences of unanticipated inflation occurred during the German hyperinflation of 1922–23, at the end of which the inflation rate was 600 percent per month. In 1919 a farmer sold a piece of land for 80,000 marks as a nest egg for old age. All he got for the money a few years later was a woolen sweater. Elderly Germans can still recall the days in 1923 when:

> People were bringing money to the bank in cardboard boxes and laundry baskets. As we no longer could count it, we put the money on scales and weighed it. I can still see my brothers coming home Saturdays with heaps of paper money. When the shops reopened

---

[3] The repayment of mortgage debt is ignored.

after the weekend they got no more than a breakfast roll for it. Many got drunk on their pay because it was worthless on Monday.[4]

The basic case against unanticipated inflation, then, is that it redistributes income from creditors (savers) to debtors without their knowledge or consent. Conversely, an unanticipated deflation does just the opposite, redistributing income from debtors to creditors. Throughout history, farmers have been an important group of debtors who have been badly hurt by unanticipated deflation. The interest income of savers hardly fell at all between 1929 and 1933, but farmers, badly hurt by a precipitous decline in farm prices, saw their nominal income fall by two-thirds, from $6.2 to $2.1 billion.

Another example of deflation occurred in the late nineteenth century, when the price level fell fairly steadily, by a total of 64 percent, between 1865 and 1896. While much of this deflation came to be anticipated, a remaining portion was unanticipated. A main issue in U.S. economic history during this period was the "free coinage of silver," which would have added a great amount of silver to the predominantly gold-based money supply, raising the growth rate of money and moderating or even ending the decline in prices. Savers and the "Eastern monied interest" benefited from unanticipated deflation and wanted the money supply strictly tied to gold. William Jennings Bryan, speaking for farmers and other debtors, decried this "cross of gold" in a famous speech delivered to the Democratic National Convention in 1896:

> You shall not press down upon the brow of labor this crown of thorns. You shall not crucify mankind on a cross of gold.

11-4 ANTICIPATED INFLATION AND AGGREGATE DEMAND

The redistributional effects of inflation disappear if the actual inflation rate (p) remains equal to the expected rate of inflation (p^e), if all contracts are written in real terms, and if the tax system is completely changed to tax only real income and real capital gains. Are there any adverse consequences for society in allowing a 6 percent inflation rate to continue, as long as everyone accurately anticipates that rate? If the government refrains from placing restrictive ceilings on savings accounts that prevent small savers from receiving a sufficiently high nominal return to compensate them for inflation, the remaining losers from a fully anticipated inflation are holders of cash and checking accounts, which still pay no interest in the United States.

An increase in the expected rate of inflation tends to reduce the average household demand for real money balances, a reduction that imposes a welfare cost by making everyday transactions more inconvenient. Figure 11-1 illustrates the adjustment of nominal interest rates and real money balances

---

[4] Alice Siegert, "When Inflation Ruined Germany," *Chicago Tribune* (November 30, 1974).

AN INCREASE IN EXPECTED INFLATION CUTS HOLDINGS OF REAL MONEY BALANCES

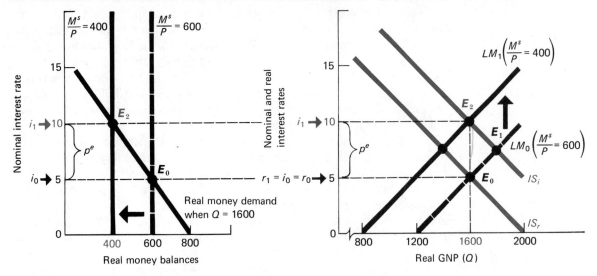

FIGURE 11-1

The Response of Real Money Demand and the Nominal Interest Rate to an Increase in Expected Inflation from Zero to 5 Percent

The economy starts at point E_0, at the crossing of the initial red IS_r line and the initial dashed black LM_0 line. An increase in expected inflation from zero to 5 percent causes the nominal interest rate to rise 5 percentage points above the real interest rate. Thus, corresponding to the initial unchanged IS_r curve drawn for the real interest rate, there is a second IS_i curve drawn exactly 5 percentage points higher in the vertical direction. Initially the economy moves from E_0 to E_1. But the higher nominal interest rate causes individuals to reduce their holdings of real balances, indicated by the movement along the money demand schedule in the left frame of the diagram from E_0 to E_2. Only when money demand has been reduced to \$400 billion, and the LM curve in the right frame has shifted left to LM_1, can both the commodity and money markets again be in equilibrium.

in response to an increase in the expected inflation rate from zero to 5 percent. Consumption, saving, and investment decisions all depend on the real interest rate r, as in the Pete Puritan-Sam Spendthrift example, so that the red IS line labeled IS_r is drawn with reference to the real interest rate (r). The IS_r curve is identical to the IS_0 curve in Chapters 4 and 5.[5] It shows all possible combinations of the real interest rate (r) and real output that keep the commodity market in equilibrium, with output and income equal to planned expenditure.

The demand for money does not depend on the real interest rate, as does

---

[5] The position of the IS curve depends on $\bar{A}$, the value of planned autonomous spending (A_p) when the interest rate is zero, and on the multiplier (k). **Review:** Section 4-3.

the demand for commodities. Instead, because government regulations hold the nominal interest rate on money equal to zero, individuals shift out of money into bonds and saving accounts whenever there is an increase in the *nominal* interest paid on these alternative assets. In 1947 the nominal interest rate was about 3 percent; holdings of money amounted to a very large 48 percent of GNP. In 1979, when the nominal interest rate on bonds was a much higher 9.6 percent, people economized on their holdings of money to earn the lucrative interest paid on bonds; holdings of money in that year amounted to only 15.8 percent of GNP.

The left side of Figure 11-1 shows a negatively sloped real money demand curve, indicating a decline in the demand for real money balances as the nominal interest rate on bonds increases. The LM_0 curve in the right frame shows the different combinations of output and the nominal interest rate consistent with equilibrium in the money market. The economy's general equilibrium occurs at the crossing point of LM_0 and IS_r at point E_0 if expected inflation is zero. Up to this point, everything is the same as in Chapters 4 and 5.

Now, however, let us assume that the Fed announces a policy of raising the money supply at 5 percent per annum, causing people to raise their expectation of future inflation from zero to 5 percent. Now the nominal interest rate rises by 5 percent. Point E_0 is no longer an equilibrium, because the inflation makes consumers and firms want to borrow and spend more money.

In the new situation of positive expected inflation we must draw a new *IS* curve in terms of the nominal interest rate (i), labeled IS_i, lying parallel to the unchanged IS_r line and above it by exactly 5 percent, the rate of expected inflation. The new IS_i curve crosses the original LM_0 curve at point E_1, where the nominal interest rate has risen to 7.5 percent and real output has risen from $1600 billion to $1800 billion.

Point E_1 is not the end of the story, because the 5 percent expected inflation reduces the real money balances which people want to hold, shown in the left-hand frame by the northwest movement from point E_0 to E_2, and in the right-hand frame by the leftward shift in the *LM* curve to the new LM_1 line drawn for a supply of real balances (M^s/P) equal to $400 billion, down from $600 billion in the initial situation.

The economy is in a dynamic long-run equilibrium only at point E_2, with output constant at $1600 billion, the real interest rate constant at 5 percent, the nominal interest rate constant at 10 percent, and both money and the price level growing at a steady fully anticipated rate of 5 percent. The only consequence of the fully anticipated inflation has been to raise the nominal interest rate from 5 to 10 percent and to reduce the real money supply from $600 billion to $400 billion.[6]

---

[6] If the initial money supply is $600 billion and grows 5 percent to $630 billion in one year, the required level of real balances of $400 billion can be achieved only if the price level rises to 1.575. An increase from 1.00 to 1.50 is required to reduce the real money supply enough to keep real output at $1600 billion, whereas the extra increase in P from 1.500 to 1.575 incorporates the 5 percent anticipated rate of inflation.

11-5 SHOE-LEATHER COSTS AND THE OPTIMUM QUANTITY OF MONEY

Why should anyone care about a reduction in real balances? Although the nominal interest rate has risen, the anticipated real interest rate has remained constant at 5 percent. By assumption, inflation actually turns out to be exactly what people expect, and so the accurately anticipated inflation has absolutely no effect on consumption, saving, and investment decisions in the commodity market. But nevertheless there is a change in the money market because the reduction in real balances induces people to make an extra effort to manage their cash. They use up "shoe leather" taking extra trips to the bank, and the welfare cost of an anticipated inflation is sometimes called the shoe-leather cost.

PEOPLE DEMAND MONEY FOR ITS CONVENIENCE SERVICES

In Figure 11-2 we have made an exact copy of the money demand schedule from the left frame of Figure 11-1. At point E_2 real balances are $400 billion, and the interest rate is 10 percent. People are voluntarily willing to hold $400 billion of money that pays no interest and know perfectly well that they are giving up 10 cents of interest income ($i = 10$) that they could earn for every dollar switched out of money into bonds. They are willing to give up the interest return on bonds to obtain the convenience of money for conducting transactions. Money, unlike bonds, can be used directly for purchases without the nuisance of time-consuming and shoe-leather consuming trips to the bank.

At point E_2, for instance, people are willing to hold $400 billion of real balances when the nominal interest rate is 10 percent, *but no more than that*. The 401-billionth dollar must be judged to provide **extra convenience services** worth less than the 10 percent paid on bonds, so that it is not held. Thus we can interpret the money demand curve as showing the extra convenience services provided by each successive dollar of money held. The first dollar, second dollar, and so on down to the 400-billionth dollar of money holdings all provide extra convenience services (ECS) worth more than the nominal interest rate sacrificed by holding money instead of bonds (i). The 401-billionth dollar and all further dollars provide ECS less than i. People hold money up to the point E_2 where the last dollar held provides ECS equal to i:

$$i = ECS$$

CONVENIENCE-VALUE-OF-MONEY COST

When inflation is zero and the nominal interest rate on bonds (i) is 5 percent, then $ECS = 5$ percent. The money market is in equilibrium at point E_0. The switch to an expected inflation rate of 5 percent and a nominal interest rate of 10 percent at point E_2 causes people to give up $200 billion of

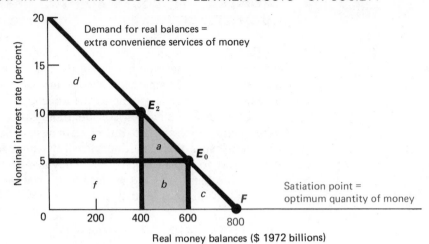

HOW INFLATION IMPOSES "SHOE LEATHER COSTS" ON SOCIETY

FIGURE 11-2

The Effect on the Demand for Real Money Balances of an Increase in the Expected Inflation Rate (p^e) from Zero to 5 Percent

At E_0 the inflation rate is expected to be zero, the nominal interest rate on bonds is 5 percent, and $600 billion of real balances are held. If instead the inflation rate is expected to be a faster 5 percent, the nominal interest on bonds shoots up to 10 percent, causing people to economize on their holdings of money to bring real money balances down to $400 billion at point E_2. The pink area under the money demand schedule shows the cost to society of losing the convenience provided by holding the extra $200 billion of money. The best situation of all is point F, where the nominal interest rate is zero (and the expected inflation rate is −5 percent). At F people hold all the money they can possibly use to facilitate their transactions (given the size of their real incomes).

real balances, each dollar of which provides *ECS* between 5 and 10 percent. What is the total value of this loss? The value of all services provided by money is the area under the demand curve for money to the left of the initial equilibrium point E_0. Comparing the old and new situations:

	Total ECS provided by all money held
Old situation at E_0 with $p^e = 0$	Areas labeled $a + b + d + e + f$
New situation at E_2 with $p^e = 5$	Areas labeled $d + e + f$
Difference = convenience value of money lost	$a + b$

The total value of the convenience services lost by the increase in anticipated inflation from 0 to 5 percent is represented by the shaded areas $a + b$.

Area of b	= 5 percent $\times$ \$200 billion	= \$10 billion
Area of triangle $a = \frac{1}{2}$ of 5 percent $\times$ \$200 billion		= \$ 5 billion
Total area $a + b$		\$15 billion

The real-world counterpart of this loss is the extra effort made by corporations and households to maintain lower cash balances when inflation occurs. Corporations try harder to synchronize cash inflows and outflows. Individuals try harder to keep their bank balances as close to zero as possible, paying all their bills on the day their paycheck arrives. The funds that otherwise would be kept in checking accounts and cash are kept in savings accounts and bonds, requiring the inconvenience of more frequent trips to deposit and withdraw cash and to transfer funds into checking accounts to cover checks just written. All these inconvenient shoe-leather consuming activities are not a transfer from one person to another, but *a real net loss to society*.

OPTIMUM QUANTITY OF MONEY

In diametric contrast to the inconvenience caused at point E_2 would be an alternative situation at point F, with a zero interest rate on bonds and savings accounts. When there was no incentive to own alternative assets to money, there would be no effort expended on trips to the savings bank nor any need to pay brokers' fees for sales of bonds. All that wasted time would be available either for working longer hours or for the enjoyment of leisure. Society is genuinely better off at point F than at point E_2, and this situation at F is called the **optimum quantity of money**. The total area of the sections labeled $a + b + c$ (\$20 billion) measures the benefit to society of moving from point E_2 to the optimum quantity of money at point F.

How can society achieve the zero nominal interest rate necessary to induce people to give up savings accounts and hold all their money in cash and checking accounts? At point F:

$$i = ECS = 0$$

Consumption, saving, and investment decisions require a real expected interest rate of 5 percent, so that achieving a zero nominal interest rate (r^e) requires a 5 percent yearly deflation:

$$p^e = i - r^e = 0 - 5 = -5$$

When no interest is paid on money and other taxes collected by the government are neglected, the optimum inflation rate is equal to minus the expected real interest rate (optimum $p = -r^e$).

OTHER DETERMINANTS OF THE OPTIMUM INFLATION RATE

The achievement of the optimum quantity of money in Figure 11-2 appears to require a 5 percent continuous and fully anticipated deflation. This outcome would be very difficult for U.S. policymakers to achieve, seeing that they have had a hard enough time ending inflation, much less creating deflation! The last time the United States experienced continuous deflation was a century ago, between 1865 and 1896.

But there is another possibility that avoids the necessity of falling prices. This possibility would allow individuals to live with inflation without suffering any cost at all from a fully anticipated inflation. The demand for money in Figure 11-2 depends on the nominal interest rate paid on alternative assets, such as bonds and savings accounts, *only because government regulations prohibit the payment of interest on currency and checking accounts.* If banks were allowed to pay any interest they choose on checking accounts, the competition between banks would drive the interest paid on those deposits to a value equal to or close to the interest rate on bonds (i). Savings accounts and even money-market mutual funds would tend to disappear, since people could earn interest and conduct transactions with a single asset, their checking accounts.

Aside from the payment of interest on money, a second factor can make the optimum inflation rate higher than minus the value of the expected real interest rate ($-r^e$). An increase in the inflation rate generates more inflation tax revenue for the government. The government must print 5 percent extra money each year to keep real balances (M^s/P) constant if there is a 5 percent inflation. In Figure 11-2 a \$400 billion total of real balances can be maintained at point E_2 in the coming year (with a 5 percent inflation) only if the government prints \$20 billion more money, an amount equal to the size of the square labeled e. This is the government's revenue from the inflation tax. If the government keeps its real expenditures constant, *it can reduce conventional income, sales, and payroll taxes by \$20 billion.* Because the effort people invest in rearranging their activities to avoid conventional taxes is thereby reduced, it is not at all clear that a little inflation is a "bad thing." In the jargon of economists, the economy reaches an optimum inflation rate when the extra inconvenience caused by the effort invested in cash management just balances the extra convenience of the smaller effort invested in avoiding conventional taxes.[7]

11-6 CASE STUDY: REDISTRIBUTION IN U.S. POSTWAR INFLATIONS

Inflation redistributes income from creditors and savers to debtors when there is a surprise — that is, when inflation proceeds faster than creditors and savers expected when they put their money into the bank or bought bonds. If savers are willing to buy a four-year certificate at a savings bank yielding 5 percent when they expect a 2 percent inflation, then their expected real rate of return is 3 percent ($r^e = i - p^e = 5 - 2 = 3$).

---

[7] A more scholarly but still short and readable presentation of this section is contained in Edward Tower, "More on the Welfare Cost of Inflationary Finance," *Journal of Money, Credit, and Banking,* vol. 3 (November 1971), pp. 850–860.

They lose if the inflation rate exceeds their expectation, because their actual real rate of return ($r = i - p$) is cut below the interest rate they expected. If inflation actually turns out to be 5 percent, not the 2 percent that savers expected, the actual real interest rate will turn out to be zero ($r = i - p = 5 - 5 = 0$).

What return did savers expect in recent years in the United States, and how badly has inflation treated them? Our first task is to determine the average expected real return (r^e) that savers demanded on their savings. The top red line in Figure 11-3 displays the nominal interest rate (i) for the period 1960–79.[8]

Directly below the nominal interest rate in the top frame is plotted an estimate of the expected inflation rate, indicated by the black line, which is identical to that plotted in Figure 10-2. It is a weighted average of recent rates of inflation, based on the idea of adaptive expectations.[9] The difference between the nominal interest rate (i) line and the expected inflation estimate (p^e) is marked off by pink shading and indicates an estimate of the expected real interest rate.

In the middle frame the estimate of the expected real interest rate is plotted directly. In each year, the height of the pink shading in the middle frame is identical to that in the top frame. The estimate of r^e fluctuates in a narrow range around 3 percent and averages out at 3.0 percent for the twenty years plotted.[10]

The redistributive effect of inflation depends on the actual real interest rate (r) — that is, the interest return people actually receive after the fact (*ex post*) on their saving minus the inflation that actually has occurred ($r = i - p$), because it is actual inflation that determines the quantity of goods people can consume with their savings at today's prices. The bottom section of Figure 11-3 shows that the actual real interest rate fell below its 3.0 percent average in the three periods when inflation accelerated, between 1965 and 1969, and a shorter but sharper period in 1973–74, and a final period during 1978–79.[11]

Although inflation redistributes income away from all savers, some have suffered more than others. Low-income families who lack the funds and expertise to buy bonds place most of their money in savings accounts, which have experienced nominal interest yields (i) considerably below the corporate bond rate displayed in Figure 11-3. Some savers have even kept their money in cash under the mattress or in cookie jars and have lost every year, because cash has a nominal interest rate of zero.

---

[8] This is the interest rate on top-grade (Aaa) corporate bonds.

[9] The hypothesis of adaptive expectations is explained and applied to the analysis of the inflation-unemployment cycle in section 8–6.

[10] This series overstates the expected real return for all savers: (1) because the income tax liability on the nominal interest receipts is neglected, and (2) because many savers kept their money in savings accounts and received nominal yields considerably below the Aaa corporate bond rate plotted as i.

[11] The actual inflation rate is the annual change in the consumption deflator, which includes the prices of food and energy, unlike the expected inflation rate, which excludes them.

ALTHOUGH THE EXPECTED REAL INTEREST RATE HAS BEEN ABOUT 3 PERCENT,
THE ACTUAL REAL INTEREST RATE HAS BEEN LESS THAN THAT IN MOST YEARS

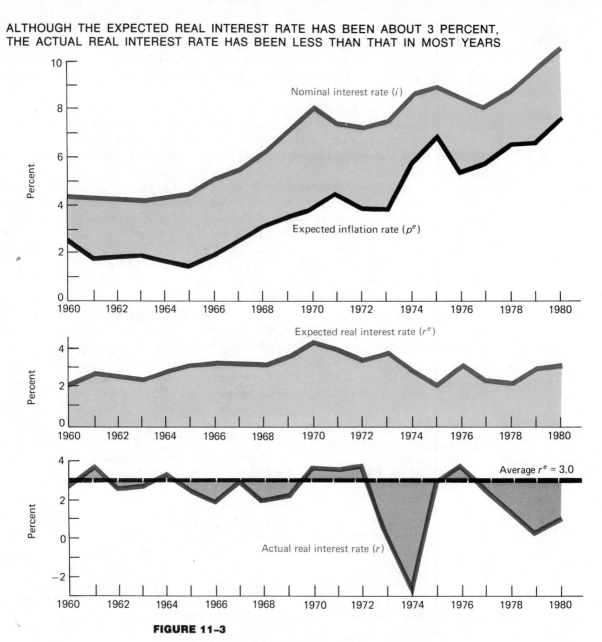

FIGURE 11–3

The Nominal Interest Rate (i), Expected Inflation (p^e),
and the Actual (r) and Expected (r^e) Real Interest Rates, 1960–80

In the top frame the red line is the nominal interest rate (i) on top-grade (Aaa)
corporate bonds. Below it the black line is an estimate of expected inflation (p^e),
the same as that displayed in the bottom frame of Figure 10–2. The pink area
between is our suggested estimate of the expected real interest rate (r^e). The middle frame displays the expected real interest rate directly. The bottom frame displays the actual (*ex post*) real interest rate, which in most years fell short of the
average 3.0 percent real rate that was expected.

342 The Consequences of Inflation

The losses displayed in Figure 11-3 are measured in percentages. How much have people lost in billions of dollars? G. L. Bach and James B. Stephenson have estimated that the postwar inflation through 1971 redistributed about $500 billion away from households.[12] Roughly another $450 billion was lost in the 1973–74 episode alone.

If the redistribution of an inflationary surprise causes savers to lose, who gains? Roughly half the gain goes to the government, and the rest is split between corporations and small businesses. Government gains because it can finance some of its spending by the revenue gained by printing the money people need to conduct their transactions at the new higher prices. But this revenue from the inflation tax reduces the government's need for conventional income, sales, and payroll taxes, thus benefiting all of us who pay federal income taxes.

EFFECTS OF INFLATION ON CORPORATIONS IN THE POSTWAR UNITED STATES

Conventional business accounting disguises many of the effects of inflation on real corporate profits. Recently Phillip Cagan and Robert E. Lipsey of the National Bureau of Economic Research have attempted to correct existing estimates of corporate profits for the effects of inflation. They distinguished four different corrections that must be made:

1. *Replacement-cost depreciation.* Business firms deduct from their profits an allowance for the depreciation (wearing out and obsolescence) of their buildings and equipment.[13] The government allows businesses to deduct each year only a fraction of the *original price paid* or "historic cost," whereas the proper deduction would be for the higher "replacement cost" based on what it would cost at today's prices to replace a given building or piece of equipment. If inflation boosts replacement cost to a much higher level than historic cost, then "true" depreciation deductions are higher than the government allows business firms to take on their tax returns, and so "true" profits are correspondingly lower. Because government rules thus force business firms to compute erroneously high levels of profit (since depreciation deductions are too low), corporation income taxes paid by business firms are too high.

2. *Capital gains.* A corporation makes a profit if it manages to increase its assets more than its liabilities — that is, to increase its **net worth.** One form of increase in the value of assets (and hence profits) is presently ignored. This is the capital gain that corporations enjoy when inflation raises the value of the land, buildings, and equipment that they own. Even if they do not sell an asset, its current market value is an

---

[12] G. L. Bach and James B. Stephenson, "Inflation and the Redistribution of Wealth," *Review of Economics and Statistics,* vol. 61 (February 1974), pp. 1–13.

[13] **Review:** Section 2-9.

asset of the corporation, and any gain in value of an asset represents an additional source of profit.

3. *Gains and losses on financial assets and liabilities.* Gains or losses on other assets and on liabilities should be counted as a profit or loss as well, since they can cause an increase or decrease in a firm's net worth, and profit is simply the change in net worth. An increase in inflation, as we have seen in Figure 11-1, tends to raise the nominal interest rate and thus decrease the value of the outstanding bonds (a liability) that the firm has issued. This, when it occurs, represents an increased profit to the firm and is equivalent to the gain made by the firm through its good fortune in issuing its debt in earlier periods of low interest rates (so that its current interest expense is lower than if it had to finance its debt today).

4. *Translation to real terms.* The first three adjustments are carried out in nominal terms, but then stated profits and all adjustments must be deflated by the GNP deflator or some other price index. This is exactly what we did in our example of Harold Homeowner in the previous section, where we found that his capital gain was $6000 in nominal terms and $5094 in real terms.

Table 11-1 shows the results of making all these corrections, including the restatement of depreciation (and inventories) on a replacement-cost basis, and the recalculation of assets and liabilities at true market prices. There are three pairs of columns, the first pair showing total profits, the second pair showing net worth, and the third pair showing the rate of return (ratio of profits to net worth). It is apparent that the effect of the adjustments is to make the rate of return much more volatile than the conventional measure, and to raise the adjusted rate in years such as 1973–74, when inflation both raised the value of corporate assets and also, through the increase in nominal interest rates, reduced the value of corporate liabilities. Comparing Table 11-1 with Figure 11-3, we see that the adjusted rate of return is highest in years such as 1973–74, when the actual real interest rate was lowest in Figure 11-3. In these years higher inflation redistributed income from households to corporations. And the adjusted rate of return is lowest in years such as 1976, when the actual real interest rate was high and a decline in actual inflation redistributed income back from corporations to households.

THE STOCK MARKET PUZZLE

One of the leading economic puzzles of the late 1970s was "Why is the stock market so low?" Notice in Table 11-1 that the inflation-adjusted net worth of corporations had increased by more than 50 percent between 1965 and 1977. Yet the Dow-Jones average hit 1000 in 1965 and as late as April of 1980 was still at 800. According to the Cagan and Lipsey study, the ratio of the market value of corporate stock to net worth fell from 1.255 in 1965 to 0.498 in 1977. Several hypotheses have been

TABLE 11-1

Effect of Adjustment for Inflation on After-tax Corporate
Profits, Net Worth, and Rate of Return, 1955–77

Billions of 1964 dollars

	Profits		Net worth		Rate of return	
	Conventional basis	After adjustment	Conventional basis	After adjustment	Conventional (1) ÷ (3)	Adjusted (2) ÷ (4)
	(1)	(2)	(3)	(4)	(5)	(6)
1955	26.5	34.9	244.0	335.9	11.6	11.4
1956	26.3	43.8	255.4	369.5	10.8	13.0
1957	24.3	23.1	263.8	381.2	9.5	6.3
1958	20.0	16.9	271.5	387.4	7.6	4.4
1959	24.8	27.9	284.3	405.9	9.1	7.2
1960	22.4	19.4	284.5	403.0	7.9	4.8
1961	21.8	13.2	301.8	411.8	7.7	3.3
1962	25.2	24.1	314.7	420.4	8.3	5.9
1963	27.5	32.2	325.0	431.5	8.7	7.7
1964	32.5	37.4	340.2	447.2	10.0	8.6
1965	38.3	51.3	355.9	469.6	11.3	11.5
1966	39.6	67.4	366.3	501.5	11.1	14.4
1967	36.5	60.3	381.4	533.6	10.0	12.0
1968	35.8	56.5	383.1	549.0	9.4	10.6
1969	31.2	78.9	386.4	593.5	8.1	14.4
1970	23.6	25.4	380.6	588.4	6.1	4.3
1971	27.0	23.4	386.9	589.8	7.1	4.0
1972	32.7	53.1	397.9	615.2	8.5	9.0
1973	39.6	103.0	393.6	668.8	10.0	16.7
1974	40.9	106.9	383.3	732.5	10.4	16.0
1975	37.3	35.2	387.2	732.7	9.7	4.8
1976	44.2	4.3	408.5	718.7	11.4	0.6
1977	46.3	92.3	413.5	764.3	11.3	12.8

Source: Phillip Cagan and Robert G. Lipsey, *The Financial Effects of Inflation* (Ballinger for National Bureau of Economic Research, 1978), Table 2-2 (columns 1 and 12) and Table 2-3 (columns 1, 3, 4, and 8).

proposed to explain the puzzle. One is the simple fact that inflation has made the corporate rate of return much more volatile and uncertain than previously, as is evident in the enormous swing in column (6) of Table 11-1 from 1973–74 to 1976. Investors are willing to pay less for the stock of a company with uncertain earnings than for that of another company with very stable earnings, and so this dislike of uncertainty has communicated itself to the stock market as a whole.

Another approach taken by Franco Modigliani of MIT and Richard Cohn of the University of Illinois is that investors have made two major errors.[14] First, they have based their evaluation of future corporate earnings using the nominal interest rate, rather than the correct real expected interest rate (such as that displayed in the middle frame of Figure 11-3) that should be used for saving and investment decisions. Second, investors appear to neglect one of the crucial adjustments made in Table 11-1. While they recognize the overstatement of profits due to the use of a historic-cost basis for depreciation, they fail to recognize the understatement of profits as inflation reduces the real value of outstanding corporate liabilities. Modigliani and Cohn conclude: "Because of inflation-induced errors, investors have systematically undervalued the stock market by 50 percent."[15]

OTHER SOURCES OF GAIN AND LOSS FROM INFLATION

In addition to redistributing income from savers to debtors, inflation has other effects that are caused by particular features of institutions in the U.S. economy.

1. *COLA clauses.* Gainers from inflation are those who have relatively complete cost-of-living escalators in their wage contracts. Because of their COLA protection, blue-collar workers—for instance, members of the steelworkers' union—have made substantial gains in relative income during the 1970s as compared to others who are not protected by COLA clauses—for instance, white-collar clerical workers. This erosion in the relative income of white-collar workers has created "a real crisis in middle-class psychology."[16]

2. *Poor versus rich old people.* People in their retirement years have been the classic losers from inflation, since inflation erodes the amount they can buy with the amount saved up during their working years. But in the 1970s this situation changed, because social security benefits paid by the government to retired individuals are completely indexed to changes in the Consumer Price Index. Thus the relatively poor old people, who live mainly on social security, have been able to stay even with inflation. But better-off old people, who had counted on supplementing their social security benefits with savings and private pension-plan income, have watched helplessly as inflation has reduced the real value of these assets.

3. *Other government programs.* While social security recipients have been able to stay even with inflation, welfare recipients have not en-

---

[14] For a biography of Franco Modigliani, see section 12-3.

[15] Franco Modigliani and Richard A. Cohn, "Inflation, Rational Valuation and the Market," *Financial Analysts Journal* (March/April 1979), pp. 3–23.

[16] Lawrence Rout, "Inflation's Brisk Pace Accentuates Variations in Who Is Hurt Most," *Wall Street Journal* (January 8, 1980), p. 34.

joyed any such complete indexing of their benefits. On the other hand, food stamp payments are indexed to changes in the price of food.

4. *Effects of tax system.* Just as corporations are not taxed on their true profits, so households are not taxed on their true income. One important error is the taxation of a saver's entire interest return on saving, whereas if the nominal interest rate is 9 percent and the inflation rate is 6 percent, only the real interest return of 3 percent should be taxed. This, after all, is the true return to saving, the return Pete Puritan received for his patience in waiting a full year to buy his bicycle. Similarly, only the real interest portion of interest payments should be deductible by borrowers, in contrast to the U.S. system where all the interest cost of a loan is deductible. Thus the U.S. tax system, together with inflation, encourages borrowing and consumption, while it discourages saving.

But in fact the situation is worse than this, because people who have funds to invest are also caused to alter their decisions by the interaction of inflation and the tax system. Some assets, particularly land and gold, yield returns in the form of capital gains rather than interest income, in contrast to savings accounts and bonds. And these capital gains are taxed at a much lower rate than ordinary income. Thus in the 1970s the prices of land and gold rose much more than the average price level, as households attempted to switch their savings into these lightly taxed assets. Holders of land and gold, as well as antiques, oriental rugs, silver, and other tangible assets, enjoyed a substantial increase in net worth as compared to others who had unwisely kept their money in bonds or savings accounts.[17] A related problem is that the taxation of nominal interest returns on bonds and savings accounts makes the real interest rates presented in Figure 11-1 too high, since in making these estimates of the real interest rate we failed to deduct the taxes paid by savers.[18]

Clearly, keeping up with inflation involves both knowledge and luck, and inflation has been unfair to many of the "losers" listed in this section. Although the tone of the following passage may seem a bit strong, it does convey the heavy cost that inflation imposes on society:

> The worst problem with inflation—even at the moderate rate of the past decade—is its disintegrating effect on the social fabric. Even those who manage to keep up with inflation, or beat it, incur a psychic cost. Economic life begins to resemble the world of Alice in Wonderland, where you must run very fast just to stay in the same place. Desperate calculation becomes necessary to achieve what a stable currency formerly guaranteed. Inevitably this added

[17] See Martin Feldstein, "The Effect of Inflation on the Prices of Land and Gold," National Bureau of Economic Research working paper no. 296, November 1978.

[18] Thus the after-tax real interest rate in a year such as 1978 or 1979 was probably negative, and this suggests that monetary policy was operating in too expansionary a direction. See Martin S. Feldstein, "Tax Rules and the Mismanagement of Monetary Policy," National Bureau of Economic Research working paper no. 422, January 1980.

element of tension in social life weakens the bonds of general good will. This general good will provides the political support for liberal designs to help the less fortunate. Inflation, therefore, erodes this support.[19]

11-7 INFLATION, THE BALANCE OF PAYMENTS, AND FLEXIBLE EXCHANGE RATES

Because of its size and the minor importance of its foreign trade, the United States can be treated as a closed economy with no international trade as we analyze the determinants of real income, inflation, and unemployment. But the consequences of inflation do include effects on U.S. economic relations with the rest of the world. Most nations are much smaller, and trade comprises a much larger part of their GNP.

The consequences of domestic economic policy depend on the system of **foreign exchange rates** that rules the price of our currency relative to other currencies. Throughout most of our history the United States has been on a system of fixed exchange rates, in which the dollar exchange rate was fixed for a long period at a single value in terms of foreign currencies, particularly the British pound sterling. Between 1949 and 1967 one American dollar would buy 0.357 of a British pound. Since 1973, however, the value of the U.S. dollar has floated, changing in its relation to other currencies from day to day. In March 1973 $1 could buy 2.81 German marks, but in February 1980 the dollar was much weaker and could buy only 1.73 German marks. When the dollar strengthens, or **appreciates,** in terms of other currencies, as in early 1980, an import from abroad with a price fixed in pounds or marks takes fewer dollars to buy, and the price of our imports declines. United States consumers benefit. The losers are U.S. exporters who find that a given pound or mark price for U.S. tractors or computers, set to compete with local companies selling their tractors and computers in Britain and Germany, brings home fewer dollars.

Conversely, a **depreciation** of the dollar, such as those in 1970–73 and 1976–79, raises the price of imports into the United States, hurting the U.S. consumer. The gainers are U.S. exporters, who find that they receive more dollars for a price set in pounds or marks. The U.S. depreciation or devaluation in the 1970–73 and 1976–79 periods raised the U.S. rate of inflation, even though the price of imports is not included in the deflator for U.S. production (GNP). The deflator was raised because the depreciation of the dollar increased the prices of goods produced in the United States by U.S. exporters who found that they could maintain fixed prices in foreign currencies while still receiving a higher price in dollars. Also, U.S. producers whose goods competed closely with imports found that they could match the price increases posted by imported goods.

---

[19] "Liberals and Inflation," *The New Republic,* January 20, 1979, p. 6.

EFFECTS OF INFLATION UNDER FIXED EXCHANGE RATES

Other countries are profoundly affected in a system of fixed exchange rates by a U.S. decision to raise its rate of monetary growth and hence its rate of inflation. Our inflation travels abroad by several routes. First, price increases by U.S. exporters create an incentive for price increases by foreigners producing exports and import-competing goods. Second, U.S. price increases will induce foreigners to shift to other suppliers and will create an incentive for U.S. residents to buy more foreign goods. Our exports will fall and our imports will rise, creating a deficit in our **balance of trade** with other countries.[20] Our deficit is their surplus, and the high demand for their exports represents an injection of aggregate demand into their domestic economies. Now, one of two reactions can occur:

1. Foreigners now hold an extra supply of dollars received as revenue on sales of goods to U.S. residents. They turn the dollars in to their central banks for domestic currency, say West German marks. If foreign central banks then attempt to sell the dollars on the foreign exchange market in exchange for their own currency, the excessive supply of dollars will drive the price of dollars down, violating our initial assumption that the exchange rate is fixed.
2. Foreign central banks can refuse to sell the excessive dollars and can hold them. Then the domestic currency — marks — remains in circulation. That is how U.S. inflation can indirectly cause an acceleration of the growth of the domestic money supplies of foreign nations, an increase in their own rates of inflation, and, ultimately, an increase in the world rate of inflation.

Both of these reactions have occurred. At first, in 1968–71, foreigners allowed their holdings of dollars to build up as U.S. inflation accelerated, substantially raising the growth rate of the world money supply and the world rate of inflation as in reaction 2. But by 1971 the situation had become untenable, dollar holdings had become excessive, and foreigners attempted to sell dollars. For a while the United States attempted to hold the value of the dollar up, but a succession of crises in the foreign exchange markets eventually led to a major devaluation of the dollar in late 1971, followed by another in February 1973. By early 1973 most countries had given up the attempt to peg their currencies to the dollar and had allowed their exchange rates to float up and down.

Summary: A decision by a large country such as the United States to raise the rate of inflation in a system of fixed exchange rates forces other countries to inflate along with us, usually against their will. The longer-run consequences of excessive domestic inflation are balance-of-trade deficits and, eventually, a devaluation of the dollar. Small

---

[20] Balance of trade = exports − imports. See the Glossary and section 19-2.

foreign countries have no ability to control their domestic inflation rate. So much of their national production is sold abroad, or competes with imports, that the national price level is like a small boat that rises automatically with the tide of world inflation.

EFFECTS OF INFLATION WITH FLEXIBLE EXCHANGE RATES

Flexible exchange rates make a substantial difference, both for the United States and for small countries. If the United States chooses a faster or slower inflation rate than other countries, it can reach this decision purely on the basis of the domestic considerations reviewed earlier in this chapter. An acceleration of U.S. inflation has no lasting consequences for U.S. export sales or import purchases. A depreciation of the dollar will offset the acceleration in domestic inflation and keep the foreign prices of U.S. goods unaffected. This in turn will prevent any direct effect on higher U.S. prices of foreign prices, as well as any indirect effect of U.S. dollar outflows into foreign central bank reserves. Small foreign nations can choose their own inflation rate irrespective of world inflation when their exchange rate is free to float.

While a floating exchange-rate system in principle allows each nation to choose its own inflation rate, it does alter the economy's response to policy actions. We have seen in section 9-4 that a decision by the United States to accommodate supply shocks can cause the dollar to depreciate if other nations pursue neutral or extinguishing aggregate demand policies, and the dollar depreciation in turn will make U.S. inflation worse. A flexible exchange-rate system also changes the relative attractiveness of monetary and fiscal expansion. A monetary expansion, by creating an excess supply of dollars, tends to cause a dollar depreciation and make inflation worse, whereas a fiscal expansion tends to appreciate the dollar. The multipliers for monetary and fiscal expansion are also affected by the response of exchange rates. We return to these issues in Chapter 19.

11-8 INDEXATION AND OTHER REFORMS TO REDUCE THE COSTS OF INFLATION

Thus far we have learned that inflation imposes substantial costs on society. Even if inflation is fully anticipated, it imposes "shoe-leather costs" on money holders, and also a redistribution between individuals resulting from the defects of our present tax system. In addition, unanticipated inflation further redistributes income from savers to borrowers.

Since inflation is so costly, it is natural that an attempt should be made to eliminate it. Three basic methods are available. First, a slowdown in aggregate demand growth can cut inflation, although this is likely to impose on society the cost of a prolonged recession (section 8-8). Second, wage and price controls can be imposed, but this is only a temporary solution that seems bound to fail in the long run (section 9-5). Third, favorable supply shifts can be created, by cutting taxes that are paid by consumers, and by reversing some of government's "self-inflicted wounds" of the 1970s (section 9-9). This last policy can succeed as a long-run solution only if it is accompanied by an "accommodating" slowdown in aggregate demand growth.

It is unlikely that any of these cures can eliminate inflation overnight. Thus there is a strong case for a fourth approach: the institution of reforms that can cut substantially the costs imposed by inflation. These reforms fall into three basic categories: the elimination of government regulations that redistribute income from savers to borrowers, the creation of an indexed bond to give savers a secure place to save, and a restatement of tax laws to eliminate the effects of inflation on real tax burdens.

REGULATION Q AND VARIABLE-RATE MORTGAGES

In the U.S. economy a major barrier that causes inflation to erode savings accounts while enriching borrowers is the fixed-rate home mortgage. Many homeowners are still paying off 5 and 6 percent mortgages, while the value of their homes in many cases is increasing at 8 or 10 percent per year.[21] Savings and loan institutions are receiving a low level of interest income on the portion of their mortgage loans that were taken out a decade ago, and for this reason they cannot afford to pay an interest rate on savings deposits that fully compensates savers for inflation. Why don't savers switch their savings to commercial banks, which have very few mortgages in their asset portfolios? The federal government protects savings and loan associations against the loss of their deposits by setting a legal **Regulation Q** ceiling on the interest rate that commercial banks can pay to holders of time deposits.

The Regulation Q rules are highly complex and allow banks to pay a wide variety of interest rates, depending on the various restrictions placed on savers. For instance, in February 1980 it was possible to earn 12.3 percent on savings deposits in a commercial bank, but only by purchasing a six-month "money-market certificate" for a minimum of $10,000. Savers with less than $10,000 but more than $1000 could earn 10.4 percent, but they had to keep their money in the bank for two and a half years without withdrawing it. Many savers protested against these complex rules by withdrawing their funds from banks and savings institutions and depositing them in **money-market mutual funds,** which allowed instant withdrawal and check-writing privileges and had minimum deposit restrictions as low as $1000. Thus the effect of Regulation Q was further to redistribute income as inflation pushed interest rates higher, hurting poor savers who did not have enough funds to qualify for money-market certificates and who were not informed about money-market mutual funds.

---

[21] A well-publicized example involves ex-President Ford, whose house in Arlington, Virginia, appreciated from $35,000 in 1955 to $137,000 in 1976.

Major reforms instituted in 1980 will help redress the imbalance between borrowers and savers in an inflationary economy by allowing variable-interest-rate mortgages and eliminating Regulation Q.[22] An acceleration of inflation will now cause mortgage interest rates to increase, allowing financial institutions to pay a higher interest rate to savers.

Even if savers were fully compensated for inflation by receiving a nominal interest rate that included a full inflation premium on their savings accounts, everyone would still suffer an erosion of purchasing power on their checking accounts and pocket cash. Inflation causes people to work harder to keep their checking account balances at a minimum, but most of this extra effort (the shoe-leather cost of inflation) will be eliminated when banks begin to pay interest on checking accounts.

INDEXED BONDS

Even though introducing variable-rate mortgages and lifting government interest-rate ceilings on savings and checking accounts will substantially cut the costs of inflation, many economists have recommended that the government go further and issue an **indexed bond** that would fully protect savers against any unexpected movements in the inflation rate. An indexed bond simply pays savers a fixed real interest rate (r_0), say 3 percent, plus the actual inflation rate (p). Thus the saver's nominal interest rate (i) would be:

GENERAL FORM   NUMERICAL EXAMPLE

$$i = r_0 + p$$

(a) $3 = 3 + 0$

(b) $13 = 3 + 10$

In the first numerical example (a), savers would receive a 3 percent return if the inflation rate were zero. If inflation suddenly accelerated to 10 percent, as in example (b), savers would find that the nominal return (i) rose to 13 percent, and they would be just as well off as without the inflation.[23]

The main disadvantage of the indexed-bond proposal is that savers might find it too attractive! Banks and savings institutions might experience a flood of withdrawals by savers eager to buy the indexed bonds. Formerly banks could not compete because of the Regulation Q interest-rate ceilings, but recent reforms now make a government indexed bond feasible at last.

---

[22] In April 1980, the Federal Home Loan Bank Board gave its permission for savings and loan associations to begin issuing a limited form of "rollover" or "renegotiable rate" mortgages, under which mortgage interest rates can be adjusted every three-to-five years. And in March 1980, Congress passed the Depository Institutions Deregulation and Monetary Control Act that gradually dismantles Regulation Q ceilings and many other regulations that limited the ability of savings institutions to compete with commercial banks.

[23] At present, savers pay taxes on all interest received. To leave them untouched by inflation, the government would have to make the inflation part of the interest return exempt from taxation.

INDEXED TAX SYSTEM

The government should not stop with indexed bonds. It should fully index the tax system — that is, raise the dollar amounts of tax credits, exemptions, standard deductions, and tax rate brackets each year by the amount of inflation that had been experienced. A 10 percent inflation would thus cause the $1000 personal exemption to rise to $1100 in the following year. Without an indexed tax system, inflation raises individual incomes and pushes taxpayers into higher tax brackets. A typical taxpayer might pay 15 percent of his income in income tax in 1981 but 15.5 percent at his higher 1982 wage, even if all his wage increase between 1981 and 1982 were eaten up by inflation. This system has been called "taxation without representation," because the share of personal income flowing to the federal government automatically is pushed up by inflation without Congressional legislation to authorize the increase.

But the government must do more than index credits, exemptions, deductions, and tax brackets in order to achieve a fully "inflation-neutral" tax system. It must end present rules that discriminate against savers and in favor of borrowers by shifting over to the taxation of real rather than nominal interest and capital gains. Just as savers should be taxed only on real interest income and real capital gains, borrowers should be allowed to deduct from their taxable income only the real portion of the interest they pay on loans. At present some borrowers are paying a negative after-tax real interest payment because inflation has ballooned the size of their tax deductions. These reforms would make an enormous difference, eliminating the present effect of inflation in the U.S. tax system of discouraging saving and encouraging borrowing and spending.[24]

As we learned in section 9-4, wage indexation (or COLA clauses) impedes the economy's adjustment to a supply shock. An oil price increase that raises the rate of inflation will cause a greater future acceleration of wage growth, the greater the degree of wage indexation. As a result, a policy decision to accommodate a supply shock will cause a permanent acceleration of inflation, while a policy decision to extinguish a supply shock will cause a deeper recession with wage indexation than without.[25] Thus most economists now endorse indexing the tax system but oppose the full indexation of wages.

---

[24] A complete catalogue of the effects of inflation is contained in S. Fischer and F. Modigliani, "Towards an Understanding of the Real Effects and Costs of Inflation," *Weltwirtschaftliches Archiv,* vol. 114 (1978), pp. 810–833.

[25] Numerical examples of the instability created by wage indexing are contained in Robert J. Gordon, "Alternative Responses of Policy to External Supply Shocks," *Brookings Papers on Economic Activity,* vol. 6, no. 1 (1975), pp. 183–206. A simple theoretical model is provided by Joanna Gray, "Wage Indexation: A Macroeconomic Approach," *Journal of Monetary Economics,* vol. 2 (April 1976), pp. 221–236.

11-9 CONCLUSION TO PART III: THE INFLATION AND UNEMPLOYMENT DILEMMA

The inflation advanced industrialized countries experienced in the 1970s originated in an excessive monetary and fiscal stimulus to aggregate demand, particularly in the mid- and late 1960s. Too much aggregate demand growth causes inflation to accelerate above the pace people expect whenever unemployment is allowed to dip below the natural unemployment rate. Governments must limit the growth in aggregate demand to keep unemployment at the natural unemployment rate, but in the 1960s the wartime financing needs of the Vietnam War pushed aggregate demand too high and unemployment too low for too long.

Monetary and fiscal policy are of little use in providing jobs to the unemployed, once the economy has reached the natural rate of unemployment. Instead structural and manpower programs must be instituted to cut the natural unemployment rate itself by better matching of workers with job openings and by reforms to reduce present incentives that favor long extended periods of low-intensity job search.

A monetary and fiscal policy that maintains actual unemployment at the natural unemployment rate will keep inflation from accelerating further if the economy is spared from supply shocks, but such a policy will do nothing to curb the expectations of further inflation that are so crucial in the persistence of actual inflation from year to year. Instead, policymakers are faced with four options. They can try to cut the inflation rate by deliberately using restrictive monetary and fiscal policy to create a recession, causing a massive waste of men and machines. They can try to use price and wage controls, but they stand little chance of succeeding without causing shortages of some products and of skilled workers. Third, they can attempt to undo the "self-inflicted wounds" of the late 1970s, government-designed mini-supply shocks that pushed up the rate of inflation. Supply-side measures that help to reduce costs and prices must be accompanied by a deceleration in aggregate demand growth. Finally, the government can loosen present financial regulations that cause inflation to erode the value of savings accounts, redistributing income from savers to debtors. It can issue an indexed bond to insulate savers from the effects of inflation, and it can redesign the tax system to make it "inflation neutral."

What should we conclude? There is no need to select a single solution to the inflation-unemployment dilemma. Multiple solutions should be pursued simultaneously. The government needs to introduce many reforms, including (1) supply-side remedies that reduce the burden of regulations, the minimum wage, tariffs and quotas against imports, and taxes that are paid by consumers through higher prices; (2) the introduction of an indexed bond and an inflation-neutral tax system that would reduce the costs of inflation; and (3) unemployment-compensation reforms that reduce turnover unemployment and manpower policies that reduce mismatch unemployment.

Vigorous pursuit of these reforms would allow a deceleration in nominal GNP growth to occur without causing nearly as much extra unemployment as would be created without any reforms.

Thus we see that economists are not devoid of solutions for stagflation and the inflation-unemployment dilemma, contrary to the accusation of some journalists that economists have run out of ideas.[26] Rather the problem is political. Most of the reforms advocated in the previous paragraph require new legislation that will raise the ire of special interest groups. I recently concluded a survey of postwar macroeconomic developments by pointing to this central problem of political inaction:

> As the U.S. entered the 1980s, a long agenda of positive and forceful economic actions lay gathering dust, awaiting the new broom of a positive and forceful politician.[27]

SUMMARY

1. Inflation is felt primarily by owners of financial assets. The financial effects of inflation are divided into two categories: the effects of a fully anticipated inflation, and the effects of unanticipated inflation.

2. An increase in the fully anticipated rate of inflation tends to reduce the average holdings of real money balances, as the cost of holding these balances—the nominal interest rate paid on alternative financial assets—increases along with the inflation rate. The extra effort made by corporations and households to maintain lower money balances is a real cost imposed on them by inflation.

3. The optimum inflation rate is reached when the extra inconvenience caused by the increase in the inflation tax is just balanced by the extra benefits of the reduction in conventional taxes.

4. The basic case against unanticipated inflation is that it redistributes income from creditors to debtors unfairly without their knowledge or consent. The gainers from unanticipated inflation are those who are heavily in debt and whose assets are primarily physical rather than financial.

5. The U.S. tax system has many rules that are stated in nominal rather than real terms. As a result, the tax system is far from "inflation neutral." The present U.S. tax system causes all types of inflation, both anticipated and unanticipated, to redistribute income from savers to borrowers. It also causes changes in relative prices, stimulating price rises in assets that offer returns in the form of lightly taxed capital gains, such as gold, land, and antiques.

---

[26] Journalists were justified in criticizing the January 1980 report of the Council of Economic Advisers, which expressed helpless pessimism regarding the inflation outlook and failed to push vigorously for the reforms listed in the preceding paragraph.

[27] Robert J. Gordon, "Postwar Macroeconomics: The Evolution of Events and Ideas," in Martin S. Feldstein (ed.), *The American Economy in Transition* (Chicago: University of Chicago Press for the National Bureau of Economic Research, 1980).

6. The actual real interest rate earned by savers was particularly low in periods of unanticipated inflation caused by supply shocks in 1973–74 and 1978–80. During these periods the true inflation-adjusted rate of return on corporate capital was relatively high, and the government also gained through its ability to finance more of its expenditures with the inflation tax rather than with conventional taxes.

7. The consequences of domestic policy depend on the system of exchange rates that determines the value of our currency relative to other currencies. In a system of fixed exchange rates, an increase in a large country's inflation rate forces smaller countries to inflate along with it. But when exchange rates are free to float, small countries can choose their own inflation rate irrespective of world inflation, because the acceleration of a country's domestic inflation will be offset by a depreciation in its currency.

8. A number of reforms have been suggested that would ease the costs of living with inflation. Among the most productive would be the introduction of variable-rate mortgages, the lifting of government interest-rate ceilings on savings and checking accounts, the issuing by the government of an indexed bond, and a recasting of the tax system in an inflation-neutral form. While indexed bonds and an indexed tax system are desirable, wage indexation should be only partial rather than complete, because wage indexation interferes with the economy's adjustment to supply shocks.

A LOOK AHEAD

Throughout the book to this point it has been assumed that aggregate demand can be controlled exactly. Monetary and fiscal policy have been assumed to be capable of setting demand growth ($\hat{y}$) at any desired value. But in the real world, life is more difficult for the policymaker: $\hat{y}$ reacts to policy changes with a lag and by an uncertain amount. As a result, many economists argue that activist government policy intervention is unwise. The next chapter sets out the main issues in the great debate on policy activism.

CONCEPTS

Indexation
Nominal and real interest rates
Anticipated and unanticipated inflation
Costs of unanticipated inflation
Costs of fully anticipated inflation
The inflation tax
Inflation premium
Variable interest-rate mortgages

Indexed bonds
Regulation Q
Expected real return (r^e)
Extra convenience services of money (ECS)
Optimum quantity of money
Optimum inflation rate
Fixed and floating exchange rates

QUESTIONS FOR REVIEW

A. Are the following statements true, false, or uncertain? Be sure you can carefully explain your answer.

1   When inflation is fully anticipated, it imposes no welfare costs on any group in society.

2   It is the expected real rate of interest, not the nominal rate, that is important in determining economic behavior.

3   Inflation redistributes income from creditors and savers to debtors only when the actual inflation rate exceeds the expected inflation rate.

4   If payment of interest were allowed on all checking accounts, the optimum rate of inflation would be increased.

5   An increase in a large country's rate of inflation will be exported to smaller countries, raising their rates of inflation.

6   If the government attempts to reduce the rate of inflation, this will redistribute income to savers from debtors, hurting those who have recently paid high mortgage interest rates to buy houses.

B. Answer the following.

1   Explain why conventional measures of corporate profits are incorrect when there is inflation.

2   Why are the adjusted measures of the corporate rate of return in Table 11-1 so volatile from year to year?

3   What are the primary dangers introduced by indexation?

4   Give some reasons why the U.S. government fails to offer an indexed savings bond.

5   At present full cost-of-living adjustments (wage indexation) cover only a small fraction of the U.S. labor force. If you were the president of a large U.S. manufacturing firm, would you favor introducing full cost-of-living adjustments for your own employees? What risks would you take by this action?

6   Which (or what combination of) the four options of handling inflation would you prefer? Explain your answer carefully.

7   Starting at point E_2 in Figure 11-1, show how the economy adjusts when there is a reduction in the expected rate of inflation from 5 to 2 percent.

8   Draw a new version of Figure 11-2, with the slope of the money demand schedule twice as steep. (That is, money demand now falls $200 billion when the interest rate increases from 0 to 10 percent). Now calculate the lost convenience value of money when inflation accelerates from 0 to 10 percent.

Part IV

Sources of Instability in the Private Economy

12 The Monetarist–Nonmonetarist Debate on Policy Activism

By week's end, Carter was ready to adopt
Richard Nixon's assertion that his economic
advisers were seldom right, but never in doubt.[1]

12-1 LINK TO PREVIOUS CHAPTERS: THE CENTRAL ROLE OF AGGREGATE DEMAND

In Part II (Chapters 3–6) we studied the determinants of the level of aggregate demand. Aggregate demand can be raised by a monetary or fiscal stimulus or by an increase in business or consumer optimism. When the private demand for consumption and investment spending falls off, an offsetting monetary or fiscal stimulus can keep aggregate demand from dropping. In the same way, a boom in private spending can be balanced by monetary or fiscal restraint.

The level of aggregate demand does not by itself tell us the level of prices or output, but rather how much nominal spending is available to be divided between the price level and real output. The division that actually occurs depends on the conditions of aggregate supply. How much output are firms willing to produce at different price levels?

Part III, especially Chapters 8 and 9, provided a dynamic analysis of aggregate demand and supply. The growth of aggregate demand ($\hat{y}$) can be controlled by the monetary and fiscal policymakers, but the division of that demand growth between inflation and output growth depends on the position of the short-run Phillips curve. A cut in demand growth ($\hat{y}$) may at first mainly affect real GNP growth and only later mainly take the form of lower inflation.

In Part III, however, we unrealistically assumed that the growth of aggregate demand could be controlled precisely. Unfortunately, policymakers cannot act as if the economy were an automobile that can quickly be steered back and forth. Rather, the procedure of changing aggregate demand is

---

[1] *Chicago Tribune* (March 16, 1980), Section 2, p. 6.

much closer to that of a captain navigating a giant supertanker. Even if he gives a signal for a hard turn, it takes a mile before he can see a change, and ten miles before the ship makes the turn. In the same way, the real-world economy has a momentum of its own, and policy shifts cannot control aggregate demand instantly or precisely.

The main subject of Part IV is the control of aggregate demand. First we ask an obvious question: Why bother? Just as the classical economists assumed that the economy has powerful self-correcting mechanisms that continuously act to steer it back to full employment without government interference (Chapter 6), so the modern school of thought called monetarism denies that the benefits of active government control of aggregate demand are worth the cost. In fact, it is a basic tenet of the monetarist position that government interference does more harm than good and actually destabilizes the economy. In this chapter we examine the monetarist case that stabilization policy (active government control of aggregate demand) is not necessary.

12-2 THE MONETARIST CONTROVERSY IS NOT ABOUT THE POTENCY OF MONETARY POLICY

In almost every episode of the past decade, monetarists offered policy recommendations that differed from their nonmonetarist opponents. In essence the monetarists usually said "Do nothing" while their opponents said "Do something." (The only exceptions to this statement were periods when the "do something" monetarist recommendations involved slowing the growth rate of the money supply to a lower number more consistent with what the monetarists believed the "do nothing" constant growth-rate target should be.) But the reasons for the differing policy recommendations had little to do with the relative potency of monetary or fiscal policy. The great irony of the debate between the monetarists and nonmonetarists is that the effect of money on unemployment and inflation is not the central issue![2]

The adjectives monetarist and nonmonetarist are confusing and deceptive labels, but we are forced to use them because of their widespread usage and acceptance by economists and journalists. The term monetarist carries the misleading implication that "only monetary policy matters."[3] Yet as

---

[2] Traditionally, macro textbooks have interpreted the monetarist debate as the strength of policy multipliers. An extended statement that attempts to reorient the monetarist debate is Franco Modigliani, "The Monetarist Controversy, or, Should We Forsake Stabilization Policy?" *American Economic Review,* vol. 67 (March 1977), pp. 1–19. An earlier paper is Milton Friedman, "Why Economists Disagree," in *Dollars and Deficits* (Englewood Cliffs, N.J.: Prentice-Hall, 1968), pp. 1–16. Friedman on pp. 6–9 shares the same orientation as this chapter, although on pp. 10–16 he places considerably more weight than we do here on the influence of money on inflation. Our orientation reflects Friedman's own influence. There remain very few economists who disagree with him that in the long run inflation is a monetary phenomenon.

[3] The term *monetarism* was introduced in Karl Brunner, "The Role of Money and Monetary Policy," *Review of the Federal Reserve Bank of St. Louis,* no. 50 (1968), pp. 9–24.

early as 1966 the chief monetarist, Milton Friedman, admitted in writing that fiscal policy could affect real output in the short run and the price level in the long run. The term nonmonetarist is even worse. As early as 1944 one of the chief nonmonetarists, Franco Modigliani of MIT, gave monetary policy a key role in his theoretical writing. None of the current leading nonmonetarists ever claimed that "money does not matter at all" for the determination of income and output.

Chapter 5 contains all the elements needed for an old-fashioned interpretation of monetarist debate. Monetary policy is potent and fiscal policy weak when the *LM* curve is steep and the *IS* curve is flat. In the extreme case of a completely vertical *LM* curve, a fiscal expansion completely crowds out an equivalent amount of private investment and leaves total real GNP unaffected. The opponents of the monetarists could not understand how it could be claimed that fiscal policy is impotent because the required vertical *LM* curve occurs only when the demand for money is unresponsive to changes in the interest rate, a condition that has been rejected by almost all economic research on the real world. The new interpretation of the monetarist debate in this chapter places no emphasis at all on the slope of the *LM* curve because none of the major monetarist conclusions depend on that slope.[4]

The real dispute between monetarists and nonmonetarists has little to do with the relative potency of monetary versus fiscal policy. Instead, their main clash concerns the location in the economy of the principal source of instability. Monetarists believe that the private economy is basically stable and that fixed policy rules are necessary to protect the economy against ill-conceived and poorly timed government actions that in the past have caused economic instability. In contrast, the nonmonetarists pinpoint private spending decisions as the main source of instability and generally support an activist government countercyclical policy (both monetary and fiscal) to achieve economic stability.

To add one irony to another, both the monetarist and nonmonetarist camps regard the period of the Great Depression as providing the most dramatic example of instability originating from, respectively, the government and the private sectors. Monetarists show how the Depression was made more severe by the 31 percent decline in the money supply that the Fed allowed to occur between 1929 and 1933, whereas nonmonetarists emphasize the 85 percent decline in private investment during the same interval.[5] Nonmonetarists add that even in the years 1936–39, when the money supply had substantially surpassed its 1929 level, real private investment was on average still 40 percent below 1929.

---

[4] **Review:** Return to Figure 6-3. An increase in government spending has no effect on real output if the price level is flexible. Thus the real question affecting the multiplier of government or private spending on real output is not the slope of the *LM* curve (which is positively sloped in Figure 6-1), where the *DD* curve of Figure 6-3 was derived, but the speed and extent of the price increase following the fiscal expansion, and the effect on private spending of that price increase.

[5] The money supply concept (*M*1) declined by 25 percent, and *M*2 by 31 percent. See Appendix B for the actual data, and the Glossary for definitions of *M*1 and *M*2.

12-3 A MONETARIST PLATFORM

The continuing disagreements between monetarists and nonmonetarists can be traced to several basic assumptions of the monetarist platform with which nonmonetarists disagree.[6]

Plank 1: *Without the interference of demand shocks introduced by erratic government policy, private spending would be stable.* The stability of private spending stems from the **permanent income hypothesis** of consumption explored in Chapter 13. Consumption, the largest component of private spending, changes only gradually as households adjust their estimate of their long-run or permanent income. Another basic stabilizing factor is the flatness of the *IS* curve due to the broad range of assets whose demand depends on the interest rate.

Plank 2: *Even if private planned spending is not completely stable, flexible prices create a natural tendency for it to come back on course.* The equilibrium to which flexible prices guide the economy is the natural rate of unemployment (U^N). Not only is U^N compatible with steady inflation, but the inflation expectations of individuals are realized when the economy is at U^N. Furthermore, many demand shocks are transitory, and their destabilizing influence on output disappears before any offsetting government policy could possibly be put into effect.

Plank 3: *Even if private planned spending is not completely stable, and prices are not completely flexible, an activist monetary and fiscal policy to counteract private demand swings is likely to do more harm than good.* All policy changes affect the economy with a long and uncertain lag, so that the effect of policy may be felt after it is needed and in some cases may occur so late that it pushes the economy in the wrong direction. Economists' forecasting abilities are too limited to

---

[6] The monetarist platform is not copied directly from any monetarist publication but is my own invention suggested by the recent drift of the continuing policy debate. It is, however, similar to the overall interpretation of Modigliani in "The Monetarist Controversy," cited in footnote 2. An extended debate between Modigliani and Milton Friedman that casts additional light on our interpretation is contained in "The Monetarist Controversy," Federal Reserve Bank of San Francisco *Economic Review Supplement* (Spring 1977). Another interpretation of the debate, which shares the interpretation of the nonmonetarist response given in the box on pp. 370–371, is James Tobin, "How Dead Is Keynes?" *Economic Inquiry,* vol. 15 (October 1977), pp. 459–468.

Early drafts of this section benefited from the detailed constructive suggestions of Milton Friedman, Allan Meltzer, and Franco Modigliani. Almost all their suggestions have been adopted together with, in some cases, their own suggested wording in an effort to make this chapter an accurate and unbiased reflection of the monetarist-nonmonetarist debate.

participants what they had really meant to say, what the issues of dispute really were, and what he thought about aspects of present policy and past history.[b]

Unlike many economists of his brilliance and reputation, Friedman chose not to participate in active policymaking in Washington. Nevertheless, his policy proposals, particularly his emphasis on maintaining steady growth in monetary aggregates, have gradually won adherents in Washington, including his old undergraduate teacher Arthur Burns, Chairman of the Board of Governors of the Federal Reserve Board during 1972–1978. One of the regional Federal Reserve Banks in St. Louis has been dominated by Friedman's disciples and has contributed much of the empirical work to support his emphasis on monetary policy as a source of economic instability.

But Friedman is no narrow monetary specialist. His broader aim has been to support individual liberty and oppose every aspect of government intervention in individual affairs, from the military draft, to compulsory social security and public education, to auto safety and drug regulations, chaotic welfare systems, fixed exchange rates, and controls on wages, prices, rents, and interest rates. His libertarian and antigovernment position is an outgrowth of themes emphasized by his teachers in graduate school in the 1930s at the University of Chicago. From the time of his return there as a teacher in the late 1940s, he was a leader of the "Chicago School" of economics, which stands in opposition to the activist government intervention espoused by most leading economists at eastern universities, largely on the grounds that many government policies hurt those they were designed to help and vice versa.

The best introduction to Friedman's views on government regulation is his classic *Capitalism and Freedom* (1962). His basic position is applied to a wide range of current problems in a collection of his *Newsweek* columns, *An Economist's Protest* (2d ed., 1975). Friedman became even better known in early 1980, when he presented his personal economic and political philosophy in a ten-episode Public Television program, "Free to Choose," and in a best-selling companion volume of the same name.[c]

Born in 1912, Friedman decided to retire from the University of Chicago in early 1977. In his last quarter at Chicago, he received the Nobel Memorial Prize in economics. He lives now in San Francisco, where he continues scholarly work on U.S. and U.K. monetary history at Stanford's Hoover Institute. Wherever he is, he is kept busy answering a flood of correspondence and writing the columns that appear in *Newsweek* every third week.[d]

---

[b] The author participated in this workshop regularly between 1968 and 1973.

[c] Milton and Rose Friedman, *Free to Choose* (New York: Harcourt Brace Jovanovich, 1980).

[d] Friedman has not been immune to criticism. See the essays by Tobin and Patinkin in Robert J. Gordon (ed.), *Milton Friedman's Monetary Framework* (Chicago: University of Chicago Press, 1974). Also see several of James Tobin's collected essays, cited in his biography in this chapter.

---

much less serious problem than the raw numbers suggest and show that a substantial portion of unemployment is voluntary (a position explored in section 10-6).[8] Nevertheless, monetarists generally refuse to accept as a characterization either disregard for unemployment or excessive concern for inflation.

---

[8] A classic monetarist attempt to reinterpret the meaning of an increase in unemployment is Milton Friedman, "Unemployment Figures," *Newsweek*, October 20, 1969, reprinted in his *An Economist's Protest*, 2d ed. (Glen Ridge, N.J.: Thomas Horton, 1975), pp. 105–107. An extended answer to Friedman's article is Robert J. Gordon, "The Welfare Cost of Higher Unemployment," *Brookings Papers on Economic Activity*, vol. 4, no. 1 (1973), pp. 133–195.

Franco Modigliani

Born in Rome in 1918, Modigliani emigrated to the United States at the outbreak of World War II. It did not take him long to make his mark. In his classic article, "Liquidity Preference and the Theory of Interest and Money," he presented the first formal theoretical analysis that integrated monetary factors into Keynesian analysis.[a] In retrospect it is ironic that Modigliani, now considered one of the two or three leading "nonmonetarists," presented the first modern analysis of the role of money in the Keynesian system.

Several of Modigliani's other articles rank among the most influential of the postwar era. He invented (with R. Brumberg) the "life-cycle" hypothesis of consumption, which shares with Friedman's "permanent income hypothesis" the ability to explain why the marginal propensity to consume is inversely proportional to income at any given moment, but remains steady over long historical periods as society becomes richer (see Chapter 13). With various co-authors he wrote several seminal articles and a book on a mathematical approach to production and employment scheduling in business. With Merton Miller of the University of Chicago he proved the controversial "Modigliani-Miller" theorem of corporate finance, which states that the value of a corporation is independent of its ratio of debt to equity. More recently his interests have spread even wider into international finance and capital theory.

Modigliani's career shifted from a theoretical to an empirical orientation with the advent of rapid electronic computers and with his move to MIT in 1962. Aided by a succession of bright MIT students, Modigliani, together with Albert Ando of the University of Pennsylvania, designed and built an elaborate computer model of the U.S. economy, in which he attempted to incorporate empirical estimates of the several channels by which money influences income. Recently

Courtesy of Franco Modigliani

Modigliani and others have used the model, now renamed "MPS," to attack the pro-monetarist conclusions of Friedman's monetarist disciples, and to confirm that both monetary and fiscal policy changes influence the level of real GNP.[b]

Unlike many emigrants, Modigliani has retained his connection with his home country. Many of his articles have been written in Italian, and he has recently studied the latest evidence on wage behavior and the consumption function in Italy.

Modigliani is almost unique among contemporary economists in the contagious enthusiasm he conveys to his students about a wide range of topics in economics and his generosity in granting co-authorships to those who help him investigate them. Modigliani has succeeded in increasing his stature by his feverish energy in scrutinizing a wide range of propositions, including his recent explanation of why stock market prices are so low (section 11-6, p. 346).

---

[a] "Liquidity Preference and the Theory of Interest and Money," *Econometrica*, vol. 12 (January 1944), pp. 45–88.

[b] MPS=MIT-Penn-Social Science Research Council. Quarterly forecasts with the model are produced by Albert Ando and others at the University of Pennsylvania.

In some recession situations of high unemployment, as occurred in 1975 in the United States, the monetarist distaste for activist policy would appear to condemn the economy to a longer recession than the alternative non-monetarist approach of monetary or fiscal stimulation. Yet monetarists deny that their recommendation reflects a choice between more or less unemployment now, but only between a lesser reduction in unemployment now and a greater increase in unemployment later. Why? They distrust the political process, which is said to throw up great obstacles to the achievement of sensible economic policy. The economy is bound to overshoot any target, they would argue, and politicians are unlikely to have the courage to apply the brakes to the economy soon enough to allow a "soft landing" at the target unemployment rate. Instead, the economy will be allowed to expand too far and too rapidly, inflation will accelerate, and the Federal Reserve will be forced to cause another recession and bout of unemployment to fight the renewed acceleration of inflation.

In the end the basic conflicts in policy recommendations by economists do not originate in irreconcilable analytical differences that call into question the scientific claims of economics. Most economists now accept the basic theoretical framework summarized in the *IS-LM* analysis of income determination (Chapters 3–6) and the Phillips-curve analysis of Chapter 8 based on shifting expectations of inflation. The dispute over planks 1 and 3 is not a matter of right or wrong but of differences in emphasis, perhaps the most important of which is the greater nonmonetarist willingness to trust the government to follow the advice of economists, as contrasted to the fundamental distrust of the political process exhibited by monetarists.[9] Plank 2 on the flexibility of prices remains in dispute because the historical data do not send strong signals that would allow economists to predict the speed of adjustment of inflation to higher unemployment. Finally, the disagreement over plank 4, on the importance of the short run as opposed to the long run, reflects not only differing value judgments but also differing degrees of optimism regarding the payoff of short-run policy shifts.

12-4 SOURCES OF INSTABILITY IN PRIVATE PLANNED SPENDING

The basic aim of stabilization policy is to keep the actual unemployment rate equal to the natural rate of unemployment (U^N) — the unemployment rate that is consistent with a continuation of inflation at its present rate

---

[9] What is the fundamental cause of this contrast? There is a chicken-and-egg problem of determining which of these statements is closer to the truth: (1) Does the preponderance of non-monetarists in important policymaking posts in Washington lead them to greater faith in the ability of the government to do the right thing? (2) Or does the absence of monetarists in leading policy positions reflect their own unwillingness to associate themselves with policymaking functions that they feel are inherently destabilizing?

James Tobin

Born in 1918, James Tobin became a superstar in the economics firmament soon after he emerged with his Ph.D. from Harvard in 1947. Noted for his role in opening up new areas of research and discussion in monetary economics, Tobin in recent years has become the outspoken arch-opponent of Milton Friedman's analysis of monetary problems and of his opposition to activist government intervention.

Tobin, who has been a professor at Yale throughout his career, differs from Keynes and Friedman in that he has never been sole author of a book. His fame stems from his articles written for a wide range of publications, and particularly his scholarly papers. After beginning his career with a series of articles on issues in the Keynesian theory of consumption and wages, and on problems in estimating statistical demand functions for food, he turned to monetary theory. Among his most noted articles are three written in the 1950s: "The Interest-Elasticity of Transactions Demand for Cash," which showed that the interest-sensitivity of the demand for money could be derived independently of Keynes' speculative motive; "Liquidity Preference as Behavior Towards Risk," which introduced the crucial idea of risk aversion into the economic analysis of asset management

Camera Press/NYT Pictures

and the demand for money; and "A Dynamic Aggregative Model," one of the first models of economic growth.

In the 1960s Tobin continued to convert economic loose ends into brilliantly concise analysis. He wrote classic articles on how the government debt should be managed and how the government debt affects the demand for money; what

without any acceleration or deceleration. Real GNP should be kept equal to the economy's natural real GNP level—the amount that the economy can produce each year when its unemployment rate is kept equal to U^N. Natural real GNP, illustrated as the black line at the top of Figure 12-1, grows each year by about 3 percent, as technological progress, capital accumulation, and growth in the labor force all work together to raise the amount the economy can produce when unemployment is equal to U^N.

How successfully has actual real GNP (Q) been kept equal to natural GNP (Q^N)? The postwar record illustrated in Figure 12-1 is decidedly mixed. Although mass unemployment has been avoided, and no repetition of the Great Depression has been experienced, nevertheless Q has diverged repeatedly from Q^N, sometimes for many years in the same direction. Between 1957 and 1974 Q was continuously below Q^N, reaching shortfalls of 5 percent in the recessions of 1958 and 1961. On the other hand, between 1966 and 1969 the reverse was true. For four straight years Q overshot and remained 3 percent or more too high. The worst year of all was 1975, when makes commercial banks different from other financial institutions; how government policy should attempt to influence the nation's output growth rate; and how money affects the long-run growth of the economy.

Tobin has not confined his attention to the narrow area of monetary economics. Unlike Friedman, he went to Washington and participated in the economic policymaking process as a member of the President's Council of Economic Advisers in 1961–62 and as a consultant to the Council for many years thereafter. He took a particular interest in the economic status of black Americans and in the poverty problem in general. Though he disagrees with Milton Friedman on many issues in monetary economics, he shares with Friedman early support for the idea of a guaranteed annual income in the form of the negative income tax.

As an articulate exponent of government activism to achieve economic stability, and one of the original designers of the Kennedy-Johnson economic philosophy, Tobin was placed on the defensive in the late 1960s and early 1970s by the Monetarist Counterrevolution. Several of his scholarly articles during this period were critiques of the work of Milton Friedman. While many of Tobin's criticisms were valid, nevertheless his advocacy of government activism tended to be undermined by the continuing mistakes of government policy, including the "self-inflicted wounds" of the late 1970s, which Tobin himself opposed.

The high water mark of Friedman's monetarism was reached in 1973. Then supply shocks and the new problems they presented eroded support for the neutral "do nothing" aggregate demand policy supported by monetarists and provided new arguments for an activist policy to provide accommodation of supply shocks. No economist was a more effective advocate than Tobin of the position that the Federal Reserve had made a serious mistake in trying to extinguish the 1974 supply shock and that the 1975 recession represented an unnecessary waste of resources. Tobin's advocacy of accommodative policy now must be weighed not in terms of traditional monetarist arguments but rather against the obstacles to accommodation presented in section 9-4.[a]

---

[a] A collection of Tobin's essays is contained in *Macroeconomics — Volume I* (Chicago: Markham Publishing Company, 1971). See also his exchange with Friedman in the volume cited in Friedman's biography, and also a critical review essay, Herschel I. Grossman, "Tobin on Macroeconomics," *Journal of Political Economy*, vol. 83 (August 1975), pp. 829–848.

Q dropped more than 6 percent below Q^N, and by 1980:Q2 real GNP had fallen 5 percent below Q^N.

GOVERNMENT SPENDING

Three expenditure components that contributed to unstable actual output growth are illustrated in Figure 12-1. Monetarists are correct that much of the postwar instability has been contributed by uneven changes in real government expenditures on goods and services (G). Any component of total real spending tends to destabilize total GNP if it grows appreciably faster or slower than the annual growth of natural real GNP. But real government spending (G) has grown in fits and starts. The most notable episode of erratic growth occurred during the Korean War, when G increased by 74 percent in the interval 1950–53. The Vietnam War buildup caused another period of rapid growth, 24 percent between 1965 and 1968. On the other hand, G hardly grew at all between 1968 and 1979.

BOTH GOVERNMENT AND PRIVATE SPENDING CONTRIBUTED TO ECONOMIC INSTABILITY IN THE POSTWAR ERA

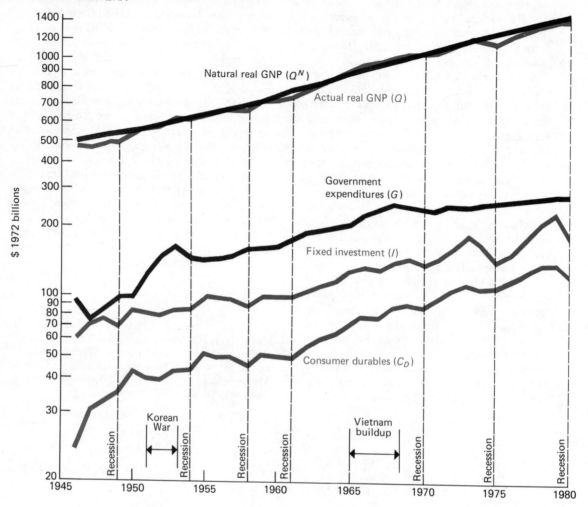

FIGURE 12–1

Actual and Natural Real GNP and the Real Values of Government Spending, Fixed Investment, and Consumer Durable Expenditures, 1946–80

Fluctuations in government spending (G) were about as important as shifts in fixed investment (I) and consumer durable expenditures (C_D) in contributing to economic instability. The scale is logarithmic (see p. 25, question 1), so the steeper increases and decreases in the G, I, and C_D lines than in the actual real GNP line indicate that the three spending components were more unstable than total real spending.

Sources: Actual and natural real GNP, see Appendix B; spending components (G, I, C_D), U.S. Department of Commerce; data for 1980 are for the second quarter.

Nonmonetarists protest any attempt by the monetarists to discredit stabilization policy by pointing to erratic growth in G in Figure 12-1. "Erratic G growth is just one of many reasons why we need activist stabilization policy," reply the nonmonetarists. "Wartime bursts in defense spending result from political decisions, not economic ones, and it is the job of stabilization policy to recommend offsetting actions that will keep the wartime expenditures from causing total real GNP to overshoot Q^N. Tax increases and tight monetary policy are appropriate activist actions to be taken in wartime situations."

PRIVATE SPENDING

Nonmonetarists then point to the behavior of the other two series plotted in Figure 12-1, fixed investment (I) and consumer purchases of durable goods (C_D), as evidence against plank 1 of the monetarist platform. Private spending does not tend to grow steadily each year at 3 or 4 percent, but tends to exhibit periods of a few years of boom followed by several years of slump. Fixed investment (I) grew 13.4 percent between 1954 and 1956, but then increased only 3.7 percent between 1956 and 1961. Then came an investment boom that pulled I up by 44 percent between 1961 and 1966. Another cycle occurred in the 1970s, with I first rising by 27 percent in three years, then falling right back in 1975 to its 1970 level, and then rising to a new high in 1979.

But business people who make investment decisions are not uniquely to blame for the instability of private spending. There is very little difference in Figure 12-1 between the behavior of the fixed investment series (I) and that plotted directly below, consumer expenditures on durable goods (about half automobiles, the remaining half appliances, furniture, and other products). The most notable instance of instability occurred in 1955, when C_D grew by exactly 20 percent in one year! After that year C_D growth became stagnant until 1962. It is true, as monetarists may argue, that at least some of the fluctuations in I and C_D are due to disturbances introduced by the government. For instance, controls on consumer credit held down C_D during the Korean War, and their elimination partly caused the 1955 spending boom.

The instability of fixed investment and consumer durable spending lies at the heart of the nonmonetarist case in favor of an activist stabilization policy. Short, sharp fluctuations in private planned spending would not be terribly serious if they lasted only six or nine months. But the behavior of I and C_D in Figure 12-1 indicates that periods of boom or bust tend to persist. Both I and C_D were weak between 1958 and 1961 and both were strong through most of the 1960s.

Plank 2 of the monetarist platform states that even if private spending is unstable, flexible prices will come to the rescue. When private demand is too high, prices will rise to choke off undesirable spending, and when private demand is weak, prices will fall (or at least rise slower) to stimulate spending. This monetarist proposition was examined quite carefully in Chapter 8, where we found that it takes many years for inflation to slow down when private demand is weak. In the seven years between 1957 and 1964 when actual real GNP was below natural output, the inflation rate fell by only 3 percentage points at an annual rate. Nonmonetarists ask, "Why should we patiently wait for five years for the slowdown in inflation to stabilize real output? Even if stimulative monetary and fiscal policy take as long as one year to affect spending, that time lag beats the monetarist recommendation that we play a long waiting game."

12-5 STABILIZATION TARGETS AND INSTRUMENTS IN THE ACTIVISTS' PARADISE

THE NEED FOR MULTIPLE INSTRUMENTS

When the driver of a car has a destination to reach on a map, he is trying to hit two targets: a particular latitude (north-south position) and a specific longitude (east-west position). To reach these two targets, he needs two basic instruments in his car, an engine to move him forward or back and a steering wheel to move him left or right. Similarly, an airplane pilot attempts to maintain three targets: latitude, longitude, and altitude. In addition to an engine and a steering wheel, he needs a third instrument (his elevators) to move him up or down. An airplane lacking any device to move up or down might achieve the desired longitude and latitude, but it would fail miserably in achieving its desired altitude.

Stabilization policy attempts to achieve several targets. Just as for an automobile or an airplane, each target requires at least one instrument of stabilization policy. Several examples of this principle have become evident in earlier chapters. We learned in Chapter 5 that the money-supply instrument could not simultaneously achieve both a target level of real GNP and a target interest rate. Both monetary and fiscal policy must be manipulated together to achieve an intersection of the IS and LM curves at a given combination of the interest rate and real GNP. Then in Chapter 8 we learned that monetary and fiscal policy together cannot achieve any desired level of real GNP after all. The long-run level of Q^N is limited to the output the economy can produce at the natural rate of unemployment (U^N). Any higher level of real GNP achieved by monetary and fiscal policy will result in higher prices rather than higher real GNP after a transition period.

Monetary and fiscal policy acting together are the two main instruments that control adjusted demand growth ($\hat{y}$) and the interest rate.[10] In the long run the unemployment-rate target is beyond the control of monetary and

[10] The nominal interest rate (i) consists of an inflation component (p) and a real interest-rate component (r): $i = r + p$. In the long run, inflation must be equal to adjusted demand growth. The real interest rate can be influenced by fiscal policy; high deficits tend to raise the real interest rate, and vice versa.

fiscal policy. A permanent reduction in unemployment requires a permanent drop in the natural rate of unemployment, which requires in turn a separate instrument. That instrument is the mixture of manpower policy tools discussed in Chapter 10—reform of unemployment compensation, training subsidies to firms, and so on.

But we are not finished yet. Fiscal policy really consists of two types of **policy instruments:** government spending and tax rates. A given government deficit can be achieved with high spending and high tax rates or low spending and low tax rates. Thus within fiscal policy the mixture between spending and tax rates determines yet another target of policy, the division of total real output between public and private spending.

So far we are up to four instruments and four targets:

Instruments	*Targets*
Manpower policy	Unemployment rate
Monetary policy	Inflation rate
Government spending	Interest rate
Tax rates	Division of real GNP between public and private spending

A more complete illustration of the principles of economic policy is given by Figure 12-2. The goal of economic policy is economic welfare, represented by the box in the upper right corner of Figure 12-2. Social welfare can be thought of as simply happiness, the things that individual members of society want—stable prices, full employment, and a high standard of living.

TARGETS, INSTRUMENTS, AND STRUCTURAL RELATIONS

Looking left from the social welfare box in Figure 12-2 we find a box that lists the main policy **target variables** that influence social welfare. Some are more important than others. The health of the balance of payments and the level of the foreign exchange rate are not very interesting in themselves unless foreign factors begin to prevent the achievement of other domestic goals, as in the 1970s in Britain, Italy, and other countries. The distribution of income is a target quite different from the others; any policy shift that raises the income of one group at the expense of others (rich versus poor; creditors versus debtors) is bound to be controversial and lead to political conflict. Almost every proposal for a change in tax rates excites disagreement because of its implications for the distribution of income. The interest rate is not listed separately as a target variable because its level is mainly relevant for growth in natural output. Low real expected interest rates stimulate investment and the growth of capital inputs, in turn raising the growth rate of real GNP.[11]

---

[11] An introduction to these and other targets is Arthur M. Okun, "Conflicting National Goals," in Eli Ginzberg (ed.), *Jobs for Americans* (Englewoods Cliffs, N.J.: Prentice-Hall, 1976).

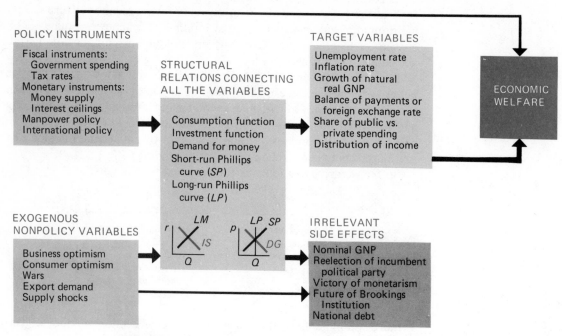

FIGURE 12–2

A Flow Chart Showing the Relation between Policy Instruments, Policy Targets, and Economic Welfare

Both policy instruments and exogenous nonpolicy variables are ingredients fed into the structural relations that connect the exogenous (policy and nonpolicy) variables with the endogenous (target and nontarget) variables. Total economic welfare at the upper right depends on the achieved values of the target variables, and thus it depends in turn on the decisions of policymakers on the settings of the policy instruments.

In the upper left corner of Figure 12-2 is a list of some of the policy instruments that the government can use to try to achieve the targets. The upper left instrument box is linked with the upper right target box through the large central box containing the structural relations that link the variables. The DG, SP, and LP curves of Chapter 8 summarize the main relations that link money, taxes, and government spending to unemployment and inflation. But those curves can be shifted as well by several exogenous factors not under the direct control of policymakers, as by a burst of business or consumer optimism or higher export sales (shifting the DG line upward) or a supply shock (shifting the SP line upward). Wars have also been listed in the exogenous rather than the instrument box, because the level of government spending in wartime is almost always set in accord with the goals of military strategy rather than economic stabilization, and in fact wars almost always represent an undesirable interference with the goals of stabilization policy.

376 The Monetarist–Nonmonetarist Debate on Policy Activism

Exogenous and instrument variables are ingredients in the structural economic relations in the middle box and yield particular values of the target variables — unemployment, inflation, and the others. Other variables are also affected, called irrelevant in the lower right rectangle because they are not major determinants of social welfare. No one cares about the level of nominal GNP ($Y = PQ$), but people do care about the inflation rate and unemployment rate that a particular level of nominal spending in part determines. Other irrelevant side effects may be the victory or defeat of politicians, of economic theories, and of academic institutions; these are irrelevant consequences for society as a whole, even if the individuals involved may care a lot about the outcome.

MONETARISM AND THE ACTIVISTS' PARADISE

Monetarists oppose activist countercyclical swings in the money supply and think that the economy will be better off with a **constant growth rate rule** (CGRR) for the money supply.[12] They have also argued for a constant rule for fiscal policy, a flexible exchange rate to meet the international target, and numerous measures to raise the economy's efficiency (eliminating minimum wages, tariffs, and other forms of government price-fixing and intervention).

What do monetarists respond when faced with the instability of government and private real spending plotted in Figure 12-1? This looks like fairly convincing evidence of the weakness of planks 1 and 2 of the monetarist platform (the stability of private spending and the ability of flexible prices to correct any instability). At this stage monetarists move on to plank 3, which says that stabilization policy may do more harm than good. "Nonmonetarist economists," they claim, "require a utopian set of assumptions about the economy if they expect an activist stabilization policy to do more good than harm."

The utopian "activists' paradise" is a hypothetical world in which activist policy could achieve almost perfect control over total aggregate demand. It has these main characteristics:[13]

---

[12] When he received his Nobel Prize in December 1976, Milton Friedman remarked that it was no thanks to him that the Central Bank of Sweden, which donated the money for his prize, still exists. "My monetary studies have led me to the conclusion that central banks could profitably be replaced by computers geared to provide a steady rate of growth in the quantity of money. Fortunately for me personally, and for a select group of fellow economists, that conclusion has had no practical impact . . . else there would have been no Central Bank of Sweden to have established the award I am honored to receive. Should I draw the moral that sometimes to fail is to succeed?" (Quote from the mimeographed text of the remarks, provided by the author.)

[13] The term *activists' paradise* and its major characteristics originate in Arthur M. Okun, "Fiscal-Monetary Activism: Some Analytical Issues," *Brookings Papers on Economic Activity,* vol. 3, no. 1 (1972), pp. 123–163. The rest of this chapter relies heavily on the late Arthur Okun's analysis of the arguments for and against activism. The author's tribute to the unique talents of Okun appears in *Brookings Papers on Economic Activity,* vol. 11, no. 1 (1980), pp. 1–5.

1. Ability by policymakers to forecast perfectly future changes in the private demand for and supply of goods and services.
2. Ability by policymakers to forecast perfectly the future effect of current changes in monetary and fiscal policy.
3. Possession by policymakers of policy instruments that powerfully affect aggregate demand.
4. Absence of any costs of changing policy instruments.
5. No political constraints on using the policy instruments for the desired purposes.

In the following sections we will find that there is reason to doubt the validity of several of the characteristics necessary for activist stabilization policy to achieve perfect control over aggregate demand. The argument for activist government intervention must be that imperfect activist control is better than the monetarist approach, not that activist control is perfect.

12-6 CASE STUDY: THE PERFORMANCE OF U.S. FORECASTERS IN THE 1970s

The first characteristic of the activists' paradise is the ability of forecasters to foresee perfectly future changes in demand and supply. The ability to look into the future is required by the time lag in the effect of policy changes. An increase in the money supply in December 1981 may not have its main influence on spending until the fall of 1982. Thus policymakers must be able to look ahead to determine whether private demand in the fall of 1982 is likely to be too high or too low.

United States forecasters experienced some dramatic failures in the 1970s, as illustrated in Figure 12-3. The diagram compares the actual growth rate of nominal GNP (y), real GNP (q), and the GNP price deflator (p) with the change predicted one year in advance of the illustrated date by five well-known forecasting organizations. Most of these forecasters sell their forecasts to business firms and have every incentive to take account of all relevant factors that might affect the economy in the coming year.

As an example, in the upper left corner of the diagram we see that in the year ending in the first quarter of 1971 (1971:Q1) nominal GNP actually increased by 7.2 percent (the red actual y line), whereas the median forecast made one year earlier in 1970:Q1 had been for an increase of 6.2 percent (this is the value for predicted y plotted for 1971:Q1). Through the middle of 1972 forecasts of nominal GNP growth (y) made a year earlier were fairly accurate, but then began a five-quarter period when actual y substantially exceeded the previously forecasted values. The maximum error occurred in the year ending in 1973:Q1, when actual y was 12.2 percent compared to a forecast growth of 9.9 percent.

Was poor forecasting responsible for the excessive aggregate demand growth that pushed the actual unemployment rate in the bottom frame well below the natural rate of unemployment between late 1972 and early 1974? Although the high growth rate of y was not predicted well, much of the error in the first three quarters of 1973 was accounted for by the failure to foresee the acceleration of inflation. The portion of nominal income growth (y) left over after taking out inflation—real output growth (q)—was fairly well predicted for the year ending in 1973:Q3, as was the unemployment rate for that quarter. Thus the overshooting of the economy in 1973, as reflected in the decline of actual unemployment (U) well below the natural rate (U^N), was caused not by bad forecasting, but by the unwillingness or inability of policymakers to restrain aggregate demand growth.

FAILURE OF FORECASTING

The real failure of forecasting occurred in early 1974. At that time the year-ahead forecasts for 1975:Q1 overpredicted y and q by record amounts. As a result, inflation was the only major problem that was forecast as requiring policy action. Unemployment was predicted to rise only slightly. Because inflation was predicted to be high, the forecasts suggested to policymakers that restraint rather than stimulation of aggregate demand was appropriate.

Yet what happened? Real GNP growth turned out to be -4.8 percent in the year ending in 1975:Q1, as opposed to the $+2.2$ percent forecast, and unemployment soared during that year from 5.0 percent in 1974:Q1 to 8.9 percent in 1975:Q2. Although there is no way to prevent a supply shock from raising both unemployment and inflation simultaneously, most nonmonetarist economists feel in retrospect that some policy stimulus should have been applied in 1974.

THE RECORD IN THE LATE 1970s

After 1975 forecasting errors were much smaller than in 1973–75. Real GNP growth was predicted with particular accuracy, having a mean absolute error between 1976:Q2 and 1979:Q2 of only 0.6 percent. Inflation and nominal GNP growth errors were larger (1.1 and 1.6 percent, respectively) and went in the same direction, with the actual values of both lower than predicted in 1976 and higher than predicted in 1978–79. Neither the extent of the acceleration of inflation in 1978–79, nor the extremely rapid growth of nominal GNP, was foreseen four quarters earlier. It is quite likely that policymakers would have shifted earlier from stimulus to restraint if they had been able to foresee the actual behavior of inflation and nominal GNP growth.

If Okun's law is working properly, it should be easy to forecast the unemployment rate, once a forecaster has made his forecast for growth in both actual and natural real GNP. Notice that the actual unemployment rate turned out to be lower than forecast throughout 1978 and 1979. Why? Since actual real GNP growth was forecast quite accurately, the problem was that forecasters failed to predict the slowing of natural real GNP growth that occurred as a result of the puzzling slowdown in the growth of labor productivity in the late 1970s (see Chapter 18).

REASONS FOR FORECASTING ERRORS

Why did forecasting errors occur? Any economic forecast that is more than a simple guess requires three main ingredients, all of which are depicted in Figure 12-2:

1. First, a guess must be made about the settings of the various policy instruments. Often forecasters make several forecasts. An initial control forecast is made that assumes that policy remains unchanged — for instance, that tax rates remain fixed, that government spending equals the most recent administration estimate for the federal government budget, and that the growth rate of the money supply is the same over the following year as it has been during the past year. Then additional forecasts may be made that vary these policy assumptions in specified ways.
2. Second, a guess must be made about the values of the nonpolicy exogenous variables. Among these, as depicted in Figure 12-2, are export demand, supply shocks, and any special aspects of business and consumer optimism that might invalidate the consumption function and investment function of the forecasting model.

FIGURE 12–3 (facing page)

Actual and Predicted Values of the Unemployment Rate (U) and of the Growth Rates of Nominal GNP (y), Real GNP (q), and the GNP Deflator (p), 1971–79

For each of the four variables plotted, the pink areas show the periods when the actual value was higher than the predicted value, and the gray shading shows the periods when the actual value was lower than the predicted value. The most important forecasting error was an underprediction of inflation throughout 1973 and 1974. Because nominal GNP was predicted with fair accuracy, most of the errors in forecasting inflation caused errors in forecasting real output in the opposite direction. In 1978–79, in contrast, both inflation and nominal GNP growth were underpredicted so that real GNP growth was predicted quite accurately.

Sources: Errors are from Stephen S. McNees, ''The Forecasting Record for the 1970s,'' *New England Economic Review* (September/October 1979), Table 5, p. 50. Corresponding actual values were provided by McNees, who calculated the median error from the four-quarter-ahead forecasts of these five forecasters: (1) Data Resources, Inc., (2) Chase Econometric Associates, Inc., (3) the MAPCAST group at the General Electric Company, (4) the Wharton Econometric Forecasting Associates, Inc., and (5) the median forecast from a survey conducted by the American Statistical Association and the National Bureau of Economic Research.

FORECASTERS DO NOT LOOK BACK FONDLY ON THEIR PERFORMANCE IN THE 1970s

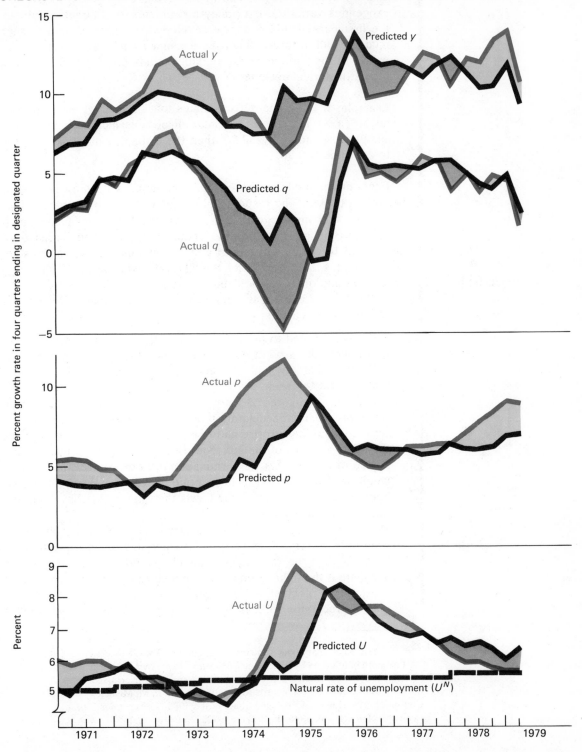

3. Third, there must be a structural model that ties together the structural exogenous variables, the policy instruments, and target variables. In the first part of this book we developed a simple version of such a model. Modern forecasting uses **econometric models** that estimate the values of the parameters by statistical study on electronic computers of past historical episodes.

Example: If the computer calculates that on average in past postwar history a $1 increase in after-tax disposable income increased consumption spending by $0.90, then the estimated marginal propensity to consume is 0.90.

Econometric models must estimate numerical values for a large number of parameters: the response of money demand to changes in the interest rate and income (the *LM* curve); the response of consumption spending to changes in disposable income and wealth and the response of investment to changes in output and various financial variables (the *IS* curve); the response of inflation to real GNP given expected inflation (the *SP* curve); and other relationships as well.

In the 1974–75 episodes, each of these three elements contributed to the failure of forecasters:

1. Forecasters failed to predict accurately the main instrument of monetary policy, the growth rate of the money supply. The money supply (*M*1) grew scarcely at all between June and December 1974, an event that was not foreseen.
2. As shown in Figure 12-3, forecasters failed miserably in predicting the unprecedented acceleration of inflation in 1974. Part of this error resulted from the surprise nature of the 1974 supply shocks that raised the relative prices of oil and food. But another part resulted from the failure to foresee that the termination of price controls in April 1974 would lead to a period of large price increases as firms attempted to boost their prices back to the levels that they would have charged in the absence of controls.
3. How flawed were the econometric structural models? So far there has been little systematic research that would answer this question.[14] My guess is that the forecasters' models would have been reasonably adequate if the tight setting of the monetary instruments and the 1974 acceleration of inflation had been accurately foreseen. But in every postwar recession forecasters have failed to foresee the sharpness of

---

[14] An early paper that reviews the first stages of the 1974–75 recession is Arthur M. Okun, "A Postmortem of the 1974 Recession," *Brookings Papers on Economic Activity,* vol. 6, no. 1 (1975), pp. 207–221. Okun's paper does not perform any retrospective tests that would reveal the sources of errors in econometric forecasts. See also F. M. Mishkin, "What Depressed the Consumer: The Household Balance Sheet in the 1973–75 Recession," *Brookings Papers on Economic Activity,* vol. 8, no. 1 (1977), pp. 123–164.

the recession drop in real GNP, primarily because they do not have accurate methods of forecasting the exact timing of the involuntary inventory accumulation and subsequent production cuts by businesses when their sales fall.

FORECASTING AND ACTIVISM

Does the forecasting record of the 1970s support the nonmonetarist case for activism or the monetarist case for a monetary rule? Despite the large errors made, forecasters almost always managed to forecast correctly one year in advance whether unemployment would be above or below the natural unemployment rate (U^N). A nonmonetarist policymaker who slowed the growth of aggregate demand during the quarters when unemployment was forecast to fall below U^N and stimulated the economy when unemployment was forecast to be above U^N would have stabilized unemployment, as compared to an alternative monetarist policymaker who simply maintained a fixed predetermined growth rate of aggregate demand (y).[15] The major flaw in this argument is that there was no agreement in the early 1970s on the value of U^N. Most policy discussions assumed that it was safe to push unemployment down to the range of 4.5 percent—a rate that now appears to have been too low.

We also have to be careful to interpret correctly the situation in 1978–79. Even though the actual unemployment rate remained above the natural rate of unemployment in Figure 12-3, nevertheless inflation accelerated. Although this was partly due to supply shocks in food and oil as well as government-caused "self-inflicted wounds," nevertheless part of the acceleration of inflation may have been caused by excessive aggregate demand growth. There is some evidence that even when U remains above U^N, excessively rapid nominal GNP growth can cause an acceleration of inflation.[16]

Can one conclude that policymakers should conduct stabilization policy as if their forecasts were correct? As Arthur Okun made the case, "So long as forecast errors are distributed symmetrically on the up side and the down side, the middle of the target is the place to aim even though the bull's eye will not always be hit."[17] But again uncertainty about the effects of policy actions temper this conclusion; policymakers should not attempt to close the entire gap between current income and the target level.

---

[15] We will see in Chapter 15 that the monetarist prescription that calls for stabilization of the growth rate of money does not automatically lead to stabilization of the growth of aggregate demand.

[16] Robert J. Gordon, "A Consistent Characterization of a Near-Century of Price Behavior," *American Economic Review,* vol. 70 (May 1980), pp. 243–249.

[17] Okun, "Fiscal-Monetary Activism: Some Analytical Issues," *Brookings Papers on Economic Activity,* vol. 3, no. 1 (1972), summary, p. 8.

12-7 UNCERTAINTY ABOUT THE INFLUENCE OF POLICY

Chapters 3–5 developed a set of multiplier formulas indicating the size of the change in real GNP that would result from a change in a policy instrument, such as tax rates, government spending, or the money supply. But the *IS-LM* models summarized in those chapters were very simple, In practice, each builder of econometric models chooses a different way of elaborating the *IS-LM* textbook model to make it more realistic. Some estimate separate equations for several components of consumption spending; others for only one. Each model differs on many other choices—for instance, which interest rate to relate to the demand for money and to the demand for investment goods. These small differences add up to quite substantial disagreement about the multipliers for changes in different policy instruments.

In the early chapters of this book we also simplified the exposition of income determination by ignoring the time lag between changes in policy instruments and the resulting effect on the target variables. An essential part of the monetarist case against activism is that the lags in the effects of policy changes are likely to be both long and variable.[18]

DISAGREEMENT OVER DYNAMIC MULTIPLIERS

Figure 12-4 illustrates several sets of **dynamic multipliers** calculated from various econometric models of the economy. The horizontal axis is successive quarters after the policy change. For each model the graph shows the cumulative total change in real GNP (Q) caused by a sustained $1 billion increase in real government spending. For instance, the MPS model yields a multiplier that starts out only a bit above 1.0. Because government spending is part of GNP, the multiplier would be exactly 1.0 if there were no stimulus at all to consumption or investment spending in the initial quarter of the increased government spending. Then the MPS multiplier rises to a peak of about 2.4 after seven quarters, reflecting the stimulus of higher income to both consumption and investment. Later, however, the multiplier begins to fall.

What should policymakers do if they predict that the economy needs $15 billion of stimulus to aggregate demand four quarters from now because unemployment is forecast to be higher than desired at that time? The Brookings multiplier for the four-quarter effect is 2.8, implying that an increase in government spending of 15/2.8 or $5.38 billion is needed. At the other extreme, the St. Louis model says that the multiplier after four quarters is only 0.5,

---

[18] The most extensive discussion of the monetarist position is Milton Friedman, "The Lag in Effect of Monetary Policy," *Journal of Political Economy,* vol. 69 (October 1961), reprinted in *The Optimum Quantity of Money and Other Essays* (Chicago: Aldine, 1969), pp. 237–260.

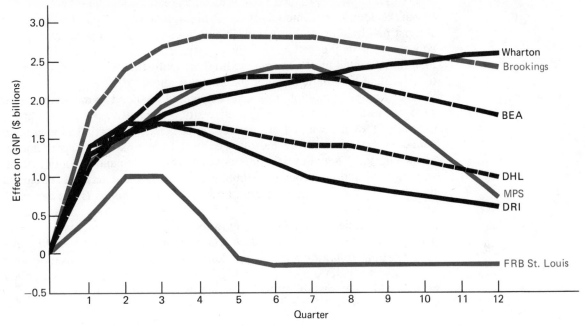

Key to models:

BEA: Bureau of Economic Analysis, U.S.
  Department of Commerce
Brookings: Brookings Institution
DHL: University of Michigan
DRI: Data Resources, Inc.

FRB St. Louis: Federal Reserve Bank of St. Louis
MPS: MIT-Penn-Social Science Research Council
Wharton: Wharton Mark III, University of
  Pennsylvania

FIGURE 12–4

**Change in Real GNP Induced by a Permanent $1 Billion Increase
in Real Government Nondefense Spending: Estimates of Seven
Econometric Models**

Each line corresponds to the estimate of a different econometric model. For instance, the line labeled Brookings indicates that, according to the Brookings model, a $1 billion increase in real government nondefense spending causes an increase in real GNP by $1.8 billion in the first quarter, $2.4 billion in the second quarter, and so on. A peak is reached at $2.8 billion in quarters 4–7, after which the impact declines.

Source: Gary Fromm and Lawrence R. Klein, "A Comparison of Eleven Econometric Models of the United States," *American Economic Review,* vol. 63 (May 1973), Table 5, p. 391.

---

implying that an increase in government spending of 15/0.5 or $30 billion is needed. The other models produce multipliers between these extremes.

Although leading nonmonetarists claim to have discredited the St. Louis techniques, the other models still leave policymakers highly uncertain about the size of the policy stimulus needed.[19] Multipliers for other policy instruments, not shown in Figure 12-4, also indicate considerable divergence between the econometric models. Though **multiplier uncertainty** does not make activist policy intervention impossible, it does require that policymakers be conservative in the settings of their instruments, taking a smaller action than that dictated by the average multiplier. Unfortunately it is very difficult to determine how much smaller the stimulus should be.[20]

The "humped" multiplier pattern, as yielded by the MPS model in Figure 12-4, raises another problem. The effects of a stimulative policy may linger long after they are wanted or needed. An anticipated shortfall of aggregate demand next quarter may be followed by an anticipated excess in subsequent quarters. A policy stimulus now may boost demand by only a small amount next quarter, when the stimulus is needed, and it may boost demand by a lot five to eight quarters from now, *when the stimulus is not desirable and in fact restraint is required.* Some economists have shown that a humped multiplier can lead to wild gyrations in policy instruments, as policymakers struggle to offset lagged effects of their own actions![21] Adding this complication to the others, policymakers are required to act conservatively and to aim to offset only part of swings in private demand, lest their policy actions add extra instability to the economy.

12-8 COSTS AND IMPRECISION IN THE SETTING OF POLICY INSTRUMENTS

In subsequent chapters we will examine some of the problems in changing policy instruments. It is easy in textbooks and undergraduate examinations to speak loosely about changing government spending, tax rates, and the money supply. But actual policymakers operate in a more complicated world. "Government spending on *what?*" they will ask. Leaf raking? Jet fighter planes? If we need more leaves raked or fighter planes now, why

---

[19] The best analyses of the St. Louis multiplier controversy are unfortunately not very comprehensible for undergraduates unless they have taken an introductory course in econometrics. See Alan S. Blinder and Robert M. Solow, "Analytical Foundations of Fiscal Policy," in *The Economics of Public Finance* (Washington, D.C.: Brookings Institution, 1974), pp. 63–78. Also Franco Modigliani and Albert Ando, "Impacts of Fiscal Actions on Aggregate Income and the Monetarist Controversy: Theory and Evidence," in Jerome Stein (ed.), *Monetarism* (Amsterdam: North-Holland, 1976), pp. 17–42.

[20] See William Brainard in his "Uncertainty and the Effectiveness of Policy," *American Economic Review,* vol. 57 (May 1967), pp. 411–425. Brainard's formula suggests that the expected gap between actual and target GNP should be closed by only a fraction of the gap, but that fraction depends on correlations that we are most unlikely to know. An earlier analysis is Milton Friedman, "The Effects of a Full-Employment Policy on Economic Stability: A Formal Analysis," *Essays in Positive Economics* (Chicago: University of Chicago Press, 1953), pp. 117–132.

[21] Robert S. Holbrook, "Optimal Economic Policy and the Problem of Instrument Instability," *American Economic Review,* vol. 62 (March 1972), pp. 57–65.

didn't we need them yesterday separately from the requirements of stabilization policy? Almost by definition, the use of spending increases or decreases to stabilize the economy means introducing government programs that were not previously thought to be justified on their own merits or, when policy restraint is required, cutting back on programs that were previously thought desirable.

These disadvantages lead most activist economists to espouse tax changes as the main fiscal instrument of stabilization policy. But there are still details to be resolved. Should taxes be changed for rich people, poor people, or both? Should corporate taxes be altered as well? Should tax changes be temporary or permanent?

The use of monetary policy for stabilization purposes raises problems as well. Some of these problems are faced even by monetarists. Their recommendation that policymakers do nothing but stabilize the growth rate of the money supply raises the question—which definition of the money supply? Activists need also to remember that a slowdown in monetary growth introduced when aggregate demand is forecast to be too high is likely to raise interest rates and possibly disrupt financial markets, drastically cut homebuilding expenditures, and even bankrupt building contractors.

12-9 ACTIVISM, POLITICS, AND THE TIME HORIZON

So far, the proponents of activism concede that the artificial assumptions of the activists' paradise are unrealistic. But they argue that forecasting uncertainty, multiplier uncertainty, lags, and costs and imprecision in the setting of policy instruments call for caution in setting stabilization policy, not its outright abandonment. They feel that the monetarist emphasis on a fixed rule for monetary growth creates too much danger that the economy will be allowed to drift away from policy targets over substantial periods of time. Monetary growth was actually quite stable during the 1970s, but this fairly close adherence to a monetarist rule did not prevent unprecedented instability in inflation and unemployment.

Here the debate between monetarists and nonmonetarists turns to the relationship between planks 3 and 4 of the monetarist platform. The inherent obstacles to an effective activist policy combined with the political realities that often cause irrational government behavior (plank 3) lead monetarists to prefer to leave the private economy alone. Even though sluggish price adjustment may imply that the private economy may take a long time to correct deviations of actual unemployment from the natural unemployment rate, monetarists are willing to wait. Their long time horizon leads them to emphasize long-run consequences and to deemphasize short-run flaws in the performance of the economy (plank 4). Milton Friedman has written most explicitly on the relationship between the long-time horizon of monetarists and their distaste for government intervention:

The man who has a short time perspective will be impatient with the slow workings of voluntary arrangements in producing changes in institutions. He will want to achieve changes at once, which requires centralized authority that can override objections. Hence he will be disposed to favor a greater role for government. But conversely, the man who favors a greater role for government will thereby be disposed to have a shorter time perspective. Partly, he will be so disposed because centralized government can achieve changes of some kinds rapidly; hence he will feel that if the longer term consequences are adverse, he—through government—can introduce new measures that will counter them, that he can have his cake and eat it. Partly, he will have a short time perspective because the political process demands it. . . . In the political process, an entrepreneur must first get elected in order to be in a position to innovate. To get elected, he must persuade the public in advance. Hence he must look at immediate results that he can offer the public. He may not be able to take a very long time perspective and still hope to be in power.[22]

The monetarists are correct that in some past episodes the absence of fixed rules allowed government actions to destabilize the economy. Perhaps the most famous episode was the failure of President Johnson to recommend a tax increase to finance the upsurge of government expenditures during the Vietnam War buildup. A rule that required a balanced budget would have forced Johnson to recommend the tax increase he resisted in 1966 for political reasons. Similarly, the economy was allowed to reach too low an unemployment rate in 1966–69, partly because the Federal Reserve accommodated the tax cuts of 1964–65 by creating enough extra money to moderate the higher interest rates that the tax cuts would otherwise have caused. A monetary rule would in retrospect have prevented the creation of the extra money and thus avoided much of the acceleration of inflation in the late 1960s. There would have been a short-run leap in interest rates that would have created a political outcry in 1964–65, but less than the outcry that accompanied the even greater leaps of 1966 and 1969.

Activists agree with the proponents of rules that monetary accommodation in the 1950s and 1960s caused money to move in the same direction as undesired movements in demand and aggravated economic instability. They agree that in some (not all) episodes a rule would have been better. But then they part company with the monetarists by supporting an activist counter-cyclical policy, the exact opposite of accommodation. Activists would move money in the opposite direction to undesired swings in aggregate demand.

At this point in the debate many economists are willing to turn the floor over to the politicians and their "bosses," the voters. Will the government usually act irresponsibly, as the monetarists predict, overlooking the careful prescriptions of activist advisers in order to win votes in the next election

---

[22] Milton Friedman, "Why Economists Disagree," in *Dollars and Deficits* (Englewood Cliffs, N.J.: Prentice-Hall, 1968), p. 8.

even at the cost of destabilizing the economy? This is a motive many feel was responsible for the undesirable acceleration in monetary growth that occurred in 1972 during President Nixon's reelection campaign. Or can activist economists trust politicians to place economic welfare first, even at the cost of lost votes that may be caused by a timely tax increase or monetary squeeze? There can be no final victor in the monetarist-nonmonetarist debate, because ultimately the nonmonetarists must stake their confidence on the willingness of politicians to do what is needed to stabilize the economy rather than what is politically expedient, a confidence that some politicians may deserve and others may not.

SUMMARY

1. In earlier chapters we assumed that the growth of aggregate demand could be controlled precisely by the monetary and fiscal policymakers. We now recognize that in the real-world economy, policy shifts cannot control aggregate demand instantly or precisely.

2. Most economists recognize the possibility of slippage between policy shifts and the response of demand, but they disagree on the merits of an activist stabilization policy as compared to a policy based on fixed rules.

3. The monetarist-nonmonetarist debate centers on the location in the economy of the principal source of economic instability. Monetarists believe that the private economy is basically stable and that fixed policy rules are necessary to protect the economy from ill-conceived and poorly timed government actions that in the past have caused economic instability. In contrast, the nonmonetarist group considers private spending to be the primary source of instability and hence supports an activist government countercyclical policy to achieve economic stability.

4. Although they recognize the problems introduced by forecasting uncertainty, multiplier uncertainty, lags, and costs and imprecision in the setting of policy instruments, the proponents of activism nevertheless favor caution in setting stabilization policy rather than its outright abandonment. Some monetarists admit that sluggish price adjustment may prolong the adjustment of the economy to insufficient or excess demand, but they are more interested in long-run consequences than short-run transition periods.

5. Both sides agree that monetary accommodation aggravated economic instability in the 1950s and 1960s, when the Fed allowed money to move in the same direction as undesired movements in demand. The monetarists point out that in most of these episodes a rule would have been better than actual policy; the nonmonetarists counter by claiming that an activist countercyclical policy (the opposite of accommodation) would have outperformed both what actually happened and the proposed monetarist fixed rules. But the nonmonetarists have yet to prove that such an activist policy would have been politically feasible.

A LOOK AHEAD

Do decisions made in the private sector stabilize the economy, insulating it from instability stemming from government actions or outside events? Or do private decisions add additional instability that establishes a need for an activist government policy? In the next three chapters we will examine the theory of consumer spending, private investment, and the demand for money. We will find support for the proposition that consumer spending on nondurable goods adds stability to the economy, but that consumer and business spending on durable goods introduces instability.

CONCEPTS

Stabilization policy
Monetarists
Nonmonetarists
Policy targets
Policy instruments

Dynamic multipliers
Econometric forecasts
Multiplier uncertainty
Long and variable lags

QUESTIONS FOR REVIEW

1   When the economy is experiencing slack demand, monetarists are usually not willing to accept the long-run costs of higher inflation for the short-run gains in the form of lower unemployment that would result from an expansionary policy. Are the gains from temporary increases in output limited to the short run? Are the costs of inflation limited to the long run? Explain.

2   How can both the monetarists and the nonmonetarists find support for their positions in the erratic growth of government expenditures? Which side do you feel has the stronger case? Why?

3   Must econometric forecasts be precisely correct to be useful for activist countercyclical policy? Why or why not?

4   What problems do long and variable lags present to the policymaker? If lags are long and fixed (rather than long and variable), do any problems remain?

5   For policymaking, is the shape of the dynamic multiplier path of monetary and fiscal changes important or only the size of the total cumulative effect? Explain.

6   In numerous instances in the postwar economy a monetarist rule would have been superior to the policy actually carried out. Can we therefore conclude that we should follow the monetarists' prescription and forget activist policy? Explain.

7   During the 1970s monetary growth was relatively stable, yet at the same time the inflation and unemployment rates experienced an unprecedented instability. Can we therefore conclude that we should follow the nonmonetarist prescription of activist policy and forget the monetarist rule?

8   If policymakers had correctly foreseen the four-quarter-ahead values of y, q, p, and U plotted in Figure 12-3 for 1974–75 and 1978–79, how might they have altered aggregate demand policy in each episode — toward more stimulation or toward more restrictiveness?

9   Assuming that a new wave of defense spending in early 1980, following the Russian invasion of Afghanistan, caused defense spending to be $10 billion higher in real terms in 1980:Q2, how much higher would real GNP be in 1981:Q2? Calculate the answer for the following models, using the information in Figure 12-4:

     a. MPS   b. St. Louis   c. Brookings

13 Instability in the Private Economy: Consumption

Economists become upset when they learn
that we aren't spending money as they've
planned for us.

—Eliot Marshall[1]

13-1 CONSUMPTION AND ECONOMIC STABILITY

The dispute between monetarist rules and nonmonetarist activism was summarized in Chapter 12 in the form of a monetarist platform. That platform says in essence that (1) the private economy would be basically stable if the government would only leave it alone and (2) government intervention does more harm than good. In this and the next chapter we carefully study the validity of the first part of the monetarist platform. Here we ask, "Does personal consumption spending contribute to economic stability by damping down instability in other forms of spending, or does consumption add extra instability of its own?" In Chapter 14 we study the sources of instability in private investment spending.

In the elementary theory of income determination of Chapter 3, consumption spending is a purely passive element. The level of consumption spending was assumed there to be some fixed amount plus a fixed fraction of personal disposable income. In that simple theory did consumption add to economic stability or make stability harder to achieve? In one sense consumption behavior made GNP more unstable, because any $1 change in autonomous planned spending had a multiplier effect as extra consumption was induced by higher income, leading to a total change in GNP of several dollars. On the other hand, the passively induced changes in consumption were always completely predictable. If a decrease in private investment had a multiplier of 3.0, so that a $1 decrease in investment caused a $3 total decrease in GNP (the extra $2 consisting of a passively induced drop in consumption), a stable level of spending could be achieved by an exactly

---

[1] "False Prophets," *New Republic* (October 1, 1977), p. 50.

and 1975–79, the last observation, income per family increased by a factor of more than four, from roughly $4200 to $17,300 at 1978 prices.[4] And yet the feared increase in the saving ratio has not occurred! The saving ratio in 1975–79 was actually below that in 1898–99. In fact, the saving ratio in Figure 13-2 was amazingly stable in the range of 4.5–7.5 percent during the 1910–1979 period, with the two main exceptions of low saving during the Great Depression and high saving during World War II.

Clearly Keynes' assumption that the saving ratio increases as society becomes richer must be modified in a way that retains the observed cross-section increase in the saving ratio when poor people are compared to rich people at a given time. The two most important hypotheses that resolve the apparent conflict between the historical time-series evidence of a fairly constant saving ratio and the cross-section evidence of a steadily increasing saving ratio with higher income are (1) the **permanent-income hypothesis** developed in the 1950s by Milton Friedman and (2) the **life-cycle hypothesis** developed at about the same time by Franco Modigliani and collaborators.

13-3 THE PERMANENT-INCOME HYPOTHESIS

Imagine that you have a job and receive your take-home pay of $800 on the first day of each month. Strictly speaking, your income on the first day of each month is $800, and your income on each of the remaining days of the month is zero. According to the simple Keynesian consumption function, you should do all your consumption spending on the first day of the month and consume absolutely nothing during the rest of the month!

Of course people do not consume their entire income on their payday, but set aside part of their pay to buy groceries and other items during the rest of the month. Why? People can eat only so much on one day and prefer to eat more or less the same amount each day of the month instead of cramming in a whole month's food in one day. In other words, individuals who have an unstable income pattern will be happier if they consume a constant amount each day rather than allowing their consumption to change each day with their changing income.

People can achieve the desirable stable consumption pattern if they consume a fraction not of their actual income but rather of their expected income over a period of time. A farmer may have experienced an annual income in recent years of $3000, $17,000, $9000, and $11,000. Because his income has averaged out at $10,000, his best guess for his expected income next year is $10,000.[5] Let us assume on average that he wants to spend 90

---

[4] Average family income from the *Economic Report of the President* (January 1980, Table B-25) is extrapolated backward by the growth in real GNP per capita.

[5] It is easy to construct examples in which inflation and real economic growth cause people to expect a higher income next year than their average income of the last few years.

percent of his expected income and save the remaining 10 percent. Then his planned consumption will be $9000 and saving $1000. If the harvest turns out to be bad and his actual realized income falls to a paltry $5000, achieving the $9000 consumption plan would require withdrawing $4000 from savings, to be returned in years of good harvests.

Milton Friedman first proposed the hypothesis that an individual consumes a constant fraction (k) of his expected income, which Friedman called **permanent income (Q^p):**[6]

GENERAL FORM   NUMERICAL EXAMPLE FOR THE FARMER

$$C = kQ^p \qquad C = 0.9(\$10{,}000) = \$9000 \qquad (13.2)$$

The individual marginal propensity to consume out of permanent income (k) depends on individual tastes and on the variability of income (farmers and others with variable income need higher savings accounts to support them during bad years). In addition k depends on the interest rate, since people should be willing to save more on average if they receive a higher rate of interest on their savings accounts.[7]

REVISING THE ESTIMATE OF PERMANENT INCOME

The permanent-income hypothesis summarized in equation (13.2) does not say that individuals consume exactly the same amount year after year. Every year new events occur that are likely to change each individual's guess about his permanent income. For instance, an individual, after several years in which his expected income turned out to be a correct guess, might find that in good years his income has increased. Gradually he will revise his estimate of his average expected income and will find that he can increase his stable consumption level.

Friedman's permanent-income hypothesis consists of the assumption in equation (13.2) that individuals consume a constant portion of their permanent income. But this is not enough, because an additional assumption is required to indicate how individuals arrive at a guess about the size of their permanent income. Friedman proposed that individual estimates of permanent income for this year (Q^p) be revised from last year's estimate (Q^p_{-1}) by some fraction (j) of the amount by which actual income (Q) differs from Q^p_{-1}:

GENERAL FORM   NUMERICAL EXAMPLE

$$Q^p = Q^p_{-1} + j\,(Q - Q^p_{-1}) \qquad \begin{aligned} Q^p &= 10{,}000 + 0.2\,(15{,}000 - 10{,}000) \\ &= 11{,}000 \qquad\qquad (13.3) \end{aligned}$$

---

[6] Milton Friedman, *A Theory of the Consumption Function* (Princeton, N.J.: Princeton University Press, 1957), especially Chapters 1–3, 6, and 9.

[7] Because of the limitations of the alphabet we are once again forced to duplicate the use of letters. The k here is completely unrelated to the k used in Chapters 3 through 5 to represent the multiplier.

Milton Friedman

"If Milton Friedman had not existed, it would have been necessary to invent him," wrote his fellow *Newsweek* columnist, Paul Samuelson. For many years, Friedman was a brilliant and outspoken gadfly who challenged from the outside many of the most cherished propositions of establishment economics and helped to keep economics a lively and controversial subject. In the last decade, Friedman has had the satisfaction of seeing many of his long-held beliefs adopted as part of the mainstream.

Friedman's scholarly activity as a professor has centered in monetary economics. Starting his work in the late 1940s when fiscal policy was in its prime and monetary policy was viewed as impotent, Friedman almost single-handedly restored money to the center of the macroeconomic analysis. In his 850-page treatise (co-authored with Anna J. Schwartz) *A Monetary History of the United States* (1963), he argued that U.S. business cycles were attributable to excessive fluctuations in the supply of money, and that the Federal Reserve was responsible for the severity of the Great Depression because it allowed the money supply to drop by almost one-third between 1929 and 1933. Almost as influential was Friedman's *A Theory of the Consumption Function* (1957), which held that short-run changes in income had a much smaller impact on consumption spending than in Keynesian theory, implying that the economy's inherent stability was greater than had been realized (see Chapter 13). In his presidential address to the American Economic Association, Friedman introduced the then heretical natural-rate hypothesis of unemploy-

Camera Press/NYT Pictures

ment, which has since been accepted by most economists (see Chapter 8).[a]

Much of the scholarship responsible for the renaissance of money took place in Friedman's Money and Banking workshop at the University of Chicago, where for twenty-five years (1952–1976) graduate students and visitors presented papers to receive Friedman's suggestions, approval, or disapproval. The workshop was almost always stimulating, even if the paper being presented was not, in which case Friedman would explain to confused

[a] "The Role of Monetary Policy," *American Economic Review,* vol. 58 (March 1968), pp. 1–15.

Some critics have accused monetarists of heartless disregard of unemployment, since their policy recommendations oriented to a gradual slowdown in the inflation rate appear to imply a long period of high unemployment.[7] Indeed, Milton Friedman and other monetarists have argued that the unemployment data, properly interpreted, show unemployment to be a

---

[7] The duration of high unemployment required to reduce the inflation rate depends on the slope of the short-run Phillips curve, the speed of adjustment of expectations, and the type of demand management policy that policymakers pursue. Two examples are illustrated in Figure 8-11.

The Monetarist Platform and the Nonmonetarist Response

The Monetarist Platform

Plank 1: Without the interference of demand shocks introduced by erratic government policy, private spending would be stable.

Plank 2: Even if private planned spending is not completely stable, flexible prices create a natural tendency for it to come back on course.

Plank 3: Even if private planned spending is not completely stable, and prices are not completely flexible, an activist monetary and fiscal policy to counteract private demand swings is likely to do more harm than good.

Plank 4: Even if prices are not completely flexible, so that the economy can wander away from U^N in the short run, there can be no dispute regarding the increased flexibility of prices, the longer the period of time allowed for adjustment.

The Nonmonetarist Response

Plank 1: Shifts in business and consumer attitudes and expectations represent a substantial source of economic instability that should be countered by offsetting monetary and fiscal policy actions.

Plank 2: Prices are relatively inflexible downward, as illustrated by the failure of prices to decline during the last half of the decade of the 1930s despite extraordinarily high unemployment.

Plank 3: Although there is no denying that monetary and fiscal policy have been destabilizing in particular past episodes, economic knowledge is now sufficiently advanced to allow countercyclical monetary and fiscal policy actions to stabilize the economy in the face of destabilizing swings in private demand.

Plank 4: The period of time required for flexible prices to bring the economy automatically back to U^N is intolerably long, and there is no reason for government policymakers to tolerate the persistence of high unemployment and low levels of output that occur in the meantime.

short-circuit this lag in the effect of policy. Further, uncertainty in the effect of policy changes adds an additional source of disturbance which makes the economy less stable than would occur with rules which limit changes in policy.

Plank 4: *Even if prices are not completely flexible, so that the economy can wander away from U^N in the short run, there can be no dispute regarding the increased flexibility of the price level the longer the period of time allowed for. adjustment.* Furthermore, it is unwise to base policy changes on short-run considerations, because the long run is a succession of short runs. It is best to set a growth rate for the money supply compatible with steady inflation or even zero inflation in the long run and avoid the temptation to tinker with the economy in the short run. In economic jargon, monetarists have a relatively low rate of "time preference," putting little emphasis on short-run events and paying primary attention to the consequences of present actions in the future.

offsetting $1 increase in government spending. Consumption did not add to instability in this case, because the multiplier effect of private investment was exactly offset by the multiplier effect of government spending.

This chapter introduces a major amendment to the simple consumption theory developed in Chapter 3. Individuals do not base their consumption solely on their disposable income at each instant of time. Individuals who want to achieve an even consumption spending pattern over a period of years, or over their lifetime, will not consume much of a transitory income increase that they expect to disappear next year. They will raise their consumption spending much more if they receive an increase in income that they expect to be permanent.

This hypothesis, called the **permanent-income hypothesis** (PIH) of consumption spending, is of major importance. Since consumption does not respond completely to every short-run "blip" in income caused by movements in investment or government spending, the PIH cuts the multipliers of Chapter 3 down below the values calculated there and helps to insulate the economy from destabilizing shocks. Thus the PIH helps to bolster plank 1 of the monetarist platform, supporting the monetarist case that the economy can be trusted to stabilize itself. Unfortunately, however, the PIH is not the whole story of consumption behavior. Several additional ingredients must be added before we can gain a complete understanding of fluctuations in consumption.

13-2 THE CONFLICT BETWEEN THE TIME-SERIES AND CROSS-SECTION EVIDENCE

One of the major innovations in Keynes' *General Theory* was the multiplier, which followed directly from the assumption that consumption behaved passively. Keynes' description of consumption behavior begins with the idea that there is a positive marginal propensity to consume that is less than unity: "The fundamental psychological law . . . is that men are disposed, as a rule and on the average, to increase their consumption as their income increases, but not by as much as the increase in their income."[2]

Keynes' second main idea is that there is a specific amount that individuals will consume independent of their income, so that it is possible for saving actually to be negative if disposable income is very low. Denoting consumption as C, and disposable income as Q_D, the Keynesian consumption function can be written:

$$C = a + cQ_D \qquad (13.1)$$

---

[2] See John Maynard Keynes, *The General Theory of Employment, Interest and Money* (New York: Macmillan, 1936), Book III. The idea of the multiplier was first introduced by R. F. Kahn, "The Relation of Home Investment to Unemployment," *Economic Journal* (June 1931), but Keynes was the first to fit the multiplier into a general economic model of the commodity and money markets.

The hypothetical Keynesian consumption function and saving ratio are plotted in the top two frames of Figure 13-1. In the top frame, look to the lower left corner and find the value of consumption (a) that occurs when disposable income is zero. Then move your eye from left to right up the red $C = a + cQ_D$ line. Consumption (C) rises less rapidly than disposable income (Q_D), since the marginal propensity to consume (c) is less than 1.0. Consumption starts out greater than Q_D, equals Q_D at the income level Q_{D_0}, and then is less than Q_D. Everywhere to the right of Q_{D_0} the shortfall of consumption below disposable income allows room for a positive amount of saving. For instance, the income level Q_{D_1} is divided into the consumption level C_1 and the saving level S_1.

Moving down to the middle frame of Figure 13-1, we find plotted the saving/income ratio, S/Q_D. To the left of the income level Q_{D_0}, saving is negative; to the right of Q_{D_0}, saving is positive.[3] As people become richer, according to the hypothetical Keynesian relation in the middle frame, they save a larger share of their disposable income.

The actual data plotted in the bottom frame of Figure 13-1 confirm Keynes' hypothesis for a **cross section** of Americans who were polled on their income, saving, and consumption behavior. Very poor people do not save at all but instead "dissave," consuming more than they earn by drawing on accumulated assets in savings accounts. As we move rightward from the poor to the rich, we find that the saving/income ratio increases, just as in the hypothetical relationship of the middle frame.

SECULAR STAGNATION DID NOT OCCUR

Figure 13-1 raises a potentially serious problem for the economy. If people save more as they become richer, then one presumes that society will

---

[3] The shape of the saving/income curve depends on the relative values of parameters a and c.

FIGURE 13–1 (facing page)

The Relation between Disposable Income (Q_D), Consumption Spending (C), and the Ratio of Saving to Income (S/Q_D)

The top frame repeats the consumption function introduced in Chapter 3. At levels of disposable income below (to the left of) point Q_{D_0}, people consume more than their income. To the right of Q_{D_0} consumption is less than income, and the shaded pink difference between income and consumption, the amount of saving, is a steadily growing fraction of disposable income. In the middle frame the share of saving in disposable income is plotted, a negative fraction to the left of point Q_{D_0} and a positive and growing fraction to the right. The bottom frame plots actual data on the relation of saving to disposable income from a survey of consumers. Notice the close correspondence between the theoretical diagram in the middle frame and the actual data in the bottom frame.

Source (for bottom frame): I. Friend and S. Schor, "Who Saves?" *Review of Economics and Statistics*, vol. 41 (May 1959), p. 217, Table 2, columns 5 and 6.

THE PERCENTAGE OF INCOME THAT IS SAVED RISES AS INCOME GOES UP

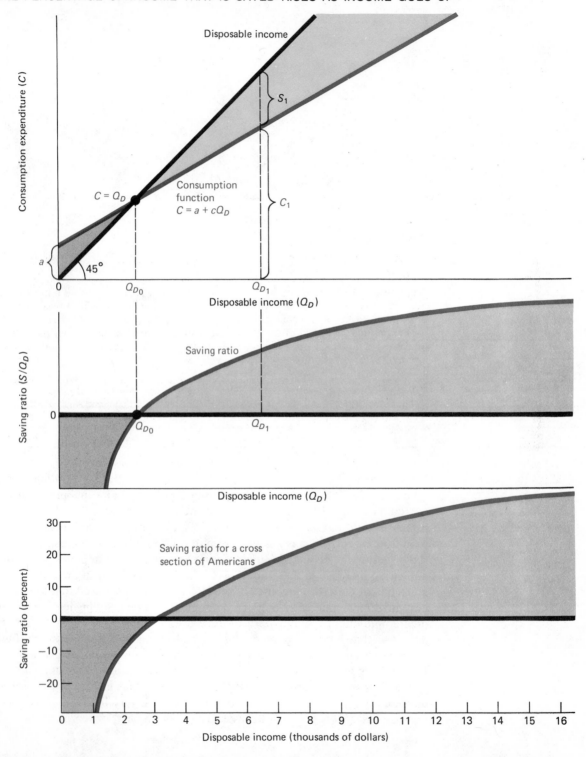

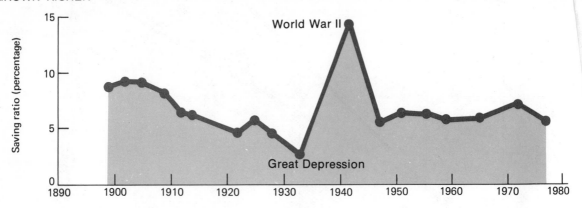

AMERICANS HAVE NOT SAVED A GREATER SHARE OF THEIR INCOME AS THEY HAVE GROWN RICHER

FIGURE 13–2

Ratio of Saving to Disposable Income (S/Q_D), Averages over Business Cycles, 1898–1979

The low level of saving during the Great Depression is consistent with our theory (compare Figure 3–2). The high level of saving during World War II was a special event caused by the unavailability of consumer goods. Leaving out these two extreme periods, the ratio of saving to disposable income was fairly constant. Notice that the ratio in 1975–79 was very close to its value in 1910. Observations plotted are averages over complete business cycles.

Sources: 1898–1929 and 1949–69: Paul A. David and John L. Scadding, "Private Savings: Ultrarationality, Aggregation, and 'Denison's Law,'" *Journal of Political Economy,* vol. 82 (March/April 1974), Table 4; 1930–48 and 1970–79: Bureau of Economic Analysis, U.S. Department of Commerce.

save more as economic growth raises average incomes. According to the figures in the bottom frame, the doubling of real family incomes that occurred between 1948 and 1978 from about $8600 to $17,600 (in 1978 prices) should have increased the saving rate from only 10 percent to more than 20 percent. Because saving in equilibrium must equal investment plus the government deficit, the increase in the saving ratio appears to require a massive increase in the ratio of investment to income or in the ratio of the government deficit to income. In the late 1930s it was feared that the economy might stagnate with high unemployment forever if saving leakages from high-employment income were to exceed investment plus the government deficit at that level of income. This fear of permanent stagnation and high unemployment due to oversaving was called the "secular stagnation hypothesis," where the word *secular* in this context means long-run.

Look now at Figure 13-2, which plots the actual historical **time-series** data on the saving rate achieved on average during each of the major business cycles of this century. Between 1898–99, the first observation plotted,

and 1975–79, the last observation, income per family increased by a factor of more than four, from roughly $4200 to $17,300 at 1978 prices.[4] And yet the feared increase in the saving ratio has not occurred! The saving ratio in 1975–79 was actually below that in 1898–99. In fact, the saving ratio in Figure 13-2 was amazingly stable in the range of 4.5–7.5 percent during the 1910–1979 period, with the two main exceptions of low saving during the Great Depression and high saving during World War II.

Clearly Keynes' assumption that the saving ratio increases as society becomes richer must be modified in a way that retains the observed cross-section increase in the saving ratio when poor people are compared to rich people at a given time. The two most important hypotheses that resolve the apparent conflict between the historical time-series evidence of a fairly constant saving ratio and the cross-section evidence of a steadily increasing saving ratio with higher income are (1) the **permanent-income hypothesis** developed in the 1950s by Milton Friedman and (2) the **life-cycle hypothesis** developed at about the same time by Franco Modigliani and collaborators.

13-3 THE PERMANENT-INCOME HYPOTHESIS

Imagine that you have a job and receive your take-home pay of $800 on the first day of each month. Strictly speaking, your income on the first day of each month is $800, and your income on each of the remaining days of the month is zero. According to the simple Keynesian consumption function, you should do all your consumption spending on the first day of the month and consume absolutely nothing during the rest of the month!

Of course people do not consume their entire income on their payday, but set aside part of their pay to buy groceries and other items during the rest of the month. Why? People can eat only so much on one day and prefer to eat more or less the same amount each day of the month instead of cramming in a whole month's food in one day. In other words, individuals who have an unstable income pattern will be happier if they consume a constant amount each day rather than allowing their consumption to change each day with their changing income.

People can achieve the desirable stable consumption pattern if they consume a fraction not of their actual income but rather of their expected income over a period of time. A farmer may have experienced an annual income in recent years of $3000, $17,000, $9000, and $11,000. Because his income has averaged out at $10,000, his best guess for his expected income next year is $10,000.[5] Let us assume on average that he wants to spend 90

---

[4] Average family income from the *Economic Report of the President* (January 1980, Table B-25) is extrapolated backward by the growth in real GNP per capita.

[5] It is easy to construct examples in which inflation and real economic growth cause people to expect a higher income next year than their average income of the last few years.

percent of his expected income and save the remaining 10 percent. Then his planned consumption will be $9000 and saving $1000. If the harvest turns out to be bad and his actual realized income falls to a paltry $5000, achieving the $9000 consumption plan would require withdrawing $4000 from savings, to be returned in years of good harvests.

Milton Friedman first proposed the hypothesis that an individual consumes a constant fraction (k) of his expected income, which Friedman called **permanent income (Q^p):**[6]

GENERAL FORM	NUMERICAL EXAMPLE FOR THE FARMER	
$C = kQ^p$	$C = 0.9(\$10,000) = \$9000$	(13.2)

The individual marginal propensity to consume out of permanent income (k) depends on individual tastes and on the variability of income (farmers and others with variable income need higher savings accounts to support them during bad years). In addition k depends on the interest rate, since people should be willing to save more on average if they receive a higher rate of interest on their savings accounts.[7]

REVISING THE ESTIMATE OF PERMANENT INCOME

The permanent-income hypothesis summarized in equation (13.2) does not say that individuals consume exactly the same amount year after year. Every year new events occur that are likely to change each individual's guess about his permanent income. For instance, an individual, after several years in which his expected income turned out to be a correct guess, might find that in good years his income has increased. Gradually he will revise his estimate of his average expected income and will find that he can increase his stable consumption level.

Friedman's permanent-income hypothesis consists of the assumption in equation (13.2) that individuals consume a constant portion of their permanent income. But this is not enough, because an additional assumption is required to indicate how individuals arrive at a guess about the size of their permanent income. Friedman proposed that individual estimates of permanent income for this year (Q^p) be revised from last year's estimate (Q^p_{-1}) by some fraction (j) of the amount by which actual income (Q) differs from Q^p_{-1}:

GENERAL FORM	NUMERICAL EXAMPLE
$Q^p = Q^p_{-1} + j\,(Q - Q^p_{-1})$	$Q^p = 10,000 + 0.2\,(15,000 - 10,000)$
	$= 11,000 \qquad (13.3)$

---

[6] Milton Friedman, *A Theory of the Consumption Function* (Princeton, N.J.: Princeton University Press, 1957), especially Chapters 1–3, 6, and 9.

[7] Because of the limitations of the alphabet we are once again forced to duplicate the use of letters. The k here is completely unrelated to the k used in Chapters 3 through 5 to represent the multiplier.

The behavior described in equation (13.3) is sometimes called the "error-learning" or "adaptive" hypothesis of expectation formation. If actual current income and last year's permanent (expected) income are the same, no change is made in the estimate of permanent income for this period. If, on the other hand, actual income Q exceeds Q^p_{-1}, then this period's estimate Q^p will be raised. In the numerical example an actual income outcome of $15,000, compared to Q^p_{-1} of $10,000, causes this period's Q^p to be raised to $11,000.[8] A person who has a widely fluctuating income (farmers, door-to-door salespeople) will pay little attention to his actual income (Q) and will thus have a smaller value of j than a college professor or government worker who has a relatively stable income.

Now we can see that an individual will allow his consumption to respond modestly to changes in actual income, because consumption depends on permanent income, and in turn permanent income in equation (13.3) depends only in part on this period's actual income. When we substitute (13.3) into (13.2), we obtain the following relationship between an individual's current consumption (C), this period's actual income (Q), and last period's estimate of permanent income (Q^p_{-1}):

$$C = kQ^p_{-1} + kj\,(Q - Q^p_{-1}) \tag{13.4}$$

For instance, if k is 90 percent and j is 20 percent, as in the above numerical examples, then the marginal propensity to consume out of a change in actual income is kj, or 18 percent (0.9 times 0.2 equals 0.18). In contrast, the marginal propensity to consume out of permanent income is k, the much higher value of 90 percent.

RECONCILING THE CONFLICT BETWEEN CROSS-SECTION AND TIME-SERIES DATA

Figure 13-3 illustrates how the permanent-income hypothesis can reconcile the apparent conflict between the cross-section data in Figure 13-1, where rich people have a higher saving ratio than poor ones, and the time-series data in Figure 13-2, where society does not appear to have raised its saving ratio as it has become richer. The solid red line running up through point A and point F lies everywhere at a vertical position equal to k times disposable income (Q). But consumption can equal kQ only if permanent income Q^p were exactly equal to actual income (Q). Thus the line running through A and F is labeled the long-run schedule, because it indicates the level of consumption only when actual income has remained at a particular

---

[8] Exactly the same hypothesis for the formation of expectations was introduced in Chapter 8 in the discussion of inflation expectations (see section 8-8). Equation (13.3) can be rewritten in the form used in Chapter 8:

$$Q^p = jQ + (1-j)Q^p_{-1}$$

This says that permanent income in this period is a weighted average of actual income and last period's permanent income.

THE SAVING RATIO IS CONSTANT ALONG THE LONG-RUN SCHEDULE, BUT NOT ALONG THE SHORT-RUN SCHEDULE

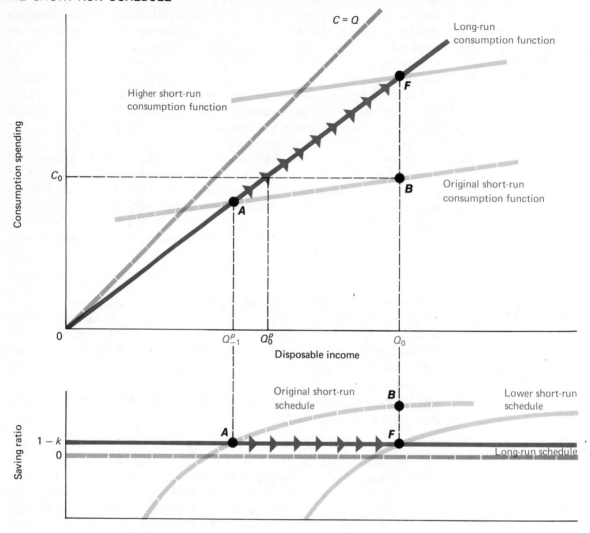

FIGURE 13–3

The Permanent-Income Hypothesis of Consumption and Saving

In both frames the long-run schedule shows that consumption and saving are fixed fractions of income in the long run, when actual and permanent income are equal. But short-run gains in actual income, as at point *B*, are not fully incorporated into permanent income. Thus consumption increases only a small amount (compare points *B* and *A*) and at *B* most of the short-run increase in income is saved. The same gain in income maintained permanently causes the short-run schedule to follow the arrows along the long-run schedule to point *F*.

level long enough for individuals to have adjusted fully their estimated permanent income to the same level.

What happens in the short run, when actual income can differ from permanent income? The flatter dashed red schedule running between A and B is the short-run schedule and plots equation (13.3). When current income (Q) is exactly equal to last period's permanent income (Q^p_{-1}), the short-run schedule intersects the long-run schedule at point A. But during a good year when an individual's income is at the high level Q_0, his current estimate of permanent income (Q^p) rises above last period's estimate (Q^p_{-1}) by a fraction (j) of the excess of actual income over last period's estimate ($Q_0 - Q^p_{-1}$). And the higher value of Q^p raises consumption by k times the increase in permanent income.

Thus consumption at point B lies vertically above point A by the fraction kj (18 percent in the numerical example) times the horizontal distance between Q^p_{-1} and Q_0. With the short-run marginal propensity to consume (kj) so far below the long-run propensity (k), any short-run increase in income goes disproportionately into saving and raises the saving-income ratio, as illustrated in the bottom frame of Figure 13-3 at point B.

THE RICH AND THE POOR

Milton Friedman used a diagram similar to Figure 13-4 to illustrate why wealthy people on average save more than poor people. Among the wealthy are many people (including, perhaps, some people who on average are poor) who are having a good year, farmers with bumper crops, executives in profitable firms who have just received high bonuses, movie stars who have just completed a popular film, and this year's champion used-car salesman. Because a disproportionate number of wealthy individuals report incomes above their own individual estimates of their permanent income, they save more than average.

Among the poor, however, are many people who are having a bad year, including farmers with diseased crops, executives who have just been fired, and show business people whose popularity has waned. These individuals formerly had estimated that their permanent income level was high; now they try to maintain relatively high consumption by saving little or even dissaving.

SAVING BEHAVIOR IN THE LONG RUN

As for the observed time-series behavior of the nationwide savings ratio over this century, the Friedman permanent-income hypothesis has the following explanation. We can now interpret Figure 13-3 as the relation between actual consumption and actual income for the whole economy, rather than for one individual. When income increases temporarily, the saving ratio goes up, as from A to B in the bottom frame; when income declines below normal, the saving rate drops or even becomes negative. Thus in booms the saving ratio is predicted to be high on average and in recessions low on average.

The long-run constancy of the saving ratio can be explained by the gradual upward adjustment of permanent income as actual income grows. When a high income level such as Q_0 occurs only once, as at point B, it is considered unusual, and saving is high. But when the high income level Q_0 has persisted for a long time, individuals gradually raise their estimates of their permanent income, shifting upward the short-run consumption schedule in the top frame of Figure 13-3 and shifting down the saving schedule in the bottom frame. When estimated permanent income finally reaches Q_0, the short-run consumption schedule in the top frame will have shifted upward, following the arrows, to the flat short-run schedule line through point F. The saving schedule in the bottom frame will have shifted downward, following the arrows, to the new line through point F.

> **Summary:** Estimates of permanent income are continually raised, as actual income outstrips previous levels, causing the saving ratio and the relationship between consumption and income to follow along the long-run schedules, as marked by the arrows in Figure 13-3. Thus in the long run the saving ratio is roughly constant. But in the short run a temporary increase in income raises the saving ratio and a temporary decrease reduces the saving ratio because permanent income does not adjust completely to each change in actual income.

13-4 THE LIFE-CYCLE HYPOTHESIS

About the same time that Friedman wrote his book on the permanent-income hypothesis, Franco Modigliani of MIT and collaborators devised a somewhat different way of reconciling the positive relation between the saving ratio and income observed in cross-section data and the constancy of the saving ratio observed over long periods in the historical time-series data.[9] Modigliani and Friedman both began from the argument that individuals prefer to maintain a stable consumption pattern rather than to allow consumption to rise or fall with every transitory oscillation of their income. But Modigliani carried the stable-consumption argument further than Friedman and suggested that people would try to stabilize their consumption over their entire lifetime.

In Figure 13-4 the horizontal axis shows various ages, with the age at

---

[9] Franco Modigliani and R. E. Brumberg, "Utility Analysis and the Consumption Function," in K. K. Kurihara (ed.), *Post-Keynesian Economics* (New Brunswick, N.J.: Rutgers University Press, 1954). Also A. Ando and F. Modigliani, "The 'Life Cycle' Hypothesis of Saving: Aggregate Implications and Tests," *American Economic Review,* vol. 53 (March 1963), pp. 55–84.

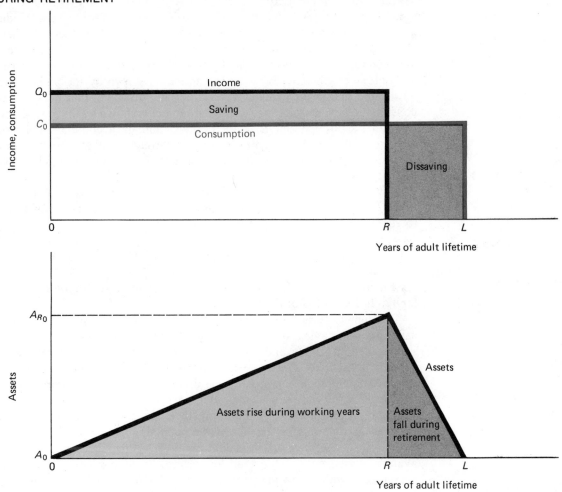

FIGURE 13–4

The Behavior of Consumption, Saving, and Assets under the
Life-cycle Hypothesis

Under the life-cycle hypothesis particular attention is paid to the relation between
the length of the lifetime (L) and an individual's age at retirement (R). The
length of the retirement period is $L - R$. In the upper frame a constant amount
(C_0) is consumed every year of one's life, as indicated by the red line. A constant
amount of income Q_0 is earned each year until retirement. During the working
years until R, income exceeds consumption, as shown by the saving that occurs
in the pink area. Then consumption exceeds the zero income during retirement
and is financed by dissaving, as shown by the gray area. In the bottom frame the
black line shows the growth of assets from the initial level (A_0) to the maximum
level at retirement (A_R), followed by a decline in assets back to zero at death.

retirement marked by R and the age at death marked by L. An individual is assumed to maintain a constant level of consumption (C_0) every year of his life. Income, however, is earned only during the R working years. If there are no assets initially, as shown by the zero level of initial assets (A_0) in the bottom frame, then the only way individuals can manage to consume without any income during their retirement is to save during their working years. The amount saved, income minus consumption, is shown by the pink shading during the period up to time R, and then the dissaving that occurs when consumption exceeds income during retirement is shown by the gray shading from time R through time L. In the bottom frame the accumulation of assets occurs steadily during the working years through time R, at which point assets reach their maximum level A_R, after which point assets fall back to zero at time L.

How are consumption and income related when there are no initial assets? Total lifetime consumption of C_0 per year for L years is constrained to equal total income Q_0 per year for R years:

$$C_0 L = Q_0 R \quad \text{or} \quad C_0 = \left(\frac{R}{L}\right) Q_0 \tag{13.5}$$

As Figure 13-4 is drawn, R is four-fifths of L, so consumption per year is limited to four-fifths of Q_0.[10]

The simple version of the life-cycle hypothesis can explain the positive association of saving and income, since those in working ages have higher values of both saving and income than those who are retired. But at the same time the time-series constancy of the saving ratio can be explained by the fact that if each historical era is divided into the same proportions of working and retired people, and each age group has the same saving behavior in generation after generation, then the saving ratio should be unchanged as time passes. In fact, if the population is constant, and if each person saves nothing over his lifetime as a whole, then the nationwide average saving ratio would tend to be zero. Positive saving would be observed only with a growing population, which cuts the fraction of the population in the dissaving retirement generation *relative to* those of working age.

The life-cycle hypothesis shares with Friedman's permanent-income hypothesis the implication that the saving ratio should rise in economic

---

[10] There are several simplifications in Figure 13-4 and equation (13.5) involving the treatment of interest income. Assuming that interest is earned on asset holdings at rate i, then total income is equal to wage income in real terms (W) plus real interest income (rA). Thus (13.5) becomes:

$$C_0 L = W_0 R + \sum_{t=0}^{L} rA_t$$

Thus total income increases gradually through time R and then decreases to zero but is nevertheless positive during the retirement period. To reflect the fact that consumption depends on total income, including both wage income and earnings from the holding of assets, the symbol Q (for total real income) rather than W is used in (13.5) in the text. The official definition of income overstates Q, since it includes the entire income from assets, including that portion of the nominal return $(i - r)$ needed to maintain intact the real value of assets.

boom years and fall in recession years. A temporary increase in income to-day will be consumed over one's entire lifetime. For instance, imagine a person who believes he has forty years left to live and receives an unexpected increase in income this year of $4000 that he does not expect to receive again. His total lifetime consumption goes up by the $4000 and his actual consumption this year goes up by only 1/40 of that amount, a mere $100. In each succeeding year an additional $100 would be spent, for a total of $4000 over the remaining forty years of life. Thus, in an economic boom widely expected to be temporary, an unexpected bonus of $4000 would lead to only $100 extra of current consumption and $3900 extra of saving. On the other hand, if the $4000 income increase is expected to be repeated for each of the next forty years, then $4000 extra can be consumed this year and again in each of the next thirty-nine years and the saving ratio will not rise.

THE ROLE OF ASSETS

The Modigliani theory provides an important role for assets as a determinant of consumption behavior. Let us assume that initially a person has an endowment of assets of A_1, but he plans to use these assets to raise his consumption through his lifetime rather than to leave the assets to his heirs. Then, as shown in Figure 13-5, consumption can be higher for a given level of income (Q_0), and saving can be lower, since the initial asset endowment provides more spending power. Now total lifetime consumption equals total lifetime income from work plus the available assets:

$$C_1 L = A_1 + Q_1 R \quad \text{or} \quad C_1 = \frac{A_1}{L} + \frac{R}{L} Q_1 \qquad (13.6)$$

When we divide (13.6) by Q_1, we have:

$$\frac{C_1}{Q_1} = \frac{A_1}{LQ_1} + \frac{R}{L} \qquad (13.7)$$

Figure 13-5 is oversimplified by assuming that the initial endowment of assets is received at the beginning of the working life. Actually increases in the value of assets occur throughout one's life, and so one would expect the response of annual consumption to a change in asset value to be larger than the coefficient of $(1/L)$ in equations (13.6) and (13.7). If the start of work occurs at age 25, and people retire at 65 but live until 75, then $L = 50$ and $1/L = 0.02$. Modigliani's empirical research has estimated that a $1 increase in real asset values raises real consumption this year by about $.06, which would indicate that people use a fifteen-year horizon over which to spend an increase in real assets.[11]

---

[11] Several issues that are usually discussed in more advanced courses in economics are relevant here. First, is all the money supply part of the public's net wealth or only the portion of the money supply that is a liability of the central bank? Second, is part or all of the public debt a part of the public's net wealth?

AN INITIAL ENDOWMENT OF ASSETS RAISES CONSUMPTION AND REDUCES SAVING

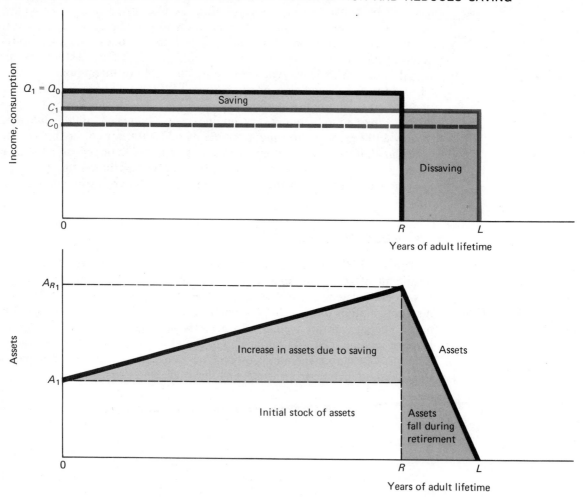

FIGURE 13-5

Consumption, Saving, and Assets under the Life-cycle Hypothesis
When There Is an Initial Stock of Assets

This diagram is identical to Figure 13–4, but here there is an initial stock of assets A_1, in contrast to the initial stock of zero in the previous diagram. If we continue to assume that dissaving during retirement runs the stock of assets down to zero, then the existence of A_1 makes more total consumption possible with a smaller amount of saving. This is shown by an upward shift from the previous level of consumption (C_0) to a new higher level (C_1). The pink saving area is now smaller, as is the pink area in the bottom frame showing the increase in assets due to saving.

We learned in Chapter 6 that the economy's self-correcting forces are enhanced when real consumption spending depends on real assets or real wealth. If a drop in spending cuts the price level, the level of real wealth is raised, and this helps to arrest the decline in spending.[12] In the other direction, if an increase in spending raises the price level, the level of real wealth declines, which helps to dampen the original stimulus to spending.

Thus, ironically, nonmonetarist Modigliani's life-cycle hypothesis helps to support plank 1 of the monetarist platform of Chapter 12. Private spending is stabilized because transitory increases in disposable income that are not expected to last a lifetime have only a modest influence on current consumption. In addition, the real-asset effect stabilizes the economy through the effect of higher prices in cutting real assets and dampening spending. Overall, the life-cycle hypothesis helps to reduce the current marginal propensity to consume, cut the multiplier, and insulate the economy from unexpected changes in investment, exports, or other types of spending.

13-5 CASE STUDY: PERMANENT INCOME, RECESSIONS, AND CONSUMER DURABLES

Both the permanent-income and life-cycle hypotheses (PIH and LCH) provide an explanation of the positive cross-section relation between the saving ratio and income. Both predict that a short-run drop in total income, as during a recession, will cause the saving ratio to drop, and a short-run increase in income will cause the saving ratio to increase. Over the long run, both predict that the short-run consumption schedule will shift upward, maintaining an approximately constant saving ratio.

The behavior of the saving ratio in postwar business cycles is plotted in Figure 13-6 for the entire period between 1946 and 1980. The data are quarterly, so that the short-term wiggles in the saving ratio are clearly evident. Each postwar recession is marked off by gray shading, with the left side of the shading labeled P to designate the *peak* quarter marking the beginning of the recession and the right side labeled T to designate the *trough* quarter marking the end of the recession.

THE SAVING RATIO IN POSTWAR RECESSIONS

Several wiggly lines are plotted in Figure 13-6. At first let us concentrate on the bottom line set off by pink shading, the saving ratio itself.[13]

---

[12] Review the Pigou effect discussed in section 6-6.

[13] In this diagram the saving ratio is calculated as personal saving (S) divided by personal income (Q^p). Personal income is in turn equal to disposable income — the normal denominator of the saving ratio — plus personal tax payments. This slightly different definition of the saving ratio is used here because we will be interested in the next section in the division of personal income between personal taxes, saving, and consumption.

UNITED STATES POSTWAR SAVING BEHAVIOR IS CONSISTENT WITH THE PIH AND LCH ONLY IF ATTENTION IS PAID TO THE BEHAVIOR OF TAXES AND CONSUMER DURABLES

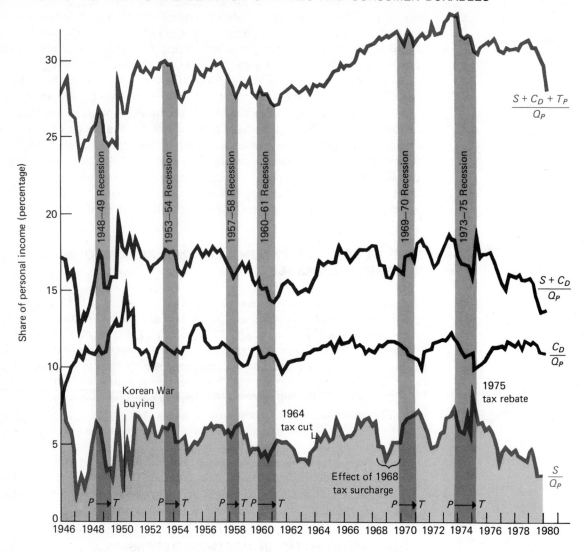

FIGURE 13–6

The Relation of Saving (S), Consumer Durable Purchases (C_D), and Personal Tax Payments (T_P) to Personal Income (Q_P), 1946–80

The bottom line marked off by pink shading is the ratio of saving (S) to personal income (Q_P). Although predicted by theory to drop during recessions and increase in expansions, the S/Q_P ratio does not do so. Part of the reason is that consumers do part of their saving by purchasing consumer durable goods (C_D). Thus the ($S + C_D)/Q_P$ ratio shows more of a tendency to decline in recessions. The red line at the top is described in the next section.

Source: Survey of Current Business, various issues.

Both the permanent-income and life-cycle hypotheses predict that in recessions and the early stages of recoveries, when actual income is low relative to permanent income, the saving ratio should be *below average*. Then in boom periods when actual income is high, the saving ratio should be *above average*. But in Figure 13-6 this predicted **procyclical** fluctuation in the saving ratio does not emerge clearly.[14] The only recessions in which there was a clear drop in the saving rate occurred in 1948–49 and 1960–61. The exceptions to the theoretical predictions of the PIH and LCH appear to be much more numerous than the confirming episodes.

Clearly, the theoretical predictions need to be amended to provide an adequate explanation of postwar saving behavior. In this and the next section we examine several additional factors that help to explain some of the puzzles in Figure 13-6.

SPECIAL EVENTS

The erratic behavior of the saving ratio in the early postwar period can largely be explained by the special nature of the termination of World War II and the outbreak of the Korean War. During World War II, a high saving ratio had been forced by rationing of consumer goods. In 1946 rationing was ended and consumers rushed to buy the goods that they had been prevented from buying during the war. From a wartime high of 25.5 percent in 1944, the saving rate plummeted to a postwar low of only 1.3 percent in 1947:Q2.

Only two years after consumers had finished their first postwar buying boom, the Korean War began in late June 1950. Fearing that rationing would be reimposed, consumers rushed out to buy again, stocking up on all categories of goods. In the first quarter after the outbreak of war (1950:Q3) the saving rate dived to its second lowest postwar value, 2.1 percent.

CONSUMER DURABLE EXPENDITURES

Both the permanent-income and life-cycle hypotheses are based on the desirability of maintaining a roughly constant level of enjoyment from consumption goods and services. For consumer *services* and *nondurable* goods such as haircuts and donuts, the enjoyment and the consumer spending occur at about the same time. But consumer *durable goods* are different. A television set is purchased at a single instant of time but produces enjoyment for many years thereafter. Thus, the PIH and LCH sug-

---

[14] A procyclical variable is one that fluctuates in the same direction as total income over the business cycle, rising in booms and falling in recessions. **Countercyclical** behavior is just the opposite; a countercyclical government spending policy would raise spending during recessions and reduce spending in boom years.

gest that it is not purchases of consumer durable goods that are kept equal to a fixed fraction of permanent income but rather the services (enjoyment) received from consumer durables.

If there is an increase in permanent income, people will want not only to increase their expenditures on nondurable goods but also to increase the services of durable goods. To obtain these services, however, they must purchase more durable goods. Imagine that there is an increase in actual income of $2000, which causes an increase in permanent income of half as much, or $1000. People want to consume 60 percent of their permanent income in the form of nondurable goods and services, so that purchases of these types of consumption rise by 60 percent of $1000, or $600. People are also assumed to want to maintain a stock of durable goods equal to 1.5 times their permanent income, so they must make durable-goods expenditures of $1500 in response to the increase in Q_P of $1000.

Now notice what has happened:

(1) Increase in actual income	$2000
(2) Increase in permanent income	$1000
(3) Increase in nondurable consumption spending [equals 0.6 of (2)]	$ 600
(4) Increase in durables expenditures [equals 1.5 of (2)]	$1500
(5) Total increase in consumption spending [equals (3) plus (4)]	$2100
(6) Saving, or actual income minus consumption [equals (1) minus (5)]	$−100

Result: Even though both desired nondurable spending and the desired stock of durables were calculated according to the permanent-income hypothesis (PIH), the saving ratio does not exhibit the procyclical behavior that occurred in Figure 13-3. Instead of rising with higher income, saving actually falls. The reverse occurs when income drops.

Thus countercyclical fluctuations in the saving ratio do not contradict the PIH or LCH but confirm them. Both theories predict that the sum of saving and consumer durable purchases should increase in relation to personal income in booms and fall in recessions, as indeed occurs in the example. But consumer durable purchases are highly unstable, rising when actual income rises and falling when actual income is constant so that no increase in the stock of durable goods is desired. Thus durable purchases (1) are simultaneously consistent with the PIH and LCH but (2) constitute a source of demand fluctuations in the private economy.

Turning back now to Figure 13-6, we notice that the upper black wiggly line plots the ratio of the sum of saving and consumer durable purchases to personal income $(S + C_D)/Q_P$. In each recession, with the single exception of 1969–70, there appears to have been at least some drop in this total ratio, as predicted by the PIH and LCH. The main remaining puzzles to be explained are the low level in the total ratio in 1968–69 relative to the 1969–70 recession, the short, sharp drop in the total ratio in 1972, and the decline in 1979.[15]

13-6 CASE STUDY: TEMPORARY TAX CHANGES AND THE SAVING RATIO

According to the permanent-income hypothesis, a drop in this month's actual income does not cut consumption unless people believe that the decline in actual income will persist, in which case permanent income declines. In the life-cycle hypothesis such a drop in current income does not cut consumption unless a person has some reason to conclude that his lifetime income has declined. For this reason a change in actual current disposable income caused by a tax change announced by the government to be *permanent* should cause a bigger change in consumption than a tax increase announced as *temporary*.

What would happen to consumption and to the saving ratio if a temporary tax surcharge were assumed by individuals to be a short-lived event with no effect at all on permanent income? Then consumption spending (C) would stay the same, because according to the PIH, consumption depends only on permanent income. People would pay for the temporary tax surcharge entirely by saving less, and so the ratio of saving to personal income (S/Q_P) would fall by exactly the increase in the ratio of taxes to personal income (T/Q_P).

TAX CHANGES IN POSTWAR U.S. HISTORY

We can begin to understand several puzzling episodes of saving behavior if we compare the movements of the ratios S/Q_P and T/Q_P, as in Figure 13-7. Several episodes plotted there illustrate sharp movements in the tax ratio (T/Q_P) that are almost totally offset by movements of the saving ratio (S/Q_P).

The two most important examples occurred in mid-1968, when Congress passed the temporary tax surcharge belatedly proposed by President Johnson to finance Vietnam War spending, and in mid-1975, when a temporary tax rebate was declared to help revive the economy.[16] Individuals must have been led by the term *temporary surcharge* in 1968 to hold unchanged their estimates of their permanent income. Thus the

---

[15] In the recessions of 1948–49, 1953–54, 1957–58, 1960–61, and 1973–75, the lowest value of $(S + C_D/Q_P)$ occurred either during the recession or within a quarter or two afterward. The 1969–70 recession was the exception.

[16] The word *belatedly* refers to the long delay between the acceleration of Vietnam spending in late 1965 and the proposed tax increase that President Johnson finally introduced in 1967.

THE SHARE OF INCOME SAVED APPEARS TO BE A MIRROR IMAGE OF THE SHARE OF
INCOME COLLECTED AS PERSONAL TAXES

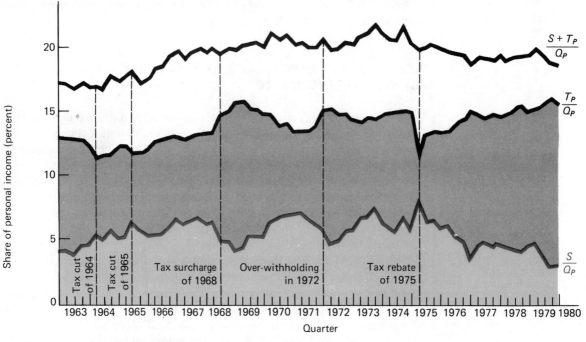

FIGURE 13–7

The Relation of Saving (S) and Personal Tax Payments (T_P)
to Personal Income (Q_P), 1963–80

The lower line shaded in pink is identical to that in the previous figure, the ratio
of saving to personal income (S/Q_P). The middle line is the ratio of personal tax
payments to personal income (T_P/Q_P). Notice how the movements of the S/Q_P
ratio are almost a mirror image of T/Q_P.

Source: Survey of Current Business, various issues.

mid-1968 increase in the T/Q_P ratio in Figure 13-7 is completely offset
by a drop in the S/Q_P ratio. Because the sum of the saving and tax ratios
remained constant, we can conclude that the tax surcharge totally failed
to achieve its aim of dampening consumption. In fact there was very
little further movement in the sum of the saving and tax ratios (the top
line in Figure 13-7) during the ten quarters following the imposition of the
surcharge. The saving ratio fell suddenly in 1968 and then gradually
rose in the next two years as the surcharge was removed.

Another dramatic example of the effect of a temporary tax change occurred in early 1975, when individuals received a rebate of up to $200
per family on their income tax liability. Much of the rebate went into

saving, at least initially, as indicated by the upward blip in the S/Q_P ratio in 1975:Q2, the same quarter as the downward blip in the T_P/Q_P ratio. The 1975 tax changes also included some permanent elements, which individuals may have treated as calling for an adjustment in their permanent income rather than in their saving ratio. In the last half of 1975 the saving ratio returned to the average level of 1973 and 1974, so that the permanent portion of the 1975 tax cut appears to have succeeded in stimulating consumption.[17]

Another episode occurred in 1964 and 1965, when permanent tax cuts were introduced in two stages. The saving rate did not remain unaffected. An increase in saving almost completely offset the tax cuts when they occurred (in 1964:Q2 and 1965:Q3), and there was only a minor subsequent decline in the saving ratio.[18]

The effects of tax changes and consumer durable purchases are combined in the red line at the top of Figure 13-6. This ratio of saving plus consumer durable purchases plus personal taxes to personal income ($S + C_D + T_P)/Q_P$ is predicted by the PIH and LCH to rise in expansions and to decline in recessions. Its behavior is smoother than the black line directly below because, by adding in personal taxes, we have eliminated erratic ups and downs in saving caused by changes in tax rate. The top red line displays marked declines in each postwar recession except 1969–70, when the drop was moderate.

$(S + C_D + T_p)/Q_p$ *Ratio*

Recession	Trough quarter	Percentage-point decline, peak to trough
1948–49	1949:Q2	−2.7
1953–54	1954:Q3	−2.8
1957–58	1958:Q2	−2.2
1960–61	1961:Q1	−1.8
1969–70	1970:Q4	−0.8
1973–75	1975:Q2	−2.5

[17] The most comprehensive recent study of the effect of temporary tax changes is Alan S. Blinder, "Temporary Income Taxes and Consumer Spending," *Journal of Political Economy,* February 1981. Blinder suggests that over a one-year planning horizon, temporary taxes are estimated to have only from 20 to 60 percent of the impact of a permanent tax change of the same magnitude, and rebates are estimated to have only between 10 and 50 percent of the impact. He attributes to the 1975 tax rebate both the high savings rate that occurred in 1975:Q2 and the drop in the savings rate that occurred in late 1976 and early 1977.

[18] One final episode marked in Figure 13-7 is not discussed in the text. At the beginning of 1972 the Internal Revenue Service issued new withholding tables that resulted in a substantial increase in the amounts withheld from paychecks, without any accompanying change in tax liability. The PIH would have expected all the effect of this event to be soaked up by a drop in the saving ratio, since people could look forward to larger refunds in early 1973. Indeed, the saving ratio did drop substantially in mid-1972, although the lack of response of saving at the beginning of 1972 differs from the simultaneity of the offset that occurred in the 1968 and 1975 episodes.

13-7 CASE STUDY: THE LOW SAVING RATE IN THE UNITED STATES IN 1979-80

As the 1970s came to an end, there was widespread concern among observers of the U.S. economy. A paramount problem was the slow growth in labor productivity and in natural real GNP, a topic we examine in Chapter 18. A related problem was the low rate of saving in the United States, which restricted the funds available for business investment; this low level of investment in turn reduced the growth in the U.S. capital stock and explained part (but not all) of the slow productivity growth phenomenon. This low rate of saving can be partly explained by the role of assets, which are important in the Modigliani life-cycle theory of section 13-4. In the late 1970s consumer assets increased as real house prices surged; this stimulated consumption and reduced conventionally measured saving.

THE PUZZLE OF LOW SAVING IN 1979-80

A universal forecast in 1979 was that the acceleration of inflation due to the doubling of oil prices (see section 9-7) would cause a steady decline in real disposable income and consumption and lead to a milder version of the recession of 1974-75. Yet the beginning of the much-heralded recession was delayed until January 1980, and it seemed clear that the behavior of the consumer was the main reason. We have noticed in Figures 13-6 and 13-7 that the saving rate declined in 1979:Q4 and 1980:Q1 to its lowest value since 1950. And this is true even if we add in consumer durables and taxes, as is done in the upper red wiggly line in Figure 13-6. There the ratio of saving plus consumer durable expenditures plus personal tax payments to personal income declined by over a percentage point in 1980:Q1 below the average values of 1976, 1977, and 1978:

	$\dfrac{S}{Q_P}$	$\dfrac{S + C_D + T_P}{Q_P}$
1976	5.0	30.6
1977	4.2	30.7
1978	4.2	30.9
1980:Q1	2.9	29.2

This represented a decline in saving and a corresponding increase in consumption of about $30 billion.

A common explanation of the low saving rate centered on the role of capital gains on houses. This view was put forth by Alan Greenspan, who was Chairman of the Council of Economic Advisers under President Ford and founder of the consulting firm Townsend-Greenspan. Greenspan argued that total consumer saving is not just the narrow concept of disposable income minus consumption, as measured in the National Income and Product Accounts. Instead, real saving consists of anything that increases a consumer's real net worth (or real net wealth). Since real net wealth equals real assets minus real liabilities, saving equals the increase in real assets minus the increase in real liabilities.

During the period after 1975 American consumers enjoyed large increases in the real value of their homes, a major component of their real assets. But these real capital gains on housing were not included in the official measures of saving. Thus much of "true" saving was overlooked. Stated another way, consumers were able to maintain their consumption expenditures in late 1979 because their net wealth was high. As Modigliani's life-cycle hypothesis would have predicted, an increase in real net wealth would tend to increase real consumption relative to real disposable income. Although they cannot directly spend their home equity, consumers can obtain needed funds by refinancing their home mortgages or by obtaining second mortgages, then using the cash proceeds to make normal consumption purchases.

It is important to note that these real capital gains were the result of the change in a *relative* price, that of residential houses. Thus this stimulus to consumption, which we may call a "relative asset price effect," differs from the real balance (Pigou) effect of Chapter 6. The Pigou effect tends to cut consumption when the aggregate price level increases relative to the value of nominal assets. The relative asset price effect tends to raise consumption by boosting the value of nominal assets (residential houses) relative to the aggregate price level.

How important is this explanation of the falling saving rate? Table 13-1 validates several elements of the argument. Column (4) indicates that the relative price of houses has been increasing, particularly between 1976 and 1978. And columns (2) and (3) show that net increases in household mortgage debt have been rising in relation both to personal income and to the value of construction of new residential housing. This suggests that a substantial share of the increase in mortgage debt, *which is not needed to purchase new housing, may be "left over" to finance consumption expenditures*. The main problem evident in Table 13-1 is in timing. The big jump in mortgages came as early as 1976, while the dramatic decline in the saving rate did not occur until late 1979.

INFLATION, SAVING, AND THE REAL RATE OF RETURN

Much discussion of the low U.S. saving rate has concentrated on the influence of inflation. We noted in Figure 11-1 that bursts of supply-shock inflation in 1973–74 and 1978–79 had reduced the actual real interest rate earned by savers. Can this be the explanation of low saving in 1979? Unfortunately, inflation itself cannot be blamed. The first episode of supply-shock inflation was accompanied by relatively *high* saving rates in 1973–74, in contrast to the low saving rates experienced in 1978–79.

TABLE 13-1

Savings and the Extension of Mortgage Debt,
Selected Periods, 1968–80

Year or quarter	Saving as percent of personal income	Net increase in mortgage debt as percent of		Relative price of housing in percent
		Personal income	Residential investment	
	(1)	(2)	(3)	(4)
1968	5.6	2.5	51.7	95
1970	6.3	1.8	40.2	97
1972	5.2	4.4	68.9	100
1974	6.2	3.1	67.2	105
1976	5.0	4.4	93.3	108
1978	4.2	6.0	99.4	121
1979:Q2	4.5	6.2	107.6	124
1980:Q1	2.9	4.5	85.8	125

Source (by column): (1) *Economic Report of the President,* January 1980, Table B-21. (2) Tables B-21 and B-24. (3) Tables B-21 and B-14. (4) Ratio of deflator of residential nonfarm investment to personal consumption deflator, from Table B-3.

Even as a theoretical matter the effect of inflation on saving is not clear. On the one hand inflation makes it more expensive to wait to buy consumption goods next year and tends to boost consumption this year (*cutting* saving). This is the destabilizing "expectations effect" of Chapter 6. But inflation also erodes the real value of savings accounts and other forms of wealth, forcing individuals to save *more* to restore the value of their wealth. There is no way of predicting which effect will dominate. And recent research suggests that there is no systematic impact of inflation or the real interest rate on saving behavior.[19]

13-8 CONCLUSION: CONSUMPTION AND THE CASE FOR ACTIVISM

If all consumption spending consisted of nondurable goods and services, the permanent-income hypothesis and life-cycle hypothesis both would strengthen the case of monetarists that the private economy is basically stable if left alone by the government. Consumption would respond only

---

[19] In a paper that received much publicity and scrutiny, Michael Boskin had appeared to show that a decrease in the real after-tax return on saving caused a significant decline in saving. See his "Taxation, Saving, and the Rate of Interest," *Journal of Political Economy,* vol. 86, part 2 (April 1978), pp. S3–S27. Now it appears that Boskin's results are questionable, and that more careful testing reveals no relation between saving and the after-tax real rate of return. See E. Philip Howrey and Saul H. Hymans, "The Measurement and Determination of Loanable-Funds Saving," *Brookings Papers on Economic Activity,* vol. 9, no. 3 (1978), pp. 655–685.

partially to temporary bursts of nonconsumption spending, so that the economy's true short-run multipliers would be smaller than those calculated in Chapters 3–5. Both the PIH and LCH predict that consumers dampen the decline of the economy in a recession by cutting their saving rate and dampen the subsequent expansion by raising their saving rate. Both the PIH and LCH are able to reconcile the observed cross-section increase in the saving ratio that occurs with higher incomes with the long-run historical constancy of the aggregate saving ratio.

Our study of the historical data began with several puzzles that the PIH and LCH did not appear able to explain. The saving ratio in the postwar United States has not fallen in every recession, and it has declined in some prosperous periods. In addition to special events connected with the end of World War II and the outbreak of the Korean War, two major factors help to reconcile the actual behavior of the saving ratio with the PIH and LCH. First, the share of consumer durable expenditures in disposable income falls in recessions and can offset part or all of the drop in the saving ratio that one would otherwise expect. The sum of the saving ratio and the consumer durable expenditures ratio exhibits the expected decline in almost all postwar recessions.

The second source of puzzling shifts in the saving ratio is the effect of temporary changes in tax rates. If temporary tax changes fail to alter permanent income, then the tax changes will be offset by movements in the saving ratio. It is ironic that the PIH, first developed by the chief monetarist, and the LCH, first developed (in collaboration with others) by one of the principal nonmonetarists, both imply that temporary tax changes introduced to implement an activist fiscal policy may be ineffective. From our study of saving behavior, the widespread nonmonetarist faith in the efficacy of temporary tax changes as a central tool of an activist stabilization policy does not appear to be warranted. On the other hand, the nonmonetarist case for policy activism is strengthened by the procyclical fluctuations in consumer durable purchases, because this source of instability in the private economy may need to be offset by countercyclical government policy.

SUMMARY

1. A major area of dispute between monetarists and nonmonetarists is the stability of private spending decisions. Friedman's permanent-income hypothesis (PIH) and Modigliani's life-cycle hypothesis (LCH) are based on the assumption that individuals achieve a higher level of total utility (well-being) when they maintain a stable consumption pattern than when they allow consumption to rise or fall with every transitory fluctuation in their actual income. Individuals can achieve the desirable stable consumption pattern by consuming a stable fraction of their permanent or lifetime income.

2. If all consumption consisted of nondurable goods and services, both the PIH and the LCH would strengthen the case of monetarists that the private economy is basically stable if left alone by the government. Consumption would respond only partially to temporary fluctuations of nonconsumption spending, so that the economy's short-run multipliers would be smaller than the simple theoretical multipliers of Chapters 3–5. Consumers would dampen the decline of the economy in a recession by reducing their saving rate, and they would similarly moderate the subsequent economic expansion by raising their saving rate.

3. Both hypotheses can reconcile the observed cross-section increase in the saving ratio that occurs for higher incomes with the observed long-run historical constancy of the aggregate saving ratio.

4. Both hypotheses have important implications for fiscal policy. For example, a tax change announced as permanent should cause a bigger change in permanent income, and hence in consumption expenditures, than another equal-sized tax change announced as temporary. Thus temporary tax changes introduced to implement an activist fiscal policy may be rendered ineffective by offsetting movements in the saving ratio.

5. An additional consideration in explaining observed consumption and saving behavior is that consumer durable expenditures should be treated as a form of saving, not as current consumption. Sharp increases in income tend to go mainly into saving, which means that consumer durable expenditures treated as a form of saving may be very responsive to transitory income changes. Thus the PIH and LCH may be valid, but still consumer durable purchases are a source of instability in the private economy.

A LOOK AHEAD

If consumers purchased only nondurable goods and services, the PIH and LCH theories would predict that consumer behavior stabilizes the economy. An offsetting factor is the procyclical movement of consumer durable purchases. Although this is consistent with the PIH and LCH, nevertheless it tends to aggravate booms and recessions. In the next chapter we will find that business-fixed investment fluctuates procyclically for reasons very similar to those used in this chapter to explain consumer durable spending. Both durable purchases by consumers and investment purchases by businesses thus introduce instability into the private economy, leading nonmonetarists to claim that an activist stabilization policy is justified.

CONCEPTS

Transitory versus permanent income	Procyclical
	Countercyclical
Permanent-income hypothesis of consumption (PIH)	Time-series versus cross-section evidence

Life-cycle hypothesis of
   consumption (LCH)
Consumer durable expenditures

Temporary versus permanent tax
   changes
Real capital gains on housing

QUESTIONS FOR REVIEW

1   Reconcile the positive cross-section relationship between income and
    the saving ratio with the observed historical constancy of the saving
    ratio.

2   How would you expect the short-run marginal propensity to consume
    to differ for farmers and university professors?

3   The growth rate of the U.S. population has declined in the past two
    decades. What effect would you expect this slowing to have on the
    aggregate saving ratio under the life-cycle hypothesis?

4   Why are estimates of permanent income continually changing?

5   Under the LCH, individuals try to smooth out their consumption over
    their lifetimes, yet we continually observe large positive bequests
    given by people to their children. Can you explain why most in-
    dividuals do not run their assets down to zero when they die, but
    rather leave assets as bequests to their heirs?

6   Under the LCH would you expect to observe the same marginal pro-
    pensity to consume out of a one-time temporary $5000 increase in in-
    come for an individual at age thirty as for the same individual at age
    fifty? Explain.

7   Why should consumer durable expenditures be considered as separate
    from nondurable expenditures? How does this distinction alter the ap-
    pearance of saving and consumption behavior?

8   How do permanent as opposed to temporary tax changes alter saving
    and consumption behavior? Can you account for the observed use of
    temporary tax changes in stabilization policy?

9   In which situation, A or B, do you think the aggregate saving rate
    would be higher? Explain carefully.

	Percentage rate of price change on	
	Existing houses	All other goods
A.	10	10
B.	20	10

14 Instability in the Private Economy: Investment

The economy is always straining to get to
the full employment limit, but by the mere
fact of being there for a time, it is projected
downward again.[1]
—Richard M. Goodwin

14-1 INVESTMENT AND ECONOMIC STABILITY

We found in Chapter 13 that the permanent-income and life-cycle hypotheses of individual consumption behavior explain the partial insulation in the short run of aggregate consumption spending from changes in other types of spending. But what are the sources of changes in these other types of spending? Real GNP in 1979 was divided among the major types of real expenditures as follows:

Personal consumption expenditures	64.6%
Gross private domestic investment	15.0
Government purchases of goods and services	19.2
Net exports	1.2
	100.0

In addition to consumption, the major types of expenditures are investment and government spending. Postponing our discussion of government spending and other aspects of fiscal policy to Chapter 17, we concentrate here on private investment.

The instability of private investment spending (together with that of consumer durable purchases treated in Chapter 13) forms the essential core of the nonmonetarist case for policy activism. The private economy can be blown off course by too much or too little investment. Even if the permanent-income hypothesis temporarily insulates consumption spending on nondurable goods and services from the effect of unstable investment, there is

---

[1] "A Model of Cyclical Growth" in E. Lundberg (ed.), *The Business Cycles in the Post War World* (London: Macmillan, 1955).

no tendency for investment itself to come promptly back on course. Sooner or later households begin to incorporate into their permanent income the change in actual income caused by the altered output of investment goods. In postwar recessions and expansions investment has maintained its record of instability. These are the changes in real gross private domestic investment during postwar business cycles:

Quarters			Percentage change	
Peak	Trough	Peak	Peak to trough	Trough to peak
1948:Q3	1949:Q2	1953:Q2	−26.0	44.5
1953:Q2	1954:Q2	1957:Q3	−10.4	25.1
1957:Q3	1958:Q2	1960:Q1	−19.0	46.1
1960:Q1	1961:Q1	1969:Q4	−20.8	71.6
1969:Q4	1970:Q4	1973:Q4	− 5.2	38.7
1973:Q4	1975:Q1	1980:Q1	−36.4	51.3

In this chapter we review a very simple theory that explains why investment spending is more likely to exhibit pronounced fluctuations than to remain constant. In so doing, we confirm an important nonmonetarist criticism of the monetarist platform. Aggregate private spending, although partially insulated by the permanent-income hypothesis of consumption, exhibits marked and persistent fluctuations as a result of the instability of private investment. The discussion of private investment in this chapter only justifies a need for activist policy, refuting plank 1 of the monetarist platform in Chapter 12. Nothing here demonstrates that an activist stabilization policy can be successful; nothing here denies plank 3 of the monetarist platform.

In Chapter 13, according to the permanent-income hypothesis, households try to maintain a constant ratio of their consumer durable stock to permanent income. This creates sudden bursts of durable purchases when an upward revision of permanent income causes the desired durable stock to increase. In this chapter the same **accelerator hypothesis** is extended to investment in plant, equipment, and housing.[2]

---

[2] Examples of plant and equipment investment are these:

Nonresidential plant (structures)	Equipment
Factories	Electronic computers
Oil refineries	Jet airplanes
Office buildings	Typewriters
Shopping centers	Cash registers
Private hospitals	Telephone switchboards
Private universities	Tractors

The principles developed in this chapter apply also to investment in residential housing, both single-family homes and multifamily apartment buildings.

14-2 THE ACCELERATOR HYPOTHESIS OF NET INVESTMENT

Business firms must continually evaluate the size of their factories and the numbers of their machines. Will they have too little capacity to produce the output that they expect to be able to sell in the forthcoming year, causing lost sales and dissatisfied customers? Or, perhaps, will capacity be excessive in relation to expected sales, causing a wasteful burden of costs to pay maintenance workers and interest expense on the unneeded plant and equipment? The accelerator theory of investment relies on the simple idea that firms attempt to maintain a fixed relation between their stock of capital (plants and equipment) and their expected sales.

ESTIMATING EXPECTED SALES

Clearly the first key ingredient in a business firm's decision about plant investment is an educated guess about the likely level of sales. Table 14-1 provides an example of how a hypothetical firm, the Mammoth Electric Company, estimates expected output and determines its desired stock of electric generating stations. The estimate of expected sales (Q^e) is revised from the estimate of the previous year (Q^e_{-1}) by any difference between last year's actual sales outcome (Q_{-1}) and what was expected:

$$Q^e = Q^e_{-1} + j\,(Q_{-1} - Q^e_{-1})$$
$$= j\,Q_{-1} + (1-j)Q^e_{-1} \tag{14.1}$$

This so-called adaptive or error-learning method of estimating sales expectations is exactly the same as we previously encountered in the formation of expectations of inflation and of permanent income.[3]

The error-learning method is illustrated in Table 14-1, where j is assumed equal to 0.5. In period 2 the previous period's sales (Q^e_{-1}) were expected to be $10 billion but turned out actually to be $12 billion ($Q_{-1}$). The revision of expected sales can be calculated from equation (14.1):

$$Q^e = 0.5(Q_{-1}) + 0.5(Q^e_{-1})$$
$$= 0.5(12) + 0.5(10)$$
$$= 11$$

Thus in period 2 expected sales are $11 billion, as recorded on line 2. But then another mistake is made, because in period 2 actual sales turn out to be $12 billion again instead of the expected $11 billion. Once again expectations for the next period are revised.

---

[3] The formation of expectations of inflation was the subject of section 8-6. The calculation of permanent income was discussed in section 13-3.

TABLE 14-1

Workings of the Accelerator Theory of Investment for the Hypothetical Mammoth Electric Company (All figures in $ billions)

		Periods					
	Variable	0	1	2	3	4	5
1.	Actual sales (Q)	10.0	12.0	12.0	12.0	12.0	12.0
2.	Expected sales $(Q^e = 0.5Q^e_{-1} + 0.5Q_{-1})$	10.0	10.0	11.0	11.5	11.75	11.87
3.	Desired stock of electric generating stations $(K^* = 4Q^e)$	40.0	40.0	44.0	46.0	47.0	47.5
4.	Net investment in electric generating stations $(I_n = K^* - K^*_{-1})$	0.0	0.0	4.0	2.0	1.0	0.5
5.	Replacement investment $(D = 0.10K_{-1})$	4.0	4.0	4.0	4.4	4.6	4.7
6.	Gross investment $(I = I_n + D)$	4.0	4.0	8.0	6.4	5.6	5.2

THE LEVEL OF INVESTMENT DEPENDS ON THE CHANGE IN OUTPUT

The next step in the accelerator theory is the assumption that the stock of capital — that is, plant and equipment — that a firm desires (K^*) is a multiple of its expected sales:

GENERAL FORM   NUMERICAL EXAMPLE

$$K^* = v^*Q^e \qquad\qquad K^* = 4.0Q^e \qquad\qquad (14.2)$$

For example, Mammoth Electric in Table 14-1 wants a capital stock that is always four times as large as its expected sales. Notice that the desired capital stock on line 3 of the table is always exactly 4.0 times the level of expected sales on line 2. What determines the multiple v^*, which relates desired capital to expected sales? As we will see, in calculating v^* firms pay attention to the interest rate and tax rates. Their chosen value of the multiple v^* reflects all available knowledge about government policies and the likely profitability of investment.

Net investment (I_n) is the change in the capital stock (ΔK) that occurs each period:

$$I_n = \Delta K = K - K_{-1} \qquad\qquad (14.3)$$

In the example in Table 14-1, we assume that Mammoth Electric always

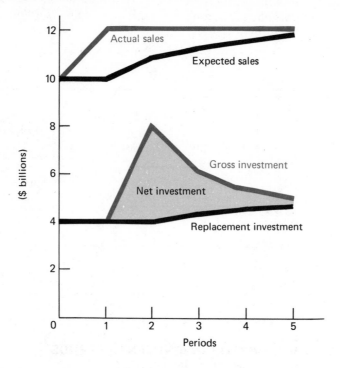

FIGURE 14–1

The Behavior of Actual Sales, Expected Sales, Gross Investment, Net Investment, and Replacement Investment for the Mammoth Electric Company Described in Table 14–1

In period 1 actual sales increase, but expected sales do not begin to respond until period 2. Net investment shoots up in period 2, as Mammoth Edison purchases equipment needed to service the higher expected level of sales. Expected sales continue to grow in periods 3, 4, and 5, but more slowly. Thus net investment actually declines from its peak in period 2.

manages to acquire new capital quickly enough to keep its actual capital stock (K) equal to its desired capital stock (K^*) in each period:

$$I_n = K - K_{-1} = K^* - K^*_{-1} \qquad (14.4)$$

Line 4 in the table shows that net investment (N) is always equal to the change in the desired capital stock in each period, which in turn from equation (14.2) is 4.0 times the change in expected sales:

$$I_n = K^* - K^*_{-1}$$
$$= v^*(Q^e - Q^e_{-1}) = v^* \, \Delta Q^e \qquad (14.5)$$

The accelerator theory, first proposed by J. M. Clark in 1917, says that the *level* of net investment (I_n) depends on the *change* in expected output (ΔQ^e). When there is an acceleration in business and expected output increases, net investment is positive, but when business decelerates and expected output stops increasing, net investment actually falls. And if expected output were ever to decline, net investment would become negative.

Total business spending on plant and equipment includes not only net investment—purchases that raise the capital stock—but also replacement purchases that simply replace old decaying plant and equipment or plant and equipment that has become obsolete. Line 5 of Table 14-1 assumes that each year 10 percent of the previous year's capital stock needs to be replaced. The total or gross investment (I) of Mammoth Electric, the amount recorded in the national income accounts of Chapter 2, is the sum of net investment (I_n) and replacement investment (D), and is written on line 6 of the table.

Figure 14-1 is an illustration of the Mammoth Electric example from Table 14-1. The level of actual sales is plotted as the top red line. Underneath, total gross investment is shown as the zigzag line that rises from $4 billion to $8 billion, only to fall in period 3 and afterward back toward the original level. Replacement investment is initially at the level of $4 billion, rising gradually as the capital stock increases. Net investment is the pink shaded area, which first increases in size and then shrinks. Overall, the accelerator theory explains why a firm's gross investment is so unstable, at first rising and then falling even when actual sales increase permanently.

14-3 CASE STUDY: THE SIMPLE ACCELERATOR AND THE POSTWAR U.S. ECONOMY

The relation between gross investment (I) and GNP (Q) for the economy as a whole is, according to the accelerator hypothesis, the same as for an individual firm. In the special case when expected sales are always set exactly equal to last period's actual sales $Q^e = Q_{-1}$, so that $\Delta Q^e = \Delta Q_{-1}$. This allows us to rewrite (14.5) as:

$$I_n = v^* \Delta Q_{-1} \qquad (14.6)$$

Net investment (I_n) equals a multiple of last period's change in sales (ΔQ_{-1}). Equation (14.6) is the simplest form of the accelerator theory and was invented when J. M. Clark in 1917 noticed a regular relationship between the level of boxcar production and the previous change in railroad traffic.[4]

---

[4] J. M. Clark, "Business Acceleration and the Law of Demand," *Journal of Political Economy*, vol. 25 (March 1917), pp. 217–235.

Perhaps no other equation in this book summarizes so succinctly the inherent instability of the private economy. Any random event — an export boom, an irregularity in the timing of government spending, or an upward revision of consumer estimates of permanent income — can change the growth of real sales and alter the level of net investment in the same direction.

Figure 14-2 compares real net investment (I_n) with the change in real output (ΔQ) in the postwar U.S. economy.[5] Unfortunately, equation (14.6) appears to be much too simple a theory to explain completely all historical movements in U.S. net investment. True, most peak years in net investment coincided with (or followed by one year) peak years in real GNP growth—1950, 1956, 1960, 1966, 1973. And trough years in net investment coincided with (or followed by one year) trough years in real GNP growth—1949, 1952, 1954, 1958, 1961, 1971, 1976. Furthermore, five years of high net investment (1965–69) followed seven years (1962–68) in which real GNP growth dipped below average only once.[6] Also, six years of low net investment (1958–63) followed eight years (1954–61) during which real GNP growth rose above average only twice. But overall, Figure 14-2 reveals quite an imperfect relationship.

There appear to be two main problems with the simple accelerator theory of equation (14.7), judging from the historical U.S. data plotted in Figure 14-2:

1. Net investment does not appear to respond to accelerations and decelerations in real GNP growth with a uniform speed. For instance, the response of net investment was much faster to the 1974–75 drop in real GNP than to the slowdown in GNP growth in 1967–70. It is as if an automobile's engine responded in a split second to some movements of the accelerator but took minutes to respond to other movements of the pedal.
2. The overall level of net investment relative to real GNP (I_n/Q) does not have a consistent historical relationship to real GNP growth ($\Delta Q/Q$). In the following four periods, real GNP growth was quite similar but the net investment ratio (I_n/Q) was quite different:

Average over period	$\Delta Q/Q$	I_n/Q
1947–54	3.29%	1.15%
1955–64	3.63	0.30
1965–74	3.40	1.51
1975–79	3.32	−0.59
Total postwar, 1947–79	3.44	0.72

[5] To adjust for the steady growth in the size of the economy, both I_n and ΔQ are divided by real GNP (Q). Thus the actual variables plotted are the share of real net investment in real GNP (I_n/Q) and the percentage growth rate of real GNP ($\Delta Q/Q$).

[6] Average real GNP growth over the 1947–79 period plotted in Figure 14-2 is 3.45 percent.

THE UPS AND DOWNS OF NET INVESTMENT ARE NOT PERFECTLY RELATED TO CHANGES IN REAL GNP

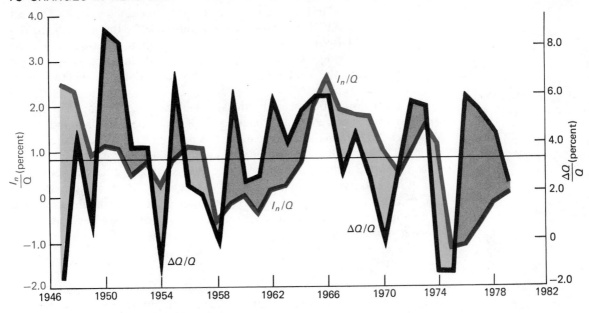

FIGURE 14-2

The Relation of the Net Investment Share (I_n/Q) to the Growth Rate of Real GNP ($\Delta Q/Q$) in the U.S. Economy, 1947–79

The net investment share does not have a perfect or simple relationship with the growth rate of real GNP. But the period when the net investment share was high, during 1965–69, followed five years of high average output growth. The period when the net investment share was very low, during 1958–63, followed a period of low real output growth between 1952 and 1961.

Source: Net investment share (I_n/Q) is real nonresidential fixed investment divided by real GNP minus capital consumption allowances divided by nominal GNP. All figures are from the *Economic Report of the President,* 1980.

14-4 THE FLEXIBLE ACCELERATOR

The simple accelerator theory of equation (14.7) depends on several restrictive and unrealistic assumptions. A more realistic version of the theory, called the **flexible accelerator,** can be obtained if we loosen several of these restrictive assumptions:

1. The simple accelerator assumed that this period's expected output was always set equal to last period's actual output. But the error-learning or adaptive hypothesis states that in general only a fraction of expected out-

put is based on last period's output, and the rest conservatively carries over whatever was expected last period.

2. The simple accelerator assumes that the desired capital stock (K^*) is set equal to a constant (v^*) times expected output (Q^e). But actually the desired capital-output ratio (v^*) may vary substantially, depending on the cost of borrowing, the taxation of capital, and other factors; we will postpone until the next section a detailed consideration of the factors that make v^* change.

3. The third assumption made by the simple accelerator is that firms can instantly put in place any desired amount of investment in plant and equipment needed to make actual capital this period (K) equal to desired capital (K^*). Actually, some kinds of capital take a substantial period to construct. Buildings sometimes take two or three years between conception and completion. Some types of electric utility generating stations can take as long as eight years to complete.[7] Further, installing too much new investment at one time would be excessively costly, because firms supplying capital goods might raise their prices and the installation activity might disrupt the flow of production.

Thus net investment in the real world does not always close the whole gap between desired capital and last year's capital stock, but only a fraction of it.

To summarize, the relationship between economywide gross investment and output depends on at least four major factors:

1. *The fraction of the gap between desired capital and last period's actual capital that can be closed in a single period.* The higher this fraction, the more current investment responds to an acceleration in last period's output.

2. *The response of expected output to last period's error in estimating actual output.* The higher this response is, the more expected output and hence investment responds to any unexpected acceleration in last period's actual output.

3. *The proportion of the capital stock that is replaced each year.* For long-lived types of capital, such as office buildings, only a fraction of buildings is replaced each year, and so total investment in office buildings is very sensitive to changes in output. When output stagnates, as in the late 1950s, few new office buildings are needed and there is little need for replacement, so that gross investment is low. But in years of booming output, as in the mid-1960s, the large net investment in new office buildings swamps the small replacement investment, and gross investment may rise by a factor of five or ten. Exactly the opposite effect works for short-lived types of capital.

A further complication is that the proportion of the capital stock re-

---

[7] At the other extreme, a shop that opens for business today in a large city could probably obtain delivery of needed equipment—cash register, calculating machine, typewriter, postage meter, furniture—in a day or two.

placed may not remain the same from year to year. The assumption that the replacement fraction is constant has been used in much econometric research.[8] But more recent studies have confirmed the obvious fact that firms are not forced to replace old capital on a fixed schedule.[9]

4. *The desired ratio of capital to expected output* (v^*). Investment responds more to changes in expected output in capital-intensive industries (those with a high v^*, such as electric utilities, oil refining, and chemicals) than in labor-intensive industries (those with a low v^* such as textiles, apparel, and barber shops).

In the next section we investigate the determinants of the desired capital-output ratio and the policy instruments with which the government can affect the size of v^*.

14-5 THE COST OF CAPITAL AND THE DESIRED CAPITAL-OUTPUT RATIO

From the previous discussion of the accelerator theory, a monetarist might conclude that investment spending does not add any extra instability not already present in the economy. If actual output were maintained at a steady pace, business firms would be able to form accurate expectations about future sales, and investment would not exhibit the pronounced up-and-down cycles observed in the past. Thus, the monetarist might conclude, investment spending does not add anything to the case for activist government policy intervention.

But, the nonmonetarists might respond, this sanguine attitude ignores the fact that v^*, the desired capital-output ratio, may vary and can have just as powerful an effect on investment as an acceleration of real output. A given percentage increase in v^* can raise the desired capital stock, and hence investment, by as much as the same percentage increase in expected output.[10]

THE USER COST OF CAPITAL

A business firm is willing to undertake an investment project only when it expects that a profit can be made. Just as we learned in Chapter 7 that an extra unit of labor will not be hired unless its marginal product—the extra output it produces—equals or exceeds its real wage, the same principle applies to capital equipment. An extra unit of capital will not be purchased

---

[8] See especially the work of Dale Jorgenson, beginning with his "Capital Theory and Investment Behavior," *American Economic Review,* vol. 53 (May 1963), pp. 247–257.

[9] A study that confirms the procyclical behavior of replacement investment is Martin S. Feldstein and David Foot, "The Other Half of Gross Investment: Replacement and Modernization Expenditures," *The Review of Economics and Statistics,* vol. 53, no. 1 (February 1971), pp. 49–58.

[10] See equation (14.2).

unless the expected **marginal product of capital** (*MPK*) is at least equal to the real **user cost of capital** (*u*):

GENERAL FORM   NUMERICAL EXAMPLE

$$MPK = u \qquad\qquad 14 = 14 \qquad\qquad (14.7)$$

Both the marginal product and the real user cost can be expressed as percentages. The marginal product of capital consists of the dollars of extra output each year produced by an extra piece of plant or equipment, divided by the cost of the equipment. If the purchase of an extra machine costing $100,000 allows a firm to produce $14,000 extra output each year, then *MPK* would be 14 percent.[11]

> *The user cost of capital is the cost to the business firm of using a piece of capital for a period of time, expressed as a fraction of the machine's purchase price. The user cost might be 14 percent, consisting perhaps of a 4 percent annual real interest rate and a 10 percent depreciation rate.*[12]

What does equation (14.7) have to do with the profitability of a business firm? When *MPK* is 15 percent and user cost is only 14 percent, then the extra revenue generated by a new machine exceeds its cost, and the firm's profits are increased. On the other hand, when *MPK* is only 13 percent and user cost is the same 14 percent, the extra revenue is insufficient to pay the costs of the new machine, and profits go down if the machine is purchased. Only if policymakers can find some way of reducing user cost to 13 percent will the new machine be purchased.

The effect of a reduction in user cost on the desired capital-output ratio is illustrated in Figure 14-3. Initially the user cost is u_0; the capital-output ratio v_0^* will be chosen. Why? A smaller amount of capital, to the left of E_0, would mean giving up some of the profits indicated by the dark gray area that measures the difference between the marginal product of capital and the user cost. But to purchase a larger amount of capital, to the right of E_0, would cause losses. The pink and red areas indicate the loss made by purchasing extra units of capital that have an insufficient *MPK* to pay for their user cost.

Now let us assume that the user cost is cut, perhaps by a new government investment incentive. Additional units of capital will now be purchased to bring the capital-output ratio rightward to v_1^*. The reduction in user cost has made available extra profits, indicated by the light gray area, and it has eliminated the losses indicated by the pink area. Only if the capital-output ratio exceeds v_1^* will the marginal product of capital (*MPK*) be insufficient to balance the new lower user cost.

---

[11] As is always true in economics, the marginal product of a single input measures the extra output produced by an extra unit of that input if the quantity of other inputs is held constant.

[12] Depreciation is part of user cost, because the portion of the machine wearing out must be replaced if *MPK* is to remain unaffected.

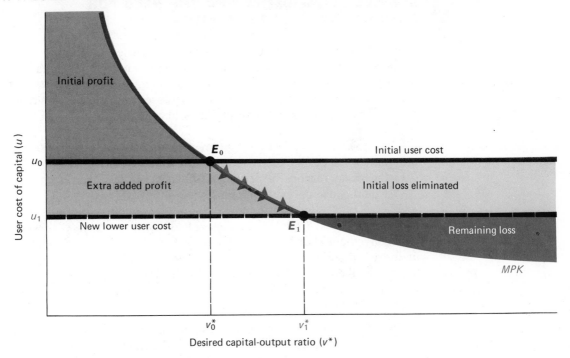

FIGURE 14–3

The Effect of a Drop in the User Cost of Capital (u) on the Desired
Capital-Output Ratio (v^*)

Initially the economy is at point E_0. Firms are making a profit on their capital
stock indicated by the dark gray area. Any further investment will not be undertaken, because it would create losses indicated by the pink and red areas. But if
the user cost can be reduced from u_0 to u_1, the economy will move from point E_0
to E_1. The initial pink area of potential losses is eliminated, and the light gray area
of added profit is gained.

*By using monetary and fiscal policy instruments, the user cost of
capital can be cut. Firms can thus be induced to adopt more capital-
intensive methods of production, and the opposite is true as well. Just
as an increase in the wage rate can cause firms to replace marginal
workers with extra machines, an increase in capital's user cost can
cause firms to substitute away from elaborate machines toward more
labor-intensive techniques of production.*[13]

---

[13] For instance, textile firms in the United States typically use fancier machines and fewer
workers to produce given products than those in less developed countries where the wage rate
is lower and the user cost of capital is higher.

14-6 BUSINESS CONFIDENCE AND THE NEED FOR ACTIVIST POLICY INTERVENTION

Remember that any increase in investment caused by a reduction in u is temporary, just as is the increase in investment caused by an increase in output. After the initial burst of investment spending caused by a lower u, firms will find their actual capital stock moving closer to the higher desired level, and they can cut back on their additions to capital.

> **Review:** In Figure 14-1 a permanent increase in actual sales causes only a temporary increase in investment. In exactly the same way for the same reasons, a permanent decrease in the user cost of capital would cause only a temporary boom in investment.

In Chapters 3 and 4 the terms *business* and *consumer confidence* were used as a convenient shorthand to refer to factors that could push output in an undesired direction when government spending and the money supply were fixed at a given level. In the flexible accelerator theory of investment summarized here, the confidence of business firms may influence investment spending in three ways:

1. Investment depends on the fraction of an increase in last period's actual output that is incorporated into expected output and hence into desired capital and investment. When business people lack confidence in the future, they may refuse to extrapolate a quarter or a year of increasing output, believing instead that any increase in output is bound to be temporary.
2. The user cost of capital (u) includes the borrowing costs that business firms expect to have to pay if they undertake an investment project. If businesses are pessimistic, they may overestimate the true borrowing cost that they are likely to face, making their estimate of u too high and their desired capital stock too low.
3. Perhaps most important, business firms can only guess the likely marginal product of new investment projects. It is the expected marginal product that matters. If business has recently been bad, a condition experienced by many business firms in 1930–33, or as recently as 1975–76, firms may currently have more capital than they may need. Some present capital may presently be underutilized, and future capital investments may be unprofitable, having close to a zero marginal product for the foreseeable future.

Any event, whether political or economic, that causes a drop in business confidence can cause a sharp drop in the level of investment. In the extreme case, the Great Depression of the 1930s, a collapse in business confidence dropped the desired capital stock far below the actual inherited capital stock. Not only did businesses refuse to add to their capital stock, but they allowed net investment to become negative by refusing to replace worn-out and obsolete equipment. Gross domestic private investment plummeted from \$55.9 billion in 1929 to \$7.9 billion in 1932 (both in 1972 prices), but despite the low levels of gross investment in the 1930s, much capital remained underutilized. The overhang of too much inherited capital depressed investment for a full decade.

CYCLES OF OVERBUILDING

Periods of excessive business overoptimism in U.S. history have periodically been followed by overbuilding, underutilized capital, and extensive pessimism. The cycle repeated itself in the late 1960s and early 1970s, leaving the United States in the mid-1970s with a substantial underutilization of some types of capital. The overbuilding of apartments was particularly severe in mid-1976:

> In Chicago, new apartment construction has just about ceased. In Atlanta, where there is at least a three-year supply of unsold condominiums overhanging the market, mortgage companies are auctioning off high-rise units to the public at two-thirds their original asking price. . . . The current problems stem from overbuilding in the early 1970's. . . . Soon the market was saturated and investors were caught in a squeeze. "During the past few years," says a Chicago builder, "there's been no return on investment."[14]

In Atlanta the overbuilding of office buildings had also reached an extreme stage:

> About 9 million of the city's 36 million sq. ft. of office space is vacant. . . . Says architect-developer John C. Portman, . . . "The city has three years' supply of office space, in my opinion. In the case of some of the poorer developments, it may take five years to work out."[15]

When a builder says that his city has "three years' supply" of office buildings, he means that there is no justification for any new construction of office buildings until three years of economic growth has created the demand to fill the previously constructed vacant buildings. If this situation is widespread, the low level of construction investment—working through the investment multiplier of Chapter 3—may prevent or delay the economic boom that is needed to create the conditions for a future recovery of investment. In the 1930s, investment never did recover to its 1929 level; in 1939 investment was only \$33.6 billion in 1972 prices, compared to the \$55.9 billion level achieved in 1929. The real problem was nonresidential building for offices and factories; this never exceeded even half its 1929 level throughout the 1930s.

The episode of overbuilding in the mid-1970s was less severe. The saturation of the Chicago and Atlanta real estate markets had ended by 1978. In

---

[14] "The Great High-rise Bust," *Newsweek* (August 30, 1976), p. 5.
[15] "Atlanta's Building Boom Overshoots Its Mark," *Business Week* (December 13, 1976), p. 92.

1979 there were twenty new office building projects underway in Chicago, although the Atlanta revival was more modest. Nevertheless, it took five full years for the 1973 level of nonresidential investment to be exceeded in late 1978. And as of 1980:Q1, the share of real nonresidential structures investment in GNP was just 3.5 percent, compared to previous peak values of 3.7 percent in 1973 and 4.3 percent in 1966.

Keynes placed major emphasis on the role of business confidence in determining the level of investment. In the following passage he stresses that investment decisions are based on estimates of the future "yield" (or marginal product) of extra capital, which may be little better than a guess. Faced with identical information and uncertainty, business people may go ahead with an investment project when they feel optimistic but postpone the same project when they feel pessimistic:

> The outstanding fact is the extreme precariousness of the basis of knowledge on which our estimates of prospective yield have to be made. Our knowledge of the factors which will govern the yield of an investment some years hence is usually very slight and often negligible. If we speak frankly, we have to admit that our basis of knowledge for estimating the yield ten years hence of a railway, a copper mine, a textile factory, the goodwill of a patent medicine, an Atlantic liner, a building in the City of London amounts to little and sometimes to nothing; or even five years hence. In fact, those who seriously attempt to make any such estimates are often so much in the minority that their behavior does not govern the market.[16]

14-7 USER COST AND THE ROLE OF MONETARY AND FISCAL POLICY

Government policymakers cannot change the state of business confidence merely by delivering pious speeches. But they can directly determine the user cost of capital (u), one of the major determinants of gross investment. The user cost of capital depends on several factors, which can be introduced in two steps. First, let us neglect the effect of taxation. A capital good that is purchased at a given real price imposes three types of cost on its user in the absence of taxation.

1. *An interest cost is involved in buying a capital good.* Either money must be borrowed at the nominal interest rate (i) or else an investor loses the interest (i) he would receive by investing in a savings account the funds that he uses to buy the investment good.
2. *Physical deterioration affects the ability of every capital good to produce, and in addition some capital goods become obsolete.* The **depreciation rate** indicates the annual decline in value of the capital good due to physical deterioration plus obsolescence.

---

[16] Keynes, *General Theory*, pp. 149–150.

3. *Some used capital goods may depreciate but may simultaneously have a market value that increases.* This paradox can occur when inflation continuously raises the price of new capital goods, "dragging along" the price of used capital goods.

Policymakers cannot alter the relative price of capital goods, which depends on the technical factors that influence innovations and productivity change in capital goods industries compared to the economy as a whole. Similarly, they cannot change the rate of physical decay and economic obsolescence summarized in the depreciation rate. But the real interest rate is under the control of policymakers. As we learned in Chapter 5, a fiscal policy stimulus raises the real interest rate and hence crowds out investment. A monetary policy stimulus, on the other hand, reduces the real interest rate and raises investment. A change in the monetary-fiscal policy mix toward easier monetary policy and tighter fiscal policy cuts the real interest rate and user cost, thus raising investment.

TAXATION AND INVESTMENT BEHAVIOR

So far taxation has been ignored. But fiscal policy can have a major effect on investment by altering the user cost. Three basic fiscal tools are available:

1. *The U.S. government levies a corporation income tax on corporate profits.* Firms make investment decisions by equating the marginal product of capital with the real user cost of capital *before* taxes. But savers care about the level of their income *after* taxes. Thus to provide savers with a given market return, an investment project must pay a higher before-tax interest rate (and hence incur a higher user cost) when the corporation tax is high than when it is low.
2. *Firms can cut their corporation tax by deducting the value of depreciation of plant and equipment.* The amount of depreciation they can deduct depends on rules set out by the U.S. Treasury Department. Whenever the Treasury depreciation rules are liberalized, as occurred in 1954, 1962, and 1964, more of corporate profits are protected from tax, thus cutting the user cost of capital.
3. *Since 1962 some investment in the United States has been eligible for an investment tax credit.* In 1980 business firms could take 10 percent of the value of the equipment investment and deduct that amount from their corporation income tax. Naturally this reduced the user cost of capital, as long as the firm was making profits and was subject to tax.

These three fiscal instruments provide much more flexibility in conducting stabilization policy than would be available if the government were limited to controlling the economy by varying the level of government spending and the personal income tax rate. For instance, government spending can be restrained and the personal income tax rate raised to slow down an economy that is experiencing too much aggregate demand, but at the same time any of the investment-related fiscal instruments can be liberalized if it is believed that the economy has too little investment and too much consumption.

14-8 THE ACCELERATOR AS A SOURCE OF INSTABILITY IN OUTPUT AND INTEREST RATES

The accelerator theory creates a favorite paradox of macroeconomics teachers. We became accustomed in Chapters 4 and 5 to an association of low interest rates with high investment and high interest rates with low investment. This inverse relationship between investment and interest rates has been confirmed in this chapter, because a low level of the real interest rate reduces the user cost of capital, which in turn raises the desired capital stock and hence the level of gross investment. Yet a predominant feature of business cycles in almost every nation is a positive correlation between business investment and interest rates. United States business investment fluctuates procyclically, reaching peaks in years of high output and troughs during recessions or soon after the business-cycle trough. But at the same time, interest rates also fluctuate procyclically, so that years of low interest rates are usually associated with low investment, not high investment.

How can the positive relationship between investment and interest rates be explained? The accelerator theory provides the answer. Figure 14-4 repeats the *IS-LM* analysis of Chapter 5. The *LM* curve maintains an unchanged position whenever the real money supply (M/P) is fixed. The *IS* curve fluctuates whenever there is a change in the investment purchases that business firms choose to make at a constant real interest rate.

A long list of factors can make the level of gross investment, and hence the *IS* curve, change for a given interest rate. Included are (1) an increase in actual output due to some factor unconnected with the investment process, (2) a change in the extent to which a current output change is predicted to continue in the future, (3) a previous episode of overbuilding that makes the actual capital stock high relative to the current desired stock, (4) a shift in demand toward shorter-lived equipment, (5) a change in the relative price of capital goods, and, finally, (6) an alteration in fiscal incentives that alters the before-tax user cost of capital. A change in any of these elements shifts the level of investment that occurs at a given interest rate and, through the miltiplier, shifts the level of total output.

Figure 14-4 illustrates two *IS* curves, IS_0 and IS_1. The movement back and forth between the two *IS* curves reflects any of the elements in the previous paragraph that change the desired capital stock (for a given real interest rate) and thus cause an increase or decrease in gross investment. The positive relationship between investment and interest rates is explained in Figure 14-4 by the constant level of the real money supply, which keeps the *LM* curve fixed at LM_0. That positive relationship suggests that the depressing effect of low output on investment, working through the accelerator, dominates the stimulative effect of low interest rates on investment, at least in the short run.

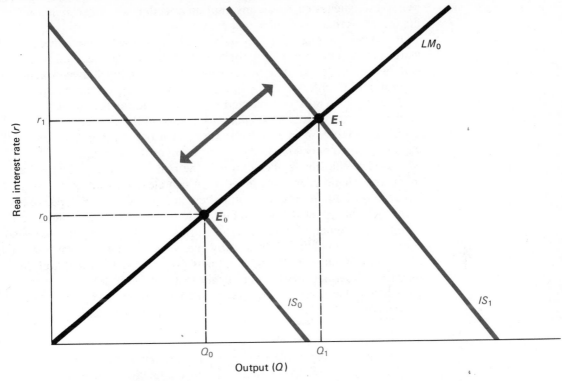

FIGURE 14–4

Effect on Output and the Interest Rate of a Shift in the Level of Investment Relative to the Interest Rate

Shifts in business confidence or in user cost can shift the red *IS* curve back and forth between IS_0 and IS_1. As a result, the interest rate will be high when investment is high, and vice versa. This conclusion assumes that the real money supply, which fixes the position of the *LM* curve, remains unchanged.

14-9 CONCLUSION: INVESTMENT AND THE CASE FOR ACTIVISM

A major source of disagreement between monetarists and nonmonetarists is the need for an activist stabilization policy. Monetarists argue that the private economy is basically stable if freed from the destabilizing influence of government intervention, whereas nonmonetarists emphasize sources of instability in the private sector that require government intervention to maintain stability in total output. We concluded in Chapter 13 that consumption spending on nondurable goods and services appeared to bolster the case of the monetarists. Both the permanent-income hypothesis and life-cycle hypothesis suggested that consumption spending on those items tends to fluctuate less than disposable income.

But this chapter appears to swing the case in the opposite direction, toward the nonmonetarist proposition that the private economy contains sources of instability that tend to make any equality between actual and natural output an infrequent coincidence rather than a frequent occurrence. The basic problem is summarized by the accelerator theory of investment. Any event that causes a *permanent* increase in the desired capital stock—whether an increase in expected output or a reduction in the user cost of capital—causes only a *temporary* burst of investment spending.

Added to the simple accelerator is the realistic element of lagged adjustment. In a single year extra investment can close only a fraction of the gap between desired and previous actual capital, because some types of investment (particularly structures) require a long delay between conception and completion. A period when business firms are overoptimistic may lead to excessive overbuilding, followed by many years when vacant apartments and office buildings are the rule and new projects are the exception. Making matters worse, households may begin to incorporate into their permanent income a slump in actual income caused by a prolonged deterioration in investment spending.

Summary: Investment spending may experience sustained booms or slumps lasting several years resulting from fluctuations in confidence and lags between the conception and completion of investment projects. Policymakers can resist a destabilizing recession in total output, but only by introducing an activist policy stimulus. Left alone, the private economy is prone to long booms and slumps in private investment, leading either to accelerations of inflation (as in the mid-1950s and mid-1960s) or to long periods of wasteful unemployment (as in the 1930s, early 1960s, and mid-1970s).

SUMMARY

1. The major source of instability in consumption spending is contributed by consumer expenditures on durables, which can exhibit large fluctuations in response to income changes. This chapter adds private investment spending as an additional source of instability, with the potential of causing major changes in GNP in response to small shocks.

2. The simple accelerator theory of investment relies on the idea that firms attempt to maintain a fixed relation between their stock of capital and their expected sales. Thus the level of net investment—the change in the capital stock—depends on the change in expected output. The accelerator theory explains why the gross investment of most firms is relatively unstable, at first rising and then falling in response to a permanent increase in actual sales.

3. The flexible accelerator theory recognizes that net investment in the real world usually closes only a portion of any gap between the desired and actual capital stocks. Furthermore, the desired capital-output ratio may change, altering investment with a powerful accelerator effect.

4. The accelerator theory implies that any event that causes a permanent increase in the desired capital stock, whether arising from an increase in expected output or from a reduction in the user cost of capital, causes only a temporary rise in investment spending. Thus investment spending may experience sustained booms or slumps lasting several years, resulting from fluctuations in business confidence and lags between the conception and completion of investment projects.

5. Government policymakers can directly alter the user cost of capital. Fiscal and monetary policy can change the real interest-rate component of user cost. Taxation can affect the user cost of capital through changes in the corporation income tax, depreciation deductions, and the investment tax credit. But the use of these policy instruments cannot eliminate all fluctuations in investment expenditures, because most policy measures operate only with lagged effects.

A LOOK AHEAD

In this chapter and the last we have examined sources of instability in the private economy originating in the commodity market — that is, in the market for goods and services. Another potential source of instability is in the money market. Is the private demand for money stable and predictable, or unstable and hard to predict? This is the subject of Chapter 15.

CONCEPTS

Simple accelerator hypothesis
Flexible accelerator hypothesis
Actual capital stock versus desired
  capital stock
Net investment versus replacement investment

Desired capital-output ratio
User cost of capital
Marginal product of capital
Depreciation deductions
Investment tax credit

QUESTIONS FOR REVIEW

1   How do changes in the user cost of capital alter net investment?

2   How can monetary and fiscal policy alter the user cost of capital?

3   Why is business and consumer confidence important? In what way(s) does it enter the flexible accelerator analysis?

4   There is an asymmetry in the adjustment of the inherited capital stock to the desired capital stock. This is a result of the lower limit of zero on gross investment, which prevents net investment from falling below the amount by which depreciation causes the actual capital stock to shrink. Can you explain how this factor might influence the economy's ability to recover from a depression without government stimulus?

5   Can you explain why gross investment in short-lived types of capital is more stable than gross investment in office buildings? Try to write down an explanation for gross investment in truck tires.

6   "Stable monetary and fiscal policy would eliminate output fluctuations caused by the government. Thus there would be no shocks causing investment to fluctuate." Evaluate this statement.

15 The Demand for Money and the Choice of Monetary Instruments

Unemployment develops . . . because people want the moon;—men cannot be employed when the object of desire (i.e., money) is something which cannot be produced and the demand for which cannot be readily choked off. There is no remedy, but to persuade the public that green cheese is practically the same thing, and to have a green cheese factory (i.e., a central bank) under public control.

—John Maynard Keynes[1]

15-1 THE DEMAND FOR MONEY AND THE EFFICACY OF FISCAL POLICY

The basic theory of income determination developed in Chapters 3–6 was based on a simple economic model consisting of two markets: a commodity market in which goods and services are bought and sold, and a money market in which the interest rate adjusts to induce households and firms voluntarily to hold the supply of money provided by the government. In those earlier chapters the demand functions for commodities and money were taken to be stable and predictable, so that stabilization of real output at the desired level was a simple matter of setting the monetary and fiscal policy instruments at particular values. But now we have seen (in Chapters 13 and 14) that the demand for the two major types of commodities demanded by the private sector—consumption goods and investment goods— depends on a wide variety of factors, including the state of consumer and business confidence, and thus the demand for commodities may not be completely stable or predictable.

In this chapter we shift from the commodity market to the money market and study the determinants of the demand for money. In Chapter 5 we were first introduced to the relationship between the efficacy of policy changes and the sensitivity of the demand for money to changes in the interest rate. We can review our conclusions with the aid of Figure 15-1, which reproduces the *IS* and *LM* curves that were used extensively earlier in the book. Once again the (real) interest rate is on the vertical axis and the level of real output is on the horizontal axis. The *IS* curve shows all the combinations of the interest rate and real output that maintain equilibrium in the commodity

---

[1] *General Theory*, p. 235.

THE SHORT-RUN EFFECT OF GOVERNMENT SPENDING ON REAL OUTPUT DEPENDS ON THE INTEREST SENSITIVITY OF THE DEMAND FOR MONEY

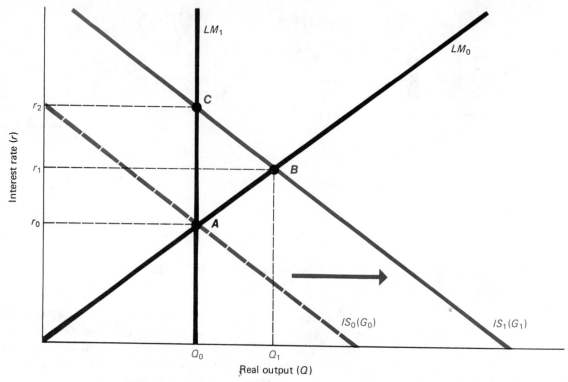

FIGURE 15–1

Two Alternative Responses of Real Output and the Interest Rate to an Increase in Government Spending from G_0 to G_1

An increase in government spending from G_0 to G_1 shifts the IS curve rightward from IS_0 to IS_1. The economy's movement in the short run (while real money balances are fixed) depends on the slope of the LM curve. When money demand is sensitive to changes in the interest rate, the economy moves from A to B. When money demand is completely insensitive to changes in the interest rate, the economy moves from A vertically up to C.

market. The position of the IS curve depends on the level of government spending. The curve is at the position IS_0 when government spending equals the fixed value G_0. But when government spending is increased to G_1, the IS curve shifts rightward to IS_1.[2]

---

[2] The position of the IS curve depends also on anything other than the interest rate that affects the level of planned expenditures in the commodity market, including tax rates, investment tax incentives, real wealth, and the state of business and consumer confidence. To review the determinants of the slope and position of the IS curve, turn back to sections 4-3 and 4-4.

The *LM* curve shows all the different combinations of the interest rate and real output that maintain equilibrium in the money market. Two *LM* curves are illustrated in Figure 15-1. The curve labeled LM_0 has the normal positive slope and assumes that the demand for money is sensitive to the interest rate. The curve labeled LM_1, on the other hand, has the extreme vertical slope and assumes that the demand for money is completely insensitive to changes in the interest rate.[3]

FISCAL POLICY AND THE DEMAND FOR MONEY

Will the boost in government spending that shifts the *IS* curve rightward from IS_0 to IS_1 raise the level of real output? In the long run the higher level of government spending will just succeed in raising the price level without any effect on real output. But in the short run the effect of the fiscal stimulus on real output depends on the interest sensitivity of the demand for money. When the demand for money is interest sensitive, the LM_0 curve is valid, and the fiscal stimulus raises real output from Q_0 to Q_1. When money demand is completely independent of the interest rate, however, the LM_1 curve is valid, and then the fiscal stimulus has no effect on real output even in the short run. In this case the economy moves from *A* to *C* (not from *A* to *B*), and the fiscal stimulus succeeds only in raising the interest rate.

Not only would a vertical LM curve destroy the effectiveness of fiscal policy, it would also eliminate its rationale. Shifts in private spending that move the *IS* curve would no longer alter real output. The *IS* curve would just move up and down a fixed vertical *LM* curve. There would no longer be any need for an activist fiscal policy. Because both the need for policy intervention and the short-run efficacy of fiscal policy depend on an interest-sensitive demand for money, economists since Keynes have placed major emphasis on refining the theory of why the demand for money depends on the interest rate, as well as on empirical estimates of the size of the interest response.

<h1 style="display:inline">15-2</h1> **THE DEMAND FOR MONEY AND THE INSTRUMENTS OF MONETARY CONTROL**

A firm understanding of the determinants of money demand is necessary not only for the conduct of fiscal policy but also for the management of monetary policy. Policymakers attempting to maintain a stable level of real output are aided if the demand for money at that desired output level is stable and predictable, because then they need only set the actual supply

---

[3] To review the relationship between the interest sensitivity of the demand for money and the slope of the *LM* curve, turn back to section 4-5. This chapter neglects the distinction between real and nominal interest rates. Actually the demand for money should depend on the nominal interest rate for reasons set out in section 11-4.

of money equal to that predicted level of money demand. If, on the other hand, money demand is unstable and hard to predict, policymakers may do better to stabilize the interest rate rather than the money supply.

This point, first popularized by William Poole of Brown University, calls into question the monetarist emphasis on achieving a constant growth rate of the money supply.[4] In the top frame of Figure 15-2 the LM_0 curve remains fixed when the real money supply is fixed.[5] At first we will assume that the demand for money is entirely stable and predictable, just as in Chapters 4 and 5, so that the LM curve shifts only if the real supply of money changes. The demand for commodities, however, is assumed to fluctuate and to cause the IS curve to move back and forth between the right-hand IS_1 curve and the left-hand IS_0 curve in the top frame of Figure 15-2.

STABLE MONEY SUPPLY OR INTEREST RATE?

Will monetary policymakers at the Federal Reserve do a better job of stabilizing output, in the face of the fluctuations in commodity demand, if they hold constant the real money supply or, alternatively, hold the interest rate constant? When the real money supply is held constant, the LM curve remains fixed at LM_0, the economy moves back and forth between positions B_0 and B_1, and real output moves over the limited range between Q_0' and Q_1'.

The alternative policy of maintaining stable interest rates has the undesirable effect of allowing wider fluctuations in real output. When commodity demand is high (along IS_1), the real money supply must be allowed to rise if the interest rate is to be prevented from increasing. In other words, to stabilize the interest rate in the face of an unstable commodity demand, the Fed is forced to accommodate the additional demand for money that occurs when commodity demand is high. The stable-interest-rate policy causes the economy to fluctuate between points A_0 and A_1, and it allows real output to vary over the wider range between Q_0 and Q_1.

ACTIVIST COUNTERCYCLICAL POLICY

The top frame of Figure 15-2 demonstrates that when commodity demand is unstable, a constant-money-supply policy, which keeps movements in

---

[4] William Poole, "Optimal Choice of Monetary Policy Instruments in a Simple Stochastic Macro Model," *Quarterly Journal of Economics,* vol. 84 (May 1970), pp. 197–216. A little-known earlier reference is M. L. Burstein, *Economic Theory* (New York: Wiley, 1966), Chapter 13.

[5] A fixed real money supply (M/P) and a fixed LM curve can be achieved either with a constant nominal money supply (M) and a fixed price level (P) or with the money supply growing at the same rate as the price level ($m = p$).

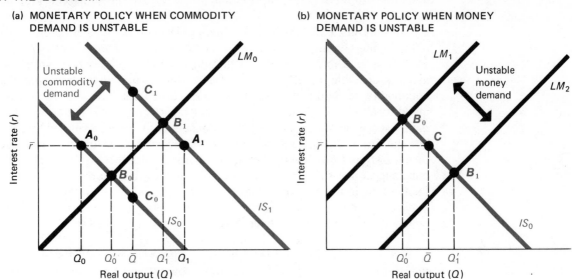

(a) MONETARY POLICY WHEN COMMODITY DEMAND IS UNSTABLE

(b) MONETARY POLICY WHEN MONEY DEMAND IS UNSTABLE

FIGURE 15-2

Effects on Real Output of Alternative Policies That Stabilize the Interest Rate or the Real Money Supply When Either Commodity Demand or Money Demand is Unstable

In the left frame the demand for commodities is unstable, fluctuating between IS_0 and IS_1. A policy that maintains a fixed real money supply and a fixed LM_0 curve leads to smaller fluctuations of output than an alternative policy that stabilizes the interest rate at $\bar{r}$ by shifting LM. The contrary is true in the right frame, where the demand for money is unstable. In this case a policy of stabilizing the interest rate at $\bar{r}$ will keep real output more stable than an alternative policy that stabilizes the real money supply. When the real money supply is held fixed, shifts in the LM curve from LM_1 to LM_2 are caused by unstable money demand, causing output to fluctuate between Q_0' and Q_1'.

real output between the bounds of points B_0 and B_1, is more stabilizing than the alternative constant-interest-rate policy, which allows output to vary between points A_0 and A_1. But a third alternative is even better. The Fed can pursue an activist countercyclical policy, reducing the money supply when commodity demand is high and raising the money supply when commodity demand is low. Now the economy will fluctuate vertically between points C_0 and C_1, and real output will not change at all. One disadvantage of a countercyclical monetary policy is evident in the diagram: the interest rate fluctuates more between C_0 and C_1 than between B_0 and B_1. Other possible limitations of a countercyclical monetary policy are the subject of the next chapter.

Not only is a constant-money-supply policy inferior to a countercyclical policy when commodity demand is unstable, as in the top frame of Figure 15-2, it is also inferior to a constant-interest-rate policy when money demand is unstable, as illustrated in the bottom frame. Now we assume that commodity demand is fixed, so that the IS curve remains at IS_0, and the demand for money is unstable and unpredictable. The LM curve does not remain fixed when the money supply is constant, as we have assumed throughout the book, but instead the LM curve moves around unpredictably between LM_1 and LM_2 even when the real money supply is constant. Thus the constant-money-supply policy recommended by the monetarists leads to fluctuations in the economy between points B_0 and B_1, with output varying between Q_0' and Q_1'. A policy of changing the money supply to maintain a constant interest rate, however, keeps the economy pinned to point C, with a fixed interest rate $\bar{r}$ and a fixed output level $\bar{Q}$.

Figure 15-2 further justifies our interest in the demand for money. If the demand for money is a stable function of output and the interest rate, as in the top frame, the Fed will do better to stabilize the real money supply than to stabilize the interest rate (although it is better still to pursue a countercyclical policy). But if the demand for money is unstable and commodity demand is stable, as in the bottom frame, the Fed will do better to stabilize the interest rate.

15-3 THE QUANTITY THEORY OF MONEY

The dominant analysis of macroeconomics before Keynes' *General Theory* was based almost entirely on the assumption of a stable demand for money. Not only was the demand for money assumed to be stable, but little or no attention was given to the dependence of the demand for money on the interest rate. Thus the entire subject of fiscal policy was neglected, as justified in the context of Figure 15-1 in the extreme case when the LM curve has the vertical slope at LM_1.

The **quantity theory of money** begins with the famous quantity equation, which is called a tautology because it is true by definition:

$$MV \equiv PQ \qquad (15.1)$$

Here M as before is the money supply, P is the price level (GNP deflator), Q is real GNP, and V is the **velocity** of money, the average number of times per year that the money stock is used in making payments for final goods and services. Equation (15.1) is a definition for the simple reason that velocity (V) is defined as (PQ/M). The right side of the equation corresponds to the transfer of goods and services between economic units, and the left side to the matching monetary payment for those goods and services.[6]

As it stands, the quantity equation is not a theory, but we can convert it into a theory by postulating that people choose to hold a constant fraction $(1/V^*)$ of their nominal income (PQ) in the form of money (M):

$$M = \frac{PQ}{V^*} \qquad (15.2)$$

As written, (15.2) appears merely to be a transformation of (15.1) that divides both sides of the earlier equation by V. The definition becomes a theory when we assume that the fraction of income that people desire to hold in the form of money $(1/V^*)$ is a constant. Starting from an initial situation in which the money supply is M_0, the price level is P_0, output is Q_0, and velocity is at the desired level, any increase in the money supply will raise nominal GNP (PQ). Why? The initial supply of money was the desired fraction $(1/V^*)$ of income, so that any additional money will be considered excess by households and firms and will be spent. Nominal GNP (PQ) will rise until the new higher money supply (M_1) is the desired fraction $(1/V^*)$ of the new higher level of spending.

In its original pre-Keynesian version, prices were generally assumed to be relatively or completely flexible, so that almost all the adjustment of nominal income (PQ) would take the form of price changes and almost none the form of quantity changes.[7] We can distinguish two versions of the quantity theory. The weak version states that, because the desired fraction of income held in the form of money $(1/V^*)$ is constant, a change in the money supply causes a proportional change in nominal GNP in the same direction. The strong version adds the assumption that all or almost all the adjustment of nominal GNP takes the form of changing prices and none or almost none the form of changing output.

---

[6] In this discussion we limit our attention to the income version of the quantity theory and ignore for lack of space the transactions version, which replaces Q in equation (15.1) by the total of transactions in the economy, including not only current goods and services, but also transactions in capital assets and intermediate goods. In that version velocity (V) is interpreted as the current value of annual transactions divided by the money supply, or the total turnover of money per year. A more complete discussion of the quantity theory, and a summary of the limitations of the transaction version, are contained in Milton Friedman, "A Theoretical Framework for Monetary Analysis," *Journal of Political Economy*, vol. 78 (March/April 1970), pp. 193–238, reprinted in Robert J. Gordon (ed.), *Milton Friedman's Monetary Framework* (Chicago: University of Chicago Press, 1974), pp. 1–62. See also Milton Friedman, "Money: Quantity Theory," in *International Encyclopedia of the Social Sciences* (New York: Macmillan, 1968).

[7] Milton Friedman has debated Don Patinkin (of the Hebrew University in Jerusalem) on the degree to which the pre-Keynesian quantity theorists allowed real output to vary in the short run. No one appears to dispute the interpretation that in both the earlier and present-day versions of the quantity theory, money is neutral in the long run — that is, money affects only nominal variables (nominal income and the price level) but not real variables. For the debate, see Gordon (ed.), *op. cit.*, pp. 114–118 and 158–162.

DETERMINANTS OF DESIRED MONEY HOLDINGS

The earlier quantity theorists did not believe that the fraction $1/V^*$ was rigidly fixed forever. They discussed a wide variety of factors that could alter $1/V^*$. Some writers emphasized that the amount of money needed for conducting transactions would change as the technology of transactions changed. In the modern era the credit card has reduced the need for money, because households can better synchronize their receipts and payments by making all their credit card payments on payday. In the pre-Keynesian era, quantity theorists discussed other changes in payments practices, the financial and economic arrangements for effecting transactions, and the speed of communication and transportation (payments are made faster by railroad than by stagecoach).

In addition to these mechanical aspects of the technology of transactions, other writers placed emphasis on important economic determinants of $1/V^*$. Money was one of many assets, and the willingness of people to hold money depended on its costs and returns as compared to those on other assets. One of the main costs of holding money is the interest that is lost by not investing the same funds in a bond or savings account. Although the dependence of the demand for money on the interest rate was implicit in the pre-Keynesian quantity theory, the meaning of this assumption was neither fully appreciated nor incorporated into formal analysis.[8]

15-4 THE KEYNESIAN TRANSACTION AND SPECULATIVE MOTIVES

Keynes in the *General Theory* divided the demand for money into two compartments. The first portion of money was held to satisfy the "transactions motive," the need to hold cash to "bridge the interval between the receipt of income and its disbursement."[9] Individuals with high incomes would need more money for this bridging than people with low incomes, and so the total demand for money for transactions purposes depended on total nominal GNP (PQ) and was written $L_1(PQ)$.

The second portion of money was held to satisfy the "speculative motive," based on the assumed role of individuals as speculators who were continually trying to make themselves richer by switching their asset holdings back and forth between money and bonds. Imagine a bond that promises to pay the holder $1 per year forever. An individual would be willing to pay a price of $1/r$ dollars for that bond. For instance, when the interest rate is 5

---

[8] Alfred Marshall and A. C. Pigou of Cambridge University were two pre-Keynesian economists who recognized that individuals kept a fraction of their total assets in the form of money, and that the attractiveness of money for asset-holding would depend on its return compared to that of other assets.

[9] Keynes, *General Theory*, pp. 195 and 199. The first portion, labeled M_1 by Keynes, also included the "precautionary motive," the need to have ready cash available for emergencies.

General Functional Forms

To simplify our exposition, we have so far used only "specific linear" forms for the behavioral equations. For instance, the demand for money in the Appendix for Chapter 5 was written as:

$$\left(\frac{M}{P}\right)^d = eQ - fr$$

This equation can be stated as: The real demand for money $(M/P)^d$ is equal to a positive number (e) times real GNP (Q) minus another number (f) times the interest rate (r). The equation tells us the specific way in which the real demand for money depends on real GNP and the interest rate.

But often in economics we are interested only in the general fact that one economic variable, say real money demand, depends on other variables, in this case real GNP and the interest rate. This general fact can be written:

$$\left(\frac{M}{P}\right)^d = L(Q, r)$$

This equation can be put into words: the real demand for money $(M/P)^d$ depends on real GNP (Q) and the interest rate (r). The capital letter L and the parentheses represent the words *depend on*, and any alphabetical letter can be used.

Why is it interesting to know simply that one variable depends on others? Figure 15-1 provides a clear example. The consequences of a shift in the *IS* curve differ depending on whether the real demand for money depends both on real GNP and on the interest rate, as assumed along the positively sloped curve LM_0 in Figure 15-1, or whether

$$\left(\frac{M}{P}\right)^d = L(Q)$$

which states that real money depends only on real GNP (Q) and not on the interest rate, as assumed along the vertical LM curve labeled LM_1.

Without further information one cannot look at these general functional forms and learn whether the assumed relationship is positive or negative. The positive relationship between real money demand and real GNP and the negative relationship with the interest rate can be written in either of two ways:

Method 1:

$$\left(\frac{M}{P}\right)^d = L(Q, \; r)$$
$$\phantom{\left(\frac{M}{P}\right)^d = L(}(+)(-)$$

Method 2:

$$\left(\frac{M}{P}\right)^d = L(Q, r); \quad L_Q > 0, L_r < 0$$

The terms to the right of the semicolon in method 2 can be put into these words: the response of the real demand for money to a change in real GNP (L_Q) is positive (> 0), holding the interest rate constant. The response of the real demand for money to a change in the interest rate (L_r) is negative (< 0), holding real GNP constant.

---

percent or 0.05, the price of the bond would be $20. Why? Simply because the interest rate (0.05) is the ratio of the return on an investment ($1) to its price ($20).[10]

If the normal interest rate is 5 percent or 0.05, then the normal bond price is $20. What would happen to the willingness of speculators to hold bonds if the actual interest rate were to drop to 0.04 and the bond price were to rise to $25? Some investors might feel that a $25 bond price was too far above

---

[10] The simple inverse relationship between the bond price and the interest rate is strictly valid only for a perpetuity, a bond that pays interest forever but that never pays off its principal. For bonds with finite maturities, say thirty years or less, the relationship between bond prices and the interest rate is slightly more complicated.

normal and that bond prices were likely to fall in the future. To avoid the risk of capital loss, the speculators might sell their bonds and hold money instead. Thus when the interest rate is low and bond prices high, the speculative demand for money tends to be large. Conversely, consider a high interest rate of 0.10 and a correspondingly low bond price of $10. Now many speculators will be eager to hold bonds instead of money, because they will believe that there is a good chance of a capital gain when bond prices go up. Thus when the interest rate is high and bond prices low, the demand for money is small.

The behavior of speculators as outlined here is the only reason put forth by Keynes to explain the sensitivity of the demand for money to the interest rate. The portion of money demand held to satisfy the speculative motive was called $L_2(r)$. Thus the total demand for money (M) was the total of the transaction demand $L_1(PQ)$ and the speculative demand $L_2(r)$:[11]

$$M = L_1(PQ) + L_2(r) \tag{15.3}$$

Keynes' equation has been criticized on several grounds. First, it is artificial to split the demand for money into two parts. In reality, as will be seen in the next section, the transactions demand depends on both real GNP and the interest rate. Second, Keynes' version erroneously implies that when the price level (P) doubles but real output (Q) and the interest rate (r) remain unchanged, the demand for money goes up by less than the price level—this error occurs because Keynes remembers to include P only in the first portion of the demand for money $L_1(PQ)$ but not in the second speculative portion $L_2(r)$.

Finally, the speculative motive itself has been criticized. The main problem is with the basic idea that speculative money holding occurs only because some investors believe that the interest rate is below normal and bond prices are above normal. This idea, however, cannot explain why the demand for money remains high over an extended period of low interest rates, such as the 1930s. As time goes by, speculators should begin to revise downward their idea of the normal interest rate. Thus the deviation between the actual and normal interest rate should gradually disappear and speculative money holding should disappear as well.

15-5 THE INTEREST RESPONSIVENESS OF THE TRANSACTION DEMAND FOR MONEY

Since the publication of Keynes' *General Theory* almost fifty years ago, his speculative motive for money holding has drifted gradually out of favor. Why should a speculator hold money during those periods when he is trying to avoid a capital loss? Other assets, particularly savings deposits, are both

---

[11] This is exactly the equation Keynes used; *General Theory*, p. 199.

free from the risk of capital loss and pay interest as well, whereas money (currency and demand deposits) does not pay interest. Surely the main feature of money that explains its use in preference to savings accounts is its acceptance in transactions.

But the abandonment of the speculative motive does not mean that the demand for money is independent of the interest rate, nor that the LM curve is vertical. In the early 1950s both William J. Baumol of Princeton and New York University and James Tobin of Yale demonstrated that the transactions demand for money depends on the interest rate. Therefore, the LM curve is positively sloped even when there is no speculative demand.[12] The basic idea is that the funds people hold for transactions, to "bridge the interval between the receipt of income and its disbursement," can be placed either in $M1$ (currency and demand deposits, which pay no interest) or in savings deposits. The higher the interest rate, the more individuals will tend to shift their transactions balances into interest-bearing savings accounts.

Baumol analyzes the money-holding decision of a hypothetical individual who receives income at specified intervals but spends it gradually at a steady rate between paydays. An example is illustrated in the left frame of Figure 15-3, where the person is assumed to be paid $900 per month ($Q$) on the first of each month. How will the person decide whether to convert all of the paycheck into currency and demand deposits ($M1$), which bear no interest, or whether to deposit part of the paycheck in a savings deposit that pays a monthly interest rate r?

COSTS AND BENEFITS OF HOLDING MONEY

As in many problems in economics, the individual compares the costs and benefits of holding $M1$ instead of the savings deposit. The main cost of $M1$ is the interest rate on savings (r) lost when $M1$ is held instead of savings deposits. The main benefit of holding $M1$ is the avoidance of what Baumol calls the "broker's fee" of b dollars charged every time (T) cash is obtained either by cashing the original paycheck or by obtaining cash at the savings bank. The broker's fee in real life includes the time and transportation expense required to make an extra trip to the savings bank to obtain cash from a savings deposit.

The number of times the broker's fee is incurred is equal to the size of the paycheck (Q) divided by the average amount of cash (C) obtained on each trip. For instance, the left frame of Figure 15-3 involves no savings account; the paycheck of $900 ($Q$) is cashed at the beginning of the month ($C = 900$), and so the broker's fee is incurred only one time ($T = Q/C = 1.0$).

---

[12] William J. Baumol, "The Transactions Demand for Cash: An Inventory Theoretic Approach," *Quarterly Journal of Economics* (November 1952). James Tobin, "The Interest-Elasticity of the Transactions Demand for Cash," *Review of Economics and Statistics* (August 1956), pp. 241–247.

In the middle frame half the paycheck is cashed on the first of the month ($C = 450$), and the other half is deposited in a savings account. Interest is lost by holding cash in an amount equal to the interest rate times the value of the average amount held in cash, which is half the value of the cash withdrawal ($rC/2$). Why? In the first half of the month the individual starts with $450 in cash and winds up with zero on the fifteenth of the month, so that his average holding is $225. Then he converts his savings deposit into cash, incurring a second broker's fee. His $450 of cash dwindles again to zero on the last day of the month, so that his average cash holding during the last half of the month is again $225. Total interest lost is the interest rate times $C/2$, or $225 in this example.[13]

In the right frame only one-third of the paycheck is initially cashed ($C = 300$), while the other two-thirds is deposited in saving. On the tenth and on the twentieth again withdrawals are made, so that the broker's fee is incurred three times ($T = Q/C = 900/300 = 3$). The interest rate lost by holding cash is once again $rC/2$.

HOW MANY TRIPS TO THE BANK?

How should the individual behave—as in the left frame, the middle frame, or the right frame, or should even more trips be made to the bank? The answer is that the combined cost of broker's fees (bT) and interest lost ($rC/2$) should be minimized:

$$\text{cost} = bT + \frac{rC}{2}, \quad \text{or}$$

$$= b\frac{Q}{C} + \frac{rC}{2} \qquad (15.4)$$

It can be shown that the average value of the cash withdrawal (C) that minimizes cost is:[14]

_____

[13] What is the area of the gray triangle in the left frame? The formula for the area of a triangle is one-half times the height times the length, or $1/2(900)(1)$, where the length is expressed in months. This equals 450. In the middle frame there are two gray triangles, each with an area $1/2(450)(1/2)$, or $1/2(450)(1)$ for both triangles taken together. This equals 225. In the right frame are three triangles, each with an area $1/2(300)(1/3)$, or $1/2(300)(1)$ for the three triangles taken together. This equals 150.

[14] Here elementary calculus is required. Cost is minimized by changing C to make the derivative of cost with respect to C equal to zero:

$$\frac{\partial(\text{cost})}{\partial C} = \frac{-bQ}{C^2} + \frac{r}{2} = 0$$

When this is solved for C, we obtain the square-root expression shown as equation (15.5) in the text.

THE HOLDING OF CASH DEPENDS INVERSELY ON THE ATTRACTIVENESS OF HOLDING SAVINGS DEPOSITS

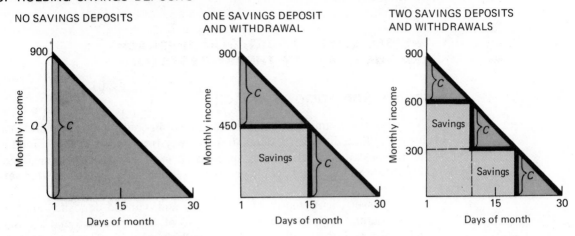

FIGURE 15-3

Alternative Allocations of an Individual's Monthly Paycheck between Cash and Savings Deposits

In the left frame the individual holds all his paycheck in the form of cash, indicated by the gray triangle, which shrinks as the paycheck is spent on consumption purchases. In the middle frame only half as much cash is held, because the individual finds it advantageous to hold half the paycheck in his savings deposit for half the month. In the right frame even less cash is held, because initially two-thirds of the paycheck is deposited into a savings account.

$$C = \sqrt{\frac{2bQ}{r}} \qquad (15.5)$$

This equation says in words that the average cash withdrawal is equal to the square root of the following: two times the broker's fee times income divided by the interest rate. A higher broker's fee (b) raises cash holdings by discouraging extra trips to the savings bank. But a higher interest rate (r) does just the opposite, reducing cash holdings as individuals shift more funds into savings deposits to earn the higher interest rate.

The Baumol (and Tobin) contributions are of major importance. They show that the interest sensitivity of the demand for money is based not on a flawed theory of speculation but on a transactions motive that is shared by almost everyone so long as money bears no interest and is the only asset that can be used for transactions. The theoretical underpinnings of the positively sloped *LM* curve are solid, implying that changes either in private spending desires or in fiscal policy will change both real output and the interest rate, at least in the short run.[15]

15-6 THE GENERALIZED PORTFOLIO APPROACH AND THE QUANTITY THEORY RESTATED

TOBIN'S PORTFOLIO APPROACH

At about the same time as the Baumol-Tobin contributions, several articles rehabilitated the asset demand for money from the criticisms aimed at the Keynesian analysis of the speculative motive.[16] In particular James Tobin showed that most people prefer to hold a balanced portfolio with several types of assets.

Some assets, particularly $M1$ (currency and demand deposits) and savings accounts, maintain the nominal value of their principal and are thus "safe" or "riskless."[17] Other assets, particularly stocks and long-term bonds, have a market value (principal) that varies in price every day, and these are called risky assets. If investors are averse to risk, which means that they do not like risk in the form of variations in asset prices, they will be unwilling to hold risky assets at all unless they are "bribed" by a higher average interest return on risky assets than on riskless assets. Otherwise, without this higher average return, why should they be willing to hold a risky asset at all and needlessly expose themselves to risk?

Faced with various safe and risky assets, with the former paying less interest than the latter, most investors make a compromise, diversifying their portfolios of assets. To choose a portfolio consisting only of risky assets

---

[15] The Baumol theory has the extra advantage of being specific, since the result in equation (15.5) provides a square-root hypothesis of money holding that can be tested against the data. Both the output elasticity and interest-rate elasticity of real money demand should be one-half. Why? Let us rewrite (15.5) in exponential form:

$$C = (2bQ)^{1/2}(r)^{-1/2}$$

Thus a one-percentage-point change in Q raises C by 1/2 percent. The most recent empirical tests for the United States have derived an income elasticity of about 0.56 and interest elasticity of -0.19. See Stephen M. Goldfeld, "The Case of the Missing Money," *Brookings Papers on Economic Activity,* vol. 7, no. 3 (1976), pp. 683–730. For more advanced treatments that allow the theoretical elasticities to differ from 1/2, see Edi Karni, "The Transactions Demand for Cash: Incorporation of the Value of Time into the Inventory Approach," *Journal of Political Economy,* vol. 81, no. 5 (September/October 1973), pp. 1216–1225; and Herschel I. Grossman and Andrew J. Policano, "Money Balances, Commodity Inventories, and Inflationary Expectations," *Journal of Political Economy,* vol. 83, no. 6 (December 1975), pp. 1093–1112.

[16] The most important of these articles was James Tobin, "Liquidity Preference as Behavior Towards Risk," *Review of Economic Studies,* vol. 25, no. 67 (1958).

[17] "Riskless" is placed in quotes because $M1$ is not free of risk when prices are flexible, since inflation causes a capital loss on holdings of $M1$. This is one of the costs of inflation emphasized in Chapter 11.

would yield a high average interest return but would expose investors to too much risk. To choose entirely safe assets would eliminate risk completely, but it would force an investor to settle for a low average return. A mixed diversified portfolio would usually be the best approach, and each person would choose a slightly different balance between risk and return.

Although the portfolio approach is very appealing as an explanation for diversifying individual portfolios, it does not explain why anyone is willing to hold $M1$ (currency and checking accounts). Investors can achieve the goal of safety by holding savings deposits, which share with $M1$ a fixed nominal principal, but which dominate $M1$ by paying interest while $M1$ pays no interest. The major contribution of the portfolio approach is to explain why most households desire a mixture of both safe time deposits and risks stocks and bonds rather than a portfolio consisting wholly of either one or the other.

FRIEDMAN'S RESTATEMENT OF THE QUANTITY THEORY

An interesting feature of the development of monetary theory in the 1950s was the simultaneous appearance of similar theories by James Tobin, a leading nonmonetarist, and Milton Friedman, the chief monetarist. Tobin's portfolio approach first introduced the role of risk aversion as an explanation for the willingness of investors to hold a portion of their portfolio in the form of safe assets. At about the same time Friedman proposed a general version of the older quantity theory, in which he treated money as one among several assets. According to Friedman's restatement of the quantity theory, the real demand for money can be written:[18]

$$\frac{M}{P} = L(Q,\, w,\, r_m,\, r_b,\, r_e,\, p) \tag{15.6}$$

Looking back at the box on page 449, we notice that our money-demand equation differs from Friedman's in several ways. The equations are similar in that ours also contains real GNP (Q) and the interest rate (r) as independent variables. The main differences are that:

1. Friedman's version splits the interest-rate variable into three parts. First is the interest rate paid on money (r_m), an increase in which naturally makes people *more* willing to hold money. The second interest-rate variable is r_b, the interest rate paid on bonds, which corresponds to the r variable that appears in our version (equation 15.4) of the demand for money function. An increase in r_b *reduces* the demand for money. The

---

[18] Friedman's approach is explained in more detail in his "The Quantity Theory of Money — a Restatement," in Friedman (ed.), *Studies in the Quantity Theory of Money* (Chicago: University of Chicago Press, 1956), pp. 3–21. A briefer version is contained in his "Theoretical Framework" in Robert J. Gordon (ed.), *Milton Friedman's Monetary Framework* (Chicago: University of Chicago Press, 1974), pp. 10–15.

third Friedman interest rate is the interest paid on equities (r_e). Although equities are more risky than money, the portfolio approach suggests that investors will strike a balance between risky and high-yielding equities versus safe and low-yielding savings deposits. Thus an increase in the yield on equities should *reduce* the demand for money.

2. Friedman views money as one way of holding wealth, including not only "nonhuman" financial wealth (bonds, stocks, money) but also "human capital" (the value of an individual's present and future earnings). He recognizes, however, that wealth held in nonhuman (financial) form is more likely to be held partially in the form of money (including savings deposits) than in human capital. Thus the fraction of nonhuman to human wealth (w) appears as an independent variable in the Friedman demand for money function.

3. Perhaps the most important difference between Friedman and Tobin is the former's emphasis on the substitution between money and commodities. When the rate of commodity inflation (p) is high, households will do well to "beat the higher prices" by purchasing goods sooner than usual (this is the "expectations effect" of Chapter 6). Because a reduction in holdings of money is one main way in which individuals can obtain the funds to purchase commodities early, a high rate of inflation (p) reduces the demand for money and appears in Friedman's demand for money function in equation (15.6).

IMPLICATIONS OF TOBIN AND FRIEDMAN APPROACH

Tobin's approach, reflected in many of the large-scale econometric models used for forecasting in the past decade, limits the effect of an increase in the money supply to those categories of spending that depend directly on reductions in the interest rate, particularly the amount of fixed investment and, perhaps, the amount of spending on consumer durables. In Friedman's approach any category of expenditures on GNP may be a substitute for money and may be stimulated by an expansion in the real money supply, even consumer nondurables and services.[19]

The portfolio approach pioneered by both Tobin and Friedman makes the demand for money a function of both income and wealth. The idea that the demand for money depends at least partly on wealth is not new. But the major implications of a wealth-dependent demand for money have been explored only in the past few years.

The major implication is for fiscal policy. An expansive fiscal policy tends to raise either the supply of money, the supply of government bonds, or both. In general, an increase in either asset raises the value of real wealth and raises the level of commodity demand through the real balance or Pigou

---

[19] In the spring of 1980 consumer spending on nondurables was cut back, partly as a result of high interest rates and partly as a result of Federal Reserve regulations intended to limit the growth of consumer credit.

effect, shifting the *IS* curve to the right.[20] But now we realize, from our study of the portfolio approach to the theory of money demand, that the demand for money depends on total wealth. Thus any stimulative fiscal policy by raising people's real wealth may raise the demand for money, shift the *LM* curve to the left, and cut back on the fiscal policy multipliers calculated in Chapters 4 and 5.[21]

15-7 CASE STUDY: THE 1974–79 MONEY DEMAND PUZZLE

The main conclusion of Figure 15-2 is that an unstable demand for money may shift the *LM* curve about unpredictably even if the real supply of money (*M/P*) is held constant. Until a few years ago most studies had found that the demand for money could be quite reliably predicted if one knew only (1) the value of real GNP, (2) the interest rate on Treasury bills, and (3) the interest rate on savings deposits.[22] But in the last few years the confidence of economists in the stability of the demand for money has collapsed. For the first time the hypothetical example depicted in the bottom of Figure 15-2 has become a reality:

> *If the demand for money is sufficiently unstable compared to the demand for commodities, a monetary policy that maintains a constant interest rate may do a better job of stabilizing real output than a policy that maintains a constant real money supply.*

The quantity theory of money in equation (15.2) was based on the idea that people want to hold a constant fraction (1/*V*) of their income in the form of money. The more modern theories all predict that the fraction 1/*V* will decline when there is an increase in the interest rate — the major cost of holding money. And indeed this has occurred during the postwar years, a time of rising interest rates (a graph illustrating the postwar increase in interest rates is presented in Figure 11-3). In the top frame of Figure 15-4, the downward-sloping line labeled 1/*V*1 plots the ratio of the money-supply concept *M*1 to nominal GNP (*PQ*) and confirms the downward drift of money holding relative to income.[23]

---

[20] The real wealth effect in the commodity market raises the effect on real output of either a decline in prices or a stimulative monetary policy measure. See section 6-6.

[21] A formal analysis of the wealth effect in the demand for money function is the subject of Alan S. Blinder and Robert M. Solow, "Analytical Foundations of Fiscal Policy," in *The Economics of Public Finance* (Washington, D.C.: Brookings Institution, 1974), pp. 45–57. See also Benjamin M. Friedman, "Crowding Out or Crowding In? Economic Consequences of Financing Government Deficits," *Brookings Papers on Economic Activity,* vol. 9, no. 3 (1978), pp. 593–641.

[22] Stephen M. Goldfeld, "The Demand for Money Revisited," *Brookings Papers on Economic Activity,* vol. 4, no. 3 (1973), pp. 577–638.

[23] Since *V*1 is defined as *PQ*/*M*1, it follows that 1/*V*1 = *M*1/*PQ*.

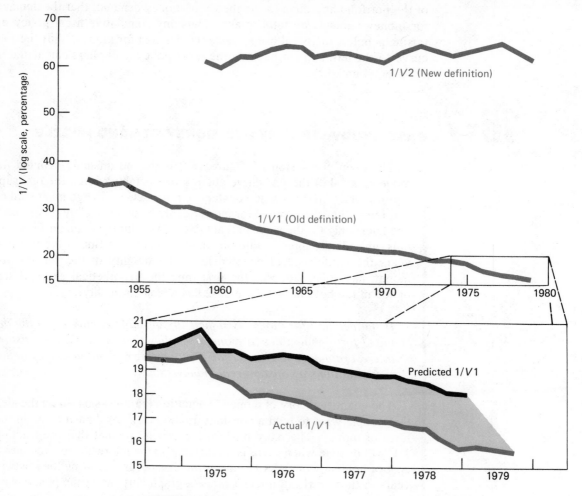

FIGURE 15–4

Actual Ratios of Money to Nominal GNP (1/*V*) for both *M*1 and *M*2, 1952–79, and Predicted Value for *M*1, 1974–79

Notice in the top frame that the demand for *M*2, as shown by 1/*V*2, was quite stable from 1959 to 1979. The demand for *M*1, as shown by 1/*V*1, exhibited an irregular decline throughout the postwar period. The bottom frame magnifies the 1974–79 experience for 1/*V*1. The sharp drop in the red line showing actual 1/*V*1 was not expected on the basis of historical behavior through the end of 1973, which would have led to the prediction that 1/*V*1 would have behaved like the solid black line.

Source: Actual 1/*V* from Appendix B. Predicted 1/*V*1 for 1974–79 from Richard D. Porter, Thomas D. Simpson, and Eileen Mauskopf, "Financial Innovation and the Monetary Aggregates," *Brookings Papers on Economic Activity,* vol. 10 no. 1, (1979), Table 1, p. 214.

The downward drift in $1/V1$ was not uniform each year. In years of rapidly rising interest rates, the decline in $1/V1$ was faster than normal, as in 1966. In recession years of falling interest rates, the decline in $1/V1$ appears to have been interrupted, as in 1954, 1958, and 1961. Indeed Stephen M. Goldfeld has succeeded in explaining almost all the movements in $M1$ and $1/V1$ during the 1952–73 period with an equation relating the real demand for $M1$ (currency and checking deposits) to real GNP, the interest rate paid on time deposits, the market interest rate on commercial paper, and last quarter's value of the real demand for $M1$.

How does the Goldfeld equation explain the postwar decline in $1/V1$? First, both interest rates (r_D and r_C) have increased through most of the postwar period, reducing the demand for money. Second, a 1 percent increase in output raises money demand in his equation by only about 0.5 percent in the long run, causing $M1/P$ to grow more slowly than Q.[24] In a recession in which interest rates and Q both decline temporarily, one would expect $1/V1$ to increase temporarily.

THE CASE OF THE MISSING MONEY

The bottom frame of Figure 15-4 is a blow-up of the top frame for the years 1974–79. Goldfeld's equation predicts a substantial increase in $1/V1$ in the worst part of the 1974–75 recession, resulting from the decline in interest rates and in Q. But the predicted behavior did not occur. During the recession $1/V1$ did not exhibit the predicted rise; then during the 1975–76 recovery $1/V1$ declined much faster than predicted. Overall, households and businesses were holding much less money than predicted in relation to their incomes and prevailing interest rates, an unpredicted shortfall of about \$30 billion in mid-1976 and \$55 billion in early 1979.[25]

Some of the shortfall can be explained by changes in banking rules that allow individuals in some states to pay for transactions with checks written on their savings accounts. And another component can be explained by the November 1978 introduction of "ATS" (automatic transfer savings) accounts that allow automatic shifting of funds from time deposits to demand deposits, thus allowing individuals to maintain their checking account balances closer to zero. Other innovations in financial markets in the late 1970s include security repurchase agreements (RPs) that provide

---

[24] When M/P grows more slowly than Q, then there is a decline in three ratios, which are equal by definition:

$$\frac{M1/P}{Q} \equiv \frac{M1}{PQ} = \frac{1}{V1}$$

[25] Goldfeld's equation is statistically estimated for the period 1952–73, and so the numerical estimates of the elasticities in his equation do not "use" any information about what happened in 1974–79. The 1974–79 predictions in Figure 15-4 are called out-of-sample or past-sample forecasts.

an opportunity for corporations to invest short-term funds in interest-earning assets, and money-market mutual funds that provide private households as well as corporations a new asset that offers high interest and at the same time allows check-writing privileges.[26] The appeal of money-market mutual funds in 1978–80 was evident in the rapid growth of these deposits from $8 billion in September 1978 to $60 billion in March 1980.

Authors differ in their explanation of the money demand puzzle. It seems clear that monetary innovations, including checkable savings deposits, RPs, and money-market mutual funds accounted for a large shift of funds away from traditional checking and time deposits. Yet the most important period of growth of these innovations occurred during 1978–80, whereas most of the $M1$ demand puzzle in Figure 15-4 emerged earlier, in 1975–76. Thus there is a portion of the puzzle that is not easy to answer and may involve the increased efficiency of corporate treasurers in managing their cash deposits.[27]

NEW MONEY DEFINITIONS AND THE APPARENT STABILITY OF $M2$ VELOCITY

In reaction to the many financial market innovations of the late 1970s, in January 1980 the Federal Reserve introduced new definitions of the money supply. Under the old definitions prevailing previously, $M1$ included currency and demand deposits, and $M2$ included $M1$ plus time deposits. Now there are a number of definitions of the money supply. The two most important, for which 1959–80 data are provided in Appendix B, are:

$M1B$. Demand deposits (excluding those of foreign and official institutions), plus currency in circulation, plus other checkable deposits at banks and thrift institutions (NOW accounts), Automatic Transfer Services (ATS) savings accounts, credit union share drafts, and demand deposits at mutual savings banks.

$M2$. Everything in $M1B$, plus most kinds of savings deposits at commercial banks and thrift institutions, money-market mutual funds, overnight repurchase agreements, and Eurodollars.

The shift from the old $M1$ (shown in Figure 15-4) to the new $M1B$ does not solve the money-demand puzzle. For instance, the new defini-

---

[26] RPs come into existence when a Treasury bill or other security is sold from a bank's portfolio to an investor—say a corporation that is looking for a high-yielding alternative to demand deposits—and then is repurchased by the bank a few days later at a lower prespecified price.

[27] Improved cash management procedures are emphasized by Porter, Simpson, and Mauskopf in the source listed in Figure 15-4. Another recent study of the demand for money is R. W. Hafer and Scott E. Hein, "Evidence on the Temporal Stability of the Demand for Money Relationship in the United States," *Federal Reserve Bank of St. Louis Review*, vol. 61 (December 1979), pp. 3–14.

tion of $1/V1$ declines between 1974:Q3 and 1979:Q4 by 17 percent compared to 20 percent for the old definition, both much more than the decline of 9 percent predicted on the basis of pre-1973 relationships. On the other hand, the velocity of the new $M2$ definition appears to be quite stable, remaining within the range for $1/V2$ of 0.60 to 0.65 for the entire two-decade period 1959–79. This suggests that much of the $M1$ demand-for-money puzzle can be explained by a movement from types of money included in $M1B$ to other types that are part of $M2$ but not part of $M1B$, especially, in recent years, money-market mutual funds.

15-8 CONCLUSION: VERDICT ON MONETARY POLICY INSTRUMENTS

A basic theme of this chapter has been that the monetarist prescription of a **constant-growth-rate rule** (CGRR) for the money supply is generally not the optimal approach to monetary policy. If the demand for money is stable and predictable but the demand for commodities is unstable, as in the top frame of Figure 15-2, then a countercyclical money-supply policy will achieve greater stability of real output than will a CGRR policy. On the other hand, if the demand for commodities is stable and the demand for money is unstable, then a constant-interest-rate policy will outperform the CGRR policy.

No clear verdict emerges from our study of the theory and evidence. The flexible accelerator theory of investment almost guarantees that the demand for investment commodities will frequently drift away from its average level (or share in GNP). In this chapter we have demonstrated that the demand for $M1$ dropped drastically during 1974–79 compared to predictions. Because the demand for both commodities and money appears to be less than perfectly predictable, it seems the Fed should adhere rigidly neither to a simple CGRR formula for $M1$ nor to a constant-interest-rate policy.

The stability of $M2$ velocity over the long 1959–79 period suggests that a monetary rule for $M2$ would be more efficient than for $M1$. But nevertheless there have been substantial swings in $1/V2$; for example, from 0.652 in 1977 to 0.619 in 1979. If monetary policy had been predicated on the assumption that $1/V2$ would remain at 0.652 over the 1977–79 period, then far too much nominal GNP growth would have been permitted. Stability in velocity during 1977–79 would have implied a 1979 nominal GNP of $2250 billion, fully 5 percent less than the $2369 billion that actually occurred. One interpretation of the policy debacle of 1978–80 is that despite relatively stable growth in $M2$, short-run movements in the velocity of $M2$ allowed nominal GNP growth that was too rapid in 1978–79 and then too slow in 1980.

There is no question that these large movements in velocity pose problems for monetarist advocates of constant-growth-rate rules and for monetarist economists attempting to forecast the future behavior of the economy. The drop in $1/V2$ in 1979 made life particularly hard for monetarist forecasters. As *Business Week* reported:

> In 1979 forecasting has become a guessing game for monetarists. . . . Of the four monetarists who have been forecasting brothers under the skin for years, . . . now Jordan predicts continued economic advance, Meltzer a mild slowdown, Heinemann a moderately severe slowdown, and Sprinkel that the U. S. is on the verge of a disastrous recession.[28]

SUMMARY

1. The smaller the interest responsiveness of the demand for money, the less real output varies in the short run in response to changes in fiscal policy and in business and consumer confidence. A zero interest response not only destroys the effectiveness of fiscal policy but also eliminates its rationale by insulating real output from variations in private spending decisions.

2. When the demand for money is stable and predictable, a monetary policy that maintains a constant money supply is preferable to one that stabilizes the interest rate. But an even better alternative is a countercyclical monetary policy, which reduces the money supply when the demand for commodities is high, and vice versa.

3. When the demand for money shifts about in an unpredictable and random fashion, but the demand for commodities is stable, a policy of maintaining a stable interest rate is preferable to maintaining a constant money supply.

4. Several theories have been developed to explain the relation between the demand for money, income, wealth, and the interest rate. The demand for money for transaction purposes depends on the interest rate, because people will take the trouble to make extra trips to the bank and keep more of their income in savings accounts (and other interest-earning assets) when the interest rate is high.

5. The portfolio approach emphasizes the household decision to allocate its wealth among money, savings accounts, bonds, and other assets. Any event that raises wealth, such as a stimulative fiscal policy, will tend to raise the demand for money. This theory suggests that fiscal policy multipliers may be smaller than in the simple theory of Chapter 5, in which the demand for money depends only on income, not on wealth.

6. In 1974–79 the demand for money declined mysteriously compared to the predictions of most economists. As a result, the actual rate of growth in demand deposits and currency ($M1$) allowed by the Federal Re-

---

[28] "Why the Forecasters Are Off Course in Plotting Monetary Policy," *Business Week* (May 7, 1979), p. 130.

serve was adequate to finance a much faster growth rate of aggregate demand than had been expected.

A LOOK AHEAD

The demands for consumer durables, investment goods, and money ($M1$) exhibit fluctuations and appear to call for an activist government stabilization policy. But the need for an activist policy approach does not guarantee that activism is desirable. On the contrary, the lags between policy actions and the economy's response may be so long and variable that countercyclical policy turns out to make fluctuations worse. Further, the response of the economy to given policy changes may be highly uncertain. In the next part of the book we will form a judgment on plank 3 of the monetarist platform, the claim that an activist countercyclical government policy may do more harm than good.

CONCEPTS

Constant-money-supply policy versus countercyclical monetary policy
Quantity theory of money
Transaction motive

Speculative motive
Portfolio approach
Velocity of money
$M1$ versus $M2$

QUESTIONS FOR REVIEW

1 What does the interest responsiveness of the demand for money have to do with the potency of fiscal policy? With the effect on real output of change in business and consumer confidence?

2 When the demand for commodities (*IS* curve) fluctuates widely but the demand for money is stable, explain why it is undesirable for the Federal Reserve to try to maintain a fixed interest rate.

3 The quantity equation is true by definition. Why?

4 What assumptions convert the quantity equation into the quantity theory?

5 Why did the quantity theorists pay little or no attention to fiscal policy?

6 If people believe that the interest rate is unusually low, will their demand for money be high or low according to the Keynesian theory of the speculative motive?

7   Relate your answer to question 6 to the concept of the liquidity trap (review section 5-3).

8   If banks were to charge a fixed fee for withdrawals from savings accounts, would this increase or decrease the demand for $M1$ (currency and demand deposits)? Explain.

9   Can you explain in words why people diversify their portfolios by holding a mixture of safe and risky assets?

10 Do you regard the portfolio approach as a convincing explanation of the demand for $M1$?

11 Explain what would have happened to nominal GNP if $V1$ in Figure 15-4 had behaved as predicted in early 1979? How would this difference in the behavior of nominal GNP have been divided between real GNP and the price level?

Part V

The Control of
Aggregate Demand

16 Federal Reserve Monetary Control and Its Limitations

There is a strong presumption . . .
discretionary actions will in general be
subject to longer lags than the automatic
reactions and hence be destabilizing even
more frequently.

—Milton Friedman[1]

16-1 INTRODUCTION

The last three chapters have developed a persuasive case against the proposition that precise control over the money supply guarantees precise control of aggregate demand. The money supply can be completely fixed, and yet aggregate demand can vary whenever anything occurs—whether an economic or political event—to change households' estimates of their permanent income and thus their consumption. Changes in investment tax incentives or business firms' expectations about the future course of output or the price of oil can alter business investment. The *IS* curve can also be shifted by changes in government spending or tax rates. Changes in consumption, investment spending, and fiscal policy alter the *IS* curve when the money supply is constant. In addition, changes in the amount of money demanded at a given level of real GNP and the interest rate can shift the *LM* curve even though the money supply is fixed.

Thus the achievement of stable growth in aggregate demand (nominal GNP) appears to require an activist countercyclical monetary policy. When either rightward shifts in the *IS* curve due to higher commodity demand or rightward shifts in the *LM* curve due to a drop in the demand for money threaten to push aggregate demand higher than desired, there is a case for a reduction in the money supply to shift the *LM* curve back to the left by the desired amount. But this recommendation brings us up against plank 3 of the monetarist platform in Chapter 12: an activist monetary policy may do more harm than good. Why? The effects of a change in the money supply on

---

[1] *Essays in Positive Economics* (Chicago: University of Chicago Press, 1953), pp. 44–45.

467

aggregate demand do not occur immediately. Economists cannot perfectly forecast future events in the economy, so that a reduction in the money supply today to cut aggregate demand because of excessive current spending might have its major restraining effects next year, by which time conditions might have changed and spending might be weak.

Until now we have assumed that the money supply can be set at any desired value. We examine in this chapter the methods by which the Fed controls the money supply. How quickly can the Fed change the money supply? How long does it take for changes in the money supply to alter spending? Finally, what are the disadvantages of an activist countercyclical monetary policy?

16-2 PRINCIPLES FOR CREATING MONEY ON A DESERT ISLAND

Readers may recall from a course in the principles of economics that the banking system can create money and that Federal Reserve actions have a multiplier effect on the total supply of money. The basic ideas of bank money creation can be illustrated here for a hypothetical community of unlucky individuals stranded on a desert island. Although many individuals are stranded, only five take part directly in our drama: the Miser, the Banker, Horace, the Used Raft Dealer, and the Economist.

Initially, the supply of money on the island is 100 gold coins held by the Miser. The Miser is afraid that someone might steal his coins and persuades the strongest man on the island to guard his coins in return for a receipt (IOU) entitling the Miser to have the coins back when desired. Starting from nothing, the strongest man has become the Banker. The balance sheet of his First Desert Island Bank can be written down in the form of a "T account," which lists assets on the left side and liabilities on the right side.

FIRST DESERT ISLAND BANK (FDIB): STAGE 1

Assets		Liabilities	
Gold coins	100	IOU to Miser	100
Total assets	100	Total liabilities	100

At first the Banker simply is doing the Miser a favor. He cannot really be said to have entered the banking business, because he has no income. He cannot spend the gold coins, because the Miser might come in at any time and claim the coins. After months of careful observation, however, the Banker concludes that the Miser never draws out more than 20 percent of the coins at any one time. The Banker separates the gold coins into two piles. The first pile contains the 20 coins needed for the Miser's withdrawals and is labeled by the Banker "required reserves." The second pile contains the unneeded coins and is labeled "excess reserves." It suddenly occurs to the Banker that he can use the unneeded excess coins to make a loan to someone, can charge interest on the loan, and thus indirectly can earn money from the coins deposited by the Miser. No longer is the Banker doing the Miser a favor; now the Miser is doing a favor for the Banker so long as the Banker fails to pay interest on the Miser's deposit.

Now the Banker's balance sheet can be written:

FDIB: STAGE 2

Assets		Liabilities	
Gold coins:		Deposit owed to Miser	100
Required reserves	20		
Excess reserves	80		
Total assets	100	Total liabilities	100

After questioning the other people on the island, the Banker finds that Horace is eager to borrow 80 gold coins to make a purchase from the Used Raft Dealer. When the loan is made, the Banker has succeeded in converting his unneeded excess reserve of 80 gold coins into an interest-paying loan — that is, a piece of paper stating that Horace owes the Banker 80 gold coins plus future interest payments.

FDIB: STAGE 3

Assets		Liabilities	
Gold coins:		Deposit owed to Miser	100
Required reserves	20		
Loan owed by Horace	80		
Total assets	100	Total liabilities	100

After the Used Raft Dealer (URD) has sold the island's only raft to Horace, he faces the same problem as the Miser. He needs a secure place to keep his 80 gold coins and brings them to the Banker. But now the Banker, much to his surprise, finds that his loan to Horace has not succeeded in getting rid of all his excess reserves! If the Banker sets aside 20 percent of the URD's 80-coin deposit, or 16 coins, as a reserve against withdrawals, his balance sheet now looks like this:

FDIB: STAGE 4

Assets		Liabilities	
Gold coins:		Deposit owed to Miser	100
Required reserves	36	Deposit owed to URD	80
(20% of deposits)			
Excess reserves	64		
Loan owed by Horace	80		
Total assets	180	Total liabilities	180

The Banker has failed in his effort to get rid of all his excess reserves. At stage 3 the Banker converted 80 of his excess reserves into a loan, but yet the 80 coins came right back. The crucial move was the decision of the URD to redeposit his 80 gold coins in the bank. After 16 of the 80 coins (20 percent) are set aside as required reserves, 64 remain.

Just as the Banker is scratching his head, wondering how to get rid of his 64 excess coins, along comes the clever Economist. "I can solve your problem," the Economist asserts confidently. "If you give me a loan of 320, I guarantee that your problem of excess reserves will disappear." "But," asks the astonished Banker, "how can I give you a loan of 320 when I only have 64 excess coins?" "Just trust me," answers the Economist.

And so the Banker follows the Economist's instructions. The Economist is given a loan of 320, which appears on the Banker's balance sheet as an asset. Because the Banker does not have enough excess reserves to give gold coins to the Economist as the proceeds of the loan, instead the Economist is given a deposit of 320:

FDIB: STAGE 5

Assets		Liabilities	
Gold coins:		Deposit owned to Miser	100
Required reserves	100	Deposit owed to URD	80
(20% of deposits)		Deposit owed to Economist	320
Loan owed by Horace	80		
Loan owed by Economist	320		
Total assets	500	Total liabilities	500

The gold coins remain in the bank. Whereas previously only 36 coins were needed as required reserves to support the 180 of deposits at stage 4, now all 100 coins are needed to back up the 500 of deposits.

REQUIRED CONDITIONS

The money supply is conventionally defined as cash held outside banks plus demand deposits (checking accounts). Initially, the island's money supply consisted only of the 100 gold coins originally held by the Miser. But now the money supply has expanded to 500, all in the form of bank deposits. The Desert Island Bank has succeeded in creating $5 of money for every $1 of cash that it initially received. Five conditions were necessary for this to occur.

1. Paper receipts claiming ownership of bank deposits must be accepted as a means of payment on a one-for-one basis—that is, a deposit representing a claim to one gold coin is accepted by sellers as equivalent to payment of one gold coin. Because people almost always want to spend an amount smaller than the total of their deposit, they must be able to spend

a portion of their deposit by writing a check or withdrawing a part of their deposit in the form of cash (gold coins in the example).

2. Any seller who receives a cash payment from the proceeds of a loan must redeposit the cash into his own account at the same bank. Thus the Used Raft Dealer redeposited 80 gold coins in stage 4 above.

3. When sellers receive payment in the form of checks written on bank accounts, they must redeposit the check in their own bank account in the same bank. Although the Economist may write checks on his account of 320 held at stage 5 of the above example, the bank's deposits will not change if each recipient of a check from the Economist brings the check back to the bank and starts his own account.

4. The Bank must hold some fraction of its reserves in the form of cash (20 percent in gold coins in this example).

5. Someone must be willing to borrow from the bank at an interest rate that at least covers the bank's cost of operation. If the bank could find no appropriate lending opportunities at either stage 3 or stage 5 — that is, if neither Horace nor the Economist had been willing to borrow — the bank could not have created money.

THE MONEY-CREATION MULTIPLIER

If all five conditions are met, then the entire process of money creation can be summed up in a simple equation. We let the symbol H denote **high-powered money** — that is, the quantity of the type of money that is held by banks as reserves. In the example, H consists of the 100 gold coins, which are "high-powered" because they generate the multiplier expansion of money by the First Desert Island Bank. The symbol D represents the total of bank deposits. The symbol e represents the fraction of deposits that banks decide to hold as reserves. The demand for high-powered money to be held as reserves (eD) is then equal to the supply of high-powered money (H):

GENERAL FORM	NUMERICAL EXAMPLE	
$eD = H$	$0.2(500) = 100$	(16.1)

The same equation can be rearranged (dividing both sides by e) to determine the size of the stock of deposits (D) relative to the quantity of high-powered money (H) and the bank reserve-holding ratio (e):

GENERAL FORM	NUMERICAL EXAMPLE	
$D = \dfrac{H}{e}$	$500 = \dfrac{100}{0.2}$	(16.2)

The money-creation multiplier is $1/e$, or $1/0.2 = 5.0$ in the numerical example. This is the second usage of the word *multiplier* in this book. In Chapters 3–6 we examined the factors determining the income-determination multiplier. In its simplest version, that multiplier in Chapter 3 was written:

$$\frac{\text{income-determination}}{\text{multiplier}} = \frac{\text{autonomous planned spending } (A_p)}{\text{marginal propensity to save } (s)}$$

An increase in autonomous planned spending (A_p) is multiplied in Chapter 3 because spending creates income, a fraction of which *leaks out* into saving and taxes and the remainder of which goes into additional spending. The multiplier process ends only when the total of extra induced leakages has become equal to the original increase in A_p.

The intuitive reasoning behind the money-creation multiplier is the same. An increase in high-powered money (H) is multiplied here because the initial deposit of H becomes reserves of the bank, a fraction of which *leaks out* into required reserves and the remainder of which is lent out and comes back as additional deposits of the stores and business firms that receive the loan proceeds. The money-creation multiplier process terminates only when the total of extra induced leakages into required reserves has used up the original increase in H.

Now it is time to recognize that some of the five conditions describing money creation on the desert island may not be accurate descriptions of the real world.

Condition (2) required that any seller receiving a cash payment from the proceeds of a loan must redeposit the cash into the bank, as did the Used Raft Dealer at stage 4. If the cash does not come back to the bank, the multiplier process of money creation cannot occur at that bank. If the cash is redeposited at another bank, then the second bank will find itself with excess reserves, allowing the multiplier process to proceed.

Conditions (2) and (3) can be revised to apply to any group of banks, say all the banks within the United States. As long as sellers receiving loan proceeds in the form of either cash or checks redeposit the funds in a U.S. bank, then the money-creation multiplier in equation (16.2) remains valid for the U.S. banking system as a whole.

CASH HOLDING

The money-creation multiplier is changed, however, if everyone wants to hold not only demand (checking) deposits at banks but some pocket cash as well. Imagine that everyone wants to hold a fixed fraction (c) of his deposits, say 5 percent, in the form of cash.[2] Then this source of cash holding adds an extra amount (cD) to the total demand for high-powered money. In a revised desert-island example, the demand for gold coins, the only form of high-powered money, might be 20 percent of deposits for bank reserves

---

[2] The cash fraction c has nothing whatsoever to do with the marginal propensity to consume (c) of Chapter 3. At this stage we have run through the alphabet once and are requiring some letters to perform double duty.

$(eD = 0.2D)$, and in addition 5 percent of deposits for pocket cash $(cD = 0.05D)$.

The total demand for high-powered money $(eD + cD)$ can be equated to the total supply (H):

GENERAL FORM		NUMERICAL EXAMPLE		
Demand	*Supply*	*Demand*	*Supply*	
$eD + cD$	$= H$	$0.2D + 0.05D = 100$		(16.3)
or $(e + c)D = H$		or	$0.25D = 100$	

Dividing both sides by $(e + c)$, we can solve for deposits:

$$D = \frac{H}{e + c} \qquad D = \frac{100}{0.25} = 400 \qquad (16.4)$$

In words, the total of deposits is equal to the supply of high-powered money (H) divided by the fraction of deposits that leaks into reserves (e) plus the fraction that leaks into pocket cash (c).

Although specialized courses in monetary economics develop complicated formulas that relate the U.S. money supply to high-powered money and numerous other factors, for our purposes equation (16.4) is an entirely adequate explanation.[3] We can modify (16.4) slightly by recognizing that the total money supply (M) includes not only deposits (D) but also cash (including currency and coins) held in an amount equal to the cash-holding ratio times deposits (cD):

$$M = D + cD = (1 + c)D \qquad (16.5)$$

Substituting for D in (16.5) from (16.4), we obtain:

$$M = (1 + c)D = \frac{(1 + c)H}{e + c} \qquad (16.6)$$

GOLD DISCOVERIES AND BANK PANICS

The supply of money depends only on the three terms that appear here in (16.6): the supply of high-powered money (H), the cash-holding ratio (c), and the ratio of deposits that the banks hold in the form of reserves (e). In an economy in which all high-powered money (H) consists of gold, then the rate of increase in the total supply of money may depend on the economics of gold mining. Because in the long run a sustained acceleration in monetary growth causes an acceleration in inflation, some historical episodes of inflation have been caused by gold discoveries. The inflow of gold into Spain following the discovery of America caused prices to double in the sixteenth century. More moderate price increases followed the gold discoveries in California in 1848 and Alaska in 1898.

---

[3] Students interested in a more detailed treatment of the money-supply process should consult Albert E. Burger, *The Money Supply Process* (Belmont, Calif.: Wadsworth, 1971).

Before the establishment of the Federal Reserve in 1914, the U.S. economy was at the mercy of capricious changes in the money supply stemming not only from the influence of gold discoveries on the growth of H, but also from episodes in which the cash-holding ratio (c) and the reserve ratio (e) fluctuated dramatically. During banking panics, which occurred about once a decade and culminated in the serious panic of 1907, depositors began to fear for the safety of their deposits and began withdrawing their deposits, converting them into cash. This raised the cash-holding ratio (c) and cut the money supply. To deal with the tide of withdrawals, banks in turn began to try to bolster their reserves, raising the reserve ratio (e) and further cutting the money supply.[4] In the pre-Federal Reserve era, there was no way for the government to raise H to offset panic-induced increases in c and e. Panics caused a drop in the money supply and in aggregate demand, cutting both output and prices.

16-3 DETERMINANTS OF THE MONEY SUPPLY IN THE UNITED STATES

The Federal Reserve System (the "Fed") was established in late 1913 upon the recommendation of a commission set up to study the causes of the 1907 banking panic and to recommend solutions to prevent future panics.[5] Banks now were to hold most of their reserves in the form of deposits at the Fed. High-powered money now consisted of two major portions: (1) cash as before and (2) bank deposits at the Fed.

The exact details of monetary control by the Fed have changed in minor ways since 1913, but the basic structure has remained intact and is illustrated in Table 16-1. The table is a simplified representation of the elements of the money-supply process, with numerical examples for September 1979. The right half of the table shows the balance sheet of the nation's commercial banks. Just as in the First Desert Island Bank, bank liabilities consist of deposits owed to the depositors, with a total amount of $835.6 billion in September 1979.[6]

Bank assets are of two types. First, banks hold reserves to back up their deposits, just as the Desert Island Bank kept gold coins on hand to meet withdrawals by depositors. United States bank reserves include vault cash

---

[4] Notice in equation (16.6) that any increase in e reduces the quantity of money (M). Although c appears both in the numerator and the denominator, an increase in c reduces the money supply as long as the reserve-holding ratio (e) is less than 1.0.

[5] A spirited narration on the establishment of the Fed is in John Kenneth Galbraith, *Money* (Boston: Houghton Mifflin, 1975), Chapter 10. See also Milton Friedman and Anna J. Schwartz, *A Monetary History of the United States, 1867–1960* (Princeton, N.J.: Princeton University Press, 1963), pp. 168–172 and 189–196.

[6] Deposits include both demand deposits (checking accounts), which in most cases pay no interest, and time deposits, which pay interest at varying rates depending on the withdrawal restrictions attached to the deposit.

TABLE 16-1

Simplified Depiction of the U.S. Money Supply Process

All figures are monthly averages for September 1979 in $ billions

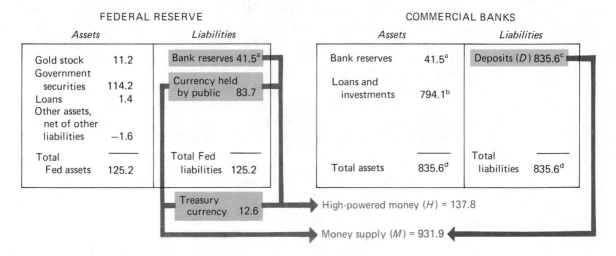

[a] Bank reserves include both deposits by banks at the Fed as well as currency and coin held by banks as vault cash.

[b] Loans and investments are calculated as deposits minus bank reserves. Since total liabilities include several other items, not shown here, this method understates loans and investments.

[c] Deposits are calculated as the old definition of $M2$ minus the currency component of $M2$ and include both demand deposits and time deposits of all banks, not just banks that are members of the Federal Reserve System. Since nonmember banks are not required to keep reserves at the Fed, the reserve ratio calculated in the text understates the true reserve ratio of member banks.

[d] Excludes negotiable time certificates of deposit issued in denominations of $100,000 or more by large weekly reporting commercial banks. Also excludes capital surplus, interbank and U.S. government deposits, and borrowings.

Source: Federal Reserve Bulletin (November 1979), Tables 1.11, 1.18, and 1.22.

---

and deposits at the Fed, both of which the banks accept as equivalent, because they can use their deposits at the Fed to obtain more vault cash if they need to accommodate an unusually large withdrawal. The other portion of bank assets consists of loans to households and business firms and investments in various types of federal, state, and local government short-term and long-term bonds.

The new element in Table 16-1, which was not present on the desert island, is the balance sheet of the Federal Reserve. The Fed's balance sheet has some similarity to that of the commercial banks, because a portion of the Fed's liabilities consists of deposits (the bank reserves that the Fed "owes" to the banks). The asset side includes both loans and investments, a tiny $1.4 billion in loans to commercial banks and a much larger $114.2 billion of investments in government bonds.

But there are differences. The Fed can issue currency, unlike the commercial banks, which are prohibited by law from doing so. The Fed's major liability item consists of currency held by the public (take a dollar bill and examine it—above George Washington's picture are the words "Federal Reserve Note" and to the left is a circle indicating the regional Fed bank responsible for issuing the note). Second, a portion of the Fed's assets consists of gold, which the commercial banks are prohibited from holding. Third, unlike the banks, which are required to keep a specified fraction of their deposits on hand in the form of reserves, the Fed does not have to maintain any fixed relation among its assets.[7]

Equation (16.6) is just as useful for studying the determinants of the U.S. money supply as of the desert island's money supply. The U.S. money supply, the old $M2$ concept, is defined as including all commercial bank deposits and includes these components that appear in Table 16-1:

Currency held by the public:
Federal Reserve currency	83.7	
Treasury currency	12.6	
Total currency		96.3

Deposits at commercial banks:
Demand deposits	273.0	
Time deposits	562.6	
Total deposits		835.6
Total money ($M2$)		931.9

The currency component of $M2$ appears in Table 16-1 in two places. The major portion is a liability of the Federal Reserve and consists entirely of the paper currency. Treasury currency is issued by the U.S. Treasury, not the Federal Reserve, and consists mainly of coins.

Equation (16.6) makes the total supply of money depend on the quantity of high-powered money (H), the bank reserve ratio (e), and the public's cash-holding ratio (c). The three components of high-powered money listed in Table 16-1 are:

Currency held by the public:
Federal Reserve currency	83.7	
Treasury currency	12.6	
Total currency		96.3
Bank reserves		41.5
Total high-powered money (H)		137.8

The bank reserve ratio (e) is the ratio of bank reserves to total deposits:

---

[7] Formerly, a fraction of the money supply had to be backed by gold, but this requirement was abandoned by Congress after growth in the money supply outstripped the supply of gold.

$$e = \frac{\text{bank reserves}}{\text{total deposits}} = \frac{41.5}{835.6} = 0.0497$$

The public's cash-holding ratio (c) is the ratio of currency held by the public to total deposits:

$$c = \frac{\text{currency}}{\text{total deposits}} = \frac{96.3}{835.6} = 0.1152$$

Now all the ingredients that determine the money supply can be inserted into equation (16.6):

$$M = \frac{(1+c)H}{e+c} = \frac{(1.1152)\,137.8}{0.0497 + 0.1152} = 931.9$$

NEW DEFINITIONS OF THE MONEY SUPPLY

As described at the end of section 15-7, the Federal Reserve introduced new definitions of the money supply in early 1980. While the old definition of $M2$ included currency and all commercial bank deposits, as in Table 16-1 and the preceding discussion, the new definition of $M2$ adds other important assets, particularly savings accounts at thrift institutions and money-market mutual funds. Since there is no easy way of summarizing the money-creation process in terms of the new money definitions, we have maintained our discussion in terms of the old $M2$ definition.

How are the new definitions of money explained in terms of equation (16.6)? Historically there has been quite a stable relation between savings deposits at thrift institutions and at commercial banks, so that the factors (H, e, and c) in equation (16.6) still do a good job of explaining the behavior of a broader concept of money. The inclusion of money-market mutual funds in the new $M2$ definition does not destroy the usefulness of equation (16.6), since a large fraction of the deposits in money-market mutual funds comes from transfers out of savings deposits and thus does not affect the total quantity of $M2$ under the new definition.

16-4 THE THREE INSTRUMENTS OF FEDERAL RESERVE CONTROL

Decisions by three types of economic units enter into the determination of the money supply in equation (16.6). The job of the Fed is to calculate the total M that it desires, based on its current target for aggregate demand. The Fed must also predict the public's desired cash-holding ratio (c), over which the Fed has no control. Then the Fed can adjust the two remaining variables in equation (16.6), H and e, to make its desired M consistent with the public's chosen c. The Fed has three main instruments to accomplish this task, the first two of which can be used to control H and the last of which influences e.

FIRST TOOL: OPEN-MARKET OPERATIONS

The first tool is by far the most important. The Fed can change H from day to day by purchasing and selling government bonds. In Table 16-1 the Fed's liabilities are the major component of H, and government bonds are the major asset of the Fed. By purchasing bonds, the Fed raises its assets and liabilities at the same time, thus increasing H. By selling bonds, the Fed reduces its assets and liabilities, lowering H. Any change in H caused by Fed **open-market operations** causes an even larger change in M through the money-creation multiplier.

Federal Reserve policy is decided on the third Tuesday of each month at a meeting of the Federal Open-Market Committee (FOMC) held in a large and imposing room in Washington and attended by the seven governors of the Fed and the presidents of the twelve regional Federal Reserve Banks.[8] Each meeting results in a directive sent to the Fed's open-market manager in New York, a position held in 1980 by Peter Sternlight.

Let us say that Mr. Sternlight's directive from the FOMC calls for continued moderate growth in the money supply, and that he has decided that the time has come for a $100 million increase in high-powered money (H). All Mr. Sternlight has to do is to pick up the phone and place an order with a New York government bond dealer, say Salomon Brothers, for $100 million in U.S. government bonds. The act that creates H "out of thin air" occurs when the Fed writes a $100 million check on itself to pay for the bonds. Salomon Brothers deposits the check in its account at a commercial bank, say Chase Manhattan. Just as the Desert Island Bank decided to hold a fixed fraction of its new deposits in the form of gold-coin reserves, so Chase Manhattan holds a portion of its new deposit, say $10 million, in its reserve account at the Fed.

The Chase Manhattan does not let Salomon Brothers' remaining $90 million deposit sit idly as excess reserves. Why? Because reserves earn no interest. To earn interest, the Chase loans out the $90 million immediately, say to Sears Roebuck, which needs money temporarily to restock its inventories. Sears takes its $90 million check from the Chase and deposits it immediately in the Sears Bank in Chicago, which must put $9 million (10 percent of $90 million) into its reserve account at the Fed. But now the Sears Bank has $81 million remaining to be lent out or invested and decides to buy $81 million in new bonds just issued by the City of Chicago. And the process continues, creating bank deposits again and again at each stage, just as on the desert island.

Thus Mr. Sternlight has "created money," not just the original $100 million, but a sizable multiple of $100 million. Yet at no stage has he made anyone wealthier, nor has he given anyone a gift. Salomon Brothers has $100 million more in its bank account, but owns $100 million less in government

---

[8] All twelve regional presidents attend, but only five (chosen on a rotating basis) may vote.

bonds. Sears has $90 million more in its bank account, but now owes $90 million to the Chase. The City of Chicago has $81 million more in its bank account, but now owes $81 million to the Sears Bank, which holds its bonds.

Sternlight's action influences not only the total supply of money but also the interest rate. When he buys the original $100 million in bonds, his action tends to raise bond prices and reduce the interest rate on bonds.

> **Review:** An important lesson in Figure 15-2 is that the Fed cannot simultaneously control both the interest rate and the money supply. Mr. Sternlight's bond purchase that raises the money supply shifts the *LM* curve to the right, moving the economy's equilibrium position southeast down the *IS* curve and thus reducing the interest rate. Similarly, the Fed cannot sell a bond and reduce the money supply without raising the interest rate. The Fed can reduce the money supply without increasing the interest rate only if fiscal policy (by cutting spending or raising tax rates) moves the *IS* curve to the left at the same time.

Sometimes the Fed must engage in open-market operations even when it has no desire to raise or lower the money supply. For instance, during a Christmas shopping season, the public needs more cash for transactions and raises its desired cash-holding ratio (*c*). Without Fed action this increase in the denominator of the money-supply equation (16.6) would reduce the money supply. Banks would use the reserves to provide cash to the public and would have fewer reserves left over to support deposits, so that the money supply would shrink by a multiple of the public's cash withdrawals. The Fed can avoid this shortage by conducting a "defensive" open-market purchase of bonds, providing banks with the extra reserves they need to handle the public's cash withdrawals.[9]

SECOND TOOL: REDISCOUNT RATE

Banks decide how much to borrow from the Fed by comparing the interest rate charged by the Fed, the **rediscount rate,** with the interest rate the banks can receive by investing the funds received from the Fed. Federal Reserve loans tend to be high when the interest rate on short-term investments, such as the interest rate on Treasury bills, is substantially above the Fed's rediscount rate, as in March 1980. And Fed loans tend to be low when the Treasury bill rate is low relative to the rediscount rate, as in June 1980. The situation in September 1979 depicted in Table 16-1 was in between with an intermediate amount of Fed loans.[10]

---

[9] For further discussion see William Poole, "The Making of Monetary Policy: Description and Analysis," *Economic Inquiry,* vol. 13 (June 1975), pp. 253–265.

[10] The rediscount was raised from 10.5 to 11 percent on September 20, 1979.

	Treasury bill rate	Fed rediscount rate	Fed loans to banks
September 1979	10.2	10.5	$1.4 billion
March 1980	15.5	13.0	$2.8 billion
June 1980	6.7	11.0	$0.4 billion

Because $100 million in Fed loans provide banks with $100 million in bank reserves, as does a $100 million open-market purchase, the Fed can control high-powered money (H) either by varying the rediscount rate or by conducting open-market operations. Monetary control can be achieved with either instrument and does not require both. In the first two decades after the Fed was established in 1913, the rediscount rate was the main instrument used by the Fed, whereas in the postwar years open-market operations have been the central instrument. The only justification for continuing the practice of lending by the Fed is the possible need for help by individual banks suffering from an unexpected rush of withdrawals, although these cases are rare and could be handled individually. Many economists have criticized the Fed for continuing its lending, because in periods of high interest rates the Fed tends to keep its rediscount rate low enough to induce substantial borrowing by banks, and this in turn reduces the precision of the Fed's day-to-day control over H.

THIRD TOOL: RESERVE REQUIREMENTS

Unlike the desert island, where the Banker chose voluntarily to keep 20 percent of his deposits on hand in the form of gold-coin reserves, in the United States, commercial banks that are members of the Fed must keep a specified fraction of their deposits as **required reserves.** Bank reserves can be held in the form of reserve accounts at the Fed or as vault cash (currency and coin). **Reserve requirements** vary with different types of deposits and with the size of the member bank.[11]

As is evident in equation (16.6), the Fed can raise the money supply by reducing bank reserve requirements (e), or vice versa. Thus a reduction in e accomplishes just the same increase in the money supply as an open-market purchase of the appropriate amount. Why does the Fed need to retain its control over reserve requirements? The only real justification is that a high level of reserve requirements can come in handy in wartime when the government needs to run a large budget deficit. In World War II, for instance, the government would have been required to pay very high interest rates to induce the public voluntarily to finance its entire deficit. To avoid this tactic, the government sold a large quantity of bonds to the Fed, causing H to

---

[11] The power to change reserve requirements came in 1933, two decades after the establishment of the Fed.

double between 1940 and 1945.[12] To minimize the inflationary pressure created by the large wartime increase in H, the Fed maintained bank reserve requirements at a level much higher than at present.

Compare the components of equation (16.6) at the end of World War II with the situation in September 1979:[13]

| | Percentage | | $ Billions | |
	c	e	H	M
September 1945	24.88	16.11	43.0	131.0
September 1979	11.52	4.97	137.8	931.9

From 1945 to 1979, H increased by 220 percent, whereas M increased by 611 percent. This growth was made possible by a sharp increase in the money-creation multiplier because of a decline in both components (e and c) of the denominator of the money-supply equation (16.6). The reserve ratio (e) dropped from 16.11 to 4.97 percent. In addition the cash-holding ratio dropped from 24.88 to 11.52 percent.[14]

16-5 CASE STUDY: MONETARY CONTROL IN THE 1930s

It appears from the preceding section that the Fed has more policy instruments than it really needs. Because any desired change in M can be achieved by raising or lowering H through open-market purchases or sales, the rediscount rate and reserve requirement tools appear to be unnecessary. Yet possession of three policy instruments does not guarantee effective monetary control.[15] The Great Depression of the 1930s illustrates two problems: (1) the need during 1929–33 for defensive open-market operations to protect the money supply from undesirable changes in e and c, and (2) the difficulties of interpretation and management introduced by **excess reserves** of banks during 1934–40.

In a previous case study (section 6-8) we found that the collapse in aggregate demand during 1929–33 caused a decline in both the price level

---

[12] Imagine that the government writes a $100 check during the war to pay a soldier's wages. The Fed actually writes the check and debits the government's account at the Fed (part of the Fed's liabilities). To restore the previous balance in its account at the Fed, the government sells the Fed a $100 bond, for which the Fed "pays" by adding $100 to the government's balance.

[13] Source for 1945: Milton Friedman and Anna J. Schwartz, *A Monetary History of the United States, 1867–1960* (Princeton, N.J.: Princeton University Press, 1963), Tables A-1 and A-2. Division between required and excess reserves from *Historical Chart Book* (Federal Reserve, 1967), p. 6. Data for 1976 from the same source as Table 16-1.

[14] Only part of the decline in reserve requirements listed above has been due to explicit Federal Reserve actions. Part has come from the relatively fast growth of time deposits, which have always had lower reserve requirements than demand deposits.

[15] The Fed has other instruments, the power to set interest-rate ceilings on bank deposits and to set minimum down payments and maximum repayment intervals for installment loans.

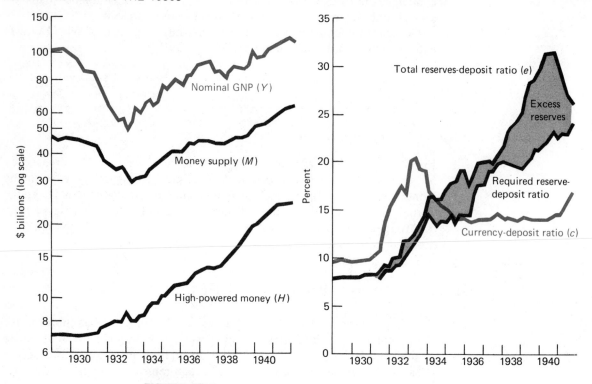

FIGURE 16-1

Nominal GNP, the Money Supply, and Its Determinants, Quarterly, 1929–41

The 35 percent collapse in M between late 1929 and early 1933 cannot be blamed on the behavior of high-powered money, which actually increased over the same interval. Instead the explanation, shown in the right frame, lies in the massive drain of high-powered money into cash and bank reserves. In the late 1930s, much of the increase in high-powered money was absorbed by excess reserve holding, indicated by the gray-shaded area in the right frame.

Source: See Appendix C.

and in real output. After 1933 real output recovered, but not by enough to reduce unemployment below 14 percent during the entire period 1934–40. The top frame in Figure 16-1 plots the dramatic 1929–33 decline in nominal GNP (Y) and the partial recovery that left Y in 1940 below the 1929 level.[16]

---

[16] A 1940 level of Y well above the 1929 value would have been necessary in 1940 to attain a 5 percent unemployment rate, because both the labor force and productivity had grown in the interim. The gap between actual and natural real GNP in 1940 was about 18 percent.

The 54 percent decline of Y between 1929:Q3 and 1933:Q1 was accompanied by a 30 percent reduction in M, as illustrated in Figure 16-1. The great irony of these years is that the Fed, originally created in 1913 to provide an elastic supply of bank reserves to protect against massive increases in the cash-holding ratio (c) during banking panics, failed in 1929–33 to accommodate the increased demand for H by the banks and the public. The right frame of Figure 16-1 shows that both components of the denominator of the money-supply equation, the bank-reserve ratio (e) and the public's cash-holding ratio (c), increased dramatically, but nevertheless H was only slightly higher at the 1933 trough of the Depression than at the 1929 peak. Compare the situation in 1929:Q3 and 1933:Q2, where the following numbers are plotted:

	Percentage		$ Billions		
	c	e	H	M	Y
1929:Q3	9.3	7.6	7.1	46.3	106.3
1933:Q2	20.4	12.3	8.0	29.9	54.6

Massive open-market purchases would have been necessary to prevent the 1929–33 decline in M, given the radical increase in e and c. But the observed behavior of e and c would not have occurred if the Fed had more vigorously purchased bonds. The public's higher cash-holding ratio (c) was mainly due to fear induced by several waves of bank failures that began in 1930. In turn, a part of the higher bank reserve ratio occurred as banks attempted to bolster their liquidity to lower the risk of failure. Had more high-powered money been available, fewer banks would have failed, and both c and e would have been lower. The Fed's performance during the 1929–33 period can only be described as inept, for reasons that Milton Friedman attributes to passivity in the absence of strong political or intellectual pressure from outside the Fed and of a strong leader inside the Fed.[17]

After 1933 the money supply grew almost continuously. By 1940:Q2 the money supply was 16 percent higher than in 1929:Q3, although nominal GNP still fell short of its 1929 peak. The individual components of the money-supply equation were quite different in 1929 and 1940, however:

	Percentage				$ Billions	
		e				
	c	Required	Excess	Total	H	M
September 1929	9.3	7.6	–	7.6	7.1	46.3
June 1940	13.8	21.8	9.5	31.3	21.1	53.7

[17] Milton Friedman and Anna J. Schwartz, *A Monetary History of the United States, 1867–1960* (Princeton, N.J.: Princeton University Press, 1963), pp. 407–419.

High-powered money tripled between 1929 and 1940, but M increased by only 16 percent. Why? Only a small part of the discrepancy is explained by the increase in the public's cash-holding ratio. Much more important is the quadrupling of the bank reserve ratio. Although the Fed directly caused a portion of the increase in e through its increase in reserve requirements (its third tool) in 1936 and early 1937, about 30 percent of bank reserves in 1940 were excess—that is, more than required by the Fed as a backing for deposits.

Why did the banks hold such a huge quantity of excess reserves? Figure 16-1 suggests that developments can be separated into three stages. Between late 1933 and early 1936 the total e ratio increased while the required e ratio remained constant, a discrepancy that Milton Friedman attributes to the voluntary demand by banks for excess reserves to protect themselves against future failure, as a reaction to the failures of 1930–33. In 1936 the Fed attempted to eliminate excess reserves in the belief that they were truly excess and not desired by the banks. In Friedman's interpretation the banks reacted by attempting to reestablish their previous levels of excess reserves, causing a slight contraction of the money supply in 1937 and a sharp recession in 1937–38. The increase in excess reserves between 1938 and 1940 is attributed by Friedman to a "second shift in preferences" by banks to favor excess reserves.[18]

Friedman's position is not universally held. An alternative interpretation of the 1938–40 episode is that banks did not have enough profitable lending opportunities to use all the reserves provided by the Fed.[19] Since short-term investments were yielding virtually nothing, with the U.S. Treasury bill rate ranging between 0.05 and 0.01 percent (one one-hundredth of one percent!), banks had nothing to lose by holding excess reserves. In a careful statistical study of this period, James A. Wilcox demonstrated that the money-creation multiplier was gravitating fairly rapidly toward zero, with banks holding larger and larger proportions of additional H as excess reserves due to the declining attraction of investing in the next-best alternative, Treasury bills. Wilcox shows in particular that the 1938–40 explosion in H (due mainly to an inflow of gold from Europe) did not cause a proportionate rise in M, because bankers believed that extending loans was unattractive at prevailing interest rates.

---

[18] Friedman and Schwartz, *op. cit.*, pp. 538–540. Recent studies of reserve holding in the 1930s include John L. Scadding, "An Annual Money Demand and Supply Model for the U.S.: 1924–1940/1949–1966," *Journal of Monetary Economics,* vol. 3 (January 1977), pp. 41–58. Also Karl Brunner and Alan Meltzer, "Liquidity Traps for Money, Bank Credit, and Interest Rates," *Journal of Political Economy,* vol. 76 (January/February 1968), pp. 1–35. See also Peter A. Frost, "Banks' Demand for Excess Reserves, *Journal of Political Economy,* vol. 79 (July/August 1971), pp. 805–825.

[19] During the entire 1933–41 period the Fed was entirely passive with the single exception of the 1936–37 increase in reserve requirements. All the increase in high-powered money between 1933 and 1940 is from an increase in U.S. gold holdings, built up mainly by the flight of capital from Europe connected with the outbreak of World War II.

Friedman's hypothesis is rejected because there is no way of quantifying a voluntary shift in bank preferences that can explain the enormous holdings of excess reserves in 1938–40.[20]

This debate is central to a proper interpretation of the 1938–40 period. In Friedman's view, excess reserve holdings were desired, so that monetary policy retained its potency, and the Fed could have raised nominal GNP by creating more H, which in turn would have raised M. In the opposing view held by Wilcox and others, any extra H would mainly have further raised excess reserve holding rather than the money supply. Monetary policy would have been "pushing on a string," impotent to return the economy to full employment without the aid of fiscal policy.

16-6 CASE STUDY: MONETARY CONTROL IN SELECTED POSTWAR EPISODES

Since World War II no problems of monetary control have been as serious as those in the Great Depression. The public's cash-holding ratio (c) has remained relatively stable, except for seasonal bulges at Christmas, and the public has been protected from the fear of bank failures by the Federal Deposit Insurance Corporation (FDIC), which guarantees holders of deposits against loss in case of bank failure. Excess reserves have also disappeared because the interest rate obtainable by banks on short-term investments has been significantly above the zero return on excess reserves, quite unlike the 1938–40 situation. Thus the Fed has been able to predict e and c with relative accuracy, allowing any target for the money supply to be achieved by altering H through appropriate open-market operations.

The Fed's main problem in the postwar era has not been in setting the money supply at a target level, but in deciding what that target should be. We learned in Chapter 15 that there are at least two monetary variables the Fed may choose to control—the interest rate and the money supply—but that in most situations the Fed cannot control both monetary variables simultaneously. There is a further problem, because the Fed must also choose which of the various definitions of the money supply to control. Once a control variable has been chosen, a further choice must be made: whether to maintain stability (a constant interest-rate level or steady growth in money) or to use the control variable countercyclically.

We limit this case study to the behavior of $M1$ during three important postwar periods. The first is the 1957–61 interval, during which actual real GNP (Q) continuously remained below natural real GNP (Q^N) and the actual unemployment rate remained above the natural rate of

---

[20] James A. Wilcox, "Excess Reserves in the Interwar Period," unpublished doctoral dissertation, Northwestern University, February 1980.

unemployment. The second is the 1964–71 period, during most of which actual real GNP (Q) exceeded natural real GNP (Q^N), causing the acceleration in inflation that has bedeviled policymakers ever since. The third interval is the turbulent decade of the 1970s, in which the problem of supply shocks posed new difficulties for monetary policy. In each period we want to ask whether the Fed's monetary control stabilized or destabilized the economy. Would a monetarist rule calling for a constant growth rate of money have performed better than the monetary policy actually pursued?

MONETARY POLICY DURING 1956–61

Our examination of each of the three periods is based on three diagrams, starting with Figure 16-2. The top frame shows the four-quarter percentage growth rates of nominal GNP and $M1$, with periods of positive growth in $M1$ indicated by pink shading and negative growth (an absolute decline in the level of $M1$) indicated by gray shading. The bottom frame compares the real GNP ratio (Q/Q^N) with the real money supply, $M1/P$. Our criterion for evaluating policy is that stabilization of the economy would have been achieved by maintaining the Q/Q^N ratio as close as possible to unity—at this level actual and real GNP are equal, and there is no tendency for inflation to accelerate or decelerate.

It is only fair to admit that in evaluating the conduct of monetary policy, we are taking advantage of hindsight. Policymakers in 1956 were not familiar with the concept of natural real GNP, a magnitude we have calculated with full knowledge of all accelerations and decelerations of inflation during the entire postwar period. They knew only that during 1956 inflation was proceeding and monetary restriction was appropriate. Thus during 1956 nominal $M1$ growth was slow, and the real supply of money ($M1/P$) declined steadily.

It was in 1957 that the Fed made a serious mistake. The Q/Q^N ratio began to drop, as the monetary tightness of the previous year began to take effect. But instead of moderating the downward pressure, the Fed intensified it. Nominal $M1$ growth was actually allowed to become negative in late 1957, and the decline in real $M1/P$ continued even though a precipitous decline in the real GNP ratio was under way. Thus the Fed appears to have acted procyclically in 1957, aggravating the 1957–58 recession.

This perverse behavior was repeated in 1959–60. After nominal $M1$ had been allowed to increase fairly rapidly during 1958 to stimulate the economy's recovery, monetary growth came to a halt in late 1959. In retrospect we can see that the Q/Q^N ratio did rise fairly close to 1.0 during mid-1959 and might have continued to increase if the economy's progress had not been interrupted by a steel strike. Thus the Fed's shift to moderate monetary growth is understandable, but the intensity of its

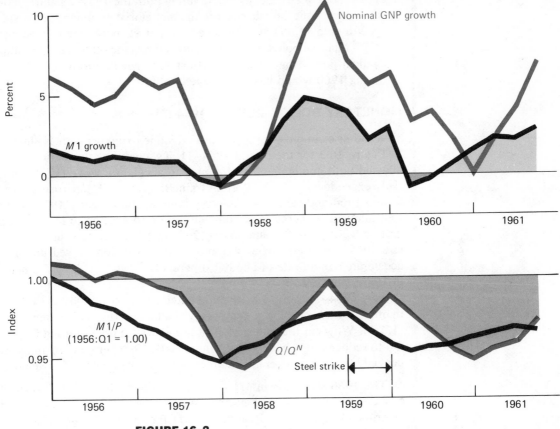

FIGURE 16–2

The Behavior of Nominal and Real $M1$, Nominal GNP,
and the Real GNP Ratio, 1956–61

Actual real GNP was below natural real GNP continuously from early 1957
through 1961, as shown by the gray shading. Notice as the Q/Q^N ratio was col-
lapsing in late 1957 in the bottom frame, growth in the nominal money supply in
the top frame was allowed to become negative, as indicated by the gray shading.
The same thing occurred again in early 1960.

Source: Appendix B, with the old $M1$ definition used for nominal and real $M1$.

1959 policy reversal is not. In early 1960 the Fed allowed both $M1$ and
$M1/P$ to decline. Throughout 1960 the real money supply ($M1/P$) was
below its mid-1959 level, aggravating the 1960–61 recession and helping
John F. Kennedy to squeeze by Richard M. Nixon in the election of 1960.

Summary: During the 1956–61 period, the Fed allowed the money supply to move procyclically, aggravating both the 1957–58 and 1960–61 recessions. It is hard to dispute the monetarist argument that a steady growth rate of $M1$ would have resulted in more stable behavior of Q/Q^N than the policies actually followed. On the other hand, a countercyclical policy that achieved fastest $M1$ growth during late 1957 and during 1960 would have been even better.[21]

MONETARY POLICY DURING 1964–71

Another example of procyclical Fed money-supply policy is illustrated in Figure 16-3 for the period 1964–71. Twice during this period the Fed allowed both nominal and real money to accelerate while Q/Q^N substantially exceeded 1.0. In the bottom frame the red Q/Q^N line rose above 1.0 in mid-1964 and remained at a very high level until early 1970. Yet the Fed allowed both real and nominal money to accelerate in two stages, first between mid-1965 and early 1966 and then between early 1967 and late 1968. The Fed's excessive monetary expansion caused inflation to accelerate from a rate of about 1.0 percent in 1964 to about 5.0 percent in 1970.

The 1964–71 period was punctuated by two periods of monetary tightness, each causing a temporary decline in the real money supply ($M1/P$). Why did the first period of monetary tightness during late 1966 fail to reduce Q/Q^N back to 1.0, whereas the 1969 period of tightness succeeded? Two fundamental differences between the episodes stand out:

1. The 1966 reduction in $M1/P$ was short-lived. By 1967:Q3 $M1/P$ had exceeded its previous high reached in 1966:Q2. In contrast the 1969 crunch lasted longer. Real money $M1/P$ remained below its early 1969 peak for nine quarters.
2. The stance of fiscal policy was completely different. In 1966–67 real government expenditures were rising very rapidly, whereas in 1968–71 they were falling. In terms of our previous theoretical analysis, in 1966–67 the IS curve was moving rightward up the LM curve, causing the crowding out of investment.[22] During 1969–70, however, both the IS and LM curves were moving to the left.

MONETARY POLICY DURING 1971–80

Nominal $M1$ growth was more stable in the 1970s than in the previous two episodes, but nevertheless the real GNP ratio and inflation were both

---

[21] In Figure 15-2 a countercyclical policy causes the economy to move between points C_0 and C_1 when the IS curve shifts back and forth, as compared to movements between points A_0 and A_1 caused by a procyclical money-supply policy. See p. 445.

[22] A case study of this period was presented in section 5-7.

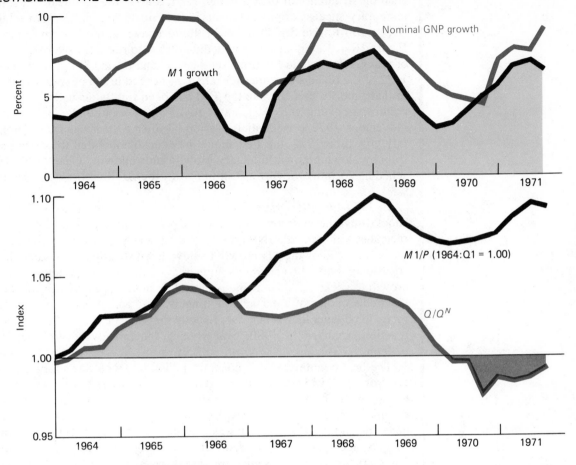

FIGURE 16–3

The Behavior of Nominal and Real $M1$, Nominal GNP,
and the Real GNP Ratio, 1964–71

The real GNP ratio in the bottom frame was above 100 percent continuously from early 1964 to late 1969, as shown by the pink shading. The Fed contributed to the acceleration of inflation by twice accelerating the growth in the money supply in 1965–66 and 1967–68, as shown in the top frame, instead of continuing the late 1966 restriction of monetary growth until the real GNP ratio had been pushed back down to 100.

Source: Appendix B. The new $M1B$ definition is used for real and nominal $M1$.

more unstable.[23] And almost without exception, monetary policy worsened the instability of the economy. First, early in the decade in 1972, the temporary success of price controls in holding down inflation allowed the Q/Q^N ratio to rise rapidly above 1.00, as shown in the bottom frame of Figure 16-4. Yet monetary policy did nothing to resist the overexpansion of real GNP, instead "pouring on the gas" and raising $M1$ growth in late 1972 to the highest four-quarter rate experienced in the postwar years up to that time. In this episode the Fed has been rightly accused of playing politics, boosting the Q/Q^N ratio to its peak around the time of the November 1972 presidential election. Rather than accelerating monetary growth in 1972, the Fed should have accommodated the price controls by slowing down monetary growth, thus allowing Chapter 9's DG schedule to move downward in line with the SP line. (**Review:** Section 9-5.)

In 1974 the Q/Q^N ratio dropped precipitously as oil and food supply shocks, together with the termination of price controls, caused inflation to race ahead of nominal GNP growth. But monetary policy exacerbated the recession by allowing $M1$ growth to slow down steadily at the same time. Instead of partially accommodating the supply shock by allowing $M1$ growth to speed up, or remaining neutral by holding $M1$ growth constant, the Fed's choice of a partially "extinguishing" policy reaction made the recession deeper than otherwise. Exactly the same "extinguishing" policy reaction occurred in 1980, exacerbating the already severe 1980 recession.

The best countercyclical monetary policy to encourage a rapid recovery from the 1975 recession would have been rapid $M1$ growth in 1975–76 when Q/Q^N was low and unemployment was high, followed by a gradual tapering off of $M1$ growth as the Q/Q^N ratio approached 100 percent. Instead the Fed's policy was just the opposite, with $M1$ growth that steadily accelerated as the economy recovered. A Fed policy of slow monetary growth in 1978 and rapid monetary growth in 1980 would have stabilized the economy compared to what actually happened.

THE LOOSE CONNECTION BETWEEN GROWTH IN NOMINAL GNP AND MONEY

Even if a constant-growth-rate rule for monetary growth had been pursued in the 1970s, nominal GNP growth would not have been constant. Why? The upper red line in the top frame of Figure 16-4 shows the

---

[23] The mean and standard deviation of the four-quarter $M1$ growth rate during our three periods was as follows (the old definition of $M1$ is used before 1959, and the new $M1B$ definition afterward):

	Mean	Standard deviation
1956–61	1.6	1.48
1964–71	4.9	1.53
1971–79	6.5	1.41

THE REAL MONEY SUPPLY WAS ALMOST A MIRROR IMAGE OF THE REAL GNP RATIO
IN THE 1970s, INDICATING AGAIN THAT THE FED DESTABILIZED THE ECONOMY

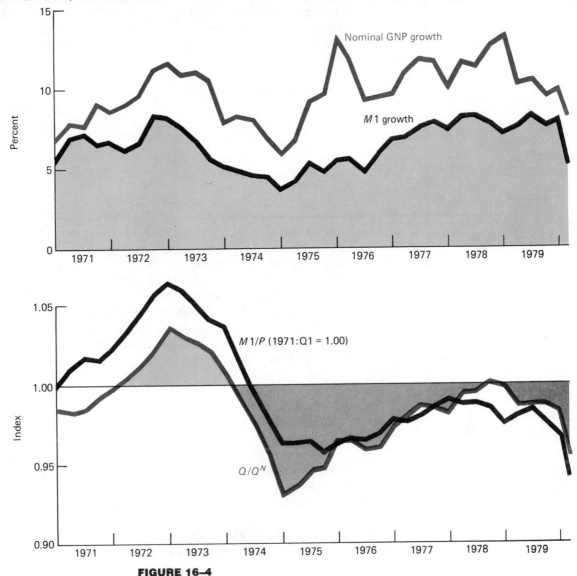

FIGURE 16–4

The Behavior of Nominal and Real $M1$, Nominal GNP,
and the Real GNP Ratio, 1971–80

Once again the Fed destabilized the economy in the 1970s. Price controls allowed
the Q/Q^N ratio to exceed 1.00 during 1972–73, but the Fed added to instability by
speeding up the growth of $M1$ in late 1972 when the Q/Q^N ratio was at its peak.
Then the reverse occurred in 1974–75 as oil and food supply shocks and the termination of controls caused inflation to accelerate and the Q/Q^N ratio to fall precipitously. Nominal $M1$ growth (top frame) and real $M1$ (bottom frame) echoed
the timing of the Q/Q^N drop, thus aggravating the recession. Yet again in 1978 $M1$
growth accelerated just as the Q/Q^N ratio came close to 1.00.

Source: Appendix B.
The new $M1B$ definition
is used for real and
nominal $M1$.

four-quarter growth rate of nominal GNP, which reflects major accelerations and decelerations in $M1$ growth but is by no means a mirror image of money. The distance between the red nominal GNP growth line and the black $M1$ growth line represents the growth of the velocity of $M1$. As shown in the table that follows, velocity growth was quite variable from year to year in the 1970s.

Four-quarter growth rate of velocity of $M1$

Four quarters ending in:

1971:Q1	1.4	1976:Q1	7.7
1972:Q1	2.0	1977:Q1	4.1
1973:Q1	3.5	1978:Q1	2.6
1974:Q1	2.8	1979:Q1	6.1
1975:Q1	2.3	1980:Q1	1.8

Why was velocity growth fast in years such as 1976 and 1979? For any given real money supply, velocity can increase whenever the IS curve of Chapters 4 and 5 is shifted right by stimulative fiscal policy or by consumer or business optimism; velocity can also increase if there is a decline in the demand for money. Thus the rapid growth in velocity in 1979 can be partly explained by the drop in consumer saving—that is, the increase in autonomous consumption that shifted IS to the right (section 13-7). And the 1976 increase in velocity is related to the downward shift in the demand for money that occurred at that time, sometimes called "the case of the missing money" (section 15-7).

Summary: The 1970s were like earlier decades in supporting the monetarists' claim that a constant-growth-rate rule (CGRR) for the money supply would have been superior to the procyclical money-growth policy actually pursued by the Fed. But nonmonetarists can likewise claim that a countercyclical monetary policy would have been even better. And nonmonetarists can put forth two additional arguments. First, the instability of velocity growth in the 1970s shows that a CGRR would not have stabilized nominal GNP growth. Second, a "neutral" CGRR policy is not necessarily the best reaction of policymakers to supply shocks, and a case can be made for at least partial accommodation to avoid a replay of the recessions of 1975 and 1980.

16-7 LIMITATIONS OF COUNTERCYCLICAL MONETARY ACTIVISM: LAGS

According to the analysis of Figure 15-2, countercyclical movements in the real money supply can achieve a more stable path of real output than a CGRR at the cost of greater fluctuations in the interest rate. The two main objections to countercyclical activism are (1) that lags prevent the monetary changes from influencing the economy until it is too late and (2) that the extra fluctuations in the interest rate caused by activism are undesirable. Monetarists have generally emphasized only the first objection.[24]

THE FIVE TYPES OF LAGS

Several types of lags intervene that prevent either monetary or fiscal policy from immediately offsetting an unexpected shift in the demand for commodities or money. There are five main types of lags, some of which are common to both monetary and fiscal policy and the rest of which are more important for one or the other:

1. The data lag
2. The recognition lag
3. The legislative lag
4. The transmission lag
5. The effectiveness lag

To explain the meaning of each lag and to estimate its length, let us take the example of the "pause" in the U.S. economic recovery that began in mid-April 1976 and extended until October.[25]

1. *The data lag.* Policymakers do not know what is going on in the economy the moment it happens. Although a few industries have sales reports with a lag of only a few days, the first sign of the 1976 pause did not appear until mid-June, when the news of a decline in employment and in real manufacturing and trade sales became known. It was not until mid-July that the quarterly GNP figures revealed that the growth rate of real GNP had dropped from an annual rate of 9.2 percent in 1976:Q1 to 4.5 percent in 1976:Q2.
2. *The recognition lag.* No policymaker pays much attention to reversals in the data that occur for only one month. The usual rule of thumb is to wait and see if the reversal continues for three successive months. If the 1976 pause had been more serious, three months of data would not have been available until late August, and a second reading on quarterly GNP growth would not have been available until mid-October.
3. *The legislative lag.* Although most changes in fiscal policy must be legislated by Congress, an important advantage of monetary policy is the short legislative lag. Once a majority of the Federal Open-Market Committee (FOMC) decides that an acceleration in monetary growth is

---

[24] See Milton Friedman, "The Lag in Effect of Monetary Policy," *Journal of Political Economy*, vol. 69 (October 1961), reprinted in his *The Optimum Quantity of Money and Other Essays* (Chicago: Aldine, 1969), pp. 237–260.

[25] The Department of Commerce "index of four coincident indicators" increased by 9.9 percent between March 1975 and April 1976, but then by only 0.2 percent between April and October 1976. Source: *Business Conditions Digest* (December 1976), Series 920.

needed, only a short wait is necessary until the next meeting of the FOMC, which occurs once every month.

4. *The transmission lag.* This lag is the time interval between the policy decision and the subsequent change in policy instruments—the money supply, government spending, or tax rates. Again, it is a more serious obstacle for fiscal policy. Once the FOMC has given its order for the open-market manager to make open-market purchases, the expansion in the money supply begins almost immediately, although the full multiple money-creation process may require one or two months.

5. *The effectiveness lag.* Almost all the controversy about the lags of monetary policy concerns the length of time required for an acceleration or deceleration in the money supply to influence real output. Milton Friedman is on record, from his extensive historical studies of U.S. monetary behavior between 1867 and 1960, as arguing that the effectiveness lag is both "long" and "variable."

A SHORT BUT VARIABLE LAG

Many estimates of the lag of monetary policy are available. Let us first develop an informal estimate of the average lag between the month of maximum monetary tightness and the subsequent onset of recession in the four major post-Korean recessions, recognizing that each recession was influenced by factors other than monetary policy.

| Business cycle peak of | Month/year of peak in: | | Average lag (months) |
	$M1/P$	Coincident indicators (CI)	
1957	4/56	2/57	10
1960	7/59	1/60	6
1969	2/69	10/69	8
1973	1/73	11/73	10
1979	3/78	3/79	12
Average	—	—	9.2

Here the dates of cyclical peaks are indicated for the real money supply $(M1/P)$—the same variable plotted in Figures 16-2, 16-3, and 16-4. Our measure of real economic activity is taken to be the government's index of coincident indicators (CI).[26] In each business cycle the peak in $M1/P$ has occurred before that in CI. The lag between the peaks in $M1/P$ and CI ranges from six to twelve months. Thus the label "short but variable" would appear

---

[26] This is an average of these four series: (1) employees on nonagricultural payrolls, (2) real personal income less transfer payments, (3) index of industrial production, and (4) real manufacturing and trade sales. We use the CI series in preference to real GNP, since the latter is not available on a monthly basis.

to be a better description of the monetary effectiveness lag than Friedman's "long but variable."

A vast amount of statistical and econometric research has been conducted to determine the timing of the economy's reaction to an increase or decrease in the money supply. Ironically, the econometric model built by the Federal Reserve Bank of St. Louis, a monetarist bastion, has a much shorter effectiveness lag of monetary policy than does the MPS (MIT-Penn-SSRC) model, designed by Franco Modigliani of MIT and other leading nonmonetarists. Thus the St. Louis results support the nonmonetarist case for countercyclical activism, whereas the MPS model supports the "long lag" monetarist argument against activism and in favor of monetary rules.

As an example, the St. Louis results indicate that virtually all the ultimate effect of a monetary change on spending has occurred by the end of four quarters. The MPS model indicates that less than half the ultimate effect has occurred by then. Thus the St. Louis results are more consistent with our crude timing table. Why do the models disagree? Unfortunately, the subject is much too complicated to be summarized here. My own suspicion is that the MPS model, despite its elaborate structure, still is overly restrictive and does not capture all the channels by which monetary policy directly influences personal consumption expenditures, thus forcing the influence of money on the economy to follow an overly roundabout and indirect route.[27]

To summarize this section on lags, let us add up the total delay between an unexpected economic pause and the arrival of stimulus from a reaction to that event by the Fed:

Time of lag	Estimated length (months)
1. Data	2.0
2. Recognition	2.0
3. Legislative	0.5
4. Transmission	1.0
5. Effectiveness	9.2
Total	14.7

Thus the economic slump that began in February 1980 could not be counteracted by the Fed until May 1981, although the variability of the effectiveness lag might shorten or lengthen the total lag by two or three months. By the time the Fed's stimulus arrived, the economy might not need additional stimulus. Or, looking at the problem in another way, the Fed would have had to forecast the 1980 slump as early as November 1978.

---

[27] The best recent study of the differences between the St. Louis and MPS models is Franco Modigliani and Albert Ando, "Impacts of Fiscal Actions on Aggregate Income and the Monetarist Controversy: Theory and Evidence," in Jerome L. Stein (ed.), *Monetarism* (Amsterdam: North-Holland, 1976), pp. 17–42.

16-8 LIMITATIONS OF COUNTERCYCLICAL MONETARY ACTIVISM: VARIATIONS IN INTEREST RATES

No one disputes that an activist countercyclical monetary policy generally causes increased fluctuations in interest rates, just as a CGRR policy causes interest rates to fluctuate more than an accommodating policy that attempts to stabilize interest rates.[28] Possible harm done by variable interest rates is an important consideration for proponents of an activist monetary policy.

Throughout this book we have referred to *the* interest rate, ignoring for the most part differences among the interest rates available on different assets. Yet a major factor bearing on the costs of monetary activism is the existence of ceilings set by the Fed that limit some interest rates but not others. The Fed's **Regulation Q** fixes ceilings on the interest rate that can be paid on commercial bank demand deposits (zero) and time deposits (a variety of ceiling rates). Similarly, the Federal Home Loan Bank sets ceiling rates for savings and loan institutions that are almost identical to those set by the Fed's Regulation Q.

During a period when the Fed allows market interest rates on short-term bills and bonds to increase, either because of a strong demand for commodities (*IS* curve moves to the right) or a decline in the real money supply (*LM* curve moves to the left), a substantial gap may open up between the interest rates on short-term bills and bonds and the interest rates on bank deposits that are held down by Regulation Q.[29] For instance, in March 1980 the Treasury bill rate reached 15.5 percent, and the long-term corporate bond rate reached 13.0 percent. Savers could also invest in money-market mutual funds (which in turn invested the funds in various high-yielding short-term assets and earned as much as 16 percent). Yet the interest rate on passbook savings accounts at commercial banks was still limited by Regulation Q to a paltry 5.25 percent. Higher interest rates were also available on certificates, but these rates were also fixed, and there were substantial penalties for savers who withdrew funds before the expiration date of the certificates.

DISINTERMEDIATION BEFORE 1978

Before 1978 such an enormous gap between the interest rate on Treasury bills and on passbook savings accounts caused a massive withdrawal of funds from commercial banks and savings and loan institutions. Any such substantial downward shift in the demand for savings deposits had a dis-

---

[28] In Figure 15-2 the accommodating policy holds the interest rate constant, the monetary rule causes fluctuations between B_0 and B_1, and the countercyclical policy causes greater fluctuations in the interest rate between C_0 and C_1.

[29] Such a situation is illustrated at point C_1 in Figure 15-2 on p. 445.

TABLE 16-2

Magnitude and Timing of Episodes of Disintermediation:
1966, 1969, and 1973–74

Date of Treasury bill interest-rate peak (month/year)	Decline in monthly change in mortgage debt between peak and trough month		Decline in real housing expenditure between peak and trough quarter	
10/66	−64.6%	(12/65 to 12/66)	−25.9%	(1965:Q2 to 1967:Q1)
12/69	−48.9	(11/68 to 11/69)	−15.3	(1969:Q1 to 1970:Q2)
8/73, 7/74	−67.0	(11/72 to 11/74)	−45.1	(1973:Q1 to 1975:Q1)

Sources: Treasury bill rate and change in mortgage debt from *Business Conditions Digest,* series 114 and 33; real housing expenditure from *Survey of Current Business.*

proportionate deflationary effect on the housing market, because savings institutions other than commercial banks (SIs) are required by law to hold almost all their assets in the form of mortgages. The supply of mortgage finance declined for purchasers of both new and used homes. The shift toward bonds and Treasury bills away from SIs was called **disintermediation.**

An outflow of funds from the SIs, a drop in mortgage finance, and a decline in housing expenditure have occurred in every postwar episode of high interest rates before 1978. Of the three most recent episodes of disintermediation—in 1966, 1969, and 1973–74—Table 16-2 indicates that the most recent was also the most severe. The twin peaks in interest rates on Treasury bills reached in the summers of 1973 and 1974 pulled billions out of SIs and forced the growth of mortgage debt to drop from an annual rate of $60 billion in late 1972 to a mere $20 billion in late 1974. With a one-quarter lag, housing expenditure also dropped precipitously, from $64.5 billion to $35.4 billion in 1972 prices.

MONEY-MARKET CERTIFICATES DEFUSED DISINTERMEDIATION IN 1978–79

In June 1978, government regulations were modified to allow commercial banks and savings institutions (SIs) to offer "money-market certificates" (MMCs). Unlike previous types of savings certificates, the new MMCs had a relatively short period of maturity (six months) and an interest rate tied to the Treasury bill rate on the date of issue. This reform meant that commercial banks and SIs could offer their customers an asset that yielded as much as a Treasury bill with the extra convenience of a familiar neighborhood banking location. MMCs had a minimum denomination of $10,000, which limited their appeal for many small savers, but Treasury bills also had minimum denominations.[30]

The introduction of the MMCs had a major impact in defusing disintermediation during 1978–79 as the interest rate of Treasury bills rose steadily. Unlike earlier episodes, the monthly change in mortgage debt did not decline through the end of 1979, despite an increase in the Treasury bill rate from 6.45 percent in January 1978 to 12.07 percent in December 1979. Although housing expenditures did decline modestly between 1978 and 1979, the drop was much less than had been predicted on the basis of previous episodes of disintermediation. It has been estimated that the MMCs generated an additional 291,000 housing starts over the period between mid-1978 and mid-1979.[31]

Although MMCs were a desirable reform, they made more difficult the task of monetary policy in 1979–80. By eliminating much of the disintermediation that would have otherwise occurred, MMCs had the effect of making residential investment much less responsive to higher interest rates. In terms of our *IS-LM* theory of income determination, the MMCs made the *IS* curve steeper by reducing the interest responsiveness of investment. Without MMCs the *IS* curve would have looked like the flatter schedule in Figure 16-5, and the introduction of MMCs rotated the *IS* curve to the steeper schedule called *IS'*. Along the old *IS* curve monetary restriction, represented by the leftward shift of *LM* from LM_0 to LM_1, would have shifted the economy's equilibrium position from E_0 to E_1. But along the new *IS'* curve the same drop in the real money supply and the same leftward shift of *LM* move the economy to point E_2.

This analysis helps to explain why the modest 1979 drop in the real money supply plotted in Figure 16-4 caused a much greater increase in short-term interest rates than the enormous 1974 drop in the real money supply. In the earlier episode the Treasury bill rate increased from 3.3 percent in early 1972 to a peak of 8.7 percent in mid-1974. In the later episode the bill rate increased from 4.4 percent at the beginning of 1977 to 15.5 percent in March 1980.[32] The high interest rate level reached in early 1980, which boosted mortgage rates as high as 18 percent, soon dried up the *demand* for housing (not the *supply* of funds, as in earlier episodes). By April 1980 the level of housing starts had fallen by 53 percent from its April 1978 peak value. High interest rates also made consumer lending unprofitable for many banks, which "shut the loan window" and helped to precipitate a 41.0 annual rate of decline in real consumer durable goods spending between 1980:Q1 and 1980:Q2.

---

[30] Both MMCs and Treasury bills were dominated by money-market mutual funds, which required a minimum deposit of as little as $1000 and offered check-writing privileges and immediate withdrawal of funds.

[31] Dwight M. Jaffee and Kenneth T. Rosen, "Mortgage Credit Availability and Residential Construction," *Brookings Papers on Economic Activity,* vol. 10, no. 2 (1979), pp. 333–376.

[32] This analysis of the 1979 situation is highly oversimplified. Another cause of high interest rates may have been an increase in expected inflation, which would have shifted *IS'* rightward as in Figure 11-1, p. 335.

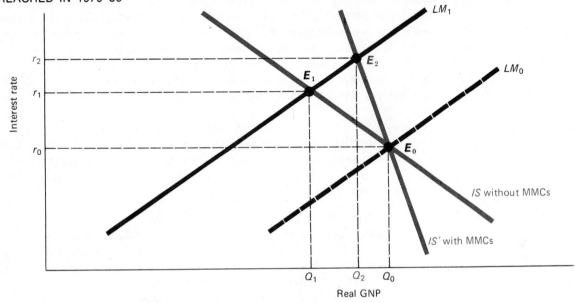

FIGURE 16–5

Effect of Restrictive Monetary Policy with and without
Money-Market Certificates (MMCs)

Here the Federal Reserve causes the LM curve to shift left from LM_0 to LM_1 by reducing the real money supply. Before the introduction of MMCs, the economy's fixed IS curve was relatively flat, owing to disintermediation in which high interest rates caused a drastic decline in housing investment. But with MMCs the response of housing to a given increase in the interest rate is much less, as indicated by the steeper IS' curve, and the economy moves to point E_2 instead of E_1.

FURTHER REGULATORY REFORMS

The high $10,000 minimum denomination of MMCs makes them unavailable to many individuals. More than before, the wealthy enjoy high returns from their saving and the poor still save disproportionately in passbook savings accounts that pay only 5.25 or 5.5 percent per year. A major reason for interest-rate ceilings on passbook savings accounts is the regulation that requires savings banks to hold all of their assets in the form of mortgages. Because mortgage loans have long maturities, many savings banks are stuck with low-yielding 5 and 6 percent mortgages lent out years ago. With this limit on the income from their assets, savings banks cannot afford to pay higher interest rates on their deposits.

Elimination of disintermediation requires a whole set of regulatory changes. Savings banks must be allowed to lend for purposes other than housing. Mortgage loans with variable interest rates should be introduced in order to sustain the flow of mortgage funds during periods of high interest rates. These and other reforms were recommended in the 1971 report of the President's Commission on Financial Structure and Regulation (the Hunt Commission), and most of them were finally enacted in the 1980 Banking Reform Act.[33] Among other things, this reform legislation gradually phases out Regulation Q ceilings on time deposits, authorizes banks to offer interest-bearing checking accounts, and allows thrift institutions to compete with commercial banks for consumer loans and credit card business. This reform is expected to make mortgage interest rates fluctuate more than in the past, since the cost of funds to thrift institutions will vary more in line with market interest rates.

Summary: When interest-rate ceilings on savings deposits are in effect, a countercyclical monetary policy has undesirable side effects. The right solution is to reform the undesirable regulations and ceilings, as in the 1980 Banking Reform Act, not to abandon countercyclical policy. A side effect of these reforms will be to reduce the welfare costs of inflation, which in Chapter 11 included the redistribution of income from savers to borrowers when inflation pushes up the nominal interest rate on bonds.

16-9 CONCLUDING ARGUMENTS ON MONETARY RULES VERSUS ACTIVISM

The postwar case studies in section 16-6 provided convincing evidence that the Fed destabilized the economy during the 1950s and 1960s, aggravating the recessions of 1957–58 and the acceleration of inflation in 1965–69. Partly as a reaction to these events themselves, and partly in response to sustained criticism by Milton Friedman and other monetarists, the Fed in January 1970 substituted monetary growth for interest rates as the primary target of monetary policy. Later, in early 1972, growth in bank reserves was substituted for "credit conditions" (interest rates) as the primary week-to-week instrument of policymaking. Nevertheless, monetary policy has continued to contribute to instability in the 1970s, as is obvious from an inspection of Figure 16-4.

What should we conclude on monetary activism? Milton Friedman has recently summarized his case in favor of the CGRR (constant-growth-rate-rule) monetary policy:[34]

---

[33] The official name of this legislation is "The Depository Institutions Deregulation and Monetary Control Act of 1980."

[34] "The Case for a Monetary Rule," *Newsweek* (February 7, 1972).

1. The past performance of the Fed
2. The limitations of our knowledge
3. The promotion of confidence
4. Neutralization of the Fed

Clearly the past performance of the Fed has been abysmally procyclical, and a CGRR would be an improvement. Adherence to a CGRR would promote confidence and prevent the Fed from succumbing to the temptation to influence election results by preelection monetary acceleration.

But all these arguments are also merits of a countercyclical policy as well. The fact that the Fed has failed to act countercyclically in the past does not prevent economists from urging it to adopt an activist countercyclical policy in the future. While there are limitations to our knowledge (Friedman's second reason) that prevent the Fed from knowing precisely how much of a change in the money supply is needed and at what exact time, nevertheless we can do better than a CGRR.[35] A stabilizing policy that temporarily slows monetary growth when forecasters predict unemployment at or below the natural rate for next year, and that temporarily accelerates monetary growth when unemployment above the natural rate is predicted, appears to be feasible with present knowledge. Lags in the effect of monetary changes appear to be less than a year in length, and forecasters in the 1970s have been able to predict accurately a year in advance the *direction* of most changes in unemployment, even though they failed badly in predicting the *magnitude* of the increase in unemployment following the 1973–74 and 1979–80 supply-shock episodes.

SUMMARY

1. A set of banks in a closed economy—one with no transfers of funds to the outside—can "create money" by a multiple of each dollar of cash that is initially received. This is true for a single bank on a desert island or for all banks in the United States taken together.

2. Among the assumptions necessary for money creation to occur are that only a fraction of the initial cash receipt is held as reserves by banks or as pocket cash by depositors and that banks loan out excess reserves to willing borrowers.

3. The deposit-creation multiplier is 1.0 divided by the fraction of an initial cash receipt that is held as bank reserves or currency. The money-creation multiplier is then the deposit-creation multiplier times 1.0 plus the currency-holding fraction. The money supply is equal to high-powered money times the money-creation multiplier.

---

[35] In studies of past episodes using both the monetarist St. Louis econometric model and the nonmonetarist MPS model, J. Phillip Cooper and Stanley Fischer have confirmed that an activist policy, in which monetary growth responds to the rate of change of unemployment, would have outperformed a CGRR. See their "Stabilization Policy and Lags: Summary and Extension," *Annals of Economic and Social Measurement* (October 1972), pp. 407–418.

4. The Federal Reserve can change high-powered money by conducting open-market operations or adjusting the rediscount rate. The Fed can also alter the required reserve ratio for banks. The final determinant of the money supply, the public's cash-holding ratio, is not under the control of the Fed but depends on the behavior of individual households and firms.

5. During the 1930s a dramatic collapse in the money supply was caused not by a decline in high-powered money, but by increases in the reserve-holding ratio and cash-holding ratio caused by a widespread and correct fear of bank failures. The Fed's control over the money supply in the late 1930s was loosened by the unwillingness of banks to loan out their excess reserves.

6. Between 1957 and 1979 the Fed destabilized the economy by reducing the money supply when the economy was weak and by accelerating monetary growth when the economy was strong.

7. There are five sources of lags between an initial change in the economy and the minimum interval before which monetary or fiscal policy can influence spending. The total length of the five lags taken together is about fourteen months for monetary policy in the United States.

8. A major disadvantage of countercyclical monetary policy is the dislocation in the economy caused by significant shifts in interest rates. An increase in the interest rate on bonds caused by restrictive monetary policy leads to an outflow of funds from savings institutions, a decline in mortgage lending, and a drop in housing starts. The severity of disintermediation was reduced by the introduction of money-market certificates in 1978 and the Banking Reform Act of 1980.

A LOOK AHEAD

Having studied some of the advantages and disadvantages of an activist countercyclical monetary policy, we now turn to consider fiscal policy. Some of the issues are the same, particularly the question of lags. But fiscal policy also raises new issues, because of the wide variety of alternative expenditure categories and types of taxes that might be chosen as fiscal policy instruments.

CONCEPTS

Required reserves
Excess reserves
Demand deposits
Money-creation multiplier
High-powered money
Cash-holding ratio
Reserve ratio

Federal Reserve System
Open-market operations
Rediscount rate
Regulation Q
Disintermediation
Money-market certificates

QUESTIONS FOR REVIEW

1   Because banks can make profits by increasing their interest-earning loans and granting the borrower a non-interest-bearing demand deposit, what prevents banks from increasing their loans without limit?

2   Starting from the situation of the First Desert Island Bank at stage 5, when its assets and liabilities are both equal to 500, calculate the effect on the bank of the following events (in each case, indicate the ultimate level of the bank's reserves, loans, and deposits after the full money-creation process has taken place):
   a. Discovery by the Miser of an additional 100 gold coins, which he deposits in the bank.
   b. The decision by the Banker to reduce his voluntary reserve ratio from 20 percent – the example used in section 16-2 – to 10 percent.
   c. The decision by all holders of demand deposits at the bank to hold 5 percent of their deposits in the form of gold coins as pocket cash.
   d. Withdrawal by the Miser of all his deposits in the form of gold coins, followed by his departure from the island.

3   Explain in words what happens when the Federal Reserve conducts an open-market sale of $100 million in bonds. What does the open-market manager do? How do banks respond? What is the ultimate effect on high-powered money and the money supply?

4   Does a reduction in the Fed rediscount rate tend to raise or lower the money supply? Is your answer affected if initially the outstanding loans from the Fed to the banks are zero?

5   Using the figures in section 16-5, what actions by the Fed would have succeeded in doubling the money supply in 1939? How much of an increase in high-powered money do you think would have been required? What conclusions do you reach about the Fed's power to end the Great Depression by itself, without any help from fiscal policy?

6   Why do you think the Fed allowed the money supply to accelerate in 1967–68 (see Figure 16-3)? Using *IS-LM* analysis, can you speculate what would have happened if the Fed had succeeded in keeping $M1$ constant?

7   What are some of the disadvantages of a monetary policy that allows interest rates to rise significantly in an effort to restrain the economy? Are these disadvantages inevitable, or can you suggest reforms that might alleviate some of the harmful side effects of high interest rates?

8   Explain why money-market certificates made interest rates higher in 1979. What are the likely consequences of the Banking Reform Act of 1980?

17

Fiscal Policy
and Its
Limitations

As to deficits, a new distinction was drawn between "deficits of
weakness" that arise out of backing into a recession and
"deficits of strength" that arise out of measures to provide fiscal
thrust to a lagging economy.
—Walter W. Heller[1]

17-1 INTRODUCTION

If a countercyclical stabilization policy is to be pursued to offset an undesirable decline or increase in the private demand for commodities, should
an activist monetary policy, an activist fiscal policy, or some combination of
the two be used? The last chapter distinguished several possible disadvantages of an activist monetary policy—lags, fluctuating interest rates, over-
concentration of policy's effects on housing, and the poor historical record
of the Fed. How does fiscal policy compare? We will see that an activist
fiscal policy is subject to criticism for some of the same reasons, particularly
lags, and for quite different reasons as well.

First, this chapter introduces important concepts frequently used in discussions of fiscal policy, including the natural employment surplus, fiscal
dividend and fiscal drag, and automatic stabilization. Before the limitations
of fiscal policy are confronted, we need to know how to measure the degree
of fiscal stimulus. As is true in most discussions of macroeconomics, our
attention is limited to the federal government; it ignores state and local
governments. Why? First, because state and local governments are limited
in the fiscal deficits they can run, and none can print money to cover their
deficits. Second, because state and local finance involves issues regarding
the migration of labor and capital among states that are best covered in
courses on public finance.

---

[1] *New Dimensions of Political Economy* (New York: Norton, 1967), p. 40.

17-2 THE NATURAL EMPLOYMENT BUDGET

For years the guiding motto of fiscal policy was to "maintain a balanced budget." Pursuit of a balanced-budget policy was considered by some politicians to constitute fiscal responsibility, and deficits were fiscally irresponsible. But this old-fashioned doctrine did considerable harm to the economy and has since been abandoned by all economists, monetarists and nonmonetarists alike. Why? Because in a recession when GNP declines, the taxable incomes of individuals and firms decline, the government's tax receipts fall, and a budget deficit emerges even if government expenditures and tax rates remain constant. To achieve a balanced budget in a recession requires an increase in tax rates or a reduction in government spending, either of which tends further to depress the economy. From the present perspective it seems unbelievable that in order to balance the budget, the Hoover administration actually raised tax rates by a major amount in 1932, when the unemployment rate was 24 percent!

The government budget surplus in real terms, as we learned in Chapter 2, is defined as real tax revenue net of transfer payments (T), minus real government spending on goods and services (G):

$$\text{surplus} \equiv T - G \qquad (17.1)$$

Tax revenues net of transfers (T) can be redefined as total real GNP (Q) times the average ratio of tax revenue net of transfers to GNP (t):

$$\text{surplus} \equiv tQ - G \qquad (17.2)$$

It is convenient to make one more change, both multiplying and dividing tQ by the same thing, the natural level of real GNP (Q^N):[2]

$$\text{surplus} \equiv tQ^N(Q/Q^N) - G \qquad (17.3)$$

The purpose of writing the surplus in the form of (17.3) is to distinguish three sources of change in the surplus: (1) **automatic stabilization** through changes in Q/Q^N, (2) **discretionary fiscal policy** through changes in t and G, and (3) economic growth that raises Q^N.

AUTOMATIC STABILIZATION

When real GNP (Q) goes up in an economic expansion, the real GNP ratio Q/Q^N rises as well and automatically boosts the government surplus by generating more tax revenues. Federal revenues from the personal and corporation income taxes are very responsive to higher income levels. The

---

[2] Earlier we defined the natural level of real GNP (Q^N) as the amount of output the economy can produce without any tendency for inflation to accelerate or decelerate.

higher surplus helps to stabilize the economy, since the higher tax revenues leak out of the spending stream and restrain the boom. Similarly, tax revenues drop in a recession, cutting the leakages out of the spending stream and helping to dampen the recession.

The automatic stabilization effect of Q/Q^N on the surplus is illustrated in Figure 17-1. The horizontal axis is the real GNP ratio Q/Q^N, and the vertical axis is the surplus. In the gray area above the zero point on the vertical axis, the government runs a positive surplus, with tax revenues exceeding expenditures. In the pink area below zero the surplus is negative, meaning that the government is running a deficit. The red upward-sloping BB_0 budget line illustrates the automatic stabilization relationship between the surplus and the output ratio Q/Q^N when the other determinants of the surplus in equation (17.3) are constant—t, Q^N, and G.

The budget line BB_0 is drawn so that the government runs a balanced budget (surplus = 0) at point A, when real GNP is at its natural level ($Q/Q^N = 1.0$). If the economy were to enter a recession and the Q/Q^N ratio were to fall from 1.0 to 0.90, the economy would move from point A to point B, where the government is running a deficit.

DISCRETIONARY FISCAL POLICY

The second source of change in the surplus comes from alterations in the tax rate (t) and government spending (G). It is evident from equation (17.3) that an increase in the average tax rate (t) raises the surplus, whereas an increase in government expenditures (G) reduces the surplus.[3] How are such discretionary changes illustrated in Figure 17-1? An increase in the tax rate shifts the red budget line upward for any given output ratio, since at a given level of output the government can collect higher tax revenues when tax rates are increased. If the original budget line BB_0 is drawn for an initial assumed tax rate t_0, then an increase in the tax rate to a higher level t_1 causes the budget line to shift upward to the new position BB_1.

> **Example:** Let us imagine that in 1931 the economy was at a point such as B in Figure 17-1, with a government deficit and an output ratio of 90 percent. Herbert Hoover was sufficiently distressed by the deficit at point B to raise tax rates, shifting the budget line upward from BB_0 to BB_1. If the higher tax rates had no depressing effect on private spending, Hoover would have achieved his goal, a budget surplus at point C along the new budget line BB_1. But our theory of Chapters 3–5 suggests that a tax increase depresses real GNP. If the tax multiplier were large enough, and the output ratio Q/Q^N were to fall far enough,

---

[3] We ignore here the automatic changes in the average tax rate caused by progressivity in the tax structure.

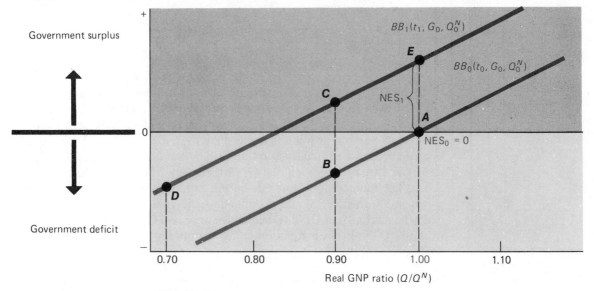

FIGURE 17-1

The Relation between the Actual Government Surplus, the Natural
Employment Surplus (NES), and the Ratio of Actual to Natural
Real GNP (Q/Q^N)

The lower budget line BB_0 shows all the levels of the government budget surplus
(or deficit) that are compatible with a given level of government expenditures
(G_0), tax rates (t_0), and the level of natural real GNP (Q_0^N). The BB line slopes
upward to the right, because as we move rightward the higher real GNP ratio
(Q/Q^N) raises government tax revenues (tQ), thus increasing the government surplus in a vertical direction. The upper BB_1 line indicates a higher government
surplus at every level of output than the lower line BB_0, because the tax rate has
been raised from t_0 to t_1, thus raising government revenues and hence the government surplus.

it is conceivable that the government might run a larger deficit at point
D than it was previously running with lower tax rates at point B!

This example illustrates the basic flaw in using the actual budget surplus
or deficit as a measure of fiscal policy's effect on the economy. Use of the
actual budget ignores the two-way interaction between the budget and the
economy: *the budget affects the economy and the economy affects the
budget.* First, the budget affects the economy through discretionary fiscal

policy, changes in G or t. But the state of the economy feeds back into the budget through automatic stabilization the dependence of the government's tax revenues on Q/Q^N.

THE NATURAL EMPLOYMENT SURPLUS

Given the inadequacies of the actual budget, what other single number can we use to summarize the effect of fiscal policy on the economy? In the diagram the fact that BB_1 is a more restrictive budget is evident from the fact that its vertical position is higher than that of BB_0. Therefore its restrictive effect can be summarized by describing the height of the budget line at some standard agreed-upon real GNP level, say when the real GNP ratio is at 1.0. The budget surplus at this output ratio can be called the **natural employment surplus** (NES) and is defined as the value of the government surplus when actual real GNP (Q) equals natural real GNP (Q^N). When we substitute $Q/Q^N = 1.0$ into equation (17.3) we obtain:

$$\text{NES} = tQ^N - G \qquad (17.4)$$

The natural employment surplus changes whenever there is a change in any of the three components on the right side of (17.4). An increase in the average tax rate (t) or in natural output itself (Q^N) raises the natural employment surplus, whereas an increase in government spending (G) has the opposite effect.

In Figure 17-1 the two budget lines BB_0 and BB_1 correspond to the two hypothetical tax rates, t_0 and t_1. The respective values of the natural employment surplus are denoted at NES_0 and NES_1 in the figure. The natural employment surplus in the diagram corresponding to each budget line is simply the vertical distance between that budget line and zero, measured at $Q/Q^N = 1.0$ on the horizontal axis. Along the lower budget line, NES_0 equals zero because tax revenues just balance government expenditures when the economy is operating with a real GNP level (Q) equal to natural real GNP (Q^N). Along the higher budget line tax rates are higher, allowing the government to run the natural employment surplus NES_1 corresponding to the vertical distance EA.

Natural employment surplus is a phrase coined for this book, corresponding to the natural-rate hypothesis developed in Chapter 8, which states that any attempt by policymakers permanently to maintain the Q/Q^N ratio above 1.0 leads to an acceleration in inflation. Government publications feature an identical concept called the *high employment surplus*, which differs only in that it is defined for a lower unemployment rate and a real GNP level higher than Q^N. At this more ambitious real GNP level, hypothetical government revenues are higher than at Q^N, and so the high employment surplus along the BB_0 budget line in Figure 17-1 is a larger amount. This target is unrealistically optimistic because it calculates government tax revenues at a high real GNP level, which if achieved and maintained permanently, would cause an accelerating inflation. Thus we reject the unrealistic "high employment" target and concentrate in the rest of this chapter on the natural employment surplus (NES).[4]

17-3 CASE STUDY: AUTOMATIC STABILIZERS BEFORE AND AFTER WORLD WAR II

The extent of automatic stabilization is measured simply by the percentage of any change in GNP that automatically leaks out of the spending stream into government tax revenue plus the percentage that is automatically injected back into the spending stream in the form of income-contingent transfers, such as unemployment benefits and welfare payments. The higher this marginal tax rate ($\bar{t}$), adjusted for transfers, the steeper is the *BB* budget line in Figure 17-1 and the greater is the change in the natural employment surplus (NES) when the real GNP ratio (Q/Q^N) rises or falls.

When we ask what fraction of a shortfall of actual output (Q) below natural real GNP (Q^N) is offset by a reduction in government tax revenues (T) below natural employment revenues (T^N), we have the following expression for the marginal tax rate ($\bar{t}$):

$$\bar{t} = \frac{T - T^N}{Q - Q^N} = \frac{\Delta T}{\Delta Q} = \left(\frac{T^N}{Q^N}\right)\left(\frac{\Delta T/T^N}{\Delta Q/Q^N}\right) \tag{17.5}$$

The first term in the right-hand expression, T^N/Q^N, is the natural employment share of real tax revenues in real GNP. The second term is the elasticity of tax revenues to changes in the real GNP ratio.[5]

The revenue share (T^N/Q^N) depends on the overall size of government and is much larger now than before World War II. The elasticity term depends on the progressivity of the tax schedule. If tax rates are proportional, then government tax revenue tends to remain at a constant fraction of GNP as long as tax rates are fixed and the elasticity term equals 1.0. But if tax rates are progressive, like those of the U.S. federal government, then government tax revenues rise by more than 1 percent for every percentage point increase in output, and the elasticity term in equation (17.5) exceeds unity.

---

[4] Finally, after many years of featuring an obsolete concept defined for a 4 percent unemployment target, the *Economic Report of the President* in January 1977 recognized explicitly that the budget concept had to be defined for a less ambitious real GNP target. The real GNP target was revised downward again in 1979 and 1980. But its new estimates of "potential" real GNP are still too ambitious (at least until policymakers manage to reduce the natural rate of unemployment along the lines discussed in Chapter 10).

[5] This elasticity is simply the shortfall of T below T^N as a percentage of T^N divided by the shortfall of Q below Q^N as a percentage of Q^N:

$$\text{elasticity} = \frac{\Delta T/T^N}{\Delta Q/Q^N} = \frac{(T - T^N)/T^N}{(Q - Q^N)/Q^N}$$

The much higher marginal tax rate in the postwar years, which has steepened the budget line and contributed so much to automatic stabilization, has been mainly due to the larger size of government and only to a much smaller extent due to an increased revenue elasticity:

	Percentage		Revenue elasticity
	$\bar{t}$	T^N/Q^N	
1932	5.5	3.9	1.41
1975	31.3	19.3	1.62

The difference between the 1932 and 1975 situations is illustrated by the two budget lines in Figure 17-2. Since we are interested in this section in the slope of the budget line rather than its vertical position, both budget lines plot on the vertical axis the difference between the real actual surplus and real natural employment surplus, expressed as a ratio to natural real GNP. Once again the horizontal axis is the GNP ratio (Q/Q^N). In 1932 the output ratio had fallen to a mere 67 percent, much lower than in any postwar year, and yet the actual surplus had fallen by only 1.8 percent of natural real GNP. Why the small decline in the surplus? The federal government was such a minor part of the economy that its expenditures in 1932 were only 3.6 percent of Q^N. Even if tax collections had fallen to zero, the actual surplus could not have fallen to more than -3.6 percent of Q^N.

In 1975 the budget line was much steeper. The real GNP ratio fell by much less than in 1932, yet the recession caused a major shortfall in the actual surplus, equal to 1.9 percent of Q^N. In 1975 the fiscal system did a much better job of automatic stabilization, insulating the economy against much of the shock of the decline in spending that occurred in the recession. The Great Depression would have been considerably less severe if the high postwar marginal tax rate ($\bar{t}$) and associated lower multiplier had been in effect during 1929–32.

The same conclusion has been reached by Bert G. Hickman of Stanford and Robert M. Coen of Northwestern, who have built a large and complex econometric model of the U.S. economy spanning the entire period between 1921 and 1966. They have calculated the following multipliers, which show the change in real GNP resulting from a $1 change in real autonomous spending after the designated number of quarters.[6]

Quarters elapsed	Multipliers for 1926–40	Multipliers for 1951–65
1	3.23	1.88
5	5.09	2.10
9	3.54	2.25

[6] Bert G. Hickman and Robert M. Coen, *An Annual Growth Model of the U.S. Economy* (Amsterdam: North-Holland, 1976), Table 9.6, p. 194.

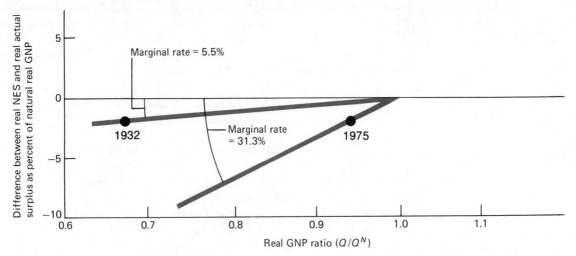

FIGURE 17–2

Change in the Federal Budget Surplus Caused by the Reduction of Actual Real GNP below Natural Real GNP in 1932 and in 1975

The vertical axis measures the difference between the actual surplus and the natural employment surplus, expressed as a ratio to natural real GNP. The horizontal axis is the output ratio Q/Q^N. Notice that in 1932 output was one-third below natural output, but the actual surplus had fallen by only 1.8 percent of natural output. In 1975 the recession was much milder, and yet the actual surplus fell by more than in 1932.

Sources: For 1932, (1) difference between actual surplus and natural employment surplus, from E. Cary Brown, "Fiscal Policy in the 'Thirties': A Reappraisal," *American Economic Review,* vol. 46 (December 1956), Table II, p. 873; (2) actual and natural output from Appendix B converted to 1947 prices (the basis used by E. Cary Brown). For 1975, see Appendix B.

After five quarters, for instance, a sustained $1.0 billion drop in the autonomous component of private consumption would lead to a $5.1 billion drop in real GNP under prewar conditions, as opposed to only a $2.1 billion drop in real GNP under postwar conditions.

17-4   FISCAL DIVIDEND AND FISCAL DRAG

FISCAL DIVIDEND

We have examined two sources of change in the budget surplus as defined in equation (17.3), automatic stabilization through changes in Q/Q^N and discretionary fiscal policy through changes in t and G. The final element in (17.3) is the natural real GNP level itself (Q^N), which tends to grow steadily from year to year, currently at a rate of about 2.5 percent annually in the United States, as a result of increased productivity and growth in the labor force. Even if the government succeeds in achieving a stable real GNP ratio of unity, the government surplus will grow from year to year when the tax rate (t) and government spending remain fixed.

> *The automatic growth in the surplus that occurs as growth in Q^N raises tax revenues is called the* **fiscal dividend.**

In Figure 17-3 the initial red budget line BB_0 has a natural employment surplus (NES_0) of zero, as indicated at point A. Automatic growth in revenues occurs if the structure of tax rates (t_0) and the level of government spending (G_0) are held fixed, while the natural real GNP level is allowed to increase over one year, say from the initial level Q_0^N to a new higher level Q_1^N. The budget line shifts leftward, from the initial line BB_0 to the new line BB_1, and as a result the natural employment surplus has risen from zero ($NES_0 = 0$) along the old line to the positive value NES_2 along the new line.[7] The fiscal dividend is the increase in NES, represented in the diagram by the distance FA, caused by the increase in natural real GNP (Q^N).

The fiscal dividend can be created not only by an increase in natural output (Q^N), as illustrated in Figure 17-3, but by inflation. An increase in the price level (P) that raises all incomes has exactly the same effect on tax revenues as an increase in Q^N of the same proportion. Because of the progressivity of the tax system, an increase in either Q^N or P raises nominal GNP, pushes people into higher tax brackets, raises tax revenues by a larger proportion than income, and thus increases the share of government revenue in GNP. This effect of inflation on tax revenues is sometimes called "bracket creep," as inflation pushes people into higher tax brackets.[8] Although an increase in P (unlike Q^N) tends to raise nominal government spending automatically, there is no increase in the share of real government spending in output. Thus inflation makes the natural employment surplus increase automatically, since the share of revenue in GNP is increased but the share of spending in GNP is not changed. In diagrammatic terms, an increase in the price level (P) shifts the budget line leftward, although not by as much as the same percentage increase in Q^N.

---

[7] Why does the budget line shift leftward when Q^N rises? Because federal revenues and the federal surplus are constant if output (Q) is constant while the tax structure and government expenditures remain unchanged. An increase in Q^N reduces the ratio (Q/Q^N) at which the zero surplus occurs from point A, where Q/Q equals unity, leftward to point A' at the new lower level of Q/Q^N caused by the increase in Q^N. For instance, if Q^N rises by 10 percent, then Q/Q^N declines from an initial 1.0 to 0.90 and the point of zero surplus moves leftward from point A to point A' in the figure.

[8] Many economists recommend indexing the tax system to prevent people from being pushed into higher tax brackets by inflation (see section 11-8). This would have the effect of automatically reducing tax rates levied on a given level of nominal household income. Under this proposal an increase in prices would no longer generate a fiscal dividend.

ECONOMIC GROWTH IN Q^N BOOSTS THE NATURAL EMPLOYMENT SURPLUS IF TAX RATES
AND GOVERNMENT SPENDING REMAIN CONSTANT

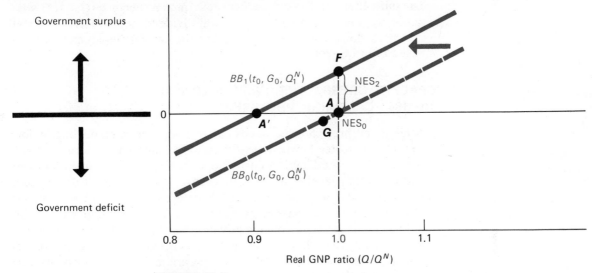

FIGURE 17–3

The Effect on the Budget Line of an Increase in Natural Real GNP
from Q_0^N to the Higher Level Q_1^N

Economic growth in Q^N raises the amount of revenue that the government can
collect at a given real GNP ratio (Q/Q^N) and at a given level of government spending (G_0) and tax rates (t_0). The higher level of revenue raises the natural employment surplus from $NES_0 = 0$ to NES_2 (the distance FA).

Example: Between 1977:Q3 and 1980:Q1 the ratio of natural employment federal revenue to Q^N was pushed up from 19.4 to 21.0 percent,
mainly as a result of a rapid inflation rate. Federal expenditure as a
fraction of Q^N changed hardly at all, decreasing from 21.7 to 21.6 percent. The result was an increase in the real natural employment surplus
from -2.3 percent to -0.6 percent of Q^N.

Thus a fiscal dividend emerges automatically as a result of growth in
natural real GNP (Q^N) or in the price level (P) if adjustments are not made in
tax rates or in real government spending. Policymakers can react to the
automatic growth of the NES and the emergence of a fiscal dividend in
three basic ways:

1. The first alternative is to allow the NES to remain positive, as at NES_2
in Figure 17-3, by holding government spending and tax rates constant.
This, as we will see later in the chapter, tends to encourage private investment.

2. The second alternative is to reduce the average tax rate, cutting revenues and shifting the budget line back down toward BB_0.
3. The third alternative is to raise real government spending (G_0). If G were raised by the full amount of the fiscal dividend, the budget line would shift back down from BB_1 to BB_0, and the natural employment surplus would return to zero.

"BRACKET CREEP," THE "NEW COLD WAR," AND 1980 CAMPAIGN PROMISES

If this set of three choices sounds familiar, we encountered it once before at the end of Chapter 5, when we discussed the mix of monetary and fiscal policy. If monetary policy is adjusted to keep the economy operating at its natural real GNP level ($Q/Q^N = 1.0$), then fiscal policy must decide each year how the fiscal dividend should be allocated. To reduce the real interest rate and encourage private investment, the natural employment surplus should be kept high. To encourage private consumption, tax-rate reductions can use up the fiscal dividend. Finally, government spending can be expanded as a share of real GNP if tax rates are maintained, since "bracket creep" continually pushes people into high tax brackets and raises the share of natural employment revenues to natural real GNP (as between 1977 and 1980).

In the 1980 presidential campaign some candidates promised both to cut taxes and to raise defense spending as a fraction of real GNP in response to the Russian invasion of Afghanistan in January 1980. Yet these same candidates promised to balance the federal budget and to reduce inflation. Were these campaign promises inconsistent? The NES was quite close to balance in early 1980, and so we can discuss this question in terms of the BB_0 line in Figure 17-3. Because the Q/Q^N ratio was about 0.98 in early 1980, the economy's situation is represented by point G.

Using the diagram, we can see that only three of the four campaign promises are consistent. As we have seen, the combined effects of growth in real GNP and in prices continuously push people into higher tax brackets. The Congressional Budget Office has recently estimated that this "bracket creep" will increase the proportion of natural real GNP taken by the federal government in taxes by about 0.8 percentage points each year from 1981 through 1985.[9] If federal expenditures are held constant in real terms over those five years at the 1979 level and if natural real GNP (Q^N) grows 2.5 percent per year, then the proportion of Q^N represented by those expenditures will fall by about 0.5 percentage points each year. Thus, the fiscal dividend will raise the federal budget surplus by about 1.3 percent of natural real GNP (0.8 plus 0.5) each year—that is, by about 5 percent of Q^N over a

---

[9] This estimate is taken from Congressional Budget Office, *Five-year Budget Projections: Fiscal Years 1981–85,* A Report to the Senate and House Committees on the Budget, February 7, 1980.

president's four-year term. This provides "room" for the fulfillment of the first three campaign promises in the following way:

1. Half of the 5 percent fiscal dividend can be used to raise real government expenditures. If all of this were to be spent on defense spending, the share of defense spending in natural real GNP could increase from 4.7 percent in 1979 to 7.2 percent in 1985, for an increase in real defense spending of 80 percent.
2. The other half of the 5 percent fiscal dividend could be used to reduce tax rates. If all of the tax-rate reductions were concentrated on social security payroll taxes, the contributions by employers and employees could both be cut by 40 percent.
3. Because the NES was close to zero in early 1980, full exhaustion of the fiscal dividend would leave it close to zero in early 1985. In terms of Figure 17-3, the fiscal dividend of 5 percent of Q^N would boost the BB line, as shown by the shift from BB_0 to BB_1. But if the fiscal dividend is completely exhausted by expenditure increases and tax reductions, the budget line stays at BB_0.

Why can only three of the four promises be kept? Because maintenance of a zero *actual* surplus in Figure 17-3 along budget line BB_0 — that is, maintaining a "balanced budget" — requires that the economy be maintained at a real GNP ratio (Q/Q^N) of unity. Yet the fourth campaign promise was to reduce inflation. We learned in Chapters 8 and 9 that a permanent and significant reduction of inflation requires acceptance of a significant recession; that is, a period when the Q/Q^N ratio remains below 1.0 for a significant period of time. Only if the government were to adopt most or all of the supply-side remedies listed at the end of Chapter 9 could the fourth campaign promise be kept, and the magnitude of the response of inflation to these supply-side cures is highly uncertain. Clearly the most helpful use of the fiscal dividend would be to concentrate it on tax cuts that directly reduce prices, particularly by devising a way for the federal government to "bribe" states to reduce their state sales taxes.

FISCAL "DRAG"

In Figure 17-3 the upper budget line BB_2 has a natural employment surplus NES_2. In a sense the surplus NES_2 acts as a "drag" on the economy because between points A' and F along the budget line BB_2, as the real GNP ratio expands toward unity, the government surplus rises toward NES_2, siphoning more and more funds out of the economy in the form of tax leakages. Walter W. Heller coined the term *fiscal drag* in the early 1960s when he was chairman of the Council of Economic Advisers.

> **Fiscal drag** *describes the emergence of a fiscal dividend that is not used up in either tax cuts or increases in expenditure.*

How can we reconcile the views of Heller, who viewed a positive surplus such as NES_2 as a drag on the economy, and those who today recommend a large natural employment surplus such as NES_2 to stimulate investment? Clearly the difference is that the second group trusts monetary policy to maintain a high real GNP ratio, whereas Heller either ignores this possibility or is so dubious of the potency of monetary expansion that he fails to mention it.[10] A policy mix of "tight fiscal, easy money" can keep the NES high but maintain an output ratio of 1.0 by keeping the money supply at a reasonably high level, as we learned in section 5-10. Heller was right in the early 1960s that a tight fiscal policy with a high NES can be a drag on the economy if monetary policy fails to provide the necessary stimulus.

17-5 FISCAL STIMULUS AND FISCAL RESTRAINT

The natural employment surplus concept is useful for two primary purposes. First, the NES tells whether at natural employment private investment exceeds or falls short of private saving. When the NES is positive, the government takes in more than it spends if the economy is operating at natural employment, compelling private investment to exceed private saving.[11] The opposite occurs when the NES is negative – the government's full-employment tax revenue falls short of government spending, so that some private saving is required to buy government bonds, thus partially crowding out private investment.

The second major use of the NES concept is to measure discretionary fiscal policy changes. In a particular episode, did discretionary fiscal policy act to stimulate or restrain the economy? The NES falls and the economy is stimulated when government spending rises or tax rates decline. The NES rises and the economy is restrained in the opposite situation, when government spending declines or tax rates are raised. Thus it seems appropriate to define fiscal stimulus and restraint as follows:

1. Fiscal stimulus occurs when the NES falls (ΔNES is negative).
2. Fiscal restraint occurs when the NES rises (ΔNES is positive).
3. Fiscal neutrality occurs when the NES is constant (ΔNES = 0).[12]

A brief review of sections 3-5 through 3-7 should convince the reader that $-\Delta$NES (minus the change in the NES) is a very crude measure of the effect of fiscal policy on total spending. If policymakers decide to stimulate the economy by raising government expenditures by \$1, that full \$1 flows

---

[10] Walter W. Heller, *New Dimensions of Political Economy* (New York: Norton, 1966), p. 65.

[11] In section 2-6 we learned that by definition the surplus $(T - G)$ equals private investment (I) minus private spending (S). This definition ignores foreign trade.

[12] Each of the three sentences should be qualified: "and Q^N remains fixed." If Q^N and G or t change together, then the value of ΔNES mixes up discretionary fiscal changes with the fiscal dividend.

directly into GNP. Then the $1 is "blown up" by the multiplier effect.[13] In contrast, if the same $1 stimulative reduction in the NES is achieved by cutting taxes by $1, the initial increase in income will not be the entire $1, but the fraction of that $1 that is spent. Any portion of the tax cut that is saved leaks out of the spending stream, cutting the multiplier.

The conclusion? A $1 change in the NES stimulates the economy more if it takes the form of a $1 increase in G than a $1 decrease in taxes. Thus a given fiscal stimulus, as measured by $-\Delta$NES, is only a crude measure of the effect of fiscal policy on the economy—a true measure would have to be weighted by the fraction of the budget change that flows directly into GNP (100 percent for spending changes, less than 100 percent for permanent tax cuts, and only a small fraction for temporary tax cuts).

Despite the defects of the natural employment surplus we will treat its changes ($-\Delta$NES) as our measure of fiscal stimulus and restraint in the case study presented in the next section. A better measure of fiscal stimulus would be changes in the weighted standardized surplus, which differs from $-\Delta$NES by placing weights of less than 100 percent on changes in NES caused by tax-rate changes and by evaluating the effect of tax-rate changes at today's output, not natural output.[14] But we prefer for expositional clarity to concentrate on the NES itself.[15]

17-6 CASE STUDY: DISCRETIONARY FISCAL POLICY IN THE POSTWAR UNITED STATES

Figure 17-4 illustrates the level of the real natural employment surplus and real actual budget surplus measured as a percentage of real GNP during the entire postwar period between 1950 and 1980. The actual surplus (black line) lies below the NES (red line) during depressed years such as 1958 and 1975–76 when the Q/Q^N ratio fell well below unity. In very prosperous years, such as 1966–69, the black actual surplus line lies above the red NES line. The maximum level of the NES was about 4.5 percent in late 1950, and the largest negative value was about 4 percent in 1975:Q2.

We can use Figure 17-4 to analyze the major discretionary fiscal policy actions taken during the 1950–80 period. On the diagram fiscal stimulus is represented by a sharp drop in the red NES line, of which the most

---

[13] See section 3-5.

[14] The best exposition of the weighted standardized surplus is in Alan S. Blinder and Robert M. Solow, "Analytical Foundations of Fiscal Policy," in *The Economics of Public Finance* (Washington, D.C.: Brookings Institution, 1974), pp. 11–33.

[15] We are interested in the NES not only because its changes represent fiscal stimulus or restraint, but also because its level measures the influence of government on the balance between natural employment saving and investment. For this second purpose the weighted standardized surplus of Blinder and Solow is useless. Fortunately, Blinder and Solow's own data suggest that $-\Delta$NES captures all the main episodes of fiscal stimulus or restraint that they measure by changes in their weighted standardized surplus. See their Table 4, p. 26.

FIFTEEN YEARS OF NES DEFICIT (1965–80) FOLLOWED A DECADE OF NES SURPLUS (1954–64)

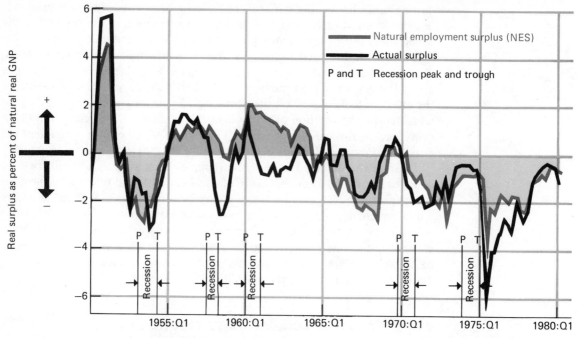

FIGURE 17–4

A Comparison of the Actual Budget Surplus and the Natural Employment Surplus (NES) for the U.S. Federal Government, 1950–80

The red NES line lies above the black actual budget line in years when the economy was weak, with actual real GNP below natural real GNP. The pink-shaded regions reflect periods when the NES was negative—in deficit—whereas the gray-shaded regions reflect quarters of a positive NES. Notice the movement of the NES into deficit during the 1965–67 escalation of the Vietnam War, followed by the movement to a zero NES as a result of the tax surcharge of 1968. The large NES deficit of 1975 reflects the tax rebate of that year.

Source: Appendix B.

obvious example occurred in 1975:Q2 as a result of a large tax rebate. Fiscal restraint is represented by a sharp increase in the red NES line, as in mid-1968 at the time of the temporary income tax surcharge.

STIMULUS AND RESTRAINT IN THE 1950s

In 1950 tax increases were legislated very rapidly after the outbreak of the Korean War, but it took time for the Defense Department to spend the money. Thus the NES rose sharply in 1950 but then fell steadily during 1951–53 as the bills came in. Defense spending peaked in early 1953 and then declined rapidly in 1953–55, causing the red NES line to rise rapidly. Although tax rates were reduced in early 1954, as some temporary Korean War taxes were allowed to expire, the stimulative impact of the tax cuts was swamped by the restrictive impact of the cuts in defense spending.

Tax rates remained unchanged between 1954 and 1964, so that all of the swings in the red NES line during this period can be attributed to the speeding up or slowing down of growth in real government spending. Notice that the Eisenhower administration can be credited with an admirable achievement of countercyclical fiscal policy in 1958 when unemployment was high, but then it promptly discredited itself by allowing a sharp movement toward restraint in 1959 and 1960, helping to abort the 1959 recovery and cause the 1960–61 recession. The Eisenhower advisers were so eager to keep the *actual* budget surplus at zero in 1959–60 that they neglected the burgeoning values of the NES. The high value of NES would have stimulated investment if monetary policy had been easy, but the combination of tight fiscal and tight monetary policy imposed "fiscal drag" on the economy. One result was the defeat of Vice-President Nixon by Senator John Kennedy in the 1960 presidential election. (The history of monetary policy during this period is summarized in Figure 16-2, p. 487.)

STIMULUS AND RESTRAINT IN THE 1960s

The high value of the NES in 1959–63 was the ammunition that Walter Heller's Council of Economic Advisers under President Kennedy used in 1962–63 to develop the concepts of "fiscal dividend" and "fiscal drag" and to convince Congress that a permanent tax reduction was needed. Finally Heller's dream came true, and tax rates were reduced substantially in March 1964. Then a second round of tax cuts in 1964 and 1965, together with the rapid growth of defense expenditures as the Vietnam War escalated in 1965–67, worked to plunge the NES into substantial deficit. The combined effect of the stimulus applied between early 1964 and early 1968 amounted to about 4 percent of GNP, and most of this represents a highly undesirable procyclical policy action, given that the Q/Q^N ratio rose above unity in late 1964.

The most important economic event of the 1960s was the Vietnam War, which was the main cause of high government deficits, rapid monetary growth, and the too-high levels of real GNP and employment achieved during 1966–69. One aggravating factor was the delay in legislating tax increases to pay for the Vietnam War. Finally, in mid-1968 government revenues were raised substantially by a 10 percent personal and corporate income tax surcharge. The NES increased from −2.8 percent of natural real GNP in 1968:Q2 to +0.2 percent in 1969:Q2. We have seen in Chapter 13 that most of the impact of the surcharge was off-set by a reduction in saving, leaving only a minor stabilizing impact. The 1970 recession did not really begin until the restraining influence of the tight monetary policy and disintermediation of 1969 was felt.

STIMULUS AND RESTRAINT IN THE 1970s

Figure 17-4 shows that the NES slid downward steadily between early 1970 and early 1973. Although the first part of this stimulative episode was appropriate as a countercyclical measure during the recession of 1970, the continuation of stimulative fiscal policy was inappropriate after the Q/Q^N ratio exceeded unity in early 1972. The initial cause of fiscal stimulus was the expiration of the temporary tax surcharge in July 1970. Then in December 1971 the president signed a tax-reduction package that, when combined with rapid increases in social security benefits during this period, pushed the NES further into deficit.

A remarkable fact about the 1972–73 period is the simultaneous timing of monetary and fiscal stimulus. We saw in Figure 16-4 that monetary growth peaked around the time of President Nixon's reelection in November 1972. And here in Figure 17-4 we can see that the NES reached its minimum level at about the same time, so that fiscal stimulus was applied in the period leading up to election. Thus both monetary and fiscal policy during this period were procyclical, aggravating the excessive aggregate demand growth that carried the Q/Q^N ratio substantially above unity.

After the election the NES was allowed to grow. In 1973 and 1974 "bracket creep" was allowed to raise the natural employment ratio of tax revenues to GNP while the ratio of expenditures to GNP held constant. The timing of this episode of restraint thus helped to aggravate the depth of the recession of 1973–75.

Alarmed by the steep decline of the economy into a serious recession in late 1974 and early 1975, Congress acted promptly to cut taxes. The 1975 stimulus consisted of both a temporary tax rebate and permanent tax reductions, accounting for the temporary drop in the NES in 1975:Q2 to a record low of −4 percent. The permanent part of the tax reduction explains why the NES in the last half of 1975 was considerably below the figure reached during most of 1974. Partly because of the promptness of congressional action, and partly by coincidence, the tax rebate was actually paid out in May 1975, the very month when unemployment reached its postwar peak of 9.0 percent.

During much of the period between the recession trough in early 1975 and 1978:Q4 when the Q/Q^N ratio peaked, the NES was allowed to rise. Thus much of the fiscal dividend that developed during this period was devoted to eliminating the NES deficit rather than to major tax cuts or increases in the share of Q^N devoted to government expenditures. The effect of bracket creep was offset in mid-1977 by congressional passage of an economic stimulus package proposed by President Carter and in early 1979 by a minor tax-rate reduction.[16]

SUMMARY: THE LESSONS OF THE 1950s WERE NOT LEARNED

An oversimplified summary of the postwar experience with discretionary fiscal policy would be:

The record of the 1950s stands out as the best. The impact of fiscal policy was destabilizing during most of the period between 1959 and 1974. Improvement occurred in the last half of the 1970s, but budgetary restriction during the 1980 recession represented a return to destabilizing practices.

The basis for this evaluation is the simple idea that fiscal restraint (a rising NES) should be applied when the economy is expanding and particularly when the Q/Q^N ratio is above 1.0. Fiscal stimulus should be applied in a recession and more generally when the Q/Q^N ratio is below 1.0, although the amount of stimulus should be lessened as Q/Q^N approaches 1.0.

In the 1950s there were two outstanding episodes of stabilizing policy: the restraining upward jump of the NES in late 1950 when the Korean War broke out, and the reduction of the NES during the 1958 recession. After that, the high level of NES aggravated the economic slack of 1958–63; the sharp stimulus during 1964–68 aggravated the overheated high levels of Q/Q^N reached during 1966–69; the restraint represented by the temporary surcharge of 1968 was appropriate but much too late; and the stimulus applied to the economy during 1971–72 was inappropriate given the high levels of Q/Q^N reached in 1972 and early 1973.

The improved record of the late 1970s begins with the prompt congressional enactment of the tax-stimulus package of early 1975, which caused a major fiscal stimulus to be applied only a few months late. Then the NES was allowed to move gradually in a restraining direction during the 1975–78 expansion. Unfortunately, in early 1980 the Carter administration began the new decade by reverting to the destabilizing practices of 1959–74. Just as a serious collapse in the Q/Q^N ratio was beginning in March 1980, a new, more restrictive budget was introduced. The NES was allowed to increase from approximate balance to positive territory during 1980, thus aggravating the needlessly severe increase in unemployment that occurred throughout the year.

---

[16] A good source for a more detailed history of fiscal policy in the early part of the postwar period is Wilfred Lewis, Jr., *Federal Budget Policy in the Postwar Recessions* (Washington, D.C.: Brookings Institution, 1962). Details of the post-1962 period are contained in U.S. House of Representatives, Committee on the Budget, *Economic Stabilization Policies: The Historical Record, 1962–76* (Washington, D.C.: U.S. Government Printing Office, November 1978). The early 1970s are reviewed in Alan S. Blinder, *Economic Policy and the Great Stagflation* (New York: Academic Press, 1979).

17-7 LAGS IN THE EFFECT OF FISCAL POLICY

Lags weaken the case for any countercyclical policy, whether monetary or fiscal, because they may prevent activist policy changes from influencing the economy early enough to help offset destabilizing shifts in spending. A stimulus designed to dampen a recession may wind up influencing the economy a year or two later, when the problem may have changed to one of restraining a boom. As in the case of monetary policy, several types of lags intervene that prevent any fiscal policy change from immediately offsetting an unexpected shift in the demand for commodities or money. The first two types of lags are shared by monetary and fiscal policy:

1. The data lag
2. The recognition lag

In section 16-7 we concluded that these lags introduce a delay of about four months between a change in economic conditions and the earliest feasible response of the policy authorities. An initial wait occurs as data are collected, and a subsequent delay interferes as analysts wait for several months to pass so that they can determine whether a reversal in the behavior of an important data series represents a transitory "blip" or a lasting alteration.

LEGISLATIVE LAG

The third source of delay, the legislative lag, is much more important for fiscal than for monetary policy. Not only the Congress, but also the president, are involved. President Kennedy's economic advisers recognized the need for a permanent income tax reduction almost immediately when they arrived in Washington in 1961, but the president did not finally agree to propose the change until mid-1962, and the Congress did not enact the necessary legislation until March 1964. In that episode Congress had a hard time accepting the radically different "New Economics" of the president's economic advisers. Walter Heller and associates in the 1961–63 period dropped any appeal for budget-balancing "fiscal responsibility" and emphasized instead the fiscal drag caused then by a high natural employment surplus in the absence of stimulative monetary policy.

Similarly, there was a long lag between the date when in early 1966 economic advisers realized that a tax increase was needed to offset expanding government expenditures on the Vietnam War and the final enactment of the income tax surcharge in mid-1968. The first problem of the advisers was to persuade President Johnson, who did not want to raise taxes and aggravate opposition to the war before the congressional elections of November 1966. Finally, in January 1967, Johnson recommended a tax increase, but final enactment by Congress was delayed a full eighteen months.

Legislative lags have been much shorter in recent episodes. Although policymaking in the 1974–75 recession was marred by President Ford's

Hoover-like plan to raise tax rates in the fall of 1974, finally in January 1975 the collapse of real GNP led the President to propose a $16 billion tax reduction. Congress responded with alacrity, passing a $21 billion tax cut only two months later. In 1977 the legislative lag was four months between President Carter's January proposal of a $31 billion two-year stimulus package and the passage by Congress in May of a $20 billion package.

TRANSMISSION LAG

The fourth source of delay, the transmission lag, varies in length for different types of fiscal policy. A change in income tax rates can alter paychecks within weeks, as soon as new withholding tax tables are printed and mailed to employers. But an increase in government spending (for example, public works expenditures) is subject to a long transmission lag because of delays necessary for designs to be created, plans to be drawn, bids to be submitted, contracts to be signed, and work to begin. The desire to minimize the transmission lag for public works projects has led to proposals for an "ever-ready" shelf of projects for which all these preliminary steps have been completed.

EFFECTIVENESS LAG

The final delay, the effectiveness lag, varies among alternative types of fiscal policy. Further, econometric models differ in their estimates of the multipliers associated with individual types of policy change. For instance, in the first quarter following a $1 billion increase in government spending, estimates of the resulting increase in nominal GNP range between $0.7 and $1.8 billion. After three quarters have elapsed, the estimates range between $1.2 and $2.7 billion.[17] Thus policymakers who want to raise spending by, say, $25 billion have no firm guidance on the exact size of the fiscal stimulus that is required.

A discussion of this subject written a few years ago would have carefully balanced the advantage of the short legislative lag of monetary policy against the short effectiveness lag of fiscal policy instruments. Monetary policy was thought to influence aggregate demand only through a roundabout process. The lag between changes in the interest rate and investment was estimated by some economists in the late 1960s to be at least eight quarters, as compared to only about two quarters for fiscal tax reductions or expenditure increases.[18]

But the evidence examined in Chapter 16 suggests that the effectiveness lag of monetary policy is much shorter, only around two to three quarters,

---

[17] *Source:* See Figure 12-4.

[18] Charles W. Bischoff, "The Effect of Alternative Lag Distributions," in Gary Fromm (ed.), *Tax Incentives and Capital Spending* (Washington, D.C.: Brookings Institution, 1971), pp. 61–130. See especially Figure 3-6, p. 114.

and is thus fully comparable with that of fiscal policy. Should we conclude that countercyclical monetary policy is superior to fiscal policy because its legislative lag is shorter and more predictable, while its effectiveness lag is not appreciably longer? Such a verdict appears premature for two reasons. First, the much more rapid response of Congress in the 1970s than in earlier decades suggests that the legislative lag, although uncertain, may not be a major obstacle to the use of fiscal policy, at least when the economy is widely agreed to be operating too far away from the natural unemployment target as in 1975. Second, the side effects of monetary and fiscal stimulus are different and must be considered in light of other policy objectives, such as those of promoting investment and economic growth and of minimizing inflation.

17-8 CHOICE OF FISCAL INSTRUMENTS: LIMITATIONS OF TAX-RATE AND EXPENDITURE CHANGES

If a countercyclical activist fiscal policy is to be pursued, which fiscal tools should be used? The number of possibilities is almost endless. Any of the following tax measures could be introduced: temporary tax credits, rebates, or surcharges; permanent changes in personal and/or corporate income tax rates; changes in the investment tax credit; liberalization of depreciation allowances; extensions of unemployment compensation; and employment subsidies. Or any one of several types of government spending can be altered: public works, grants to state and local governments, manpower training programs, and others.

The efficiency of a fiscal tool can be defined as its bang per buck, the dollars of extra nominal GNP created per extra dollar of budget deficit. If we assume that the natural employment surplus (NES) is initially at its desired level, then any discretionary fiscal change will push the NES away from its desired level. If, for instance, the objective is a $20 billion increase in GNP required to reduce unemployment, an efficient policy stimulus is one with a large multiplier effect, achieving the policy objective with, say, only a $5 billion decrease in the NES. A less efficient policy with a smaller multiplier might require a $40 billion decrease in the NES to raise GNP and reduce unemployment by the same amount.

As we first learned in Chapter 3, the multiplier effect of any change in tax rates or government spending depends on (1) the fraction of each initial dollar of deficit that is spent immediately on the first round rather than saved, and (2) the fraction of the income created from the first-round extra spending that is spent again rather than leaking out of the spending stream into saving, income taxes, and imports.[19] Component (2) is roughly the same for all types of fiscal changes, but component (1) may differ widely.

For instance, any extra dollar of budget deficit caused by a dollar of extra

---

[19] If the money supply is fixed, a higher demand for money will raise the interest rate and cause a crowding out effect on private spending. See section 5-6.

government expenditures results in a spending fraction on the first round of 100 percent. At the opposite extreme, an extra dollar of budget deficit incurred when a tax rebate is given to rich people may have a spending fraction on the first round of only 2 or 3 percent. Rich people may have all the consumption goods they want and may put almost all the tax rebate into savings.

INEFFICIENCY OF PERSONAL TAX-RATE CHANGES

Changes in personal income tax rates in 1964, 1968, and 1975 designed for stabilization purposes were largely absorbed by offsetting changes in saving, as we learned in section 13-6. Thus inefficiency is the fundamental limitation of changes in tax rates as a tool of discretionary fiscal policy. Very large shifts in the natural employment surplus (NES) may be necessary to achieve significant changes in total spending and unemployment. To achieve a given unemployment target through tax policy alone, the NES may have to be shifted from its desired level by four or five times more than if the same unemployment target were reached through changes in government spending.

Tax policy differs from the use of government spending for stabilization by temporarily shifting the short-run Phillips curve. In a recession, when a reduction in unemployment is desired, a cut in income taxes tends to shift the short-run Phillips curve downward temporarily because tax cuts enable firms to reduce the selling price of their products while maintaining intact both after-tax wages and profits. The same phenomenon works in reverse in a boom when an increase in unemployment and reduction in inflation is desired; a tax-rate increase may shift the Phillips curve upward and thus have a perverse effect, increasing the inflation rate instead of reducing it. Why? Higher taxes will partially be incorporated into business costs and prices. This upward shift in costs may outweigh the anti-inflationary contribution of the reduction in aggregate demand achieved by the tax increase.[20]

The fiscal policy tool that has been used most often for countercyclical stabilization policy—changes in personal income tax rates—thus appears to be severely flawed. It is a poor stimulus for use in recessions because so much of each dollar of extra federal deficit leaks out into saving. And it is a poor anti-inflationary device for use in booms because tax increases raise business costs and prices. Should tax policy be abandoned as a stabilization tool?

OTHER TAXES

Several tax instruments are available besides the personal income tax. Any tax or subsidy on spending, such as a sales or excise tax or an invest-

---

[20] For a theoretical analysis demonstrating that the final outcome may go either way, see Alan S. Blinder, "Can Income Tax Increases be Inflationary? An Expository Note," *National Tax Journal*, vol. 26 (June 1973), pp. 295–301.

ment credit, is ideally suited for stabilization if legislative lags are sufficiently short. Imagine that a U.S. national sales tax of 5 percent were levied on all products and that in a recession the sales tax were eliminated for six months. The temporary nature of the tax cut would aid in stimulating economic recovery, because it would induce households to make their purchases of durable and semidurable goods (autos, clothing) earlier than would otherwise have occurred.

The major disadvantages of temporary changes in sales taxes are practical. First, the effect will be perverse during congressional debate of the measure; households will delay spending during a recession if they think that proposed tax cuts will make goods cheaper in the future after congressional action. Second, there is no national sales tax in the United States that can be used for countercyclical stabilization. The federal government could subsidize state and local governments to reduce their own sales taxes during recessions, but this proposal has the disadvantage of inequity, since some states (albeit a minority) do not have a state sales tax and thus would be unable to take advantage of the federal subsidy.

Because of these limitations, sales tax changes in U.S. stabilization policy have been limited to alterations in the investment tax credit (ITC), first introduced in 1962 as a permanent stimulus to investment. Unfortunately, past attempts to use the ITC as a countercyclical stabilization tool have been ill-timed and counterproductive. The ITC was repealed in the spring of 1969, too late to offset the excessive spending and too-low unemployment of the 1966–69 period. The decline in investment spending induced by the repeal of the ITC served only to amplify the decline of spending in the 1969–70 recession. Then the credit was reintroduced in late 1971, and it contributed to the excessive spending that occurred in late 1972 and early 1973. This sad experience has led Harvard's Dale W. Jorgenson to conclude:

> The investment tax credit cannot be used as a short-run stabilization or countercyclical measure because the time lags involved are too long. Instead, it should be kept on permanently at a relatively high rate to foster the long-run goal of stimulating the growth of the capital stock.[21]

Another conflicting piece of evidence is the success in Sweden of a somewhat different stabilization tool, a countercyclical investment fund. The Swedish plan uses a powerful fiscal stick and carrot to shift investment from booms to recessions.[22] The stick is the corporation income tax, which corporations naturally try to avoid. The government encourages avoidance by allowing firms in boom years to put aside up to 40 percent of pretax profits

---

[21] "A Tax Credit to Check Inflation and Recession," *Business Week* (November 16, 1974), p. 118. We shall see in section 18-6 that Jorgenson's quotation is misleading, since the total capital stock cannot be made to grow faster unless private saving is raised or the government surplus is increased, neither of which can be accomplished by a higher investment tax credit. The credit just shifts funds to capital projects eligible for the credit from those that are not eligible.

[22] See Hans Brems, "Swedish Fine Tuning," *Challenge* (March/April 1976), pp. 39–42.

in a special fund. Investment in booms is reduced, since firms have immobilized part of their profits, which, after paying tax, they could have used for investment.

The carrot to firms is the availability of all the fund—including the profits that otherwise would have gone to the government in tax—for specific types of investment projects during certain specified recession periods. From the firm's point of view, the plan amounts to an extreme liberalization of depreciation that allows taxes to be written off even before an investment is made.

EXPENDITURE CHANGES

Changes in government expenditures are more efficient than changes in tax rates because 100 percent of the extra spending initially becomes extra GNP. The main disadvantages of spending changes as compared to tax changes are (1) delays in timing and (2) the possibility that the social value of the extra output produced may be relatively low. The timing problem is most acute. In early 1977, for instance, President Carter's advisers did not include major spending increases in the first year of their two-year stimulus package because they did not believe that it was administratively possible to spend extra billions productively within a short period. Even after the legislative lag is surmounted, there are usually long delays while projects are planned and funds allocated. In our federal system of government, there may be a further delay if the spending increase takes the form of a federal government grant that is actually spent by state and local governments.

Just as questions of equity cloud any discussion of tax-rate changes, changes in spending on public projects raise the same questions of fairness. Spending on what? Cleaner parks for Santa Monica? A new city hall for Plains? Another disadvantage of spending changes is that they are not easily reversible. Let us imagine that money is allocated even-handedly in 1981 both for cleaner parks in Santa Monica and for a new city hall for Plains. Then let us suppose that a rapid economic expansion in 1982 requires fiscal restraint. The choice of cutbacks in public works projects as a fiscal tool is bound to cause unhappiness and waste. Santa Monica residents will complain about the mess in their parks. Plains residents will complain about their half-finished city hall. Frequent changes in government spending plans can lead to a lack of confidence in the promises of government officials and considerable difficulties in hiring employees, who may fear subsequent dismissal when economic conditions change.[23]

---

[23] In an early study, S. J. Maisel found a delay of about one year between the authorization of certain federal public works projects and the awarding of contracts. See S. J. Maisel, "Timing and Flexibility of a Public Works Program," *Review of Economics and Statistics*, vol. 31 (May 1949), p. 149. A more recent study by Albert Ando and E. Cary Brown suggests that an attempt by the federal government during the 1957–58 recession to accelerate spending on construction projects did not succeed in stimulating the economy during the period when it was needed. See Albert Ando and E. Cary Brown, "Lags in Fiscal Policy," in *Stabilization Policies* (Englewood Cliffs, N.J.: Prentice-Hall, 1963).

How can funds be allocated rapidly and fairly? The Swedes solve this problem by keeping a large inventory of projects ready to be mobilized on short notice, in say one or two months. The Japanese have also developed a system of countercyclical public works expenditures that avoids lags in starting new projects and the dislocations and inefficiency caused when projects are canceled. The technique is simple—increase or decrease the speed with which a given project is completed. For instance, the 115-mile Tokyo Coastal Bay Expressway has been under construction since 1962. The Japanese central government decides each year how much money should be allocated to it, depending on the stabilization needs of the economy. No one knows when the project will be completed, because "that depends on the economy and how we control spending."[24]

17-9 CONCLUSION TO PARTS IV AND V

Two main themes have been our focus in Parts IV and V. The first is the monetarist-nonmonetarist debate on the relative merits of policy activism as opposed to fixed policy rules, particularly a constant-growth-rate-rule for the money supply. The second theme is a comparison of the relative merits of alternative policy instruments that might be used to pursue an activist countercyclical policy.

VERDICT ON ACTIVISM

In an imaginary world in which all private spending consisted of consumer expenditures on services, the case for countercyclical activism would be relatively weak. Consumers would tend to keep their consumption of services equal to a fixed (or very slowly changing) fraction of their permanent or lifetime income. Since only a small fraction of any transitory shock would be incorporated into permanent income, consumer spending and hence total private spending would be stable. If the government could manage to avoid sudden accelerations or decelerations in the growth of government spending, then total GNP could grow fairly smoothly.

This imaginary world lacks one crucial feature of the real world, the accumulation of capital, both by business firms and by consumers in the form of durable goods. The decision to accumulate durable goods is a two-stage process. First, numerous factors, including monetary and fiscal policy, influence the total stock of capital goods that each firm and consumer desires to hold. Second, firms and consumers may vary the speed at which they adjust their actual capital stock to the level that they desire. Both stages can

---

[24] The speaker is a Mr. Ito, who oversees the Japanese Construction Ministry's financial planning, as quoted in Andrew H. Malcolm, "Japan Is Battling Economic Slump with Public Works Projects," *The New York Times* (May 12, 1976), p. 57.

contribute to highly unstable rates of spending on durable goods, resulting in aggregate economic instability when durable goods industries suffer from stretches of inadequate demand followed by years of excess demand.

Monetarists do not deny that private investment tends to be unstable. In fact, they almost never mention the instability of investment inherent in the accelerator process.[25] Instead, the opposition of monetarists to counter-cyclical activism is mainly based on the poor past performance of the government, the inability of economic forecasts to look accurately far enough ahead to overcome long policy lags, and, perhaps more fundamentally, a deep distrust of government. Most proponents of activism do not deny these accusations, except the last. Nor do they insist that every small wiggle in the growth rate of output must be smoothed out. But they argue that society wastes huge amounts of resources, in the form of idle people and machines, when it pursues fixed policy rules during long slumps of investment (1930–41, 1958–63, and 1975–77). In a symmetric fashion, long booms of the 1966–69 Vietnam variety should be avoided as well. Lags between the initiation of a countercyclical policy action and the economy's response do not appear to be more than a year in duration, certainly a short enough delay to allow ample room for an activist policy to counter a three- or four-year investment slump, even if not enough room to counter a six-month economic pause.

CHOICE OF TOOLS

The second theme of Parts IV and V is the choice of tools for an activist policy. Since society has a multitude of goals, no one policy instrument is adequate. The evidence accumulated in Chapters 15–17 points to the following as desirable policy tools to achieve the principal goals, although many economists would be able to construct their own list differing somewhat in components and emphasis:

1. *Keeping the actual unemployment rate close to the natural rate of unemployment.* This target is best left to countercyclical variations in the growth rate of the money supply. Aggregate fiscal measures suffer from serious defects as countercyclical tools, particularly the low efficiency of personal tax changes and the problems of administering and allocating sudden spurts in government spending.
2. *Minimize the rate of inflation.* Two approaches to inflation fighting are emphasized in this book. First, the short-run Phillips curve can be shifted downward by supply-side policy innovations, including the reduction of tax rates that heavily influence prices, the reduction of the minimum wage, elimination of government regulation that raise business costs, and

---

[25] For an example of a monetarist analysis of the sources of the Great Depression that does not once mention the contribution of the durable goods accelerator, see Allan H. Meltzer, "Monetary and Other Explanations of the Start of the Great Depression," *Journal of Monetary Economics,* vol. 2 (November 1976), pp. 455–472.

other measures listed at the end of Chapter 9. To maintain a stable unemployment rate, these favorable supply shifts must be accompanied by an "accommodative" deceleration in the growth rate of the money supply. Second, the social cost of an ongoing inflation can be reduced by institutional reforms, particularly indexing of the tax system, issuance by the government of an indexed bond, and termination of restrictive government regulations that allow wealthy savers to enjoy high returns but limit the interest rate available to poor savers.

3. *Reduce the natural rate of unemployment.* Some of the schemes discussed in Chapter 10, such as reform of the unemployment compensation system and provision of training subsidies for low-skill workers, would help to reduce the natural rate. If successful, these programs might allow U.S. policymakers eventually to reduce actual unemployment to below 5.0 percent as compared to a minimum of 5.5 or 6.0 percent in the absence of such programs.

4. *Promote economic growth.* The United States saves less, invests less, and grows slower than most advanced industrialized countries. We consider the sources of economic growth in the next chapter.

SUMMARY

1. The actual government surplus can change for three reasons. First, changes in the output ratio Q/Q^N alter the government's tax collections even if tax rates are fixed. This response of the actual budget to the economy is called automatic stabilization. Second, the actual surplus can change through discretionary fiscal policy actions that raise or lower tax rates and government spending. Finally, the actual surplus can change through economic growth, which raises natural output (Q^N) and creates a fiscal dividend.

2. The response of the budget to the economy is called automatic stabilization, because the positive response of tax collections to changes in total real GNP raises leakages out of the spending stream when the economy is expanding, thus dampening the expansion. Similarly, leakages out of the spending stream fall when the economy is shrinking in a recession, thus helping to limit the decline in real GNP.

3. The natural employment surplus concept (NES) eliminates changes in the budget due to the automatic stabilization response of the budget to the state of the economy. The NES can change either through discretionary fiscal policy actions or through the fiscal dividend created by economic growth.

4. The NES budget concept is useful for two main purposes. First, the level of NES tells whether or not the government is running a surplus when the economy is operating at natural employment. Second, changes in the NES with the sign reversed ($-\Delta$ NES) are a crude measure of the degree of fiscal stimulus and restraint.

5. The government budget has helped to stabilize the economy to a much greater extent since World War II than before the war. The main reason is that the government is much bigger, collecting more of GNP in the form of taxes and accounting for more of total spending on goods and services. Combined with the high responsiveness of tax revenues to changes in the state of the economy, this means that almost one-third of any change in the real GNP ratio (Q/Q^N) leaks out of the spending stream, cutting the spending multiplier far below its prewar value.

6. The record of discretionary fiscal policy actions in the postwar period is mixed. Between 1959 and 1974 and again in 1980 policy was mainly procyclical rather than countercyclical and thus aggravated the instability of the economy.

7. Fiscal policy lags are more uncertain than monetary policy lags. Unlike monetary policy, in which decisions are made in a single meeting, fiscal policy changes usually require debate in Congress that may extend over many months. This legislative lag is a crucial disadvantage of using fiscal policy for short-run stabilization.

8. Fiscal policy shares with monetary policy additional lags between a turning point in the economy and the earliest possible effect of countercyclical policy. The transmission lag differs among types of fiscal policy and is long for government investment projects but short for tax changes. The effectiveness lag likewise varies among policies.

9. The variety of fiscal policies is almost limitless. An efficient fiscal tool generates a relatively large change in output for a given change in the natural employment surplus. Temporary changes in income tax are inefficient compared to permanent ones, and temporary subsidies or indirect taxes on goods and services may be more efficient than permanent changes.

A LOOK AHEAD

One of the most perplexing economic problems in the United States in the 1970s was a slowdown in the growth rate of labor productivity. This, in turn, led to a slowdown in the growth rate of natural real GNP. Although the productivity slowdown also occurred in most other countries, nowhere in the late 1970s was productivity growing as slowly as in the United States. In the next chapter we examine the sources of economic growth and recent explanations for the U.S. growth slowdown.

CONCEPTS

Actual government surplus
Natural employment surplus
Automatic stabilization
Discretionary fiscal policy
Fiscal dividend

Fiscal drag
Fiscal stimulus and restraint
Efficiency of a fiscal tool
Countercyclical investment fund
Public works projects

QUESTIONS FOR REVIEW

1   Explain why the budget line in Figures 17-1 and 17-3 slopes upward. What factors determine the steepness of the line? Can you explain why the actual U.S. budget line in Figure 17-2 was steeper in 1975 than in 1932?

2   Explain how each of the following would affect the budget line: increase in government spending to build airplanes for a rapid-deployment force; a higher federal gasoline tax; growth in natural real GNP; an increase in the price level.

3   A 1 percent change in nominal GNP generates a change in federal tax revenues of about 1.6 percent. Using this information, explain what would happen to the NES if the federal government were to keep all tax rates constant while maintaining a fixed fraction of government spending in nominal GNP.

4   Turn back to Figure 17-4. Explain in words why the actual budget line drops so much more than the NES line between early 1974 and early 1975. Why does the actual budget line lie above the NES line in 1966? Why are the two lines roughly equal in 1979?

5   Is the change in the natural employment surplus (NES) an accurate measure of fiscal stimulus or restraint when the government conducts a balanced budget expansion that raises government spending and tax collections by the same amount?

6   Since either monetary or fiscal policy can alter output, why do we not rely exclusively on one or the other?

7   What are the main side effects of fiscal policy, other than altering total spending? Of monetary policy?

8   What factors help explain why the efficiencies of various fiscal policies differ?

9   Even after it has been decided that increased (or decreased) government spending is the appropriate way to eliminate a difference between actual and natural real GNP, what decisions must still be made? What do these decisions depend on?

APPENDIXES TO CHAPTER 17
1. The Burden of the Public Debt

A defender of a continually balanced budget, such as California's governor Jerry Brown, implies that it is not legitimate for a government to pursue a discretionary fiscal policy that involves running deficits in recessions. "Surely the increase in the government debt caused by the government's failure to 'pay its bills' creates a burden on the future taxpayers who must pay interest on the debt," he might assert. How are we to assess the argument that government deficits create an extra burden of the public debt, thus mitigating their virtues as devices to stabilize the economy?

THE BURDEN OF THE AT&T DEBT

The burden of the public debt is a topic that has taken up a vast amount of space in the economic literature, and yet the most important ideas are very simple.[1] When the government fails to collect sufficient tax revenues to pay for its expenditures, it finances its deficit by selling bonds to the public. The government must pay interest on these bonds for many years in the future. Extra taxes must be levied on future taxpayers to cover these interest payments. At first glance government deficit spending appears to be similar to deficit spending by the telephone company, AT&T, which fails to collect sufficient revenues from telephone service to pay for all its new plant and equipment. It finances its deficit by selling bonds to the public. What is the difference between the "burden of the AT&T debt" and the "burden of the public debt"?

No one has ever accused AT&T of creating a burden on future generations by issuing bonds, and for good reason. Like any other corporation, AT&T is in business to make a profit for its stockholders. It attempts to estimate the future rate of return on each planned investment project; that is, the annual future profit likely to be contributed by each project divided by its cost.[2] When each project is ranked in order of its rate of return, AT&T is ready to make its investment decisions. Projects with rates of return greater than the interest rate that AT&T must pay to sell bonds (AT&T's borrowing rate, say r_0) are approved. Projects with a rate of return below the borrowing rate (r_0) are rejected.

The contribution to revenue and expenses of the marginal AT&T project is summarized on the first line of Table 17-A. Net of all operating expenses (labor, materials, fuel, and so forth), the marginal project generates a rate of return (r_0) just equal to the borrowing rate (r_0), and thus it contributes zero to net profit.[3] There is no burden on present or future generations. Individuals currently living make voluntary purchases of AT&T bonds without compulsion. Workers and firms voluntarily build AT&T telephone ex-

---

[1] The most accessible collection of articles is contained in J. M. Ferguson (ed.), *Public Debt and Future Generations* (Chapel Hill: University of North Carolina, 1964). Undergraduates are warned that delving into the complexities of this book is best undertaken by those working on an advanced senior thesis or independent study.

[2] See the example of the ranking of investment projects in Figure 4-1. We choose AT&T because in an average year it singlehandedly accounts for more than half the U.S. corporate bond issues.

[3] This discussion neglects explicit consideration of corporation and personal income taxes. The AT&T rate of return on line 1 can be calculated after payment of corporate income taxes. Although personal income taxes must be paid on interest payments to individuals by both AT&T and the government, this factor makes no essential difference in the discussion.

TABLE 17-A

Comparison of Consequences of AT&T Debt with That of Public Debt

	(1) Rate of return	(2) Interest payment	(3) Net of interest return
1. AT&T marginal investment project	r_0	r_0	0
2. Government marginal investment project	r_0	r_0	0
3. Government deficit-financed consumption expenditure	0	r_0	$-r_0$

changes and new installation equipment because they are paid with the money that AT&T raises from the bond purchasers. Thus in the present generation everyone acts voluntarily in his own best interests and there is no burden on anyone.

In future generations the bondholders receive the interest payments that induced them to purchase the bonds in the first place. Where does AT&T obtain the money to pay the interest payments? By definition the marginal investment project creates exactly enough revenue (over and above operating costs) to pay the interest costs. Thus in future generations everyone is acting voluntarily. The investment projects create extra revenue for AT&T that pays the interest to keep the bondholders happy.

INVESTMENT VERSUS CONSUMPTION

If AT&T bonds do not create a burden for present or future generations, what is meant by the burden of the public debt allegedly created when the government issues bonds? The entire discussion depends on the way the government spends the proceeds of the bond floated to finance its deficit. If the government spends the proceeds on an investment project that yields a return to society sufficient to pay the interest costs on the bonds, then there is no future burden. In this case the government is acting exactly as does AT&T. But if the government spends the proceeds on consumption (for example, ammunition that is used up in a war), then there is no future benefit to pay for the future interest payments, leaving future generations with a net burden.

Government investment projects, such as the construction of government hospitals, schools, and public universities, generate a future rate of return.

The return does not take the form of a monetary profit, since the government is not in business to make a profit; rather the return consists of the benefits to future society created by the project. Assuming that a hospital is utilized to cure sick patients, society is better off to have the hospital than to let patients go uncured in the absence of the hospital. The hospital's rate of return is the annual stream of benefits to society (net of the hospital's operating costs) divided by the cost of the hospital.

If the government chooses to invest only in projects yielding future benefits to society that on an annual basis equal or exceed the government's borrowing rate, then the bonds floated to finance government investment projects are exactly analogous to AT&T bonds. As illustrated on line 2 of Table 17-A, the marginal government investment project generates a future rate of return in the form of future benefits to society that just suffice to pay the interest on the government bonds. If the interest rate on government bonds—like that on AT&T bonds—is r_0, and the social rate of return of the government investment project is the same rate r_0, then there are no future burdens on society. The AT&T bond and the government bond are identical.[4]

The main difference between AT&T bonds and government bonds is that people pay voluntarily to receive telephone service, automatically generating revenue to pay the interest on AT&T bonds without compulsory taxation, whereas the government must raise taxes to pay the interest on its bonds.[5] No burden on future taxpayers exists if they are the same individuals who benefit from the government investment project. For a local road or rapid transit project financed by local property taxes, there is a presumption that the beneficiaries and the taxpayers are the same people. For federal projects this assumption may be invalid. Benefits may be concentrated on certain constituencies (the often-publicized flow of federal dollars to the sunbelt), whereas taxes are widely dispersed across all households. In this case no aggregate burden is created by government deficit spending to finance investment projects but rather a redistribution from some members of future generations to others.

The true and unambiguous burden on future generations is created by government deficit spending that pays for goods that yield no future benefits—for example, current maintenance of parks and streets. As illustrated on line 3 of Table 17-A, absolutely nothing is generated in the future as a rate of return; all benefits accrue in the present and none in the future. The

---

[4] Problems involved in the choice of the interest rate ("the social discount rate") that should be used in evaluating government investment projects have been elegantly analyzed by A. C. Harberger in "Our Measuring the Social Opportunity Cost of Public Funds," in his *Project Evaluation* (Chicago: Markham, 1972), Chapter 4, pp. 94–122.

[5] The alternative of floating more bonds to pay the interest cost on the original bonds is ignored. If the growth rate of real GNP exceeds the real interest rate on the government debt, then the government can finance its interest cost by issuing new bonds without raising the ratio of the value of outstanding bonds to GNP.

government must pay interest to keep bondholders happy, just as AT&T must pay interest, yet in current government deficit-financed consumption, there is no future benefit or income to pay the interest. Future taxpayers are forced to hand over extra payments to the government to cover the interest cost on the debt, and the taxpayers receive no benefit in return.

> **Example:** In the fiscal year 1981 (ending September 30, 1981), interest on the public debt is estimated at $67.2 billion, or about $817 per household.[6] Unless the government uses deficit financing to cover these interest payments, it must cover them by raising taxes. Thus 1981 taxpayers are turning over to the federal government $817 per household. What is their benefit in return? Part of the deficit was incurred to build post offices in the Great Depression of the 1930s and other public buildings in recent years, but most of the present benefits of past deficits are intangible—present freedom here and in some foreign countries as a result of deficits incurred in past wars.

THE MONETARY-FISCAL MIX DURING PERIODS OF HIGH UNEMPLOYMENT

The possibility that fiscal stimulus during a recession will create a burden for future generations raises an obvious question: why not stimulate the economy via tax cuts or increased government expenditure financed not by a higher public debt but by a higher money supply? In terms of Chapters 4–5, why not shift the *LM* and *IS* curves rightward at the same time, rather than shifting the *IS* curve alone rightward, with the resulting increase in interest rates? Government deficits financed by money creation create no burden for future generations, because no interest is paid by the government on the high-powered money that it creates. In this situation the government bonds issued by the Treasury are purchased by the Federal Reserve. The Federal Reserve earns the interest on the bonds and returns it to the Treasury, so that no taxes need to be levied to pay the interest cost. In terms of our discussion in Chapters 15 and 16, this constitutes just one more argument in favor of countercyclical monetary policy.

2. The Optimal Natural Employment Surplus

Current deficits incurred to finance government consumption impose a burden on future generations, as indicated in Table 17-A. Can an argument be made that to avoid this burden the government should consistently run a positive natural employment surplus, relying on monetary stimulus to maintain real GNP at the natural level and prevent fiscal drag? If a desirable or optimal level of private investment is defined as that which would occur

---

[6] Estimate of fiscal 1981 interest from *Economic Report of the President,* January 1980, Table B-69, p. 285. Data on households (families plus unrelated individuals) are for 1978, from *ibid.,* Table B-25, p. 232.

without interference of the government, how can the natural employment surplus be adjusted to allow society to attain its optimal level of investment?

TAXATION OF CAPITAL AS AN ARGUMENT FOR A POSITIVE NATURAL EMPLOYMENT SURPLUS

The basic argument for a positive natural employment surplus appears in Figure 17-A.[7] The horizontal axis measures the amount of investment and saving, and the vertical axis measures the interest rate. The downward-sloping I line illustrates the dependence of the demand for investment goods on the interest rate. A reduction in the interest rate increases the demand for investment goods as firms find that additional investment projects can earn a future return sufficient to cover reduced interest costs. The upward-sloping S line illustrates the dependence on the interest rate of the supply of saving. An increase in the interest rate induces individuals to sacrifice consumption now and raise saving in order to obtain more consumption goods in the future.

In the absence of any government spending or taxation, the private economy operates at point A, with a level of investment and saving (I_0) that maximizes welfare. Why? At point A the future return on investment (the vertical distance r_0) exactly compensates savers for their sacrifice of current consumption, measured as the vertical height of the S line. Investment projects made possible by saving produce a future return just high enough to provide the extra future consumption goods that "bribe" savers to sacrifice current consumption.

What is wrong with an alternative position, say the investment level I_1? At I_1 the return on the marginal investment project is the vertical distance r_1, but the value to savers of sacrificing current consumption goods for future consumption goods is the smaller vertical distance r_1', the height of the saving line S at point B'. An additional \$1 of saving and investment produces future consumption goods in an amount that substantially exceeds the value placed by savers on the sacrifice of a dollar from current consumption, and society can gain by shifting current consumption into additional saving and investment.[8]

---

[7] The diagram in Figure 17-A and the entire argument of this section rely heavily on Martin J. Bailey, "The Optimum Full Employment Surplus," *Journal of Political Economy,* vol. 80 (July/August 1972), pp. 649–661.

[8] In the jargon of economists, the amount of future consumption next year (C_{+1}) required by savers voluntarily to sacrifice \$1 of consumption today is 1.0 plus the **rate of time preference** (ρ). Thus:

$$1 + \rho = \frac{C_{+1}}{C}$$

or

$$\rho = \frac{C_{+1}}{C} - 1$$

Thus investment is at an optimal level in Figure 17-A at point A, where the marginal return on investment (r_0) equals the rate of time preference (ρ), the vertical height of the saving line.

HOW A GOVERNMENT SURPLUS CAN OFFSET THE DISTORTION OF INVESTMENT DECISIONS CAUSED BY INCOME TAXES

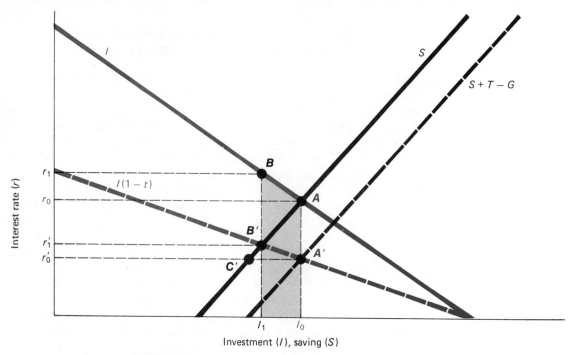

FIGURE 17-A

Effect of an Income Tax and of a Government Surplus on Investment and Saving

In the absence of taxation the amount of saving and investment is determined at point A, where the solid black saving schedule (S) intersects the downward-sloping red investment schedule (I). The introduction of an income tax cuts the after-tax return on investment projects to the lower dashed red $I(1 - t)$ line, and the amount of investment is now determined at point B'. The effect of taxation is thus to cut investment from I_0 to I_1. A government surplus generates additional saving, which raises the economy's total supply of saving to the black dashed $S + T - G$ line, and this extra saving allows investment to return to its initial level I_0 at point A'.

Example: Imagine that individuals currently receive an interest rate (r_1') of 5 percent on their saving. This means that they are willing to sacrifice $1 of current consumption for a return of $1.05 in future consumption goods obtained one year later. If the return on investment (r_1) is 10 percent, then an extra dollar of current saving produces $1.10 in extra consumption goods next year, enough to pay savers the $1.05

they require and still leave $0.05 as a net gain for society. In this situaation society will be better off if it continues to cut back current consumption and add extra dollars of saving and investment until the return on investment equals the return required by savers.

Taxation of income from capital interferes with the economy's ability to obtain the optimal investment level I_0 in Figure 17-A. Savers do not obtain the entire profit produced by investment projects. Instead, the government siphons off a substantial portion of capital income through the corporation income tax and the individual income tax on income from dividends, interest, and rent. The after-tax income from added investment is measured in Figure 17-A by the line labeled $I(1 - t)$, which lies below the I line by a fraction equal to the tax rate (t). If the tax rate is 50 percent, the vertical position of the $I(1 - t)$ line is everywhere exactly 50 percent of the I line. Now only a fraction of the return on capital is available to reward savers, and the level of investment cannot exceed I_1, the amount savers are willing to provide for an after-tax return of r_1'.

Since I_0 is the optimum amount of investment, and only I_1 takes place because of taxation, the best government policy is to run a natural employment surplus equal to the shortfall of investment below the optimum ($I_1 - I_0$). The dashed line labeled $S + T - G$ illustrates the total supply of private saving plus the government surplus required to return investment to the optimum level I_0. Now at point A the before-tax rate of return on capital is r_0, yielding an after-tax return to savers of r_0'. Private saving induced by the return r_0' is indicated at point C' along the original S saving schedule. The government surplus, the distance $C'A'$, provides the extra saving needed to achieve the optimum level of investment I_0.

THE BALANCE-OF-IGNORANCE PRINCIPLE AS AN ARGUMENT FOR DEFICIT SPENDING

This argument indicates that the government should run a natural employment surplus, in contrast to the natural employment deficits actually achieved during most of the period between 1965 and 1980 (see Figure 17-4). Is there any offsetting argument for a full-employment deficit? A government investment project financed by deficit spending, requiring a bond issue, creates no burden if those who benefit from the future payoff of the project are exactly the same people who have to pay the future taxes required to finance the interest payments on the bonds. If a current government investment project creates future benefits for a known group, say a sewer improvement project for a town, then financing the project by current taxation of town residents or by a bond issue paid by future town residents creates no impact on the saving or consumption behavior of anyone. Town residents voluntarily pay taxes in return for the higher standard of living made possible by better sewers.

In contrast to the sewer example, in which the recipients of future benefits are known and certain, Martin J. Bailey[9] of the University of Maryland points out that some government projects have future benefits whose recipients are unknown and uncertain; for example, veterans' hospitals.[10] If the government runs a balanced budget, then every government investment project with uncertain benefits must be financed by current taxation. Today's taxpayers pay their tax bills by reducing current consumption below the optimal amount, because uncertainty prevents them from being able to foresee the future benefits of the project. The government can avoid the undesirable current reduction in consumption by financing such projects by deficit spending, financing the interest on the bonds by future taxes whose incidence is uncertain.

Bailey labels his conclusion the "balance-of-ignorance" principle. Government projects that yield a stream of future benefits should be financed by issuing a bond whose interest payments are paid by taxes having the same time profile as the project's benefits. The government deficit each year would equal the increase in the stock of projects eligible for deficit finance — that is, those with uncertain benefits. Future consumers would pay taxes balanced by the enjoyment of benefits received from the government projects, while present consumers would be unaffected by either project benefits or current taxation.

Thus the balance-of-ignorance principle argues for a natural employment deficit, in direct contrast to the capital-taxation argument that supports a natural employment surplus. If the two opposing arguments were of exactly the same practical importance, their net effect would cancel out and the optimum natural employment surplus would be zero. Indeed, in Bailey's own numerical example, the net recommendation is for a natural employment surplus close to zero.[11]

---

[9] Bailey, *op. cit.*

[10] Current veterans do not know how sick they will be in future years. Also, young members of the population do not know whether they will be future veterans because future wars and the likelihood that the military draft will be reinstated are uncertain.

[11] Bailey, *op. cit.*, p. 659.

Part VI

Economic Growth and the Open Economy

18 Economic Growth and the Productivity Slowdown

In essence the question of growth is nothing new but a new disguise for an age-old issue, one which has always intrigued and preoccupied economics: the present versus the future.

— James Tobin[1]

18-1 STANDARDS OF LIVING AS THE CONSEQUENCE OF ECONOMIC GROWTH

In 1870 average real GNP per person in the United Kingdom was about 20 percent higher than in the United States. But by 1979 average real GNP per person in the United States was almost 75 percent higher than that in the United Kingdom. How was this possible? Faster **economic growth,** meaning a higher average annual growth rate of real GNP per person, allowed the United States to overtake the United Kingdom around 1890 and to move ahead by a growing distance between 1890 and 1950. Although the United Kingdom kept pace with the United States after 1950, it was never able to close the gap.

And that gap between the level of average real GNP per person in the two countries makes an enormous difference in their relative standards of living. Since the comparisons are made in a way that holds constant the prices of goods and services in the two countries, the average American can purchase all the goods and services bought by the average U.K. resident and still have 73 percent more left over for additional spending. At 1979 prices, this surplus of additional spending power available to the American and not to the U.K. resident amounted to $5000 per person, or about $13,385 per household. And this difference is the result of a faster U.S. economic growth rate between 1870 and 1979 that seems a puny and insignificant difference — 1.93 percent per year for the United States as compared to 1.24 percent for the United Kingdom.

It is the power of compound interest that makes minor differences in economic growth rates sustained over a long period build up into

---

[1] "Economic Growth as an Objective of Government Policy," *American Economic Review,* vol. 54 (May 1964), p. 1.

substantial differences in relative living standards. As another example, in 1955 the United Kingdom enjoyed a living standard that was 14 percent higher than that of West Germany. But a West German economic growth advantage between 1955 and 1979 of 3.70 percent compared to 2.06 percent for the United Kingdom converted the 1955 situation into a totally different relationship in 1979, when the West German average per-person real GNP level was 28 percent higher than the British.

It is easy to see why economic growth is such a fascinating topic. High rates of economic growth make it possible to have more of everything— higher defense spending and welfare benefits with plenty left over for more private consumption of goods and services. In contrast, a society with a low rate of economic growth suffers continual strife as difficult choices must be made about the allocation of a slow-growing pie; in this unfortunate society more defense spending may mean higher taxes or a cut in welfare benefits.

Interest in the subject of economic growth has gone through two phases in the postwar years. After the Soviet launching of the first space satellite in 1957, Americans feared that their standard of living would be overtaken by the Soviet Union's rapid economic growth. Then in the 1960s the achievement of relatively rapid U.S. economic growth gradually diminished concern and interest in the topic of growth. But in the late 1970s the U.S. performance faltered. Growth in real GNP per worker almost vanished, and no one has yet come up with a complete explanation of the slowdown. Thus we have two main concerns in this chapter. First, we want to identify the main determinants of the rate of economic growth. Second, we want to review the many possible explanations suggested for the slowdown of U.S. economic growth in the late 1970s. We will also compare the recent growth experience of the United States with that of other countries, all of which have experienced growth slowdowns but not to so low a rate of growth of real GNP per worker as in the United States.

We will find that one key determinant of growth, both in theory and in practice, is the percentage of total GNP that is saved and invested. Since high current saving tends to lead to faster growth in the future, U.S. economists were concerned about the record low rate of household saving in 1979 and 1980. And political discussions of policy to foster more rapid economic growth increasingly emphasized the need to introduce additional tax incentives to encourage additional saving and investment.

18-2 CASE STUDY: THE GROWTH EXPERIENCE OF SEVEN COUNTRIES OVER THE LAST CENTURY

Figure 18-1 shows the level of per-person GNP in seven leading industrial countries for selected years over the last century. The figures are expressed in 1979 U.S. dollars and are based on a careful study that con-

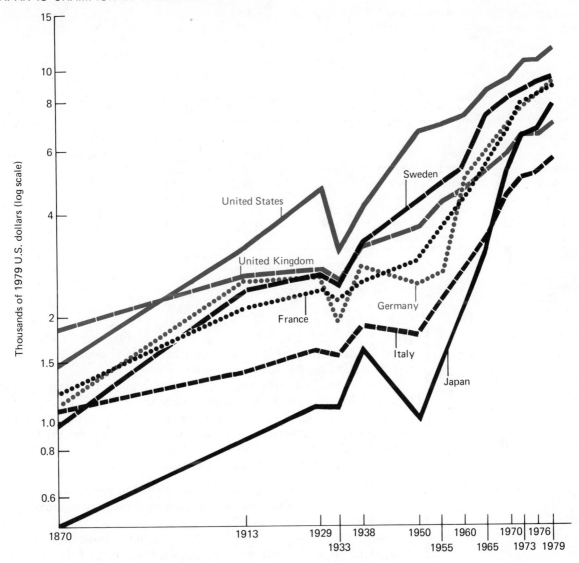

FIGURE 18–1

Per-Person GNP in 1979 U.S. Dollars for Seven Countries, 1870–1979

Notice that the United Kingdom (red dashed line) had the highest per-person income level in 1870, but its slow growth during the century now places it second from the bottom. Japan (solid black line) was the champion, rising from last place in the early years to a level above the United Kingdom in 1979. Note also how France and West Germany (black and red dotted lines) have remained almost tied for the past century, and that both have raced past the once-mighty but now faltering United Kingdom.

Source: Appendix C.

The Growth Experience of Seven Countries over the Last Century **545**

TABLE 18-1

Level and Growth Rate of Per Capita Real GNP, in 1979 Dollars
for Seven Countries, 1870–1979

Country	Level in thousands of 1979 dollars		Average annual growth rate in percent				
	1870	*1979*	*1870–1979*	*1870–1913*	*1913–1955*	*1955–1973*	*1973–1979*
	(1)	(2)	(3)	(4)	(5)	(6)	(7)
United States	1456	11,750	1.93	2.00	1.72	2.34	1.70
Sweden	972	9,520	2.11	2.20	1.65	3.53	1.52
Germany	1138	9,068	1.92	1.58	1.26	4.08	2.58
France	1209	9,004	1.86	1.31	1.29	4.35	2.40
Japan	478	7,809	2.60	1.40	1.26	8.69	2.85
United Kingdom	1838	7,067	1.24	0.99	1.04	2.42	0.99
Italy	1009	5,631	1.59	0.78	1.15	4.55	1.78

Source: Appendix C.

verts the prices actually paid by inhabitants of other countries into the prices that would have been paid by U.S. residents, with an adjustment made for differences between countries in the provision of free services (health, education) by the government.[2]

Table 18-1 summarizes some of the most important information contained in Figure 18-1, including the values in 1979 U.S. prices of per-person GNP in both 1870 and 1979, as well as the growth rates of per-person GNP during selected intervals. In the table countries are listed in order of 1979 per-person GNP. Several major conclusions can be drawn from an inspection of the figure and companion table:

1. All nations have enjoyed substantial growth in per-person GNP; in the United States there was an increase by a factor of 8, from $1456 in 1870 to $11,750 in 1979.
2. Figure 18-1 is plotted on a logarithmic scale. (**Review:** Question 1, p. 25.) This means that the slope of each line indicates the economic growth rate; a steep line means fast growth and a flat line indicates slow growth. For most countries 1950–73 was the period of fastest growth, and all countries have experienced a growth slowdown since 1973.
3. Differing growth rates among countries have led to changes in relative positions. Japan's growth has been most rapid, particularly between

---

[2] The source of the price comparisons is the major international study headed by Irving B. Kravis of the University of Pennsylvania. See Irving B. Kravis et al., *A System of International Comparisons of Gross Product and Purchasing Power* (Baltimore: Johns Hopkins Press, 1975).

1955 and 1973, with an incredible growth rate of 8.7 percent per annum. Japan overtook Italy in 1967 and the United Kingdom in 1973.

4. The United Kingdom's loss of relative position has been continuous over the entire century. In each subperiod listed in Table 18-1 the United Kingdom had a growth rate at the bottom or next to the bottom of the group. The United Kingdom was overtaken by the United States in 1890, by Sweden during World War II, by France and Germany in 1960, and by Japan in 1973. The only consolation for the British is that a continuation of the 1973–79 trend would require thirty more years for the Italians to catch up and put the British into bottom place.

5. The United States is something of a "has-been" in the growth race, owing its high living standard to its superior growth performance before 1950. In particular, the United States gained an advantage in its freedom from wartime destruction as compared to some European nations. But since 1950 the U.S. advantage has eroded, with the United States at the bottom of the growth league during 1955–73.

18-3 THE THEORY OF ECONOMIC GROWTH

The theory of economic growth has filled many academic journals with highly mathematical articles. Yet the basic ideas are very simple. We begin by dividing up output growth into two categories: (1) growth of **factor inputs,** such as labor and capital, and (2) growth in output relative to growth in factor inputs. This converts the question of how to achieve faster growth into two subquestions: how to achieve faster growth in factor inputs, and how to achieve faster growth in output relative to inputs.

Throughout most of this book we have examined the causes and consequences of changes in the ratio of actual real GNP to natural real GNP, the ratio Q/Q^N. But now we are interested in changes in economic conditions over long periods during which the Q/Q^N ratio may be expected to be roughly constant. Thus our theory of economic growth refers to the growth of natural real GNP (Q^N), and we assume that over periods of a decade or more, actual real GNP will be roughly equal to natural real GNP.

THE PRODUCTION FUNCTION

How much real GNP (Q) can be produced at any given time? This depends on the total available quantity of the two main factor inputs, capital (K) and labor (N), and the behavior of output per average available factor input, which we call A (for "autonomous" growth factor).[3] The relationship between Q, K, N, and A is given by the **production function:**

---

[3] The use of the symbol A in this context and the decomposition of real GNP growth into growth in labor, capital, and the "residual" A dates back to the seminal paper by Robert M. Solow, "Technical Change and the Aggregate Production Function," *Review of Economics and Statistics,* vol. 39 (August 1957), pp. 312–320.

$$Q = AK^b N^{1-b} \qquad Q = AK^{0.25} N^{0.75} \qquad (18.1)$$

In words, this production function states that real GNP is equal to an autonomous growth factor (A), expressed as an index, multiplied by a geometric weighted average of an index of capital (K) and of labor (N). The weights, b and $1 - b$, add up to unity and also represent the elasticity of real GNP to an increase in either factor.[4] For instance, in our numerical example if all variables are indexes initially at 1.0, a 4 percent increase in labor input will cause a 3 percent increase in real GNP. Initially:

$$1.0 = 1.0 \, (1.0^{0.25} \; 1.0^{0.75})$$

After a 4 percent increase in labor input:

$$1.03 = 1.0 \, (1.0^{0.25} \; 1.04^{0.75})$$

Thus the elasticity of real GNP with respect to a change in labor input is 0.75 (= 3/4).

Several other characteristics of the production function are evident. First, an equal percentage increase in both factors, capital and labor, raises real GNP by the same percentage. This characteristic, called **constant returns to scale**, occurs because the sum of the weights (b and $1 - b$) add up to unity. When both factor inputs increase by 4 percent, we have:

$$1.04 = 1.0(1.04^{0.25} \; 1.04^{0.75}) \quad \text{(after 4 percent increase in } K \text{ and } N)$$

A second characteristic is the direct one-for-one response of real GNP to the autonomous growth factor A. If A increases by 4 percentage points, while capital and labor input remain fixed at 1.0, real GNP increases by the same 4 percentage points:

$$1.04 = 1.04(1.0^{0.25} \; 1.0^{0.75}) \quad \text{(after 4 percent increase in } A)$$

Up to this point our production function has described changes in the *level* of Q in response to changes in A, K, and N. What determines the *growth rate* of real GNP? As before, we designate percentage rates of growth by using lower-case letters, and we recall the rule that the growth rate of a product of several variables is the sum of the growth rates of the individual components. Thus the growth-rate version of our production function is:[5]

---

[4] *Elasticity* is a term introduced in every economic principles course and refers to the percentage change in one variable in response to a 1 percent change in another variable. In the next sentence, the elasticity of real GNP with respect to labor input is 0.75, because a 4-percentage-point change in labor causes a 3-percentage-point change in real GNP.

[5] The growth-rate relationship in (18.2) can be derived from (18.1) if we use calculus. First, we take the logarithm of both sides of (18.1):

$$q = a + bk + (1 - b)n \qquad q = a + 0.25k + 0.75n \qquad (18.2)$$

In words, this states that the growth rate of real GNP (q) equals the growth rate of the autonomous growth factor (a) plus a weighted average of the growth of capital input and labor input (k and n), with respective weights of b and $1 - b$.

> **Exercise:** Calculate the percentage growth rate of real GNP (q) for the following combinations of the percentage growth rates a, k, and n:

a	k	n	q
0	0	4	—
0	4	4	—
4	0	0	—
4	4	4	—

We can simplify our basic expression if we recognize that economic growth involves the growth of real GNP *per person;* that is, the growth rate of real GNP minus the growth rate of the population. If labor input and the population are both growing at the same rate n, then the growth rate of real GNP per person is equal to $q - n$. Let us subtract n from both sides of equation (18.2):

GENERAL FORM

NUMERICAL EXAMPLE

$$q - n = a + bk + (1 - b)n - n \qquad q - n = a + 0.25k + 0.75n - n \quad (18.3)$$
$$= a + b(k - n) \qquad\qquad\qquad = a + 0.25(k - n)$$

This states that growth in real GNP per person equals the autonomous factor a plus the growth of capital per person.

So far the theory of growth tells us simply that the main sources of growth are an autonomous factor a and growth in capital per person. But this is not very helpful, because it does not tell us what makes a or the growth in capital per person differ among countries or among historical eras. Growth theory tells us almost nothing about a, but we can increase our understanding of the determinants of growth in capital per person by examining basic relationships between saving, investment, and growth in capital.

$$\log Q = \log A + b \log K + (1 - b) \log N$$

Then we take the derivative of each logarithm with respect to time:

$$\frac{d \log Q}{dt} = \frac{d \log A}{dt} + b \frac{d \log K}{dt} + (1 - b) \frac{d \log N}{dt}$$

This expression is identical to (18.2) in the text when we recall our convention of using lower-case letters to designate the percentage growth rate of a variable — that is, the time derivative of its log. For instance,

$$q = \frac{d \log Q}{dt}$$

SAVING AND THE GROWTH OF CAPITAL PER PERSON

First we know from Chapter 2 that under special conditions (no government deficit and balanced foreign trade) saving equals investment:

$$S = I \qquad (18.4)$$

Second, total investment (I) can be divided into net investment (I_n) and replacement investment (D):

$$I = I_n + D \qquad (18.5)$$

Third, replacement investment can be assumed to be a fixed fraction (the "depreciation rate" d) of the capital stock (K):

$$D = dK \qquad (18.6)$$

Finally, net investment is equal to the change in the capital stock from one period to the next (ΔK):

$$I_n = \Delta K \qquad (18.7)$$

These elements can be combined if we substitute from (18.4), replacing I with S on the left-hand side of (18.5), and if we substitute from (18.6) and (18.7) to replace I_n and D on the right-hand side of (18.5):

$$S = \Delta K + dK \qquad (18.8)$$

As our next step, we can divide both sides of (18.8) by the capital stock (K) and multiply the left-hand side (S/K) by Q/Q:

$$\frac{SQ}{QK} = \frac{\Delta K}{K} + d$$

This can be simplified if we allow s to designate the ratio of total real saving to real GNP (S/Q), and if we recall that the percentage change in capital ($\Delta K/K$) is designated by the lowercase letter k:[6]

$$s\frac{Q}{K} = k + d$$

Finally, let us solve this expression for k, and subtract n from both sides of the equation:

GENERAL FORM   NUMERICAL EXAMPLE

$$k - n = s\frac{Q}{K} - d - n \qquad 0.03 = 0.15\left(\frac{2}{3}\right) - 0.06 - 0.01 \qquad (18.9)$$

---

[6] The average propensity to save in Chapter 3 is equal to s, the marginal propensity to save, only when there is no autonomous consumption. Here, for convenience, we use s to designate the average propensity to save (or average saving rate), without implying that there is no autonomous consumption.

We are interested in the growth of capital per person ($k - n$) because it is one of the two main determinants of real GNP per person. And equation (18.9) tells us that $k - n$ in turn depends on the average saving rate (s), the output-to-capital ratio (Q/K), the depreciation rate d, and the population growth rate n. Its commonsense interpretation is that the total available amount of saving relative to the capital stock (sQ/K) can be used for three purposes—replacing old capital (d), equipping new workers with capital (n), or allowing the capital stock to grow faster than the growth in labor input ($k - n$). Using the numerical example, if the saving ratio is 0.15 and the Q/K ratio is 2/3, then the available amount of saving is 0.10 of the capital stock. This is divided up by allocating 0.06 to replacing old capital, 0.01 to equipping new workers, and 0.03 to growth in capital per worker.

The policy implications of equation (18.9) are straightforward. The growth in capital per worker depends on four determinants, but three of them cannot be affected by policy. The Q/K ratio depends on the nature of the production function, the depreciation rate (d) depends on the types of capital purchased in the past and how long they last, and the growth rate of labor input or population (n) depends on birth and death rates over which the government has little control.[7] Thus an increase in the growth of capital per person depends on achievement of an increase in the saving rate.

THE SAVING RATE AND THE MONETARY-FISCAL MIX

The concept of saving that is relevant in the previous discussion is total saving available for private investment. In our examination of leakages and injections in section 2-9 we found that this concept of total available saving can be broken down into the following components:

$$
\begin{array}{l}
\text{Household personal savings } (S_P) \\
+ \text{ business saving } (S_D + S_B) \\
+ \text{ government surplus } (T - G) \\
- \text{ trade surplus } (X - M) \\
\hline
= \text{ gross domestic private investment } (I)
\end{array}
$$

Thus policymakers can take several approaches to stimulate available saving and thereby growth in capital per person ($k - n$). Household personal saving and business saving can be boosted by tax incentives, or the government surplus can be raised by a shift in the mix of policy toward a tighter fiscal

---

[7] A more advanced point in the theory of growth is that a higher saving rate cannot permanently raise the growth rate of per-person real GNP. Why? Imagine a one-shot increase in the saving rate in equation (18.9) from s_0 to s_1. This will initially raise $k - n$. Now capital is growing faster, and output per head will grow faster by $b (k - n)$. As long as b is less than 1.0, the growth in output will be increased by less than the growth in $k - n$, and so the ratio Q/K will begin to fall. This decline will continue until the product sQ/K has returned to its initial value. In fact, without growth in the autonomous factor (a), $k - n$ cannot be positive permanently.

and easier monetary policy (section 5-10). We postpone discussion of the trade surplus to the next chapter.

So far our main emphasis has been on how to raise growth in capital per person, one of the two basic determinants of growth in real GNP per person. How can the other main determinant, the growth rate in the autonomous factor (a), be influenced? We shall see that, while part of a is outside the scope of policy action, another part of a is influenced by many different government policies, including environmental legislation, support for research and development, and others.

18-4 CASE STUDY: SOURCES OF U.S. GROWTH

Why has the United States grown faster at some times than at others? And why have some nations grown faster than others? For the past two decades Edward F. Denison has been engaged in painstaking research to identify the sources of the growth in real GNP of the main industrialized countries. Denison's method involves finding numbers that correspond to the main elements of equation (18.2), which is repeated here for convenience:

GENERAL FORM

NUMERICAL EXAMPLE

$$q = a + bk + (1 - b)n \qquad q = a + 0.25k + 0.75n \quad (18.2)$$

Denison's method involves estimating the magnitude of the main elements q, b, k, and n. Then the final element a is calculated as a residual.

SOURCES OF GROWTH IN THE UNITED STATES

Table 18-2 illustrates the main components of Denison's method for the United States in two time periods, 1929–48 and 1948–73. The first line lists the percentage growth rates of real national income, which differs from real GNP growth (q) only by excluding depreciation and indirect business taxes.[8] Next, Denison must calculate the weights (b and $1 - b$) to be applied to the growth in capital and labor input. His b weights are based on the share of labor and capital in total national income; thus b is set equal to the fraction of national income consisting of income of all types of capital (corporate profits, interest, rent) while $1 - b$ is set equal to the fraction consisting of compensation of employees.[9] In calculating the growth rate of capital (k), Denison makes straightforward use of government data and arrives at the results shown on line B1 in Table 18-2. The figures 0.10 percent and 0.71 percent represent the weight b (about 0.2) times the growth rates of capital (k) during the two periods.

---

[8] **Review:** Figure 2-6.
[9] Income of the self-employed is allocated partly to labor and partly to capital.

TABLE 18-2

Sources of Growth of Real National Income in the United States,
Selected Periods, 1929–73 (contributions to growth rates
in percentage points)

	1929–48	*1948–73*	*Difference:* *(2) − (1)*
	(1)	(2)	(3)
A. Real national income	2.49	3.65	1.16
B. Total factor input	1.52	2.13	0.61
1. Capital	0.10	0.71	0.61
2. Labor	1.42	1.42	0.00
a. Employment	1.01	1.22	0.21
b. Hours of work	−0.22	−0.24	−0.02
c. Education	0.38	0.41	0.03
d. Other	0.25	0.03	−0.22
C. Output per unit of input	0.97	1.52	0.55
1. Movement from farms and small business	0.28	0.29	0.01
2. Economies of scale	0.21	0.32	0.11
3. Miscellaneous	0.02	−0.19	−0.21
4. Residual: "advances in knowledge"	0.46	1.10	0.64

Source: Edward F. Denison, *Accounting for Slower Economic Growth* (Washington, D.C.: Brookings Institution, 1979), Table 8-1.

The next section of the table shows the contribution to economic growth of labor input growth divided up into several categories. First, Denison calculates the growth in employment. Then he makes adjustments for increases or decreases in the quality of labor and for hours worked per employee. The major quality adjustment is for increased education: using information on how much more college graduates earn than high school graduates, Denison treats one college-graduate employee as representing more labor input than one high-school-graduate employee. Further adjustments are made in the "other" category on line B.2.d, of which the most important is the effect on production of the shift in the labor force toward a larger share of women and teenagers and a smaller share of adult men.[10] Each of the components of the "labor" category in section B.2 of the table is shown after multiplication by the $1 - b$ weight (about 0.8).

The bottom part of Table 18-2 shows additional estimates that link part of the autonomous growth factor (a) to specific causes. For instance,

---

[10] This shift is shown in Table 10-2.

line C.1 lists the addition to economic growth caused by the movement of workers from farms where their productivity was relatively low to urban jobs where their productivity was higher. Line C.2 shows an estimate of the effect of "economies of scale," the benefits of growing market size that allow greater specialization of firms, longer production runs, and larger transaction sizes. After a final estimate of various miscellaneous factors, Denison arrives at his "residual," which he calls an estimate of the contribution to growth of advances in knowledge. This is calculated by subtracting from output growth in line A the total contribution of factor input growth in line B and the other growth sources listed in lines C.1, C.2, and C.3.

Now we are in a position to explain why the rate of economic growth in the United States was faster in the 1948–73 period than in 1929–48. The contribution of labor input was exactly the same in each interval (line B.2). About half the acceleration in growth was caused by faster growth in capital (line B.1) and the other half by a greater contribution of the "residual," which presumably incorporates the impact of inventions, better organization, research, and other factors not specifically taken into account in the rest of the table. It is fairly easy to explain why capital growth was so small during 1929–48, since the Great Depression of 1929–41 depressed the demand for new capital goods, and then during World War II investment had to be postponed in order to concentrate resources on war production.

THE UNITED STATES COMPARED TO WEST GERMANY AND JAPAN

Although the United States grew faster in 1948–73 than in the previous two decades, 1929–48, the postwar growth experience of West Germany and Japan was an even more impressive accomplishment. Figure 18-1 illustrates how rapidly West Germany and Japan caught up to and exceeded their previous levels of per-person real GNP relative to the United States and United Kindgom. At least as far as economic growth was concerned, defeat in World War II seems to have been preferable to victory.

The sources of growth in the three countries are shown in Table 18-3. Although the time periods are different, nevertheless the comparisons are interesting. It appears that almost no part of the faster growth experience of West Germany and Japan can be attributed to faster growth in labor input, and this is true with or without adjustments for hours of work and education. Instead, West Germany and Japan can attribute their faster growth to three main factors. First, their capital input grew much more rapidly, owing to their higher rates of saving and investment. This suggests that U.S. policymakers attempting to stimulate growth might do well to adopt some of the incentives to saving and investment already used by the Germans and Japanese. Second, West Germany and Japan benefited from a much more substantial movement of workers out of agriculture than did the United States, where this movement had taken

TABLE 18-3

Sources of Economic Growth,
United States Compared to
West Germany and Japan

	United States, 1948–73	West Germany, 1950–62	Japan, 1953–71
A. Real national income	3.65	6.27	8.81
B. Total factor input	2.13	2.78	3.95
1. Capital	0.71	1.41	2.10
2. Labor	1.42	1.37	1.85
a. Employment	1.22	1.49	1.14
b. Hours of work	−0.24	−0.27	0.21
c. Education	0.41	0.11	0.34
d. Other	0.03	0.04	0.16
C. Output per unit of input	1.52	3.49	4.86
1. Decline of agriculture and self-employment	0.29	1.01	0.95
2. Residual (mainly economies of scale and contribution of advances in knowledge)	1.23	2.48	3.91

Source: Table 18-2 and Edward F. Denison and William K. Chung, *How Japan's Economy Grew So Fast* (Washington, D.C.: Brookings Institution, 1976), Table 4-8.

place in earlier decades. Third, West Germany and Japan recorded much greater contributions of advances in knowledge. This may have been partly because of their ability to copy American techniques, and partly because more of their research effort went into private production rather than the design of military hardware.

18-5 CASE STUDY: EXPLANATIONS OF THE SLOWDOWN IN PRODUCTIVITY GROWTH

The calculations in Table 18-3 do not extend beyond 1973, because in the period since 1973 the growth process in the United States and most other industrialized countries has experienced a marked change. Growth in real GNP per capita has decelerated almost everywhere, as we have already seen in Table 18-1. Growth in real GNP per hour has slowed down even more sharply, particularly in the United States.

Table 18-4 compares the growth of labor productivity during the period 1948–73 with the recent shorter period 1973–78. Notice that the recent rate of productivity growth of about 1 percent per year is much slower than the previous rate of about 3 percent per year. Why has this slow-down occurred? No question has created more puzzlement among macro-

TABLE 18-4

Contributions to the Slowdown in U.S. Productivity Growth, 1973–78 Compared to 1948–73 (in percentage points)

	1948–73	1973–78	Difference: (2)−(1)
	(1)	(2)	(3)
A. Labor productivity	3.00	1.09	−1.91
B. Total factor input	1.16	0.17	−0.99
1. Capital	0.97	0.29	−0.68
2. Labor	0.19	−0.12	−0.31
C. Other factors	1.84	0.92	−0.92
1. Cyclical effect	0.03	−0.14	−0.17
2. Legal and human environment	−0.04	−0.34	−0.30
3. Contribution of "problem sectors"	−0.07	−0.24	−0.17
a. Mining	−0.01	−0.07	−0.06
b. Construction	−0.11	−0.14	−0.03
c. Utilities	0.05	−0.03	−0.08
4. Residual: "advances in knowledge"	1.92	1.64	−0.28

Source: Appendix C.

economists during the last few years. Edward F. Denison concluded a long and detailed investigation by stating, "What happened is, to be blunt, a mystery."[11] Nevertheless, it seems to be possible in Table 18-4 to find enough separate explanations of the slowdown to explain it, without any need to declare it a puzzle or "mystery."

The first explanation, listed in line B.1, is that capital grew much more slowly relative to labor in the 1973–78 period than during 1948–73. As in equation (18.3), a slowdown in the growth of the capital/labor ratio $(k - n)$ causes a slowdown in the growth of the output/labor ratio $(q - n)$, which is the same as a slowdown in productivity growth. Slow capital growth, in turn, was due to the depressing effect of the 1974–75 recession on investment. Higher energy prices after 1973 may also have had an impact by making the total operating cost of capital equipment high, including both purchase price and energy usage, thus leading firms to hire more workers and use relatively less capital.

In equation (18.3) the growth in labor input does not appear by itself as a cause of productivity growth, but shifts in the type, quality, or occupation of labor input in fact do have effects on the growth rate of

---

[11] Edward F. Denison, *Accounting for Slower Growth* (Washington, D.C.: Brookings Institution, 1979), p. 4. Our analysis in this section is not based on Denison's figures, partly because his decomposition of growth sources does not extend past 1976, and partly because of some weaknesses in Denison's methodology.

productivity. If workers become more educated, their productivity tends to grow, whereas if the composition of the work force shifts more toward teenagers who have less on-the-job experience, it is likely that average productivity will shrink. The net contribution of all these factors on line B.2 explains about 0.31 percent of the productivity slowdown, and much of this is accounted for by the reduced bonus the economy received by the movement of workers out of agriculture. Although the contribution of education to productivity growth was greater in 1973–78 than previously, this was almost canceled out by the shift in the share of younger workers in the labor force.

In sum, the smaller growth contribution of capital and labor input accounts for about half the productivity slowdown. Of the remaining slowdown in the contribution of "other factors," most can be linked to specific problems, while the rest remains unexplained. Line C.1 makes a rough calculation of the "cyclical effect" that raised productivity in 1973 to an unsustainable level, due to the fact that the Q/Q^N ratio in that year was considerably above unity, while in 1948 and 1978 the ratio was slightly below unity. The section titled "legal and human environment" reports Edward Denison's calculations of the net impact of environmental, health, and safety legislation and the greater incidence of crime in the 1970s. All of these factors raised business costs, and required some investments by business firms in response to crime or government legislation. Thus a significant fraction of capital investment during the 1973–78 period was not "productive" in the usual sense but was "mandated" by regulation or required to offset the impact of crime on business operations.

Finally, there were significant slowdowns in productivity growth in three particular sectors that have special problems. Mining productivity declined in absolute terms after the 1973 increase in energy prices, mainly because there was an increase in factor inputs involved in oil and gas drilling (a part of the mining sector) but little increase in the oil actually discovered. When more oil-drilling employees find more "dry wells," mining productivity goes down. The level of productivity in the construction industry also dropped in absolute terms for reasons that are not clearly understood but may be partially related to the difficulties of measuring output and inputs in this industry.[12] Finally, productivity growth came to a halt in the electric and gas utility industry after several decades of rapid progress. This seems to be related to a genuine halt in innovation; for years electric utilities had been able to save labor by purchasing larger and larger generators, but by the mid-1960s manufacturers found that they had reached the end of the road in devising ways to increase generator size.

How much of the productivity slowdown remains to be explained? In line C.4 the growth in the "residual" slowed from 1.92 to 1.64 percent per

---

[12] "The Productivity Drop That Nobody Believes," *Business Week*, February 25, 1980, p. 77.

year—only a minor slowdown that could be due to many reasons, including a decline in research and development and in the number of patents registered by U.S. inventors.

Will productivity growth recover in the 1980s partway back to its rapid 1948–73 pace? After the temporary impact of the 1980 recession is over, it is likely that the growth of the capital-labor ratio will accelerate. And the labor force will gradually increase in average age and experience (as the 1947–58 "baby boom" generation grows older). Some of the problems in the mining, construction, and utility industries may prove to be temporary; even a recovery of mining and construction productivity growth from negative to zero rates would give a boost to aggregate average productivity growth. Finally, a number of reforms in government policy have been recommended that, if adopted, could improve the productivity performance of the United States.

THE U.S. PRODUCTIVITY SLOWDOWN COMPARED TO OTHER INDUSTRIALIZED COUNTRIES

The productivity slowdown in the United States has not been a unique American experience, nor does it indicate that the American economy is terminally ill in comparison to other nations. As shown in Table 18-5, all seven of the largest industrialized nations experienced significant slowdowns in the rate of productivity growth in the 1973–78 period. Columns (1) through (3) show figures for economy-wide productivity, real gross domestic product per employed person.[13] The right-hand side of the table shows figures for the manufacturing sector.

The first major conclusion from Table 18-5 is that the productivity slowdown in the United States has been much less severe than in Italy and Japan. The United States and the other four nations appear to have experienced similar slowdowns in column (3) of about 1.75 percentage points per year. In column (6) the slowdown figures are more diverse, with Japan and Italy again suffering the worst slowdowns, Germany and France showing the best performance, and the United States third from the best.

Although the U.S. *slowdown* has not been unusual, nevertheless the U.S. productivity-growth performance in the 1973–78 period was abysmal, ranking lowest in column (2) and next-to-lowest in column (5). If the disparities in column (2) were to continue forever, living standards in Germany, Japan, and France would catch up to those in the United States much faster than we indicated in section 18-2. Despite their pro-

---

[13] Why are the U.S. figures shown in the first two columns of Table 18-5 lower than the corresponding figures in line A of Table 18-4? First, for comparability with other nations, the Table 18-5 figures measure productivity as output per employee rather than output per hour as in Table 18-4. Because hours per employee fell, output per employee grew less rapidly than output per hour. Second, the starting date in Table 18-5 is 1950, not 1948, and this eliminates the very rapid productivity growth achieved by the United States during 1948–50.

TABLE 18-5

Two Measures of the Slowdown in Productivity Growth, Seven Large
Industrialized Countries, 1973–78 Compared to 1950–73 (annual
growth rates in percentage points)

Countries ranked by column (2)	Real gross domestic product per employed person			Manufacturing output per hour		
	1950–73	1973–78	Difference (2) − (1)	1950–73	1973–78	Difference (5) − (4)
	(1)	(2)	(3)	(4)	(5)	(6)
West Germany	4.88	3.18	−1.70	5.81	5.12	−0.69
Japan	7.86	3.07	−4.79	9.71	3.55	−6.16
France	4.66	2.78	−1.88	5.25	4.81	−0.44
Italy	5.26	1.31	−3.95	6.58	2.63	−3.95
United Kingdom	2.57	0.95	−1.62	3.15	0.16	−2.95
Canada	2.58	0.85	−1.73	4.25	2.53	−1.72
United States	2.10	0.38	−1.72	2.66	1.65	−1.01
Average of seven countries	4.27	1.79	−2.48	5.34	2.92	−2.42

Source: U.S. Department of Labor.

ductivity slowdowns, the 1973–78 growth rate of productivity in these three countries in both columns (2) and (5) was considerably faster than the United States was able to achieve in the earlier 1950–78 period.

This case study suggests that the main concern for U.S. policymakers should *not* be in trying to understand the 1973–78 productivity slowdown, which seems to have a straightforward explanation in Table 18-4. Rather, policymakers should be concerned with the poor overall postwar productivity performance of the American economy compared to other countries and should consider reforming specific U.S. laws and regulations that tend to stifle productivity growth.

18-6 ECONOMIC GROWTH AS AN OBJECTIVE OF GOVERNMENT POLICY

Just as it is not easy to stop inflation, in the same way it is not easy to raise the growth rate of natural real GNP.[14] Sacrifices must be made, and it is not clear in every case that the benefit exceeds the cost of the sacrifice.

---

[14] The title of this section is taken from James Tobin's classic article, "Economic Growth as an Objective of Government Policy," *American Economic Review,* vol. 54 (May 1964), pp. 1–20, reprinted in his *Essays in Economics,* vol. 1 (Chicago: Markham, 1971), Chapter 16. The quote that began this chapter comes from the same article.

In the case of inflation, the basic solution of reducing the growth rate of aggregate demand requires that society suffer the cost of a recession *now* in order to gain the benefit of slower inflation *in the future*. In the case of growth, the basic solution is to sacrifice consumption *now* in order to invest more now to obtain extra consumption *in the future*. The choice in both cases—ending inflation and stimulating growth—depends on society's rate of time preference, the extra amount people would be willing to pay to have consumption goods now instead of in the future.[15]

Figure 18-2 illustrates two of the choices open to society, paths A and B. Path A reflects a "do-nothing" policy that maintains the growth rate of per-person consumption after time t_0 at the same rate as before. Path B reflects a policy that deliberately at time t_0 raises the incentive to save and invest while reducing the incentive to consume. Consumption along path B initially drops below path A by an amount shown by the gray shading. But then the higher rate of investment makes the capital stock grow faster, and so consumption begins to grow faster along path B than path A, eventually catching up at time t_1 and moving ahead thereafter. The central question for growth policy is: which path is better, A or B?

If the rate of return on extra capital investment is greater than society's rate of time preference, then $1 shifted from present consumption to investment will yield enough future consumption to be worthwhile. For instance, if the rate of return is 10 percent, $1 less of consumption today will yield $1.10 next year. If the rate of time preference is less than 10 percent, say 5 percent, this means that people are equally happy with $1.05 next year and $1 this year, so that clearly they would prefer $1.10 next year to $1 this year. In this situation, with a rate of return higher than the rate of time preference (sometimes called the rate at which individuals "discount" future consumption), society should save more and consume less, as along path B. As Martin Feldstein has written:

> The U.S. saves too little if the rate at which individuals discount
> future consumption is less than the national rate of return on
> private investment.[16]

In recent years the rate of return on private investment in the corporate sector has been about 12 percent, and the rate of time preference of individuals is less than that. How much less? We know that the *real* interest rate on corporate bonds has been roughly 3 percent for the last twenty years (Figure 11-3), and that many individuals have been willing to save despite the low 5 percent nominal interest rate available to them on passbook savings accounts (in recent years the *real* passbook interest rate has been negative). Thus it is probably an accurate description of the U.S. economy to say

---

[15] The rate of time preference is defined in footnote 8 on p. 537.

[16] Martin S. Feldstein, "National Saving in the United States," in Shapiro and White (eds.), *Capital for Productivity and Jobs* (New York: The American Assembly, Columbia University).

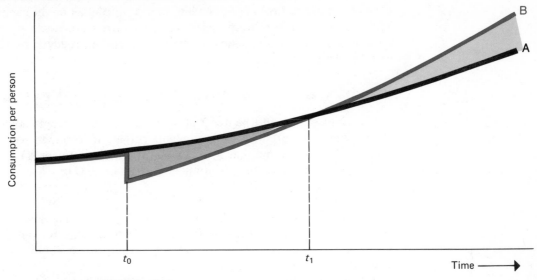

FIGURE 18-2

Two Alternative Paths of Consumption per Person

Before time t_0 both paths involve exactly the same consumption per person. Along path A consumption per person continues to grow at the same steady rate after time t_0. But along path B a policy decision is made to consume less in order to save and invest more. At first, between t_0 and t_1, consumption along path B drops below path A by an amount shown by the gray shading. Then, after t_1 (and forever thereafter), consumption along path B exceeds that along path A as shown by the pink shading.

that the United States now saves too little, because a dollar diverted from present consumption to present saving could earn a real return of about 12 percent, much more than the real return now earned by most savers. People would want to save more if they were offered a real return of 12 percent than they save now at a real return of 3 percent or less.

Why is the real rate of return to private investment so much higher than the real rate received by savers? The primary reason is the tax treatment of income from capital. Corporate profits are taxed at a rate of almost 50 percent, reducing the real rate of return from about 12 percent to about 6 percent. But then savers who hold corporate stock and receive dividends must pay personal income tax on their dividend income, reducing their return below 6 percent, say to 3 percent for an individual in the 50 percent tax bracket. Individuals can reduce their tax burden somewhat by investing in "growth" companies that offer most of the return on saving in the form of high future growth of earnings, leading to capital gains on stock that are taxed at lower rates than dividend income. Also, many individuals save through contributions to pension plans that pay little tax on the capital gains and dividends received from their holdings of corporate stock. But even in these cases the funds available to reward savers are reduced by the existence of the corporation income tax.

ECONOMIC GROWTH AND THE NATURAL EMPLOYMENT SURPLUS

Our brief survey in Chapter 2 of national income concepts immediately identifies one important way to stimulate private investment. Rearranging equation (2.10), we find that *by definition* private investment (I) is equal to private saving (S) plus the government surplus ($T - G$):

$$I \equiv S + (T - G) \tag{18.10}$$

Thus the two basic methods for stimulating investment, and hence the growth of the capital stock and future consumption, are for policymakers (1) to create incentives that raise private saving (S), or (2) to run a larger government surplus (or smaller deficit).

The outcome for economic growth of a policy shift toward a larger government surplus depends on how this shift is carried out. First, the fiscal shift toward a "tighter" policy must be accompanied by enough of a boost in the money supply to maintain unchanged the level of real GNP relative to natural real GNP—that is, the real GNP ratio (Q/Q^N). In terms of section 5-10, this would be a shift in the "monetary-fiscal policy mix" that would lower the real interest rate, which in turn would induce firms to borrow the extra funds made available by the larger government surplus.

A second feature of the fiscal shift is that its stimulus to investment will be greater if carried out in a way that reduces private consumption rather than private saving. Thus preferable methods would be through an increase in taxes on consumption goods or through a reduction in transfer payments, rather than through an increase in income taxes that would further reduce the after-tax return to private saving. Unfortunately, each of the methods that would provide the greatest stimulus to investment would tend to hurt poor people more than rich people; the political difficulties of engineering such a shift toward higher taxation of consumption and lower transfer payments may explain why so little was done in the late 1970s.

INVESTMENT INCENTIVES

Although it is extremely simple, equation (18.10) points out a fallacy in many discussions of investment incentives such as the U.S. investment tax credit. If the government were to allow firms to take a larger tax credit for new investment, firms would pay less corporate tax to the government and would have the extra funds available as part of business saving. Since S in equation (18.10) includes all forms of private saving, both household saving and business saving, the investment credit would raise S by exactly the amount by which government tax receipts (T) declined, leaving no change on the right-hand side of (18.10). Since there would be no increase in the supply of funds available for investment, there would be no increase in aggregate private investment. Instead, firms would invest more in projects eligible for the investment tax credit and less in other projects. Investment in machinery and equipment would grow, since these items are eligible for the tax credit, while investment in residential and nonresidential structures would decline.

INCENTIVES TO PRIVATE SAVING

In addition to measures taken to raise the government surplus, equation (18.10) points to incentives for private saving as the second main way to stimulate private investment. Total private saving consists of business saving (both depreciation and retained earnings) and private household saving. Numerous economists have called attention to reforms that could stimulate the supply of both forms of private saving.

Private business saving. Two types of reforms have been suggested that would stimulate business saving. The first would simply eliminate the corporate income tax. If corporations were to pay out as higher dividends their extra profits obtained by the elimination of the corporate income tax, then the government could tax back part of the funds through the personal income tax (which is levied on dividends). But extra profits that were retained by corporations would automatically become part of private saving (S) and would be available for private investment. While many economists endorse an elimination of the corporation income tax, Congress has not moved in this direction because of the substantial revenue losses that would be involved, and a revenue offset in the form of higher taxes on consumption or wage income would generate strong opposition by groups of consumers and workers.[17]

A more popular reform would be to eliminate the effects of inflation on the corporate income tax. An "indexed tax system" (see section 11-8) would allow corporations to take larger depreciation deductions based on the current replacement costs of assets rather than their lower historical cost, thus raising business saving and reducing government tax collections. Other reforms in an indexed tax system would stimulate household saving and reduce borrowing to finance consumption, including the taxation of real interest returns (that is, the actual interest rate earned minus the inflation rate) and real capital gains (the actual percent capital gain per year minus the annual rate of inflation over the time the asset was held).

Private household saving. One of the most interesting differences between the United States and other large industrialized countries is the small fraction of disposable income saved by U.S. households:

---

[17] A comprehensive discussion of alternative forms of business taxation is Charles McLure, *Must Corporate Income Be Taxed Twice?* (Washington, D.C.: Brookings Institution, 1979).

	Personal saving as a percent of personal disposable income, five-year average, 1973–77
Japan	24.9
France	17.3
West Germany	15.2
United Kingdom	14.1
Canada	10.3
United States	6.7

There are many disincentives to private saving in the United States that are shared by other countries, but there are differences as well. Perhaps the most important disincentive in the United States is the tax system, which is not indexed and imposes the full personal income tax rate on the nominal rate of return on saving rather than on the real rate. Since the full nominal interest rate on borrowed funds is deductible, the system discourages saving and encourages borrowing. For a taxpayer in the one-third marginal tax bracket, the 18 percent interest rate on his credit-card balance becomes only 12 percent after tax, and only 2 percent in real terms if the inflation rate is 10 percent. For a saver in the same situation, the real return on a saving certificate with a 12 percent nominal yield is actually *minus* 2 percent $[12 \times (1-0.33) - 10 = -2]$.

Other countries avoid this disincentive to saving by partially or completely exempting interest income from taxation, and even in the case of West Germany by offering a government subsidy for household saving.[18]

Other factors contributing to the low U.S. saving rate are:

Regulation Q ceilings and government savings bonds. Through its Regulation Q ceilings, the government until recently limited the interest rate on passbook savings accounts to only a bit more than 5 percent, clearly yielding a negative real rate of return even without taking taxation into account. No such interest-rate ceilings exist in West Germany, a nation with a much higher personal saving rate than the United States. And the government issues savings bonds that pay only a 7 percent interest rate while its economists forecast inflation of 8 or 10 percent, a policy that Robert M. Solow of MIT has called "one of the major swindles of all time on low- and middle-income wage earners."[19]

Inflation and real assets. While individuals are taxed on the interest and dividends they receive from investment in financial assets, they are taxed little if at all on returns from "real assets" — that is, new and used goods such as gold, silver, art, stamps, coins, and oriental rugs. The faster the inflation rate, the faster the prices of these objects tend to increase, and

---

[18] See Burkhard Strumpel, "Saving Behavior in Western Germany and the United States," *American Economic Review,* vol. 65 (May 1975), pp. 210–216; also Henry C. Wallich and Mabel I. Wallich, "Banking and Finance," in H. Patrick and H. Rosovsky (eds.), *Asia's New Giant* (Washington, D.C.: Brookings Institution, 1976), Chapter 4.

[19] *Business Week,* December 11, 1978, p. 93.

yet these inflation-induced capital gains tend to escape taxation (either because goods are not sold, or if sold the capital gains are not declared on the tax return, or if declared are taxed at a lower rate than ordinary income). Thus inflation tends to lure people into purchasing objects rather than financial assets, lowering the saving rate.[20]

Social security benefits. When individuals can look forward to social security benefits to provide for consumption during their retirement years, they will have less incentive to save for their retirement. Martin S. Feldstein of Harvard has placed major emphasis on the social security system as a cause of the low rate of personal saving in the United States. While some critics think that Feldstein's estimates of this effect are too high, it does seem plausible that a partial reason for the high saving rate in Japan is the more modest level of social security benefits available there.

Other International Differences. The relatively high personal saving rates in some other countries, particularly West Germany and Japan, have other causes as well. The high Japanese saving rate has been partially attributed to the system of paying out large wage bonus payments twice a year. Another factor that West Germany and Japan share is the wartime destruction of personal wealth, which has led to high savings rates as individuals have attempted to reconstitute their desired ratio of wealth to income. In addition, mortgages require higher down payments than in the United States. This, together with relatively high housing prices, encourages personal saving. Finally, some writers have claimed that high savings rates in West Germany and Japan are caused by cultural differences in the form of a puritanical streak and aversion to borrowing.

CONCLUSION

The achievement of more rapid economic growth in the United States will require more government saving in the form of a higher natural employment surplus and more private business and household saving. Tax reforms to stimulate business and personal saving are politically difficult, simply because rich people save proportionately more of their incomes than poor people. Thus any measure to reduce the taxation of income from capital and raise the taxation of consumption or wage income would tend to benefit rich people and be opposed by poor people and many members of the middle class, although Regulation Q and the low interest rates paid on savings bonds now hurt poor savers much more than rich savers.

How can we resolve the paradox that the United States not only has a less equal distribution of income than Sweden, Japan, or Germany, but also saves

---

[20] Saving is defined as disposable income minus consumption. When individuals "save" by making purchases of new durable consumption goods, this is not considered saving in the national income and product accounts. Purchases of used assets involve transfers of funds among members of the population without entering the national income accounts (except for markups and commissions by sales people).

and invests less? To avoid making inequality worse, a delicate fiscal reform will be required that raises transfers to the poor and increases incentives for business and private saving, while at the same time paying the bill by a reduction in transfer payments paid to the nonpoor (mainly social security) or by an increase in taxation on the consumption of nonpoor individuals. A drastic reform that would accomplish many of these objectives would be to shift from our present combination of a corporate and personal income tax to a progressive consumption tax — that is, a tax that taxes household consumption, in contrast to the present system, which taxes all income, whether it is consumed or saved.[21]

SUMMARY

1. Divergences between the economic growth rates of individual nations sustained over long periods of time can create substantial differences in living standards. Although Britain had the highest level of real GNP per capita in 1870 among the seven nations displayed in Figure 18-1, by 1979 Britain was second from the bottom as a consequence of its slow rate of economic growth during the intervening century.

2. The production function explains real GNP as depending on the quantity of factor inputs (capital and labor) and on an autonomous growth factor that reflects the influence of research, innovation, and other factors. An increase in the growth rate of real GNP per person requires either an increase in the growth rate of capital per person or an increase in the growth rate of the autonomous growth factor.

3. The achievement of faster growth in capital per person requires a higher ratio of saving to income. This, in turn, requires either a higher government surplus or tax incentives to boost the share of national income going into business and household saving.

4. The growth rate of labor productivity in the United States increased between 1929–48 and 1948–73 but then slowed markedly in the 1973–78 period. The most important causes of the productivity-growth slowdown were the slower growth of capital per head, the diversion of some investment from productive to nonproductive use through the effect of government environmental, health, and safety legislation, and the contribution of three "problem" sectors (mining, construction, and utilities).

5. The United States has not been alone in experiencing a slowdown in productivity growth. The extent of the slowdown in Japan and Italy was greater than in the United States, but nevertheless the growth rate of productivity in the United States (both before and after 1973) ranked at or near the bottom of the group of industrialized countries.

---

[21] An excellent recent compendium on this issue is Joseph A. Pechman (ed.), *What Should Be Taxed: Income or Expenditure?* (Washington, D.C.: Brookings Institution, 1980).

6. Economic policy should stimulate saving if the real rate of return on private investment is less than the rate at which individuals discount future consumption (the rate of time preference).

7. Among the factors that account for the low saving rate in the United States as compared to other countries are low regulated interest-rate ceilings on some types of savings accounts and savings bonds, taxation of nominal rather than real interest income and tax-deductibility of nominal rather than real borrowing costs, the ability of individuals to escape from taxation by investing in real objects rather than financial assets, and the adverse effect of the social security system on private saving.

A LOOK AHEAD

This chapter concludes our study of macroeconomic policy in a closed economy. We will examine in Chapter 19 the constraints on domestic policy imposed by foreign trade and capital movements. Economic policy in an open economy depends greatly on whether the foreign exchange rate is fixed or flexible and requires a different interpretation of the role of monetary and fiscal policy than that developed for the closed economy.

CONCEPTS

Economic growth
Production function
Factor inputs
Autonomous growth factor
Constant returns to scale

Sources of growth
Output per unit of input
The "residual"
Rate of time preference

QUESTIONS FOR REVIEW

1 Why do differences in the rate of economic growth lead to differences in the "league table" of living standards? If you have a scientific calculator, you should be able to use the following information to determine whether the ranking of real GNP per person of the three countries in 1980 has changed from that in 1970:

Country	1970 rank	1970 real GNP per person	1970–80 economic growth rate
A	1	$10,000	2.0%
B	2	8,000	3.0%
C	3	7,500	5.0%

2   If the production function is characterized by constant returns to scale, what happens to real GNP when labor and capital inputs both double? What happens when labor and capital inputs double *and* the autonomous growth factor (A) also doubles in size?

3   Why do Denison and other researchers use the observed shares of capital and labor income as estimates of the weights on capital and labor in the production function (b and $1 - b$)?

4   Assume that there is no growth in the autonomous growth factor ($a = 0$). If $b = 1/2$, $s = 0.2$, $Q/K = 0.5$, $d = 0.08$, and $n = 0.02$, calculate the growth rate of real GNP per person. Show how each of the following changes would alter your answer:
    a. A reduction of b from 1/2 to 1/3
    b. An increase in s from 0.2 to 0.25
    c. A reduction of d from 0.08 to 0.06
    d. A reduction of n from 0.02 to 0.01

5   How would each of the following affect the growth rate of real GNP per head?
    a. An elimination of Regulation Q ceilings
    b. A shift to a tighter fiscal and easier monetary policy
    c. Indexation of the tax system
    d. An increase in the number of productive new inventions submitted to the U.S. patent office
    e. A reduction in the birth rate

6   Explain, using the framework of section 18-3, how the higher price of energy in the 1970s might affect the growth of real GNP per person.

7   If the level of real GNP is held fixed by monetary policy at some given amount, which of the following will provide the greatest stimulus to saving?
    a. Increase in the personal income tax rates paid by the rich
    b. Increase in the personal income tax rates paid by the poor
    c. Introduction of a federal retail sales tax

19

Policy in an International Setting

Business fortunes are made on the ability
to forecast such changes in the values of
national currencies, while political
futures become frayed as a result of these
changes.
—Robert Z. Aliber[1]

19-1 INTRODUCTION

With only a few exceptions, the rest of the book has covered macroeconomic theory and policy for a closed economy, one that has no flows of
goods, capital, or money to or from other nations. This chapter, though,
treats special problems of formulating policy in an open economy, one that
trades goods, capital, and money. Our attention to the closed economy in
previous chapters is at least partially justified by the orientation of this book
toward the United States, where the massiveness of the domestic economy
and the relative unimportance of foreign trade give policymakers the luxury
of ignoring the outside world.[2] In very small countries where foreign trade
makes up a large share of domestic production and consumption, much of
our closed-economy analysis is irrelevant. In extreme cases there is virtually
no role for domestic macroeconomic policy, because the price level and real
GNP depend almost completely on what happens in other nations.

Most industrialized nations face an intermediate situation between the
closed-economy autonomy of Chapters 3–18 of this book and the pure open-
economy helplessness of policymakers in very small countries. In this intermediate case, domestic policy decisions matter, but at the same time the
domestic policy environment is strongly influenced by events in the rest of
the world. In the 1970s, for instance, all nations have faced the problem of

---

[1] *The International Money Game* (New York: Basic Books, 1973), p. 4.

[2] Actually, the U.S. economy is more dependent on international trade than is commonly
believed: (1) One out of six manufacturing jobs produces for export. (2) One out of three acres
of U.S. farmland produces for export. (3) Nearly one out of three dollars of U.S. corporate
profits derives from the international activities, exports, and investments of corporations.
Source: New York Times (June 13, 1977), p. 46.

world inflation, which has fed into each domestic economy by raising the prices of imports, of exports, and of the domestic goods that are closely competitive with imports and exports. The United States has found itself more and more influenced by external events during the past decade.

Despite this common external environment, however, the economic performance of individual nations has varied widely, partly as a result of different domestic policy reactions. The annual percentage rate of inflation (of the GNP deflator) between 1972 and 1979 was as high as 16.0 percent for Italy and as low as 4.9 percent for West Germany, with other countries distributed in between:

	1972–79 inflation rate
Italy	16.0
United Kingdom	14.2
Canada	9.6
France	9.6
Japan	8.3
United States	7.5
West Germany	4.9

INTERNATIONAL MONETARY ECONOMICS

In this chapter we introduce some of the main themes of open-economy macroeconomics, sometimes called international monetary economics. Goods, services, and capital flow among nations. Problems arise when inflows do not balance outflows. If a nation buys more imports than the combined value of the exports it sells and capital it borrows, how is it to pay for the difference, called the deficit on its **balance of payments?** It must pay in a form of money that other nations find acceptable, such as gold or U.S. dollars, of which it keeps a stock, called its **international reserves,** to be used as a contingency when there is a balance-of-payments deficit. Problems arise when the stock of international reserves runs low, just as a family faces difficulties when it runs out of money.

The theme of this chapter is that there are two main methods of adjustment to an imbalance between international receipts and expenditures. The most straightforward is a system with a flexible **foreign exchange rate,** the amount of another nation's money that residents of a country can obtain in exchange for a unit of their own money. In mid-1980 a resident of the United Kingdom could obtain $2.30 in U.S. dollars for one unit of its own money, the pound sterling. If the United Kingdom faces a balance-of-payments deficit, without enough dollars to pay for its international expenditures on imports and capital outflows, its foreign exchange rate tends to drop to bring the demand and supply for the pound sterling back into balance.

The second method of adjustment occurs if the foreign exchange rate of the pound is held fixed and prevented from dropping. The U.K. policymakers must find some other way of inducing foreigners to raise their demand for pounds and to induce British citizens to reduce the supply of pounds that they are offering to foreigners to pay for imports. The prices of British products must be made cheaper, and so the British inflation rate must be reduced, raising all the problems of inflation adjustment that we examined in Chapters 8 and 9.

Just as we learned in Part III that the sluggish adjustment of wages and prices makes it difficult to slow down inflation in a closed economy such as that of the United States, we will find here that sluggish price adjustment inhibits the adjustment of open economies to a balance-of-payments surplus or deficit under a system of fixed exchange rates. Partly as a result, the world has shifted from the fixed-exchange-rate system that was in effect between the end of World War II and early 1973 to a new system in which exchange rates are flexible and change every day. We will see that the flexible-exchange-rate system does not solve all problems of balance-of-payments adjustment or completely insulate individual economies from the rest of the world.

19-2 FLOWS OF GOODS, SERVICES, CAPITAL, AND MONEY

Not only does the U.S. Department of Commerce keep track of the total flows of goods and services in the U.S. domestic economy in its national income and product accounts (reviewed in Chapter 2), but it also is the official record keeper for U.S. international transactions. Table 19-1 summarizes international inflows and outflows during 1979, including goods and services sold by Americans to foreigners and purchased from foreigners, income earned on foreign assets, gifts and transfers, loans and borrowing, and the flows of international reserves that "pay" for any imbalance. The data in Table 19-1 are sometimes called the balance-of-payments (BP) statistics, even though they include not only the net balance between inflows and outflows, but also the individual components of the flows.

THE BALANCE OF PAYMENTS

Table 19-1 is divided into three sections. The top (white) section is the **Current Account,** including flows of goods, services, and transfer payments. The middle (gray) section is the **Capital Account,** including borrowing and lending by banks and purchases of U.S. private assets by foreigners and foreign assets by U.S. individuals and by the U.S. government. The bottom (pink) section of Table 19-1 shows how the balance-of-payments (BP) surplus or deficit is financed. The table is arranged so that the sum of all the items in the right-hand Balance column is zero. If the total of the items in the Current Account and Capital Account sections is positive, as in 1979, then the United States is running a BP surplus (see line 9) and there must be an exactly equivalent negative financing item to offset the surplus (see line 12).

TABLE 19-1

U.S. International Transactions, 1979 ($ millions)

Line number	Items	Credits (+)	Debits (−)	Net credit (+) or debit (−)	Balance
	CURRENT ACCOUNT				
	1. Exports and imports of goods and services				
	a. Goods	+182,074	−211,524	−29,450	
	b. Current services	+ 38,376	− 35,908	+ 2,468	
	c. Income on foreign assets	+ 65,862	− 33,548	+32,314	
	d. *Balance on goods and services*	+286,312	−280,980		+ 5,332
	2. Net transfers				
	a. Government grants			− 3,488	
	b. Government pensions and private remittances			− 2,161	
	c. *Net unilateral transfers*				− 5,649
	3. Balance on current account				− 317
	CAPITAL ACCOUNT				
	4. Long-term borrowing (+) or lending (−)	+ 15,273	− 33,509	−18,236	−18,236
	5. Basic balance on current account and long-term capital				−18,553
	6. Nonliquid short-term private capital flows			− 1,600	− 1,600
	7. Liquidity balance				−20,153
	8. Liquid foreign capital flows			+35,704	+35,704
	9. Official reserve transactions balance				+15,551
	METHOD OF FINANCING				
	10. Reduction in U.S. official reserve assets (+)			− 1,107	
	11. Increase in foreign official assets in the United States (+)			−14,444	
	12. Total financing of deficit				−15,551

Note: Line 6 includes the statistical discrepancy.
Source: Adapted from *Survey of Current Business*, March 1980, Table 1, p. 54.

Every figure in Table 19-1 is preceded by a plus or minus. Plus items are credits, any transactions that provide the United States with an additional supply of foreign money. Examples of current account credits are exports of wheat, travel by foreigners on U.S. airlines and ships, and income earned by U.S. holdings of assets abroad (for example, the Ford Motor Company, H. J. Heinz, and many other firms own factories in foreign countries). Examples of capital account credits are investments by Arab sheikhs in the U.S. stock market and construction of a Japanese-owned Honda assembly plant in Pennsylvania. In each of these cases, U.S. households or firms are paid in foreign money — British pounds sterling, Japanese yen, and many others — and a demand for dollars is created as the U.S. recipients take the foreign money they have received to their banks and turn it in for the U.S. dollars they want.

Minus items are debits, the opposite of credits, and are any transactions that provide foreigners with an additional supply of dollars. Examples of current account debits are imports of Scotch whiskey and French wine, travel by Americans on foreign-owned airlines and ships, and dividends paid to Arab sheikhs who own stock in U.S. companies. Capital account debits occur when General Motors builds a factory abroad or when an American deposits funds in a Swiss bank account.

What was the situation of the United States in 1979? Total credits exceeded total debits, so that the United States ran a balance-of-payments (BP) surplus. After we examine the main sources of the surplus, we will learn how in the bottom pink part of Table 19-1 the United States managed to satisfy the excess demand for dollars by foreigners.

THE CURRENT ACCOUNT

The first line of Table 19-1 states that U.S. exports of goods (a credit that supplies the United States with foreign money) were $182,074 million. Imports of goods far exceeded exports of goods by $29,450 million. Two of the reasons the United States imported so much in 1979 were its heavy dependence on imported oil ($61,000 million) and automobiles ($25,600 million). The deficit in the trade of goods was more than offset by a surplus on services and income on foreign assets. Despite the large debit caused by U.S. travel abroad, a surplus was earned on current services, thanks to fees and royalties for foreign use of U.S. inventions and patents and to foreign customers of U.S. banks, insurance companies, lawyers, and other services. A surplus of more than $32 billion was earned from income on foreign assets, because U.S. investments abroad are much higher than foreign investments in the United States. In 1979 particularly large profits were earned by U.S. oil companies operating abroad.

The sum of the first three lines (1.a, 1.b, and 1.c) is called the balance on goods and services (line 1.d), sometimes called **net exports** of goods and services. This balance is a component of GNP and directly contributes to production and employment.[3] A deterioration in this balance causes just as serious a decline in production and employment as would have been caused by a drop by the same amount in private investment or government spending.[4]

The United States did not retain the excess of foreign money earned from its surplus on goods and services, but gave it away in the form of transfer payments. Most of this (line 2.a) was in the form of government grants, or

---

[3] Net exports were introduced as a component of GNP in section 2-5. The total amount of net exports (foreign investment) recorded in Figure 2-6 differs slightly from the balance on goods and services in Table 19-1 because of minor differences in definitions.

[4] The statement in the text needs to be qualified, because the BP figures cited in Table 19-1 are nominal (stated in current dollars), whereas production and employment depend on real shifts in the balance on goods and services.

foreign aid. The remainder consisted of a variety of items (line 2.b), including government pensions to employees who have retired abroad and private remittances, including gifts from Americans to their children and other relatives living overseas. Transfers are flows of money without any corresponding return flow of goods and services and hence make no contribution to GNP.

The total balance in the white portion of Table 19-1 is called the balance on current account, and it summarizes all the current transactions, those which do not involve the transfer of assets or liabilities. In 1979 the U.S. current account balance was a relatively small minus number, −$317 million, in contrast to the much larger deficit of the previous year. Any surplus or deficit on current account must be exactly balanced by capital transactions in the gray block of the table or by financing items in the pink area. For the United States in 1979, the current account was almost in balance, so that a capital account inflow was what accounted for our overall balance-of-payments surplus.

THE CAPITAL ACCOUNT

Foreign lending by the United States is a debit item, because we supply dollars to foreigners as we buy assets in other nations, whereas investment by foreigners in the United States is a credit item. The United States has traditionally incurred a deficit on long-term capital account (line 4) because the United States is a relatively wealthy country that is better endowed with capital than with labor. It is quite natural that the return on capital investments should be higher in other countries that have less capital and that U.S. firms would be attracted to send capital abroad to earn these high returns.[5]

Short-term capital movements refer to lending and borrowing of short duration. Examples are investments by foreigners in U.S. 90-day treasury bills (a credit) and loans by U.S. banks to finance U.S. exports (a debit). Combining lines 6 and 8, the United States in 1979 ran a very large surplus on short-term capital movements, so that the overall BP was in surplus on line 9 despite a deficit in the basic balance on line 5. Why the split between lines 6 and 8? Some experts prefer to tally up the BP deficit excluding the effect of line 8's short-term foreign deposits in U.S. banks on the argument that these deposits are volatile and may be withdrawn at any time. A counterargument is that these deposits should not be counted as part of the U.S. BP deficit, because they are already treated as debit items in the accounts of foreign nations, preventing the total world BP from netting out to zero. Further, these deposits are not necessarily volatile and subject to immediate withdrawal; many are needed for commercial transactions by foreigners.

---

[5] Both free trade and free capital movements cause a redistribution of income between domestic labor and capital and between different types of U.S. workers. The nature of these redistributions is beyond the scope of this book and is treated in courses on international trade. See Richard E. Caves and Ronald Jones, *World Trade and Payments*, 3rd ed. (Boston: Little, Brown, 1981).

SIGNIFICANCE OF THE OFFICIAL RESERVE TRANSACTIONS DEFICIT

These considerations lead to the choice of line 9 as the fundamental U.S. BP measure. The name **official reserve transactions** (ORT) **balance** refers to the fact that only movements of international reserves by governments and official agencies are excluded from the components of the ORT balance on lines 1 through 8. Thus any changes in international reserves serve as a means of financing the ORT surplus or deficit, as illustrated for 1979 in lines 10 and 11.

The United States holds its international reserves in two main forms, (1) gold, and (2) its reserve position at the International Monetary Fund (analogous to reserves that banks hold at the Federal Reserve). One way for the United States to cover a deficit is to draw down its holdings of gold; this method was the dominant means of financing deficits between 1957 (when the U.S. gold stock was $22.8 billion) and 1968 (by which time the gold stock had fallen to $10.9 billion). In 1979 U.S. reserve assets increased, one of the two methods used to finance the 1979 BP surplus.

The United States has an advantage over other nations, which all hold U.S. dollars as part of their international reserves. The demand for international reserve dollars by other nations allows the United States to finance its deficit in some years without drawing down its own reserve assets. How? When foreign central banks demand extra dollars to add to their official international reserves, this extra demand for dollars counts as one way the United States can finance its deficit. This method of financing a deficit would appear as a "plus" item on line 11.

But in 1979 line 11 shows a minus item, meaning that foreign central banks drew down their official reserves of dollars in order to finance the massive short-term private capital inflow into the United States (line 8). Unlike many years of the past decade when the United States financed its deficit through additions to official reserve holdings by foreign central banks, in 1979 high U.S. interest rates lured in a large amount of short-term private capital and allowed the U.S. to run a BP surplus.

COLLAPSE OF THE FIXED-EXCHANGE-RATE SYSTEM

During the last years of the fixed-exchange-rate system, the period between 1968 and 1973, the United States was able to run virtually any ORT deficit it desired. How? Foreign governments that had an excess supply of dollars received from the U.S. deficit, as a result of the excess of U.S. debits over credits, were prevented from cashing in their dollars for gold, because the United States in 1968 and thereafter refused to pay out any more of its gold stock. Japanese merchants could sell their excess dollars to the Japanese Central Bank in return for yen, but the Japanese Central Bank could not get rid of its excess dollars because the United States refused to accept them. To make matters worse for Japan, the increased supply of yen now held by Japanese merchants constituted an increase in the domestic money supply and added to domestic Japanese inflation.

Adjustments were necessary to eliminate the Japanese BP surplus that provided the excess dollars. The two basic alternatives, examined later in this chapter, were to change the exchange rate between the Japanese yen and the U.S. dollar or to allow the Japanese economy to experience a higher inflation rate (which would make its exports more expensive and induce higher Japanese imports as well).

Both the Japanese and the Germans attempted to postpone the necessity of changing their exchange rate with the dollar. Eventually in 1971 and 1972 these countries were so inundated with unwanted U.S. dollars that they allowed their exchange rate to appreciate.[6] By early 1973 the fixed-exchange-rate system had collapsed and a new system of flexible exchange rates was introduced, which allowed exchange rates to change considerably more from day to day and month to month than previously had been acceptable. The current system does not, however, allow the exchange to fluctuate by enough to eliminate all changes in international reserves. Most countries still experience either a surplus or deficit in their balance of payments, as exhibited by the U.S. surplus for 1979 in Table 19-1.

IS A BP DEFICIT HARMFUL?

Is a U.S. BP deficit, as occurred in 1978 and many earlier years, harmful to the economy? The very large deficits incurred in 1971–72 clearly exceeded the demand for added dollar reserves by foreign nations and had the effect of forcing extra inflation on them. But surprisingly enough, a modest BP deficit is a healthy and natural phenomenon and could continue for a long time without adverse consequences. Why?

1. The method of computing the BP statistics is misleading because the U.S. capital outflow is treated as a debit but there is no offsetting credit for the assets that U.S. individuals and firms acquire overseas. Thus at the end of 1978 the U.S. owned $450.1 billion in assets abroad, swamping the $373.3 billion of foreign holdings of U.S. assets (including dollars held as reserves).
2. Foreign holdings of U.S. dollars as international reserves can grow only if the United States runs an ORT deficit. Yet most of these deficits are caused fundamentally by the acquisition of foreign factories, stocks, and bonds by U.S. investors. Thus the United States for many years has been operating as a giant bank or financial intermediary, simultaneously borrowing from the foreign governments that hold their international reserves in the form of bank deposits and short-term government securities in the United States and lending back to foreign nations by buying up

---

[6] Japanese official holdings of dollars leaped from $3.2 billion at the end of 1970 to $16.5 billion at the end of 1972.

long-term foreign assets. The United States comes out ahead in this operation if it earns a higher rate of return on its foreign assets than it pays out in interest on its reserves.[7]

Summary: In most recent years (unlike 1979) the United States ran a deficit in its official reserve transactions balance. But this was almost entirely accounted for by a long-term capital outflow, financed by increased foreign holdings of the U.S. dollar as international reserves. This deficit did not change the net wealth of the United States, but simply its liquidity, because it involved the acquisition of long-term assets in trade for short-term liabilities.

19-3

THE MARKET FOR FOREIGN EXCHANGE

When an American tourist steps into a taxi at the London airport, the driver will expect to be paid in British currency, not American dollars or German marks. To obtain the needed British currency, the tourist must first stop at a bank (in his original U.S. airport or at the London airport upon arrival) and buy British pounds in exchange for U.S. dollars. Banks that have too much or too little of given types of foreign money can trade for what they need on the foreign exchange market. Unlike the New York Stock Exchange or the Chicago Board of Trade, where the trading takes place in a single location, the foreign exchange market consists of hundreds of dealers who sit at desks in banks, mainly in New York and London, and conduct trades by phone. In London, 256 banks are authorized to deal in foreign currencies.

The results of the trading in foreign exchange are illustrated for four foreign nations in Figure 19-1. Each section of the figure illustrates the exchange rate, expressed in terms of U.S. cents per unit of foreign currency. The data expressed are quarterly, and thus they conceal additional day-to-day and month-to-month movements. Major changes occurred during the years plotted; there is a notable contrast between the appreciation (increased dollar price) of the West German mark and Japanese yen as compared with the depreciation (reduced dollar price) of the Canadian dollar and the depreciation followed by appreciation of the British pound.

---

[7] The hypothesis that the United States plays the role of a financial intermediary, borrowing at short term and lending at long term, was first proposed in Emile Despres, Charles P. Kindleberger, and Walter S. Salant, "The Dollar and World Liquidity: A Minority View," *Economist* (London), vol. 218 (February 5, 1966). See also Walter S. Salant, "Capital Markets and the Balance of Payments of a Financial Center," in William Fellner, Fritz Machlup, Robert Triffin, et al., *Maintaining and Restoring Balance in International Payments* (Princeton, N.J.: Princeton University Press, 1966), Chapter 14.

SINCE 1970 THE DOLLAR HAS MOVED IN DIFFERENT DIRECTIONS AGAINST FOUR FOREIGN CURRENCIES

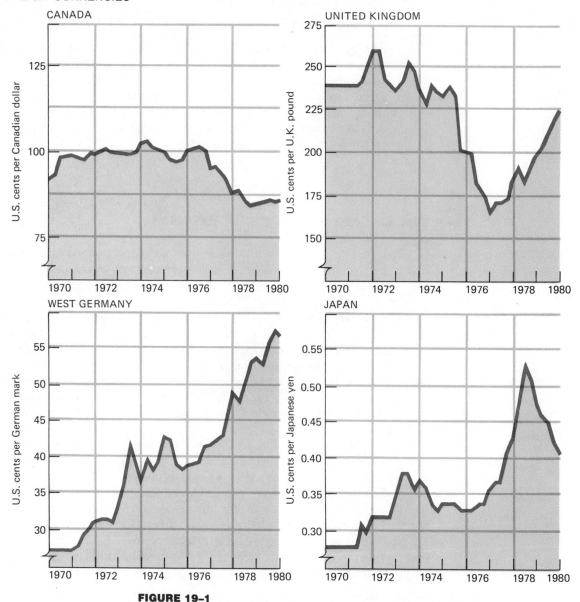

FIGURE 19-1

Foreign Exchange Rates of Four Major Industrial Nations Expressed as U.S. Cents per Unit of Foreign Currency, Quarterly, 1970–80

Each foreign exchange rate displays quarter-to-quarter fluctuations together with a trend that lasts several years or more. The Canadian dollar fluctuated within a narrow range until late 1976 but then plunged by about 15 percent. The British pound plummeted in 1975 and 1976 but then recovered almost back to its 1970 value. Both the German mark and Japanese yen appreciated between 1970 and late 1978, but in 1979 the mark continued to rise while the value of the yen dropped by 20 percent.

Source: International Financial Statistics, various issues.

THE DEMAND FOR AND SUPPLY OF FOREIGN EXCHANGE

The factors that determine the foreign exchange rate and influence its fluctuations can be summarized on a demand-supply diagram like that used in elementary economics to analyze many problems of price determination (for instance, the explanation of the price of wheat, real wage rate, return on capital, and other microeconomic problems). In Figure 19-2 the vertical axis measures the dollar price of the British pound, the same concept as is plotted in the upper right frame of Figure 19-1 for the actual 1970–79 behavior of the pound. The horizontal axis shows the number of pounds that would be demanded or supplied at different prices.

Currencies such as the U.S. dollar and the British pound are held by foreigners who find dollars or pounds more convenient or safer than their own currencies. For instance, sellers of goods or services may be willing to accept payment in dollars or pounds, but not in the Finnish markka or the Malaysian ringgit. Thus a change in the preference by holders of money for a currency such as the British pound will shift the demand curve for pounds and influence the pound's exchange rate.

All currencies, whether or not they are demanded as a means of money holding, have a demand that is created by a country's exports and a supply generated by a country's imports. Figure 19-2 and Table 19-1 are connected. The British have a balance-of-payments statement that contains entries for the same items as the American BP statement in Table 19-1. British credits for exports create a demand for the pound. So, too, do credits generated by foreigners who invest in British factories, who repay previous loans, who send to Britain dividends and interest payments on British overseas investments, and who are attracted by high British interest rates to put money into British savings accounts and government securities. Thus the demand curve for pounds D_0 in Figure 19-2 is labeled with two of the credit items that create the demand (British exports, capital inflows). In the same way, the supply curve of pounds S_0 depends on the magnitude of the debit items — mainly British imports and capital outflows.

What explains the slopes of the demand and supply curves as drawn in Figure 19-2? Imagine that a British automobile costs 3000 pounds. If the exchange rate is $2 per pound, as at point A, an American would have to pay $6000 for the automobile. A decline in the exchange rate from $2 to $1.50, however, would cut the dollar price from $6000 to $4500 if the British domestic price remained fixed at 3000 pounds. If the demand for British automobiles in the United States is price elastic, so that a decline in price raises the quantity purchased, the demand for British pounds will rise as the exchange rate falls and the number of British automobiles purchased goes up. The demand curve D_0 will be vertical only if the price elasticity of American demand for British imports is zero — that is, completely insensitive to changes in price.

The supply curve of pounds S_0 depends on the price elasticity of British demand for imports from the United States. First, imagine that the price elasticity is zero. Will the supply curve be vertical? The answer, surprisingly,

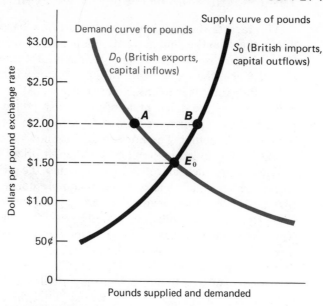

FIGURE 19–2

An Illustration of the Determination of the Price in Dollars
of the British Pound Sterling

The demand curve D_0 slopes downward and to the right, reflecting the increased
demand for pounds induced by depreciation (a lowering in the pound's price). The
supply curve S_0 is assumed to slope upward, although this does not always occur
(see text). The equilibrium price of the pound in the diagram is assumed to be
$1.50, at the crossing point of the D_0 and S_0 curves.

is no. Imagine that a U.S. auto sells for $6000, and the British always buy
one auto regardless of its price. Then at an exchange rate of $2 per pound,
the British will spend 3000 pounds on the auto. But at the lower exchange
rate of $1.50, an expenditure of 4000 pounds will be necessary to obtain the
same automobile. Thus with a completely inelastic demand for imports, the
British supply curve of pounds will have a negative slope, opposite that depicted in Figure 19-2. The supply curve will be vertical if the price elasticity
of demand for imports is -1.0, so that expenditures in pounds are independent of the exchange rate.[8] Only if the price elasticity is greater than unity
(in absolute value) will the supply curve slope positively, as drawn in Figure
19-2.

---

[8] The price elasticity of demand, a concept used in most elementary economics courses, is
defined as:

DETERMINATION OF THE FOREIGN EXCHANGE RATE

The foreign exchange rate is determined where the demand curve D_0 crosses the supply curve S_0 in Figure 19-2. As the curves are drawn, the equilibrium exchange rate is $1.50 per pound at point E_0. At a higher exchange rate, say $2, the supply of pounds exceeds demand by the distance AB. British imports and capital outflows exceed the demand for pounds created by British exports and capital inflows. In order to induce foreigners to accept their pounds, the British will have to accept a lower exchange rate, $1.50. If the British government wants to maintain the higher exchange rate of $2, it can do so only by exchange market intervention. It must buy up the excess supply of pounds from the foreigners who have received payments in pounds from British purchasers of imports. What does the government use to obtain these pounds from foreigners? This is the purpose of its international reserves (holdings of gold and U.S. dollars). If the government does not intervene, or if it runs out of international reserves so that it cannot intervene, the foreigners holding excess pounds will sell them on the foreign exchange market, driving the price down to $1.50.

There is a possibility that the exchange market is unstable, if the supply curve is negatively sloped and flatter than the demand curve. Imagine as an example that the demand curve is vertical and the supply curve has a negative slope. At the crossing point of the two curves demand and supply are equal, but the equilibrium is not stable. Why? If the exchange rate falls slightly below the crossing point, supply will exceed demand, driving the exchange rate down continuously. In the same way an increase in the exchange rate above the crossing point will cause demand to exceed supply, driving the exchange rate up continuously.

The condition required for a decline in the exchange rate to raise the demand relative to the supply is called the Marshall-Lerner condition. It states that (ignoring the negative signs of the elasticities) the sum of the elasticities of the demand and supply curves must exceed 1.0.[9] If the sum of the elasticities is less than 1.0, a decline in the exchange rate will raise the supply relative to the demand and worsen the trade balance. Table 19-2 shows some

---

$$\text{elasticity} = \frac{\text{percentage change in quantity}}{\text{percentage change in price}}$$

When the elasticity is -1.0, the percentage change in quantity is equal to and opposite in sign to the change in price, so that revenue (= price × quantity) does not change. For the American automobile, a drop in the exchange rate from $2 to $1.50 would raise the price of the car from 3000 to 4000 pounds, an increase in price of 33 percent, and would cause a reduction in quantity purchased from 1.0 to 0.67 autos. Total British expenditure originally was 3000 pounds (1.0 autos times 3000 price) and in the new situation is still 3000 pounds (0.67 autos times 4000 price).

[9] The Marshall-Lerner condition is named after Alfred Marshall, *The Pure Theory of Foreign Trade* (1879) and Abba P. Lerner, *The Economics of Control* (New York: Macmillan, 1946). The condition given in the text ignores the possibility of changes in the domestic prices charged by the producers of exports. For more complicated versions of the condition, see Joan Robinson, "The Foreign Exchanges," in *Essays in the Theory of Employment* (Oxford: Blackwell, 1947).

TABLE 19-2

	American demand elasticity for British exports	Slope of demand curve for pounds	British demand elasticity for imports	Slope of supply curve for pounds	Sum of demand and supply elasticities	Effect of drop in exchange rate on trade balance
1.	−1.0	−1.0	0.0	−1.0	−1.0	None
2.	0.0	Vertical	−1.0	Vertical	−1.0	None
3.	0.0	Vertical	0.0	−1.0	0.0	Worsens
4.	−1.0	−1.0	−1.0	Vertical	−2.0	Improves

examples with different combinations of elasticities of the demand and supply curves for the British case.

On line 1 both the demand curve and supply curve have the same negative slope, so that a change in the exchange rate alters supply and demand by exactly the same amount and thus has no effect on the trade balance (balance on goods and services). On line 2 the borderline situation again occurs, this time with elastic import demand and inelastic export demand. On line 3 the Marshall-Lerner condition is not satisfied; both demand elasticities are zero and the supply curve slopes negatively while the demand curve is vertical, so that a depreciation in the exchange rate raises the supply of pounds more than demand, worsening the trade balance. Finally, line 4 exhibits the favorable situation with a sum of elasticities of −2.0, so that an exchange-rate depreciation raises the demand more than the supply and improves the trade balance. According to most estimates, the sum of the two elasticities does in fact exceed 1.0 in the long run, so that line 4 can be considered the normal case.

19-4 CASE STUDY: DETERMINANTS OF EXCHANGE RATES IN THE LONG RUN

The most important factor determining the level of exchange rates is the fact that in open economies the prices of traded goods *should be the same everywhere,* after adjustment for customs duties and the cost of transportation. This is called the **purchasing-power-parity (PPP) theory** of the exchange rate. It can be written as follows:[10]

---

[10] A review of the theory, limitations, and applications of the PPP approach is contained in Lawrence H. Officer, "The Purchasing-Power-Theory of Exchange Rates: A Review Article," *International Monetary Fund Staff Papers*, vol. 23 (March 1976), pp. 1–60.

$$\text{domestic price } (P) = \frac{\text{foreign price } (P')}{\text{foreign exchange rate } (F)}, \quad \text{or} \quad P = \frac{P'}{F} \qquad (19.1)$$

As an example of a situation when PPP is satisfied, consider a bushel of wheat selling for $3 on the world market and for 2 pounds in Britain, with an exchange rate (F) of $1.50 per pound:

NUMERICAL EXAMPLE

$$P = \frac{P'}{F} = \frac{\$3}{\$1.50/\text{pound}} = 2 \text{ pounds}$$

If PPP were not satisfied, an unsustainable situation would be created. For instance, if the British price of wheat were only 1.50 pounds, then foreigners would be able to obtain wheat in Britain cheaper than the $3 world price. They would pay:

$$\text{price of British wheat to foreigners}$$
$$= PF$$
$$= (1.50 \text{ pounds})\left(\frac{\$1.50}{\text{pound}}\right) = \$2.25$$

Foreigners would rush to Britain to buy up all the cheap British wheat, and the higher demand would push up the British price into equality with the $3 world price.

As written in equation (19.1), the PPP approach is a theory for determining the domestic price, given foreign prices and the exchange rate. But the same equation can be turned around to state the PPP theory of exchange rates:

$$F = \frac{P'}{P} \qquad (19.2)$$

This states that if the world price level (P') increases faster than the domestic price level (P), there is an increase in P'/P and the exchange rate appreciates. In the wheat example, if a worldwide inflation were to raise the price of wheat from $3 to $4, but there were no inflation in Britain to alter the fixed 2-pound price of British wheat, the British exchange rate would increase from $1.50 per pound to $2 per pound:

$$F = \frac{P'}{P} = \frac{\$4}{2 \text{ pounds}} = \$2 \text{ per pound}$$

Exactly the opposite would occur if British prices were to rise faster than foreign prices. If British inflation were to double the price of British wheat from 2 to 4 pounds, whereas foreign prices remained fixed at $3, the British exchange rate would depreciate from $1.50 per pound to $0.75 per pound:

$$F = \frac{P'}{P} = \frac{\$3}{4 \text{ pounds}} = \$0.75 \text{ per pound}$$

PPP IN ACTION: 1966–79

Another way of writing equation (19.2) is to express the exchange rate and the two prices in terms of rates of growth, written as a lowercase letter for each variable:[11]

$$f = p' - p \qquad (19.3)$$

In words, this states that the rate of change of the foreign exchange rate (f) equals the difference between the foreign inflation rate (p') and the domestic inflation rate (p). For Canada and the United States this relationship is almost exactly correct for the interval between 1966 and 1979:

	Annual rate of change of Canadian-U.S. exchange rate		Annual rate of change of U.S. GNP deflator		Annual rate of change of Canadian GNP deflator
Theory:	f	$=$	p'	$-$	p
Actual for Canada:	-0.6	$\cong$	6.1	$-$	6.8

The relation does not hold exactly in each year, partly because the balance of trade is not in long-run equilibrium each year.

The PPP theory contains an essential kernel of truth: that nations that allow their domestic inflation rate (p) to exceed the world rate will experience a depreciation of their exchange rate, and vice versa. But there are numerous exceptions to the relationship, because the demand for and supply of foreign currency depends on factors other than the simple ratio of domestic and foreign aggregate price indexes. Consider the same relationship of (19.3) for Japan and the United States over the 1966–79 interval.

	Annual rate of change of Japan-U.S. exchange rate		Annual rate of change of U.S. GNP deflator		Annual rate of change of Japanese GNP deflator
Actual for Japan:	$+3.9$	$\neq$	6.1	$-$	6.8

How can we explain the appreciation of the Japanese exchange rate (dollars per yen), knowing that Japanese inflation was 6.8 percent per annum, faster than U.S. inflation? At least three crucial factors can cause the behavior of the exchange rate to differ from the simple difference between foreign and domestic inflation rates:

---

[11] The growth rate of a ratio such as P'/P is equal to the growth rate of the numerator (p') minus the growth rate of the denominator (p).

1. *Technology and natural resources.* Imagine that the Japanese and U.S. inflation rates were absolutely identical over some time period. Then, according to PPP, there should have been no change in the Japanese exchange rate over the same period. But imagine also that over this period the Japanese produced several new products that U.S. firms and households imported in great numbers, such as color television sets and videotape recorders, without any similar addition of new products sold by U.S. exporters. As a result there would be an increased U.S. demand for the yen to pay for the color television sets and videotape recorders and no change in the supply of yen. The price of the yen would have to increase (appreciate) to keep the foreign exchange market in equilibrium.

   Discoveries of natural resources have the same effect on the exchange rate as applications of new technology. With identical inflation rates in Britain and the United States, the British exchange rate would be bound to appreciate as a result of the discovery of oil in the North Sea. British oil imports would fall, cutting the supply of pounds, and Britain might eventually be able to export some of its oil, raising the demand for pounds. Indeed, the British pound did appreciate for this reason between 1977 and 1979, even though inflation in the United Kingdom was faster than in the United States.

2. *Capital movements.* The exchange rate depends not just on the products exported and imported by a country, but also on the demand for its money by foreigners. Customers from all over the world send funds to Switzerland for deposit in anonymous numbered bank accounts. Why? Because tax authorities cannot identify the owners of the accounts, making such deposits attractive to criminals, tax evaders, and other individuals who are eager to keep their financial operations secret. Partly as a result, Switzerland enjoyed a substantial appreciation of its exchange rate over the 1966–79 interval, despite a rate of inflation approximately equal to that of the United States:

	Annual rate of change of Swiss-U.S. exchange rate		*Annual rate of change of U.S. GNP deflator*		*Annual rate of change of Swiss GNP deflator*
Actual for Switzerland:	+7.7	≠	6.1	—	5.6

A nation with an attractive currency, such as Switzerland, can enjoy a low rate of domestic inflation because the higher prices of imports charged by foreigners are offset by exchange-rate appreciation, which makes a growing number of dollars available per Swiss franc. But problems are created for exporters, such as producers of Swiss watches. Export prices in dollars will tend to increase at the Swiss domestic inflation rate (5.6 percent per annum between 1966 and 1979) plus the growth rate of the exchange rate (a 7.7 percent change per annum in the dollars needed to purchase one Swiss franc).

3. *Government policy.* Even if there are no changes in technology, no discoveries of natural resources, and no capital movements, the PPP relationship of equation (19.3) still may not hold. Governments can interfere in several ways. First, a trade surplus generated by low domestic inflation may not cause an appreciation if the government gives the surplus away by supporting a large defense establishment overseas or by making large grants of foreign aid to other nations. Such government actions partly explain why the United States ran an overall balance-of-payments deficit in the early 1960s despite a large trade surplus and a low domestic inflation rate. Second, a government facing a trade surplus may decide to stimulate the domestic demand for imports by cutting customs duties. Third, a government may try to prevent the exchange rate from appreciating by barring or taxing capital inflows, a tactic used by Germany in the early 1970s. In contrast, the United States in the 1960s tried partially to offset a balance-of-payments deficit, caused mainly by Vietnam war spending, by taxing capital outflows. Finally, a government may cause its currency to appreciate by running a domestic policy of tight money and high interest rates, as in the United States in March 1980 and in the United Kingdom throughout late 1979 and most of 1980.[12]

All these factors can interfere with the operation of the PPP relationship, but they do not change the basic validity of its prediction that, under a *flexible*-exchange-rate system, a nation that allows its domestic inflation rate to accelerate relative to foreign inflation will experience a depreciation in its exchange rate. Under a *fixed*-exchange-rate system, a nation that allows its domestic inflation rate to accelerate relative to foreign inflation will experience a growing deficit in its balance of trade. Eventually the government will be unable to sustain the exchange rate at an artificially high level and a devaluation will be forced, like that of Britain in 1967 when the pound was allowed to drop from $2.80 to $2.40.

19-5 DETERMINANTS OF EXCHANGE RATES IN THE SHORT RUN

INELASTIC SHORT-RUN SUPPLY AND DEMAND

Why do governments intervene to limit the fluctuations of their exchange rates rather than allowing the exchange rate to adjust freely according to PPP? The basic problem is that without government intervention drastic

---

[12] This last example, together with the effect of North Sea oil, explains why the British pound appreciated in 1980 to $2.30, above the example used in Figure 19-2.

up-and-down movements in exchange rates may be necessary to equate demand and supply in the short run, and these fluctuations in turn can cause undesirable movements in domestic prices and output. The most important cause of large fluctuations in exchange rates is the low elasticity of demand for imports and exports, particularly in the short run.

A nation may face two sets of demand and supply curves for foreign exchange. In the short run the supply and demand elasticities may be close to zero, but in the long run the elasticities may be substantial. The transition from the short run to the long run is illustrated in Figure 19-3. The demand and supply curves indicated by the solid lines, D_1 and S'_1, are valid in the long run. At an initial exchange rate of \$1.50, Britain is running a trade deficit shown by the distance between the D_1 and S'_1 curves, the distance $E_0 F$. After enough time has passed, the British trade deficit can be eliminated at point E_1 if the exchange rate is allowed to decline to \$1.25.

But what happens in the short run, before British producers have time to increase their production of exports and import substitutes? The relevant schedules reflecting inelastic short-run demand and supply are the dashed red d_1 and dashed black s_1 curves. A decline in the exchange rate to \$1.25 will widen the trade deficit to the distance HG, the distance between d_1 and s_1. No reduction in the exchange rate, no matter how drastic, can bring the trade deficit into balance in the short run. The British government will be forced to intervene to keep the exchange rate from falling below \$1.25 by buying up the excess pounds that foreigners have obtained from the import purchases of British firms. Only by patient waiting will the needed improvement in the trade balance occur. If the exchange rate is held at \$1.25 by the government, the demand and supply curves will slowly change their shape. The s_1 curve will pivot clockwise until it becomes the S'_1 curve. The d_1 curve will pivot counterclockwise until it becomes the D_1 curve. And the trade balance will gradually shrink from the large amount HG to zero at point E_1.

The right frame of Figure 19-3 illustrates the evolution of the trade balance as time passes. Now the trade balance is plotted in a vertical rather than in a horizontal direction. The initial trade balance is the distance $E_0 F$. After the exchange rate depreciates to \$1.25, at first the trade balance widens to the distance HG, and then it narrows to eventually reach zero at E_1. The red line running between E_0, H, and E_1 has the shape of the capital letter J, tipped over on its side. Thus the situation of a trade balance that deteriorates in the short run following a depreciation in the exchange rate is called the **J-curve phenomenon.**[13]

Summary: The *J*-curve phenomenon partly explains why the worldwide flexible-exchange-rate system in the 1970s has exhibited such

---

[13] Evidence on the *J* curve is presented in Rudiger Dornbusch and Paul Krugman, "Flexible Exchange Rates in the Short Run," *Brookings Papers on Economic Activity,* vol. 7, no. 3 (1976), especially on pp. 558–566. The authors conclude that "there is a significant price responsiveness, but adjustment lags are important and run to years, not quarters" (p. 566).

LOW ELASTICITIES OF DEMAND AND SUPPLY IN THE SHORT RUN CREATE THE *J*-CURVE PHENOMENON

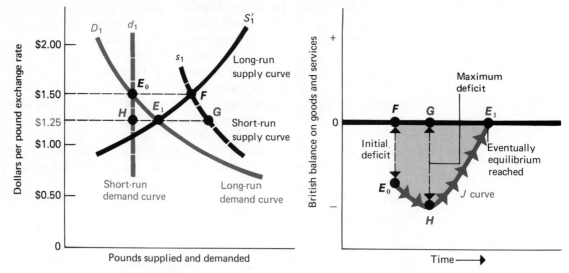

FIGURE 19–3

Response of the Balance on Goods and Services to a Devaluation in the Exchange Rate from $1.50 to $1.25, in Both the Short Run and the Long Run

Initially we assume that intervention by the British government holds the exchange rate at $1.50 in the left frame. The trade deficit will be the distance between the solid red demand curve D_1 and the solid black supply curve S_1', or the distance E_0F. In the long run an equilibrium with a zero trade balance can be obtained at an exchange rate of $1.25, but, in the short run, the trade balance will get worse when the exchange rate drops from $1.50 to $1.25. Because demand and suppy are inelastic, the short-run curves are the dashed lines d_1 and s_1, and the trade balance widens to the distance HG. The right frame shows the evolution of the trade balance over time, at first widening from E_0F (now plotted in the vertical direction) to HG, and then disappearing at point E_1.

sharp short-run changes in exchange rates. Small changes in the supply and demand curves for foreign exchange may require drastic changes in exchange rates in the short run. The actual value of the exchange rate then depends on the extent of government intervention. Since governments quite frequently may change their idea of the correct long-run equilibrium exchange rate, the rate at which they intervene is likely to be quite variable. Finally, private speculators also form expectations about the exchange rate, and they will raise their demand for a currency that they think is about to appreciate.

MAJOR EXCHANGE-RATE MOVEMENTS IN THE 1970s

The major sources of long-run changes in exchange rates are: differences among countries in the development of technology and natural resources; differences in inflation rates; and the differing attractiveness of various currencies for investors of funds. Since each of these three sources tends to change gradually over the course of time, why can't governments simply intervene and peg the exchange rate to the slowly evolving long-run equilibrium rate? Were the wide swings in the exchange rates depicted in Figure 19-1 for the 1970s really necessary?

The trouble is that no one, either inside the government or in the private sector, has discovered a reliable way to figure out what the exchange rate should be. Expectations of future exchange rates, as reflected in the forward exchange rate negotiated for future sales and purchases of foreign exchange 90 or 180 days in the future, have been extremely inaccurate estimates of the actual outcome. The main theories of exchange-rate determination do not seem to work. The purchasing-power-parity (PPP) theory states, for instance, that when the Japanese inflation rate is 1 percentage point slower than the U.S. inflation rate, the yen should appreciate at a rate of 1 percent per year. Yet Figure 19-1 reveals much larger fluctuations in the dollar-yen rate in one direction, followed by a reversal.

If the government cannot estimate the right equilibrium value of the exchange rate, it does not know how to conduct a policy to stabilize the exchange rate in the short run at the correct equilibrium rate. Nor do private speculators who buy and sell foreign currencies appear to have any better idea. As Henry Wallich, a governor of the Federal Reserve System, described the problem:

> The market certainly knows a wrong rate when it sees one. As for the "right rate," there seems to be a rather wide range upon which views are quite loosely held. This is evidenced, for instance, by the way in which spot and distant forward rates often move together, although the facts affecting the spot rate today might seem to be irrelevant to the spot rate in a distant future. There seems to be little of the stabilizing speculation that theoreticians have relied upon to push rates back to equilibrium after they have been knocked off balance.[14]

The failure of private speculators to maintain the day-to-day exchange rate at the equilibrium value does not constitute an automatic argument for intervention by government. Governments appear to be no better at forecasting than private dealers. Further, heavy intervention tempts governments to maintain a disequilibrium exchange rate to try to achieve other policy goals. In early 1977, for instance, both Germany and Japan attempted

---

[14] Henry Wallich, "What Makes Exchange Rates Move?" *Challenge*, vol. 20 (July/August 1977), p. 40.

to keep their exchange rates from appreciating, despite massive trade surpluses. Then in the summer of 1977, under pressure from U.S. officials, the value of the German mark and Japanese yen was finally allowed to rise. Three economists associated with the U.S. Treasury Department have recently concluded:

> Historical experience clearly demonstrates the relevant choice is neither between imperfect markets and ideal government speculation nor between ideal private market speculation and misguided government intervention, but between imperfect private and imperfect government speculation.[15]

19-6 BALANCE-OF-PAYMENTS ADJUSTMENT WITH FIXED EXCHANGE RATES

So far we have examined determinants of the foreign exchange rate in the long run and short run, but we have not paid any attention to interactions between the exchange rate, the balance of payments, and the domestic level of output and employment. For this analysis it is useful to return once again to the *IS-LM* curve diagrams developed in Part II. It is possible to superimpose on the *IS-LM* diagram a balance-of-payments line (*BP*), which shows the relationship of the balance of payments to the domestic interest rate and real output. This allows us to analyze the effects on the economy and balance of payments of changes in monetary policy, fiscal policy, and the foreign exchange rate.

THE *BP* CURVE

The U.S. balance of payments is divided in Table 19-1 into three sections: (1) the current account, (2) the capital account, and (3) financing items. The balance of payments (BP) is said to be in equilibrium when the financing items equal zero, implying that the balance on current account exactly cancels the balance on capital account. For instance, the overall BP can be in equilibrium when there is a current-account surplus and equivalent capital-account deficit, or vice versa. When the current account and capital account do not cancel each other, there is an overall BP surplus or deficit. An overall BP surplus is financed by an inflow of international reserves, which consist of gold and certain important foreign currencies, particularly the U.S. dollar. An overall BP deficit is financed by paying out reserves or by borrowing from other countries or from international agencies.

How are the current account and capital account related to the domestic economy?

---

[15] Dennis Logue, Richard Sweeney, and Thomas D. Willett, "Speculative Behavior of Foreign Exchange Rates During the Current Float," U.S. Department of the Treasury, Assistant Secretary for International Affairs Research Office, Discussion Paper 77/2, p. 19.

The current account consists of exports and imports of goods and services and unilateral transfers. Three of the most important determinants of the current-account balance are the level of domestic output (Q), the domestic price level relative to the foreign price level (P/P'), and the foreign exchange rate (F). When the price ratio P/P' and the exchange rate (F) are fixed, then an increase in domestic output causes the current account to deteriorate. Why? Export sales depend on output in other countries and are thus independent of domestic real output. But purchases of imports depend on domestic real output, because people buy more of all types of goods, both domestic and imported, when their real income (Q) increases.

The capital account includes both long-term and short-term capital flows. Many firms and individuals have a choice about the location of their bank accounts and holdings of short-term securities. If no changes in foreign exchange rates are expected, then investors will shift their funds to countries that have the highest interest rates.

The dashed red BP curve drawn through points J, E_0, and K in Figure 19-4 shows all the combinations of the interest rate (r) and real output (Q) consistent with overall balance-of-payments equilibrium. In the gray area above the BP line, the balance of payments is in surplus because an increase in the interest rate causes an increased capital inflow. In the pink area below the BP line, the balance of payments is in deficit, because a decrease in the interest rate leads to a smaller capital inflow or increased outflow. If policymakers want to avoid losing their international reserves, they must keep the economy out of the pink area. But if they want to avoid building up extra reserves that are not needed, they must keep the economy out of the gray area.

Everywhere along the BP line the balance of payments is in equilibrium. At point J real output is relatively low, so that imports are low and the current account is in surplus. To offset this and keep the overall balance (the sum of the current and capital account) equal to zero, the capital account must run a deficit. This adjustment requires a relatively low interest rate, so that funds will flow abroad to seek a higher return. Point K illustrates the opposite situation. Relatively high real output pulls in imports and causes the current account to run a deficit. To offset the deficit, the capital account must run a surplus, requiring a relatively high interest rate to attract funds from abroad. At point E_0, an intermediate situation, both the current and capital accounts are balanced, as is the overall balance of payments.

As with any market equilibrium curve in this book, we must ask several questions about BP to understand it fully:

1. *What makes BP slope upward?* The BP line has a positive slope because higher interest rates improve the capital account, requiring higher income to make the current account deteriorate by the offsetting amount needed to keep the overall balance of payments in equilibrium. If capital is perfectly mobile, all of it flows out of the country if the domestic interest rate should fall even slightly below the foreign interest rate, say r'. And if the

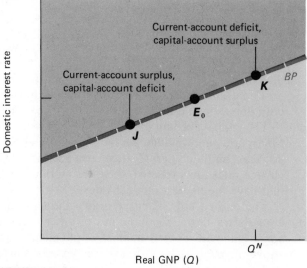

FIGURE 19–4

The *BP* Curve, Showing Different Combinations of Domestic Output
(*Q*) and the Domestic Interest Rate (*r*) Where the Balance of
Payments Is in Equilibrium

In the gray area the balance of payments is in surplus, and in the pink area there
is a deficit. Points *J*, E_0, *K*, and every other point along the red dashed *BP* line
represent situations of balance-of-payments equilibrium. At point *J* real output is
low, depressing imports and leading to a current-account surplus. To offset this,
the capital account must be in deficit, which can occur if the domestic interest
rate is low and funds flow abroad seeking a higher interest return. At point *K* real
output is high, raising imports and causing a current-account deficit. To offset
this, a high domestic interest rate is required to attract sufficient foreign funds to
generate a capital-account surplus.

---

domestic interest rate rises even slightly above the foreign interest rate
r' when capital is perfectly mobile, the country is flooded with capital
inflows. Thus in the case of perfect capital mobility, the *BP* line would be
horizontal and lie at the level of the foreign interest rate r'.

At the other extreme, if capital is completely immobile, there is no
capital account at all. The overall balance of payments can be in equilibrium only when the current account is balanced. In this case the dashed
red *BP* curve would be a vertical line running through E_0.

2. *What causes the BP curve to shift its position?* As is true of all diagrams,
the red balance-of-payments equilibrium curve will shift if there is a
change in any variable other than those plotted on the axes, the interest
rate (*r*) and real output (*Q*). For instance, the *BP* line in Figure 19-4 is
drawn on the assumption that both the ratio of domestic to foreign prices

(P/P') and the exchange rate (F) are fixed. A decline in P/P' will make domestic goods cheaper and improve the trade balance for any given level of output, thus moving the BP line to the right. This shift in BP increases the size of the gray surplus area and raises the payments surplus at every level of output. In the same way, a depreciation in the exchange rate will shift the BP line rightward.[16] And an appreciation of the exchange rate will shift BP to the left.

Government intervention can also cause the BP curve to shift. Anything that improves the current account for a given value of real output (Q) will shift the BP curve to the right. In addition to a reduction in the price ratio (P/P') or the exchange rate (F), a rightward shift in BP can be caused by an increase in customs duties on imports or subsidies to exports. Similarly, anything that improves the capital account at a given interest rate will shift the BP line rightward. Examples are taxes or prohibitions on capital outflows.

BALANCE-OF-PAYMENTS ADJUSTMENT WITH A FIXED PRICE LEVEL AND EXCHANGE RATE

Figure 19-4 provides no information on precisely what the economy's level of real output, interest rate, and its balance of payments will be. The BP equilibrium curve merely shows numerous possible combinations of output and the interest rate that are compatible with balance-of-payments equilibrium. Which of these combinations will occur? In Chapter 4 we learned that the economy's level of real output and interest rate occurs at the intersection of its commodity-market and money-market equilibrium schedules, the IS and LM curves. Now in Figure 19-5 we combine the new BP curve with IS and LM curves to determine where the economy will operate and how it will adjust to balance-of-payments surplus or deficit.

The BP equilibrium curve from Figure 19-4 is drawn again in the left frame of Figure 19-5 and is labeled BP_0. The red IS_0 line shows all the combinations of real output and the interest rate compatible with equilibrium in the commodity market. Earlier we learned that expansive fiscal policy can move the IS curve to the right. In addition, because the balance of payments on current account (net of transfer payments) is part of the demand for commodities, or expenditures on GNP, anything that improves the current account balance for a given level of real output will shift the IS curve to the right. One such event would be a decrease in domestic prices relative to foreign prices (P/P')—this would raise the domestic production of export goods and cut imports. Similarly, a depreciation in the exchange rate would stimulate the current account balance and shift the IS curve rightward.[17]

---

[16] The rightward shift in BP will occur only after the temporary J-curve deterioration in the current account has ended and the current account has begun to improve.

[17] The elementary theory of income determination in an open economy with exports and imports is reviewed in the Appendix to Chapter 3.

In Figure 19-5 three *LM* curves are drawn. Each shows different combinations of real output and the interest rate at which the demand for and supply of money are equal. Recall that the position of the *LM* curve depends on the size of the real money supply—that is, on the ratio of the nominal money supply (M^s) to the price level (P). An increase in M^s/P shifts the *LM* curve to the right, and vice versa. Whereas in earlier chapters the money supply was determined solely by decisions of the Federal Reserve, now in addition the size of the money supply and hence the position of the *LM* curve depend on the balance of payments.

Let us assume that the economy is initially at point E_1 in the left frame, at the intersection of the fixed red IS_0 line and the black LM_1 money-market line. Because E_1 lies in the gray area above the *BP* curve, the balance of payments is in surplus, and the central bank adds to its holdings of international reserves. The assets of the central bank are increased, which tends to increase the money supply and thus shift the *LM* curve to the right.[18] The rightward shift in *LM* will continue until the balance-of-payments surplus is eliminated, which occurs when the *LM* curve crosses the *BP* line at point E_0.

Exactly the opposite shift in *LM* occurs if the economy begins at point E_2 (the crossing point of IS_0 with LM_2), which lies in the pink area where the balance of payments is in deficit. The central bank finances the deficit by supporting the current foreign exchange rate of its own currency, using up some of its international reserves. The loss of reserves cuts the assets of the central banks and thus reduces the money supply, shifting the *LM* curve leftward from LM_2 back toward LM_0. The shift in *LM* continues until the balance of payments returns to equilibrium along the *BP* line at point E_0.

The shift in the *LM* curve that achieves balance-of-payments equilibrium occurs automatically, without policymakers doing anything. What remains for policymakers to do? The noteworthy fact about the equilibrium position E_0 is that output Q_0 is undesirably low, lying well below the natural real GNP level (Q^N). How can expansive monetary or fiscal policy simultaneously achieve Q^N together with balance-of-payments equilibrium along the *BP* line? Clearly, monetary policy is impotent. Starting from equilibrium at point E_0 along the LM_0 curve, any expansion in the money supply will push *LM* to the right toward LM_2. But this will just cause a loss in international reserves that will push *LM* back leftward to LM_0 again.

---

[18] In Chapter 16 we learned that the money supply is a multiple of high-powered money, which with a few minor adjustments equals the assets of the central bank (the Federal Reserve in the United States). The assets of the central bank consist mainly of domestic government bonds and international reserves (gold in the United States, gold and dollars elsewhere). In principle a central bank can prevent the money supply from rising in response to an inflow of international reserves resulting from a balance-of-payments surplus. How? There are several methods of "sterilizing" a reserve inflow, of which the most obvious is an open-market sale of government bonds. If reserves increase by $1 billion, then a $1 billion sale of bonds cancels any effect on high-powered money or the money supply. Another method would be for the central bank to raise legal reserve requirements of the commercial banks, which tends to cut the

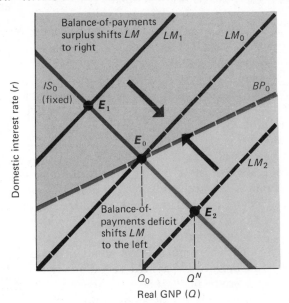

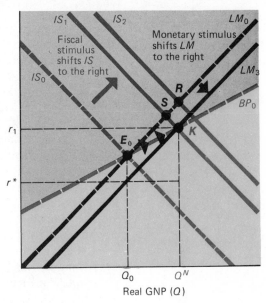

FIGURE 19-5

Adjustment of the Balance of Payments with a Fixed Price Level and Exchange Rate

In the left frame the economy automatically gravitates to point E_0, where the balance of payments is in equilibrium along the BP_0 line and the money and commodity markets are also in equilibrium along LM_0 and IS_0. The money supply will adjust automatically through gains or losses of international reserves to reach E_0 from any other starting point such as E_1 or E_2. In the right frame a coordinated monetary and fiscal expansion can keep the balance of payments in equilibrium and at the same time achieve the natural level of real GNP Q^N at point K.

In an open economy with fixed prices and exchange rates, monetary expansion is impotent to achieve natural real GNP (Q^N) from a starting point such as E_0 for more than a short transition period. Open-market purchases by the central bank will raise the money supply only

number of dollars of money supply that can be created per dollar of high-powered money. Many foreign central banks are limited in their ability to sterilize by open-market sales because their portfolios of government bonds are relatively small and they have been reluctant to change bank reserve requirements.

temporarily, but then will lead to losses of international reserves that bring the money supply back to its original value.[19]

If monetary policy cannot achieve an increase in output because of the leak of international reserves abroad, then economic expansion requires a fiscal stimulus. In the right frame of Figure 19-5 we continue to assume that the price level and the exchange rate are fixed. Nevertheless Q^N can be achieved at point K, where the balance of payments is in equilibrium.[20] It is not enough for fiscal policy alone to stimulate the economy. A rightward shift in the IS curve to position IS_2 will achieve the desired increase in output to point R, where real GNP is at Q^N. But R lies in the gray area above the BP line, indicating a balance-of-payments surplus. Point K is superior because not only is natural real GNP achieved, but the balance of payments is in equilibrium as well. Point K lies at the intersection of the IS_1 and LM_3 schedules and can be reached from a starting point of E_0 by a combined fiscal stimulus that shifts the IS curve from IS_0 to IS_1, together with a monetary stimulus to shift the LM curve from LM_0 to LM_3.[21]

Although expansive fiscal policy is essential for the simultaneous achievement of natural real GNP and a balance-of-payments equilibrium, nevertheless point K in Figure 19-5 may not be the best possible situation. The fiscal policy stimulus requires some combination of a cut in tax rates or an increase in government expenditure, raising the government deficit. The higher government deficit (an increase in the supply of government bonds relative to the demand for them) pushes up the interest rate and allows the economy to enjoy a higher level of real GNP without a deterioration in the balance of payments. But at the same time some private investment may be crowded out, leading to a situation at point K with too much government spending and private consumption or both and too little private investment.

In drawing our positively sloped BP line, we have assumed that capital is only imperfectly mobile between nations. The BP curve is a horizontal

---

[19] A corollary is that any country with a balance-of-payments problem has only itself to blame. Just as an expansion in holdings of domestic bonds by the central bank (accomplished through open-market purchases) causes a loss of reserves, so a country can accumulate extra reserves by reducing its holdings of domestic bonds. An extreme version of this theory with perfect capital mobility and instantaneous equality between foreign and domestic prices implies that the central bank has no control at all over its own money supply. See Harry G. Johnson, "The Monetary Approach to Balance-of-Payments Theory," in Jacob A. Frenkel and Harry G. Johnson (eds.), *The Monetary Approach to the Balance of Payments* (Toronto: University of Toronto Press, 1976). See also Harry G. Johnson, "The Monetary Approach to Balance of Payments Theory: A Diagrammatic Analysis," *The Manchester School*, vol. 43 (September 1976), pp. 220–74.

[20] Turn back to Figure 19-4, where an identical point K is plotted.

[21] If monetary and fiscal expansion are applied simultaneously, then the economy can move immediately from the initial position E_0 to the desired point K. If fiscal policy is applied alone, K is reached in two stages. First fiscal policy expands the economy to point S, where a balance-of-payments surplus causes international reserves to flow in; this in turn gradually raises the money supply and shifts the economy from S to K.

A FISCAL STIMULUS NO LONGER RAISES THE INTEREST RATE WHEN CAPITAL IS PERFECTLY MOBILE

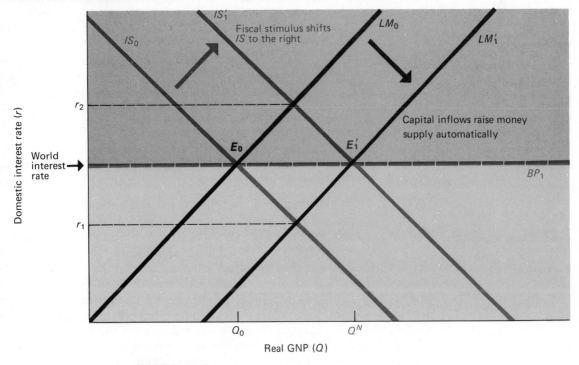

FIGURE 19-6

Effect of a Fiscal Stimulus on Real GNP and the Interest Rate When Capital Is Perfectly Mobile

Now the BP line is horizontal. Why? With perfectly mobile capital even the slightest increase in the domestic interest rate above the world interest rate causes capital to flood in. The balance of payments can be in equilibrium only when the domestic interest rate is exactly equal to the world interest rate, as along the flat BP_1 line. Now a fiscal stimulus that moves IS rightward from IS_0 to IS_1' can raise real output without increasing the interest rate. Inflows of capital provide international reserves that boost the money supply, shifting LM rightward from LM_0 to LM_1'.

line at the level of the world interest rate if capital is perfectly mobile, because a domestic interest rate even a fraction higher than the world interest rate would cause an infinite amount of capital to flood in. This result is illustrated by the BP_1 line in Figure 19-6. In this case a fiscal expansion from IS_0 to IS_1' can push the economy to Q^N along the horizontal BP line. The money supply will be lifted automatically by capital movements from LM_0 to LM_1' to prevent any increase in the domestic interest rate. As a result there is no crowding out effect and the full Chapter 3 multiplier occurs.

In the case of imperfectly mobile capital illustrated in the right frame of Figure 19-5, the interest rate at point K increases compared to the initial interest rate at E_0. In the case of perfectly mobile capital (Figure 19-6) with a horizontal BP line, the interest rate is not affected by a fiscal expansion designed to raise output to the natural level at E_1'. But what if a lower interest rate is desired? Let us assume that the interest rate designated $r*$ in Figure 19-5 is necessary to achieve the right blend of consumption, investment, and government spending. How can the lower interest rate $r*$ be reached, while maintaining natural real GNP (Q^N) and an equilibrium in the balance of payments?

BALANCE-OF-PAYMENTS ADJUSTMENT WITH FLEXIBLE PRICES AND A FIXED EXCHANGE RATE

The first method of improving the situation should be familiar. As in many areas of macroeconomics, problems tend to disappear if the price level is perfectly flexible. The beneficial effects of a drop in the domestic price level relative to foreign prices (P/P') are illustrated in Figure 19-7. Once again we assume that capital is only imperfectly mobile, so that the BP curve slopes upward. Each of the three curves (IS, LM, and BP) is affected by the drop in prices. First, lower prices make exports more attractive to foreigners and also cause domestic purchasers to switch from imports to domestically produced goods. The balance on goods and services (part of GNP) improves. This extra injection of spending shifts the IS curve rightward from IS_0 to IS_0'. Similarly, the improvement in the current account shifts the BP line rightward from BP_0 to BP_0'. Finally, the position of the LM curve depends on the ratio of the nominal money supply (M^s) to the price level (P). With lower prices M^s/P rises and the LM curve shifts rightward from LM_0 to LM_0'.

The economy's new equilibrium position is at point E_0', with a higher output and lower interest rate than at the initial E_0. Two automatic mechanisms guarantee that the three curves will all cross at the new position E_0'. First, the term *price flexibility* means that the price level will continue to fall until the economy reaches natural real GNP. This makes the IS_0' and BP_0' curves shift rightward until they cross at Q^N. Second, the LM curve must cross point E_0'. If not, the balance of payments will be in surplus or deficit and the nominal money supply will expand or contract until the LM curve reaches E_0'.

Thus flexible prices can achieve natural real GNP automatically, without any need for a coordinated monetary-fiscal expansion, as was necessary in the right frame of Figure 19-5. This is the same conclusion reached in Chapter 6 for a closed economy: when the price level is perfectly flexible, policymakers can "go fishing" with the assurance that the price level will automatically adjust to keep actual real GNP at the natural level Q^N. The only remaining role for policymakers is to choose the desired interest rate. If the optimal interest rate is $r*$ in Figure 19-7, but flexible prices push the interest rate to r_0', a combination of fiscal restraint and monetary stimulus can push

FLEXIBLE PRICES CAN AUTOMATICALLY ACHIEVE THE NATURAL REAL GNP LEVEL AND BALANCE-OF-PAYMENTS EQUILIBRIUM

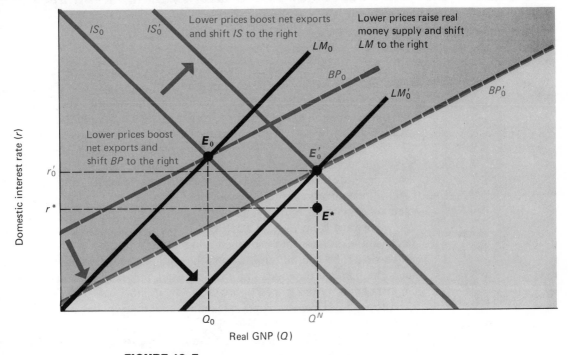

FIGURE 19–7

Effect on Real GNP, the Interest Rate, and the Balance of Payments of a Decline in Domestic Prices Relative to Foreign Prices (P/P')

Lower prices cause all three curves to shift to the right. More exports will be sold, and fewer imports bought, which raises the current-account balance. This shifts both IS and BP rightward. And the lower price level raises the real money supply (M^s/P), thus shifting the LM curve rightward.

the economy to the best position of all, E^*. Price flexiblity will work to keep the balance of payments in equilibrium at E^*.

In contrast, if capital is perfectly mobile and the BP curve is a horizontal line, as in Figure 19-6, there is no role for policymakers at all. The interest rate is fixed at the level of the world interest rate. Starting out from the lower output level at point E_0, flexible prices by themselves will guarantee that the economy will reach natural real GNP (Q^N) at point E_1'. The drop in prices will shift the IS curve rightward as export sales are stimulated and import sales are inhibited. And the reduction in the price level will raise the real money supply and shift LM rightward until the economy reaches E_1'.

19-7 THE ROLE OF POLICY UNDER FLEXIBLE EXCHANGE RATES

EFFECTS ON REAL GNP

If we continue to assume perfect capital mobility, Figure 19-6 is equally relevant for an analysis of the economy's adjustment when the foreign exchange rate is flexible. Whereas previously a monetary expansion was impotent, because a rightward shift from LM_0 to LM_1' would cause a capital outflow and a loss of international reserves, this no longer happens under flexible exchange rates. There is no automatic influence of a balance-of-payments deficit or surplus on the money supply because the flexibility of exchange rates keeps the balance of payments in equilibrium at all times.

On the contrary, monetary policy becomes a potent policy tool with flexible exchange rates. Initially, an increase in the nominal money supply shifts LM rightward from LM_0 to LM_1'. But this in turn induces a capital outflow, because the interest rate is pushed down in the short run to r_1 by a monetary expansion. The capital outflow cuts the exchange rate, which in turn stimulates the balance on goods and services; this increase in exports relative to imports shifts the IS curve rightward from IS_0 to IS_1'.

Although flexible exchange rates make monetary policy more potent than under fixed exchange rates, fiscal policy becomes less potent. In Figure 19-6 a fiscal expansion will initially shift the IS curve to the right. But the temporary increase in the interest rate to r_2 will induce a capital inflow and an appreciation of the exchange rate. Exports will become more expensive and their sales will fall. Imports will become more attractive. This decline in net exports (exports minus imports) will shift the IS curve backward toward IS_0. Since this process will continue as long as the interest rate is above the world interest rate, we conclude that in an open economy with a flexible exchange rate fiscal policy loses control of the IS curve.

The only effect of a fiscal expansion is on foreign countries, which enjoy an increase in net exports and domestic income as a result of the appreciation in the currency of the country illustrated in Figure 19-6. In the same way, the potency of monetary expansion under flexible exchange rates is offset by the negative effect on net exports and domestic income in foreign countries. The influence of a monetary expansion will be transmitted abroad if foreign nations react by raising their own money supplies. Thus the effect of monetary expansion, taking into account the reaction of other nations, may be to induce a worldwide expansion of the money supply. Since the world is a closed economy, a worldwide monetary expansion would then have exactly the same effects as those analyzed in Chapter 8. There would be an expansion in both real GNP and the price level if the worldwide economy were initially below Q^N, but a monetary expansion that occurs when the economy is initially at Q^N would give only a transitory boost to real GNP.

THE OPEN-ECONOMY PHILLIPS CURVE

How does a system of flexible exchange rates affect the choice of policy-makers in the United States and other large countries between monetary and fiscal expansion in situations when output is low and unemployment is high? In the real world fiscal expansion is not completely impotent. Though a rightward shift in the *IS* curve does tend to raise the real interest rate, attract foreign capital, and thus lead to an appreciation of the exchange rate, it may take a substantial length of time for the appreciation to cut net exports by enough to offset the effect of the fiscal expansion. Just as the *J*-curve phenomenon in section 19-5 suggests that a nation's trade balance may improve temporarily following a depreciation in the exchange rate, so it also implies that a fiscal expansion, which causes an exchange-rate appreciation, may temporarily improve the trade balance.

Because fiscal expansion tends to cause the exchange rate to appreciate and monetary expansion causes a depreciation, domestic policymakers find that the short-run Phillips-curve relationship between inflation and unemployment now depends on the type of stimulus chosen. Previously in the closed-economy analysis of Chapter 8 the short-run increase in inflation associated with a given increase in real GNP did not depend on the choice of policy instruments. Consider in Figure 19-8 an economy starting at point A, with Q well below Q^N. The black short-run Phillips curve corresponds to our previous analysis of the closed economy and shows the short-run increase in inflation that will be induced by a policy stimulus that raises real GNP by a given amount, say to point B.

The same increase in Q will have a different inflationary effect in an open economy with flexible exchange rates. A fiscal expansion, which causes the exchange rate to appreciate, will tend to moderate the inflationary effect of the same reduction in unemployment. Why? An appreciation means that domestic residents have to pay fewer units of their own currency to buy an imported good selling for a given number of units of foreign currency. A Mercedes-Benz selling for 45,000 marks costs an American $22,500 if a dollar buys only 2 marks, but the dollar price drops to $15,000 if suddenly the dollar appreciates to a rate of 3 marks per dollar. The effect of the appreciation alters not only the prices of imports, but also the dollar prices of some exports and some domestically produced goods that compete with imports. An increase in real GNP in the short run now pushes the economy along the red path from A to D in Figure 19-8.

A monetary stimulus has just the opposite effect. The exchange rate tends to depreciate, because of the increased supply of domestic money. Prices of imports, exports, and import substitutes go up. An increase in real GNP pushes the economy along the red path between A and C in Figure 19-8. And the situation may be even worse than indicated by the red path between A and C, which describes the short-run trade-off while holding constant people's expectations of future inflation. If individuals learn that monetary

IN AN OPEN ECONOMY THE SHORT-RUN PHILLIPS CURVE IS FLATTER FOR A FISCAL THAN FOR A MONETARY STIMULUS

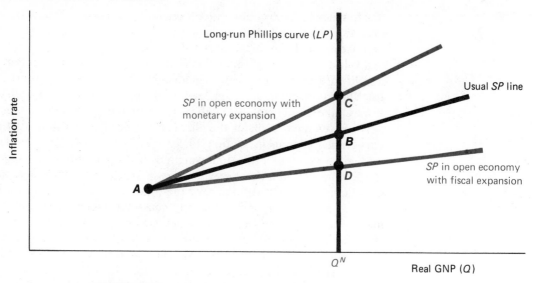

FIGURE 19-8

Comparison of Conventional Closed-Economy Short-run Phillips Curve with Two Alternative Curves for an Open Economy with Flexible Exchange Rates

In a closed economy an increase in real GNP starting from point *A* causes inflation to increase along the path marked between *A* and *B*. In an open economy with flexible exchange rates an increase in real GNP generated by fiscal expansion causes the exchange rate to appreciate and the inflation rate to be moderated by smaller price increases of imports and exports. A monetary expansion has the opposite effect, causing the exchange rate to depreciate, prices of exports and imports to rise, and domestic inflation to accelerate relative to the closed-economy case.

expansion implies more domestic inflation, caused by a currency depreciation, their inflation expectations will shift the short-run Phillips curve up *above* the red line running through *A* and *C*.

Combined with the *J*-curve phenomenon, which states that following an exchange-rate depreciation the trade surplus (part of GNP) temporarily deteriorates, monetary expansion may not only make inflation worse, but may cause real GNP to fall and unemployment to become worse as well. The disadvantages of monetary policy are paralleled by corresponding advantages of fiscal policy, which can temporarily moderate the inflation rate with a possible temporary improvement in the trade surplus. Many economists believe that it is important to insulate domestic inflation from the disruptive influence of exchange-rate movements and that any policy stimulus consists of a balanced monetary and fiscal expansion while holding the exchange rate constant. A tax cut or spending increase should therefore be accommodated by faster monetary growth, a recommendation that conflicts with the monetarist preference for a constant-monetary-growth-rate rule.

19-8 CONCLUSION: INTERNATIONAL POLICY PROBLEMS OF THE 1980s

HAS NATIONAL MONETARY INDEPENDENCE BEEN ACHIEVED BY THE FLEXIBLE-RATE SYSTEM?

The old system of fixed exchange rates collapsed in 1971–73 when nations having a surplus, particularly Germany and Japan, lost their monetary independence. To keep their currencies from appreciating, they had been forced to buy massive amounts of dollars. These dollars tended to raise the domestic money supply of Germany, Japan, and other nations more than the amount desired by their domestic central banks, thus contributing to a worldwide acceleration of inflation in 1973. Flexible exchange rates were attractive to these countries as a way of untying their money supplies from the influence of the United States. If American monetary growth was excessive, the dollar would depreciate while the mark and yen appreciated, allowing Germany and Japan to maintain lower inflation rates than the United States. This monetary independence had previously been stymied by massive inflows of reserves that their central banks had been forced to accumulate to keep their exchange rates fixed.

In the long run a flexible-exchange-rate system does permit a country to choose an inflation rate that differs from that of its main trading partners. The contrast between the low inflation rate enjoyed by Germany since 1973, compared to the much higher inflation rates of Italy and the United Kingdom, provides evidence of the advantages of flexible rates for nations attempting to avoid inflation. If there were a permanent long-run trade-off between inflation and real GNP, other nations might be able to use their monetary independence in a flexible-exchange-rate system to achieve more real GNP at the cost of higher inflation. But because the long-run Phillips curve in fact appears to be vertical, it may not be possible for nations to "buy" higher real GNP for more than a short transition period by their willingness to suffer high inflation, leaving no obvious advantages of flexible rates for countries with high inflation.

If the flexible-exchange-rate system is advantageous to those nations with a taste for low inflation rates, what are the offsetting costs? We have seen that, in the short run, exchange rates tend to fluctuate widely around their long-run equilibrium levels. Such fluctuations may inhibit the growth of foreign trade and capital movements, although as yet there is little evidence that the post-1973 flexible-exchange-rate system has had any such effect. Another problem is that adjustment may eventually be costly when a country allows its currency to become overvalued or undervalued relative to long-run equilibrium. Depreciation for an overvalued currency requires that resources be shifted toward export industries, and also may cause transitional unemployment in other nations. But these adjustment costs are probably not as serious under the flexible-rate system as under the old system of fixed exchange rates, which by the late 1960s had allowed exchange rates to become badly out of line.

VICIOUS AND VIRTUOUS CIRCLES

The adjustment lags summarized as the *J*-curve phenomenon pose a dilemma for countries with weak economies, as for Britain and Italy in the 1970s, which were both experiencing high unemployment and above-average inflation simultaneously. High inflation leads speculators to expect that the long-term equilibrium exchange rate is declining according to the purchasing-power-parity theory, and accordingly the actual value of the exchange rate is bid down. This depreciation aggravates the inflation problem by raising the prices of imports, exports, and import substitutes, and may even temporarily worsen unemployment, if the *J*-curve phenomenon is strong. Thus a vicious circle develops, with inflation causing depreciation, which causes further inflation, all without any major stimulus to real output or employment. Even though the British pound appreciated during 1977–79 as North Sea oil began to flow, there was little improvement in the U.K. inflation and unemployment situation, and the danger of a renewed vicious circle was still present.

Strong countries with below-average inflation rates benefit from a corresponding virtuous circle, with low inflation causing appreciation, which causes inflation to slow still further. Eventually changes in the exchange rate do help to improve a depreciating country's trade performance. But economists have been gradually raising their estimates of the adjustment lags and of the importance of factors other than prices alone that influence the success of a nation's export sales performance or its ability to compete with imports. Until the increase in oil prices occurred in 1979, Germany had enjoyed a massive surplus of exports over imports, despite an effective appreciation of the mark of more than 40 percent between early 1973 and early 1977. Apparently German suppliers provide goods of high quality with prompt delivery and have a sufficient monopoly of these desirable talents to be able to sell goods even at the higher prices forced by appreciation.[22]

THE DILEMMA OF SLOW ADJUSTMENT

During the 1970s the value of the U.S. dollar fell relative to the German mark and the Japanese yen. Americans are all worse off and the Germans

---

[22] A further assessment of the vicious-circle problem is contained in William J. Fellner, "The Payments Adjustment Process and the Exchange Rate Regime: What Have We Learned?" *American Economic Review*, vol. 55 (May 1975), pp. 148–151.

and Japanese are all better off as a result. Why? The first reason is obvious — imported goods are now more expensive for Americans and less expensive for Germans and Japanese, and this handicaps Americans in attaining higher living standards while stimulating the growth of living standards in Germany and Japan. The second reason is less obvious — the decline in the dollar has boosted the prices of imports and "import-substitutes" (goods that compete with imports), pushing up the U.S. rate of inflation relative to that in Germany and Japan. This further weakens the dollar and strengthens the mark and the yen.

How can the United States escape from this vicious circle? The 1970–78 drop in the value of the dollar compared to the mark and yen should have been balanced by an excess of U.S. inflation over German and Japanese inflation, according to the purchasing-power-parity doctrine that we studied in section 19-4. But there we found that the dollar has dropped more, and the mark and yen have risen more, than can be accounted for by differences in inflation rates. This means that, since the dollar has fallen in value more than the excess inflation in the United States, U.S. exports should be good bargains and German and Japanese exports should be poor bargains. Customers in other nations should be shifting from German and Japanese to U.S. goods, thus helping to arrest the decline in the dollar and the rise of the mark and the yen. Unfortunately, this has not happened. The current-account balances of Germany and Japan were much more healthy than that of the United States over the 1970–78 period during which exchange rates changed so much:[23]

	1970–78 average, $ billions		
	Current account	Net private capital account	Total
United States	−64	−62	−126
West Germany	+37	+ 4	+ 41
Japan	+40	− 4	+ 36

If the United States had not had such a large current-account deficit, or had not exported so much private capital, there would have been a greater demand for dollars. The higher intersection point of the demand and supply curves for dollars would have prevented part of the depreciation of the dollar. Americans would be better off and would have a lower rate of inflation. What forces have impeded the process of adjustment, allowing the Germans and Japanese to continue to run a surplus on current account despite the high price of their exports and the cheapness of goods available to them to import?

Part of the answer comes from the simple national income definitions of Chapter 2. Since exports (X) are an injection into the spending stream, while

---

[23] Higher oil prices in 1979 pushed the current account of both Germany and Japan into deficit, but they retained their very strong surplus in trade of manufactured goods.

imports (H) are a leakage out of the spending stream, the definition that injections must equal leakages becomes:

$$I + G + X = S + T - H$$

or   (19.3)

$$X - H = S - I + T - G$$

In words, this last line can be stated:

current account = private saving − private investment + government surplus

A basic difference between the United States and the other two nations, Germany and Japan, is that U.S. private saving has been small enough to make the right-hand side of (19.3) negative, whereas German and Japanese private saving has been strong enough to make the right-hand side positive.

> *Thus the low level of private household saving in the United States is a fundamental source of two chronic American problems — the low rate of productivity growth as examined in section 18-6, and the current-account deficit and dollar depreciation examined in this section. Increases in the U.S. government surplus and tax incentives to encourage private saving would help alleviate both problems.*

The current account in Germany and Japan has been strong not only because of high levels of private saving, but also because private investment dropped more than in the United States during the 1970s. Especially in Japan the marked slowdown in real GNP growth after 1973 brought about a decline of investment demand through Chapter 14's accelerator principle. Private investment fell less and recovered sooner after the 1973–75 recession in the United States, because aggregate demand policy was more stimulative. Economists do not agree on the reasons for the more rapid U.S. recovery. Some, such as Yale's James Tobin, think that Germany and Japan needlessly restricted demand growth in their economies during the 1975–78 period because of excessive concern about inflation and insufficient concern about the consequences of their restrictive policy on the level of worldwide real GNP. Others, such as Harvard's Jeffrey Sachs, claim that the rigidity of real wages in Germany and Japan made their aggregate supply curves more nearly vertical (like Chapter 7's QQ line) and made policymakers in these nations unable to stimulate real GNP and investment more than they did.[24]

---

[24] **Review:** The SS short-run supply curve of Chapter 7 becomes vertical when the expected price level adjusts to the actual price level; if all wage rates quickly respond to changes in the price level, then the aggregate supply curve may be vertical even in the short run. The relation of real-wage rigidity to macroeconomic adjustment in the 1970s is explored in Jeffrey Sachs, "Wages, Profits, and Macroeconomic Adjustment: A Comparative Study," *Brookings Papers on Economic Activity,* vol. 10, no. 2 (1979), pp. 269–319.

If the Germans and Japanese saved too much relative to their level of investment in the late 1970s, why did they not simply export their surplus savings in the form of a capital-account private outflow? While some Japanese and German companies have exported capital to the United States by building new factories, the institutional nature of the domestic banking system in these countries discourages capital exports. On the other hand, U.S. banks are well established overseas, as are many U.S. multinational corporations, so that the value of the U.S. dollar is further depreciated by capital outflows.

THE LIMITATIONS OF AGGREGATE DEMAND POLICY

A major theme of this book has been the shifting emphasis in macro-economics from demand management to supply-side policies. Our examination of international macroeconomics in this chapter suggests additional reasons why control of aggregate demand growth cannot by itself solve the world's problems of excessive inflation and slow real GNP growth. The United States by itself cannot use faster growth in its money supply to raise the growth rate of world real GNP if other nations such as Germany and Japan keep their monetary growth rates at a more moderate pace. Unilateral monetary stimulus by the United States will cause a depreciation of the dollar and extra inflation inside the United States. Faced with supply shocks such as those of 1979 and 1980, when OPEC more than doubled the price of oil, a policy of full accommodation by the United States is of limited use if other nations do not pursue an accommodative policy. In Chapters 9 and 10 we emphasized supply-side policies, such as a reduction in cost-boosting taxes and government regulation, as a way of introducing favorable supply shocks. In Chapters 18 and 19 we add the importance of an increase in the U.S. natural employment surplus and in incentives to private saving as a means of increasing the growth rate of productivity and of improving the U.S. current account.

While the feasibility of U.S. demand management policies depends on the policies chosen in other nations, innovative supply-side policies can be undertaken independently of foreign opinion. Just as adverse supply shocks make everything worse, reducing real GNP and aggravating inflation, so policy-induced favorable supply shocks can "make everything better." If so, why have politicians been so slow to adopt many of the supply-side policies advocated in this book? While some of their economic benefits may seem obvious, each raises political difficulties. After a decade of expanding environmental, health, and safety legislation, it is hard to throw the machinery into reverse. After a decade of ballooning government transfer payments that have stimulated consumption and sapped private saving, it is hard to contemplate a period during which real transfer payments grow more slowly than real GNP. It seems appropriate, therefore, to end the second edition of this textbook with an observation from the first edition that seems just as relevant now as when it was first written in 1977:

It is fitting that we end our book about macroeconomics on this humbling note. Despite our improved understanding of the economic factors that brought the world to its mid-1970s situation of unprecedented inflation and unemployment, the design of a solution cannot be extricated from political factors of which economists have only a modest understanding and over which they exercise even less control.

SUMMARY

1. The international transactions of any nation are divided into the three categories—*current* transactions involving the export or import of goods and services, together with unilateral transfer payments; *capital* transactions involving long-term and short-term borrowing and lending; and *financing items* required to offset any deficit or surplus on the current and capital accounts taken together.

2. If governments allowed the exchange rate of their currency to fluctuate from day to day to eliminate any imbalance on current and capital account, no financing items would be necessary. But if a government intervenes to maintain a fixed exchange rate, then there is likely to be a surplus or shortage of foreign exchange, which in turn causes an increase or decrease in the government's stock of international reserves (or, when the reserves run low, borrowing from abroad).

3. In the absence of government intervention, the foreign exchange rate tends to appreciate when there is an increased demand for a currency due to higher exports or capital inflows. The rate tends to depreciate when there is an increased supply of a currency due to higher imports or capital outflows.

4. In the long run, the main determinants of the exchange rate between the currencies of two nations are their relative inflation rates, their comparative rates of innovation and technological change, their comparative rates of discovery of natural resources, and the balance of flows of capital and government transfer payments between them.

5. In the short run, the exchange rate can fluctuate widely around the long-run equilibrium exchange rate, because the price elasticities of imports and exports may be smaller in the short run than in the long run, and because neither the government nor private speculators have enough knowledge to stabilize the exchange rate at its long-run equilibrium level.

6. When the exchange rate is fixed, monetary policy by itself cannot stimulate real output, if the balance of payments is initially in equilibrium. Fiscal and monetary policy must be used together to achieve simultaneously the natural level of real GNP together with equilibrium in the balance of payments.

7. When prices are flexible and the exchange rate is fixed, the economy tends to arrive automatically at natural real GNP with its balance of payments in equilibrium, and changes in fiscal policy are necessary only if a change in the interest rate is desired.

8. In a system with flexible exchange rates, monetary policy becomes more potent by causing a depreciation which reinforces a monetary stimulus, while fiscal policy becomes less potent by causing an appreciation which works to offset a fiscal stimulus.

9. While monetary policy becomes more potent under a system of flexible exchange rates, the short-run inflation–real GNP trade-off becomes worse for monetary than for fiscal policy.

CONCEPTS

Open economy versus closed economy
Balance-of-payments surplus or deficit
Foreign exchange rate
Appreciation versus depreciation
International reserves
Current account versus capital account

Official Reserve Transactions Deficit
Purchasing-power-parity theory of the exchange rate
J-curve phenomenon
BP line
Fixed-exchange-rate system
Flexible-exchange-rate system

QUESTIONS FOR REVIEW

1   In which of the categories of Table 19-1 would you classify the following international transactions of the United States?
   a. Purchase of a $100,000 Caterpillar tractor from the Peoria, U.S.A., factory by an Italian road-building contractor.
   b. Short-term loan to the Italian contractor by the First National Bank of Chicago to finance the tractor.
   c. Purchase of a $450 round-trip ticket to London on British Airways by a student at Pennsylvania State University.
   d. A $100 gift sent by a recent Irish immigrant in the United States by mail to his mother in Dublin.
   e. Purchase of an old Chrysler factory at New Stanton, Pennsylvania, by the Volkswagen company of Germany for $40 million.
   f. A $100 million increase in the holdings of short-term U.S. government bonds by the Bank of England (the central bank of the United Kingdom).

2   What method of financing its balance-of-payments deficit is available to the United States, but not to other countries? Does the availability of this special method make U.S. citizens better off?

3   Explain the nature of the dilemma of a nation facing a balance-of-payments deficit, when the sum of its import and export price elasticities is less than 1.0. How does this problem help to explain exchange-rate movements in the 1970s?

4   Explain why the exchange rate of the Japanese yen appreciated between 1966 and 1979 relative to the U.S. dollar, despite the higher inflation rate in Japan than in the United States.

5   Explain in words why the *BP* line in Figure 19-4 slopes upward to the right. Under what circumstances would it be horizontal?

6   When exchange rates are fixed, is monetary or fiscal policy a more potent method for controlling real output? Why?

7   When exchange rates are flexible, is monetary or fiscal policy a more potent method for controlling real output? Why?

8   If a nation operating under flexible exchange rates desires to cut its excessively high unemployment rate by a given amount, will its inflation rate increase more if it chooses monetary policy to achieve its economic expansion or if it chooses fiscal policy?

9   Between 1973 and 1980 economic growth in many industrialized nations was well below the growth rate before 1973. What are some of the reasons for this worldwide situation?

10   In your library try to find out what has happened to inflation and the growth rate of real GNP in Japan, Germany, and other countries since 1979. See sources such as *International Financial Statistics* (International Monetary Fund) or *Main Economic Indicators* (OECD). Both are published every month.

Appendixes

Appendix A
Conceptual Problems in the Measurement of Income and Prices

Introductory Note: This supplement can be read either immediately after Chapter 2 or else after the rest of the book. It is designed to deepen the student's understanding of the differences between GNP as currently measured and national welfare and to introduce the student to problems in achieving a better measure of welfare as well as to problems in measuring prices. Although these are interesting questions currently under active investigation by economists inside and outside the federal government, they are not crucial to the understanding of the rest of the book, and so this discussion has been placed here at the end. For instance, an improved measure of economic welfare may decline less during a recession than the current official measure of GNP, but improved measurement does not eliminate our need for a good theory of recessions and how to avoid them. Similarly, the annual increase in our price indexes may be overstated as a consequence of measurement error. However, this has been true for many decades and does not lessen our need for an explanation of the much faster inflation rate of the past decade compared to previous eras.

A-1 FROM NET NATIONAL PRODUCT TO NET NATIONAL WELFARE

WELFARE CONCEPTS OF CONSUMPTION AND INVESTMENT

The U.S. National Income and Product Accounts (NIPA) are the official data on gross national product (GNP), net national product (NNP), and all the other magnitudes depicted in Figure 2-6 and described in the main part of Chapter 2. The NIPA are widely admired for their detail, consistency, and timeliness compared to the national accounts of other nations. Nevertheless, the accounts have been subject to criticism for many years as inadequate measures of economic welfare.

For instance, real NNP as currently measured is the same in two different years, if the net quantity of currently produced goods and services sold on the market is identical, even when pollution has increased between the two years and as a result true welfare has decreased. Similarly, an increasing crime rate from the first year to the second may be accompanied by higher market purchases of guard dogs, burglar screens, and more comprehensive insurance policies as well as higher government expenditures for larger and better equipped police forces — all of which raise NNP even if true welfare has remained the same or declined. In fact, some critics have claimed that NNP is so irrelevant a measure of welfare that economic growth (growth in NNP) actually does more harm than good.

Recall that total final product (GNP) includes all currently produced goods and services that are sold on the market but not resold. Net national product (NNP) differs from GNP only in its exclusion of currently produced investment goods that replace obsolete and worn-out capital goods. To achieve a better approximation to the annual increase in the nation's well-being or welfare, it has been suggested that we switch from the current NNP concept to "net national welfare" (NNW). The concept NNW is defined as consumption and net investment, but differs from NNP because consumption and net investment are treated differently.

The consumption part of NNW measures the enjoyment of services by households. Some household expenditures that do not provide enjoyment are included in NNP, but excluded from NNW. For instance, commuting is a necessary evil that helps to produce household income, but is not enjoyed itself. Purchases of durables (houses, autos, TV sets), now included in NIPA consumption, are instead counted as gross investment in the NNW approach. TV sets only contribute to consumption or enjoyment as they are used. Finally, NNW consumption includes several important intangible items that are not sold on the market and are not in NNP, but that add to welfare (leisure time) or reduce welfare (congestion and pollution).

The net investment part of NNW includes all net additions to the stock of assets that yield goods and services. This includes not only business structures, equipment, residential housing (which are already in NNP), but also several extra items: additions to the stock of consumer-owned assets (autos, TV sets, education, health) and government-owned assets (schools, national parks). Net investment equals gross purchases of assets minus capital consumption, the portion of the existing capital stock that is used up or consumed due to obsolescence or physical wear and tear.

STEP-BY-STEP FROM NNP TO NNW

William D. Nordhaus and James Tobin, economists at Yale University, have attempted to calculate a rough measure of net national welfare,

NNW.[1] Table A-1 sets out the main components of NNP and NNW side-by-side for the year 1965, measured in the constant prices of 1958.[2] Look first at columns (3) and (4) of the table, which list the major components of the official NIPA concept of GNP (consumption, investment, and government spending), adding up to $617.2 billion in 1958 prices. The deduction of capital consumption allowances yields a total value of NNP of $563.1 billion, at the very bottom of column (4).[3]

Step 1: Identical Items. More than half the dollar value of NNP is treated identically in the welfare measure, NNW. On line 1 the pure consumption portion of NNP, for example food and haircuts, is listed as $243.2 billion as a component of NIPA final product in column (3) and as part of NNW consumption in column (6). Gross private domestic investment, for example, factories and residential housing, is listed as $99.2 billion on line 11 both as a component of NIPA final product and as part of NNW investment. The same goes for net foreign investment on line 12 and for capital consumption allowances on line 20. In addition, both NIPA final product and NNW include an imputed estimate of the services that homeowners receive from the houses they own (line 2). This imputation is calculated by government statisticians, since it does not represent something bought or sold in the market. An imputation is a transaction that does not actually take place on the market, but nevertheless represents a service that increases or decreases consumer well-being.

Step 2: Intermediates and Regrettables. The conventional NIPA measure of final product excludes intermediate goods, items that are ingredients in final goods purchased by households, business firms, and the government (recall the discussion of Figure 2-2). Our NNW measure excludes some additional items, which, although purchased by consumers or government and not resold, nevertheless are mere ingredients in producing the services that households enjoy and are not the objects of enjoyment themselves.

One easy example consists of consumer purchases made only because they are tools necessary to earn an income, including uniforms and the costs of commuting. They are listed on line 4 of Table A-1 as a component of NIPA final product and again to the right as an intermediate good excluded from NNW. Other consumer expenditures that are not separated out in the table, but which might be excluded from NNW include the costs of anticrime devices and insurance. These purchases are not made because they are enjoyed, but only because they are viewed as necessary to protect

---

[1] William D. Nordhaus and James Tobin, *Is Growth Obsolete?* (Washington, D.C.: National Bureau of Economic Research, General Series 96, 1972). Nordhaus-Tobin call their concept Measure of Economic Welfare, or MEW. Our NNW total in Table A-1 is identical to their sustainable MEW, except that we do not concur in their deduction from net investment of a large growth requirement to be set aside to guarantee continued steady future growth.

[2] A good term paper project for an interested student would be to construct an estimate of NNW for a recent year, using Appendix A in Nordhaus-Tobin *op. cit.* as a guide to sources.

[3] Compare these totals with Figure 2-6. Notice the tremendous growth in all the magnitudes between 1965 and 1979, due both to real economic growth and to inflation.

TABLE A-1

Relation of NIPA Net Income Product (NNP) to a Measure of Net National Welfare (NNW)

(1965 Totals in 1958 Prices, $ billions)

	Sources of data (1) Market purchases	(2) Imputations	National income and product (NIPA) (3) Components	(4) Totals	(5) Extra intermediates and regrettables excluded from NNW	Components of welfare (NNW) (6) Consumption	(7) Investment
1.	Pure consumption		243.2			243.2	
2.	Consumer durables		60.9				60.9
3.	Education and health		30.1				30.1
4.	Commuting and personal business		30.9		30.9		
5.		Dwelling services	32.0			32.0	
6.		Other capital services				62.3	
7.		Leisure time				626.9	
8.		Nonmarket work				295.4	
9.		Urban congestion				−34.6	
10.				Total consumption = 397.1			
11.	Gross domestic investment		99.2				99.2
12.	Net foreign investment		6.2				6.2
13.				Total investment = 105.4			
14.	Government consumption		1.2			1.2	
15.	Government gross investment		50.3				50.3
16.	Government regrettables and intermediates		63.2		63.2		
17.		Government capital services				16.6	
18.				Total government = 114.7			
19.				Gross nat. prod. = 617.2			
20.		NIPA capital consumption		−54.7			−54.7
21.		Extra capital consumption					−92.7
22.				Net nat. prod. = 563.1		1243.0	99.3
23.							
24.						Net national welfare = 1342.3	

Source: Author's rearrangement of William D. Nordhaus and James Tobin, *Is Growth Obsolete?* (Washington, D.C.: National Bureau of Economic Research, General Series 96, 1972). Tables A.1, A.4, A.5, A.16, and A.17.

the consumer assets (houses, cars, boats, TV sets) that do yield services or enjoyment.[4]

Somewhat more controversial is the exclusion from NNW of the majority of government purchases. Just as consumer expenditures on locks and other anticrime devices can be viewed as necessary evils that do not add to welfare, so government expenditures on police and fire protection can be viewed as intermediate goods useful only as a means of protecting consumer assets.[5] And if police are a necessary evil, so are defense expenditures. The increased level of international tension in the postwar world has required a much higher level of military spending than in 1890 or 1925, even though our level of national security (a component of welfare) is no higher than before. Just as an increase in the crime rate requires greater expenditures on locks and police to maintain the same level of welfare as before, in the same way a deterioration in the international political atmosphere requires higher military expenditures than before just to keep welfare constant. The item labeled Government regrettables and intermediates on line 16 of Table A-1 isolates the $63.2 billion counted as part of final product in the NIPA accounts, but is shown again to the right as excluded from NNW. Only a small portion of government expenditures are included in the consumption part of NNW on line 14, basically government provision for cheap postage stamps (through financing of the postal service deficit) and for cheap recreation (through below-cost or no-cost charges for national, state, and city parks).

Step 3: The Treatment of Capital. New net national welfare includes the consumption of enjoyable services and net additions to capital. Why? Compare two nations, say Britain and West Germany, which had roughly the same level of real consumption per person in 1970. Since West Germany added about twice as much to capital as Britain in that year, that is, its net investment was twice as high, West Germany should be regarded as being better off, because higher additions to capital would allow it to enjoy a higher level of consumption in the future. Nations that shift resources from the provision of present consumption to net investment, which provides future consumption, should not be regarded as making themselves worse off. For this reason both consumption and net investment are included in both NNP and NNW.

---

[4] In this case, and in several others that follow, the Nordhaus-Tobin estimates summarized in Table A-1 represent only a partial and incomplete attempt to calculate NNW. A more comprehensive approach is the Total Income System of Accounts (TISA) currently being developed by Robert Eisner and his students at Northwestern. Preliminary estimates of TISA are available but were judged too complex for textbook presentation. Another source is Nancy Ruggles and Richard Ruggles, *The Design of Economic Accounts* (Washington, D.C.: National Bureau of Economic Research, 1970).

[5] Here is an example of government purchases that are substitutes for consumer purchases. If the government spends more on police and fire protection, the consumer may spend less on locks and fire insurance. If so, our income determination multipliers developed in Chapters 3 and 4 are reduced.

The main difference in the welfare approach is the much broader class of goods treated as investment. Investment in business structures and equipment, residential construction, and net foreign investment (lines 11 and 12) all are included as investment in both NNP and NNW, with capital consumption subtracted in the same way in both approaches (line 20). In addition, consumer purchases of autos, TV sets, and other durable goods are treated as investment in NNW (line 2). Once purchased and in operation, consumer durables provide a flow of services (the annual enjoyment provided by an automobile or TV set), which is included as part of NNW consumption on line 6.

Many consumer expenditures on education and health (line 3) should also be treated as investments. Teenagers go to college and some adults go to night school with the expectation that their expenditures on books, tuition, and lab fees will provide them with additional knowledge and will allow them to earn higher incomes in the future. These expenditures add to the nation's stock of human capital and are just as valid a component of national wealth as our stock of factories and machines. Health expenditures either cure present illnesses or prevent future illnesses and can be treated as raising the level of health capital, thus raising the future level of production and consumption (although some health expenditures admittedly have no effect on either current or future health).

The government makes many expenditures that add to the nation's wealth and allow more production and consumption to be enjoyed in the future. Examples are federal support of school, hospital, highway, and mass transit construction, as well as expenditures for the development of nuclear power for electricity generation and for agricultural research. This portion of government expenditures, presently counted as part of GNP but not as an addition to wealth, is listed as Government gross investment on line 15.

We cannot count all expenditures on investment goods as additions to wealth. If $500,000 worth of machinery is purchased, but half the new machinery simply replaces $250,000 of old machinery that had become obsolete or worn out, the net addition to the nation's capital stock or net investment is $250,000.[6] In the case of machinery, the total expenditure of $500,000 is entered as part of Gross domestic investment on line 11 of the table and the consumption of capital as old machines become obsolete and wear out is entered as a minus item on line 20. The welfare approach simply adds in an extra entry on line 21 for depreciation on those goods that are considered investment in the NNW accounts—consumer durables, consumer expenditures on education and health, and government gross investment.

The Nordhaus-Tobin approach to the measurement of NNW in Table

---

[6] This sentence is correct if the values are measured in constant prices and if the measurement of prices adequately takes account of all differences in quality between new and old machines. More on the problems of price measurement follows.

A-1 does not exhaust the possibilities for treatment of items as investment and capital. Additional items that might be included are child-rearing expenses of parents, since better education of children at home raises their achievement at school and ultimately their income-earning potential. Another possible category is consumer and business expenditures for moving employees from city to city. These moves in many cases are part of the process by which individuals find jobs better suited to their own capabilities and the economywide matching of jobs and workers is improved (see Chapter 9). Since this process increases future incomes, it should in principle be treated as investment.[7] Finally, business expenditures on research and development create new products that consumers value (jet airlines) or that increase the potential (or natural) level of attainable production (computer-controlled machine tools) and should be considered as investment adding to the nation's stock of research and development capital.

Step 4: Addition and Subtraction of Intangibles. One of the most important components of consumer enjoyment is never bought or sold on the marketplace. Yet without it consumers would have little incentive to work hard and accumulate possessions. Puzzled? This mysterious component is leisure time, the portion of the week spent in activities other than work, sleep, and housework. What fun would boats and fishing poles provide if there were no time to enjoy them? The production of leisure services can be viewed as a production activity requiring the input of two basic ingredients, a durable good (boat, fishing pole) and household leisure time.

How much is this time worth? Ask yourself why most people only have one job requiring roughly 40 hours per week of work. Why don't they take an extra job requiring another 20 or 30 hours of work? Leaving aside the possibility that they can't find such an extra moonlighting job because the economy is weak, the basic reason for the refusal to take an extra job is the value of the leisure time that would be sacrificed. Since we observe that most people refuse second jobs, we deduce that their leisure time must be worth at least the wage rate on such jobs. Hence the best simple estimate of the value of each hour of leisure time is the wage rate. The imputation of the 1965 value of leisure time in Table A-1, line 7, is an immense $626.9 billion, larger than the entire NIPA concept of GNP of that year!

But we are not finished. In most households a great deal of time is spent on housework. Many women are on the borderline between staying at home and making the decision to accept a job, and more and more each year enter the labor force to work. The borderline nature of the decision suggests that the work women do in the home is valuable and should be considered part of NNW—after all, if housework and child rearing did not produce something of value, all women would long since have entered the labor

---

[7] In the NIPA accounts, consumer expenditures on moving are counted as pure consumption (line 1), while business reimbursements of moving expenses are treated as an intermediate good and are excluded from NNP.

force. Line 8 in Table A-1 registers the value of housework, with each hour (as in the case of leisure) valued at the wage rate.[8]

Finally, one last correction must be made that reduces welfare. On average, inhabitants of cities and metropolitan areas earn more than those who live in the country. When people migrate from the farm to the city, as they have done throughout our history, conventionally measured GNP is raised by the increase in market wages received in the city. But at least part of the higher urban wage is a payment made to offset unpleasant aspects of city life—congestion, pollution, noise, litter, and lack of access to nature. Line 9 in Table A-1 subtracts an estimate of this cost of urban living based on a statistical study by Nordhaus and Tobin of wage rates in urban and rural areas.

Step 5: NNW and Its Historical Growth. The grand total of the components of NNW for 1965 consists of $1243.0 billion of consumption and $99.3 billion of net investment or a total NNW of $1342.3 billion.[9] This is much more than double the total official estimate of NNP for the same year. As the table shows, most of the difference is due to the huge imputations for the value of leisure and housework time. This source of difference explains why between 1929 and 1965 per-person NNW grew so much more slowly (0.98 percent per year, compounded) than did per-person NNP (1.75 percent per year).

The largest difference between the two concepts, leisure time, is not assumed to grow at all in value per person. Yet an argument could be made that leisure time is now more valuable, because recreational equipment is better and more widely owned and, in particular, air and auto travel have opened access to vacation and weekend locations that have made leisure more pleasant. Thus the growth rate of NNW is probably an underestimate.

The Nordhaus-Tobin method of calculating the leisure and housework component of NNW uses the current wage rate to value each hour of leisure time and housework. Thus, during the Great Depression when millions were out of work, their increased hours of leisure are treated as just as valuable to them as the income that they received from work! This is unreasonable and fails to explain why everyone was so unhappy during the Great Depression. An improved concept of NNW would value hours of

---

[8] This overstates the value of housework, since a housewife compares the value of staying at home not with the before-tax wage rate (assumed in Table A-1), but rather with the wage rate after subtraction of all taxes and commuting expenses. I estimate the value of home time for married women to be only 40 percent of the average hourly wage in my "Welfare Cost of Higher Unemployment," *Brookings Papers on Economic Activity,* vol. 4, no. 1 (1973).

[9] The close reader of Nordhaus-Tobin will notice that their deduction for the investment growth requirement has been omitted. This is the portion of investment needed to sustain the inherited rate of output growth. Taking aside the question of population growth, their procedure is peculiar. Why should Japan be penalized by a growth requirement deduction for its additions to capital that allow it to grow faster and enjoy a higher level of future consumption than other countries that invest less?

leisure caused by involuntary unemployment at an hourly rate much below the current wage rate.

CONCLUSION ON THE WELFARE MEASURE

When can we look forward to official NIPA estimates that come closer to a measure of welfare? A long-planned major revision of the NIPA concepts was published in early 1976, but all changes were minor. Not one of the changes in treatment outlined in Table A-1 was adopted. Why? Because traditionally the Bureau of Economic Analysis in the U.S. Department of Commerce, which is the branch of the federal government responsible for compilation of the NIPA estimates, has emphasized precision at the expense of conceptual merit. Since many of the major changes in the NNW measure of Table A-1 involve imputations for services that are not bought and sold on the market, they must of necessity involve reliance on economic theory and some guesswork. Accountants who specialize in the careful transcription of figures on market transactions will naturally balk at the prospect of working with a welfare concept (NNW) that actually includes a larger value of imputations than of market transactions.

Another argument can be made in favor of the retention of the present concept of NNP based on market transactions: NNP is a better indication than NNW of the total amount of job-creating economic activity. For instance, when the nation fights a war, NNP goes up and extra jobs are created, but NNW does not increase because military expenditures are treated as regrettable intermediate goods excluded from NNW. Even if economists can eventually convince the federal government to begin compiling an official set of data on NNW, most would nevertheless recommend that publication of NNP statistics be continued as well.

A-2 PROBLEMS IN THE MEASUREMENT OF PRICE DEFLATORS

As outlined in the last section of Chapter 2 and in the numerical example of Table 2-3, the price deflator for GNP is simply a weighted average of many different individual price indexes. If the individual component price indexes increase on average between two successive years, then the GNP deflator will increase and indicate that inflation has occurred between the first year and the second. While the procedure for weighting causes minor difficulties, most of the serious problems involved in price measurement involve the accuracy of the individual price indexes themselves.[10] The basic

---

[10] A recent evaluation of weighting problems is contained in Steven D. Braithwait, "The Substitution Bias of the Laspeyres Price Index: An Analysis Using Estimated Cost-of-Living Indexes," *American Economic Review,* vol. 70 (March 1980), pp. 64–77.

flaw is that the goods and services whose prices are being compared in two different years should be identical in quality. Yet it is difficult and sometimes impossible to hold quality constant when measuring price change.

HOLDING QUALITY CONSTANT

The basic principle to be observed is that price comparisons between two different years are to be made for goods that are identical in quality. When a newer, higher quality model is introduced at a higher price, as when refrigerators were first equipped with automatic defrosting, we do not want to treat the entire price increase as contributing to inflation, because the higher quality of goods and services (the automatic defroster) is something real that raises real GNP. In many cases it is easy to hold quality constant when measuring the prices of individual products because exactly the same models with exactly the same specifications are sold in two successive years. But in other cases the attempt to hold quality constant raises significant and sometimes even insurmountable problems.

Quality Change in Existing Products. For some products, for instance washing machines, refrigerators, and automobiles, there are years in which all models change in quality. How then can prices be compared? Economists have developed techniques for measuring the value of changes in quality. Unfortunately, these new techniques for quality adjustment have been used only recently and sporadically by the Bureau of Labor Statistics, the branch of the federal government responsible for the compilation of most of the individual price indexes on which the GNP deflator is based.[11] For instance, a great effort appears to be made to correct automobile prices for the effect of quality change, but much less is done for office machinery and machine tools. Thus the official data that show that the prices of automobiles have increased less over the postwar era than the prices of machines may not reflect actual facts, but rather inconsistent techniques of measurement. Further, methods of measurement are steadily improving, which suggests that the price data for earlier historical periods are less accurate than those for recent years. If so, and if quality on balance has been improving rather than deteriorating, then the acceleration of inflation in the period since 1965 is understated in the official data (that is, the bias in the official inflation rate measure may overstate inflation more before 1965 than since).

When New Products Are Introduced. Some new products perform the same function as an older product, in which case a price comparison can be made. For instance, the electronic calculators introduced in 1970 for about $200 can multiply and divide, just as did the old rotary electric cal-

---

[11] A wide variety of techniques for the measurement of quality change are reviewed and utilized in my book, *The Measurement of Durable Goods Prices* (Washington, D.C.: National Bureau of Economic Research, forthcoming). An earlier collection of essays is Zvi Griliches (ed.), *Price Indexes and Quality Change* (Cambridge, Mass.: Harvard University Press, 1971).

culators sold in 1970 for $1000. This appears to represent a price decline of 80 percent. Actually the true price decline was much more, because the new electronic calculators perform given operations much faster than the older models and also perform operations that formerly had to be done by hand (for instance, placement of the decimal). Incredibly, despite the occurrence in this case of a price decline of 90 percent or more, the official government price data failed to register any price decline at all![12]

Other cases where a large price decrease occurred, but was ignored by government statisticians, include the replacement of piston airliners by jets and the development of more durable synthetic fibers. Unfortunately, some kinds of new products are so different that a measurement of quality change is impossible. How can television be compared to radio? Color television to black and white TV? How can the freedom allowed by the automobile be compared to the limitations of train travel?

TRANSACTION VERSUS LIST PRICES

Most price indexes of consumer products are compiled from the reports of government field agents who go out and record the actual selling prices of individual items. But the prices of investment goods, both structures and equipment, may not fully reflect actual selling prices. In the case of structures, the government indexes are not (with a few exceptions) based on actual price quotations at all, because it is all but impossible to find structures that are identical in quality. Instead, the prices of structures are taken to be averages of wage rates and the prices of construction materials, a procedure that ignores improvements in labor productivity and fluctuations in the profits of construction contractors. Thus government price indexes for structures do not reflect the price reductions that occur in periods of weak demand when contractors are willing to slash profit margins to stay in business.

The price indexes for machines are collected from mail reports sent in by manufacturers. Unfortunately, firms report the list prices of equipment; rarely do they report the discounts that they allow in recessions and premiums that they sometimes charge in prosperous periods. (Often the discounts and premiums take the form of the changing availability of free delivery and other services.) This flaw in the government's price collecting procedures implies that the overall GNP deflator understates the true decline in transaction prices during recessions and exaggerates the true decline in real output. Nevertheless, this deficiency is relatively minor and it does not lessen the importance of gaining an adequate understanding of the causes of inflation and recession.

---

[12] In the official jargon, the new price index for electronic calculators was "linked" to the old one for rotary electric calculators. In the month of the linkage no price change was assumed to occur, although since then the official index has mirrored the rapid decline in the prices of electronic calculators.

Appendix B
Time Series Data
for U.S. Economy,
1900-1980

Introductory Note: All data in this appendix are current through the fourth quarter of 1980. In this printing all data back to 1929 incorporate the revisions of the National Income and Product Accounts announced in the *Survey of Current Business*, December 1980, pp. 13-33. The estimates of the real natural employment surplus have also been revised to correspond to estimates in F. deLeeuw *et al.*, "The High-Employment Budget: New Estimates, 1955-80," *Survey of Current Business*, November 1980, pp. 13-43.

TABLE B-1

Annual Data (Revised), 1900–1980

	Nominal GNP (Y)	GNP deflator (P)	Real GNP (1972$) (Q)	Natural real GNP (1972$) ($Q^N$)	Unemployment rate (U)	Natural unemployment rate (U^N)	Money supply (Old M1)	Money supply (New M1B)	Money supply (Old M2)	Money supply (New M2)
1900	19.5	15.78	123.3	129.3	5.0	3.4	—	—	6.6	—
1901	21.5	15.60	137.6	134.7	4.0	3.4	—	—	7.5	—
1902	22.5	16.18	138.9	139.4	3.7	3.4	—	—	8.2	—
1903	23.8	16.30	145.8	144.4	3.9	3.4	—	—	8.7	—
1904	23.8	16.51	144.0	149.4	5.4	3.4	—	—	9.2	—
1905	26.2	16.92	154.7	154.7	4.3	3.5	—	—	10.2	—
1906	29.9	17.32	172.6	160.1	1.7	3.5	—	—	11.1	—
1907	31.7	18.07	175.4	165.8	2.8	3.5	—	—	11.6	—
1908	28.9	17.95	160.9	171.6	8.0	3.5	—	—	11.4	—
1909	33.5	18.55	180.5	177.7	5.1	3.5	—	—	12.7	—
1910	35.4	19.07	185.6	183.9	5.9	3.5	—	—	13.3	—
1911	35.9	18.86	190.4	190.4	6.7	3.5	—	—	14.1	—
1912	39.5	19.63	201.2	197.1	4.6	3.5	—	—	15.1	—
1913	39.7	19.55	203.1	201.4	4.3	3.5	—	—	15.7	—
1914	38.7	19.94	194.1	205.8	7.9	3.5	—	—	16.4	—
1915	40.1	20.85	192.4	210.3	8.5	3.5	12.5	—	17.6	—
1916	48.4	23.34	207.6	214.9	5.1	3.5	14.7	—	20.9	—
1917	60.6	28.99	208.9	216.6	4.6	3.5	17.1	—	24.4	—
1918	76.6	32.66	234.6	224.4	1.4	3.6	19.0	—	26.7	—
1919	84.2	37.23	226.3	229.2	1.4	3.6	21.8	—	31.0	—
1920	91.8	42.41	216.4	234.3	5.2	3.6	23.7	—	34.8	—
1921	69.8	35.34	197.5	239.4	11.7	3.6	21.5	—	32.8	—
1922	74.3	32.49	228.8	244.6	6.7	3.6	21.7	—	33.7	—
1923	85.3	33.28	256.4	250.0	2.4	3.6	22.9	—	36.6	—
1924	84.9	33.21	255.8	259.1	5.0	3.6	23.7	—	38.6	—
1925	93.4	33.68	277.2	268.7	3.2	3.6	25.7	—	42.0	—
1926	97.3	33.13	293.7	278.5	1.8	3.7	26.2	—	43.7	—
1927	95.2	32.45	293.3	288.7	3.3	3.7	26.1	—	44.7	—
1928	97.3	32.97	295.0	299.3	4.2	3.7	26.4	—	46.4	—
1929	103.4	32.87	314.6	310.3	3.2	3.7	26.6	—	46.6	—

TABLE B-1

Annual Data (Revised), 1900–1980 (continued)

	Nominal GNP (Y)	GNP deflator (P)	Real GNP (1972$) (Q)	Natural real GNP (1972$) (Q^N)	Unemployment rate (U)	Natural unemployment rate (U^N)	Money supply (Old M1)	Money supply (New M1B)	Money supply (Old M2)	Money supply (New M2)
1930	90.7	31.8	285.6	318.8	8.9	3.7	25.8	—	45.7	—
1931	76.1	28.9	263.5	327.6	16.3	3.7	24.1	—	42.7	—
1932	58.3	25.7	227.1	336.6	24.1	3.8	21.1	—	36.0	—
1933	55.8	25.1	222.1	345.9	25.2	3.8	19.9	—	32.2	—
1934	65.3	27.3	239.1	355.4	22.0	3.8	21.9	—	34.4	—
1935	72.5	27.8	260.5	365.2	20.3	3.8	25.9	—	39.1	—
1936	82.7	30.0	295.5	375.2	17.0	3.8	29.5	—	43.5	—
1937	90.9	29.3	310.2	385.5	14.3	3.9	30.9	—	45.7	—
1938	85.0	28.7	296.7	396.1	19.1	3.9	30.5	—	45.5	—
1939	90.9	28.4	319.8	407.0	17.2	3.9	34.2	—	49.3	—
1940	100.0	29.1	344.1	418.2	14.6	3.9	39.7	—	55.2	—
1941	125.0	31.2	400.4	429.7	9.9	3.9	46.5	—	62.5	—
1942	158.5	34.4	461.7	441.5	4.7	3.9	55.4	—	71.2	—
1943	192.1	36.1	531.6	453.6	1.9	4.0	72.2	—	89.9	—
1944	210.6	37.0	569.1	466.1	1.2	4.0	85.3	—	106.8	—
1945	212.6	37.9	560.4	479.0	1.9	4.0	99.2	—	126.6	—
1946	209.8	44.0	476.9	492.1	3.9	4.0	106.5	—	138.7	—
1947	233.0	49.5	470.4	506.1	3.9	4.0	111.8	—	146.0	—
1948	259.5	53.0	489.6	519.5	3.8	4.1	112.3	—	148.1	—
1949	258.3	52.5	492.1	533.7	6.1	4.1	111.2	—	147.5	—
1950	286.5	53.6	534.8	548.8	5.2	4.1	114.1	—	150.8	—
1951	330.7	57.1	579.3	566.5	3.3	4.1	119.2	—	156.5	—
1952	348.0	57.9	600.8	584.9	3.0	4.2	125.2	—	164.9	—
1953	366.8	58.8	623.5	603.8	2.9	4.2	128.3	—	171.2	—
1954	366.8	59.6	616.0	623.5	5.6	4.2	130.3	—	177.2	—

1955	400.1	60.9	657.5	643.7	4.4	4.3	134.5	—	183.7	—
1956	421.7	62.8	671.5	664.9	4.1	4.3	136.0	—	186.9	—
1957	444.0	65.0	683.8	687.5	4.3	4.3	136.8	—	191.8	—
1958	449.6	66.0	681.0	712.7	6.8	4.3	138.4	—	201.2	—
1959	487.9	67.6	721.7	732.1	5.5	4.3	143.6	141.0	210.5	292.2
1960	506.5	68.7	737.2	757.8	5.5	4.4	143.5	141.0	212.6	303.1
1961	524.6	69.3	756.6	786.9	6.7	4.4	146.5	143.9	223.7	323.4
1962	565.0	70.6	800.3	815.2	5.6	4.4	149.7	147.4	236.7	348.6
1963	596.7	71.7	832.5	842.0	5.6	4.5	154.1	151.9	252.0	377.9
1964	637.7	72.8	876.4	872.9	5.2	4.6	160.2	157.8	267.8	407.6
1965	691.0	74.4	929.3	901.8	4.5	4.7	167.1	164.5	289.2	440.6
1966	756.0	76.8	984.8	941.9	3.8	4.8	174.7	172.0	311.7	469.6
1967	799.6	79.1	1011.4	982.5	3.8	4.9	181.5	178.8	335.5	502.3
1968	873.4	82.5	1058.1	1016.6	3.6	4.9	194.3	191.3	365.6	544.5
1969	944.0	86.8	1087.7	1051.8	3.5	5.0	206.5	202.7	389.8	578.3
1970	992.7	91.4	1085.6	1090.3	5.0	5.1	214.5	210.3	406.0	600.8
1971	1077.7	96.0	1122.4	1133.9	6.0	5.2	228.9	224.4	453.1	673.6
1972	1185.9	100.0	1185.9	1175.3	5.6	5.3	245.0	240.4	501.0	757.9
1973	1326.4	105.7	1255.0	1220.3	4.9	5.4	263.3	257.9	549.1	833.4
1974	1434.2	114.9	1248.0	1261.8	5.6	5.4	277.7	270.5	595.4	885.2
1975	1549.2	125.5	1233.9	1305.5	8.5	5.4	289.5	282.9	641.0	969.4
1976	1718.0	132.1	1300.4	1353.4	7.7	5.5	304.2	298.6	703.8	1097.0
1977	1918.0	139.8	1371.7	1401.5	7.0	5.5	324.5	321.0	777.6	1239.0
1978	2156.1	150.0	1436.9	1447.1	6.0	5.5	352.3	347.3	847.0	1349.3
1979	2413.9	162.8	1483.0	1487.8	5.8	5.6	371.0	374.5	914.4	1468.1
1980	2626.5	177.4	1480.9	1525.0	7.2	5.6	—	397.8	—	1600.2

TABLE B-2

Quarterly Data (Revised), 1947–1980

	Nominal GNP (Y)	GNP deflator (P)	Real GNP (1972$) (Q)	Natural real GNP (1972$) (Q^N)	Unemployment rate (U)	Natural unemployment rate (U^N)	Money supply (Old M1)	Money supply (New M1B)	Money supply (Old M2)	Money supply (New M2)	Actual federal surplus	Natural employment surplus
1947.Q1	225.1	48.3	466.0	502.5	3.9	4.0	109.8	—	143.3	—	—	—
1947.Q2	229.3	48.8	469.5	503.9	3.9	4.0	111.6	—	145.4	—	—	—
1947.Q3	233.6	49.7	470.2	507.3	3.9	4.0	112.6	—	147.0	—	—	—
1947.Q4	244.0	51.3	475.7	510.8	3.9	4.0	113.1	—	148.3	—	—	—
1948.Q1	250.0	52.1	479.4	514.2	3.7	4.1	113.1	—	148.7	—	—	—
1948.Q2	257.5	52.7	488.3	517.7	3.7	4.1	112.1	—	147.9	—	—	—
1948.Q3	264.5	53.7	492.9	521.2	3.8	4.1	112.2	—	148.1	—	—	—
1948.Q4	265.9	53.4	497.9	524.8	3.8	4.1	111.8	—	147.8	—	—	—
1949.Q1	260.5	52.9	492.6	528.3	4.7	4.1	111.2	—	147.3	—	—	—
1949.Q2	257.0	52.4	490.3	531.9	5.9	4.1	111.4	—	147.7	—	—	—
1949.Q3	258.9	52.3	494.8	535.5	6.7	4.1	111.0	—	147.4	—	—	—
1949.Q4	256.8	52.3	490.8	539.2	7.0	4.1	111.0	—	147.4	—	—	—
1950.Q1	267.6	52.2	512.6	542.8	6.4	4.1	112.0	—	148.6	—	-4.7	—
1950.Q2	277.1	52.7	526.4	546.2	5.6	4.1	113.7	—	150.5	—	7.8	—
1950.Q3	294.8	54.2	543.8	550.9	4.6	4.1	114.9	—	151.6	—	16.6	—
1950.Q4	306.3	55.1	556.3	555.3	4.2	4.1	115.9	—	152.5	—	17.3	—
1951.Q1	320.4	56.8	564.4	559.7	3.5	4.1	117.1	—	153.8	—	18.3	—
1951.Q2	328.3	57.0	575.9	564.2	3.1	4.1	118.2	—	155.0	—	8.4	—
1951.Q3	335.0	57.0	587.9	568.8	3.2	4.1	119.7	—	157.1	—	1.0	—
1951.Q4	339.2	57.6	589.1	573.3	3.4	4.1	121.9	—	159.9	—	-1.7	—
1952.Q1	341.9	57.6	593.7	577.9	3.1	4.2	123.5	—	162.2	—	.2	—
1952.Q2	342.1	57.6	594.3	582.5	3.0	4.2	124.5	—	163.8	—	-3.7	—
1952.Q3	347.8	57.9	600.5	587.2	3.2	4.2	125.8	—	165.8	—	-7.5	—
1952.Q4	360.0	58.6	614.6	591.9	2.8	4.2	127.1	—	167.9	—	-3.7	—
1953.Q1	366.1	58.8	623.2	596.6	2.7	4.2	127.6	—	169.2	—	-4.5	—
1953.Q2	369.4	58.8	628.3	601.4	2.6	4.2	128.4	—	170.8	—	-6.2	—
1953.Q3	368.4	59.0	624.4	606.2	2.7	4.2	128.6	—	171.8	—	-5.8	—
1953.Q4	363.1	58.7	618.2	611.1	3.7	4.2	128.7	—	172.9	—	-11.8	—
1954.Q1	362.5	59.4	610.5	616.0	5.3	4.2	129.1	—	174.3	—	-10.6	—
1954.Q2	362.3	59.6	608.1	621.0	5.8	4.2	129.4	—	175.9	—	-6.7	—
1954.Q3	366.7	59.5	616.9	625.9	6.0	4.2	130.6	—	178.3	—	-5.1	—
1954.Q4	375.6	59.8	628.4	630.9	5.3	4.2	132.0	—	180.2	—	-1.9	—

Quarter												
1955.Q1	1.6	1.8	—	182.2	—	133.5	4.3	4.7	636.0	644.1	60.3	388.2
1955.Q2	5.0	4.9	—	183.4	—	134.3	4.3	4.4	641.1	653.2	60.7	396.2
1955.Q3	2.6	4.8	—	184.3	—	134.9	4.3	4.1	646.2	663.2	61.0	404.8
1955.Q4	5.5	6.5	—	185.0	—	135.1	4.3	4.2	651.4	669.5	61.4	411.0
1956.Q1	10.9	6.6	—	185.5	—	135.6	4.3	4.0	656.6	666.8	61.9	412.8
1956.Q2	10.6	5.8	—	186.4	—	135.9	4.3	4.2	661.9	670.2	62.4	418.4
1956.Q3	7.9	5.2	—	187.2	—	136.0	4.3	4.1	667.7	670.7	63.1	423.5
1956.Q4	9.2	6.3	—	188.4	—	136.6	4.3	4.1	673.5	678.4	63.7	432.1
1957.Q1	6.4	4.6	—	190.0	—	136.9	4.3	3.9	679.6	683.5	64.4	440.2
1957.Q2	4.9	2.8	—	191.4	—	136.9	4.3	4.1	684.4	684.1	64.7	442.3
1957.Q3	5.9	2.8	—	192.7	—	137.0	4.3	4.2	691.6	688.5	65.3	449.4
1957.Q4	3.5	-1.3	—	193.2	—	136.2	4.3	4.9	694.4	679.1	65.4	444.0
1958.Q1	.5	-7.5	—	195.2	—	136.1	4.3	6.3	698.6	665.5	65.6	436.8
1958.Q2	-2.5	-11.9	—	200.0	—	137.6	4.3	7.4	708.2	669.9	65.8	440.7
1958.Q3	-4.6	-12.1	—	203.5	—	139.0	4.3	7.3	719.0	685.9	66.2	453.9
1958.Q4	-6.2	-10.0	—	205.9	—	140.7	4.3	6.4	724.9	702.5	66.5	467.0
1959.Q1	.3	-2.9	286.6	208.8	139.9	142.6	4.3	5.8	723.9	711.5	67.0	477.0
1959.Q2	3.8	1.6	291.0	210.5	141.0	143.8	4.3	5.1	728.8	726.2	67.6	490.6
1959.Q3	1.6	-1.8	294.9	211.6	142.1	144.5	4.3	5.3	731.6	721.2	67.8	489.0
1959.Q4	4.1	-1.5	296.1	211.0	140.9	143.6	4.3	5.6	744.0	727.9	68.0	495.0
1960.Q1	14.3	7.7	297.2	210.1	140.4	143.0	4.4	5.1	748.8	740.7	68.4	506.9
1960.Q2	11.8	4.2	299.9	210.3	140.2	142.8	4.4	5.2	755.3	738.4	68.6	506.3
1960.Q3	10.6	1.4	305.3	213.4	141.6	143.9	4.4	5.5	760.2	737.7	68.9	508.0
1960.Q4	10.4	-1.1	309.8	216.4	141.7	144.2	4.4	6.3	766.7	732.1	69.0	504.8
1961.Q1	8.4	-4.3	314.8	219.2	142.2	144.8	4.4	6.8	776.2	737.7	68.9	508.2
1961.Q2	5.9	-5.1	320.7	222.4	143.4	146.0	4.4	7.0	783.4	750.1	69.2	519.2
1961.Q3	5.8	-3.9	326.2	225.2	144.2	146.9	4.4	6.8	790.2	759.6	69.5	528.2
1961.Q4	4.7	-2.2	331.8	228.0	145.6	148.3	4.4	6.2	797.7	779.0	69.7	542.6
1962.Q1	-1.8	-5.6	338.9	231.8	146.6	149.2	4.4	5.6	806.3	789.2	70.2	554.2
1962.Q2	0	-4.1	345.9	235.8	147.5	149.8	4.4	5.5	814.3	798.4	70.5	562.7
1962.Q3	.4	-3.2	351.3	237.7	147.4	149.5	4.4	5.6	818.5	805.5	70.6	568.9
1962.Q4	0	-4.1	358.4	241.4	148.2	150.4	4.4	5.5	821.6	808.0	71.1	574.3
1963.Q1	3.4	-1.9	366.3	245.9	149.7	151.8	4.5	5.8	829.1	815.0	71.4	582.0
1963.Q2	7.9	1.9	374.2	250.0	151.1	153.3	4.5	5.7	836.2	826.7	71.5	590.7
1963.Q3	5.7	1.2	381.9	253.8	152.6	154.8	4.5	5.5	847.6	839.8	71.7	601.8
1963.Q4	3.4	-.2	389.3	258.2	154.1	156.4	4.5	5.6	855.2	848.6	72.2	612.4
1964.Q1	-1.9	-3.0	395.8	261.1	155.2	157.3	4.6	5.5	864.9	864.2	72.4	625.3
1964.Q2	-8.7	-6.7	402.5	264.6	156.3	158.8	4.6	5.2	872.0	873.7	72.6	634.0
1964.Q3	-4.2	-2.4	411.7	270.0	158.9	161.4	4.6	5.0	876.0	880.9	73.0	642.8
1964.Q4	-2.8	-1.0	420.2	275.4	160.9	163.4	4.6	5.0	878.5	886.8	73.2	648.8

	Nominal GNP (Y)	GNP deflator (P)	Real GNP (1972$) (Q)	Natural real GNP (1972$) (Q^N)	Unemployment rate (U)	Natural unemployment rate (U^N)	Money supply (Old M1)	Money supply (New M1B)	Money supply (Old M2)	Money supply (New M2)	Actual federal surplus	Natural employment surplus
1965.Q1	668.8	73.8	906.7	887.4	4.9	4.7	164.5	162.1	281.0	428.5	4.6	2.2
1965.Q2	681.7	74.1	919.7	895.0	4.7	4.7	165.8	163.1	285.5	435.7	3.9	−.9
1965.Q3	696.4	74.6	934.1	908.0	4.4	4.7	167.7	165.0	291.3	444.1	−3.0	−11.1
1965.Q4	717.2	75.0	956.8	916.7	4.1	4.7	170.5	167.9	299.0	454.0	−3.4	−14.7
1966.Q1	738.5	75.7	975.4	928.8	3.9	4.8	173.2	170.8	305.3	462.5	.6	−11.2
1966.Q2	750.0	76.6	979.3	936.6	3.8	4.8	175.3	172.7	310.8	468.3	1.3	−10.5
1966.Q3	760.6	77.0	987.9	945.5	3.8	4.8	175.0	172.1	313.8	471.3	−3.2	−16.6
1966.Q4	774.9	77.8	996.6	956.9	3.7	4.8	175.2	172.5	316.7	476.2	−5.9	−18.4
1967.Q1	780.7	78.3	997.8	968.6	3.8	4.9	176.9	174.3	323.2	484.0	−12.8	−24.0
1967.Q2	788.6	78.5	1004.2	976.1	3.8	4.9	179.5	176.6	330.1	495.5	−13.2	−24.6
1967.Q3	805.7	79.3	1016.2	989.6	3.8	4.9	183.5	180.7	339.2	509.5	−13.6	−24.3
1967.Q4	823.3	80.1	1027.3	995.6	3.9	4.9	186.2	183.4	349.6	520.3	−13.0	−24.5
1968.Q1	841.2	81.2	1036.6	1002.1	3.7	4.9	188.7	186.0	353.8	529.3	−12.1	−21.7
1968.Q2	867.2	82.1	1055.7	1014.3	3.6	4.9	192.2	189.3	360.7	538.1	−14.9	−26.0
1968.Q3	884.9	82.8	1068.2	1022.7	3.5	4.9	196.2	193.0	368.8	549.0	−3.1	−16.8
1968.Q4	900.3	84.0	1071.8	1027.4	3.4	4.9	200.2	197.0	378.9	561.8	.4	−13.3
1969.Q1	921.2	85.0	1084.2	1039.4	3.4	5.0	203.9	200.6	386.4	571.2	13.4	−.5
1969.Q2	937.4	86.1	1088.8	1047.1	3.4	5.0	206.1	202.4	390.5	576.5	13.4	.9
1969.Q3	955.3	87.5	1092.0	1057.1	3.6	5.0	207.3	203.1	390.6	580.3	7.4	−3.2
1969.Q4	962.0	88.6	1085.6	1063.8	3.6	5.0	208.5	204.5	391.7	585.2	4.9	−2.6
1970.Q1	972.0	89.9	1081.4	1074.2	4.2	5.0	210.4	206.5	393.2	587.3	−1.4	−4.1
1970.Q2	986.3	91.1	1083.0	1085.2	4.7	5.0	213.1	208.9	400.2	593.1	−14.5	−13.1
1970.Q3	1003.6	91.8	1093.3	1094.2	5.2	5.1	215.8	211.2	410.3	603.5	−16.2	−14.4
1970.Q4	1009.0	93.0	1084.7	1107.6	5.9	5.1	218.7	214.4	420.2	619.1	−21.9	−12.9
1971.Q1	1049.3	94.4	1111.5	1121.5	5.9	5.1	222.4	218.4	434.6	640.4	−19.6	−13.3
1971.Q2	1068.9	95.7	1116.9	1133.0	5.9	5.2	228.0	223.6	450.4	666.6	−24.8	−17.9
1971.Q3	1086.6	96.5	1125.7	1138.8	6.0	5.2	231.8	226.9	459.3	684.6	−24.6	−18.2
1971.Q4	1105.8	97.4	1135.4	1142.1	6.0	5.2	233.3	228.6	468.0	702.9	−22.8	−19.2

Quarter												
1972.Q1	1142.4	98.7	1157.2	1157.4	5.8	5.3	237.5	233.5	481.9	725.2	−13.0	−11.5
1972.Q2	1171.7	99.4	1178.5	1171.6	5.6	5.3	242.3	237.7	494.1	744.3	−19.9	−20.7
1972.Q3	1196.1	100.3	1193.1	1179.1	5.6	5.3	247.4	242.3	507.4	768.5	−10.5	−14.9
1972.Q4	1233.5	101.5	1214.8	1193.1	5.3	5.3	252.9	248.1	520.5	793.4	−23.7	−31.2
1973.Q1	1283.5	102.9	1247.1	1205.0	4.9	5.4	257.6	253.3	532.5	813.8	−8.4	−21.6
1973.Q2	1307.6	104.7	1249.0	1213.7	4.9	5.4	261.7	256.4	543.4	827.9	−6.8	−17.4
1973.Q3	1337.7	106.4	1256.8	1224.3	4.8	5.4	265.3	259.3	554.1	840.3	−2.4	−15.6
1973.Q4	1376.7	108.7	1267.0	1238.2	4.8	5.4	268.7	262.4	566.5	851.6	−3.7	−14.0
1974.Q1	1387.7	110.6	1254.7	1241.6	5.0	5.4	272.7	266.8	580.1	868.7	−4.2	−11.8
1974.Q2	1423.8	113.3	1256.3	1257.3	5.2	5.4	276.5	269.2	590.9	880.0	−9.4	−8.2
1974.Q3	1451.6	116.2	1248.6	1269.6	5.6	5.4	279.4	271.3	600.4	889.6	−7.2	−3.8
1974.Q4	1473.8	119.6	1232.4	1278.7	6.6	5.4	282.2	274.7	610.0	902.4	−18.7	−6.5
1975.Q1	1479.8	122.7	1206.3	1285.8	8.2	5.5	282.6	276.7	618.6	920.1	−37.1	−14.2
1975.Q2	1516.7	124.2	1221.0	1297.9	8.9	5.5	287.8	280.8	634.3	954.3	−79.7	−55.8
1975.Q3	1578.5	126.4	1248.4	1314.7	8.5	5.5	292.9	285.9	650.3	989.1	−52.7	−29.8
1975.Q4	1621.8	128.7	1259.7	1323.7	8.3	5.5	294.6	288.2	660.7	1014.0	−51.3	−30.7
1976.Q1	1672.0	129.9	1287.2	1335.0	7.7	5.5	296.7	292.3	677.0	1046.0	−51.0	−28.6
1976.Q2	1698.6	131.1	1295.8	1344.5	7.5	5.5	302.8	296.9	694.8	1080.0	−36.8	−22.7
1976.Q3	1729.0	132.7	1303.3	1362.2	7.7	5.5	306.1	299.8	710.6	1110.0	−38.9	−23.4
1976.Q4	1772.5	134.8	1315.4	1371.9	7.8	5.5	311.1	305.5	732.8	1152.0	−41.8	−27.2
1977.Q1	1839.1	136.6	1345.9	1384.3	7.4	5.5	314.4	312.6	751.0	1192.0	−27.9	−15.9
1977.Q2	1893.9	138.9	1363.4	1394.9	7.2	5.5	321.1	318.0	768.3	1225.0	−30.7	−22.1
1977.Q3	1950.4	140.8	1385.8	1409.0	6.9	5.5	328.5	323.2	788.0	1254.0	−37.1	−33.6
1977.Q4	1988.6	142.9	1391.5	1417.7	6.6	5.5	334.1	330.2	802.9	1285.0	−36.7	−34.1
1978.Q1	2032.4	144.9	1402.3	1429.4	6.2	5.5	340.3	336.7	819.3	1309.0	−33.7	−31.2
1978.Q2	2129.6	148.6	1432.8	1441.2	6.0	5.5	350.4	344.4	836.5	1334.0	−18.4	−18.7
1978.Q3	2190.5	151.4	1446.7	1453.0	6.0	5.5	357.3	350.7	856.9	1361.0	−15.1	−16.2
1978.Q4	2271.9	155.0	1465.8	1465.0	5.8	5.5	361.1	357.2	875.1	1393.0	−11.5	−15.0
1979.Q1	2340.6	158.2	1479.9	1474.1	5.7	5.6	359.9	361.5	881.3	1415.0	−7.3	−11.3
1979.Q2	2374.6	161.2	1473.4	1483.2	5.8	5.6	367.2	371.2	900.6	1451.0	−5.0	−3.5
1979.Q3	2444.1	164.2	1488.2	1492.4	5.8	5.6	376.1	380.6	927.5	1489.0	−9.3	−5.8
1979.Q4	2496.3	167.5	1490.6	1501.6	5.9	5.6	380.9	384.5	948.1	1517.3	−14.6	−7.3
1980.Q1	2571.7	171.2	1501.9	1510.9	6.2	5.5	—	390.2	—	1544.8	−21.2	−9.6
1980.Q2	2564.8	175.3	1463.3	1520.3	7.3	5.5	—	387.9	—	1565.9	−37.9	−9.9
1980.Q3	2637.3	179.2	1471.9	1529.7	7.6	5.6	—	401.0	—	1626.6	−41.4	−10.8
1980.Q4	2732.3	183.8	1486.5	1539.1	7.5	5.6	—	411.9	—	1663.3	−37.9	—

Appendix C
Data Sources
and Methods
for Appendix B

C-1 ANNUAL VARIABLES

1. Nominal GNP (Y):

   1900–08: *Long-term Economic Growth, 1860–1970* (Washington, D.C.: U.S. Department of Commerce, 1973), series A7, linked in 1909 to:

   1909–28: *Long-term Economic Growth, 1860–1970*, series A8, linked in 1929 to:

   1929–46: *Survey of Current Business* (Washington, D.C.: U.S. Department of Commerce, October 1978), Table A.

   1947–79: *Economic Report of the President, 1980* (Washington, D.C.: U.S. Government Printing Office, 1980), Table B–1.

2. Implicit GNP deflator (P):

   1900–79: Obtained by dividing nominal GNP (Y) by real GNP (Q), then multiplying by 100; that is, $P = 100 \times (Y/Q)$.

3. Real GNP (Q):

   1900–08: *Long-term Economic Growth, 1860–1970*, series A1, linked in 1909 to:

   1909–28: *Long-term Economic Growth, 1860–1970*, series A2, linked in 1929 to:

   1929–46: *Survey of Current Business*, October 1978, Table A.

   1947–77: *Economic Report of the President, 1980*, Table B-2.

4. Natural real GNP (Q^N):

   1900–54: Q^N is calculated as the geometric interpolation between the Q^N values of the benchmark years of 1901, 1912, 1923, 1929, and 1950. Thus, between benchmark years 1901 and 1912, the one year growth rate of Q^N (q^N) is calculated as

   $$q^N = \left(\frac{Q^N_{1912}}{Q^N_{1901}}\right)^{\frac{1}{11}} - 1.0$$

Benchmark values for 1901, 1912, 1923, 1929, and 1950 are estimates of output producible at an adjusted unemployment rate, UA, of 5 percent. Q^N for the benchmark years is estimated as: $Q^N = (Q) \times [1.0 + 2 \times (UA - 0.05)]$ where Q is actual real GNP, the parameter 2 is an approximation of the relationship between changes in the unemployment rate and actual output during the 1900–1929 period, and UA, the adjusted unemployment rate, is obtained by dividing the number of unemployed persons by the civilian labor force net of self-employed persons.

1955–78: Jeffrey M. Perloff and Michael L. Wachter, "A Production Function-Nonaccelerating Inflation Approach to Potential Output: Is Measured Potential Output Too High?" in K. Brunner and A. H. Meltzer (eds.), *Three Aspects of Policy and Policy-making: Knowledge, Data, and Institutions*, vol. 10 of a supplementary series to the *Journal of Monetary Economics*, 1979, 113–164. The "$QPOT_1$" series from Perloff and Wachter was supplied by Michael Wachter and was extrapolated to 1977–78 by extending the 1976–77 rate of growth.

1979: Estimated by the author. For 1979 natural output was computed using a 2.5 percent growth rate beginning in 1979:Q1 as suggested in the *Economic Report of the President, 1980*, p. 89.

5. Unemployment rate (U):

1900–39: *Long-term Economic Growth, 1860–1970*, series B1.

1940–70: *Long-term Economic Growth, 1860–1970*, series B2.

1971–79: *Economic Report of the President, 1980*, Table B-29.

6. Natural unemployment rate (U^N):

1900–56: U^N is calculated as the linear interpolation between the U^N values of the benchmark years of 1902, 1907, 1913, 1929, 1950, and 1956.

U^N for the benchmark years of 1902, 1907, 1913, 1929, and 1950 is calculated as $U^N = 5.0 \times (U/UA)$ where U is the published unemployment rate and UA is an unemployment rate that adjusts for self-employment. UA equals the number of unemployed divided by the civilian labor force net of self-employed persons. The assumed 5.0 rate for UA, assumed to be consistent with long-run equilibrium, reflects the value of UA observed in late 1950, when the economy was operating at its natural rate of unemployment. Changes in U^N before 1950 reflect only changes in the U/UA ratio.

1956–76: As estimated by Robert J. Gordon, "Structural Unemployment and the Productivity of Women," in K. Brunner and A. Meltzer (eds.), *Stabilization of Domestic and International Economy*, vol. 5 of a supplementary series to the *Journal of Monetary Economics*, 1977, p. 189–191 (line 5).

1977–79: Estimated by the author.

7. Money supply (old $M1$):

1915–46: Historical Statistics of the United States, *Colonial Times to 1970* (Washington, D.C.: U.S. Department of Commerce, 1975), series 414.

1947–79: *Federal Reserve Bulletin*, various issues.
8. Money supply (new $M1B$):
   Unpublished data provided by the Federal Reserve Bank of New York.
9. Money supply (old $M2$):
   1900–46: Historical Statistics of the United States, *Colonial Times to 1970*, series 415.
   1947–79: *Federal Reserve Bulletin*, various issues.
10. Money supply (new $M2$):
    Unpublished data provided by the Federal Reserve Bank of New York.

C-2 QUARTERLY VARIABLES

1. Nominal GNP (Y):
   1947:Q1–1979:Q4: *Survey of Current Business*, January 1980, Table A, pp. 36–37.
   1980:Q1–1980:Q2: *Survey of Current Business*, August 1980.
2. GNP implicit price deflator (P):
   1947:Q1–1980:Q2: Obtained by dividing nominal GNP (Y) by real GNP (Q), then multiplying by 100; that is, $P = 100 \times (Y/Q)$.
3. Real GNP, (Q):
   1947:Q1–1979:Q4: *Survey of Current Business*, January 1980, Table B.
   1980:Q1–1980:Q2: *Survey of Current Business*, August 1980.
4. Natural real GNP (Q^N):
   1947:Q1–1980:Q2: The quarterly values are derived by linear interpolation between the annual values.
5. Unemployment rate (U):
   1947:Q1–1980:Q2: *Business Conditions Digest* (Washington, D.C.: U.S. Department of Commerce), April 1979 and various issues, series 43.
6. Natural unemployment rate (U^N):
   1947:Q1–1980:Q2: The quarterly values are derived by linear interpolation between the annual values.
7. Money supply (old $M1$):
   1947:Q1–1979:Q4: *Federal Reserve Bulletin*, various issues.
8. Money supply (new $M1B$):
   Unpublished data provided by the Federal Reserve Bank of New York.
9. Money supply (old $M2$):
   1947:Q1–1979:Q4: *Federal Reserve Bulletin*, various issues.
10. Money supply (new $M2$):
    Unpublished data provided by the Federal Reserve Bank of New York.
11. Actual federal government surplus in 1972 dollars:
    1947:Q1–1980:Q1: Unpublished printout provided to the author by the Federal Reserve Bank of St. Louis, converted by the author to real terms by dividing by the GNP deflator.

12. Natural employment surplus in 1972 dollars:

1947:Q1–1980:Q1: Figures on nominal "high employment expenditures" (E^H) and "high employment revenues" (R^H) were provided by the Federal Reserve Bank of St. Louis. "Natural employment revenues" were calculated by adjusting the St. Louis estimate for the difference between our estimate of natural real GNP (Q^N) and the official government estimate of "high employment real GNP" (Q^H), which we believe to be unrealistically optimistic. Government revenues are estimated to fall by 1.62 percent for any 1 percent change in real GNP, as shown in Figure 17–2 for 1975. Thus the real natural employment surplus is calculated as:

$$\text{real NES} = \frac{R^H - 1.62 R^H (Q^H - Q^N)/Q^N - E^H}{P}$$

C-3 VARIABLES USED IN FIGURES BUT NOT LISTED IN APPENDIX B

Figure 8-12. The vertical axis plots the four-quarter rate of change of an adjusted wage index first used and described by the author in his "Inflation in Recession and Recovery," *Brookings Papers on Economic Activity,* vol. 2, no. 1 (1971), pp. 153–154. This index adjusts changes in average hourly earnings for changes in overtime pay and the interindustry mix of employment, and in addition includes fringe benefits and employers' social security contributions. The index has been kept up to date using the sources described in the 1971 reference.

Figure 10-2. The expected rate of inflation (p^e) is the annual average of the fitted value of a regression of the one-quarter change of the "stripped" personal consumption deflator on twenty lagged values of itself and a dummy for the Nixon price controls. The estimated coefficient on the controls variable is then used to add back in the effect of the controls to the fitted values, so that the estimate of p^e reflects the assumption that expectations did not adjust for the effect of the controls. This seems to be supported by the behavior of the corporate bond rate in Figure 11–2.

Figure 11-2. The interest rate displayed is Moody's Aaa corporate bond rate, from the *Economic Report of the President, 1980,* Table B-64, p. 278. The expected rate of inflation is the same as that used in Figure 10-2.

Figure 16-1. Nominal GNP is from the quarterly data bank developed in Robert J. Gordon and James A. Wilcox, "Monetarist Interpretations of the Great Depression: An Evaluation and Critique," in K. Brunner (ed.), *Contemporary Views of the Great Depression* (Hingham, Mass.: Martinus-Nijhoff, 1980). The money supply includes currency and all commercial bank deposits and is from Milton Friedman and Anna J. Schwartz, *A Monetary History of the United States, 1867–1960* (Princeton, N.J.: Princeton University Press, 1971). High-powered money, the currency-deposit ratio, and the total reserves-deposit ratio are from the same source. Excess reserves are from James A. Wilcox, "Excess Reserves in the Interwar Period," unpublished doctoral dissertation, Northwestern University, February 1980.

Figure 18-1. The calculations start with 1970 U.S. per capita GNP in 1979 prices, calculated from the *Economic Report of the President, 1980.* Real income per capita across nations was not compared on the basis of market exchange rates, which can be very misleading. Instead, the comparison for 1970 is based on an extremely careful study which involved traveling to each nation to collect data on their prices for goods identical in quality to those in each other nation. Adjustments were made for services provided free by the government in some countries but not in others, e.g., free national health care in the United Kingdom. See Irving B. Kravis, Alan W. Heston, and Robert Summers, "Real GNP *Per Capita* for More Than One Hundred Countries," *Economic Journal,* vol. 88 (June 1978), Table 4, column (5), pp. 236–237. Figures for other years were obtained as follows: 1950–79. The 1970 dollar figures were extrapolated forward and back by GNP per capita data obtained from *International Financial Statistics,* 1950–1979. The postwar figures were linked in 1953 to those compiled for 1870–1960 in Angus Maddison, *Economic Growth in the West* (New York: The Twentieth Century Fund, 1964), Appendixes A and B.

Table 18-3. Lines A, B. J. R. Norsworthy, Michael J. Harper, and Kent Kunze, "The Slowdown in Productivity Growth: Analysis of Some Contributing Factors," *Brookings Papers on Economic Activity,* vol. 10, no. 2 (1979), Table 10, p. 415. The effect of pollution abatement capital is added back in to line B in order to avoid double counting with line C.2. Line C.1. The ratio of Q/Q^N grew by 3 percent between 1948 and 1973, and then fell by 3 percent between 1973 and 1978. This was converted to an annual growth rate and then multiplied by 0.23, the elasticity of productivity growth to a cyclical change in output growth, from Robert J. Gordon, "The End-of-Expansion Effect in Short-run Productivity Behavior," *Brookings Papers on Economic Activity,* vol. 10, no. 2 (1979), Table 1, column (3), p. 452. Line C.2. From Edward Denison, same source as listed for Table 18-2. Line C.3. Unpublished Bureau of Labor Statistics worksheets supplied to the author by Martin N. Baily.

Glossary of Major Concepts

Note: Numbers in parentheses indicate the chapter and section where each term is first introduced. Words and phrases in the text set in boldface type are those defined in this list. The glossary does not include every word listed in the Concepts section at the end of each chapter, particularly those whose use is confined to a single chapter.

Accelerator hypothesis (14–1). The theory that the level of net investment depends on the change in expected output, because firms are assumed to attempt to maintain a fixed ratio of desired capital to expected output.

Adaptive expectations (7–4, 8–6). A hypothesis that claims economic units base their expectations for next period's values on an average of actual values during previous periods.

Adjusted demand growth or **adjusted nominal GNP growth** (8–7). The growth rate of actual nominal GNP minus the growth rate of natural real GNP. In the long run, must equal the inflation rate.

Adjusted real GNP growth (8–7). The difference between the growth rates of actual and natural real GNP. Must be zero in the long run.

Aggregates (1–1). The total amount of an economic magnitude for the economy as a whole. Example: **GNP** is an economic aggregate.

Aggregate demand (1–5). Total (nominal) spending on goods and services by all economic units in the economy. See **Nominal GNP.**

Aggregate demand curve (6–2). The schedule that indicates the combinations of the price level and output at which the money and commodity markets are simultaneously in equilibrium.

Aggregate supply (1–5). The total amount that business firms are willing to produce at the current price level. The study of aggregate supply asks how changes in **nominal GNP** are divided between changes in prices and changes in **real GNP.**

Aggregate supply curve (6–8). A short-run schedule that indicates the amount of output supplied at any price level, given a fixed expected price level.

Appreciation (11–7). A rise in the value of one nation's currency relative to another nation's currency. Example: The appreciation of the American dollar relative to the British pound in the 1970s means $1 buys more British pounds than before.

Automatic stabilization (3–appendix, 17–2). A feature of any economy in which tax receipts depend on income; the economy is stabilized by the **leakage** of tax revenues from the spending stream when income rises or falls.

Autonomus (3–2). A magnitude which is independent of the level of income. Example: Autonomous consumption spending.

Average propensity to consume (3–2). The ratio of consumption expenditures to disposable income. See **Marginal propensity to consume.**

Average propensity to save (3–2). The ratio of personal saving to disposable income. See **Marginal propensity to save.**

Balanced-budget multiplier (3–7). The ratio of the change in equilibrium real income to the change in government expenditure when government expenditure and tax revenues are raised by an equal amount.

Balance of payments (11–7, 19–1). The total of an economy's external trade in goods, securities, and money. When the balance of payments runs a surplus, a nation gains foreign-exchange reserves. With a deficit the nation loses reserves.

Balance of trade (11–7). The difference between exports and imports. When a nation's exports exceed its imports, it has a balance of trade surplus; when its imports exceed exports, it has a balance of trade deficit. Also called **net exports.**

Base year (1–2). The year with which a magnitude is compared in the calculation of an index. Example: The **implicit GNP deflator** is a price index which currently is calculated using 1972 as the base year.

Bears (5–3). Individuals who think stock and bond prices are likely to decline. In the **liquidity trap,** everyone is a bear.

Capital account (19–2). The portion of the balance of payments which includes direct investment and trade in both long-term and short-term securities.

Capital consumption allowances (2–9). Amount of capital stock used up in the process of production due to obsolescence and physical wear. See **Depreciation.**

Capital gain (11–3). Any increase in the value of a physical or financial asset. If you buy a share of stock for $20 and sell it six months later for $25, your capital gain is $5.

Closed economy (1–6). Economy in which there are no flows of labor, goods, or money to and from other nations.

Commodity market (3–1). The aggregate market for goods and services (GNP).

Comparative statics (7–1). A technique of economic analysis in which a comparison is made between two equilibrium positions, ignoring the behavior of the economy between the two equilibrium positions, either the length of time required or the route followed during the transition between the initial and final positions.

Constant-growth-rate rule (CGRR) (12–5, 15–8). A policy (recommended by many monetarists) which advocates a constant percentage rate of the money supply in order to prevent the Federal Reserve from destabilizing the economy.

Constant returns to scale (18–3). An increase of x percent in each factor input (e.g., labor and capital) is accompanied by an x percent increase in output.

Consumer expenditures (2–2). Purchases of goods and services by households for their own use.

Consumption function (3–2). The relationship between the amount households desire to consume and their disposable income.

Cost-of-living agreements (COLA clauses) (7–6). Provisions in wage contracts for an automatic increase in the wage rate in response to an increase in a price index, usually the Consumer Price Index.

Countercyclical (13–5). An adjective describing any economic variable which fluctuates in the opposite direction as real output over the business cycle. See **Procyclical.**

Cross-section (13–2). Data which cover several categories, each at the same point in time. Example: Cross-section studies of the income-consumption relation often gather consumption data for the various income classes during a single year.

Crowding out effect (5–6). A term which describes the decrease in one component of spending when another component of spending rises. Example: When government expenditure rises, the interest rate rises, depressing investment spending. This fall in investment is the amount which has been crowded out.

Current account (19–2). The portion of the balance of payments which includes exports and imports of goods and services, as well as transfers and gifts.

Deflation (1–3, 6–1). A sustained downward movement of the aggregate price level.

Deflator (6–1). See Implicit GNP deflator.

Demand-pull inflation (7–7). Inflation caused by a continuous rightward shift of the aggregate demand curve.

Depreciation (2–9). Same as **capital consumption allowances.**

Depreciation (9–4, 11–7, 19–3). A decline in the value of one nation's currency relative to another nation's currency. Example: The depreciation of the American dollar relative to the German mark in the 1970s means $1 buys fewer marks than before.

Depreciation rate (14–7). The annual percentage decline in the *value* of a piece of a capital due to physical deterioration and obsolescence. Example: If your new car purchased for $5000 is worth only $4000 after one year, then its depreciation rate over that year is 20 percent.

Discretionary fiscal policy (17–2). A deliberate policy which alters tax rates and/or government expenditure in an attempt to influence real output and unemployment.

Disequilibrium (7–6). An economy that is not in a state of **equilibrium**; e.g., an economy in which demand is not equal to supply. This occurs when prices and wages are slow to respond to excess demand and supply. A classic example was the Great Depression, when the supply of labor was far in excess of the demand for labor.

Disintermediation (16–8). The term used to describe the shift of funds out of savings banks when the interest rate on stocks and bonds increases. An important cause of disintermediation is the **Regulation Q** ceiling which prevents savings banks from raising their interest rate on deposits to compete with the higher returns available on bonds.

Dynamic multipliers (12–7). The amount by which output is raised during each of several time periods after a $1 increase in autonomous spending. Example: The econometric models discussed in section 12-7 have dynamic multipliers for a change in government spending, which generally rise through the first year, peak in the second year, and decline steadily thereafter.

Econometric models (12–6). A group of equations, each one representing a different relation in the economy, in which the parameters are estimated by the statistical study of past historical episodes. All the equations of an econometric model can be solved simultaneously to determine the levels of inflation, unemployment, other variables of interest, and what changes would occur with differing economic policies.

Economic growth (18–1). The study in economics of the causes and consequences of sustained growth in **natural real GNP**. Different rates of economic growth, maintained over long periods of time, can drastically change the order of nations' standings in the league table of living standards, as in Table 18-1.

Economic model (5–appendix). A graphical or mathematical representation of an economy, usually consisting of two or more graphical schedules or algebraic equations. Example: The *IS* and *LM* **curves** of Chapters 3–6 combine to form an economic model which determines the equilibrium levels of real income and the interest rate. The same information is contained in the algebraic version in the appendix to Chapter 5.

Equilibrium (3–4). A state in which there exists no pressure for change. Example: The commodity market is in equilibrium when the demand for commodities equals the supply of commodities.

Ex ante (3–4). A term that describes planned expenditures (before they actually take place); before the fact. Example: Ex ante inventory accumulation is planned inventory accumulation. See **Ex post.**

Excess reserves (16–5). The amount of reserves held by a bank in excess of its **required reserves.**

Exchange rate. See **Foreign exchange rate.**

Expectations effect (6–6). The decline in commodity demand during a price deflation due to the expectation that future prices will be lower, leading to a postponement of purchases to take advantage of lower prices in the future.

Expected real interest rate (11–2). The real rate of return which people expect to pay on their borrowings or earn on their savings after deduction of the expected rate of inflation from the nominal interest rate. Example: If people receive a 10 percent nominal return on their savings and expect a 7 percent inflation rate, the expected real interest rate is 3 percent. See **Real interest rate.**

Exports (2–5, 19–2). Exports of country A are goods and services produced in country A and shipped to residents of another country. See **Imports.**

Ex post (3–4). A term that describes the actual expenditures that have resulted after the fact. Example: Ex post inventory accumulation is actual inventory accumulation. See **Ex ante.**

Extra convenience services (11–5). The convenience of money compared to bonds and other assets for conducting transactions. Money is immediately and universally accepted for purchases and payments, whereas bonds and other interest-bearing financial investments are not, forcing bond-holders to convert their bonds into money before making transactions.

Factor inputs (18–3). The economic elements that directly produce real GNP, especially labor and capital (structures and equipment). Other types of factor input are research and development, education, and specialized training. The relation of output to factor inputs is given by the **production function.**

Final good (2–3). Part of **final product.** See **Intermediate good.**

Final product (2–3). All currently produced goods and services that are sold through the market but are not resold. Same as **Gross national product.**

Fiscal dividend (17–4). The automatic growth in the federal government surplus generated by growth in the natural rate of output.

Fiscal drag (17–4). A fiscal dividend which is not eliminated by tax cuts or expenditure increases.

Fiscal policy (1–6). Government policy that attempts to influence target variables by manipulating government expenditures and tax rates.

Fixed investment (2–4). All final goods purchased by businesses which are not intended for resale. Example: Buildings, machinery, office equipment.

Flexible accelerator (14–4). The theory that the desired ratio of capital to expected output may be affected by the user cost of capital. The flexible accelerator hypothesis also usually maintains that only a portion of any gap between the actual and desired capital stock will be made up in any one period.

Flow magnitude (2–2). Economic magnitude which moves from one economic unit to another at a specified rate per unit of time. Examples: **GNP, Personal income.**

Foreign exchange rate (11–7, 19–1). The amount of another nation's money that residents of a country can obtain in exchange for a unit of their own money. For instance, in November, 1977, residents of the United Kingdom could obtain $1.74 in U.S. dollars for one pound sterling.

General equilibrium (4–7). A situation of simultaneous equilibrium in all the markets of the economy.

GNP. See **Gross national product.**

GNP gap (5–3). The difference between natural real GNP and actual real GNP.

Government deficit (2–6). Excess of government expenditures over tax revenues.

Gross (2–9). An adjective that usually refers to magnitudes which include capital consumption allowance. Example: Gross national product. See **Net.**

Gross national product (GNP) (1–2). The market value of all currently produced goods and services during a particular time interval that are sold through the market but are not resold.

High-powered money (16–2). The sum of currency held by the nonbank public and bank reserves. This money is high-powered, because it is capable of supporting bank deposits equal to a multiple of itself, when held by banks as reserves.

Implicit GNP deflator (1–2, 2–10). The economy's aggregate price index. Defined as the ratio of **nominal GNP** to **real GNP.**

Implicit price deflator (1–2). See **Implicit GNP deflator.**

Imports (2–5, 19–2). Imports of country A are goods and services consumed in country A but produced elsewhere. See **Exports.**

Indexed bond (11–8). A bond which pays a fixed real interest rate to its holder. Its nominal interest rate is equal to the fixed real interest rate plus the actual inflation rate.

Indirect business taxes (2–9). Taxes on business levied as a cost of operation. Examples: Sales, excise, and property taxes.

Induced consumption (3–2). The portion of consumption spending that responds to changes in income ($= cQ$).

Induced saving (3–2). The portion of saving that responds to changes in income ($= sQ$).

Inflation (1–2, 7–7). A sustained upward movement in the aggregate price level which is shared by most products.

Inflation rate (1–3). The rate of change of an economy-wide price index per unit of time.

Inflation tax (11–3). The extra revenue which the federal government receives when it raises the nominal money supply in response to higher prices.

Injection (2–6). That part of income which is spent on nonconsumption goods. Example: Private investment, government spending. See **Leakage.**

Intermediate good (2–3). Any good which is resold by its purchaser either in its present or in altered form. See **Final good.**

International reserves (19–1). The internationally acceptable assets which each nation maintains to pay for any deficit in its balance of payments. The main types of international reserves are gold, the U.S. dollar, and special drawing rights.

Inventory investment (2–4). Changes in the stock of raw materials, parts, and finished goods held by business.

Investment (2–4). The portion of final product which adds to the nation's stock of income-yielding assets (inventories, structures, and business equipment) or which replaces old, worn-out assets.

IS curve (4–3). The schedule that identifies the combinations of income and the interest rate at which the commodity market is in equilibrium; everywhere along the *IS* curve, the demand for commodities equals the supply of commodities.

J-curve phenomenon (19–5). The tendency for a nation to run a larger excess of imports over exports in the short run following a depreciation of its exchange rate, followed later by reduced trade deficit.

Keynes effect (6–6). The stimulus to aggregate demand generated by a decline in the rate of interest caused by the rise in the real money supply (caused in turn either by a higher nominal money supply or lower price level).

Leakage (2–6). That part of income which leaks out of the spending stream and is not available to be spent on consumption goods. (See **Injection**.) Examples: Income taxes, personal savings.

Life-cycle hypothesis (13–2). The theory that people try to stabilize their consumption over their entire lifetime. The life-cycle hypothesis predicts that young and old households will consume in excess of their income and that those in the middle-aged groups will save to support themselves during their retirement.

Liquidity trap (5–3). A situation in which the interest rate is believed by all to be at its minimum possible value and the price of bonds is as high as it is likely to go. Because people uniformly expect that bond prices will fall, they hold no bonds and there is no one from whom the Federal Reserve can purchase bonds in order to lower the interest rate and stimulate the economy.

LM curve (4–5). The schedule that identifies the combinations of income and the interest rate at which the money market is in equilibrium; everywhere along the *LM* curve the demand for money equals the supply of money.

Long-run equilibrium (7–5). A situation in which

aggregate demand equals aggregate supply, and in addition, expectations turn out to be correct. See **Short-run equilibrium.**

M1 (15–7). The narrowly defined money supply; the public's holding of currency and checking accounts.

M2 (15–7). The broadly defined money supply; the sum of currency and checking accounts held by the public (*M*1) plus savings deposits held at commercial banks and thrift institutions plus accounts at money-market mutual funds.

Macroeconomics (1–1). The study of the major economic totals or aggregates.

Marginal leakage rate (3–7, 3–appendix). The fraction of income which is not spent on consumption; the fraction of income that flows into savings, income tax payments, and import purchases.

Marginal product of capital (14–5). The dollars of extra output in constant prices which a firm can produce over a specified period by adding an extra unit of capital, divided by the total cost of that capital. The marginal product, like the user cost of capital, is expressed as a percent. Example: If an extra $1000 machine produces an extra $150 worth of output in a year when no additional labor is hired, the marginal product of that piece of capital is 15 percent.

Marginal product of labor (7–2). The dollars of extra output in constant prices which a firm can produce by adding an extra hour of labor.

Marginal propensity to consume (3–2). The change in **consumption expenditures** that results from an extra dollar of income; the fraction of an extra dollar of **personal disposable income** that households spend on consumption goods and services.

Marginal propensity to save (3–2). The change in **personal saving** induced by a $1 change in **personal disposable income.**

Market (5–1). The process in which producers supplying a good or group of goods come together with the purchasers demanding that good. The interaction of supply and demand determines the market price. The market for assets (such as government bonds) determines the price of the asset and hence its yield or interest rate.

Monetarists (1–7). A group of economists who are opposed to government intervention in the economy and who disagree with nonmonetarists on several major issues. See also sections 12–2 and 12–3.

Monetary policy (1–6). Government policy conducted in the United States by the Federal Reserve Board that attempts to influence **target variables** by changing the money and/or interest rates. See **Fiscal policy.**

Money-market mutual funds (11–8). Institutions that accept deposits by mail from individuals and companies and invest those funds in a variety of short-term financial securities that are normally not available for purchase by individuals. These funds give households the opportunity to earn high and secure yields and at the same time to write checks on the deposits. Included in the new definition of *M2.*

Money supply (1–7, 4–5). The main policy instrument of monetary policy. The money-supply concept *M1* consists of currency held by the public and all checking accounts (demand deposits). See also *M2.*

Multiplier (3–5). The ratio of the change in income to the change in **autonomous spending,** which causes the change in income.

Multiplier uncertainty (12–7). The uncertainty about the exact numerical values and timing of spending multipliers; used as an argument against an activist stabilization policy. Example: Since each **econometric model** produces different estimates of policy multipliers, policymakers are uncertain as to the time value of each multiplier and therefore of the actual effect of policy changes.

National income (2–9). The income that originates in the production of goods and services; net national product less indirect business taxes.

National Income and Product Accounts (NIPA) (2–3). The official United States government economic accounting system which keeps track of GNP and its subcomponents.

Natural employment surplus (NES) (17–2). The difference between tax revenue and government expenditure which would be generated if the economy were operating at the natural rate of output.

Natural rate of interest (5–3). The rate of interest at which the *IS* curve intersects the level of **natural real GNP.**

Natural rate of unemployment (1–3). The minimum sustainable level of unemployment below which inflation tends to accelerate. At this rate of unemployment, there is no tendency for inflation to accelerate or decelerate.

Natural real GNP (1–3). Estimate of the amount the economy can produce when actual unemployment is equal to the **natural rate of unemployment.** In this situation, there is no tendency for inflation to accelerate or decelerate.

Net (2–9). An adjective which usually refers to magnitudes that exclude the capital consumption allowance. Net investment is the amount by which the capital stock changes over a specified period. See **Gross.**

Net exports (2–5, 19–2). Excess of exports over imports.

Net foreign investment (2–5). Excess of exports over imports or net exports.

Net national product (2–9). Net market value of goods and services produced per unit of time; GNP less **capital consumption allowances.**

Net tax revenue (2–6). Taxes collected minus transfer payments.

Net worth (11–6). For a household or firm, the total of its assets minus the total of its liabilities. Sometimes called net wealth.

Nominal (1–2). An adjective which modifies any economic magnitude measured in current prices. Example: **Nominal GNP** is the current dollar value of GNP.

Nominal GNP (1–2). The value of **gross national product** in current (actual) prices.

Nominal interest rate (11–2). The interest rate actually charged by banks and earned by bondholders; the market interest rate. Example: When a customer pays 12 percent interest on an auto loan, the nominal interest rate is 12 percent.

Nonmonetarists (1–7). See **Monetarists** and sections 12–2 and 12–3.

Normative economics (1–6). An individual's recommendations regarding an optimal or desirable state of affairs. See **Positive economics.**

Official reserve transactions (ORT) **balance** (19–2). The balance-of-payments surplus or deficit concept which includes all trade in goods and securities; any such deficit must be offset by an outflow of international reserves.

Okun's law (10–2). The name given to the close relationship in the postwar United States between the unemployment rate (U) and the ratio of actual to natural real output (Q/Q^N). According to the original version of Okun's law, a 1 percentage point rise (drop) in the unemployment rate is associated with roughly a 3 percent decrease (increase) in Q/Q^N. Now, however, it appears that there is a 2 rather than a 3 percent decrease (increase) in Q/Q^N.

OPEC (1–4, 7–7). An abbreviation for the Organization of Petroleum Exporting Countries, the "oil cartel" that raised oil prices in 1973–74 and in 1979–80, thus administering a **supply shock** to the rest of the world.

Open economy (1–6). Economy in which there are flows of labor, goods, bonds, and/or money between nations.

Open-market operations (16–4). Purchases and sales by the Federal Reserve's selling of government bonds used to influence the supply of high-powered money, the money supply, and interest rates. When the Federal Reserve wishes to raise the money supply, it buys bonds, paying with high-powered money, resulting in a higher money supply.

Optimum quantity of money (11–5). The stock of money which minimizes the costs in terms of fees and inconvenience of conducting transactions.

Parameter (3–4, 5–appendix). A parameter is taken as given or known within a given analysis. Example: In the consumption function, $(C = a + cQ_D)$, autonomous consumption (a) and the marginal propensity to consume (c) are parameters. Many exercises in economics involve examining the effects of a change in a single parameter.

Permanent income (13–3). The average income which people expect to receive over a period of years, often estimated as a weighted average of past actual income.

Permanent income hypothesis (PIH) (12–3, 13–1). The theory that consumption spending depends on the long run average (permanent) income which people expect to receive. Example: If people's incomes rise and fall with the business cycle, then their actual incomes will be above their permanent income in booms and below in recessions. Their saving will rise and fall with their actual income.

Personal disposable income (2–9). The income available to households for consumption and saving; personal income less tax payments.

Personal income (2–9). The income received by households from all sources (interest, wages, transfers); national income less corporate undistributed profits, corporate income taxes and social security taxes, plus transfer payments.

Personal saving (2–4). That part of personal income which is neither consumed nor paid out in taxes.

Pigou effect (5–5, 6–6). The direct stimulus to autonomous consumption spending that occurs when a price deflation raises the real money supply and thus wealth. Also called the real balance effect.

Policy instruments (1–6, 12–5). Elements of government policy which can be manipulated to influence **target variables.** Examples: Personal income tax rate, money supply.

Positive economics (1–6). The attempt scientifically to describe and explain the behavior of the economy.

Price index (2–10). A weighted average of prices in the economy at any given time, divided by the prices of the same goods in a **base year.** Example: The Consumer Price Index is the ratio of an average of the prices of consumer goods in each month to the average prices of the same goods in 1967, the base year.

Procyclical (13–5). An adjective describing any economic variable which fluctuates in the same direction as real output, rising during a boom and declining during a recession. See **Countercyclical.**

Production function (18–3). A relationship, usually written in algebra, that shows how much output can be produced by a given quantity of **factor inputs.**

Productivity (8–9). A general term that most often means the average amount of output (real GNP) produced per employee or per hour. New machines and inventions tend to raise the productivity of labor by helping workers to produce more.

Purchasing-power-parity (PPP) **theory** (19–4). The theory that the prices of identical goods should be the same in all countries, differing only by the cost of transport and any import duties.

Pure fiscal policy shift (5–6). A shift in policy that involves changes in government spending and/or tax rates while the money supply is held constant.

Pure monetary policy shift (5–6). A shift in policy that involves changes in the money supply while government spending and tax rates are held constant. See **Pure fiscal policy shift.**

Quantity theory of money (15–3). The theory that money is demanded to conduct transactions and that to facilitate these transactions people hold a constant fraction of their nominal income in the form of money. The strong version of the theory assumes also that real output is fixed, so price changes are proportional to changes in the money supply.

Rate of return (4–2). The annual dollar earnings of an investment good divided by its dollar cost.

Rate of time preference (17–appendix). The extra

amount a consumer would be willing to pay to be able to obtain a given quantity of consumption goods now rather than one year from now.

Real (1–2). An adjective which modifies any economic magnitude measured in the constant prices of a single base year. Opposite of **nominal.**

Real balance effect (5–5, 6–6). Also see **Pigou effect.**

Real GNP (1–2). The value of gross national product in constant prices.

Real interest rate (11–3). The interest rate people actually pay on their borrowings or receive on their savings after allowing for inflation rate. This equals the nominal interest rate minus the actual inflation rate. Example: When the nominal interest rate is 12 percent and actual inflation is 10 percent, the real interest rate is 2 percent.

Real output (1–2). Same as real GNP; total production measured in constant prices. Also the same as real income.

Real wage (7–3). The value of the nominal wage in terms of the goods and services it can purchase; the nominal wage divided by the price level. A competitive firm will tend to hire workers up to the point where the marginal product of labor equals the real wage.

Recession (8–8). A period of declining real economic activity, often defined as a period during which real GNP falls for two quarters or more. A recession begins after the preceding expansion has reached its "peak" and continues until the economy reaches its "trough," after which a "recovery" begins.

Rediscount rate (16–4). The interest rate which the Federal Reserve charges banks when they borrow funds.

Redistribution effect (6–6). The effect on commodity demand caused by the redistribution of income from debtors to creditors during a price deflation. If debtors cut their consumption more than creditors raise theirs, then aggregate consumption falls.

Regulation Q (11–8, 16–8). The Federal Reserve Board requirement which sets an upper limit on the nominal interest rate commercial banks can pay to holders of time deposits. A similar regulation limits the allowable interest rates payable on deposits by savings and loan institutions.

Required reserves (16–4). The reserves banks must hold according to Federal Reserve regulations; banks' deposits times the reserve ratio. Example: A bank with $100 million in deposits has required re-

serves of $10 million when the reserve ratio is 10 percent. In the U.S., reserves can be held either as cash in the vault or as reserve deposits at the Federal Reserve.

Reserve requirements (16–4). The rules which stipulate the minimum fraction of deposits that banks must maintain as required reserves.

Saving. See **Personal saving.**

Saving function. See **Consumption function.**

Self-correcting forces (6–1). Inherent forces in the economy, particularly price flexibility, that propel it toward the natural output level without any government intervention.

Short-run equilibrium (7–5). A situation in which **aggregate demand** equals short-run **aggregate supply,** given the current state of expectations (expectations do not have to be realized in short-run equilibrium, as is required for long-run equilibrium).

Short-run Phillips curve (8–2). The schedule relating unemployment to the inflation rate achievable given a fixed expected rate of inflation.

Spending responsiveness (4–4). The dollar change in planned autonomous spending divided by the percentage point change on the interest rate which causes it.

Stabilization policy (1–6). A general term for monetary and fiscal policies. Any policy that seeks to influence the level of aggregate demand.

Stagflation (8–7). A situation which combines stagnation (zero or negative output growth) with inflation.

Stock (2–2). An economic magnitude in the possession of a given unit or aggregate at a particular point in time. Examples: The capital stock, the money supply.

Supply shock (1–5, 7–7). A change in the amount of output which firms are willing to produce at a given price level. Examples: Crop failures caused by droughts and the 1973–74 and 1979–80 increases in oil prices. See also sections 7–7 and 8–10.

Target variables (1–6, 12–5). Aggregates whose values society cares about; society's economic goals. Examples: Inflation, unemployment.

Time-series (13–2). Data which cover a span of time. Example: The behavior of consumption and income since 1900 constitutes time-series evidence that income and consumption are related.

Total labor force (10–3). The total number of those

employed and unemployed. Excludes those not working who do not seek work.

Transfer payments (2–3). Payments made for which no goods or services are produced in return. Examples: Welfare and social security.

Unanticipated inflation (11–3). That portion of actual inflation which people did not expect; actual inflation minus expected inflation. Example: If people expect inflation to be 10 percent per year, but the actual rate is 12 percent, the unanticipated inflation rate is 2 percent.

Undistributed corporate profits (2–9). That portion of corporate profits that remains with firms after stockholder dividends and corporate income taxes are paid. Also called retained earnings.

Unemployment rate (1–3, 8–1). The number of jobless individuals who are actively looking for work (or are on temporary layoff), divided by total employment plus unemployment.

Unintended inventory investment (3–4). The amount by which businesses are forced to accumulate inventories above their plans when the economy's planned expenditures fall short of production and income.

User cost of capital (14–5). The cost to the firm of using a piece of capital for a specified period, expressed as a percent of the total cost of the capital. The user cost is influenced by the interest and depreciation rates and by the tax treatment of investment, depreciation, and corporate profits.

Value added (2–3). The increase in value of inputs which is imparted by a particular stage of the production process.

Variables (5–1). Magnitudes that can change. Consumption, GNP, and the money supply are all variables.

Velocity (4–6, 15–3). The ratio of nominal income (PQ) to the money supply (M); the average number of times per year that the money stock is used in making payments for final goods and services. The inverse of velocity (M/PQ) is the amount of money held relative to nominal income.

Index

Guide to Symbols

(continued)

Symbol	Chapter where introduced	Explanation
N	14	Net real private investment.
NES	17	Natural employment surplus.
NNP	2	Real net national product: $NNP = GNP - S_D$
p	8	Inflation rate.
p'	19	Foreign or world inflation rate.
p^e	8	Expected inflation rate.
P	2	Implicit price deflator for gross national product: $P = Y/Q$
P'	19	Foreign or world price level.
P^e	7	Expected level of a price index.
PPI	2	Producer price index.
q	8	Growth rate of real GNP.
q^N	8	Growth rate of natural real GNP.
$\hat{q}$	8	Deviation of actual from natural real GNP growth: $\hat{q} = q - q^N$
Q	2	Real income or real GNP.
Q_D	2	Real disposable personal income.
Q_N	2	Real national income: $Q_N = NNP - R_B$
Q_P	2	Real personal income: $Q_P = Q_N - S_B - R_C - R_S + F_G$
Q^e	14	Real expected sales.